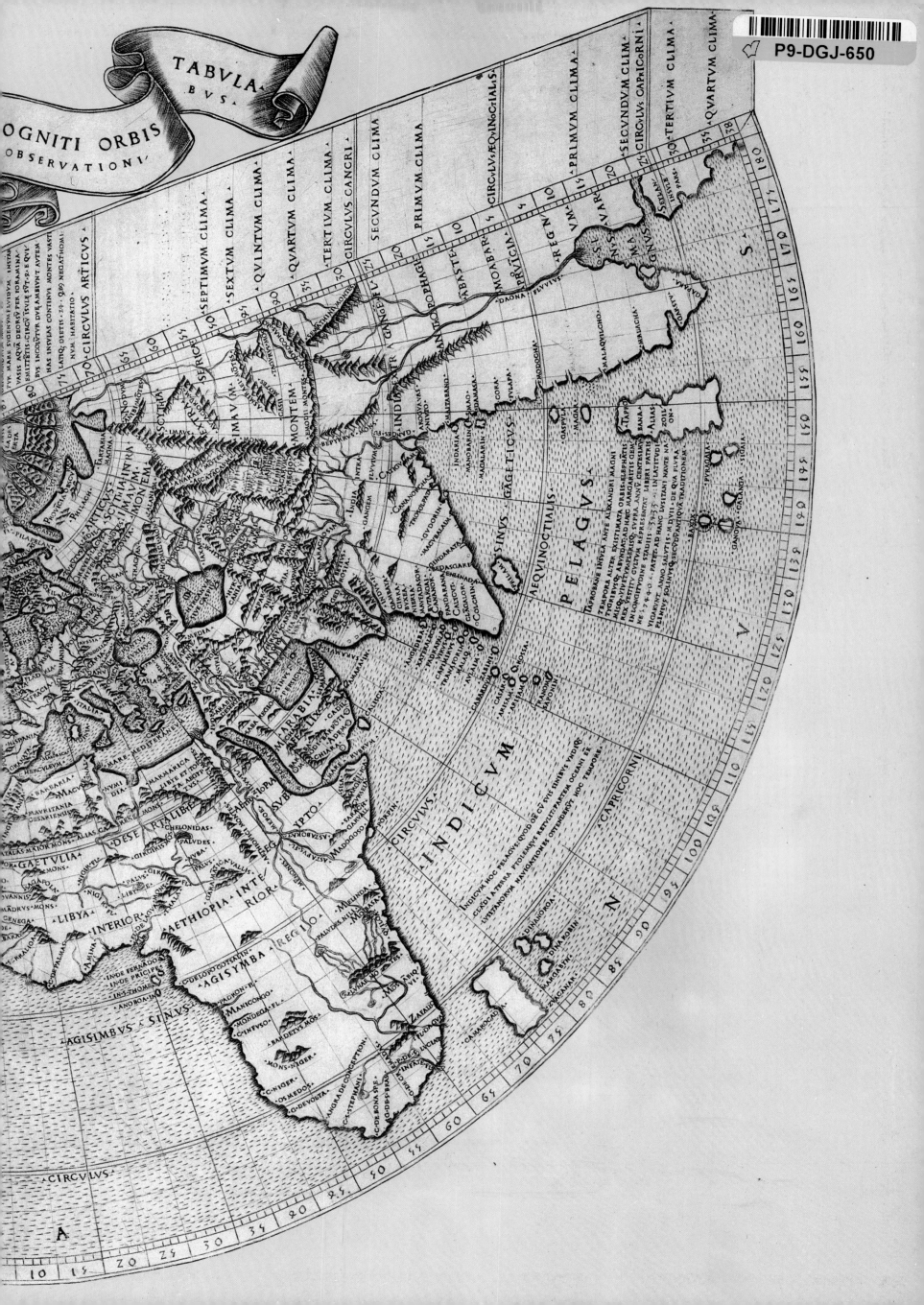

THE TIMES
Atlas of World
EXPLORATION

Atlas of World

THE TIMES

EXPLORATION

3,000 Years of Exploring, Explorers, and Mapmaking

Edited by
FELIPE FERNÁNDEZ-ARMESTO

CONSULTANT EDITORS:
Kirti Chaudhuri
Geoffrey Parker
G V Scammell
Glyndwr Williams

HarperCollins*Publishers*

This book is produced in Great Britain by Times Books

LIBRARY OF CONGRESS CATALOG CARD NUMBER
91-55000

Editorial direction
Thomas Cussans
Andrew Heritage

Ian Castello-Cortes
Ailsa Heritage
Mandy Keyho
Anita Roberts

Cartographic direction
Alison Ewington

Martin Brown
Karen Tait

Design
Ivan Dodd

Tracy Enever

Place names consultant, index
Pat Geelan

Technical glossary
H.A.G. Lewis OBE

Original cartography
CHK Datamap, Oxford

Typesetting
Swanston Graphics Ltd, Derby

Colour processing
Colourscan, Singapore

Printed and bound in Italy by
Mondadori, Verona

Library of Congress Cataloging-in-Publication Data
The Times atlas of world exploration/edited by Felipe Fernández-Armesto,
    consultant editors, Geoffrey Parker et al.
        p.   cm.
    'Published in Great Britain by Times Books'. – T.p. verso.
    Includes bibliographical refereces and index.
    ISBN 0-06-270032-4: $75.00
    1. Discoveries (in geography)—History—Maps.   2. Explorers—
History—Maps.   I. Fernández-Armesto, Felipe.   II. Parker,
Geoffrey, 1943-   .   III. Times Books (Firm).   IV. Title: Atlas of World Exploration.
G1036.T5   1991   <G&M>
912—dc20   91-55000
                                                             CIP
                                                             MAP

ISBN 0-06-270032-4

91 92 93 94 95   10 9 8 7 6 5 4 3 2 1

The publishers wish to thank Professor George Winius;
Marrianne Behm; Lesley Branscombe; Ruth Duxbury;
John Goss; Anthony Livesey; Ian Smith; Jeanne Radford

CONTRIBUTORS

EDITOR

FELIPE FERNÁNDEZ-ARMESTO
Director, Oxford Comparative Colonial History
Project; Visiting Professor of Maritime History
THE JOHN CARTER BROWN LIBRARY,
BROWN UNIVERSITY

CONSULTANT EDITORS

KIRTI CHAUDHURI
Professor of the Economic History of Asia
SCHOOL OF ORIENTAL AND AFRICAN STUDIES
UNIVERSITY OF LONDON

GEOFFREY PARKER
Distinguished Professor of History and Chair
UNIVERSITY OF ILLINOIS AT URBANA-
CHAMPAIGN

G V SCAMMELL
Fellow of Pembroke College
UNIVERSITY OF CAMBRIDGE

GLYNDWR WILLIAMS
Professor of History
Queen Mary and Westfield College
UNIVERSITY OF LONDON

CONTRIBUTORS

J ANTHONY ALLAN
Professor of Geography
SCHOOL OF ORIENTAL AND AFRICAN STUDIES
UNIVERSITY OF LONDON

TERENCE ARMSTRONG
Emeritus Reader in Arctic Studies
UNIVERSITY OF CAMBRIDGE

RICHARD A BARTLETT
Professor of History Emeritus
THE FLORIDA STATE UNIVERSITY

C A BAYLY
Professor of Modern Indian History
UNIVERSITY OF CAMBRIDGE

ALAN V BRICELAND
Associate Professor of History
VIRGINIA COMMONWEALTH UNIVERSITY

ROY C BRIDGES
Professor of History
UNIVERSITY OF ABERDEEN

IAN BROWN
Senior Lecturer in Economic History
SCHOOL OF ORIENTAL AND AFRICAN STUDIES
UNIVERSITY OF LONDON

NIGEL CALDER FRAS FRGS

AVERIL CAMERON
Professor of Late Antique and Byzantine Studies
KING'S COLLEGE LONDON

SIR HUGH CORTAZZI
Former British Ambassador to Japan

ALAN FROST
Reader in History
LA TROBE UNIVERSITY, MELBOURNE

ROBERT HEADLAND
Archivist and Curator
SCOTT POLAR RESEARCH INSTITUTE
UNIVERSITY OF CAMBRIDGE

CLIVE HOLLAND
Research Associate
SCOTT POLAR RESEARCH INSTITUTE
UNIVERSITY OF CAMBRIDGE

DR GENNADI LEONOV
Curator of Tibetan and Mongolian Art
THE HERMITAGE MUSEUM
LENINGRAD

CHARLES W POLZER SJ
Curator of Ethnohistory
ARIZONA STATE MUSEUM

DAVID B QUINN
Emeritus Professor of Modern History
UNIVERSITY OF LIVERPOOL

MORRIS ROSSABI
Professor of History
COLUMBIA UNIVERSITY
CITY UNIVERSITY OF NEW YORK

LOUIS DE VORSEY
Professor Emeritus of Geography
UNIVERSITY OF GEORGIA

CONTENTS

INTRODUCTION

EXPLORERS WERE IN THE FIRST WAVE – and deserve to be placed in the first rank – of the makers of the modern world. They found and reported the routes that linked once-sundered cultures and brought mutual awareness to almost all the communities that inhabit our planet. This book is an attempt to map their routes and set their work in its historical contexts.

Most path-finding was undertaken with primitive technology and at the mercy of the elements. The Atlas therefore proceeds geographically, from area to area of an unfolding world, tracing maritime routes determined by winds and currents and land routes limited by the severities of climate and the lie of the land. Late in the story – in most respects not before the end of the 19th century – new technology enabled explorers to move into new environments. The Atlas follows them to the coldest, remotest and most impenetrable regions of the globe in the awareness that the story is not over yet, and that there remain recesses of the planet, within its crust and under its seas, to be penetrated and mapped.

In this Atlas, routes are considered to have been explored if and when they find their way onto a map or are reported in a form on which maps can be based. Modern maps on which explorers' routes have been traced are shown, wherever possible, beside period maps or cartographic documents which help the reader to share the explorers' own mental images of what they explored. In consequence, *The Times Atlas of World Exploration* is in a secondary sense an atlas of the evolution of Man's world-picture.

Today, an agreed world map is a common resource of mankind. It was pieced together slowly and often painfully over a long period, mainly in the last 500 years. Previous civilizations derived their images of the world from dogmas of cosmography, from inductive reasoning, from revelation, from inherited tradition, or from the elaboration of theory. We owe ours today largely to the practical contributions – often gathered at hazard in hostile environments and reported over vast distances – of the empirical observers whom we call explorers.

Since the 15th century, the girdling of the world with routes of access and of empire has been largely a European enterprise. Yet most long-range exploration has depended on the local and regional knowledge of the unsung native heroes of earlier path-finding. It could, moreover, easily have been from any one of a number of world civilizations that the decisive initiatives in world exploration came. The Atlas accordingly opens with a survey of the achievements in exploration of these civilizations by the 15th century, the period after which Europe became the dominant power in world exploration. Whether accompanied by superior technical resources – as in China and Islam – or made in the face of technical shortcomings – as in Mesoamerica and Peru – their achievements emerge as heroic and spectacular.

The path-finders who are the subject of this Atlas were succeeded by 'scientific' explorers, who followed with geological, botanical, zoological and anthropological fieldwork. It is not possible to cover the whole range of 'exploration' in this extended sense in a single work, but some of the main landmarks are signposted in special panels interspersed throughout the Atlas. Other panels cover related topics which demand to be highlighted: the development of the technology available to explorers and the mental and moral effects of some of the new knowledge they revealed about the world – its shape, its size, and the diversity and unity of nature and of mankind.

The main coverage of the Atlas begins with a chronology. This sets the major achievements in exploration, region by region, in the broader context of world history. It ends with a glossary, which explains technical terms and provides biographies of explorers, cartographers, geographers and sponsors of exploration, and a detailed index.

Previous attempts to cover the history of world exploration comprehensively and coherently have been defeated by problems of definition and selection, by the variety and scale of the material, and by the difficulty of uniting the different disciplines needed to master the subject. This Atlas is the outcome of an approach radically new to the history of exploration but belonging to the *Times Atlas* tradition of visual presentation amplified by expert texts. It has been produced as a genuinely collaborative project in which contributors of unimpeachable scholarship have worked with cartographers of uncompromising professionalism.

Felipe Fernández-Armesto
April 1991

EUROPE	ASIA	AFRICA	REST OF THE WORLD

EUROPE

BC
c.2000
Use of sail on seagoing vessels (Aegean)

c.750
Greek city-states begin to found settlements in Black Sea and Mediterranean

early 6th century
Thales of Miletus establishes many early principles of physical geography and hydrology

c.600
Anaximander of Miletus produces the first Greek map

c.445
The History of Herodotus

c.340
Aristotle establishes basis of formal scientific and astronomical observation and enquiry and shows the world to be round.

c.310
The Greek Pytheas of Marseilles sails north from the Mediterranean, circumnavigating Britain and possibly reaching Iceland or Norway

c.240
Eratosthenes draws up map of known world, and estimates circumference, tilt and size of Earth and distance from Moon and Sun

58–49
Julius Caesar's campaigns in Gaul and Britain

AD
c.20
Strabo's *Geography*, 17-volume account of the geography and history of the known world

c.150
Ptolemy's *Geography* establishes Ptolemaic system of geography and cosmology

c.170
Guide to Greece by Pausanius, a detailed gazetteer of major cities and shrines of the Greek world

4th century
Peutinger Table, a Roman road map, published

711
Muslim invasion of Spain

793
Viking raids begin

862
Novgorod founded by Rurik the Viking; Varangian trade network to Black Sea becomes established

c.1290
Carte Pisane, oldest surviving European portolan chart

1416
Henry the Navigator founds base for explorations at Sagres; later added naval arsenal, observatory and school of navigation

1453
Ottoman Turks capture Constantinople: end of Byzantine Empire

1477
Publication of Ptolemy's *Geography* in Europe

1492
Martin Behaim's terrestrial globe shows approximate position of Eurasia and Africa

1494
Treaty of Tordesillas divides New World between Portugal and Spain

ASIA

BC
c.1200
Development of Vedic cosmographical schemes

c.800
Trading routes from China to Central Asia developed – the beginnings of the Silk Road

5th century
Publication of earliest known Chinese geography, the *Shu Ching* (Historical Classic)

325–24
Alexander commissions Nearchus to sail from the Indus to the mouth of the Tigris

1001–945
Emperor Mu undertakes his legendary travels to 'the four remote corners of the world'

510
The Persian Scylax of Caria commissioned by Darius I to navigate and report on the Indus

334
Alexander the Great (of Macedon) invades Asia Minor; conquers Egypt (332), Persia (330), reaches India (329)

c.138
Chang Ch'ien explores Central Asia; his reports include information on regions as far away as Egypt

AD
1st century
Roman links with China along the Silk Roads established

c.85
Roman contacts with Taprobane (Ceylon) established

c.250
Lodestone compass in use (China)

399–414
Fa Hsien, a Buddhist pilgrim, journeys to India, where he spends ten years

622
Hegira of Mohammed; beginning of Islamic calendar

632
Death of Mohammed: Arab expansion begins

c.800
Division of Japan into 68 provinces; first maps of Japan made from c.900

c.100
Publication of *The Periplus of the Erythraean Sea*, a Roman handbook to navigation in the Indian Ocean

c.360
Chinese merchants said to have reached the Euphrates

607
First recorded Japanese diplomatic mission to China

629–45
Hsüan Tsang journeys across Central Asia

760
Arabs adopt Indian numerals and develop algebra and trigonometry

from c.900
Development of Islamic practical geographical tradition

1154
Publication of al-Idrisi's *Kitab al-Rudjar* (Book of Roger); including a detailed world map

c.1220
Chao Ju-Kua writes *Chu Fan Chih*, an account of the South China Sea

1253
William of Rubruck reaches Karakorum

1325–49
Travels of Ibn Battuta to Africa, the Near and Middle East, Central Asia, India, Ceylon and China

1405–33
Cheng Ho undertakes seven state-sponsored voyages, visiting 30 countries around the Indian Ocean

1206
Mongols under Genghis Khan begin conquest of Asia; the 'Mongol Peace' later permits unhindered travel along the Silk Road

1246
John of Piano Carpini almost reaches Mongol capital, Karakorum

1275
Marco Polo arrives in China; he returns to Europe in 1295

1341
Mission of John of Marignolli to Peking

1414–37
Niccolò de Conti travels across the Indian Ocean, possibly as far as present-day Vietnam

1487–90
Pero de Covilhão travels across the Indian Ocean

1498
Vasco da Gama enters the Indian Ocean and reaches India

AFRICA

BC
c.3500
Invention of wheel and sail (Egypt)

c.600
Legendary Phoenician circumnavigation of Africa, sponsored by the Pharaoh Necho

480
Hanno, from Carthage, said to have sailed south along the Atlantic coast of Morocco founding settlements and possibly reaching as far as present-day Sierra Leone

AD
42
Seutonius Paulinus, later Governor of Britain, crosses the Atlas Mountains to the River Ger

44
Mauretania (Morocco) annexed by Rome

641
Arabs conquer Egypt and begin conquest of North Africa

c.1330
Portuguese and Spanish discoveries of Azores, Canaries and Madeira begin

1375
Catalan Atlas includes map of West Africa

1434
Portuguese voyages along the west coast of Africa, sponsored by Henry the Navigator, begin

1469–75
Voyages of Fernão Gomes

1482–85
Voyages of Diogo Cão

1487
Bartolomeu Dias rounds Cape of Good Hope

1493–94
Pero de Covilhão penetrates Ethiopia

1497
Vasco da Gama rounds Cape of Good Hope

REST OF THE WORLD

BC
c.4000
Settlement of Melanesia by immigrants from Indonesia begins

c.1500
Settlers of Melanesia reach Fiji, later spreading to western Polynesia

AD
c.300
Settlement of eastern Polynesia (Marquesas)

c.400
Settlement of Easter Island

c.600
Settlement of Society Islands (Tahiti) and Hawaiian Islands

c.750
Settlement of New Zealand by Polynesians

c.1000
Vikings colonize Greenland and discover Markland, Helluland and Vinland

c.1100
Migration of the Mexica-Aztecs begins

1325
Rise of Aztecs in Mexico: Tenochtitlán founded

c.1400
Expansion of Inca Empire (Peru)

1492–93
Columbus's first Atlantic voyage

1493–96
Columbus' second Atlantic voyage

1497
John Cabot reaches Newfoundland

1498–1500
Columbus's third Atlantic voyage

EUROPE	ASIA	AFRICA	AMERICAS		REST OF THE WORLD
			1500 Pinzón's voyage to Brazil. Cabral secures Brazil for Portugal. Gaspar Corte-Real's voyage to Newfoundland. La Cosa world map (now lost), the first to show the New World	**1501** Coelho and Vespucci coast south from Cape São Agostinho	
			1501–2 Voyage of Bastidas and La Cosa	**1502** Contarini map: oldest surviving map of the New World	
	1509 First Portuguese voyage to Malacca	**1505** Portuguese establish trading posts in East Africa	**1502–4** Columbus's fourth Atlantic voyage	**1508** Voyage of Pinzón and Solís	
	1512–13 Abreu and Rodrigues launch expedition to the Moluccas	**1511–16** António Fernandes explores Monomotapa			
	c.**1514** First Portuguese reach China		**1513** Ponce de León explores coast of Florida; Gulf Stream discovered. Balboa crosses the isthmus of Darien to the Pacific		**1514** First Spanish voyages in the Pacific
	1515–16 Tomé Pires reaches China and attempts to establish diplomatic relations		**1517** Hernández de Córdoba explores north and west coasts of Yucatán	**1516** Solís enters River Plate estuary	
1520 Johann Schöner's map of the world in two hemispheres			**1519** Hernán Cortés begins conquest of Aztec Empire. Pineda explores north and west coasts of Gulf of Mexico	**1518** Grijalva follows south and west coasts of Gulf of Mexico	
	1521 Magellan reaches the Moluccas			**1520** Magellan discovers the Strait named after him and enters the Pacific	**1520–21** Magellan makes the first crossing of the Pacific
1522 Return of *Victoria*, Magellan's flagship, to complete first circumnavigation					**1522** Voyage of Andagoya towards Peru
c.**1525** Introduction of potato from South America to Europe			**1524** Verazzano traces east coast of North America. Spanish conquests of Guatemala, Honduras and Nicaragua.		
				1526–29 Sebastian Cabot's exploration of River Plate region	**1527** Álvaro de Saavedra makes first crossing of Pacific from New Spain
			1528–36 Narváez's expedition to Florida and Alvar Nuñez's march from the Mississippi to Mexico	**1530** Expeditions of Alfinger and Federmann in Lake Maracaibo region	
			1531 Diego de Ordas's expedition to the Orinoco	**1531–35** Francisco Pizarro's conquest of Peru	
			1533–34 Benalcázar's conquest of Quito	**1534–35** Cartier explores Strait of Belle Isle and St. Lawrence	
			1535 Alonso de Herrera reaches Meta rapids. Almagro's march to Chile	**1536** Pedro de Mendoza's expedition to River Plate	
			1536–37 Gonzalo Jimémez de Quesada's expedition to Bogotá	**1536–38** Hohermuth's expedition to the Llanos	
			1537 Francisco César's expedition to Antioquia. Foundation of Asunción	**1537–39** Federmann's expedition to Bogotá	
			1538–39 Benalcázar's expedition to Bogotá; El Dorado myth begins	**1538–43** Hernando de Soto's wanderings in North America	
			1540 Valdivia's invasion of Chile	**1541** Coronado's expedition to Kansas	
		1541 João de Castro compiles guide to the Red Sea	**1541–42** Alvar Núñez's march to Asunción	**1541–46** Hutten's expedition in the Llanos region	
1543 Copernicus publishes *Of the Revolution of Celestial Bodies*	**1543** Portuguese reach Japan		**1542** Orellana's navigation of the Amazon	**1543** Expedition of Rojas Gutiérrez and Mendoza to Tucumán	**1542** Jean Rotz draws his World Chart, on which Australia may be represented (Java-la-Grande)
		1546 Destruction of Mali Empire by Songhay	**1545** Discovery of silver mines in Peru and Mexico	**1548** Members of Irala's expedition reach Peru from Paraguay	
	1557 Portuguese established at Macao (China)		**1553** Gonzalo Hurtado de Mendoza arrives in Chile		**1553–54** Willoughby and Chancellor initiate a search for Northeast Passage
					1565 Andrés de Urdaneta pioneers a viable return route from the Philippines to New Spain across the northern Pacific
				1566 Martín de Póveda's march from Chachapoyas to Bogotá	**1568** Álvaro de Mendaña discovers the Solomon Islands
1570 *Theatrum Orbis Terrarum* published by Ortelius; first world atlas on Ptolemaic principles. Invention of plane table for mapping	**1571** Spanish conquer Philippines; Manila founded	**1571** Portuguese create colony in Angola	**1574–81** Journeys of Quadramito and Mendo in southern Chile		
	1576 Observatory in Byzantium built	**1576** Luanda founded by Portuguese		**1576–78** Frobisher reaches Frobisher Bay in Baffin Island,	
	1581–82 Yermak begins Russian conquest of Siberia	**1578** Battle of Al Kasr al Kabir: Moroccans destroy Portuguese power in north-western Africa	**1579** Francis Drake founds New Albion in California. De Gamboa's survey of southern Chilean islands	**1584–93** Antonio de Berrio's explorations of Orinoco basin	
			1585–87 Davis's search for Northwest Passage		**1595** Mendaña and Pedro Fernández Quirós discover the Marquesas and Santa Cruz Islands
1595 Mercator publishes *Atlas Sive Cosmographicae*	**1595** Dutch begin to trade in East Indies and Sunda Islands		**1598** Expedition of Juan de Oñate between the Pacific and the plains		**1596–97** Barents discovers Bear Island and Spitsbergen and winters in Novaya Zemlya

EUROPE	ASIA	AFRICA	AMERICAS	AUSTRALASIA & OCEANIA	POLAR REGIONS
1600 Foundation of English and Dutch (1602) East India Companies. Publication of Gilbert's *De Magnete*, analysing electric, natural and terrestrial magnetism	**1601** First voyage of East India Company ships under Lancaster				
	1602 Dutch East India Company ejects Portuguese from Moluccas		**1603–35** Journeys of Samuel de Champlain		
			1605 French settlement in Nova Scotia	**1605** Quirós discovers Espiritu Santo and believes it is the unknown southern continent	
			1607 First permanent English settlement in America (Jamestown, Virginia)	**1606** Willem Jansz discovers the Gulf of Carpentaria and makes the first known landing by Europeans on Australia, on the western side of Cape York. Luis Váez Torres sails through the Torres Strait	
			1608 Samuel de Champlain founds Quebec		
1609 Telescope invented (Holland)					
1609–19 Publication of Kepler's laws of planetary motions					
c.1610 Galileo (1564–1642), Descartes (1596–1650), major advances in astronomy, cosmology and physics	**1611** Hendrik Brouwer initiates southerly route across the Indian Ocean to Bantam		**1610** Hudson sails through Hudson Strait to the southern extremity of Hudson Bay, which he and others take to be the Pacific		**1611** Spitsbergen becomes the base for new European whaling industry in the Arctic
			1612–13 Button explores west coast of Hudson Bay and concludes it landlocked on the west		
1615 Invention of triangulation	**1614** First English trading settlement in India founded at Surat	**1613** Fr. António Fernandes explores Ethiopia	**1616** Bylot and Baffin sail through Davis Strait	**1616** Willem Schouten and Isaac Le Maire discover Cape Horn	
	1619 Foundation of Batavia (Jakarta) by Dutch: start of Dutch colonial empire in East Indies	**1618** Pedro Paez reaches the source of the Blue Nile	**1620** Puritans land in New England (*Mayflower*)	**1619** Frederik de Houtman sights the western coast of Australia in c.33°S latitude, and follows it north to c.27°S latitude	
1625 Colonial Office established in London	**1624** Dutch traders established in Formosa		**1624** Dutch found New Amsterdam (New York)	**1627** Frans Thyssen and Pieter Nuyts chart parts of the south-western coast of New Holland (Australia)	
1643 Toricelli invents the barometer	**1641** Dutch capture Malacca from Portuguese		**1637–39** Fr. Domingo de Brieva and companions navigate Amazon in both directions	**1642–43** Abel Tasman circumnavigates New Holland, discovering and taking possession of parts of Tasmania, New Zealand and some of the Fijian and Tongan islands	
	1648 Semen Dezhnev sails through Bering Strait without realising the proximity of North America		**1647** Miguel de Ochogavia's navigation of the Orinoco	**1644** Tasman charts the northern coasts of New Holland from the Gulf of Carpentaria to North West Cape, showing it to be one landmass	
1650 Publication of *Geographia Generalis* by Varenius, the first modern standard geographical textbook	**1649** Russians reach Pacific coast and found Okhotsk		**1650** Amazon expedition of Antônio Rapôso		
c.1650 Huygens develops theory of centrifugal force and satellite motion; invention of pendulum motion for clocks		**1652** Foundation of Cape Colony by Dutch			
1662 Royal Society founded in London and (1666) Académie Française in Paris	**1661** Jesuits John Grueber and Albert d'Orville reach Lhasa from China	**1659** French found trading station on Senegal coast	**1663** Antonio de Monteverde's navigation of the Orinoco		
1664 French East India Company founded			**1664** New Amsterdam taken by British from Dutch		
			1667–69 Juan Álvarez Maldonado's journey in Manú valley		
			1670 Hudson's Bay Company formed by Prince Rupert		
1671 Newton constructs reflecting telescope			**1673** Marquette sails down the Wisconsin River and part of the Mississippi		
1675 Royal Observatory established at Greenwich			**1678** Louis Hennepin is the first to see and describe the Niagara Falls		
1679 Newton's calculations of the lunar orbit			**1682** La Salle explores Mississippi and claims Louisiana for France		
1687 Publication of Newton's *Principia Mathematica*, outlining the mathematical principles of natural philosophy, including dynamics and the laws of motion				**1688** William Dampier visits the north-west coast of New Holland, and is the first Englishman to give a detailed account of the land and its people	
1689 Halley's chart of tradewinds published	**1689** Treaty of Nerchinsk establishes spheres of influence in Central Asia between Russia and China				
	1690 English found Calcutta				
1693 Halley composes first scientific astronomical tables	**1697** Chinese occupy Outer Mongolia		**1693** Gold discovered in Brazil	**1699** Dampier explores more of the west and north-west coasts of New Holland	**late 17th century** Mapping of Spitsbergen by European whalers largely complete

EUROPE	ASIA	AFRICA	AMERICAS	AUSTRALASIA & OCEANIA	POLAR REGIONS
1702 Halley publishes chart of tides in the English Channel 1704 Publication of Newton's *Opticks*					
			1718 New Orleans founded by the French 1720–22 Pierre François Xavier de Charlevoix travels up the St. Lawrence to the Illinois river 1724–29 Great Survey of Rivera and Barreiro	1721–22 Jacob Roggeveen discovers Easter Island and some of the Samoan group	
	1728 Vitus Bering sails through the Bering Strait 1733–42 Great Northern Expedition under Vitus Bering makes detailed surveys of north coast of Russia and Siberia		1731–44 La Vérendrye discovers Manitoba and the Dakotas 1735 Departure of La Condamine's scientific expedition to Peru 1742 Antonio de Lima opens new route from Mato Grosso to River Madeira. João de Sousa traces course of River Tapajós. Journeys of the brothers Vérendrye		1738–39 Bouvet de Lozier probes fringe of Antarctic pack-ice
1735–44 Measurement of arc of meridian variously attempted by Maupertius, Clairaut and Camus					
1752 Publication of French chart of English Channel with isobaths	1751 China overruns Tibet, Dzungaria and Tarim Basin (1756–59) 1751 French gain control of Deccan and Carnatic 1757 Battle of Plassey: British defeat French 1761 Capture of Pondicherry: British end French power in India		1760 New France conquered by British: Quebec (1759) and Montreal (1760)		
1762 Harrison's chronometer, enabling more accurate calculation of longitude				1764 John Byron crosses the Pacific 1766–68 Samuel Wallis discovers the Society Islands (Tahiti); Carteret sails farther south in the Pacific than any European before him and finds no hint of Terra Australis 1768 Louis Antoine de Bougainville reaches Tahiti 1768–71 James Cook sails into the Pacific, observes the Transit of Venus at Tahiti, charts the coast of New Zealand, discovers and charts the eastern coast of New Holland and confirms the existence of Torres Strait	
1771 Publication of French land-map showing contours			1766–68 Surveying expeditions of Rubí and La Fora		
		1772 James Bruce rediscovers the source of the Blue Nile		1772–75 Cook makes a circuit of the southern oceans in high latitudes, ending the hope of a habitable southern continent. He discovers or re-discovers many islands in the Pacific, including the Marquesas, the New Hebrides, New Caledonia and Norfolk Island 1778–79 Cook, Charles Clerke and James King discover the Sandwich Islands (Hawaii), explore the north-west coast of North America from Vancouver Island to Unimak Pass, sail through Bering Strait to the edge of the pack-ice, and coast north-eastern Asia; January 1779, death of Cook in Hawaii	1772–75 Cook makes first crossing of Antarctic Circle
			1776 American Declaration of Independence		
1784 First American commercial expedition to China					
1785 First aerial voyages by hot-air and hydrogen balloons 1787 Patrick Miller invents steamboat				1785–88 La Pérouse sails the Pacific; his ships are wrecked on the reefs of Vanikoro 1788 Arthur Phillip transports 759 convicts to New South Wales to found a colony at Sydney	
		1788 The African Association formed in London to pioneer the methodical exploration of the continent		1789–95 Alejandro Malaspina sails to the Pacific on an extensive voyage of surveying, collection and reporting	1790s US and British sealers begin to visit sub-Antarctic islands
1792–98 Measurements of arc of meridian in France to obtain length of the metre: origin of metric system	1796 British conquer Ceylon 1798 Napoleon invades Egypt and Palestine and initiates first comprehensive attempts to map both regions	1796 Mungo Park reaches Niger 1798 Hornemann reaches Murzuk	1791–95 George Vancouver undertakes an extensive survey of the north-west coast of America; 1791, discovers Snake Island 1799–1804 Alexander von Humboldt and Bonplaid's voyages from the mouth of the Orinoco to Bogotá and Quito	1798 Bass and Matthew Flinders circumnavigate Tasmania, showing it to be an island	

EUROPE

1807
Abolition of slave trade by Britain

1830
Foundation of Royal Geographical Society in London

1833
Slavery abolished in British Empire

1845–48
Publication of *Physikalischer Atlas*, the most comprehensive early example of a physical geography illustrated by thematic maps

1848
Slavery abolished in French colonies

1850
First use of camera for mapping from tall buildings, kites and balloons (France)

1858
Nadar obtains first photographs from hot-air balloons

1859
Darwin publishes *The Origin of Species*

1862
Completion of Humboldt's *Kosmos*

1876
King Leopold's Brussels Geographical Conference begins partition of Africa

1887
Imperial British East Africa Company founded

1895
First publication of *The Times Atlas*

ASIA

1802
Trigonometrical survey of India begun under William Lambton

1809
Ulrich Seetzen visits Mecca

1815
Johann Burckhardt penetrates Mecca

1846
French monks Evarist Huc and Joseph Gabet make brief visit to Lhasa

1853
First railway and telegraph lines in India

1854–62
Wallace undertakes detailed investigation of the Malay Archipelago

1862–63
William Palgrave explores eastern and central Arabia

1865–66
Nain Sinh sent to Tibet by Great Trigonometrical Survey

1866–68
French Mekong River Expedition

1870–74
Nikolai Przhevalsky makes first of five scientific and geographical expeditions of Central Asia

1899
Gombozhab Tsybikov penetrates Tibet

AFRICA

1823–24
Denham and Clapperton reach Lake Chad

1826
Laing reaches Timbuktu but dies

1828
Caillié reaches Timbuktu

1830
The Lander brothers discover the mouths of the River Niger

from 1835
'Great Trek' of Boer colonists from Cape, leading to foundation of Transvaal (1852) and Orange Free State (1854)

1849
David Livingstone reaches Lake Ngami

1851
Heinrich Barth reaches Lake Chad

1853–56
Livingstone crosses Africa, discovers Victoria Falls (1855)

1858
Burton and Speke discover Lake Tanganyika; Speke discovers Lake Victoria

1859
Livingstone discovers Lake Nyasa

1862
Speke reaches source of the Nile

1869–75
Gustav Nachtigal travels across the Sahara

1871
Livingstone meets Stanley at Ujiji

1873
Livingstone dies. Cameron crosses Africa from east to west;

1875
Stanley circumnavigates Lake Victoria; confirms source of Nile

1876–77
Stanley travels down the Congo to the Atlantic

1883–84
Joseph Thomson travels from Mombasa to Lake Victoria

1888
Teleki discovers Lake Rudolf

AMERICAS

1804–6
Lewis and Clark lead their Corps of Discovery from St. Louis to the Pacific

1807–11
David Thompson makes the first overland journey to the Pacific coast

1826–27
Jedediah Strong Smith makes the first crossing of the Sierra Nevada

1831
Robert Fitzroy explores Patagonia and Tierra del Fuego

1837
Tebenkov's *Atlas of Alaska*

1840
The Geological Survey of Canada established

1842
John Charles Frémont's first expedition to the Far West

1853
Trans-continental railway surveys begin

1867–68
US Geological survey established

1869
First trans-continental railroad completed (U.S.)

1890
Foundation of National Geographical Society in Washington D.C.

1895
Development of instruments for measuring on stereoscopic aerial photography

AUSTRALASIA & OCEANIA

1800–3
Baudin and Flinders chart the Australian coast

1813
Blaxland, Lawson and Wentworth cross the Blue Mountains

1817–22
Phillip Parker King explores the Australian coast on five voyages

1823
Oxley surveys coast from the Brisbane River to Port Curtis

1824
Hamilton Hume and William Hovell travel south from Lake George to Port Phillip

1828–30
Charles Sturt traces sections of the Macquarie, Darling, Murrumbidgee, Lachlan and Murray Rivers

1831–36
Thomas Mitchell discovers 'Australia Felix'

1837–39
George Grey explores coastline between Perth and Shark Bay

1840
The British annex New Zealand (Treaty of Waitangi)

1841
Edward Eyre crosses the Nullarbor Plain

1845–46
Mitchell discovers sections of the Warrego, Belyando and Barcoo Rivers

1847–48
Edmund Kennedy traces the Barcoo to its junction with the Thompson river, then travels from Rockingham Bay up to Cape York

1855–56
Augustus Gregory traces the Victoria River, and crosses to the east coast at Port Curtis

1858–62
Stuart becomes the first to cross the continent from south to north

1860–61
Robert Burke leads an expedition to cross Australia from south to north. Of the four who press up from Cooper's Creek, only one survives

1872–76
Giles explores the desert areas of central and western Australia

1873
Peter Warburton goes from Alice Springs to the western coast at the Oakover River

1879
Alexander Forrest explores from Port Hedland north to the Fitzroy river, then east to the Overland Telegraph line at Birdum

POLAR REGIONS

1819–20
Parry discovers entrance to Northwest Passage (Lancaster Sound)

1819–21
Bellingshausen circumnavigates Antarctica

1823
Weddell explores Weddell Sea

1839–43
James Ross explores Ross Sea, Ross Ice Shelf and Victoria Land, Antarctica

1845–48
Franklin expedition disappears off King William Island

1847–59
Over 20 expeditions search for Franklin and discover much of Canadian Arctic archipelago

1850–54
McClure establishes existence of Northwest Passage

1872–74
Weyprecht and Payer discover Zemlya Frantsa-Iosifa (Franz Josef Land)

1878–79
Nordenskiöld completes first navigation of Northeast Passage

1888
Nansen makes first crossing of Greenland

1897
de Gerlache explores Antarctic Peninsula and is first to winter in Antarctica

EUROPE	ASIA	AFRICA	AMERICAS	AUSTRALASIA & OCEANIA	POLAR REGIONS
					1900 Cagni attempts to reach North Pole; reaches record 86°34'N
					1901–4 Scott's first Antarctic expedition; he reaches 82°17'S
			1903 First successful flight of petrol-powered aircraft (Wright Brothers)		**1903–6** Amundsen completes first successful navigation of Northwest Passage
	1904 British expedition under Francis Younghusband establishes British influence in Tibet				**1907–9** Shackleton's first Antarctic expedition; he reaches 88°23'S
					1908 Frederick Cook claims to reach North Pole (21 April)
1908 Development of instruments for mechanically plotting from aerial photography					**1909** Peary claims to reach North Pole (6 April)
					1910–12 Amundsen reaches South Pole (14 December 1911)
					1910–13 Scott's second Antarctic expedition; he reaches South Pole (17 January 1912); party dies during return
					1911–14 Mawson's Australasian Antarctic Expedition.
1914 Outbreak of First World War; development of photo interpretation and cameras able to take photographs with constant overlap, development of submarine echo-sounding (later developed into sonar); development of radio	**1914** German concessions in China and Colonies in Pacific taken over by Japan, Australia and New Zealand	**1914–15** British and French conquer German colonies, except German East Africa			**1914–17** Shackleton's second Antarctic expedition; his ship *Endurance* sinks in Weddell Sea.
					1929–31 Mawson explores Mac Robertson Land
	1930–31 Bertram Thomas crosses the Empty Quarter of Arabia				**1930–32** Ushakov's expedition explores Severnaya Zemlya (Russian Arctic)
					1932 Schmidt on the *Sibiryakov* makes first one-season voyage through Northeast Passage
		1935 Italy invades Ethiopia			**1935** Ellsworth makes first flight across Antarctica
					1937 First ice station established (*North Pole 1*, USSR)
	1941–45 War in East Asia leads to defeat of Japan, and dismemberment of Japanese empire	**1940–43** Desert wars leading to expulsion of Axis forces from North Africa by Allied troops	**1939–45** Aerial photography used for mapping inaccessible terrain	**1941–45** War in the Pacific leads to acquisition of detailed geographical knowledge of many island groups	
			1946 First electronic computer built; development of computerized photogrammetry (1960–70) and electronic distance measuring (1960–70), replacing triangulation		
1950 Publication of *Morskoi Atlas* (USSR), the first detailed atlas of the oceans and seas					**1952–53** First US ice station established in Arctic (*T-3*)
		1954–62 Nationalist revolt in Algeria			**1955–58** Fuchs and Hillary make first surface crossing of Antarctica
1957 USSR launches first satellite (Sputnik)		**1957** Beginning of decolonization of sub-Saharan Africa, Gold Coast (Ghana) becomes independent			**1957–58** International Geophysical Year.
1958 First accurate determination of flattening of Earth at Poles (UK)					**1958** USS *Nautilus* crosses beneath Arctic ice-cap
1959–60 First photographs of far side of Moon (USSR)			**1960** First World Geodetic System, permitting unification of surveys and mapping	**1960** Bathyscape *Trieste* reaches deepest ocean bed, in Marianas Trench	
1961 First man in space: Gagarin (USSR)			**1960–69** Photographic exploration of Moon by Ranger Surveyor Orbiter satellites		**1961** Antarctic Treaty introduced to preserve Antarctica for peaceful scientific research, signed originally by 12 nations, many others have since acceded
			1965 Mariner probe transmits data from Mars		
			1966 Second World Geodetic System, making use of satellite photography		
1967 Publication of *The Times Atlas of the World* (comprehensive edition)			**1969** First man lands on moon: Armstrong		
			1972 Earth Resources Technology Satellite (renamed Landsat) launched		
			1981 First re-usable Space Shuttle flight		**1977** Soviet ice-breaker *Arktika* reaches North Pole
1986 Launch of world's first permanently manned space station (USSR)					
1986 European Space Agency's SPOT satellite launched					
1987 Development of satellite geodesy			**1987** Development of satellite geodesy replacing traditional methods of surveying		
	1990–91 Gulf crises; UN coalition forces liberate Kuwait from Iraqi occupation, using high-quality satellite data and aerial reconnaissance imagery, and advanced direction finding, target positioning and detection technology		**1990** *Voyager* unmanned space probe mission completed; last planetary encounter (Neptune). Development of hand-held position finders		

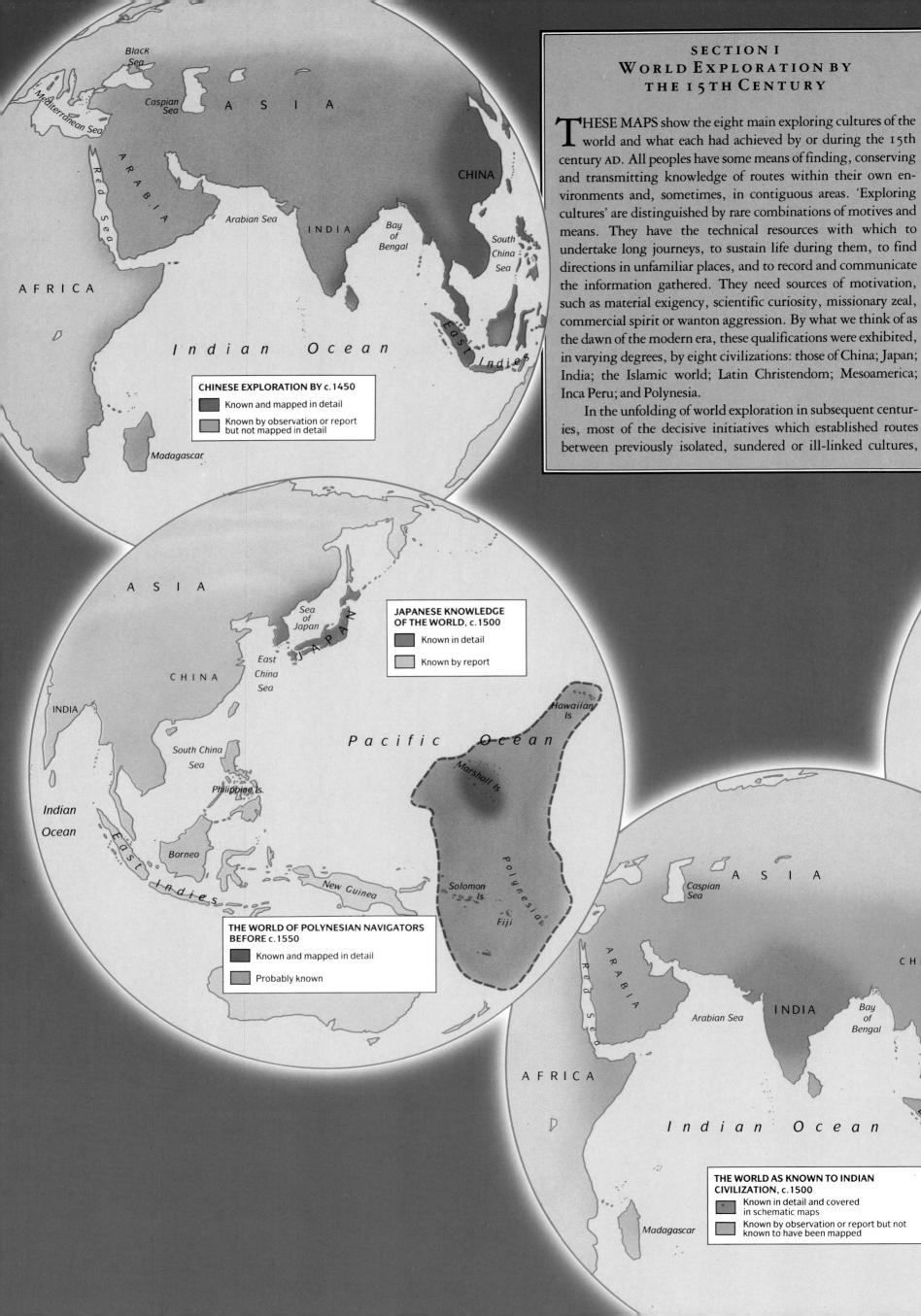

THESE MAPS show the eight main exploring cultures of the world and what each had achieved by or during the 15th century AD. All peoples have some means of finding, conserving and transmitting knowledge of routes within their own environments and, sometimes, in contiguous areas. 'Exploring cultures' are distinguished by rare combinations of motives and means. They have the technical resources with which to undertake long journeys, to sustain life during them, to find directions in unfamiliar places, and to record and communicate the information gathered. They need sources of motivation, such as material exigency, scientific curiosity, missionary zeal, commercial spirit or wanton aggression. By what we think of as the dawn of the modern era, these qualifications were exhibited, in varying degrees, by eight civilizations: those of China; Japan; India; the Islamic world; Latin Christendom; Mesoamerica; Inca Peru; and Polynesia.

In the unfolding of world exploration in subsequent centuries, most of the decisive initiatives which established routes between previously isolated, sundered or ill-linked cultures,

CHINESE EXPLORATION BY c.1450

　Known and mapped in detail

　Known by observation or report but not mapped in detail

JAPANESE KNOWLEDGE OF THE WORLD, c.1500

　Known in detail

　Known by report

THE WORLD OF POLYNESIAN NAVIGATORS BEFORE c.1550

　Known and mapped in detail

　Probably known

THE WORLD AS KNOWN TO INDIAN CIVILIZATION, c.1500

　Known in detail and covered in schematic maps

　Known by observation or report but not known to have been mapped

and which built up the world-map familiar today, came from Latin Christendom or its colonies. It was not an outcome that could have been foreseen at the start, when the Chinese seemed to be best equipped for a world-exploring role. Their practical achievements in exploration exceeded those of all rivals.

Some of these rivals were almost equally well-equipped. Transport of similar quality and many of the same direction-finding techniques were available in India and in Islam; Islam had the additional advantage, shared with Christendom, of access to the Graeco-Roman legacy of geographical knowledge. The Japanese seem to have been inhibited more by lack of curiosity than of means. Other cultures were subject to grave technical limitations: in Mesoamerica there was no means of long-range navigation, in Peru, no maps; the Polynesians, surrounded by the vast Pacific, may have attained the limits of the world accessible to them with the technology at their disposal. Yet the record of these societies shows how much can be achieved in defiance of technical insufficiency. At a crucial time, Latin Christendom was to develop a unique combination of exploring impetus and technical prowess that enabled its explorers rapidly to catch up with and surpass the achievements of their counterparts elsewhere.

I

MESOAMERICA, c.1500
- Known and mapped in detail by the Aztecs
- Known by observation or report but not known to have been mapped

ISLAMIC KNOWLEDGE OF THE WORLD BY c.1500
- Well-established heartlands of Islam
- Known by observation or report

THE INCA WORLD, c.1510
- Known in detail and linked by paved roads
- Probably known by observation or report but not reached by the road-system

EXPLORATION FROM LATIN CHRISTENDOM BY 1492
- Known and mapped in detail
- Known by observation or report

1
CHINA
C. 1700 BC – AD 1443

TO A UNIQUE *degree, the internal exploration of China appears to have been a deliberate and self-conscious activity. Prehistoric man in China seems to have been a restless and prodigious explorer. There is general agreement that Neolithic cultures evolved in the forested valleys of northern China and along the flood plains of the Yellow River between the fourth and second millennia* BC. *These cultures subsequently expanded north and west through present-day Kansu Province as far as Sinkiang in Chinese Turkestan and east through present-day Honan Province to Shantung on the Yellow Sea.*

From around 1700 BC, *with the development of the Chinese Bronze Age and the rise of the powerful and centralizing Shang dynasty, the colonization of much of the rest of modern China followed. With further population growth in the ancient heartland of China – Szechwan and the more northern provinces – new settlements were established to the east and south.*

The settlement of the Yangtze Delta and the Pearl River on the southern maritime frontier was a gradual process of exploration undertaken both by ordinary farmers and state-sponsored military expeditions that lasted more then 1,500 *years. The development of a more rigid state system and the unification in turn of various warring principalities into an imperial order were underpinned above all by the economic pull stemming from sophisticated urban consumption and demand.*

A

A LEFT *Hsüan Tsang shown on his 7th-century pilgrimage to India, from a 10th-century coloured woodcut. In his left hand he holds a fly-whisk to drive away demons, in his right the* khakkhara, *the symbol of a Buddhist monk; he carries sacred texts on his back. An image of Buddha watches over him.* B BELOW *Priests, officials and prostrating figures observe the return of Hsüan Tsang to China. The monk was said to have returned with 75 Buddhist texts; here, pack horses carrying them are led into a temple. The black-clad figures on the right are carrying gifts.*

B

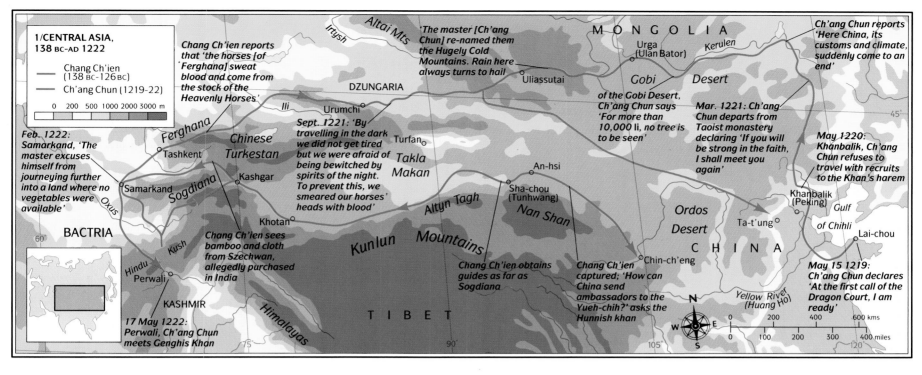

1/CENTRAL ASIA,
138 BC-1222

1/CENTRAL ASIA, 138 BC-1222

Chang Ch'ien (138 BC-126 BC)
Ch'ang Chun (1219-22)

0 200 500 1000 2000 3000 m

Chang Ch'ien reports that 'the horses [of Ferghana] sweat blood and come from the stock of the Heavenly Horses'

'The master [Ch'ang Chun] re-named them the Hugely Cold Mountains. Rain here always turns to hail

MONGOLIA

Urga (Ulan Bator)   Kerulen

Uliassutai

Gobi   Desert

Ch'ang Chun reports 'Here China, its customs and climate, suddenly come to an end'

Irtysh   Altai Mts

DZUNGARIA

Ili   Urumchi

Feb. 1222: Samarkand, 'The master excuses himself from journeying further into a land where no vegetables were available'

Ferghana   Chinese Turkestan

Tashkent

Kashgar

Samarkand   Sogdiana   Oxus

BACTRIA

Hindu   Kush   Perwali

KASHMIR

17 May 1222: Perwali, Ch'ang Chun meets Genghis Khan

Himalayas

Khotan

Sept. 1221: 'By travelling in the dark we did not get tired but we were afraid of being bewitched by spirits of the night. To prevent this, we smeared our horses' heads with blood'

Turfan

Takla Makan

Chang Ch'ien sees bamboo and cloth from Szechwan, allegedly purchased in India

Altyn Tagh

Kunlun   Mountains

T I B E T

of the Gobi Desert, Ch'ang Chun says 'For more than 10,000 li, no tree is to be seen'

An-hsi

Sha-chou (Tunhwang)   Nan Shan

Chang Ch'ien obtains guides as far as Sogdiana

Chang Ch'ien captured; 'How can China send ambassadors to the Yueh-chih?' asks the Hunnish khan

Mar. 1221: Ch'ang Chun departs from Taoist monastery declaring 'If you will be strong in the faith, I shall meet you again'

Ordos Desert

Ta-t'ung

Chin-ch'eng

C H I N A

Yellow River (Huang Ho)

May 1220: Khanbalik, Ch'ang Chun refuses to travel with recruits to the Khan's harem

Khanbalik (Peking)   Gulf of Chihli

Lai-chou

May 15 1219: Ch'ang Chun declares 'At the first call of the Dragon Court, I am ready'

0 200 400 600 kms
0 100 200 300 400 miles

A T ANY rate until the 15th century AD, the Chinese were accomplished and successful explorers of the wider world. Exploration of Central Asia is said to have begun with the mission to Bactria of Chang Ch'ien in 138 BC. He was sent as the Emperor's ambassador to seek allies against the nomadic Hsiung-nu, the Huns. Captured en route, he remained a prisoner for ten years before escaping to continue his task, crossing the Pamir Mountains and the River Oxus, only to be rebuffed by the barbarians. He returned via Tibet, again eluding captors, after an absence of 12 years.

His report, which included information on Central Asia and the Middle East perhaps as far away as Egypt, stimulated imperial missions in all directions, including an unsuccessful attempt to find a way to Bactria around Hunnish territory. In the same period, it was recorded that, 'specimens of strange things began to arrive from every direction'. The trade routes Chang Ch'ien discovered became melded into a continuous 'Silk Road', with caravans journeying from China to Persia from 106 BC. From the 1st century AD, having overcome Parthian hostility, Chinese traders opened direct commerce with Roman Syria.

Exploration along Central Asian routes was not pressed

1 ABOVE *Chang Ch'ien in the 2nd century BC and Ch'ang Chun 1,400 years later were both engaged in missions to nomadic masters of the Asiatic Steppelands. For mounted travellers, the routes were easy to follow but only when the insecurities of Steppeland politics permitted. Whereas Chang Ch'ien was twice imprisoned by the Huns, Ch'ang Chun travelled the breadth of the steppes under Mongol escort.*
C BELOW *A 7th-century fresco from the Ch'ien-fo-tung cave-temples near Tunhwang in western China illustrates the peaceful nature of long-distance travel in a well-regulated empire.*

C

further until the 13th century, when Mongol conquests brought much of the length of the Silk Roads under unified political control (*see* ch.31). In 1219 Genghis Khan ordered Ch'ang Chun, a Taoist sage then already 71 years old, whose 'long years in the caverns of the rocks' had brought a reputation for sanctity and enlightenment, to report on Central Asia. With an escort of 20 Mongols and 19 disciples, he set out in fear of his life but successfully completed an arduous journey from the Chinese border into the depths of Afghanistan in 14 months, including four months spent in winter quarters in Samarkand before returning. Chinese members of the Khan's entourage were able to go even farther and to transmit home first-hand accounts of Persia. The conditions of peace which Mongol conquest brought to the Steppeland highways to the West made possible the Jerusalem pilgrimage of Rabban Sauma, a Nestorian Christian of Peking, in c.1280. In the service of the Mongol Khan Arghun, he continued on to various Western courts but was never able to return to China.

In the direction of India – though there were trading contacts at least from the time of Chang Ch'ien in the 2nd century BC, and diplomatic exchanges with the Kushans towards the end of the 1st century AD – exploration was dominated by

Buddhist monks. The first recorded pilgrimage was that of Fa Hsien, who set out from the valley of the Yellow River in AD 399. His long route, skirting the great mountains of Central Asia to the north, set a pattern for later travellers. He crossed the Gobi Desert to the Tien Shan mountains before turning south to Khotan in eastern Turkestan. He reached Peshawar across the Hindu Kush after a journey lasting three years. During the ten years he spent in India he crossed the entire subcontinent and visited Ceylon before returning to Tsung-chou by sea in 414.

The golden age of such pilgrimages was in the late 7th century, when I Ching, who in 671 made his own pilgrimage by sea from Canton in a Persian ship, recorded 56 journeys: half went overland, some by Fa Hsien's route; others through Tibet and Nepal. Their spirit is best exemplified by Hsüan Tsang, the pioneer who, in 629, began 16 years of travel 'not for riches or for worldly profit or fame but only for the sake of religious truth'. His journey was vividly recounted by his disciple, Hui-li, whose account of the Gobi Desert suggests the problems of direction-finding in a trackless environment. 'Alone and abandoned he traversed the sandy waste, with no means of finding his way except by following the heaps of bones and the horse-dung … In all four directions the expanse was boundless. No trace was there of man or horse and in the night the demons and goblins raised fire-lights to confound the stars'. Fortified by the conviction that 'it is better to die in the attempt to go to the West than to live by returning to the East' Hsüan Tsang entered India over the Tien Shan and the Hindu Kush Mountains and spent two years of spiritual preparation in Kashmir before following the course of the Ganges from monastery to monastery. He followed the east coast to Madras and, from there, the west coast to the Indus. He returned to

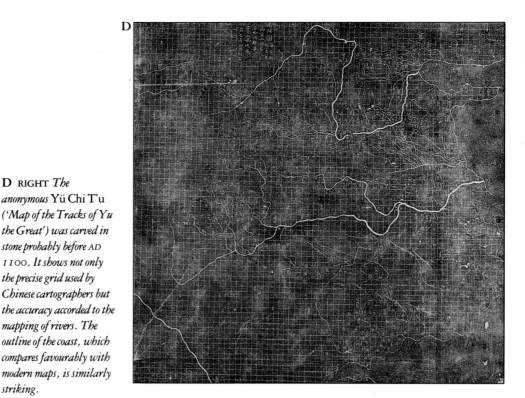

D RIGHT *The anonymous* Yü Chi T'u *('Map of the Tracks of Yu the Great') was carved in stone probably before AD 1100. It shows not only the precise grid used by Chinese cartographers but the accuracy accorded to the mapping of rivers. The outline of the coast, which compares favourably with modern maps, is similarly striking.*

China along the edge of the Takla Makan.

Explorations such as these stemmed from the tradition of state-sponsored internal exploration that began in the Western Chou dynasty (1122-770 BC). It was a process characterized by a desire both to record and to master the physical environment. The key was the management of the country's waterways, whether fast-flowing rivers or swampy lowlands. Without this, large-scale and productive agriculture would have been impossible, as would the growth of cities, which depended on surplus food production. The philosopher Mencius, for example, writing in the 4th century BC, related how Yu the Great,

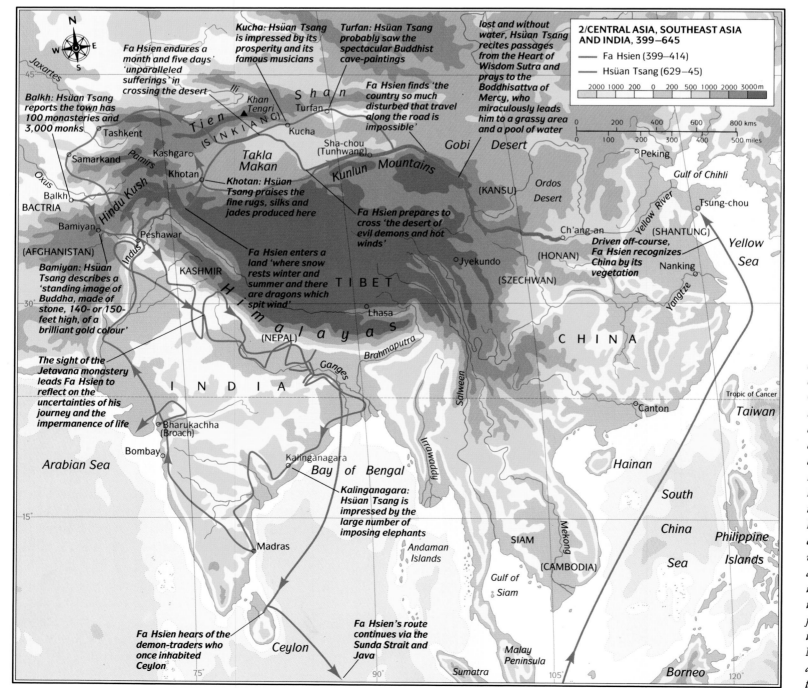

2 LEFT *Though diplomatic and commercial contacts were frequent, Chinese knowledge of routes to and within India depended mainly on the detailed and widely disseminated accounts of Buddhist pilgrims. Fa Hsien's is the earliest of those to have survived, Hsüan Tsang's the most detailed. The journey home was normally made by sea, a route later increasingly used for the journey out, though overland routes from shrine to shrine through central Asia, Nepal or Tibet remained attractive to adventurous pilgrims.*

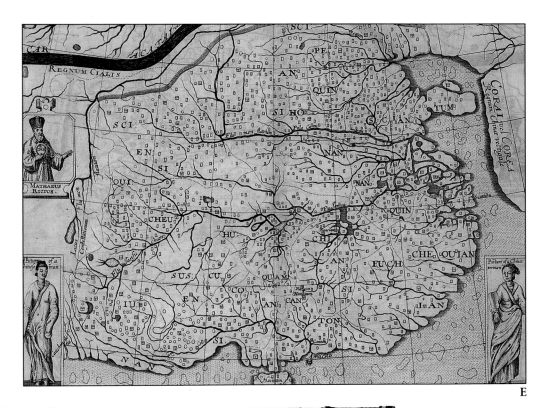

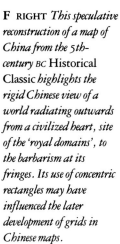

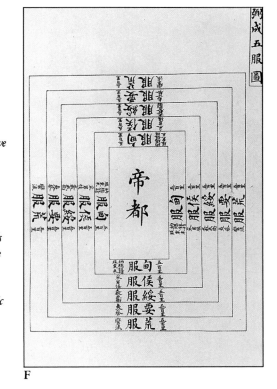

F RIGHT *This speculative reconstruction of a map of China from the 5th-century* BC *Historical Classic highlights the rigid Chinese view of a world radiating outwards from a civilized heart, site of the 'royal domains', to the barbarism at its fringes. Its use of concentric rectangles may have influenced the later development of grids in Chinese maps.*

E

F

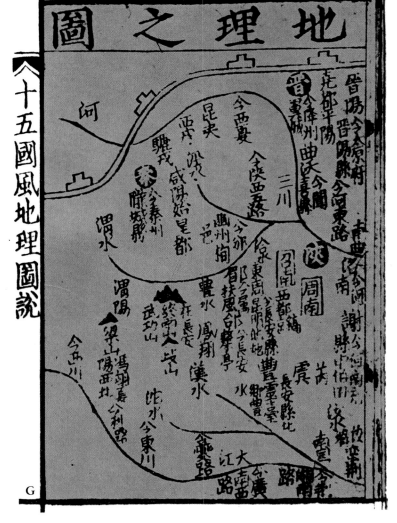

G

H

E ABOVE *This early 17th-century map, engraved for Samuel Purchas's great compendium of travel literature, is attributed by implication to the Jesuit missionary Matteo Ricci (d. 1610), whose portrait appears on the left and who may have been responsible for adding Western cartographic conventions and for re-drawing the map on a global projection. The basis of the work, however, is a map by the early 14th-century Chinese cartographer, Chu-ssu-pen; the stylised black band in the top left-hand corner derives from the prototype's method of representing the Gobi Desert, the curling palisade beneath it from the more angular and realistic representation of the Great Wall in the original.*
G ABOVE LEFT *This map of west China from the mid-12th-century encyclopaedia called* Liu Ching T'u *(Illustrations of Objects Mentioned in the Six Classics) is the oldest printed map in the world. Though schematic, the Great Wall is marked clearly, as are major rivers. The names of three provinces are shown by the white characters on black circles.* **H** LEFT *Barbarian envoys bring gifts of tribute to officials of the court. Extensive records of such gifts and of their 'tribute-bearing peoples' and their countries were compiled from the 3rd century* AD, *giving rise to a substantial body of government-held information about neighbouring countries.*

the hero-emperor, 'mastered' the water and 'caused it to flow in controlled channels'. The building of these canals, as of the country's roads, both requiring manpower on a huge scale, is evidence not just of the state's command of resources but of a sophisticated geographical understanding. The country's water systems were to remain crucial to the development of Chinese society. The great rivers were the principal means of access between the arid plains of the north and the semi-tropical, often mountainous south. These, too, were mapped and their economic and geographical features described in detail in a series of treatises, such as the 1st-century BC *Sui Ching*, or *Waterways Classic*, in which 137 rivers were described. Szechwan had been mapped by c.AD 150 and was the subject of a detailed topographical study, the *Hua Yang Kuo Chih*, or *Historical Geography of Szechwan*, by Ch'ang ch'u written in AD 347. By the late 7th century, local maps and topographies were commonplace. In 971 the emperor ordered a comprehensive survey of the empire, which by 1010 had grown to 1,566 chapters. In the 11th century, the rivers, lakes and canals of Suchow and its neighbouring districts were also mapped. This tradition of geographical and historical surveying crystallized in the form of local gazetteers, which provided huge quantities of topographical data. Grain distribution in the 13th century was assisted by comprehensive maps compiled from district and village surveys made by Yuan Hsieh, director-general of government grain stores.

Some of China's history of internal exploration was stimulated by scientific curiosity in the spirit of the legendary travels of the Emperor Mu (1001-945 BC), which were said, in a compilation perhaps of the 3rd century BC, to have reached 'the four remote corners of the world'. In the 7th century AD, for instance, long-standing curiosity about the source of the Yellow River was satisfied when a punitive expedition against a Tibetan tribe discovered it in 635 near Kyaring Nor. Liu Yüan-ting, ambassador in Tibet in 822, verified the find during a journey to Lhasa which took him across the Yellow River below Ngaring Nor and the Yangtze near the lakes of Jyekundo. The upper course of the river was finally established by an expedition sent by Kublai Khan in 1280.

Chinese attitudes to the wider world are made clear in the earliest-known Chinese geographical work, the 5th-century BC *Shu Ching*, or *Historical Classic*. In it, the world is represented as a series of concentric rectangles, with the royal palace at the centre (*see* map **F**). Radiating outwards from it are the royal capital and domains, the lands of the feudal princes, the 'zone of pacification', the 'zone of allied barbarians' and finally the 'lands of uncivilized savages'. It neatly encapsulates the Chinese view of a world centered on the emperor and increasingly barbaric as one travelled from its heart. It was a belief that was to endure essentially unchanged into the 20th century and goes far toward explaining why, for all their early sophistication and technical expertise, the Chinese never fulfilled their promise as a great exploring culture.

Thus, though regular Chinese contacts with the wider world existed from at least the middle of the last millennium BC, Chinese attitudes to the world were always ambivalent. A belief in its own superiority, in which self-esteem is hard to distinguish from complacency, allied to the rigid doctrines of Confucius, produced a society that was not only deeply resistant to change but fully confident of its own perfection: self-sufficient, isolated from the world's other great civilizations and in many respects significantly more advanced. Where they could not subdue troublesome foreigners, the Chinese either physically excluded them or bought them off through a system of tributary trade, by which foreign merchants trading with the Chinese were officially categorized as bearers of tributes to the Emperor and rewarded with Chinese goods equal or greater in value. The 3,700-mile-long Great Wall defined China's northern frontier, giving physical substance to the notion of an ideal society within and barbarian without. Similarly, technical advances such as the discovery of the magnetic compass in the 3rd century AD or the invention of printing (c. AD 730) were seen not as means of permitting further expansion so much as of buttressing the state and the rigid bureaucratic class that administered it.

Nothing illustrates this better then the Chinese attitude to astronomy, of which they were the unsurpassed masters in the Middle Ages, perfecting instruments and techniques which could have enhanced direction-finding and cartography. Yet the art was treated as a form of state-magic and underwent a sad decline in a period corresponding to the European early modern. Jesuit missionaries who re-equipped the imperial observatory in Peking in 1674 had to re-introduce to Chinese astronomers technology familiar to their ancestors, and demonstrate unsuspected practical applications of the science (see L).

Before introspection and isolationism took over, the most famous Chinese explorations of the wider world were accomplished in the early 15th century by the eunuch-admiral Cheng Ho. His achievement must be understood against the background of a long and intermittent history of contacts between the China Sea and the Indian Ocean. In AD 97, for example, Kan-ying, an ambassador bound for Roman Syria and who got as far as Parthia, brought back tales of the perils of the sea. Nonetheless, Chinese ships reached Malaya by the middle of the 4th century and Ceylon by the end of it. In 360, Chinese

I RIGHT *Chu-ssu-pen's 14th-century world atlas was remarkable for its recording of information about the China Seas and the Indian Ocean, and is the earliest known map to show Africa in roughly its true shape. The section here shows the China Seas.*
J BELOW *Chinese sea-charts, such as this 17th-century copy of a chart made as a result of Cheng Ho's voyages, were highly schematic. The chart shows the north-western Indian Ocean, with the west coast of India at the top and the southern coast of Arabia at the bottom. Such charts were nevertheless practical; the sailing routes are given compass courses and other aids to navigation; the characters next to the Arabic figures (added in the 19th century) give the altitude of the Pole Star.*
3 BOTTOM *Cheng Ho's voyages were along routes well known to merchants but were novel both in their origins – as an official venture of the Chinese empire – and in their effects: as the source of an 'overall survey' of the shores of the Indian Ocean.*

I

merchants were said to frequent the fair of Batanea on the Euphrates, having probably been carried there by Persian or Indian shipping, which increasingly seized the initiatives in Far Eastern trade in the following centuries. Persian and Arab ships were recorded in Canton from the 7th century. Excavations at Siraf, the principal port in the Persian Gulf, which became prominent at that time, have produced many Chinese porcelain fragments: the site of the mosque, built between 815 and 825, has particularly abundant remains. In c. 1220, a high-ranking Chinese official, Chao Ju-kua, wrote the *Chu Fan Chih*, a detailed account of the South China Sea and of countries of South-

J

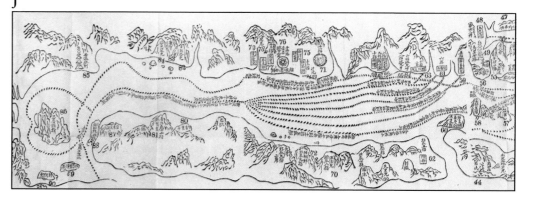

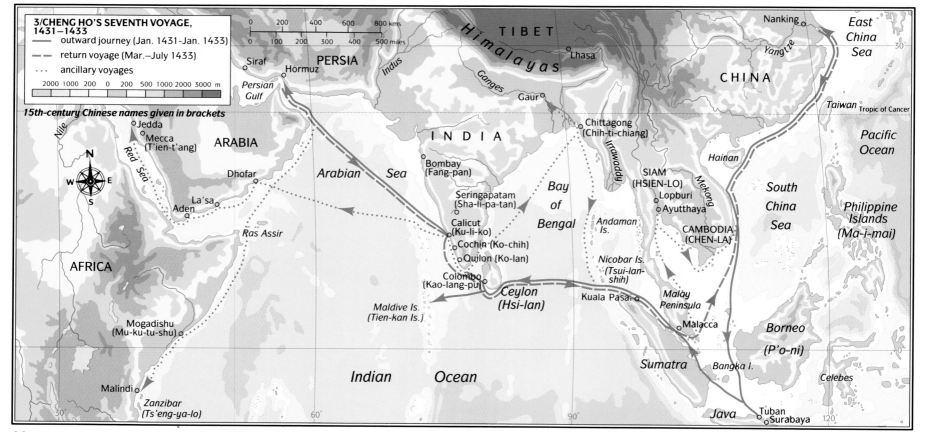

3/CHENG HO'S SEVENTH VOYAGE, 1431–1433
— outward journey (Jan. 1431–Jan. 1433)
- - - return voyage (Mar.–July 1433)
· · · ancillary voyages

2000 1000 200 0 200 500 1000 2000 3000 m

15th-century Chinese names given in brackets

Nanking
East China Sea
TIBET
Himalayas
Lhasa
PERSIA
Siraf
Hormuz
Persian Gulf
Indus
Ganges
Gaur
CHINA
Yangtze
Taiwan
Tropic of Cancer
Jedda
Mecca (T'ien-t'ang)
ARABIA
Red Sea
Dhofar
Arabian Sea
INDIA
Chittagong (Chih-ti-chiang)
Irrawaddy
Pacific Ocean
Hainan
La'sa
Aden
Bombay (Fang-pan)
Bay of Bengal
SIAM (HSIEN-LO)
Lopburi
Ayutthaya
Mekong
South China Sea
Ras Assir
Seringapatam (Sha-li-pa-tan)
Calicut (Ku-li-ko)
Cochin (Ko-chih)
Quilon (Ko-lan)
Andaman Is.
CAMBODIA (CHEN-LA)
Philippine Islands (Ma-i-mai)
AFRICA
Colombo (Kao-lang-pu)
Ceylon (Hsi-lan)
Nicobar Is. (Tsui-lan-shih)
Malay Peninsula
Borneo (P'o-ni)
Maldive Is. (Tien-kan Is.)
Kuala Pasai
Malacca
Mogadishu (Mu-ku-tu-shu)
Nile
Indian Ocean
Sumatra
Bangka I.
Celebes
Malindi
Zanzibar (Ts'eng-ya-lo)
Java
Tuban
Surabaya

N W E S

dint of prowess in war, becoming a grand eunuch and superintendent of the office of eunuchs in 1404. The series of diplomatic and exploratory missions he began the following year were in every sense unprecedented, for the imperial navy and the corps of eunuchs alike. His fleets, of up to 63 ships and with – reputedly – nearly 30,000 men, visited 30 countries around the rim of the Indian Ocean, in the course of (probably) seven voyages of about two years each, gathering intelligence, exacting tribute and, in one case, capturing a Ceylonese king. The direct encounter with Africa which his journeys added to Chinese experience astonished people at both ends of the ocean. In the preface to his own book about the voyages, Ma Huan, an interpreter aboard Cheng Ho's fleet, tells us that as a young man, when he had contemplated the season, climates, landscapes and peoples of distant lands, he had asked himself in great surprise, 'How can such dissimilarities exist in the world?'. His own travels, however, convinced him that the reality was even stranger. The arrival of the Chinese junks at Middle Eastern ports with cargoes of precious exotica caused a sensation. Ibn Taghri Birdi describes the obvious excitement at the Egyptian court when news arrived that several Chinese junks had anchored off Aden and that the captains of the ships had asked permission from the Mameluke sultan to bring up the vessels to Jedda, the port of Mecca.

Though naval demonstrations like Cheng Ho's generated no lasting enthusiasm in China, they did have permanent effects on geographical science and on trade. Excavations at Kilwa in East Africa revealed that the inside of the dome of the great mosque was lined with blue-and-white Ming bowls. In scale, the voyages were stupendous achievements. According to the best available estimate, the seventh – probably the greatest – sailed 12,618 miles, of which the 3,327 miles between Hormuz and Malacca took only 44 days, while the 1,491 miles from Calicut to Kuala Pasai were covered in an amazing time of 14 days.

east Asia and India. A century later, Chu-ssu-pen produced a passable map of the Indian Ocean, including the coast of Africa to beyond the Cape of Good Hope, though this may have been compiled from others' reports (*see* map 1).

The voyages of Cheng Ho remain among the mysteries of Chinese history. Why they were initiated in 1405 and aborted after 1433, never to be repeated, no one knows, though the Emperor Ch'eng-tsu, who was the patron of all but the last voyage, was, by Ming standards, an exceptionally aggressive, expansionist and maritime-minded leader. Cheng Ho was a Muslim of Mongol ancestry who rose in imperial service by

K ABOVE *Chinaman leading a zebra, from the* I Yu T'u Chih (Illustrated Work of Strange Countries) *of 1430.* L BELOW *From the 17th century the Chinese became dependent on Western science for the practical applications of technical expertise. In 1674, the imperial observatory in Peking was turned over to the Jesuits for reorganization.*

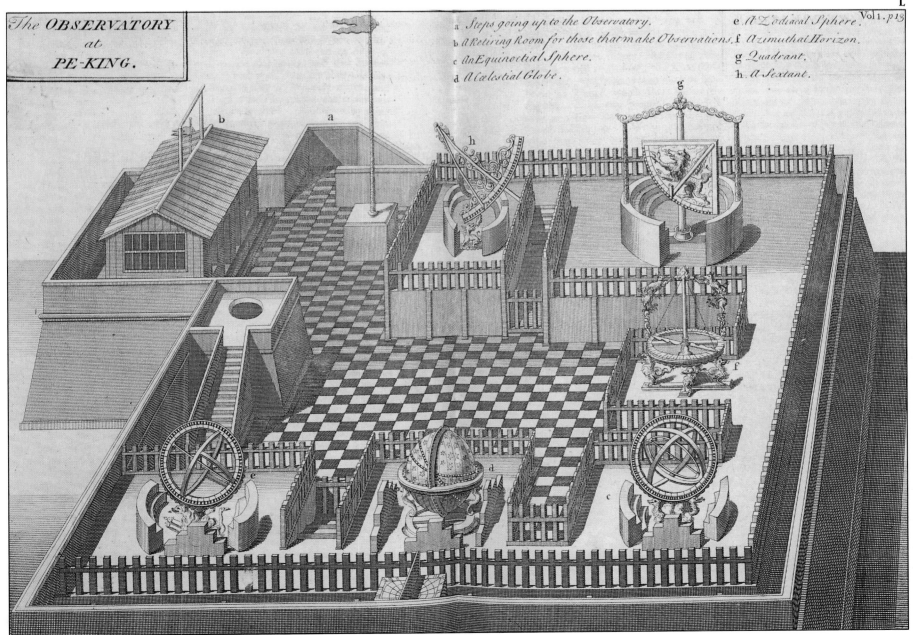

The OBSERVATORY at PE-KING.

a *Steps going up to the Observatory.*
b *A Retiring Room for those that make Observations.*
c *An Equinoctial Sphere.*
d *A Celestial Globe.*
e *A Zodiacal Sphere.*
f *Azimuthal Horizon.*
g *Quadrant.*
h *A Sextant.*

Vol.1. p.13

2

THE GRAECO-ROMAN WORLD

C.2000 BC-AD 640

FROM ABOUT *the middle of the 8th century* BC, *the small Greek city-states of the Aegean expanded rapidly east into the Black Sea and south and west across the Mediterranean. Colonies and trading links were established as far apart as southern France and the Crimea. In the 4th century* BC, *Alexander the Great was to push the limits of the Greek world far into Asia. The growth of Rome from the 3rd century* BC *fused many elements of Greek learning with Roman political, military and economic forms. Extensive knowledge of regions far beyond the boundaries of Rome – of China, the Indian Ocean, Central Asia and Africa – was assembled.*

In the Barbarian west from the 5th century AD, *much of this body of knowledge was lost. But what survived and what was later painfully re-discovered exerted a crucial influence on exploration. Islam was the immediate beneficiary of the Graeco-Roman geographical tradition; Western Europe – Latin Christendom – from the 15th century the dominant force in world exploration, the longer-term beneficiary, with much of its information filtered through Islamic and Byzantine sources. Thus, to a considerable extent the significance of Greece and Rome in exploration lay not so much in what they achieved for themselves as in the foundation – however imperfectly preserved – they established for others.*

1 RIGHT *The world-picture of the Greeks at the beginning of the 5th century* BC, *represented by this reconstruction of the world map of Hecateus of Miletus, was challenged by Herodotus, who ridiculed 'maps of the world drawn without any reason to guide them', and by Aristotle, who derided the circular form assigned to the inhabited world. Subsequent depictions adopted a form more like that of the reconstruction from Ptolemy (*A *above right).*

2 BELOW *At its greatest extent, in the 2nd century* AD, *the Roman Empire stretched from Mesopotamia in the east to Spain in the west. The aim was to secure a defensible ring around the inner provinces bordering the Mediterranean. Barbarian invasions in the west and war against the Sasanian Persians from the 3rd to 7th centuries* AD *made the frontiers impossible to sustain.*

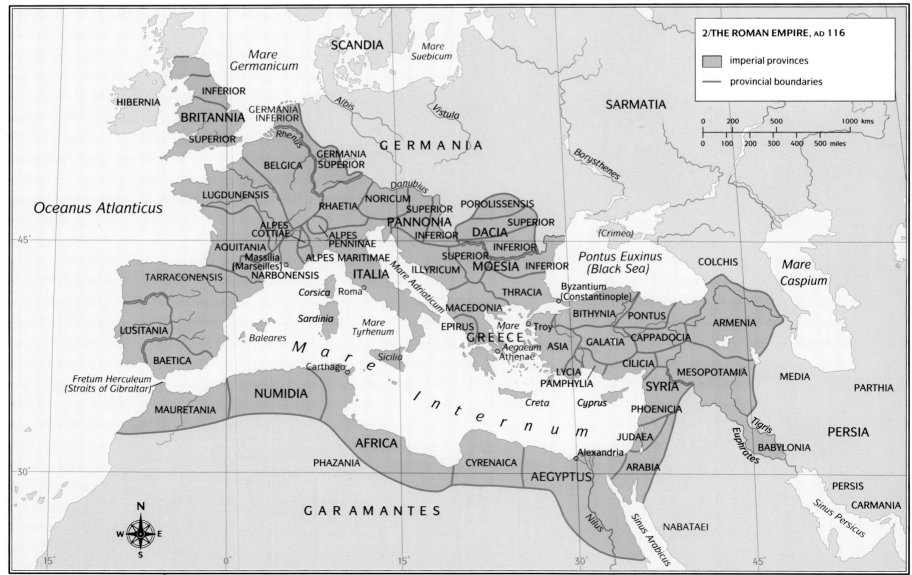

2/THE ROMAN EMPIRE, AD 116

imperial provinces

provincial boundaries

THE GREEKS produced handbooks of travel from an early date, including navigational guides and ethnographical descriptions. After Aristotle in the 4th century BC had shown that the world was round, Eratosthenes in c.200 BC and others developed the system of latitude and longitude which was applied by Ptolemy of Alexandria in his *Geography* of the 2nd century AD. But though Ptolemy's calulations appear scientific, they were based on theory rather than astronomical observation, and promulgated significant inaccuracies, such as his belief in a great southern continent – Terra Australis – linking East Africa and China. He also had little idea of Germany, Poland and central and northern Russia. Nonetheless, the *Geography* was to remain a standard source in the West until the great age of European discovery began in the mid-15th century. An important 1st-century AD geographical work by Strabo also survives. Apart from India and Persia, however, which he knew about from the campaigns of Alexander the Great, Strabo's horizons were largely Mediterranean; like Ptolemy, he knew little about central Europe and northern Asia.

The epic travels of Aristotle's pupil, Alexander the Great of Macedon, in the 4th century BC took Greek settlers as far east as Bactria and north-west India and stimulated several accounts of the regions traversed by Alexander's armies. Alexander himself had commissioned surveyors to precede his armies and to assemble information on the territories ahead. This systematic attempt to gather knowledge was evident, too, in the voyage Alexander commissioned his admiral Nearchus to make from the Indus to the Persian Gulf and the Tigris (*see map 2*).

After Alexander's death in 323 BC, his vast empire was split into successor states under the Ptolemies in Egypt and the Seleucids in Syria, Babylon and Media, in the process greatly expanding the hitherto limited horizons of the Greek world. Between 310 and 306 BC, the navigator Pytheas of Marseilles, then a Greek colony, is reported to have sailed north from the Straits of Gibraltar along the west coast of France and to have circumnavigated Britain, reaching an island he called Ultima Thule (Iceland or Norway). Unlike many ancient travellers,

A

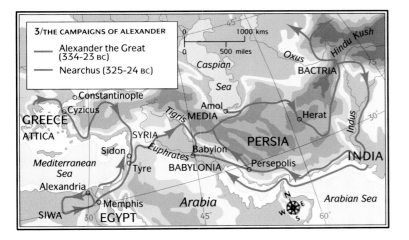

who were motivated by trading or military considerations, Pytheas seems to have had a genuinely scientific interest, taking measurements of latitude as he proceeded on his voyage.

It was only with its war against Carthage in the 3rd century BC that Rome acquired a fleet and showed an interest in the wider Mediterranean world. Subsequent contact with Greece broadened Roman horizons, but Roman interest in maps and travel came only with the development of empire and the acquisition of overseas provinces, though even then it tended to be practical rather than scientific or theoretical. The network of Roman roads, for example, was essentially military in origin, permitting Rome's armies to travel swiftly and securely. The frontier defences of the Roman empire reached their fullest development in the 2nd century AD and made use where possible of natural barriers such as rivers. It was perhaps the Emperor Augustus, who ruled from 31 BC to AD 14, who first thought in terms of a bounded empire defended by permanent military forces. He commissioned a map, since lost, from

A ABOVE *Ptolemy's 2nd-century* AD Geography *was still a standard text when Columbus discovered the New World at the end of the 15th century. None of Ptolemy's maps – if indeed he ever made any – survived the Classical era, but medieval reconstructions such as this from the 15th century exerted a considerable influence in late-medieval Europe. Ptolemy's system of latitude and longitude is conspicuous; the left-hand margin gives details of* climata, *or latitude belts. The exhaling heads represent winds, whose names are given next to them.* **3** ABOVE LEFT *Geographical knowledge in the ancient world often went hand in hand with military conquest. Alexander the Great's conquests encompassed systematic attempts at exploration and recording routes and regions and significantly expanded contemporary horizons.*

his general Agrippa. It was, however, the map of a traveller rather than of a soldier, and it does not seem to have supplied reliable military information, even for the crucial campaigns Augustus conducted in Germany.

The Roman view of the world was political and imperialistic. But if little interest was taken in the regions beyond the frontiers, much attention was paid to setting up monuments claiming the extent of the Roman control, especially if a general could claim, as Gallus did in Egypt, that he had been the first to enter and subdue them for Rome. Few Roman emperors took any interest in exploration as such, unless for military purposes, and the frontiers remained largely stable after AD 14, the chief exceptions being the conquest of Britain in AD 43 and Dacia (modern Romania) in AD 106, the latter commemorated on Trajan's Column in Rome. Augustus's posthumously published account of his achievements, the *Res Gestae*, was set up on bronze tablets in Rome and major cities. But though listing the extent of his conquests, its aim was to impress rather than inform.

From the late 2nd century AD, the repeated incursions of barbarian tribes forced the Romans to greater awareness of the world beyond their frontiers. The Emperor Marcus Aurelius in the middle of the century spent many years of his reign campaigning on the Danube, while the 3rd century AD was a time of continual warfare. By the early 5th century, Germanic tribes had penetrated Germany, Gaul and Spain, while in AD 430 the Vandals seized North Africa. But if conditions were not conducive to exploration, the spread of Christianity after the reign of Constantine the Great (AD 306-37) prompted pilgrimages to the Holy Land. A notable example was that made by the female pilgrim Egeria, who travelled to the Holy Land from Spain in AD 384 and produced a lively travel diary.

Trading contacts were maintained throughout this period as far east as India and even China, from where silk had been imported overland as early as the 1st century AD. In the west, some contact with Britain seems to have continued even after the province was abandoned in AD 410. Armies from Constantinople were able to recapture North Africa in the 6th century AD, and to fight successfully against nomads in the sub-Saharan desert of south-east Tunisia and modern Libya.

The break-up of the western empire in the later 5th century AD did not put an end to Mediterranean trade and sea-travel. It was the Arab conquests of the 630s and 640s which marked the end of the Classical era. Christianization, too, had altered perceptions of the physical world, and, though Aristotle was still taught in Alexandria in the 6th century, Cosmas Indicopleustes ('the man who had travelled to India') produced a rival *Christian Topography* in which the world was represented as flat, with heaven above and hell below.

3
JAPAN
AD 25 - 1364

1 BELOW The division of Japan into 68 provinces in the 7th century reflected the influence of China. The same imported tradition of strong central government subsequently permitted state-sponsored attempts to map the country.

2 BELOW (inset) Links with neighbouring China and Korea had to be forged in the face of consistently unfavourable conditions of navigation made more hazardous, on the longer southern route, by the risk of attack from pirates.

2/JAPAN, CHINA AND KOREA, AD 600–804
— Japanese embassies

Hokkaido
Oshima Peninsula
Matsumae
Tsugaru Strait
Sea of Japan
northern route, used 600–607
SILLA
(KOREA)
Teng-chou
Hiraizumi
Yellow Sea
Honshu
PAECHE
MUTSU
DEWA
Heian-kyo (Kyoto)
(Tokyo)
Nara
(Osaka)
CHINA
southern route, used 762–804
Hakata
Shikoku
East China Sea
Kyushu
Pacific Ocean
Yellow River
Tanegashima
Ming-chou
northern Ryukyu route, used 669–752
Amami O-shima
Ryukyu route, used 733
Okinawa

0 200 400 600 kms
0 100 200 300 miles

1/THE 68 PROVINCES OF JAPAN, C. AD 800

Yellow Sea
Sea of Japan
SADO
ECHIGO
NOTO
ETCHU
SHIMOTSUKE
KOZUKE
HITACHI
KAGA
HIDA
SHINANO
MUSASHI
SHIMOSA
OKI
ECHIZEN
KAI
KAZUSA
WAKASA
MINO
SAGAMI
INABA
TANGO
OWARI
AWA
IZUMO HOKI
TAJIMA
TAMBA
OMI
SURUGA
IZU
IWAMI BINGO HARIMA
IGA
TOTOMI
TSUSHIMA
BITCHU
BIZEN
ISE
MIKAWA
NAGATO AKI
AWAJI
SHIMA
IKI SUO
SANUKI
YAMATO
CHIKUZEN BUZEN
AWA
KII
HIZEN
IYO TOSA
Honshu
CHIKUGO BUNGO
HIGO
Shikoku
HYUGA
Kyushu
SATSUMA
OSUMI
Pacific Ocean

① MIMASAKA
② SETTSU
③ YAMASHIRO
④ KAWACHI
⑤ IZUMI

DESPITE EARLY achievements in mapping much of their own territory, the Japanese showed little interest in exploring the wider world. Their origins are obscure. They seem predominantly to be a mixture of strains from the northern part of the Asian mainland with an admixture of peoples from Southeast Asia and, probably, the South Pacific. They were not the only inhabitants of the Japanese islands. Prominent among other tribes were the Ainu on the central island of Honshu and on the northern island of Hokkaido.

The lead among the Japanese was seized in the first centuries AD by tribes from the southern island of Kyushu, whose leader claimed descent for the sun goddess Amaterasu. By the 3rd or 4th century they had won a dominant position in Japan except in the northern part of Honshu and on Hokkaido where the Ainu remained hostile. By 1500 they had extended their influence over much of northern Japan, though the province of Mutsu in the northern tip of Honshu remained remote from their influence and Hokkaido largely unknown to them.

Until 1543, when the earliest direct contacts between Japan and the West were made, first-hand Japanese knowledge of the outside world was restricted to China and Korea, though the existence of India was recognized. Links between Japan and China can be traced to the later Han dynasty (AD 25-220). In the early 5th century, the legendary Japanese Empress Jingu, having subdued the Kumaso tribes in Kyushu, is said to have led a Japanese attack against the Korean kingdom of Silla.

Over the next 200 years, Japan came increasingly under Chinese and Korean cultural influences. Confucian ideas and Chinese government practices began to be adopted in Japan from the 5th century, when the Korean scribe Wani is reputed to have journeyed to Japan bringing with him a copy of The Analects of Confucius. Buddhism also reached Japan from China in these centuries.

The first recorded official Japanese government mission to China was sent in 607. Students of Buddhism also travelled to China. But until about the 14th century contact remained intermittent. The natural hazards of the sea-passage were increased by the fragility of Japanese ships and the lack of all but the most basic navigational equipment. Primitive compasses are known to have reached Japan from China around the 11th century, though there is some evidence to suggest an earlier date.

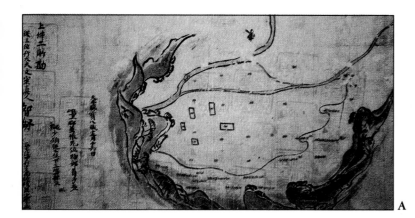

A LEFT *Oriented with east at the top, this* shōen, *or estate, map of a manor in Settsu Province is among the oldest extant Japanese maps. It dates from AD 756. Buildings are shown in the centre; wooded mountains rise up to the north, west and south.*

THE INTRODUCTION to Japan in the 7th century of Chinese forms of administration led to the eventual division of Japan into 68 provinces (*see* map 1). Attempts were made to divide farming land among cultivators and to ensure that taxes were paid by the cultivators to the government. To this end surveys of population and land were instituted and the first Japanese maps, sketch maps of estates (*shōen*), were produced (*see* map A). But the Chinese system of land tenure and taxation was never properly applied in Japan and much of the land came to be dominated by local magnates or was taken over by powerful Buddhist temples.

With the establishment in 710 of the Japanese capital at Nara and then, in 784, at Heian-kyo (present-day Kyoto) attempts to develop more reliable communications between these and other centres were made. A leading role was taken in these endeavours by the Buddhist priest Gyogi. No overall surveys were made, but Gyogi is thought to have produced some form of sketch or diagram showing the rough relationship between the provinces. None of the Gyogi-type maps gave anything like an accurate shape to the Japanese islands. In particular, the northern part of Honshu was generally compressed and

often incorrectly shown in an almost horizontal east-west position or even turning southward. An interesting feature of early Gyogi-type maps is the inclusion on some of two fabulous countries. To the south was Rasetsukoku, a country inhabited by female demons called *rasetsu* (from the Sanskrit *raksasa* or *rakshasa*) and reputed to eat shipwrecked mariners. To the north was Gando or *Kari no michi*, 'the route of the wild geese'. Hokkaido may have been intended by this name.

The exploration of the more remote parts of Japan also began in this period. From the 7th century, the Japanese had attempted to push back the Ainu – the *emishi* to the Japanese, or barbarians – in Mutsu. Military posts were established to protect the frontier as it was gradually extended north. Fujiwara no Kiyohira (1056-1128) established the main government centre in northern Honshu at Hiraizumi in what is now Iwate prefecture. Nonetheless, the northern island of Hokkaido was hardly known to the Japanese authorities before 1500 and it was certainly not properly explored. Some scattered settlements were founded on the Oshima Peninsula of the island by refugees from the civil wars in the 12th century. In the 14th century, the Ando family was granted a fief in the island, although it does not seem to have exercised any real control. In about 1442, Takeda Nobuhiro established firm control of the southern part of the island bordering the Tsugaru Straits. A castle was built at Matsumae, and for a time it gave its name not only to the fief but to the island as a whole.

The earliest Japanese missions to China in the 7th century followed a northern route round the south-west coast of Korea. Because of troubles in Korea they were later forced to take more hazardous routes to the south (*see* map 2). The shortest and most direct route, across the East China Sea from Hakata in Kyushu to ports on the mainland, was also the most hazardous. Another route involved calls at islands in the Ryukyu chain to

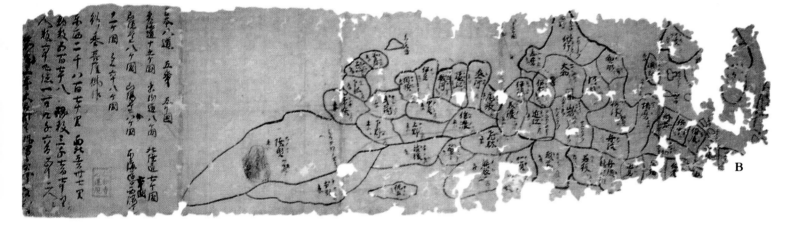

B LEFT *One of the two earliest surviving maps of Japan, both dated 1305 and both Gyogi-type. It is oriented with south at the top. Provinces, listed in the text on the left, are shown clearly; routes are marked by the faint red lines.*

C LEFT *The* Gotenjikuzu, *or Map of the Five Regions, of 1364 is one of the few surviving Japanese maps of the world. Based on traditional Buddhist depictions, it shows the 'civilized world' as centred on India and the Himalayas, which appear as snow-capped peaks in the centre of the map. Mount Sumeru, the mythical centre of the Cosmos, is depicted in whirlpool-like form just above the Himalayas. China, called the 'great Tang', is shown as relatively small. Over stormy seas from China, the Japanese islands can be made out in the lower right-hand corner.*

the south of Kyushu and then across to the Chinese coast. Shipwreck was a regular hazard and the journey was much feared. All four of the ships which accompanied the embassy of Fujiwara no Kadonomaru in 803, for example, were battered by storms and were forced to return to Japan to set out again the following year. Only two of the ships subsequently reached the Chinese mainland, and on their return in 805 only one made the Japanese coast. In 894, following the fall of the Japanese Tang dynasty, the despatch of official missions was suspended and Japanese subjects were forbidden to leave Japan. Exceptions were made for Buddhist priests, who seem not to have been discouraged by the perils of the journey.

In these early centuries trade between Japan and China was never more than intermittent. But contacts were resumed in the 14th century when the threat of Mongol invasion had passed. In 1342, when Ashikaga Takauji was Shogun (military ruler), a ship was chartered to re-open trade with China. Occasional missions were exchanged over the next 150 years and a considerable trade developed. The Japanese exported horses, swords, armour, copper, gold, lacquer, screens, fans and sulphur to China. Their imports were mainly silver and copper coins, brocade, silk, jade, pearls, porcelain, incense, books and medicines.

4
INDIA
FROM C. 1200 BC

DURING *the first millennium AD, Indian civilization was exceptionally well equipped – and, to all appearances, remarkably well poised – to contribute to world exploration. Great overland journeys were made by missionaries, such as the monk Kumárajúra, who joined disseminators of Mahayanist Buddhist teachings in China in AD 386 and, from the 5th century, by embassies from Ceylon, Kapila and the Gupta kingdom. In 641, embassies were exchanged between China and King Ciladitya, whose realm was centred on Bihar, to the latter's professed astonishment. The Chinese invaders of 646 were accompanied home by an Indian 'magician' who unsuccessfully treated the sick emperor T'ai Tsung.*

The Indian maritime tradition was equally impressive, though it barely affected the sacred geography of Vedic and early Buddhist tradition. Indian merchants, already familiar with the Persian Gulf and the Red Sea, began contacts with their Javanese and Sumatran counterparts that were strengthened in the 7th and 8th centuries by the arrival in the islands of Buddhism from Ceylon. A later southern Indian Chola king even claimed to have sent a naval expedition to Java in 1025. Indian navigators, capable of sophisticated astronomical calculations, provided the Arabs with sailing directions to these shores.

Medieval texts, such as Yaśodhara's 13th-century commentary on the Kama Sutra, compiled lists of place names, latitudes and topographical details. Descriptions of the world remained largely unchanged, except for Rajaśekh's attempt (c. 900) to imitate Chinese geography.

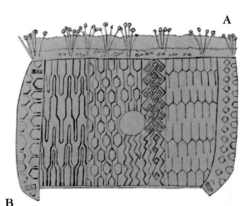

A LEFT *This Mesolithic cave-painting from Jaora in Madhya Pradesh may represent the oldest attempted depiction of the cosmos. Water-plants and fish can be detected at the top.* **B** BELOW *Navigators on an Indian ship take soundings during a pilgrimage to Mecca, from a manuscript of 1666. The use of sounding lines to measure sea depths was already ancient.*

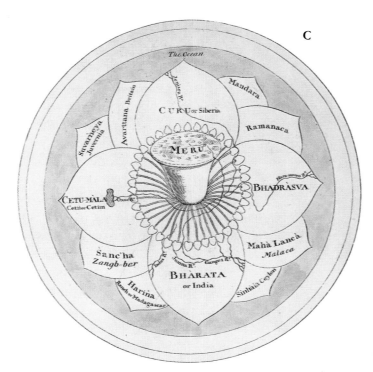

C

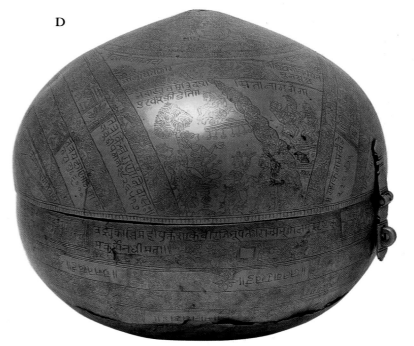

D

C LEFT *The lotus was favoured by Buddhist tradition for the depiction of the earth; it was later adopted by Hindus for maps of Vraj, the birthplace of Krishna. This illustration was made by Francis Wilford in 1805 in one of the earliest systematic studies of Indian cosmography.*
D ABOVE RIGHT *The ancient image of the 'four-continent-earth', with geographical names in Sanskrit for places in India, is engraved in brass on this* bughola, *or earth-ball, of 1571.*
E BELOW *A diagram by a Kutchi mariner of sailing courses from Socotra in the Indian Ocean for ports in the Arabian Sea. Stellar bearings, latitudes and distances are also given.*

INDIAN literature is strangely deficient in records of conscious exploration. But this silence may be misleading: a single surviving record of an exploratory voyage of the 5th century seems to belong to a tradition of geographical curiosity and map-making unattested elsewhere. The story is of a ship blown by a storm to a mountain called Srikunja. 'Hearing the account as related by the ship's captain, the prince Manohara noted down on a wooden board the details of the particular sea, direction and place. With this information the prince ordered a ship manned by an experienced captain and went out in search of the spot. Borne by a favourable wind, he reached his desired destination'. Even if the tale is fictional, the prince's exploring zeal, and the notion of recording a route in what sounds like map-form, must have been intelligible to the audience of the day. No such sailing directions or sea charts are known from before the early 16th century when Europeans arrived in India (*see* ch.29), but the recent discovery of a Kutchi-language seafar-er's manual from Gujarat has excited expectations (*see* map **F**). Though the document is of 1664 and profoundly influenced by European conventions, its charts of parts of the coast of southern India and Ceylon are thought to reflect much earlier traditions.

All that is known for certain about early Indian notions of the world is contained in cosmographical schemes. The earliest surviving Indian attempt to depict the cosmos is perhaps a Mesolithic cave painting from Jaora in Madhya Pradesh (*see* **A**), where water is indicated by wavy lines and aquatic creatures and plants, and the earth by geometric patterns. The extent to which Indian cosmosgraphical tradition reflects practical experience of the world is a matter of debate. Surviving Vedic literature of c. 1200–c. 600 BC seems almost innocent of geography. In its six- or nine-layered universe, the highest of three earths is the abode of men, its regions largely designated by tribal names, though in later texts areas are given geographical names and regions are named after the cardinal points.

The well-known world-picture of post-Vedic times, the 'Four Continent-World', seems to reflect a schematic version of a world centred on the Himalayas. Four 'island-continents' radiate from a mountainous core, the Meru or Sineru, which is surrounded by seven concentric circles or rock. The biggest, to the south, is the Jambu-Dvípa (which includes India). To the east is Bhadráva, the Buddhist name for which appears to associate it with a people of northern Bihar and part of Nepal, while the northern continent, Uttara-Kuru, may be located in Central Asia. The fourth continent, Ketumala, located in the west, was known by the apparently fanciful name of Apara-Godána.

From the 2nd century BC onwards, this picture of the world increasingly gave way to a 'Seven-Continent-World', apparently even further removed from reality. In this, each continent was surrounded by a different sea, respectively of salt, sugarcane juice, wine, clarified butter, curds, milk and water. Little influence was exerted by the world of experience, although some details reflect realities: the sun-worshipping Magas, for instance, of the milk-lapped continent of Śaka, may correspond to the inhabitants of eastern Iran, while Kuśa, in its sea of butter, may be Ethiopia. Even the most fanciful texts, such as those by Jain writers who imagine the cosmos as a series of truncated pyramids, never quite seem to lose touch with reality. The computation of the volume of the universe, for example, was a standard concern of Jain astronomy and mathematics.

Still, given the technical achievements of Indian science, and the range of travel by Indian mercenaries, missionaries, armies and merchants, interest in recording knowledge yielded by exploration remained surprisingly slight until the 16th century AD. Yet even for these late writers, geography remained essentially a learned subject rather than one based on first-hand knowledge of the wider world. Ancient and medieval India possessed all the equipment, but none of the urge, required to create an exploring culture.

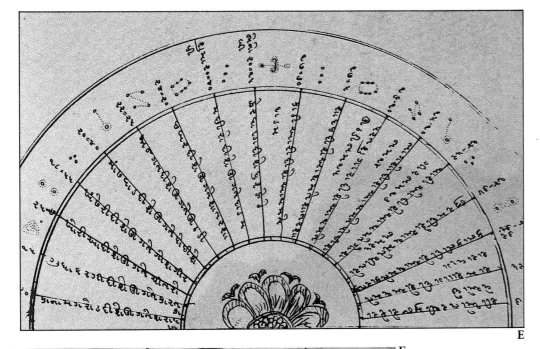

E

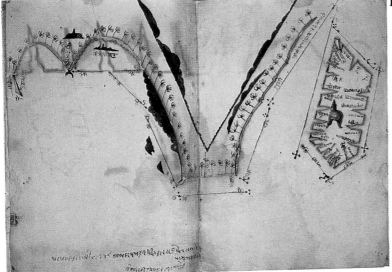

F

F LEFT *A Kutchi Gujarati chart of 1664 of the southern tip of India with Ceylon on the right. The chart is a unique survival of what was probably an ancient tradition of Indian chart-making.*

5
ISLAM
AD 622-1513

WITHIN *a century of the foundation of Islam by Mohammed in* AD 622, *the ancient civilizations of the Near East were faced by an astonishing historical phenomenon. From Sind in western India to the Straits of Gibraltar in the Mediterranean, a unified political, religious, social and economic world-system developed that drew its theoretical and practical precepts from Islam. It was to have a profound influence, permitting the civilizations of the Near East to expand rapidly across and beyond the Indian Ocean. In a burst of exploration, Muslim military conquerors, navigators and caravan-masters reconnoitred the Middle East itself, north and east Africa, the Mediterranean, the Indian Ocean, and even the South China Sea in impressive depth. In the 9th and 10th centuries, they were joined by Arab geographers and semi-professional explorers, who systematically surveyed the Islamic and non-Islamic worlds. One immediate effect was to revitalize the long-distance trade on which the Near East depended, increasing its prosperity and in turn stimulating further trade and travel.*

But the history of Islamic exploration also owed much to the importance of Mecca, the 'House of God', the annual pilgrimage to which made the Hejaz, the western coast of Arabia, among the most frequented places in the world. Scholarly hajjis, *or pilgrims, seem to have developed an urge to travel, and in many cases produced detailed descriptions of the places they visited.*

A BELOW The Book of Roger *of 1154 was conceived by the geographer al-Idrisi as a commentary on a world map, engraved on silver, for Roger II of Sicily. It was single-mindedly in the tradition of Ptolemy, attempting to describe the world in terms of 'climates' and to fix the positions of places by their supposed co-ordinates. It is oriented with south at the top.*

A

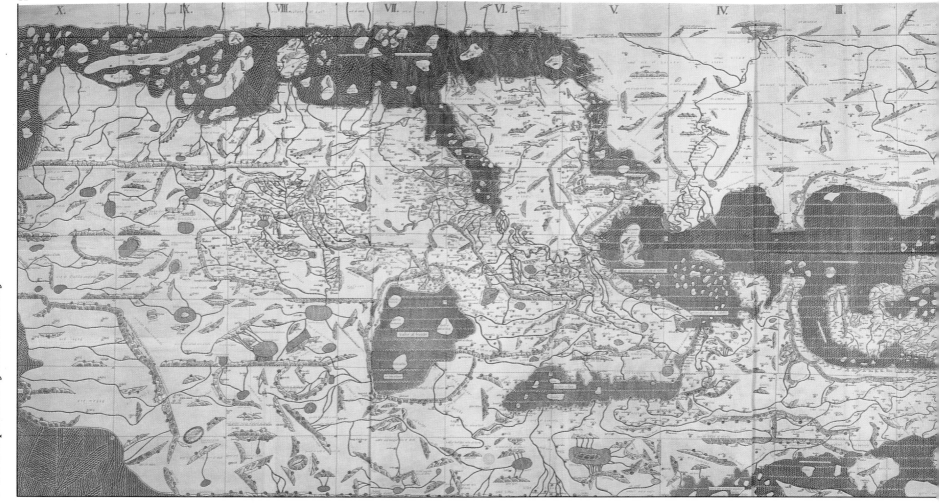

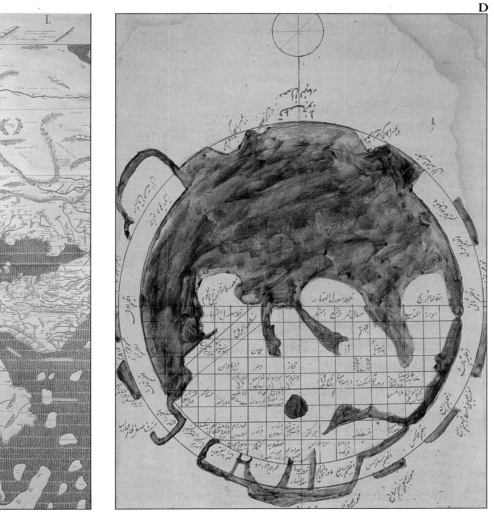

ISLAM, at least potentially, was the legatee of an enormous amount of ancient geographical wisdom. The heartlands not only of Egypt were occupied, but also those of Babylonia, whose traditions of recording geographical information are demonstrated by a stone tablet of c.400 BC in the British Museum (see B). This shows the Euphrates, and names Babylon, Assyria and Armenia in cuneiform script. In practice, however, though some Babylonian concepts influenced the world-picture of pre-Islamic Arab literature and of the Koran, Egyptian and Babylonian knowledge was irrecoverable by the time of the Arab conquests. Instead, Islamic geography built on Indian, Persian and, above all, Graeco-Roman foundations.

B LEFT *The Arabs inherited the learning of the civilizations that preceded them in the Middle East. Among them were the Babylonians, whose geographical knowledge is represented by this map, carved in stone around 400 BC, of Mesopotamia and surrounding regions. A cuneiform commentary on the map is carved above it.* C RIGHT *The observatory built for Taki al-Din in Byzantium in about 1576 was the culmination of a long tradition of practical Islamic astronomy, which contributed to direction-finding and mapping techniques.* D BELOW *After the fall of Baghdad to the Mongols in 1258, the Persian savant Al-Qazwini devoted himself to producing a synthesis of geographical knowledge. His world map shows an attempt to construct the grid of reference recommended by Ptolemy.*

Indian influence was strong in astronomy; Persia may have influenced early cartography and cosmography. But the superiority of Graeco-Roman traditions, represented in particular by Ptolemy (see ch.2), was established by the early 9th century, when the Caliph al Ma'mun assembled a circle of scholars who produced a world map and measured the length of a degree on the arc of a meridian.

Islamic geography has often been condemned as fossilized by bookish prejudices, its geographers more given to academic speculation than to gathering first-hand experience. Yet interest in incorporating observations made by travellers and traders was a constant feature of early Islamic geography. Al-Ya'qubi (d. 897), for example, was an inveterate traveller who compiled itineraries of Islam and neighbouring territories, including the Byzantine empire. Al-Mas'udi (d. 956) wrote an account (since lost) of his own travels, which reached from the Mediterranean to the Caspian Sea, as well as extant academic works. His experiences did not necessarily lead to much accurate knowledge, however, as when he denied the existence of unknown continents or postulated, on the basis of Arab ships' timbers washed ashore in Crete, the existence of a northern passage linking the Black Sea and the Pacific.

One of the most perceptive and reliable of these early Arab authors was the Syrian al-Muqaddasi (d. 1000). His great work, *The Best Description for an Understanding of all Provinces*, is not only a geographical treatise on the Islamic world but a systematic investigation of the economic resources of every major province from Syria to Khurasan. Al-Muqaddasi was especially interested in the influence of urbanization in long-distance trade. In his listing of Muslim cities and towns, al-Muqaddasi accorded geographical rank following the analogy of political administration. Capitals were treated as kings, provincial capitals as chamberlains, ordinary towns as cavalrymen and villages as foot-soldiers. The description 'metropolis' was used to designate a city where the supreme ruler of a country resided, where the state administrations were housed, where provincial governors were invested, and to which the towns of the province were referred.

The early history of Islamic exploration began with the military conquest of Iraq and the foundation of the port of

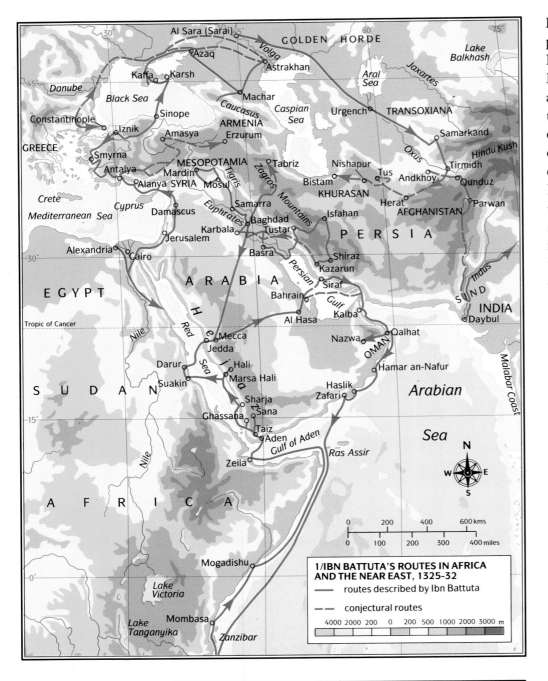

1/IBN BATTUTA'S ROUTES IN AFRICA AND THE NEAR EAST, 1325-32
— routes described by Ibn Battuta
-- conjectural routes

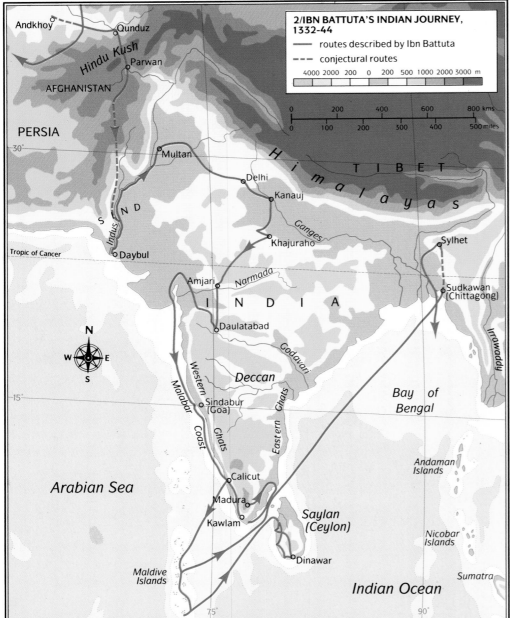

2/IBN BATTUTA'S INDIAN JOURNEY, 1332-44
— routes described by Ibn Battuta
-- conjectural routes

Basra in 638. It was a process sparked by the economic and political need to establish secure communications between the Persian Gulf and Damascus, which became the capital of the Islamic empire after 661. The surplus food production generated by the fertile alluvial flood-plains of the Nile Valley and the rich canal-irrigated lands of Mesopotamia placed a potent economic resource at the disposal of the Arab rulers. But it was one that required extensive maritime and caravan transport to exploit fully. The sailors and shipbuilders of Egypt and the Persian Gulf had long been known in antiquity for their maritime skills. It was these seafaring people, facing the Mediterranean and the Indian Ocean respectively, who were responsible for the rapid rise of a Muslim fleet engaged in both trade and warfare. From the middle of the 8th century, Muslim merchants and navigators began to trade regularly not only with Daybul, the great port near the mouth of the River Indus, but with the Malabar coast in India. The foundation of great capital cities in Iraq such as Baghdad and Samarra was an obvious stimulus to both the overland caravan trade and to maritime trade in the Persian Gulf. Evidence suggests that they developed a substantial demand for exotic products from India and China. Indeed by the third quarter of the 9th century, the number of Middle Eastern merchants living in, and trading with, China had grown substantially. When a formidable rebel warlord, Huang Ch'ao, raided Canton in 878 he was reputed to have killed 120,000 Muslims, Christians, Jews and Zoroastrians. On the other hand, the political uncertainties of the late T'ang empire in the late 9th century may have also encouraged the growth of trade in the Malayan archipelago, the cultural crossroads between China and the Middle East.

During the course of his voyages in the Indian Ocean in the early 10th century, al-Mas'udi learned that ships from Siraf and Oman in the west met those from the China Sea at Kalah Bar in the Malayan peninsula. He also provided a remarkable account of the Muslim colony on the west coast of India. 'At

1 and 2 LEFT The Travels of Ibn Battuta *recounted journeys spanning almost the whole of the Islamic world. For his journeys in Africa, see ch.11.* **E BELOW** *Like many Muslim geographers, al-Istakhri in the 10th century believed in the need to complement academic study with practical travel. The world map attributed to him shown here is nonetheless highly schematic.*

F ABOVE RIGHT *The reliability of the camel allied to the cultural unity of the Islamic world created land routes that stretched from the Maghrib to China. This 13th-century illumination depicts Arab merchants.* **G FAR RIGHT** *An Indian ship from an Iraqi manuscript of 1238. Its square sail was ideal for monsoonal winds; its hold had ample space for passengers and cargo.*

E

F

Ibn Battuta's travels were exploratory only in a limited sense: he hitched himself to caravans or maritime merchant ventures and tried to stick to Islamic communities, even on his rare sorties beyond the frontiers of Islam. It is a remarkable fact that, after the aggression of the early conquests of Islam was spent, and after the Arab commercial world had attained its desired limits in the Mediterranean and the Far East, Islamic exploration of the wider world was so fitful and slight. The most striking limitations were in maritime exploration, despite the enormous advantages derived from the proven competence and equipment of Islamic navigation.

Descriptions of the volume and direction of maritime trade in the Indian Ocean prove beyond doubt that Arab shipowners and their captains were well able to navigate the vessels out of sight of land. By the time Ahmad Ibn Majid (c.1470) came to write his navigational treatise (*see* ch.28), Arab and Indian knowledge of methods in laying down a ship's course were highly advanced. The South Indian and Arab navigators used mathematical tables and charts indicating latitudes; they also had the benefit of compasses. The position of the ship relative to latitude was fixed by calculating the altitudes of the sun and stars with a device known as a *kamal*, a type of primitive sextant. The speed of vessels could also be measured using a fairly sophisticated type of log. Sailing-directions such as those of Ibn Majid were backed by the work of outstanding shore-based astronomers. Yet for all their undoubted sophistication, the achievements of Indian Ocean navigators were not duplicated in Atlantic waters. Only rare and timid ventures seem to have been made along the Moroccan coast. When the New World became an extension of Christendom, and the Portuguese discovered an Atlantic highway to the east, the Ottoman sultans came, too late, to regret their failings. The western portion of the world map made by Piri Reis (*see* ch.9, map **C**) in 1513 bears witness to their concern at a lost opportunity.

G

that time there were ten thousand Muslims settled there [Saymur]', he wrote, 'Bayasiras and Sirafis, Omanis, Basrans and Baghdadis and those from other cities, including some outstanding merchants'.

Further evidence of the nature of the Muslim maritime world is provided by 10th-century compilations. That of Abu Zayd of Siraf purports to record impressions from as far afield as China transmitted by 'Sulayman the merchant' in the middle of the previous century. The Sirafi shipmaster Buzurg Ibn Shahriyar was similarly well acquainted with the maritime world of Siraf, Oman and Jedda. His narratives of trading voyages were often presented as fantastic sea stories.

Academic geography lost touch with exploration after the 11th century, though in the field of world geography in particular remarkable contributions were made, most notably by al-Idrisi, a Hammudi prince who joined a group of astronomers at the court of Roger II of Sicily. His *Kitab al-Rudjar* (*The Book of Roger*) was intended as a commentary on a silver planisphere compiled from Arab maps of the regions of the world. The range and boldness of Islamic travellers seems, from the 12th to the 14th centuries, to have diminished, with most surviving literature limited to the Near and Middle East. Al-Qazwini (d. 1283) was exceptional in his day as a cartographer and geographer who gathered material in extensive travels of his own, which resulted in what was perhaps the most comprehensive world geography yet produced in Arabic.

The revival of what might be called an exploring spirit in the late Middle Ages is best exemplified by Ibn Battuta of Tangier whose goal, apparently conceived on a pilgrimage to Mecca, was to travel the accessible world. His travels reached Sardinia, Granada and the Niger in the west (*see* ch.11) and, in the east, included the lands of the Golden Horde, Transoxiana, Afghanistan, India, the Maldives, Ceylon, Sumatra and China. Southward, he went by way of the Red Sea to east Africa as far

6
THE AMERICAS
C. 1500

THE RELIANCE of the first European explorers of the Americas on native guides suggests that indigenous exploration on an heroic scale had long occurred in these regions. Mesoamerica and the Andes in particular, where the sedentary civilizations of the Aztecs and the Incas developed long-range commerical and imperialistic habits, have strong claims to be considered exploring cultures similar to those of the Old World.

Although the scale of their achievements as explorers is impressive, both Aztecs and Incas were nonetheless limited by a combination of geography and technical deficiencies. The Aztecs were hemmed in by the vast desert to the north from which they traced their own provenance. Moreover, its nomadic Chichimec inhabitants were indomitable; without pack animals, and with no means of carrying food and water over long distances, the Aztecs could neither subdue nor traverse the Chichimec world. There were no comparable obstacles to the south, but Aztec knowledge of these neighbouring lands was substantial only along the routes of their armies of 'conquest' (raiders who exacted tribute before returning home).

By the arrival of the Spaniards in 1519, the Aztecs seemed to have pushed this 'imperial' system beyond the limits of its viability. Nor did the Aztecs develop a maritime vocation; the seaborne trade of their world was carried by coastal middle-men. In any case, neither the vessels available nor the sailing conditions favoured Aztec access to a wider world: unrigged canoes demanded big crews and could only carry limited supplies; while the prevailing north-easterlies beyond the Caribbean prevented long-range voyaging to the east and the immense expanse of the Pacific discouraged sailings to the west.

The Incas, in some respects, had superior resources: their balsa-rafts were handy; the llama did duty as a beast of burden. But winds and currents limited any oceanic ventures in which they might have engaged. Moreover, unlike Mesoamerican peoples, they had no knowledge of mapping. Their civilization is proof of how much can be achieved without written systems for recording information: they were able to transmit intricate knowledge of routes south into Chile and deep into the South American interior using only human memory and mnemonic devices. Still, it seems reasonable to suppose that the resources of this particular 'information technology' cannot have been infinitely elastic.

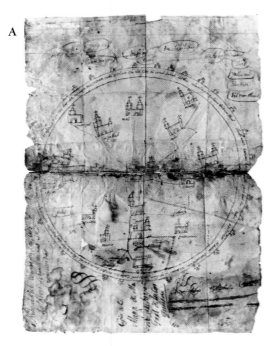

A LEFT Maya mapping traditions of much greater antiquity than those of the Aztecs survived into colonial times, to judge from this circular map of the province of Xiu, with the capital, Mani, at the centre. 1 BELOW Beyond the inner network of routes traversed by Aztec armies, where meticulous topographical mapping was possible, less detailed Aztec knowledge was gathered by trade. Cortés found Aztecs' maps inadequate beyond Cempoala 'because they usually went by sea'.

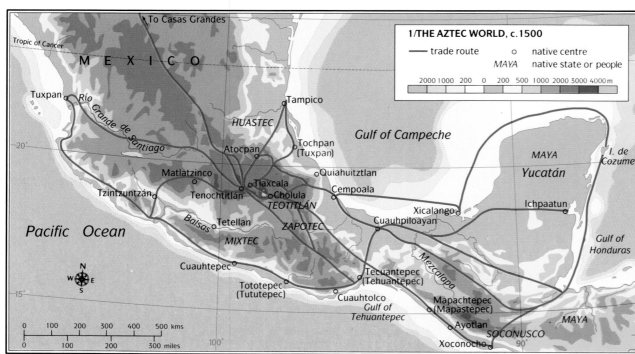

NO PRE-CONQUEST Mesoamerican maps have survived but early colonial examples in indigenous traditions supply an idea of what they were like. There were at least three types, intended, respectively, to provide records of routes of migration, trade and conquest. A fourth may perhaps have provided local information for the assessment of tribute and the fixing of boundaries. Most post-conquest maps are of this last type: native communities relied on them in making supplication to the Spanish crown for the relief of tribute or the despoliation of their neighbours. Further, Spanish cartographers relied on them in mapping New Spain (*see* ch. 10). It is not clear, however, whether they derived from an older tradition or whether they were improvised in the litigious atmosphere of the early colonial world.

Surviving records of migrations in map-form are so schematic as to be useless as pathfinding devices. Commonly, places are symbolically represented without attention to their geographical relationships, with movement shown by stylised footprints, a convention also used in pre-conquest genealogical codices. It is evident, however, that the Aztecs also had genuine route-finding maps. Cortés and the Spanish *conquistadores* found their way to Honduras with the aid of indigenous maps: the fact that this route locked into the canoe-borne trading network of the circum-Caribbean region demonstrates one of the purposes for which maps were made. A scene in the famous early colonial Aztec manuscript, *Codex Mendoza*, shows a war starting as a result of a breakdown of trade, and routes of trade seem always to have been potential routes of conquest, one object of which was to secure valuable produce by way of tribute.

In the last generation or so of Aztec history, campaigns were launched into ever-more distant territories to levy the exotic products on which the metropolitan life of the Aztec elite

was increasingly dependent. The annual tribute of Tochtepec, in the 'hot country' of the Gulf coast, for instance, included 9,600 decorated cloaks, 1,600 women's tunics, one feathered battle dress and shield, one feathered shield of gold, one feathered banner, gold hair fillets and beads, rich and rare feathers, 100 pots of liquid amber, 200 loads of cacao, 40 lip plugs and 16,000 balls of rubber. The gargantuan appetite of the Aztec empire was the source alike of its strength and its weakness, explaining both its tentacular reach and its unsustainable consumption. It is reasonable to suppose that the Aztecs had mapped in detail the areas traversed by their armies and in rough the area covered by their commerce from Honduras to Chihuahua.

The world known to the Incas was even more extensive. Conquistadores in Peru recruited guides capable of leading them over the whole world of the high Andes from Tolima to Bíobío. Yet this vast mental map was retained without written aids to memory. Andean geography and the siting of the Incas' mountain-top shrines, or *huacas*, may provide a clue to how this feat was achieved. Some vantage-points yielded views up to 100 miles in clear conditions. Pilgrimage routes led straight between huacas, like the *quipu*, strings on which the Inca recorded statistical data, held taut between knots. The longest such route, or *ceque*, led from Cuzco, the ceremonial centre of the Inca state, over 185 miles to the temple at Tiahuanaco through the 'house of the sun' at Vilcanota and the island of Titicaca, 'island of the sun', in a virtually straight line. Regular devotions practised in connection with particular huacas made the priestly corps a custodian of knowledge of a grid of sight-lines and ceques (routes) which covered the empire: the spatial relationships between the sacred sites were themselves a mnemonic device which constituted, as it were, a vast schematic map in itself on a scale of 1:1.

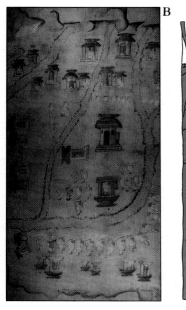

B FAR LEFT BELOW *The Lienzo de la Gran Chinantla shows the survival of native mapping techniques in Mexico in early colonial times. The area depicted is Chinantec country, with villages, rivers and mountains schematically represented.*
C LEFT *Tupac Inca Yupanqui (1471-93), legendary ruler of the Incas and depicted in this illustration from Pedre Cieza de Leon's 16th-century history of the Incas, was credited with extraordinary feats of conquest and exploration. Notice the mountain-top huaca in the background.*
D BOTTOM LEFT *Peruvian fishing-craft illustrated in Girolamo Benzoni's* History of the New World. *They are unlikely to have ventured far into the ocean without the hope of a returning wind, but Inca legends of discovered islands may relate to the Galapagos.*

2 RIGHT *The Incas did not make maps but can be said to have 'mapped' their world by covering it with roads. The inset map, based on work by R. Tom Zuidema, showing the alignment of mountain-top shrines, suggests how wide-ranging topographical information could be organized for mental recording in a society that did not need writing or mapping.*

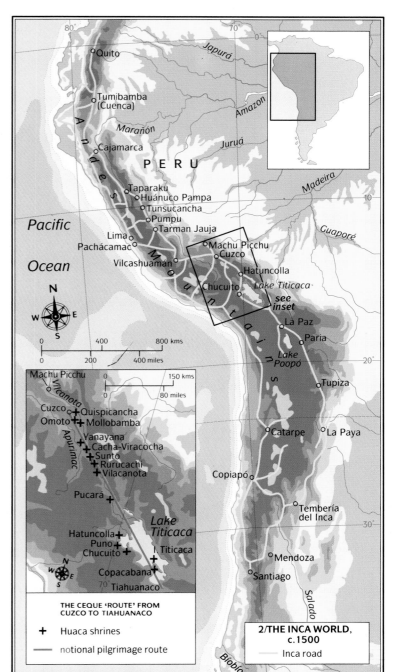

2/THE INCA WORLD, c.1500
—— Inca road

THE CEQUE 'ROUTE' FROM CUZCO TO TIAHUANACO
+ Huaca shrines
—— notional pilgrimage route

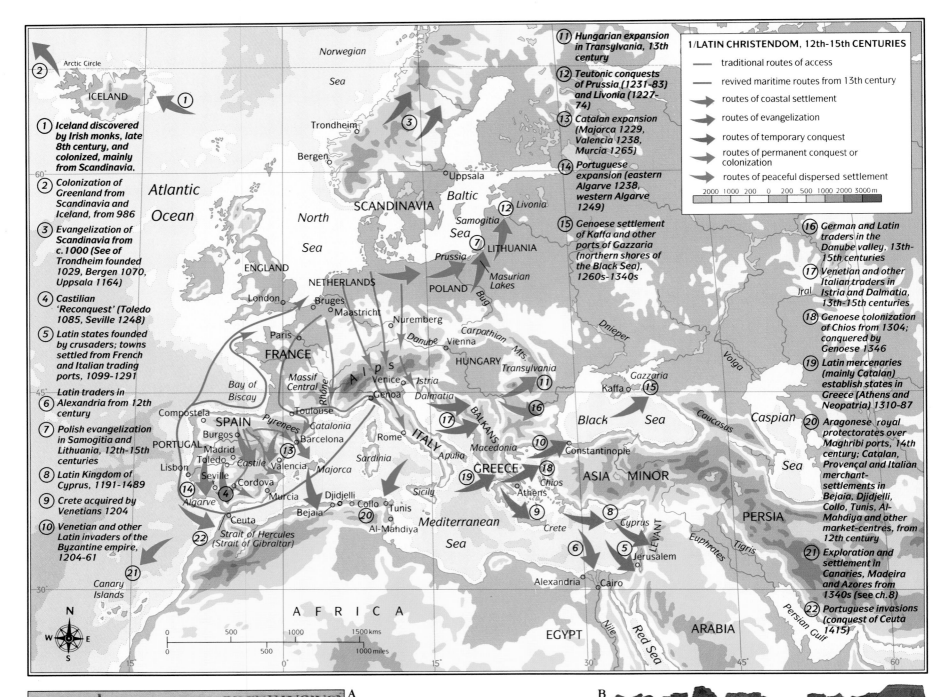

1/LATIN CHRISTENDOM, 12th-15th CENTURIES

— traditional routes of access
— revived maritime routes from 13th century
→ routes of coastal settlement
→ routes of evangelization
→ routes of temporary conquest
→ routes of permanent conquest or colonization
→ routes of peaceful dispersed settlement

2000 1000 200 0 200 500 1000 2000 3000 m

(1) **Iceland discovered by Irish monks, late 8th century, and colonized, mainly from Scandinavia.**

(2) Colonization of Greenland from Scandinavia and Iceland, from 986

(3) Evangelization of Scandinavia from c.1000 (See of Trondheim founded 1029, Bergen 1070, Uppsala 1164)

(4) Castilian 'Reconquest' (Toledo 1085, Seville 1248)

(5) Latin states founded by crusaders; towns settled from French and Italian trading ports, 1099-1291

(6) Latin traders in Alexandria from 12th century

(7) Polish evangelization in Samogitia and Lithuania, 12th-15th centuries

(8) Latin Kingdom of Cyprus, 1191-1489

(9) Crete acquired by Venetians 1204

(10) Venetian and other Latin invaders of the Byzantine empire, 1204-61

(11) Hungarian expansion in Transylvania, 13th century

(12) Teutonic conquests of Prussia (1231-83) and Livonia (1227-74)

(13) Catalan expansion (Majorca 1229, Valencia 1238, Murcia 1265)

(14) Portuguese expansion (eastern Algarve 1238, western Algarve 1249)

(15) Genoese settlement of Kaffa and other ports of Gazzaria (northern shores of the Black Sea), 1260s-1340s

(16) German and Latin traders in the Danube valley, 13th-15th centuries

(17) Venetian and other Italian traders in Istria and Dalmatia, 13th-15th centuries

(18) Genoese colonization of Chios from 1304; conquered by Genoese 1346

(19) Latin mercenaries (mainly Catalan) establish states in Greece (Athens and Neopatria) 1310-87

(20) Aragonese royal protectorates over Maghribi ports, 14th century; Catalan, Provençal and Italian merchant-settlements in Bejaia, Djidjelli, Collo, Tunis, Al-Mahdiya and other market-centres, from 12th century

(21) Exploration and settlement in Canaries, Madeira and Azores from 1340s (see ch.8)

(22) Portuguese invasions (conquest of Ceuta 1415)

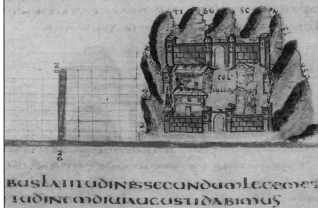

1 ABOVE *Latin Christendom was shaped by the expansion of its frontiers and internal travel and trade that united the northern and Mediterranean economic zones.* **A** LEFT *These surveyors' instructions, probably copied in the 9th century, indicate the survival of at least some knowledge of Roman mapping techniques.* **B** RIGHT *The 13th-century* Peutinger Itinerarium *is based on a Roman road map.*

AN OBSERVER *privileged to look down on the world 1,000 years ago would have seen a number of civilizations sundered by vast distances and poor communications. Asked to predict which would be most likely to produce explorers who would trace the routes between them and bring them into contact, he would have been most unlikely to nominate the European nations of Latin Christendom.*

By comparison with China, for example, Western Europe would have seemed under-populated. Its main seaway, the Mediterranean, would have appeared almost landlocked, its western bottleneck virtually stoppered by the current racing between the Strait of Hercules. Europe lacked the technical pre-requisites of long-range exploration. Ship-types, in contrast to the junks of China or the plank-sewn craft of the Indian Ocean, were unsuitable for ocean voyaging. There was no European compass, rendering open-sea navigation, under cloud and without bird-flight to follow, impossible. Similarly, there were few navigational instruments, not that Western mathematics were sophisticated enough to use them. As far as is known, there were also no marine charts; indeed cartographic techniques in general were vastly inferior to those of the Chinese. The internal exploration of Latin Christendom was at a similarly rudimentary phase, with perhaps the greatest potential advantage Westerners enjoyed – the inheritance of Greek and Roman cosmographical and geographical knowledge – largely forfeit to Islam, which possessed more of the relevant texts and exploited them more efficiently (see ch.5).

Above all, 'the West' was a small and beleaguered corner of the world, dwarfed and threatened by Islam to the south and paganism to the north. We now know that exploration is often encouraged by such under-development: the communities within Latin Christendom that created world trade in the 15th and 16th centuries – the Spanish, the Portuguese and the Dutch – occupied much the same position in relation to their neighbours – poor, peripheral and under-populated – as did the West to the Old World civilizations as a whole earlier in the Middle Ages. Necessity was a prime motive in the drive to explore. Nonetheless, the emergence of Latin Christendom as the world's great 'exploring culture', to the exclusion of better-equipped rivals, remains one of the mysteries of world history, intelligible only against a background of the region's own internal exploration in the late Middle Ages.

I N 1051 a messenger travelled north from the Pyrenean monastery of Canigou bearing news of the death of Count Wilfred of Cerdanya. All the way to Maastricht in present-day Holland he found the local speech intelligible. If he had crossed the Channel to England he would still have found monastic communities of Romance-speakers with whom he could have conversed. Beyond, in the lands of Germanic speech, Latin would have served as a means of communication with his fellow-churchmen: as far as the eastern borders of Saxony, writers revelled in the Classical heritage and the sense of a common culture shared with their brethren in the West.

The self-awareness of Latin Christendom was enormously enhanced over the following century by the Crusades. Paradoxically, however, while extending the frontier of Latin speech, social forms and worship, the creation of Crusader states in the Levant also helped to bring home to Western Europeans the smallness of their own world and the vastness of the hostile

D

C BELOW *Matthew Paris's map of an itinerary from London to Apulia is among the best 13th-century efforts to depict knowledge cartographically. Lateral relationships are ignored, however, and no attempt is made to show a network of roads.* **D** RIGHT *The Gough map of about 1360 by contrast is remarkably mature in its rendering of lateral relationships between stopping-points along the routes depicted: it remained influential into the 16th century.*

C

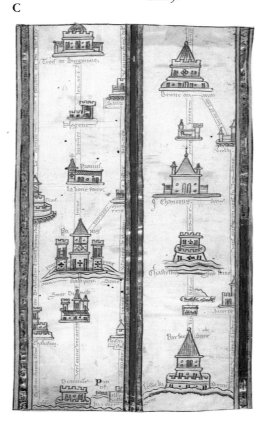

worlds beyond. Partly this was a consequence of direct knowledge of exotic climes, partly of access to Islamic geographical learning, itself based on tradition – including texts long lost in the West, such as Ptolemy's *Geography* – and knowledge of the trade routes that linked the Middle East with the Orient. The mingled covetousness and esteem with which the wider world was contemplated in Latin Christendom contrast with the complacency of the Chinese and perhaps help to explain why the less well-equipped culture was more drawn to exploration.

The Crusaders' material successes were checked in the mid-12th century and virtually obliterated by the end of the 13th. On other fronts in the same period, however, Latin Christendom made permanent gains. The inexorable logic of the winds and currents, which make the major islands of the area naturally subject to domination from the north, turned the western Mediterranean into a 'Christian lake' by the mid-13th century. All but a small corner of the Iberian peninsula was reconquered for Christendom by the 1260s. That most vital and menacing part of the pagan world – the Viking north – was absorbed without conquest by evangelization in the century after St. Olaf's conversion in about 1013. As a result, probably with help from Celtic settlers, the Norsemen's remote colonies in Iceland and Greenland became outposts of the Latin West. Conversion in the late 10th century turned the Poles into the most zealous of neophytes, much as the Saxons had become after their conquest in the early 9th century. In the 12th and 13th centuries crusades from Saxony and evangelizing missions from Poland extended the allegiance of the Roman communion eastwards to beyond the River Bug and into the Masurian lakes. Conversion of the Magyars, traditionally associated with the coronation of St. Stephen in 1000, and colonization by Italian and German traders along the Danube, extended the southern frontier to the Carpathians and the Balkans.

In the period following the consolidation of the new frontier, a single economy embracing the whole of Latin Christendom was forged by travel and trade. Geographically and historically, western Europe had two economies, a 'Mediterranean' and a 'northern'. The narrowness and remoteness (at least to northern Europeans) of the only sea-passage between them – the Strait of Hercules – made maritime links arduous. Moreover, sailing conditions along the two seaboards – the Atlantic and the Mediterranean – differed widely. There was only slightly less awkward access between the two zones by land, although the Toulouse gap, the Rhône corridor and the Alpine passes kept restricted commerce alive even in periods when commercial navigation from sea to sea was abandoned.

When Mediterranean craft resumed large-scale seaborne commerce to the north in the late 13th century, they faced enormous problems. Heavy seas, especially in the Bay of Biscay, threatened ships designed for the Mediterranean. Galleys, which carried much of the trade, had the additional disadvantage of requiring huge quantities of food and water for their large crews. The gradual integration of the northern and southern economies depended on the geographical specialization of industry and trade. The Italian merchants who carried eastern

E RIGHT *This wood-cut map of central Europe was made in Nuremberg for pilgrims to Rome in the Holy Year of 1500 perhaps by Erhard Etzlaub and almost certainly using lost maps by Nicholas of Cusa. It highlights the impressive degree to which mapped itineraries had evolved. The Alpine passes and route through Venice shown here were among the principal avenues of access between northern Europe and the Mediterranean.*

Mediterranean alum to England and English wool to Italy in the 14th century became bankers to an English king. In the 15th century, Bruges, where the raw materials for the Flemish cloth trade were bought from all over the Mediterranean, became an entrepôt 'where all the nations of the world meet'.

By haphazard means, the internal exploration of Latin Christendom and the cartographic recording of routes were developed. It was a process that was handicapped, in direct contrast to China and Japan, by the absence of a central authority to organize comprehensive mapping. The map of Latin Christendom had to be pieced together gradually from a number of sources. Two of these went back to Roman times: the map of the Roman roads preserved, among surviving medieval sources, only in the 14th-century 'Peutinger tables' in Vienna; and local surveying techniques, the continuity of which is suggested by fragmentary survivals of maps made by the 'agrimensores' – Roman land surveyors – and their successors.

F BELOW *The Venetian Pietro Vesconte's 1320 map of the Holy Land from Mario Sanudo's* Liber Secretorum Fidelium Crucis *was made with access to Islamic sources. The grid ensured accurate spatial relationships, essential for military planning.*

F

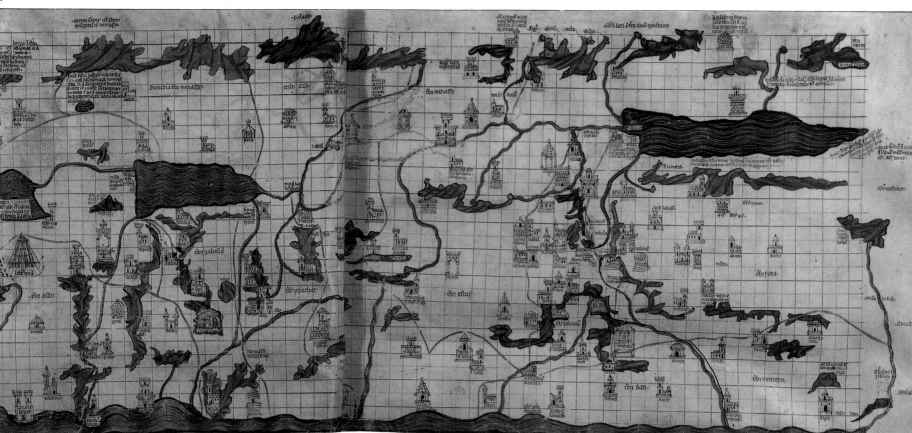

G

·BOEMIE· GERMANIE·RVSSIE·LITHVANIE·

The estate maps of wealthy medieval monasteries could cover vast areas that were sometimes widely separated from one another in the case of those foundations that attracted donations from far afield. Monastic estate management and the collective business of widespread orders gradually yielded itineraries – in essence, lists of stopping-places, such as that which the messenger of Canigou compiled in 1051. Pilgrimages and royal progresses likewise yielded route maps. Both these forms of travel were essential in medieval Europe: monarchs had to work indefatigably at fostering allegiance and dispensing justice up and down their realms, while pilgrimage, which included crusading, was a form of penance both salutary and popular and which accounted for the longest journeys made outside commerce, taking the hardiest venturers to remote shrines like Compostela in north-west Spain and the Holy Sepulchre in Jerusalem.

Itineraries in map form survive in fairly large numbers from the 13th century. As their traditional, linear patterns were displaced by the attempt to render spatial relationships accurately, so area maps evolved. A comparison of Matthew Paris's 13th-century map of the route between London and Apulia (*see* map C) with the relatively complex Gough map of about a century later (*see* map D) or the map of 1500 for pilgrims to Rome (*see* map E) demonstrates this process.

A similar evolution turned written sailing directions into marine charts during the 13th century: Jaume I of Aragon may have used a map to guide him to Majorca as early as 1228; St. Louis, voyaging to Tunis in 1270, certainly had one. The earliest surviving example (*see* map I) is of not much later date. In the 14th century these 'portolan' charts (from the Italian *portolano* or pilot book) came to include the Atlantic and northern waters. War played an even more important role in the production of area maps than trade. The maps of Palestine produced by Pietro Vesconte in the early 14th century (*see* map F) were made with strategic planning in mind; Italian generals in the 15th century would have considered their preparations deficient without access to maps (*see* map G).

Over this long period of preparation, Latin Europe had taken a series of small but significant steps in the acquisition of the technology – in ships and navigation – that would enable it to explore well beyond its immediate frontiers, for all that it remained a long way behind the Chinese, the Indians and the Arabs. But the search for the causes or origins of Europe's exploring vocation can be rewarded only be taking a very long-term view and acknowledging that the process grew, cumulatively but slowly, from modest beginnings.

I

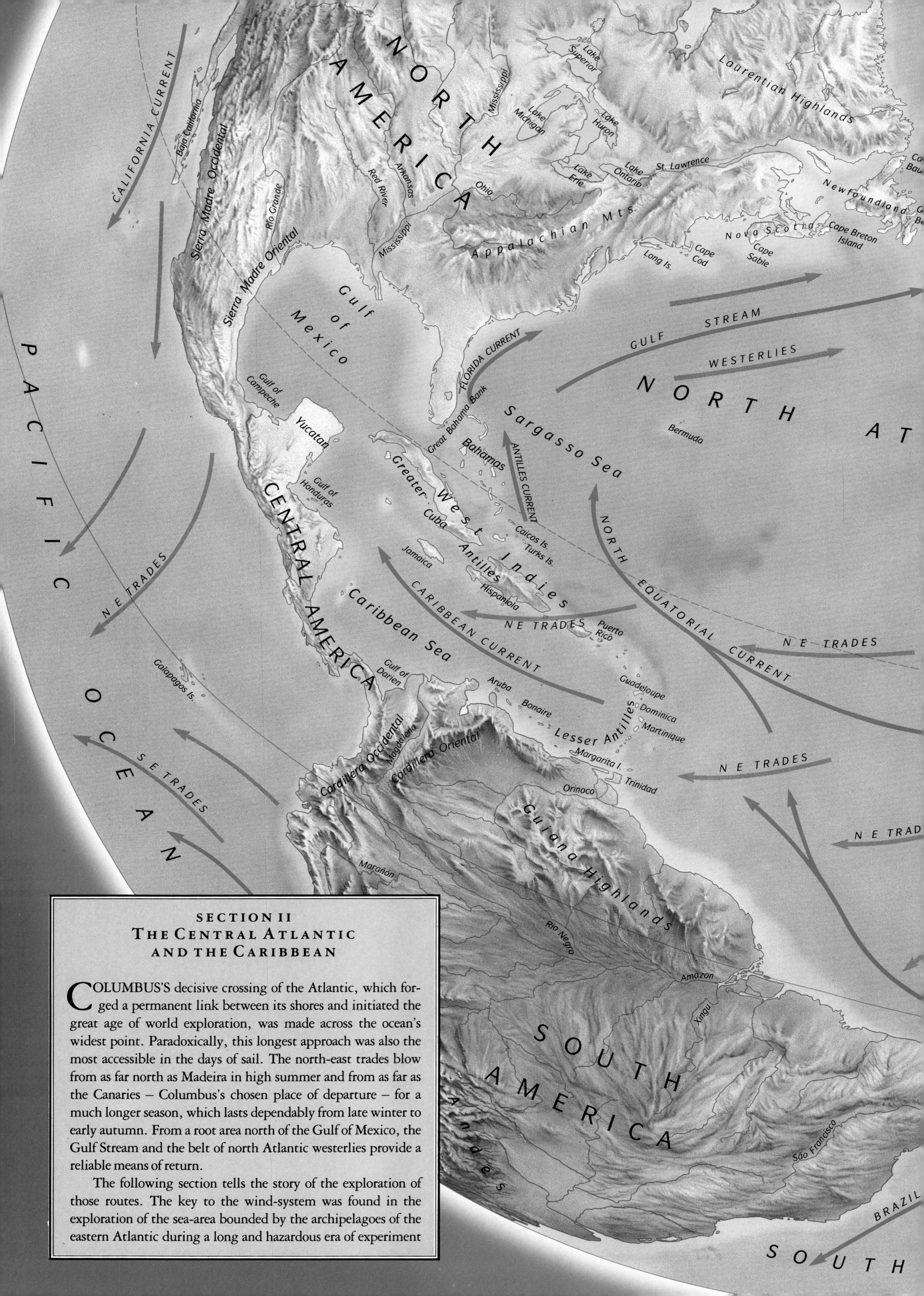

PACIFIC OCEAN

NORTH AMERICA

CENTRAL AMERICA

SOUTH AMERICA

NORTH ATL

SOUTH

CALIFORNIA CURRENT

Baja California

Sierra Madre Occidental

Sierra Madre Oriental

Rio Grande

Red River

Arkansas

Mississippi

Mississippi

Ohio

Lake Superior

Lake Michigan

Lake Huron

Lake Erie

Lake Ontario

St. Lawrence

Laurentian Highlands

Newfoundland

Nova Scotia

Cape Breton Island

Cape Sable

Cape Cod

Long Is.

Appalachian Mts.

Gulf of Mexico

Gulf of Campeche

Yucatan

Gulf of Honduras

Greater

Cuba

Jamaica

Hispaniola

Bahamas

Great Bahama Bank

FLORIDA CURRENT

Caicos Is.

Turks Is.

Puerto Rico

Sargasso Sea

Bermuda

GULF STREAM

WESTERLIES

NORTH

ANTILLES CURRENT

West Indies

Antilles

NORTH EQUATORIAL CURRENT

N E TRADES

N E TRADES

N E TRADES

N E TRADES

N E TRADES

N E TRAD

N E TRADES

S E TRADES

CARIBBEAN CURRENT

Caribbean Sea

Gulf of Darien

Cordillera Occidental

Magdalena

Cordillera Oriental

Marañón

Galapagos Is

Aruba

Bonaire

Margarita I.

Trinidad

Guadeloupe

Dominica

Martinique

Lesser Antilles

Orinoco

Guiana Highlands

Rio Negro

Amazon

Xingu

São Francisco

Andes

BRAZIL

SECTION II
THE CENTRAL ATLANTIC
AND THE CARIBBEAN

COLUMBUS'S decisive crossing of the Atlantic, which forged a permanent link between its shores and initiated the
great age of world exploration, was made across the ocean's
widest point. Paradoxically, this longest approach was also the
most accessible in the days of sail. The north-east trades blow
from as far north as Madeira in high summer and from as far as
the Canaries – Columbus's chosen place of departure – for a
much longer season, which lasts dependably from late winter to
early autumn. From a root area north of the Gulf of Mexico, the
Gulf Stream and the belt of north Atlantic westerlies provide a
reliable means of return.

The following section tells the story of the exploration of
those routes. The key to the wind-system was found in the
exploration of the sea-area bounded by the archipelagoes of the
eastern Atlantic during a long and hazardous era of experiment

Labrador Sea

Greenland

WESTERLIES

NORTH ATLANTIC DRIFT

WESTERLIES

WESTERLIES

WESTERLIES

WESTERLIES

North Sea

Elbe

BRITISH ISLES

Black Sea

Rhine

Loire

Alps

Bay of Biscay

Mediterranean Sea

Azores

ATLANTIC OCEAN

Maderia

CANARIES CURRENT

Canary Is.

N E TRADES

N E TRADES

N E TRADES

N E TRADES

N E TRADES

N E TRADES

Cape Verde Is.

Cape Verde

Senegal

Atlas Mountains

Sahara Desert

Tibesti

Hoggar

A F R I C A

Lake Chad

Sahel

Niger

Benue

Equator

Slave Coast

Tropic of Nile

Cancer

CURRENT

S E TRADES

ATLANTIC OCEAN

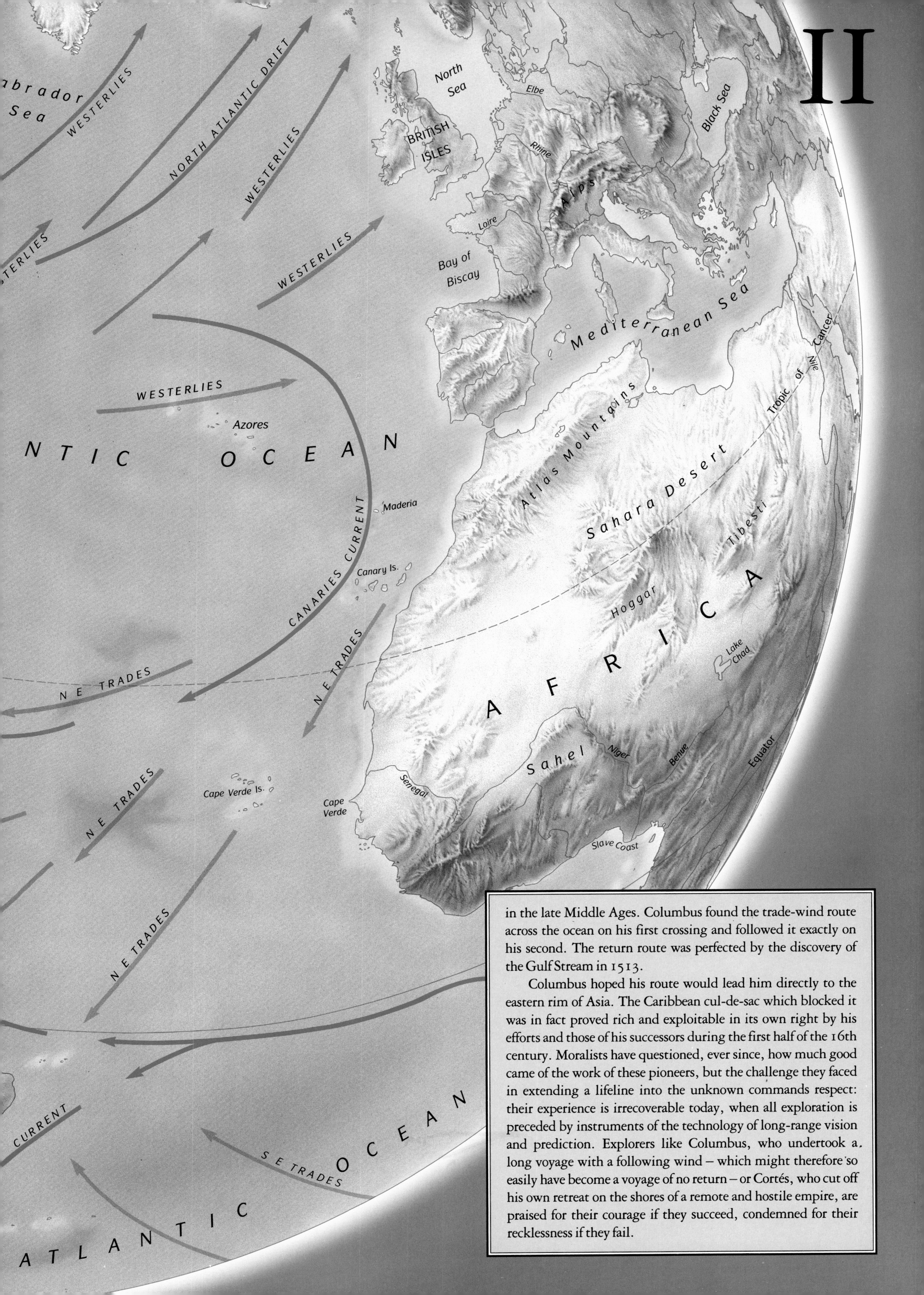

in the late Middle Ages. Columbus found the trade-wind route across the ocean on his first crossing and followed it exactly on his second. The return route was perfected by the discovery of the Gulf Stream in 1513.

Columbus hoped his route would lead him directly to the eastern rim of Asia. The Caribbean cul-de-sac which blocked it was in fact proved rich and exploitable in its own right by his efforts and those of his successors during the first half of the 16th century. Moralists have questioned, ever since, how much good came of the work of these pioneers, but the challenge they faced in extending a lifeline into the unknown commands respect: their experience is irrecoverable today, when all exploration is preceded by instruments of the technology of long-range vision and prediction. Explorers like Columbus, who undertook a long voyage with a following wind – which might therefore so easily have become a voyage of no return – or Cortés, who cut off his own retreat on the shores of a remote and hostile empire, are praised for their courage if they succeed, condemned for their recklessness if they fail.

8

THE AZORES AND THE CANARIES: THE 'ATLANTIC MEDITERRANEAN' 1330-1452

A LEFT *Atlantic islands were settings of chivalric tales or traditional fables; St. Brendan was supposed to have mistaken a gigantic whale for one of them.*
1 BELOW *Madeira and the Azores were discovered by navigators seeking westerly winds with which to return home from the Canaries and the African coast.*

IN THE *13th century, when Mediterranean navigators overcame the intimidatingly adverse current of the Strait of Hercules and began to frequent the Atlantic in large numbers, some turned northwards, to the lucrative and well-known markets of Flanders and England; others turned south into waters unsailed – so far as we know – for centuries, off the west coast of Africa. The record of only one such voyage has survived, that of the brothers Vivaldi in 1291. They presumably intended a circumnavigation of Africa rather than a transnavigation of the Atlantic, but the galleys they deployed were hardly suited to either purpose. They were never heard of again, but it is likely that there were other journeys in the same direction. It was probably in the course of such expeditions that the Canary Islands were discovered. According to Petrarch, writing in the 1340s, Genoese armed ships had sailed to the Canaries 'within the memory of my parents {patrum}'.*

Beginning in the 1330s, the archipelagoes of the eastern Atlantic were explored and mapped. Some of the Canary Islands with three islands in relative positions suggestive of the Madeira archipelago, appeared for the first time on a surviving map of 1339 (see map B). Thereafter there were so many voyages, accumulating so much knowledge, that an almost complete picture of the islands of the east-central Atlantic became available in Latin Christendom. The transformation of that picture by the time of maps reliably dated in the 1380s, in which the Canaries are shown almost complete, with the Savage Islands, the Madeira archipelago and what can be taken to be the Azores, was a remarkable achievement: hazardous to the vessels, challenging to the technology, and unparalled in the experience of sailors of the time. The result was the creation of a zone of navigation in previously unexplored waters bounded by the Azores in the north, the Canaries in the south and the Iberian and African coasts in the east (see map 1), and linked by the Atlantic wind-system. French-speaking historians have coined the phrase 'Atlantic Mediterranean' to denote this area; the term is justified, not only because the area was a 'middle sea' surrounded by mainlands and archipelagoes which constituted, for a time, the practical limits of navigation, but because it was the creation of Mediterranean mariners and came to represent an extension or transplantation of traditional Mediterranean civilization in the new oceanic environment.

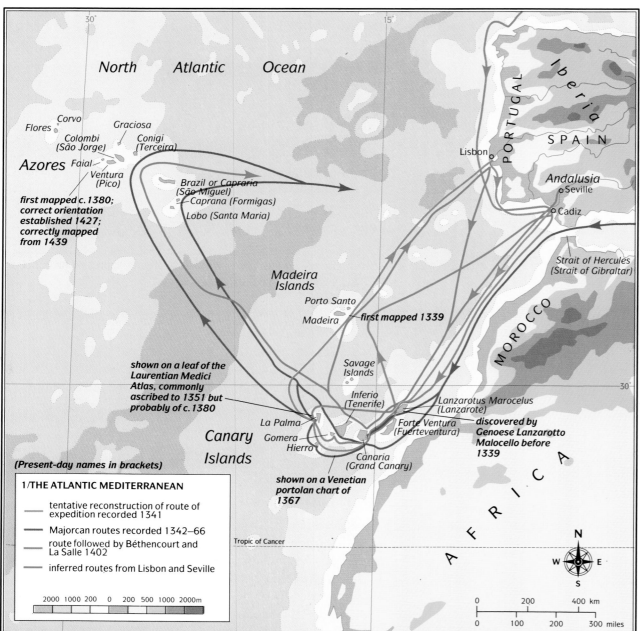

North Atlantic Ocean

Flores
Corvo
Colombi (São Jorge)
Graciosa
Conigi (Terceira)
Azores
Faial
Ventura (Pico)

first mapped c.1380; correct orientation established 1427; correctly mapped from 1439

Brazil or Capraria (São Miguel)
Caprana (Formigas)
Lobo (Santa Maria)

Madeira Islands
Porto Santo
Madeira **first mapped 1339**

shown on a leaf of the Laurentian Medici Atlas, commonly ascribed to 1351 but probably of c.1380

Savage Islands

Inferio (Tenerife)
La Palma
Gomera
Hierro
Canaria (Grand Canary)
Lanzarotus Marocelus (Lanzarote)
Forte Ventura (Fuerteventura)

discovered by Genoese Lanzarotto Malocello before 1339

Canary Islands

(Present-day names in brackets)

shown on a Venetian portolan chart of 1367

Iberia
PORTUGAL
SPAIN
Lisbon
Andalusia
Seville
Cadiz
Strait of Hercules (Strait of Gibraltar)
MOROCCO
AFRICA

Tropic of Cancer

1/THE ATLANTIC MEDITERRANEAN

━━ tentative reconstruction of route of expedition recorded 1341
━━ Majorcan routes recorded 1342–66
━━ route followed by Béthencourt and La Salle 1402
━━ inferred routes from Lisbon and Seville

2000 1000 200 0 200 500 1000 2000m

0   200   400 km
0   100   200   300 miles

N W E S

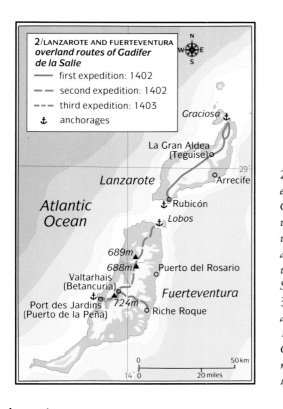

2/LANZAROTE AND FUERTEVENTURA
overland routes of Gadifer de la Salle
— first expedition: 1402
-- second expedition: 1402
--- third expedition: 1403
⚓ anchorages

N W E S

Graciosa

La Gran Aldea (Teguise)

Lanzarote

Arrecife

Atlantic Ocean

⚓ Rubicón

⚓ Lobos

689m ▲
688m ▲ Puerto del Rosario

Valtarhais (Betancuria)

⚓ Port des Jardins (Puerto de la Peña)
724m ▲ Riche Roque

Fuerteventura

0 — 50 km
0 — 20 miles

14°

2 LEFT *The first land explorations of the Canaries, the course of which were sufficiently well recorded to permit an attempt to reconstruct them, were those of Gadifer de la Salle in 1402–3.*

3 RIGHT *Boccaccio wrote a detailed account of a 14th-century voyage to the Canaries, on which the reconstruction of his voyage is based.*

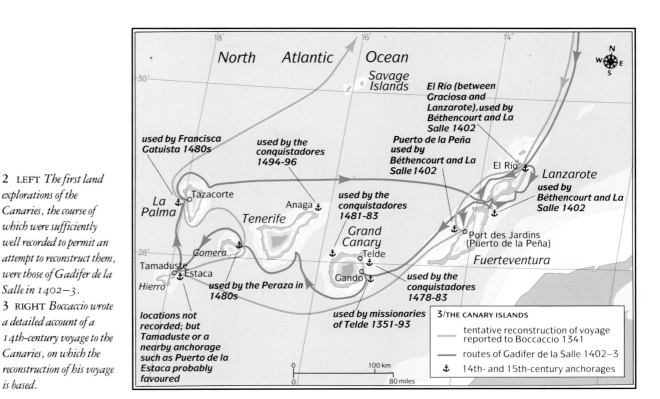

North Atlantic Ocean

Savage Islands

El Río (between Graciosa and Lanzarote), used by Béthencourt and La Salle 1402

used by Francisca Gatuista 1480s

used by the conquistadores 1494-96

Puerto de la Peña used by Béthencourt and La Salle 1402

El Río

Lanzarote

used by Béthencourt and La Salle 1402

⚓ Tazacorte

La Palma

Anaga ⚓

Tenerife

used by the conquistadores 1481-83

Grand Canary

⚓ Telde

Port des Jardins (Puerto de la Peña)

Fuerteventura

⚓ Gomera

Tamaduste ⚓ Estaca

Hierro

used by the Peraza in 1480s

⚓ Gando

used by the conquistadores 1478-83

used by missionaries of Telde 1351-93

locations not recorded; but Tamaduste or a nearby anchorage such as Puerto de la Estaca probably favoured

3/THE CANARY ISLANDS
— tentative reconstruction of voyage reported to Boccaccio 1341
— routes of Gadifer de la Salle 1402–3
⚓ 14th- and 15th-century anchorages

0 — 100 km
0 — 80 miles

THE achievement of Mediterranean sailors in opening up the Atlantic Mediterranean was the fruit of modest miracles of high-medieval technology: the compass, the portolan chart, the cog – a round-hulled, square-rigged vessel – and primitive celestial navigation. The navigators based their judgements of relative latitude on glimpsed appraisals of the height of the sun or the Pole star above the horizon. Most were 'unknown pilots'. Many known by name are recorded only or chiefly on maps: Lanzarotto Malocello, of Genoa, was recorded on the island that still bears a version of his name by a cartographer of 1339 (*see* map B); in a cartographer's note, Jaume Ferrer of Majorca was reported lost off the African coast in 1346; of the Portuguese Diogo Silves, who may have established the true lie of the Azores in 1427, the sole memorial, on a Majorcan map, was accidentally blotted by ink in the 19th century. But most of the explorers remain anonymous. However, just as their efforts can be reconstructed from the maps, so their profile can be built up from a few surviving documents. They came, to begin with, mainly from Genoa and Majorca, homes of the art of the 'conners of the sea', and – later and increasingly – from Portugal and Andalusia. They often had crusading experience, like the Poitevin adventurer, Gadifer de la Salle, who went to the Canaries in 1402 (*see* map **2**), or Joan de Mora, who was the king of Aragon's captain in Canarian waters in 1366. They were sometimes penurious noblemen escaping from a society of restricted opportunity at home. They sought 'routes of gold' like Ferrer, or 'routes of spices' like the Vivaldi, or slaves, like the Las Casas and Peraza families of Seville, who promoted a series of raids and conquests from 1393. They strove to embody chivalric fable, to win fiefs or

B BELOW LEFT *Most of the exploration of the Atlantic Mediterranean is recorded only in cartographic evidence. Dulcert's map of 1339 includes the first record of a named explorer (Lanzarotto Malocello) in the Canaries.* **C** BELOW RIGHT *Bianco's 1448 map shows the Azores arranged diagonally. Though still stylised, it is more realistic than the north–south alignment of the archipelago on earlier maps.*

create kingdoms, like the would-be conquerer of the Canaries, Luis de la Cerda, created 'Prince of Fortunia' in 1344, or la Salle's partner, Jean de Béthencourt, who had himself proclaimed 'king of the Canaries' in the streets of Seville. Or else they were missionaries, like the Franciscans of the Canarian bishopric of Telde, who sailed to and fro for nearly 40 years until, in 1393, they were massacred. They came from a world steeped in the idealisation of adventure: the Perazas' squalid wars against Stone Age savages on the island of Gomera were celebrated in chivalric verse; the coat-of-arms of the Béthencourt family was charged with wodehouses in tribute to Jean's Canarian adversaries. They bore storybook names like Gadifer and Lancelot. They aspired to fame, and most have been forgotten.

Their story can be divided into three phases. The first begins with Malocello's expedition, before 1339, and continues with prolific records of voyages to the Canaries in the 1340s, one of which – including Portuguese, Spanish and Italian participants – was the subject of an account copied by Boccaccio and dated 1341 (*see* map **3**). From 1342, a series of voyages in ships described as 'cogs', to 'islands newly found in the parts of the west' were recorded in Majorcan documents; despite gaps in the archives, these can be shown to have a more or less continuous history until the 1380s. Visits to the Azores and Madeira group can be inferred both from the nature of the wind-system, which tends to impose a daring passage out into the ocean to the north-west on traffic returning from the Canaries (*see* map **1**), and from cartographical evidence, which shows all but the two most westerly islands of the Azores to have been known to mapmakers of the 1380s.

In the second phase, from 1402 to 1405, the expedition of Béthencourt and la Salle – a gold-hunting conquest of some of the Canary Islands – made no new discoveries, but did contribute the first land exploration to be recorded in an itinerary that can be mapped (*see* map **2**). The final phase, straggling a long period from 1427 to 1452, was an exclusively Portuguese enterprise, one that established the true relationship of the islands of the Azores to one another, enabled mapmakers to fix them in roughly their true positions, and added the two remotest islands, Flores and Corvo, to the known tally.

The Atlantic Mediterranean was not just a world of islands, but of winds: discovery of the wind-system – of the outward-bound north-east trades and Canary current and of the returning westerlies – opened a causeway to European navigators that would carry Columbus to America. It was, moreover, at least in the Canary Islands, a 'brave new world' with people in it, a terrain of anthropological as well as geographical discovery, where began the continuous history of Europeans' self-revealing encounters with 'primitive' cultures.

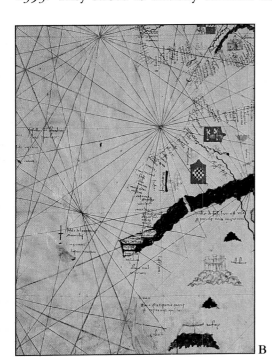

B

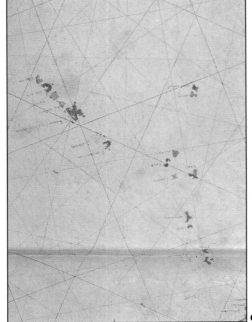

C

9 CHRISTOPHER COLUMBUS 1451/2-1506

ATLANTIC exploration before 1492 had established the ocean as exploitable space, sprinkled by cartographers with rumoured islands, even, by some cosmographers, with undiscovered worlds. Its probable dimensions, however, inhibited any attempt at transnavigation. Island-hopping to the west made no progress after the discovery of Flores and Corvo in the Azores in 1452. The remoter Atlantic could not be explored until its wind-system was decoded.

Christopher Columbus was an escapee from the clannish, socially modest Genoese weaver's household in which he was born in 1451 or 1452. He was ambitious for both social and material gain. These were aims that he pursued by a means which chivalric romance made familiar in the 15th century: seaborne deeds of renown. His explorer's vocation arose from the seafaring which he began 'at a very young age', and which, he said, 'inclines all who follow it to wish to know the secrets of this world'. Removal from Genoa to Lisbon by about 1477 and marriage, into one of the most peripheral of Portugal's noble families, may have helped to focus his ambitions. By 1489, possibly as early as 1482, he had become steeped in geographical literature. But his essential formation was as a practical navigator. By the mid-1480s, he may have accomplished, by the standard of his time, his later boast to have 'sailed all the seas that men have sailed', except the Indian Ocean (see map 1).

The single-mindedness commonly attributed to him is not borne out by the first-hand sources. He contemplated at least three projects: a search for new Atlantic islands; a quest for an 'Antipodean' world; and a westward crossing to Asia. The first scheme was plausible, but such ventures were commonplace. The second concerned a common speculation of late-medieval cosmography: that an unknown land must occupy part of the unexplored hemisphere, largely on the grounds that the ocean would otherwise be disturbingly big and the geography of the planet imbalanced. The third was universally regarded as theoretically possible, though the size of the globe was known to be sufficient to preclude an ocean crossing. Even on the most favourable informed estimates, Columbus, along his chosen latitude (that of the Canaries), would have between 5,000 and 6,750 nautical miles of ocean to cross, this at a period when the maximum distance normally traversed by a ship on the open sea on established routes was less than 800 miles. The feat seemed beyond any vessel of the time.

1 BELOW *Columbus's formation as a navigator and cosmographer before 1492 has to be pieced together tentatively from stray references in his later writings and the information of early biographers.*

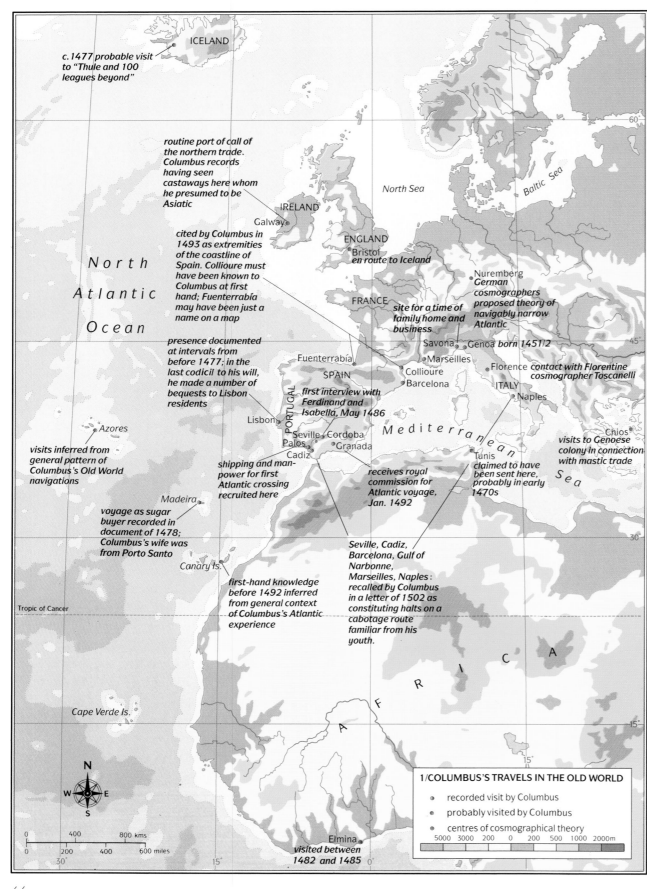

c.1477 probable visit to "Thule and 100 leagues beyond"

ICELAND

routine port of call of the northern trade. Columbus records having seen castaways here whom he presumed to be Asiatic

North Sea

Baltic Sea

IRELAND

Galway

ENGLAND
Bristol en route to Iceland

cited by Columbus in 1493 as extremities of the coastline of Spain. Collioure must have been known to Columbus at first hand; Fuenterrabía may have been just a name on a map

North Atlantic Ocean

FRANCE

site for a time of family home and business

Nuremberg
German cosmographers proposed theory of navigably narrow Atlantic

Savona
Genoa born 1451/2

Marseilles

Florence contact with Florentine cosmographer Toscanelli

presence documented at intervals from before 1477; in the last codicil to his will, he made a number of bequests to Lisbon residents

Fuenterrabía

SPAIN

Collioure
Barcelona

ITALY

Naples

first interview with Ferdinand and Isabella, May 1486

PORTUGAL

Chios
visits to Genoese colony in connection with mastic trade

Azores

visits inferred from general pattern of Columbus's Old World navigations

Lisbon

Seville Cordoba
Palos
Cadiz
Granada

Mediterranean Sea

Tunis
claimed to have been sent here, probably in early 1470s

shipping and man-power for first Atlantic crossing recruited here

receives royal commission for Atlantic voyage, Jan. 1492

Madeira

voyage as sugar buyer recorded in document of 1478; Columbus's wife was from Porto Santo

Seville, Cadiz, Barcelona, Gulf of Narbonne, Marseilles, Naples: recalled by Columbus in a letter of 1502 as constituting halts on a cabotage route familiar from his youth.

Canary Is.

first-hand knowledge before 1492 inferred from general context of Columbus's Atlantic experience

Tropic of Cancer

A F R I C A

Cape Verde Is.

N W E S

0   400   800 kms
0   200   400   600 miles

Elmina
visited between 1482 and 1485

1/COLUMBUS'S TRAVELS IN THE OLD WORLD

- recorded visit by Columbus
- probably visited by Columbus
- centres of cosmographical theory

5000 3000 200 0 200 500 1000 2000m

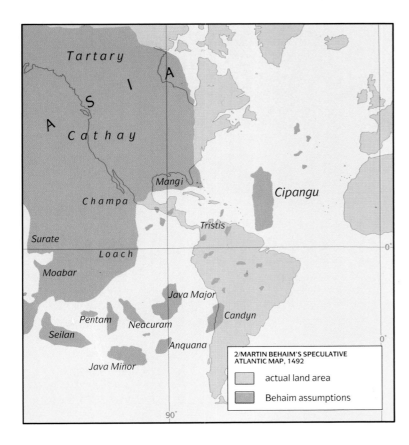

2 ABOVE *The map
Columbus had with him on
his first voyage has been lost
but must have resembled
this reconstruction based
principally on Martin
Behaim's globe. The
superimposition of the
modern outline shows why
Columbus mistook the New
World for part of Asia.*

A BELOW *Behaim's
globe of 1492 represents the
closest we can get to
Columbus's mental picture
of the North Atlantic in
maps surviving from his
time. Marco Polo's island
of Cipangu is in the lower
left-hand corner.*

COLUMBUS was determined to conquer the apparently
insuperable practical obstacles to a crossing of the Atlantic. His own writings prove beyond reasonable doubt
that by the time he made his great voyage he was personally
committed to reaching Asia, even though the terms of his commission spoke more guardedly of 'islands and mainlands in the
Ocean'. His optimism seems to have rested on three grounds.
The first was that the world was smaller than was generally
held; calculations he later recorded yielded a value 25 per cent
less than the true figure and 8 per cent less than that of any of
his contemporaries. Second, in common with many cosmographers, he supposed that the Eurasian landmass extended
much farther to the east than traditionally supposed. Finally,
he hoped to be able to break the journey *en route*, particularly at
the fabled island of Cipangu, which Marco Polo had reported
to lie 1,500 miles out into the ocean from China. All three
links in his chain of reasoning were weak: the first was demon-
strably false; the second highly suppositious; and the third reliant on the authority of Marco Polo, whose description of the
Orient was widely disbelieved.

Nonetheless, minority learned opinion was available to en-
dorse some parts of his plan. In Florence and Nuremberg, for
example, there were cosmographers who sustained, albeit to a
lesser degree than Columbus, the view that the globe was small
and the Atlantic navigable. Furthermore, Columbus was supported at the Spanish court by at least two accredited experts.
The consensus of learned opinion, however, was against him,
and he was obliged to fall back on boasted practical experience

A

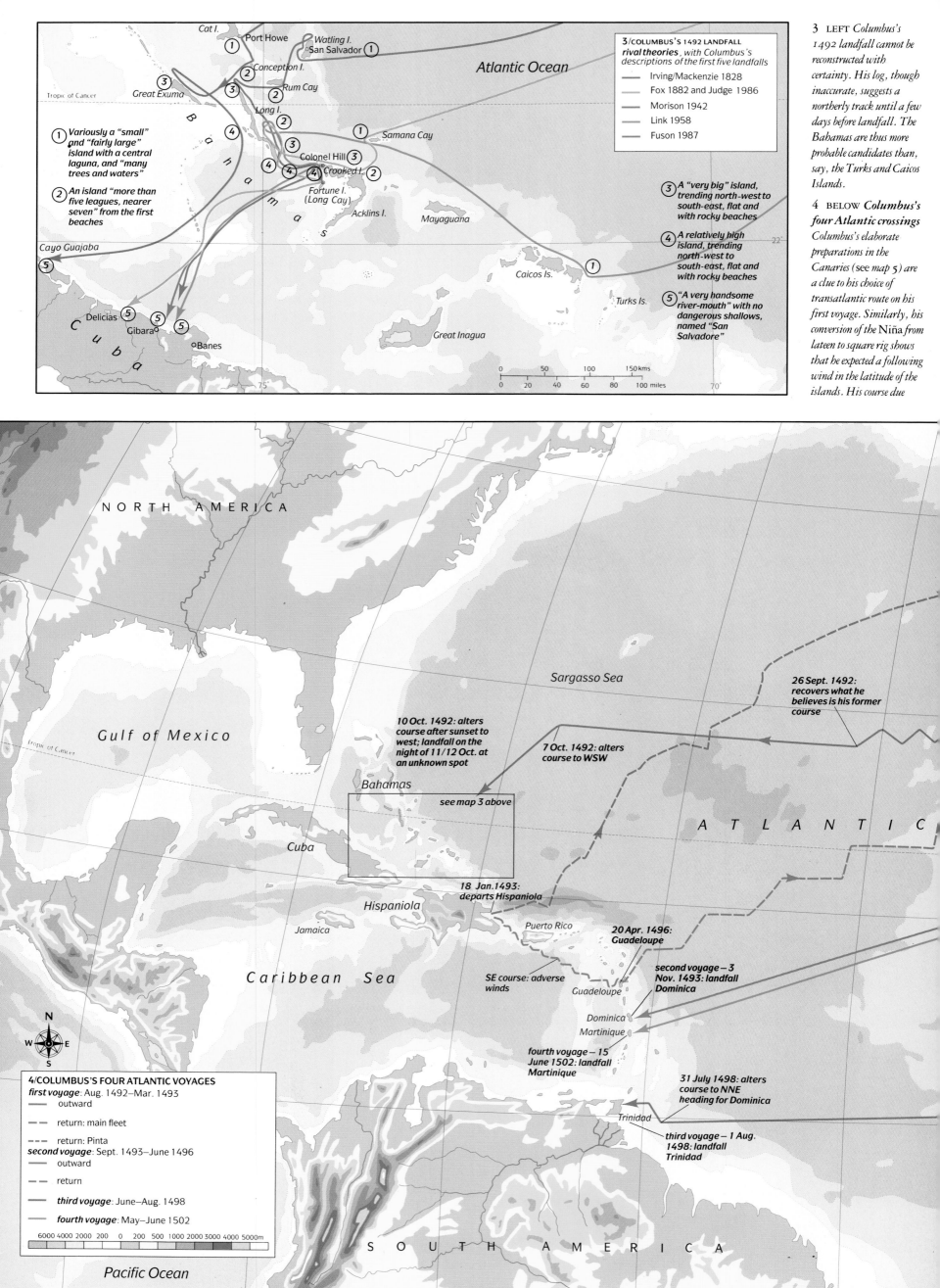

3/COLUMBUS'S 1492 LANDFALL
rival theories, with Columbus's descriptions of the first five landfalls
— Irving/Mackenzie 1828
— Fox 1882 and Judge 1986
— Morison 1942
— Link 1958
— Fuson 1987

Atlantic Ocean

Cat I.
Port Howe
Watling I.
San Salvador
Conception I.
Rum Cay
Great Exuma
Tropic of Cancer
Long I.
Samana Cay
Colonel Hill
Crooked I.
Fortune I. (Long Cay)
Acklins I.
Mayaguana
Caicos Is.
Turks Is.
Great Inagua
Cayo Guajaba
Delicias
Gibara
Banes
Cuba

① Variously a "small" and "fairly large" island with a central laguna, and "many trees and waters"

② An island "more than five leagues, nearer seven" from the first beaches

③ A "very big" island, trending north-west to south-east, flat and with rocky beaches

④ A relatively high island, trending north-west to south-east, flat and with rocky beaches

⑤ "A very handsome river-mouth" with no dangerous shallows, named "San Salvadore"

0 50 100 150 kms
0 20 40 60 80 100 miles

3 LEFT *Columbus's 1492 landfall cannot be reconstructed with certainty. His log, though inaccurate, suggests a northerly track until a few days before landfall. The Bahamas are thus more probable candidates than, say, the Turks and Caicos Islands.*

4 BELOW *Columbus's four Atlantic crossings Columbus's elaborate preparations in the Canaries (see map 5) are a clue to his choice of transatlantic route on his first voyage. Similarly, his conversion of the Niña from lateen to square rig shows that he expected a following wind in the latitude of the islands. His course due*

NORTH AMERICA

Gulf of Mexico
Tropic of Cancer

Sargasso Sea

26 Sept. 1492: recovers what he believes is his former course

10 Oct. 1492: alters course after sunset to west; landfall on the night of 11/12 Oct. at an unknown spot

7 Oct. 1492: alters course to WSW

Bahamas
see map 3 above

Cuba

ATLANTIC

Hispaniola

18 Jan. 1493: departs Hispaniola

Jamaica

Puerto Rico

20 Apr. 1496: Guadeloupe

Caribbean Sea

SE course: adverse winds

Guadeloupe

second voyage – 3 Nov. 1493: landfall Dominica

Dominica
Martinique

fourth voyage – 15 June 1502: landfall Martinique

31 July 1498: alters course to NNE heading for Dominica

Trinidad

third voyage – 1 Aug. 1498: landfall Trinidad

4/COLUMBUS'S FOUR ATLANTIC VOYAGES
first voyage: Aug. 1492–Mar. 1493
— outward
--- return: main fleet
-·- return: Pinta
second voyage: Sept. 1493–June 1496
— outward
--- return
third voyage: June–Aug. 1498
fourth voyage: May–June 1502

6000 4000 2000 200 0 200 500 1000 2000 3000 4000 5000m

SOUTH AMERICA

Pacific Ocean

to make up for his obvious deficiences in learning.

Columbus's departure depended not on learned approval –
experts rarely rule – but on political and financial backing. His
quest for patronage began to make progress in the latter half of
the 1480s, when he concentrated his efforts on the Spanish
court, where some of his fellow-Genoese were financially influential, and where a consortium, reliant on Genoese capital,
had been brought together by the exchequer official, Alonso de
Quintanilla, for another Atlantic project: the conquest of the
Canaries. This circle became the basis for financing Columbus,
with most of the money for the first voyage apparently advanced by Francesco Pinelli, Genoese banker of Seville, and Luis
de Santángel, treasury official of the crown of Aragon. Political
backing was won by Columbus's tireless self-recommendation,
winning lobbyists among the Franciscan Order, with whom
Columbus seems to have enjoyed a special rapport, and in the
entourage of the heir to the throne, where he made some of his
closest and most enduring friends. Ferdinand and Isabella were
influenced in his favour by their need for a new source of gold
to rival Portugal's African bonanza and to replace the tributes
forfeited when they conquered Granada.

*west suggests simply that he
wanted to make maximum
westing as directly as
possible and does not
support the theory that he
had prior knowledge of the
farther shore. His decision
to return well to the north
of his outward track
suggests experience of the
prevailing westerlies in the
latitude of the Azores.
Columbus's outward routes
on his second and fourth
voyages show his absorption
of the lessons of the north-
east trades. His attempts to
deviate from the wind-
system, by crossing out too
far south on his third
voyage and coming back too
far south on his second
voyage, were time-wasting
failures.*

To reach his hoped-for new lands, Columbus had first to
discover a practical route across the Atlantic. His first great –
and undisputed – achievement was the exploration of the
North Atlantic wind-system. Maritime explorers under sail in
most parts of the world have tended to prefer to make their
attempts against an adverse wind: the assurance of returning
home is at least as important as the prospect of a new discovery.
Thus most known 15th-century attempts to advance the Atlantic frontier had been made in the zone of the westerlies that
blow across the Azores. As a point of departure, the Azores had
the additional advantage of lying well to the west in a relatively
northerly latitude, promising a short passage to new lands. The
strength of the westerlies, however, defeated every attempt.
Columbus succeeded where others failed because he made his
journey from farther south, from the Canaries, where he could
ride on the north-east trades, apparently relying on the hope of
finding the westerlies for his return. His first two Atlantic
crossings demonstrated the viability of this scheme. His third,
stymied in the Doldrums, showed that he had discovered a
route of unique merit. In the new century, the discovery of the
Gulf Stream brought the only significant modification.

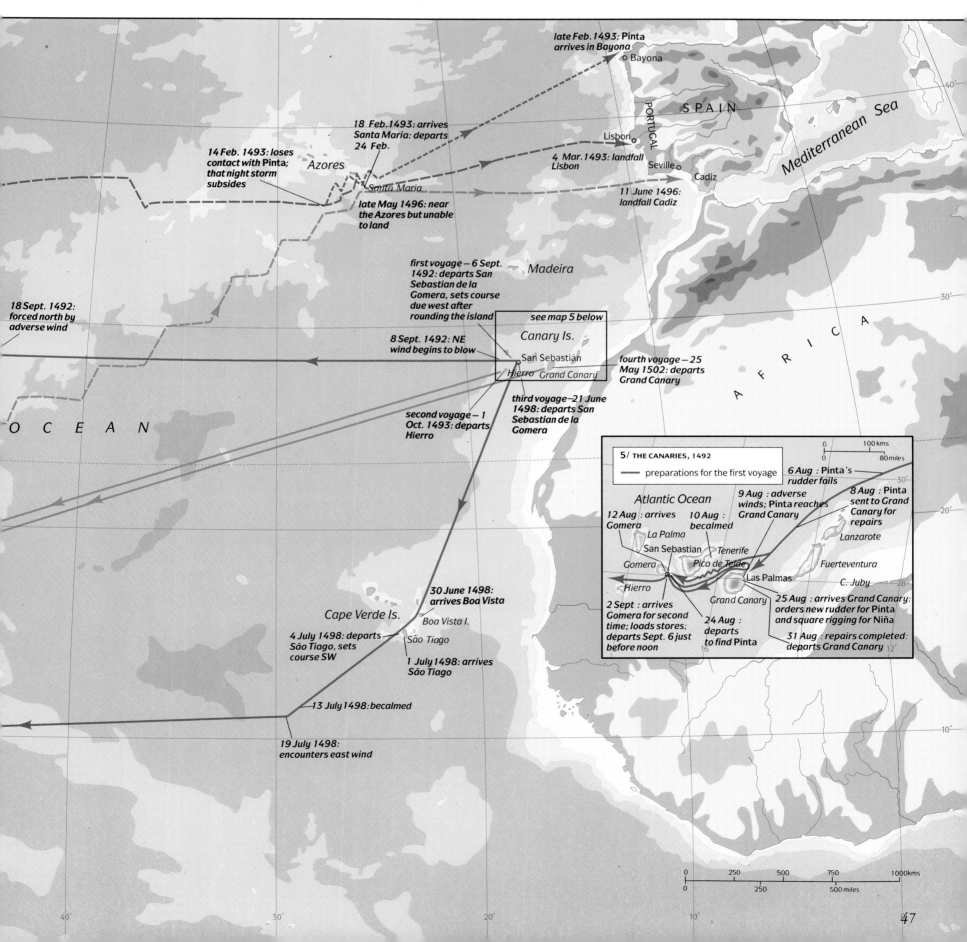

47

Columbus was as notable an explorer of coasts as of routes. His first landfall in the New World cannot be pinpointed: his sailing directions strongly suggest that it was an island – probably a fairly northerly one – in the Bahamas, but his description is too vague to justify claims in favour of particular isles (*see* map 3). Beyond the Bahamas, his routes can be reconstructed exactly. In his first three American voyages, he compiled a remarkably full picture of the rim of the Caribbean from southern and eastern Cuba to Dominica and made the first recorded discovery of the American mainland (*see* ch. 10).

He recognised it for what it was: 'a very big mainland, of which until this day nothing was known', and 'a new world' (*otro mundo*). Attempts to deprive him of the honour on the grounds that 'when he set off he did not know where he was going, when he arrived he did not know where he was and when he got back he did not know where he had been' are unworthy. He remained convinced, however, that 'this world is small' and that the new lands were close to or contiguous with Asia. His justification stemmed from wildly inaccurate computations of longitude based on the timing of eclipses.

He was not isolated in his belief. His discoveries, when first announced, were classified by some cosmographers – mainly Italians of humanist inclinations – as 'antipodean'. Others, however, were lulled by Columbus's prestige and charisma. A leading expert at the court of Ferdinand and Isabella regarded him as 'a great theorist and marvellously experienced ... an apostle and ambassador of God' who 'at the present time knows more about this than any other man'. Navigators in Columbus's wake, including Pinzón, Vespucci and Magellan (*see* ch. 13), accepted his world-picture, which was not definitely undermined by empirical evidence until Magellan's voyage across the Pacific disclosed the vastness of the globe.

B BELOW *The maps Waldseemüller made in Dieppe decisively influenced the 16th-century perception of the new discoveries. A map of 1507 imposed the name America, for example, which stuck despite Waldseemüller's recantation of it in this 1513 version, in which the priority of Columbus's discovery is re-affirmed.*

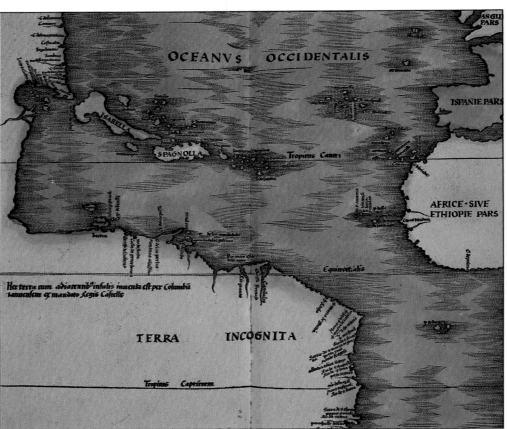

B

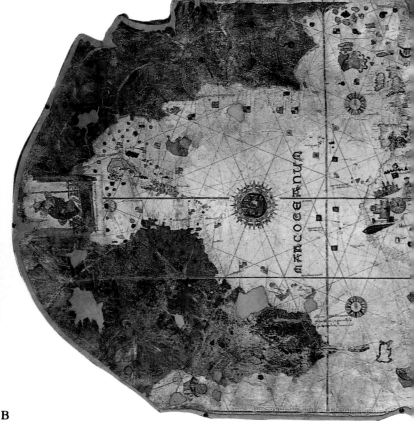

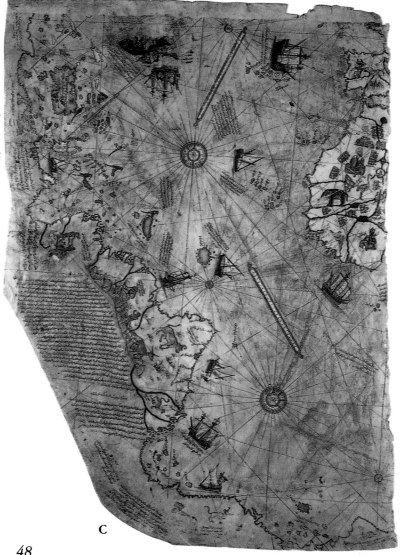

C LEFT *The Turkish Piri Reis map (1513) is important as the only surviving map made with access to Columbus's cartographical sketches; they were captured from a Spanish sailor in 1501. The map also reflects Turkish anxiety about the new discoveries, which threatened to affect the global balance adversely from the Ottoman point of view.* **D** RIGHT *The work of the Polish cartographer, Stobnicza, of about the same period shows Waldseemüller's influence on the diffusion of images of the New World.*

C

A party at court, however, never ceased to deride Columbus and to dispute his theories. The lavish rewards he claimed never materialised. Having staked his reputation on his claim to have found a route to Asia, Columbus found that royal favour was forfeit and his hard-won status at risk when he was unable to deliver the fruits of his promises. For a weaver's son turned seaman, his achievements were dazzling; but implacable ambitions condemned his last years to embittered frustration, from which he took refuge in an almost messianic self-perception as a divinely elected prophet. He died in May 1506, promising on his deathbed that 'though this sickness wracks me without mercy, I can still serve their Highnesses with service the like of which has never been seen'.

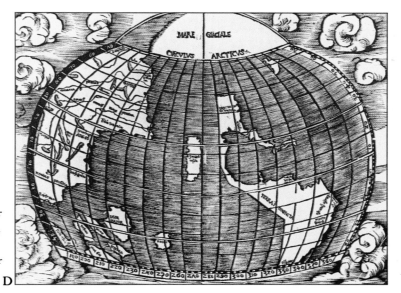

D

E BELOW *Though
evidently several years later
than 1500, the date
traditionally assigned to
it, the Juan de la Cosa
world map has resisted
attempts to impugn its
authenticity: it represents
Columbus's discoveries as
seen by a member of his
circle. The map avoids the
issue of whether there was a
passage to Asia in the
central American isthmus,
obscuring the region with
an image of Columbus's
patron saint, St.
Christopher.*

F RIGHT *The Cantino
map of 1502 shows
discoveries in the North
and South Atlantic, as
well as those of Columbus.
Its purpose seems to have
been to locate discoveries in
relation to the 1494
treaty-line dividing
Portuguese from Spanish
spheres of navigation.
Though the Caribbean and
Brazil are correctly shown
as belonging to Spain and
Portugal respectively,
Newfoundland, at the top,
here called* Terra del Rey
de portugall, *is wrongly
assigned.* G BELOW
Schoener's Mappa Mundi
*of 1520 represents an
attempt to graft the
discoveries of Columbus
and his successors onto
Behaim's conception of the
world. Though up-to-date
in its depiction of the
Caribbean and east coast of
South America, Schoener's
inclusion of a westward
passage to Asia in central
America reflects a vision
that was already
outmoded.* H BELOW
RIGHT *Though the
Cantino map was the first
to show the discoveries of
Columbus, the Contarini
map of 1506, being
printed, was the first to
bring the new world-
picture to to a wider public.*

E

F

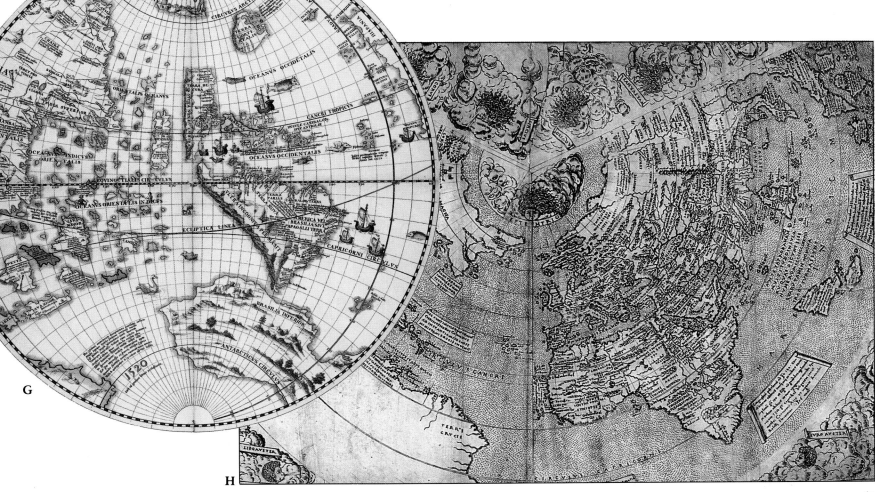

G

H

II *The Central Atlantic and the Caribbean* CHRISTOPHER COLUMBUS 1451/2–1506

10
THE CARIBBEAN
1492-1543

A BELOW *The 'Caveri' or 'Canerio' map of after 1502, derived from Cantino's, illustrates the rapid progress of New World exploration in the decade after 1492. The peninsula-like North American landmass may derive from Columbus's confusing reports of Cuba.*

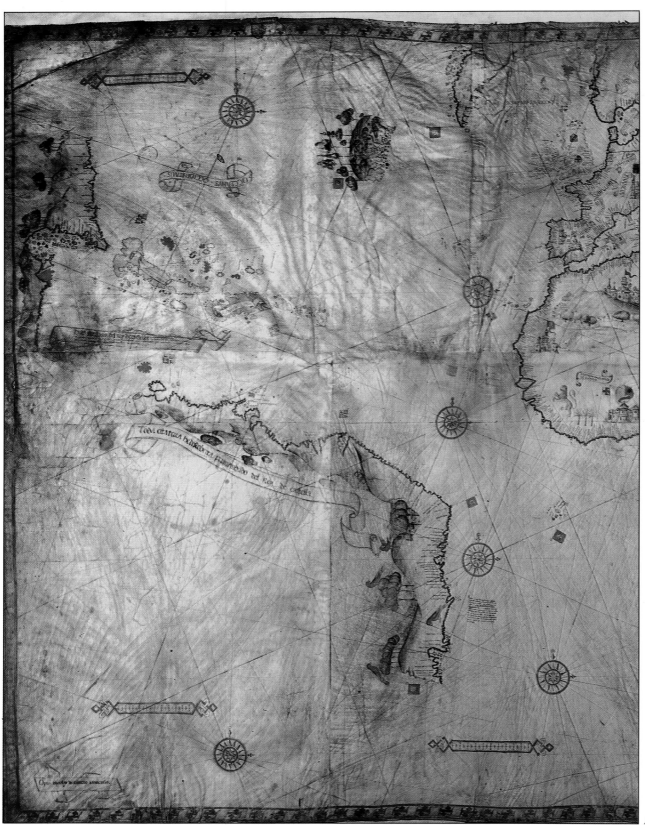

CROSSING the Caribbean, with its variable winds, perilous reefs and shoals, and tempestuous weather, was in some ways a more demanding task than crossing the Atlantic. When Columbus accomplished it, for the first time in recorded history, in June 1502, he felt that he had been guided by divine inspiration and that none of his professional pilots would be capable of finding the way again. Caribbean routes were well known to native canoe-borne traffic, but the early Spanish navigators seem to have made little or no use of native knowledge of the sea. When at the end of Columbus's fourth voyage the expedition was marooned on Jamaica, the Spaniards do not seem to have realized that help on Hispaniola was a short and familiar journey away by canoe. In the late 16th century, much Spanish Caribbean trade was borne by canoe, but indigenous skills contributed little to Spanish seaborne explorations. The Gulf Stream and the currents of the Gulf of Mexico, which must have been known to the Indians, were found by the Spaniards by accident.

The landward exploration of the Caribbean basin on the other hand, though recorded by Spaniards, had been accomplished by Indian predecessors whose expertise European discoverers adopted. In exploring the Aztec world, Cortés and his lieutenants used native maps as well as native guides. In his epic journey from Texas to Mexico, Alvar Núñez Cabeza de Vaca was led by hundreds of Indians.

The extension of European knowledge of the world from the Atlantic to the Caribbean fell into two phases: seaborne and landward. Seaborne exploration falls into two sub-divisions: the investigation of the Caribbean proper, largely the personal achievement of Columbus; and the exploration of the Gulf of Mexico, a slower and more hesitant process, not accomplished for a decade after his death. Landward exploration was slower still, beginning with Balboa in Darién in 1513, continuing with Cortés in Mexico from 1519 and not accomplished, on the northern edge of the Gulf, until the return to Mexico of Soto's ill-fated expedition in 1543.

Columbus was unequalled as a Caribbean explorer. The 'foresight' he claimed was already well developed by the start of his fourth voyage, when he sensed the onset of the hurricane that sank his enemy, Francisco de Bobadilla. Though many emulators followed, none made a comparable contribution, except perhaps the pilot Alaminos, who between 1512 and 1519 discovered the Gulf Stream and guided the conquerors of Mexico.

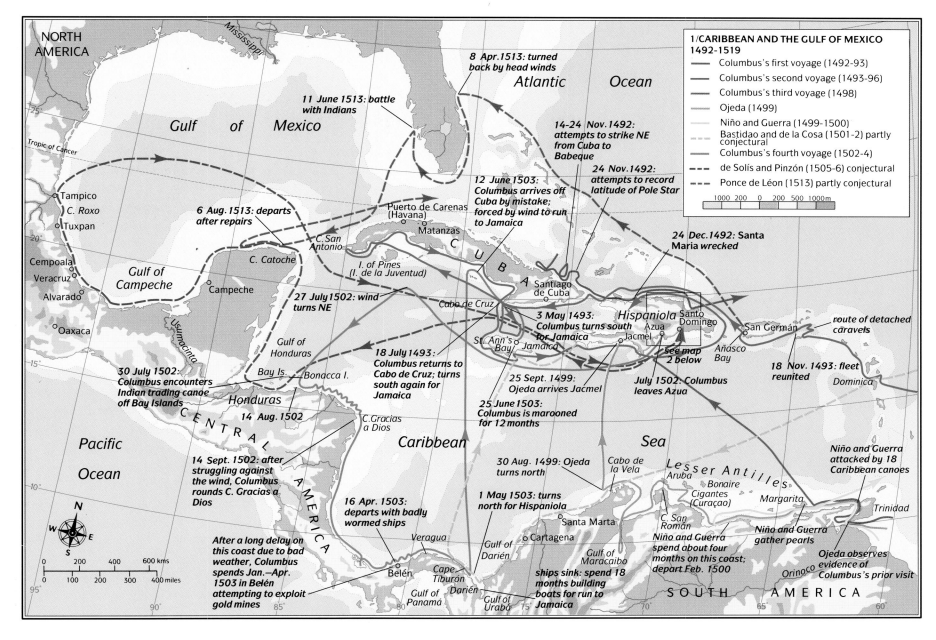

1 / CARIBBEAN AND THE GULF OF MEXICO 1492-1519
— Columbus's first voyage (1492-93)
— Columbus's second voyage (1493-96)
— Columbus's third voyage (1498)
— Ojeda (1499)
— Niño and Guerra (1499-1500)
— Bastidao and de la Cosa (1501-2) partly conjectural
— Columbus's fourth voyage (1502-4)
— — de Solís and Pinzón (1505-6) conjectural
— — Ponce de Léon (1513) partly conjectural

8 Apr.1513: turned back by head winds

11 June 1513: battle with Indians

14-24 Nov.1492: attempts to strike NE from Cuba to Babeque

24 Nov.1492: attempts to record latitude of Pole Star

12 June 1503: Columbus arrives off Cuba by mistake; forced by wind to run to Jamaica

6 Aug.1513: departs after repairs

24 Dec.1492: Santa Maria wrecked

27 July 1502: wind turns NE

3 May 1493: Columbus turns south for Jamaica

route of detached caravels

18 July 1493: Columbus returns to Cabo de Cruz; turns south again for Jamaica

30 July 1502: Columbus encounters Indian trading canoe off Bay Islands

25 Sept. 1499: Ojeda arrives Jacmel

July 1502: Columbus leaves Azua

18 Nov. 1493: fleet reunited

14 Aug. 1502

25 June 1503: Columbus is marooned for 12 months

14 Sept. 1502: after struggling against the wind, Columbus rounds C. Gracias a Dios

30 Aug. 1499: Ojeda turns north

Niño and Guerra attacked by 18 Caribbean canoes

16 Apr. 1503: departs with badly wormed ships

1 May 1503: turns north for Hispaniola

Niño and Guerra gather pearls

After a long delay on this coast due to bad weather, Columbus spends Jan.—Apr. 1503 in Belén attempting to exploit gold mines

ships sink: spend 18 months building boats for run to Jamaica

Niño and Guerra spend about four months on this coast; depart Feb. 1500

Ojeda observes evidence of Columbus's prior visit

T O THE investigation of Cuba and Hispaniola on his first voyage, Columbus on his second added the discovery of the lesser Antilles from Dominica northwards and the exploration of most of the coast of Cuba and Jamaica. He travelled in an atmosphere of febrile anxiety: in his determination to vindicate his claim to have reached Asia, Columbus imposed on his men an oath that Cuba was the mainland Chinese province of Mangi. Cuba was not circumnavigated until 1508, but Columbus's achievement in revealing so much of its nature remains remarkable. On his third voyage, in 1498, he discovered Trinidad and the mainland of South America around the mouth of the Orinoco, fixing the southern limit of the Caribbean. On his last voyage, in 1502, he made the first recorded crossing of the Caribbean from east to west, between Hispaniola and Honduras. In a rainswept epic of endeavour, he filled in the remaining outline of the western and southern shore, from Bonacca to about Cape Tiburón, before the burrowing of termites and the exhaustion of his men brought the great journey to an ignominious end, marooned on Jamaica. Among the side-effects were the discovery of Veragua, with its inaccessible but alluring deposits of gold; the encounter with the trading culture of Honduras (which would lead future *conquistadores* to the civilisations of Mesoamerica); and the establishment of the continen-

1 ABOVE *Columbus left little for emulators to accomplish: 'in-filling' of the north coast of South America; delineation of the shoreline north of Honduras; and perfection of the outlines of islands.*

tal nature of America. Columbus had already glimpsed this on his third voyage, inferring that he had discovered a mighty mainland from the volume of water deposited by the Orinoco. 'I believe,' he wrote, 'that I have discovered a new world (*otro mundo*), hitherto unknown'. Though he exaggerated its proximity to the extremities of Asia, these words constitute a solid basis for Columbus's claim to be the conscious, as well as the adventitious, discoverer of America.

Within the strict confines of the Caribbean, his achievements left successors with little to prove. Most of those who followed in early years were members of his crews or household. Although Columbus's discoveries were widely acclaimed, it was in a restricted world of professional mariners, around the mouth of the Guadalquivir in Spain, that they had their strongest reverberations. From here, in 1499, when Columbus fell from royal favour as a result of his apparent mismanagement of the rebellious garrison of Hispaniola, many of his erstwhile followers seized the opportunity to infringe his privileges. First to encroach, in May 1499, was his former lieutenant, Alonso de Ojeda, accompanied by his future confidant, Amerigo Vespucci. The expedition made initially for Margarita, which Columbus had discovered on his third voyage, and then travelled west along an unknown stretch of coast. On 9 August, they rounded

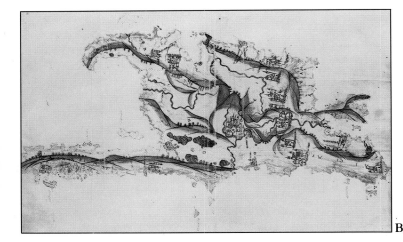

B

B LEFT *Alonso Morales, who made this 1508 map of Hispaniola, was the first, and one of the greatest, of a long line of Spanish surveyors of the 16th, 17th and 18th centuries.* 2 RIGHT *Maritime exploration was succeeded by overland journeys, such as Bartolomé Colón's 1496 crossing of Hispaniola.*

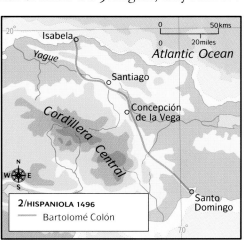

2/HISPANIOLA 1496
— Bartolomé Colón

C LEFT *Diogo Ribeiro's map of 1529, based on official records of discovery and kept by the Crown with the object of supplying continually up-dated cartographical records, shows the opening of a land route across the Isthmus to link the Caribbean with the 'Mar del Sur' – the Pacific.* D ABOVE RIGHT *A map printed in Peter Martyr's history of the New World in 1511 seems remarkably up to date, reflecting the discovery of the Yucatán peninsula by Pinzón and de Solís in 1508 and the legend of the isle of 'Bermendi' north of Cuba.*

little new to the catalogue of exploration. More adventurous, but less profitable, was the voyage headed by Rodrigo de Bastidas, in January 1500, which reached beyond the limit of Ojeda's navigation and explored the Gulf of Urabá. Between them, Columbus, Ojeda and Bastidas demonstrated the continuity of the coast of America from the Orinoco to the Bay of Honduras; meanwhile, explorers of Brazil were to extend this knowledge southward (*see* ch.13). Bastidas' fleet was obliged to run for Hispaniola because of the ravages of termites, where it sank on arrival.

The greatest effect of Bastidas' journey was perhaps the interest aroused in Urabá. Despite attempted colonization, little came of this until in 1510 an old shipmate of Bastidas, Vasco Núñez de Balboa, fled to Urabá to escape his debts. His profile of fortune-hunting and evasion was typical of the forces that drove and drew explorers. Joining the few demoralized survivors of the existing colony, he used his previous knowledge of the area to establish a personal ascendancy, and moved the settlement to the most promising available site, at Santa María de la Antigua in Darién. Seizing sole power by a *putsch*, he turned Darién into an economic success and a base for the first inland explorations of the American continent. His first march, in 1512, took him south, beyond the Caribbean basin to within sight of the Andes (*see* ch.24). His second, from September 1513 to January 1514, launched the exploration of the Isthmus of Panama (*see* map 3) and made him the first European to 'gaze on the Pacific'. In the drive from the Atlantic to the Caribbean, another world-avenue had been opened: for nearly two centuries, for journeys to the Pacific, Balboa's land route across the Isthmus was preferred to the arduous access by sea around Cape Horn.

The second important effect of renewed interest in Urabá was extension of the reconnaissance of the American coast northward from the point at which Columbus left it. After a conference to promote the exploitation of Urabá in 1508, Vincent Yañez Pinzón and Juan Díaz de Solís were commissioned by the crown in March of that year to explore an area vaguely defined as 'west of the Antilles and north of the equator'. Pinzón was a captain in Columbus's first voyage who already had a distinguished career behind him in another theatre (*see* ch.13). Díaz, whose early history is obscure, had a reputation as a leading pilot in the waters of the New World. Their course, after their departure on 29 June 1508, can only be tentatively reconstructed, but by the time they returned to Spain in August 1509, they seem to have run coastwise – looking, presumably, for a westward passage along the Nicaraguan and Honduran coasts to the Yucatán (*see* map 1). Their presumed discovery may be reflected in the depiction of this peninsula in maps of 1511, including that printed (*see* map D) in Peter Martyr's influential account of the

San Román point and made their major discovery: the Gulf of Maracaibo. A native village built over the water reminded Vespucci obscurely of Venice: hence the name Venezuela became attached to the entire coast. They reached Cabo de la Vela before the end of the month, turning north to reach Hispaniola on 5 September.

Columbus blamed Ojeda for robbing him of 'his' pearl fisheries. In fact, Ojeda missed the pearls and died in poverty. The benefit was reaped by the Guerra brothers of Triana, purveyors of hard-tack to the Indies fleets, who were well placed to muster the capital for an expedition to find new resources in Columbus's domains. The active partner in the enterprise was Pero Alonso Niño, a shipmate of Columbus, who led the pearl-fishing voyage of 1499. In the event, the enterprise contributed

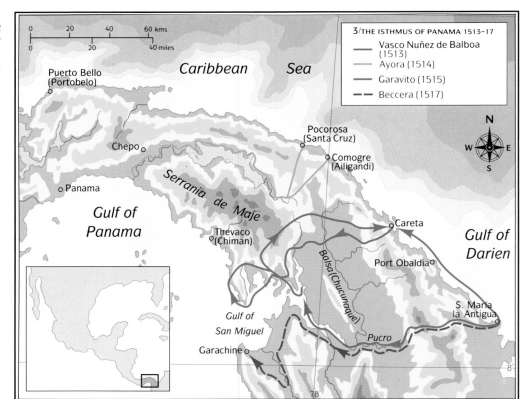

3/THE ISTHMUS OF PANAMA 1513-17
— Vasco Nuñez de Balboa (1513)
— Ayora (1514)
— Garavito (1515)
--- Beccera (1517)

3 LEFT *The discovery of the land route for the Pacific by Balboa in 1513 encouraged exploration of the Isthmus in the course of a search for the best route.*

E RIGHT *The so-called 'Garay' map (c. 1519) reflects the progress of exploration in the Gulf by Fernández de Córdoba (1517) and Alvarez de Piñeda (1519), both led by the pilot Alaminos.*

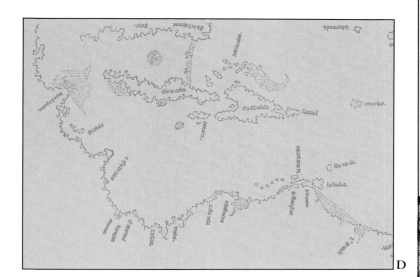

D

New World.

Although the discovery of Yucatán was not followed up – and further visitors cast themselves, without conscious mendacity, in the role of discoverers a few years later – Pinzón and Díaz can be said to have launched the next great enterprise in the Caribbean region: the exploration of the Gulf of Mexico. In February 1512, the ex-governor of Puerto Rico, Juan Ponce de León, frustrated by one of the many dismissals from office that punctuated his career, applied to the crown to search the waters north of the Bahamas. His aim was to find the fabled island of 'Bimini', or 'Bermendi', which appears on Peter Martyr's map of 1511 and which was said to house a therapeutic 'fountain of eternal youth'. This utopian image presumably derives from Classical myth, but had been confirmed by, or confused with, native rumours. He set off with two caravels on 3 March 1513, passed through the Bahamas, and on 27 March sighted what he thought was an island. On 2 April he made a landfall at what he reckoned to be 30°N. He called the 'island' Florida. The priority of his discovery has been disputed on the grounds that a land resembling Florida appears in the Cantino map of 1502 (see ch.9, map F). Perhaps more significant still was a discovery made on 21 April, when, heading south-east along the coast, his ships encountered an adverse current so fierce that it drove them back. This was the Gulf Stream (see map 1). Ponce's pilot, Alaminos, remembered it and used its power to escape from the vengeance of a thwarted superior a few years later. Its discovery was the most important single addition to the knowledge of the central Atlantic wind-system gained by Columbus.

Two tasks remained in the exploration of the Caribbean region: first, to complete the outline of the coast of the Gulf of Mexico; secondly, to explore the land limits of the Caribbean basin beyond the small tranche already covered in the Isthmus. The first was accomplished by accident (if our admittedly du-

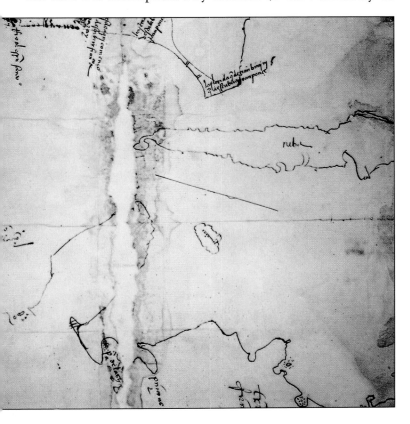

OPEN-SEA navigation was made possible by three techniques. Primitive **celestial navigation** supplied rough estimates of relative latitude from the height of the sun or the Pole Star. In **dead reckoning**, course was judged by the compass, time by the sand-glass or heavens. Leeway, the sideways track of the ship through the water, could be allowed for through simple visual observation. Columbus used **solar tables** to read latitude according to the hours of daylight, calculated by observing the movement of the Guard stars around Polaris: these complete their rotation

A

B

C

every twenty-four hours, so that by comparing their positions with a chart like that of **B** one could work out the duration of night. The figure is a mnemonic device: the divisions of the dial were named after parts of the body, for instance, 'the left arm' or 'above the right arm'.

Navigational instruments were in their infancy. Astronomers' astrolabes (**C**) made the fixing of latitudes on land increasingly accurate. In (**A**), French, of the 1540s, an expedition's chartmaker uses a mounted cross-staff for this purpose. The hand-held cross-staff, comprising only the cross-pieces and outer dial, the mariners' astrolabe and the quadrant were simple shipboard versions; defeated by the motion of the vessel, they inspired Heath-Robinson suggestions (**D**) for keeping them steady. Astronomical gadgets made navigation an increasingly esoteric art – 'a kind of prophetic vision', Columbus called it. Most sailors, unable to read or write and used to coastal navigation in which they could check their position visually, distrusted it. On Columbus's first voyage, mutineers plotted to throw him overboard as he wrestled with his new fangled astrolabe.

D

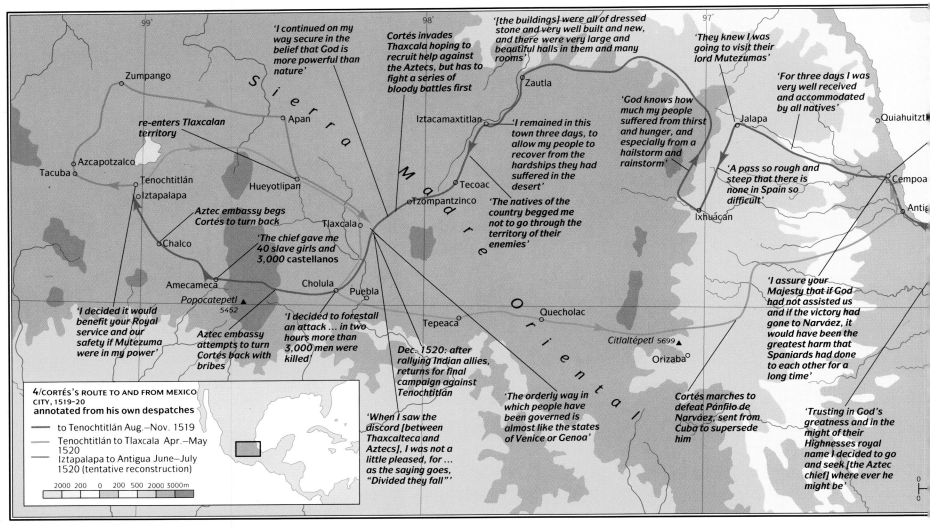

4 ABOVE *Though essentially an indigenous achievement, tracing routes known to and mapped by natives, Cortés's routes to Mexico and (5 RIGHT) Honduras were the main axes of Spanish conquest and exploration.*

bious source can be trusted) in 1517, when Francisco Hernández de Córdoba – future conqueror of Nicaragua – made a reconnaissance in force towards the mainland of Mesoamerica in an apparent attempt to trace the civilization that partnered the now well-known canoe-borne traders of Honduras. He found Yucatán in February. Supposing it an island, he attributed its discovery to himself. A Maya stone city seen early in March was given the exotic name of '*el Gran Cairo*', helping to fix an image of heathen civilization and wealth in the minds of future *conquistadores*; but a bloody battle with the Maya sent the expedition scurrying away (its pilot, Alaminos, seems to have taken the opportunity to guide them via Florida). Alaminos certainly followed part of this route in a reconnaissance the following year, which gathered promising intelligence about Mexico, and re-traced the coast of the Gulf from east to west in 1519, in an expedition mounted by one of the richest men in the Indies, Francisco de Garay. Garay's motive may have been the elusive passage to the Orient, but his ships turned back after months of frustrated endeavour among Florida's shoals and reefs. They explored the Mobile delta to a depth of six leagues and proved that Florida was part of a continent. From this expedition, or perhaps from Hernández de Córdoba's, the so-called 'Garay' map (*see* map E), the first of the Gulf of Mexico, derives.

By the time the ships arrived in Mexico, at the mouth of the River Pánuco, Cortés had already launched the landward exploration of the Caribbean basin, in the course of his conquest of Mexico. He appears as a surrogate for the native explorers who preceded him, and the unknown Indians who guided him or, in some cases, provided him with indigenous maps. This is not to detract from his importance as the communicator of native knowledge to a wider world. The routes he chose to follow, moreover, were deliberately the most challenging. His march from Cempoala to Mexico (*see* map 4), was intended to take in the lands of the Aztecs' most redoubtable enemies and most rebellious subjects; naturally, this meant traversing the most defiant fastnesses. On his second great journey of exploration, to Honduras via Tabasco and Chiapas in 1524 (*see* map 5) he engaged in a genuinely unprecedented undertaking, albeit along known routes, transporting an army of thousands through jungles and across ravines.

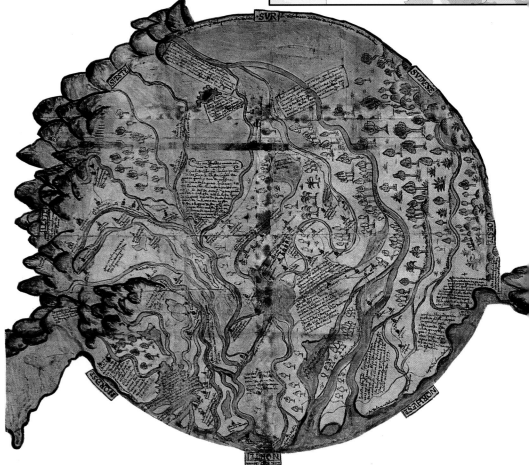

96°

set out from the
own of Cempoal,
which I renamed
evilla, on the
ixteenth of August,
with fifteen horsemen
nd 300 foot
oldiers, as well
quipped for war as
he conditions
ermitted me to
ake them'

Bay of Campeche

'I declared the ships
unfit and grounded
them ... and I
proceeded in greater
safety and with no
fear that once my
back was turned the
people I had left in
the town would
betray me'

to legitimise Cortés's
actions, his men elect
him 'in the name of
Your royal
Highnesses, chief
justice and Lord
mayor'

cruz

ellin

19°

30   40   50kms
20   30 miles

N
W   E
S

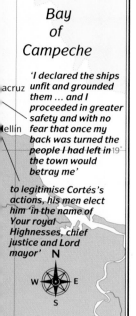

Canasoga   Guasili
Chiaha   Xuala
Coligua
Tula   Pacaha   Coste
Tanico Casqui
Quiguate   Cofitachequi
Utiangue Quizquiz Chicasa   Cosa
                                    Savannah
Ayays
Anilco   Mabila
Guasco   Aute
                            Napituca
                            Caliquen
                            Ocala
Atlantic Ocean

Mississippi

90°   80°   30°

Mocoso
Espíritu Santo
(Tampa Bay)

Gulf of Mexico

6/FLORIDA 1528–43
—— Narváez (1528–36)
—— Hernando de Soto (1538–43)
○ Indian town

N
W   E
S

0   100   200   300 kms
0   100 miles

5/GUATEMALA AND HONDURAS
—— Cortés's 1524 route
■ Maya temple sites

90°   18°

Yasuncabil

asal

Gulf of Honduras

Nito   Puerto Cortés
Naco   San Pedro Sula
Quimistán
L. Izabel

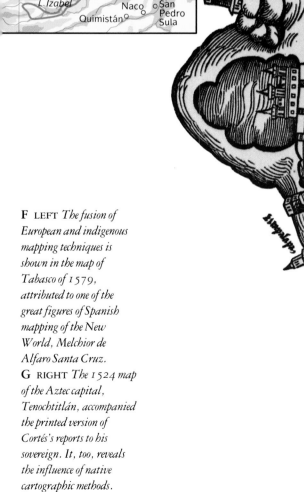

F LEFT *The fusion of
European and indigenous
mapping techniques is
shown in the map of
Tabasco of 1579,
attributed to one of the
great figures of Spanish
mapping of the New
World, Melchior de
Alfaro Santa Cruz.*
G RIGHT *The 1524 map
of the Aztec capital,
Tenochtitlán, accompanied
the printed version of
Cortés's reports to his
sovereign. It, too, reveals
the influence of native
cartographic methods.*

6 BELOW *De Soto's route
along the northern shore of
the Gulf of Mexico was
never satisfactorily
recorded. This
reconstruction is based on a
US-Government analysis.*

Less systematic, but equally heroic, was the landward exploration of the Gulf basin to the north. This can be said to have begun in April 1528, with the arrival in Tampa Bay, Florida, of Cortés's defeated rival, Pánfilo de Narváez. Cortés's success made it easy to raise capital and recruits for a force that proved fatally big, unwieldy and hungry. Dispersed by the need for food, most of the survivors fell into Indian hands. A party of three Spaniards and one negro slave, however, was led by Alvar Núñez Cabeza de Vaca into extraordinary feats of survival and exploration. By a combination of intense spirituality and remarkable therapeutic skills, Cabeza de Vaca established a reputation as a holy man among the Indians. After crossing the Rio Grande, Coahuila, Chihuahua and Sonora, he arrived in Sinaloa, in northern Mexico, with 600 native followers in his train and entered Mexico City in something like triumph on 25 June 1536. His achievement possibly encouraged Hernando de Soto, after legendary feats of arms in the conquests of Nicaragua and Peru, to attempt the subjugation of North America.

Leaving Havana with an impressive force (515 men and 237 horses), which showed that he had learnt nothing from Pánfilo's débacle, he disembarked in Tampa Bay on 25 May 1539. Three years of wanderings in the wilderness yielded distant glimpses of the geography of the new continent, with news of the Savannah River in Georgia, of the course of the Mississippi as far as Memphis, Tennessee, and of the Arkansas River in the west (*see* map 6). After Soto's death and the loss of nearly half the force, the survivors returned via the Mississippi, in ships they built themselves, in 1543.

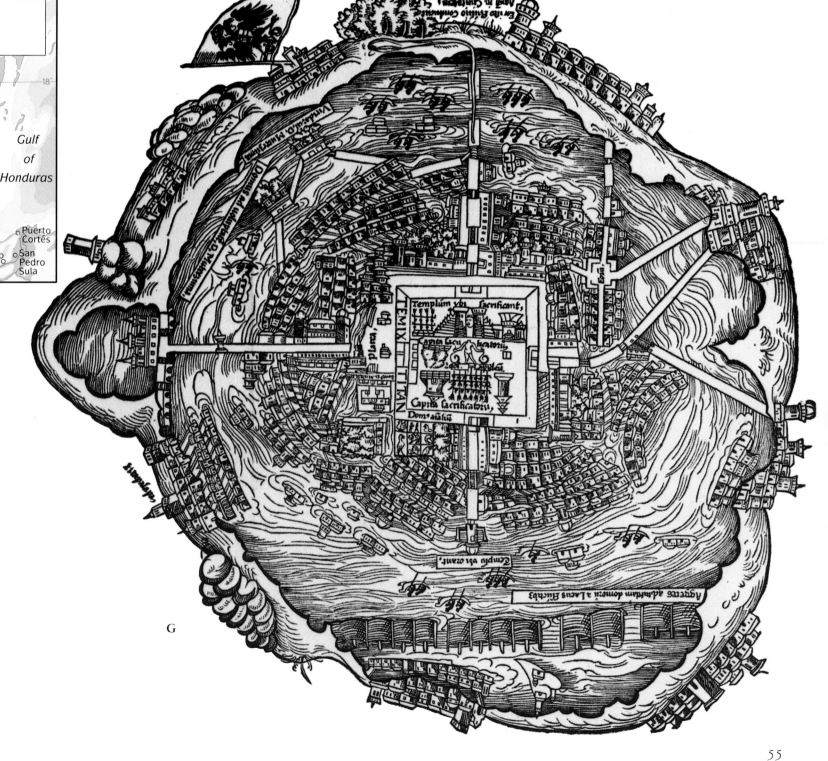

G

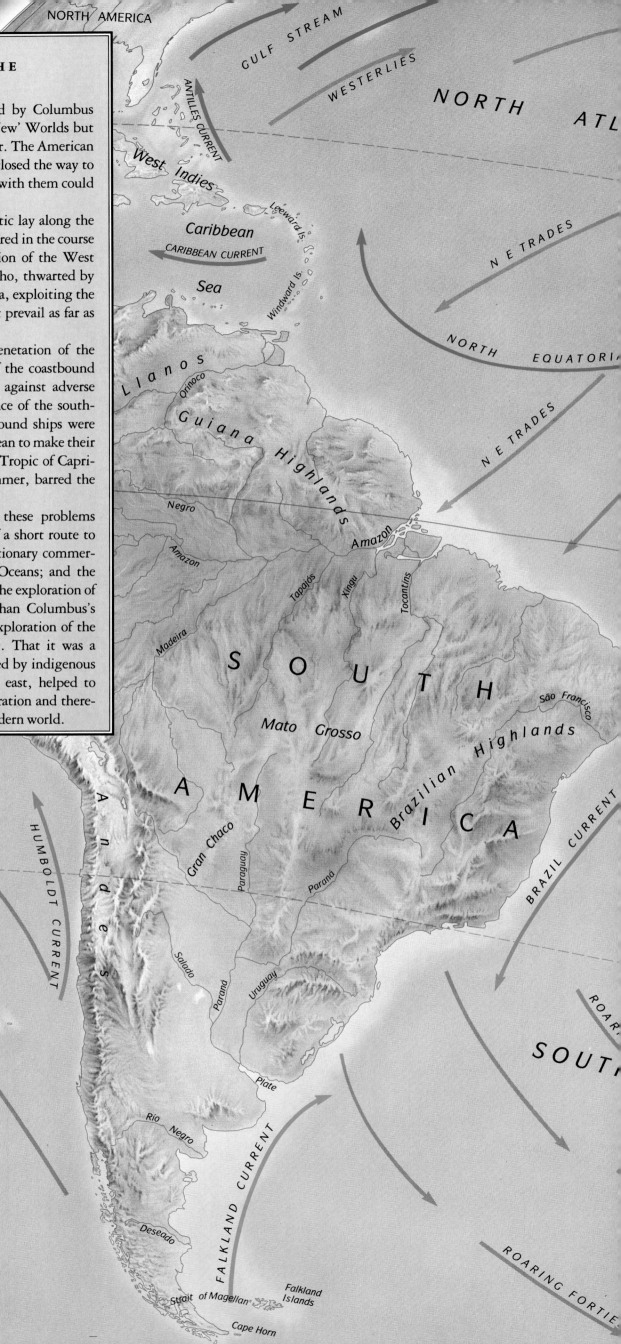

SECTION III
WEST AFRICA AND THE SOUTH ATLANTIC

THE CENTRAL Atlantic route discovered by Columbus linked the formerly sundered 'Old' and 'New' Worlds but disappointed its explorers by reaching no farther. The American hemisphere, however spectacular a discovery, closed the way to the Pacific and Indian Oceans. Maritime links with them could thus only be established via the South Atlantic.

From Europe, the way to the South Atlantic lay along the coast of West Africa. The approach was discovered in the course of the long late-medieval process of penetration of the West African gold-trade by Christian interlopers, who, thwarted by land, slowly and tentatively gained access by sea, exploiting the favourable currents and sailing conditions that prevail as far as the turn of Africa's bulge.

The map shows how difficult further penetration of the South Atlantic from this point was. Much of the coastbound route around Africa was along lee shores or against adverse currents. The strength, breadth and persistence of the southeast trade winds were such that southward-bound ships were forced to sail slanting courses deep into mid-ocean to make their southing. The high-pressure zone around the Tropic of Capricorn created a storm-trap which, in high summer, barred the way south right across the breadth of the ocean.

The perseverance required to overcome these problems yielded considerable rewards: the discovery of a short route to sub-equatorial Brazil; the creation of a revolutionary commercial route between the Atlantic and Indian Oceans; and the opening of a way – admittedly little used – to the exploration of the Pacific. Though achieved a little later than Columbus's creation of a central transatlantic route, the exploration of the South Atlantic was perhaps more significant. That it was a European achievement, neglected or abandoned by indigenous cultures and explorers approaching from the east, helped to secure Europe's preponderance in world exploration and therefore Europe's long-lasting hegemony in the modern world.

NORTH AMERICA

GULF STREAM

WESTERLIES

NORTH ATL

ANTILLES CURRENT

West Indies

N E TRADES

Caribbean

CARIBBEAN CURRENT

N E TRADES

Leeward Is.

Windward Is.

Sea

NORTH EQUATORIA

Llanos

Orinoco

Guiana Highlands

Negro

Amazon

Amazon

Madeira

Tapajós

Xingu

Tocantins

SOUTH

Mato Grosso

São Francisco

Brazilian Highlands

AMERICA

BRAZIL CURRENT

S E TRADES

Gran Chaco

Paraguay

Paraná

HUMBOLDT CURRENT

A n d e s

S E TRADES

Salado

Paraná

Uruguay

PACIFIC

Plate

ROAR

SOUTH

OCEAN

Rio Negro

FALKLAND CURRENT

Deseado

ROARING FORTIE

Strait of Magellan

Falkland Islands

Cape Horn

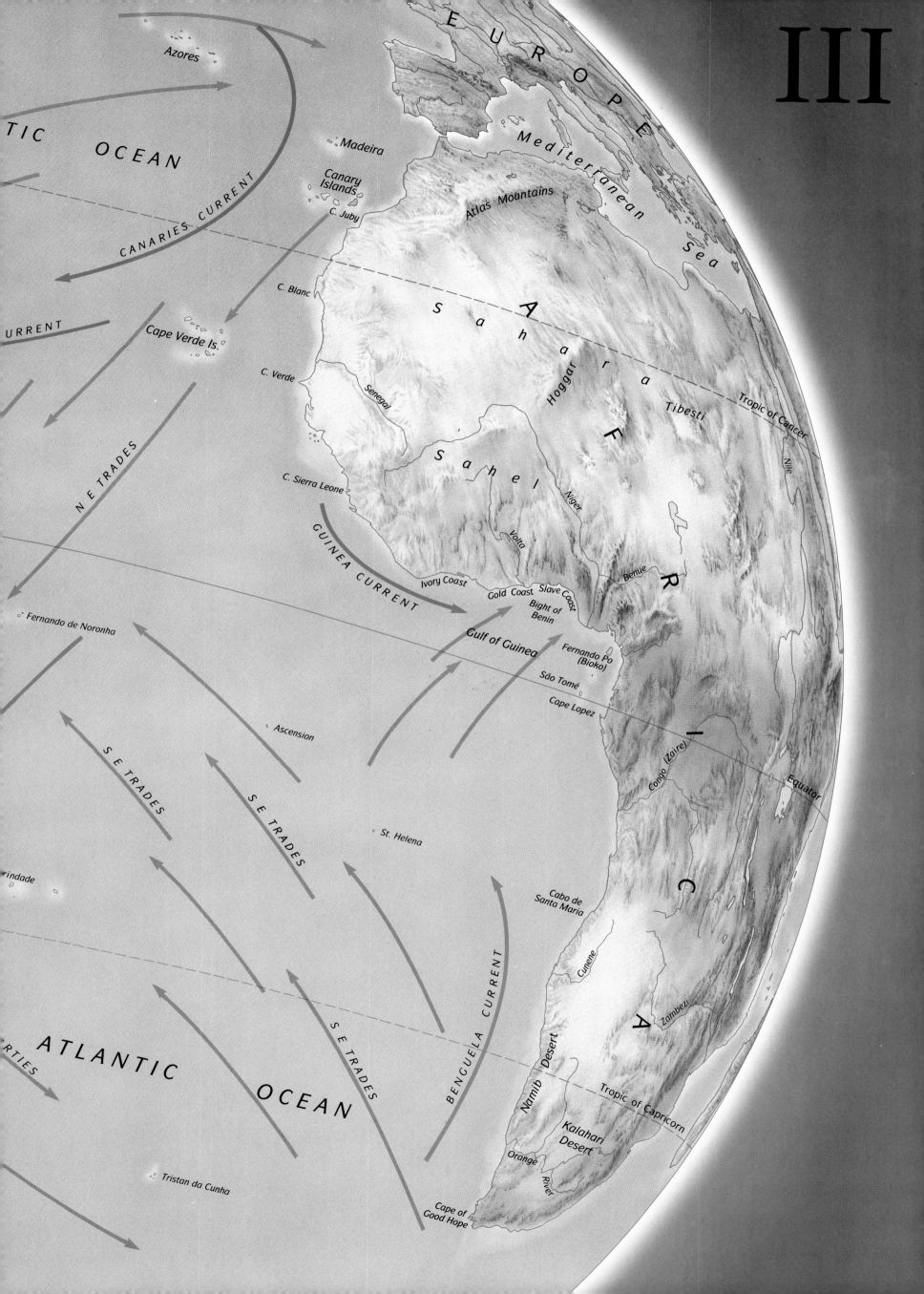

III

Azores

ATIC   OCEAN

Madeira

CANARIES CURRENT

Canary
Islands

C. Juby

CURRENT

C. Blanc

Cape Verde Is.

C. Verde

Senegal

N E TRADES

C. Sierra Leone

GUINEA CURRENT

Ivory Coast

Fernando de Noronha

Gold Coast   Slave Coast
Bight of
Benin

Gulf of Guinea

Fernando Po
(Bioko)

São Tomé

Cape Lopez

Ascension

SE TRADES

SE TRADES

SE TRADES

St. Helena

rindade

ATLANTIC

OCEAN

SE TRADES

BENGUELA CURRENT

Tristan da Cunha

rties

Cape of
Good Hope

EUROPE

Mediterranean   Sea

Atlas Mountains

S a h a r a

Hoggar

Tibesti

Tropic of Cancer

Nile

A F R I C A

S a h e l

Niger

Volta

Benue

Congo (Zaire)

Equator

Cabo de
Santa Maria

Cunene

Zambezi

Namib Desert

Tropic of Capricorn

Kalahari
Desert

Orange

River

11
WEST AFRICA: OVERLAND ROUTES
1324-1480

A BELOW *The Catalan Atlas, which displays the sumptuous and detailed picture of the peri-Saharan world imagined in late-medieval Latin Christendom, is closely related to a map known to have been made by c.1380 for the royal library of France by the Majorcan Jew, Abraham Cresques.*

ALTHOUGH *the long and laborious history of the European exploration of west Africa and the Sahara is told elsewhere (see chs. 12 and 37), it was an area which had nourished indigenous civilizations and long-range trade for centuries before the Europeans arrived. It also played a vital role in the early history of European maritime expansion, since it was precisely the wealth of the area which attracted explorers and the inaccessibility of the desert routes that encouraged seafarers to find a way round it in their ships.*

Map 2 shows the diversity of trades which inspired medieval merchants, based in the Maghrib, to develop routes across the desert, but it was west African gold which underpinned the commerce in all commodities. The source of the gold was deep in the tropical interior, around the middle and upper reaches of the Niger and the Volta. The location of the gold-source and the routes by which it was brought north were closely guarded secrets of the Black monopolists of the empire of Mali through whose lands (between the Niger and the upper Senegal) the trade passed, and of the Saharan merchants who dealt with them. Procured, according to all accounts — written perhaps from convention rather than conviction — by 'dump trade', in which goods were exchanged by being left exposed for collection, the gold generated bizarre theories about its origin: it grew like carrots; it was brought up by ants; it was mined by naked men who lived in holes. Its probable real origin was chiefly in the region of Bure, around the upper reaches of the Niger and the headwaters of the Gambia and Senegal Rivers. Some may have come from the Volta valley. The middlemen of Mali never succeeded in controlling the production of the gold, but they did control access from the south to the emporia of Walata and Timbuktu, on the fringes of the Sahara. Its 'marketing' was therefore in their hands, and they took the nuggets for their tribute, leaving the gold dust to the traders who carried it north.

The most important of the exchange trades were in salt and copper, supplemented by Maghribi and European textiles. The salt came from desert-mines, scooped by short-lived Black labour with copper tools at Taghaza and deep in the central Sahara, which the empire briefly controlled in the 14th century. In the 14th and 15th centuries, however, one red metal was exchanged for another as Moroccan and European copper made the long journey to Mali on camel-back.

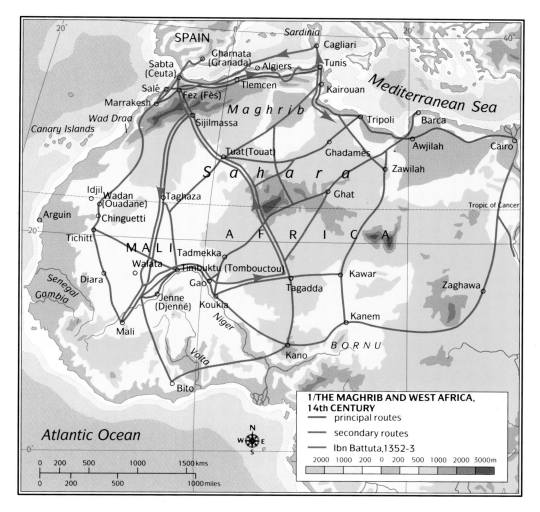

1 ABOVE *Saharan routes, first explored by the anonymous promoters of ancient caravans, were determined by the flow of trade and the distribution of oases. Travellers depended on a complex structure of caravans, routes and logistical support.*

AS THE remotest place to which the gold could reliably be traced, Mali became famous in the Mediterranean world in the 14th century. Its ruler, known as the Mansa, attained legendary proportions in 1324 when Mansa Musa undertook a spectacular pilgrimage to Mecca. He was one of three Mansas to undertake the journey; this alone indicates the substance and stability of the Mali state, as the pilgrimage took over a year. But Musa's trip was made in particularly lavish style and with conspicuous effect. It was remembered for centuries in Egypt, where the Mansa stayed for three months and distributed gold with so lavish a hand that he caused inflation; by various accounts, the value of gold in Egypt fell by between ten and 25 per cent. He gave 50,000 dinars to the sultan and thousands of ingots of raw gold to the shrines which received him and the officials who entertained him. Though he travelled with 80 or 100 camels, each weighed down with 100 pounds of gold, he was obliged to finance himself by borrowing on his homeward journey. Reputedly, he repaid his debts at the rate of 700 dinars for every 300 he had borrowed.

It was the ritual magnificence of the court of Mali, almost as much as its wealth, that impressed beholders. The Mansa exuded majesty: his stately gait; his hundreds of attendants bearing gilded staves; his indirect method of address through an intermediary; the acts of humiliation — prostration and 'dusting' of the head — to which his interlocutors submitted; the reverberant hum of strummed bowstrings and murmured approval with which his words were greeted by his audience; the capricious taboos which enjoined death for those who entered his presence in sandals or sneezed in his hearing. This exotic theatre of power had a suitably dignified setting: the Mansa's audience chamber was a domed pavilion in which an Andalusian poet sang; his bushland capital had a brick-built mosque.

The splendour did not last. By the mid-15th century, when direct contact with the outposts of Mali was briefly opened up by Portuguese penetration of the Gambia (see ch.12), Mali was in decline. For a while, however, the empire projected an enthralling image for European gold-hunters. 'So abundant is the gold which is found in his country', said a legend on the Catalan Atlas of Mali's ruler, 'that this lord is the richest and noblest king in all the land'.

Land crossings of the Sahara from starting-points in the Latin west were attempted in the 15th century. In 1413,

Anselme d'Isalguier was reported to have returned to Toulouse from Gao with three black eunuchs and a harem of Negresses, though how he could have got so far into the interior of Africa no one knows. In 1447, the Genoese Antonio Malfante got as far as Touat before turning back with garnered rumours of the gold trade. In 1470, the Florentine Benedetto Dei claimed to have been to Timbuktu and to have observed there a lively trade in European textiles. And from the 1450s to the 1480s, Portuguese merchants made frequent efforts to cut across country from Arguin.

For detailed itineraries, the unrivalled source is Ibn Battuta, who saw the empire of Mali at its height and described his routes to and from the Mansa's court. Though he was said to have 'only a modest share of the sciences' he was a conventionally well-educated scion of the Maghribi aristocracy of service who developed a passion 'to travel through the earth'. When he died, in 1368 or 1369, he left a reputation as the most travelled man who had ever lived and his stories, received with stupefaction in Fez, were embellished with repetition. The account which survives from his own hand, however, is almost entirely convincing. His Sahara crossing (map 1) was the last of his journeys, made when he had already been to China, East Africa, India and the lands of the Golden Horde, and his powers of observation were at their height.

His route south was through Sijilmassa to Taghaza, 'an unattractive village with the curious feature that its houses and mosques are built of blocks of salt'. As they crossed the empire of Mali, the salt caravans tripled or quadrupled in value. The desert had to be crossed by marches of ten nights at a stretch

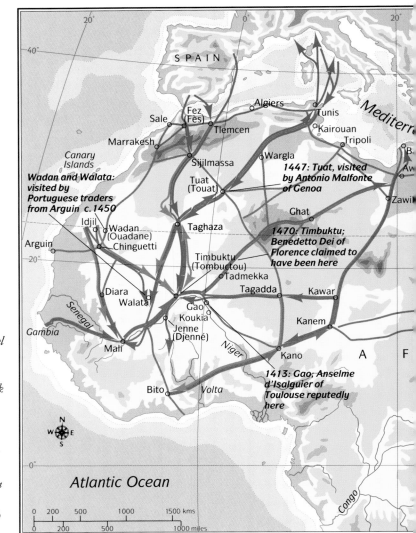

B BELOW *This illustration, probably of Mali, from a Book of Hours belonging to Manuel I of Portugal, gives a romanticized view of the world of caravans in Black Africa.* C BOTTOM *Gabriel Vallseca's ornamental portolan map (1438) shows a daunting Atlas range but a temptingly narrow Sahara traversed by camels and rimmed to the south by rich kingdoms.*

B

without water, eating 'desert truffles swarming with lice'. 'That desert is haunted by demons … There is no visible road – nothing but sand blown hither and thither by the wind'.

At Walata, Ibn Battuta encountered the first outpost of Mali officialdom. 'It was then that I repented of having come to their country, because of their lack of manners and their contempt for the whites'. Culture shock struck quickly. Ibn Battuta was disgusted by the food, not at first realizing at what precious cost millet was brought from far away. Outraged by a

C
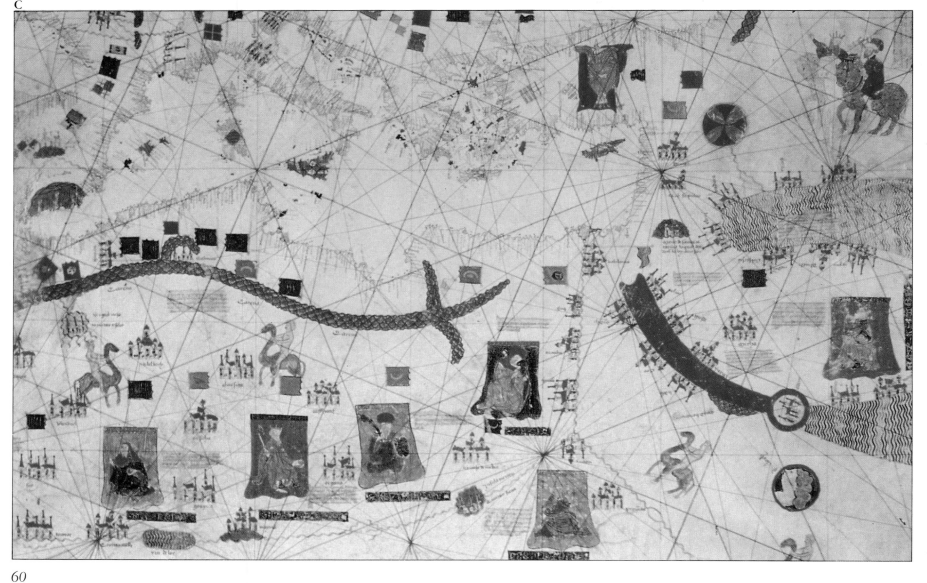

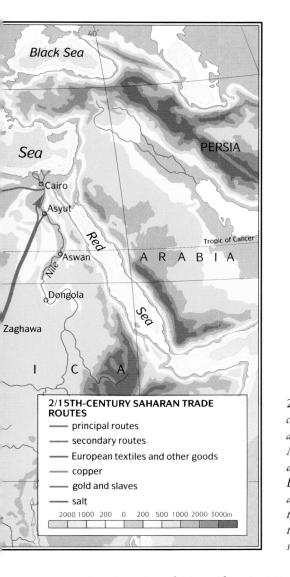

40°

Black Sea

Sea

PERSIA

Cairo

Asyut

Red

Aswan

ARABIA

Tropic of Cancer

Nile

Dongola

Sea

Zaghawa

I C A

A

2/15TH-CENTURY SAHARAN TRADE ROUTES
— principal routes
— secondary routes
— European textiles and other goods
— copper
— gold and slaves
— salt

2000 1000 200 0 200 500 1000 2000 3000m

2 LEFT *Long-range commerce in the Maghrib and west Africa in the late Middle Ages scored the desert with routes. Broadly speaking, gold and slaves went from south to north, copper, salt and textiles from north to south.*

spectator when he relieved himself in the Niger, he subsequently discovered that the man was on guard to protect him from a crocodile. The brazen womenfolk and sexual freedom alarmed him, but he was impressed to find children chained until they learned their Koran, and he praised the Blacks' 'abhorrence of injustice'.

When he reached the Mansa's court, he was annoyed by the contrast between the ruler's personal meanness and the copious displays of gold. A gold bird bestrode the Mansa's parasol; his skull cap, quivers and scabbards were of gold; but the Mansa had to be shamed into generosity ('What am I to say of you before other rulers?') and the opulent court rituals seemed ridiculous, especially the antics of the poets dressed in thrushes' feathers 'with a wooden head and red beak'. Cannibal envoys, whom the Mansa presented with a slave-girl, appeared at court to thank him, daubed with the blood of the gift they had just consumed. Fortunately, 'they say the white man is indigestible, because he is unripe'.

The return journey was more rigorous than the outward route. The oases turned white garments black, and there were only dates to eat, eked out with locusts caught before dawn. From the copper mines of Tagadda, 70 days' provisions had to be carried for the journey to Sijilmassa, beyond which the snows of the Atlas tormented the travellers to Fez.

However severe or costly, the Saharan routes were never bad enough to tempt Maghribi merchants to approach west Africa by sea. Of only three well-attested Muslim navigators south of Nul Lamta from the 12th to the 14th centuries, one – Ibn Fatima, who must have sailed before c.1280 – may have been a conscious explorer, since he is said to have written a cosmographical work and calculated latitudes and longitudes. He does not seem to have got as far as the mouth of the Wad Draa. The only overtly commercial pioneer, Muhammad ibn Ragan, in the early 14th century, vanished in the attempt, somewhere off the African coast. Part of the source of inhibition may have been legends of a 'Sea of Darkness', patrolled by monsters and rimmed by boiling tropical waters. It is equally likely, however, that the Maghribis knew that the gold-sources were well inland and supposed that a seaborne effort would prove unavailing.

THE IMAGE OF BLACK KINGSHIP

UNFORTUNATELY for the future history of race relations, Europeans discovered sub-Saharan Africa when the major Black states were in decline. The isolated and fragile civilizations of Mali, Ethiopia and Mwene Mutapa (*see* ch.29) were not exhibited to best advantage. The kingdom of the Congo (*see* ch.12) both excited and disappointed great expectations. Europe was left with a false impression of Black capabilities.

The changing image of Black kingship of Latin Christendom demonstrates this. Early in the 14th century, the example of the Mansa Musa of Mali gave Black kings enormous

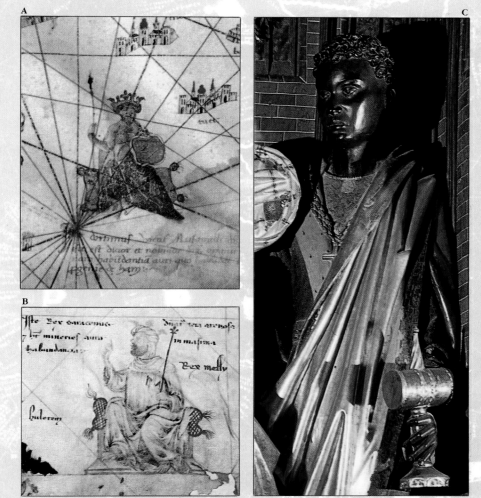

prestige. His legendary wealth, lavishly expended on a pilgrimage to Mecca, and glowing reports of his court, with its brick-built mosques and Andalusian poets, aroused the cupidity and admiration of Mediterranean cartographers. Dulcert in 1339 (**B**) showed him in Saracen garb. Long after his death, the Majorcan tradition (represented here by Gabriel Vallseca's map of the 1430s, (**D**) showed him black-faced but in European style, bearded with orb and sceptre. In the 1450s, however, the Portuguese made contact with the decadent empire of Mali and the Mansa's image began to change for the worse (**A**): cartography of the 1480s caricatured him, mocking his faded grandeur and appending grotesquely large sexual organs to his naked form.

Idealized Black kings still appeared among the Magi in altarpieces, as in the fine 15th century example from Covarrubias, Burgos (**C**), and in Portugal positive images were propagated for political reasons. In 1488, the show-baptism of a Wolof Chief, decked out with European clothes and silver plate, was a typical pantomime. The Kings of Portugal addressed those of the Congo, contacted in the 1480s, in fraternal terms. Official iconography showed them as splendid figures. They bore royal Portuguese baptismal names and were given a palace modelled on that of Lisbon. Familiarity, however, bred contempt, and the Portuguese with first-hand experience increasingly characterized Black kingdoms as savage and bestial.

12
THE WEST AFRICAN COAST
1434–1508

THE WEST African coast was genuinely unexplored territory in the late Middle Ages. The great civilizations of western Africa tended to be centred on upriver states, such as Congo and Mali, while the navigation of coastal peoples was confined to dugouts of limited range: in contrast to east Africa, there were no established seaports and no long-range trade. Similarly, though Chinese cartographers had inferred the approximate overall shape of the continent from their knowledge of the eastern seaboard, no Asiatic ships are known to have explored the west coast. Exploration was left to Europeans, whose interest was slowly awakened and falteringly sustained.

Unless the story of a Phoenician circumnaviation in the 6th century BC is credited, the first recorded attempt to coast western Africa was made from Genoa in 1291 by the brothers Vivaldi, who sought 'India by way of the Ocean'. Their attempt, like those of their few recorded successors, such as Jaume Ferrer of Majorca, who came to grief somewhere below 28°N in 1346, was defeated by the less favourable sailing conditions which prevailed beyond the reach of the Canary current.

These early, little-known and uniformly unsuccessful voyages were made in galleys, which were over-reliant on frequent victualling and watering from on shore, or in cogs, which were ill-adapted to adverse winds. In the early 15th century, the development in Portugal of the ocean-going caravel, rigged for sailing close to the wind, greatly increased the potential reach of explorers. At about the same time, strong commercial motives for undertaking the task began to make themselves felt: the desire to outflank the Saharan gold-road by opening direct access with the gold-bearing west of Africa by sea; and the prospect of creating a sea-route to the Orient, as envisaged by the Vivaldis. Hope of gain was complemented by the chivalric values of navigators and their patrons, for whom the sea was a proper medium for knightly exploits.

Despite their heroic self-perception, however, exploration was an unspectacular business: slow, tentative and often half-hearted. From the 1430s to the 1480s, it was pursued intermittently, usually as a spin-off from some other objective: at first, the conquest of the Canary Islands; later, the drive to the Orient; at times, perhaps, the quest for an ally against Islam, such as the legendary Prester John; and, more or less constantly, the search for immediately exploitable resources, especially gold and slaves.

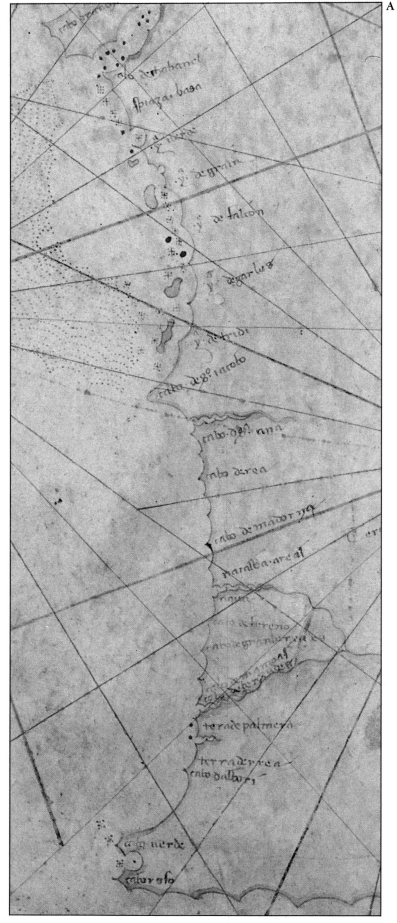

A LEFT *Andrea Bianco's chart of 1448, published in London, represents an attempt to record the range of Portuguese exploration in the Atlantic. 'Cabo Verde' is shown at the southernmost point, a little way beyond which the coast appears to trend eastward.*

probable location of the 'Cape Bojador' said to have been rounded by Gil Eannes in 1434

limit apparently assigned to Jaume Ferrer's voyage in search of the 'river of gold' 1346, according to the Catalan Atlas of c.1375–85

Cabo das Barbas (C.Branco)

C.Verde

Cabo da Varga (C.Verga)

Serra Lyoa (C.Sierra Leone)

approximate starting point of explorations under the patronage of Ferdinand Gomes 1469

recorded by Benincasa in chart of 1473

Atlantic Ocean

N
W E
S

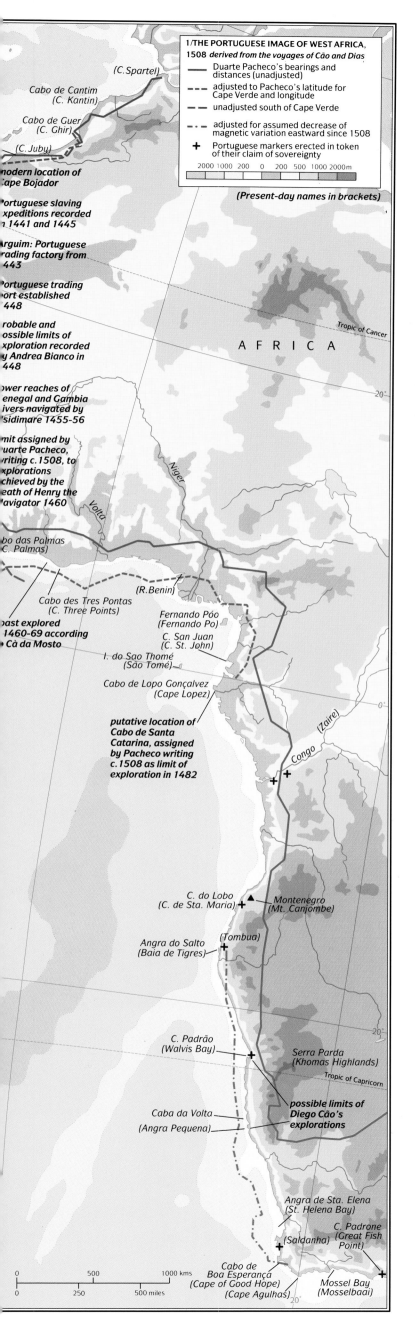

1/THE PORTUGUESE IMAGE OF WEST AFRICA,
1508 *derived from the voyages of Cão and Dias*

— Duarte Pacheco's bearings and distances (unadjusted)
- - - adjusted to Pacheco's latitude for Cape Verde and longitude
– – unadjusted south of Cape Verde
–·– adjusted for assumed decrease of magnetic variation eastward since 1508
+ Portuguese markers erected in token of their claim of sovereignty

2000 1000 200 | 0 | 200 500 1000 2000m

(Present-day names in brackets)

(C. Spartel)

Cabo de Cantim (C. Kantin)

Cabo de Guer (C. Ghir)

(C. Juby)

modern location of Cape Bojador

Portuguese slaving expeditions recorded in 1441 and 1445

Arguim: Portuguese trading factory from 1443

Portuguese trading port established 1448

probable and possible limits of exploration recorded by Andrea Bianco in 1448

lower reaches of Senegal and Gambia rivers navigated by Usidimare 1455-56

limit assigned by Duarte Pacheco, writing c.1508, to explorations achieved by the death of Henry the Navigator 1460

AFRICA

Tropic of Cancer

Niger

Volta

Cabo das Palmas (C. Palmas)

Cabo des Tres Pontas (C. Three Points)

coast explored 1460-69 according to Cà da Mosto

(R. Benin)

Fernando Póo (Fernando Po)

C. San Juan (C. St. John)

I. do Sao Thomé (São Tomé)

Cabo de Lopo Gonçalvez (Cape Lopez)

putative location of Cabo de Santa Catarina, assigned by Pacheco writing c.1508 as limit of exploration in 1482

(Zaire)

Congo

C. do Lobo (C. de Sta. Maria) — Montenegro (Mt. Canjombe)

Angra do Salto (Baia de Tigres) — (Tombua)

C. Padrão (Walvis Bay)

Serra Parda (Khomas Highlands)

Tropic of Capricorn

Caba da Volta (Angra Pequena)

possible limits of Diego Cão's explorations

Angra de Sta. Elena (St. Helena Bay)

C. Padrone (Saldanha) — (Great Fish Point)

Cabo de Boa Esperança (Cape of Good Hope) — (Cape Agulhas)

Mossel Bay (Mosselbaai)

0 500 1000 kms
0 250 500 miles

THE renowned patron of the first phase of West African exploration was Prince Henry of Portugal (1398-1460). His fame, however, rests on a number of misleading assumptions, while his common nickname of 'the Navigator' is inappropriate, at least in its modern sense, for a prince who only made two short journeys by sea in person. Henry's behaviour displayed signs of the classic syndrome of the royal cadet with serious kingly ambitions. Motivated for much of his life by a sense of unspecified 'destiny' or 'vocation', which he seems to have inferred from his horoscope, at different times he toyed with ideas of carving out a realm for himself in Moorish Andalusia, in North Africa's Maghrib, or, most persistently, in the Canary Islands. His enterprises were entrusted to a large, turbulent and expensive household of 'knights' and 'squires' who practised chivalric rituals which in no way precluded a liking for violent crime.

Henry, however, outgrew these early ventures, becoming increasingly absorbed with a scheme to tap the Saharan gold trade from bases in North Africa and the Canaries. The idea

B

may have arisen shortly after the Portuguese capture of Ceuta in 1415. Certainly, by the 1430s Henrique's interest in the Canaries had grown into an obsession well documented in surviving sources. Voyages to the neighbouring African coast, from 1434 onwards, were at first no more than a side-show, elevated only with hindsight into a great undertaking of scientific exploration. His other professed motive — expansion of the Christian faith — was never clearly confirmed by his deeds.

Henry's efforts in the Canaries came to little. Africa, on the other hand, began to yield exploitable opportunities: especially in the form of slaves and gold. His involvement in African exploration accordingly intensified. Towards the mid-1450s he began to employ professional navigators, usually Genoese, instead of relying exclusively on his entourage. In partial consequence, the lower reaches of the Rivers Gambia and Senegal were explored, contact was established with the empire of Mali, and the Cape Verde Islands were discovered. A further influence on this accelerated pace of exploration may have been the transformation of Henry's rickety finances by the demonstration that exploration could reveal profitable commodities.

The image of Henry that has dominated the historical tradition — a figure of science and romance — can be traced to a chronicler in the prince's pay but is uncorroborated by other sources. He was, however, responsible for two genuine contributions to the history of exploration: the development of the North Atlantic triangle of navigation, linking the Iberian seaboard with west Africa via the colonies he helped to promote in the Azores; and a great extension of European knowledge of the rim of Africa's bulge. Without these achievements, the relatively rapid progress of exploration in the 1470s and 1480s would have been unthinkable.

After Prince Henry's death, explorers paused, presumably deterred by lack of patronage and by the lee shores around the

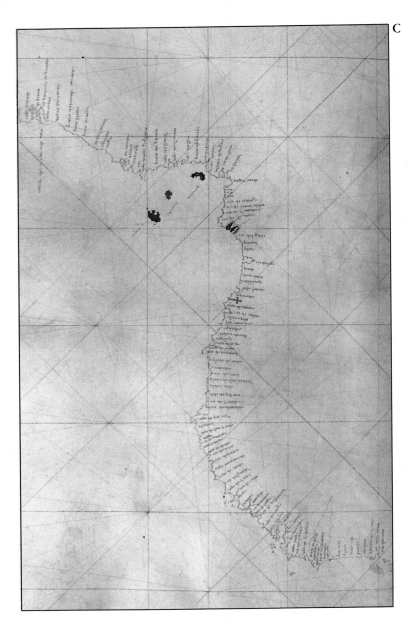

In the summer of 1487, Cão was followed by Bartolomeu Dias. Dias left Lisbon with three ships and a commission to find the ocean route around Africa. At first retracing Cão's route, he subsequently, and with great daring, turned away from the coast, perhaps in around 27° or 28°S, in search of a favourable wind. His success in encountering westerlies which carried him to a landfall some 300 miles east of the Cape of Good Hope made a major contribution to knowledge of the wind-system of the South Atlantic. The expedition seems to have been exceptionally well-provisioned, suggesting that the detour into the open ocean was planned in advance.

The discovery of ample sources of gold and slaves meant that the direct economic effects of west African exploration were potentially revolutionary. Yet in the 16th century the development of transatlantic and Indian Ocean trade largely left behind the west African world of dangerous shores, inhospitable climes, difficult access and limited rewards. Exploration had, however, yielded two benefits for the growth of man's picture of his world: the discoveries of the South Atlantic wind-system, the key which unlocked access to the Indian and Pacific Oceans (*see* ch. 13); and of the shape and southward reach of Africa, which had been speculatively anticipated on some medieval maps but which had been obscured by general uncertainty and by the popularity in the 15th century of Ptolemy's notion of an Africa linked by land to Asia at its southern extremity. The African enterprise had, moreover, taken European seamen beyond the equator for the first time to a hemisphere where, out of sight of the Pole Star, an unfamiliar heaven made new demands of celestial navigators. The early modern revolutions in the methods, range and results of navigation were thus prepared, to some extent pre-figured, in the 15th-century African voyages.

C LEFT *A remarkably detailed Venetian portolan atlas of the 1480s is particularly well informed, from Portuguese sources, about the west coast of Africa. No Portuguese map of before 1492 – if there ever was such a thing – has survived.*

D

2 BELOW *Priority in the discovery of the Cape Verde Islands has been hotly disputed, but the first clear account of them emerges from the voyage of Antoniotto di Usodimare, made under the auspices of Henry the Navigator and recorded by Alvise da Cà da Mosto. The earliest traceable explorer's route, by Diogo Afonso, exposed the full extent of the archipelago.*

turn of Africa's bulge. In 1469, the initiative was revived by the grant of the right of exploration to Ferdinand Gomes, a Lisbon merchant who had capital to inject into the enterprise. He commissioned voyages which added 3,000 miles of coastline to the area navigated by Portuguese ships and extended the range of mapping to about the latitude of Cabo de Santa Caterina (2°N), the approximate limit of navigation with favourable currents. Though Ferdinand's monopoly lasted only six years, on the face of it his explorations represented an astonishing rate of increase over the tentative efforts of Henry the Navigator. But conditions were now more propitious. The Portuguese had found a way through the most adverse of the sailing conditions that made the route to Africa so arduous, and had established a convenient route home via well-stocked island ports. Moreover, the profitability of the enterprise had been reinforced by the discovery of further saleable commercial products, in the form of ivory and malaguetta 'pepper'.

The crown rescinded Ferdinand's monopoly in 1475, perhaps in order to confront Spanish interlopers on the Guinea coast, and the navigation of west Africa became the responsibility of the senior prince of the royal house, Prince John. Henceforth, Portugal had an heir and, from his accession in 1481, a king committed to the further exploration and exploitation of Africa. Prince John seems to have conceived Atlantic Africa as a sort of 'Portuguese Main'. He had a militant and organizing mentality, forged in his war against the Spanish on the Guinea coast between 1475 and 1481. As 'Lord of Guinea' he enhanced the prestige of African enterprise at home, centralized the control of trade, and presided over an extraordinary turnover in baptisms and rebaptisms of rapidly apostasizing African chiefs. He was also the patron of heroic new feats of exploration, which dwarfed those of the eras of Prince Henry and Ferdinand Gomes: the voyages of Diego Cão (who made contact with the kingdom of Congo in 1482 and, having entered the River Zaire, established the shape of the coast to just beyond 22°S in 1485), voyages made with amazing tenacity in the face of continuously adverse winds and currents.

Santo Antão

São Vicente

São Nicolau

Sal

Boa Vista

Atlantic Ocean

São Tiago

Maio

Brava

Fogo

Praia

0   50   100   200 kms

0   50   100 miles

N W E S

2/CAPE VERDE ISLANDS, 1461-62

— Diogo Afonso

3/THE CAPE OF GOOD HOPE, 1487-88

Bartolomeu Dias
(tentative reconstruction)

+ Portuguese markers erected in
token of their claim of sovereignty

3 ABOVE *Presumably by
taking a route well out to
sea, Dias rounded the Cape
in January 1488.
According to a 16th-
century chronicler, 'he
named it Cape of Storms,
but King John ... gave it
another name, calling it
Cape of Good Hope'.*

D BELOW *The Henricus
Martellus map (c. 1489)
is perhaps the first world
map to incorporate the
Portuguese discoveries; it
was made, as stated in the
annotation under the bulge
of Africa, 'according to the
description of the
Portuguese'.*

ATLANTIC EXPLORATION yielded anthropological as well as geographical discoveries. At first, the line that divided man from the rest of creation seemed
indistinct: Breydenbach's late 15th-century pilgrim guide, for instance,
showed a hominoid baboon next to a camel (E). When the aboriginal Canary Islanders were
first recorded (c. 1340) and the Black societies of west Africa first reported (c. 1440), both
were relegated to the nether links of the chain of being with the mythical 'wild man' – a

commonplace symbol of savagery opposed to civility – shown (A) in a 14th-century
vault-painting from Granada in his traditional role as raptor of a lady and adversary of a
knight. Columbus expected to find monstrous, sub-human races on his arrival in the New
World, though assumed that their primitiveness would at least ensure some use as slaves.
Indeed, until the Pope pronounced definitively in the 1530s there was room to doubt
whether the American Indians were fully human. Further doubts about the unity of
mankind were raised by the discovery of the Hottentots in Africa. Some of the earliest
European images of them, however, such as Sebastian Cabot's of 1544 (B), depict clearly
civilised characteristics: use of tools, classical equipoise, conversation and shame.

This slow revolution in man's perception of man had been started by the discovery of the
Canary Islanders, whose unclad state and Stone Age culture divided learned opinion
between those attracted by their 'sylvan innocence' and those repelled by their 'bestiality'.
De Bry's late 16th-century image (in which islanders gather dew from the 'magic' tree of
Hierro) reflects gradual romanticisation (C). Black cultures had a similar initial impact:
the realistic detail of (D) is from a Genoese map of the later 15th century. But their more
radical challenge to European assumptions about natural order proved harder to absorb.

65

13
ROUTES OF THE SOUTH ATLANTIC
1497-1619

IN THE *history of exploration, no change has ever been so conspicuous as the sudden extension within a single generation after 1492 of the range of European navigation to encompass the entire girth of the globe. The avenue of access to remoter oceans was the wind-system of the South Atlantic. Until it was explored, the Indian and Pacific Oceans could not be approached by ships from Europe. The earliest recorded voyages to South America, beginning with Columbus's third ocean crossing in 1498, struggled through the Doldrums or used the north-east trades before working their way along the coast. The discovery of the sub-equatorial system was made by Bartolomeu Dias in 1487, when he met the South Atlantic westerlies that took him around the Cape of Good Hope (see ch. 12). This encouraged successors to make ever-wider sweeps into the South Atlantic. The results included the huge arc described by Vasco da Gama on his way to the Indian Ocean in 1497 and the Portuguese landfall in Brazil in 1500.*

Reconnaissance of the east coast of sub-equatorial South America, from Cabral's voyage of 1500 to Magellan's of 1519, defined the western shore of the South Atlantic and demonstrated that its routes could lead west as well as east. The westward option, however, was never very attractive. The environment south of the River Plate was hostile. Furthermore, zones of calms and cross-winds had to be negotiated, and although Schouten and Le Maire in 1615 were willing to take a long, diagonal course across the South Atlantic, most found the shortest route, to the bulge of Brazil, demanding enough.

The explorers of the area can be treated in three groups: first, the anatomisers of the wind-system and of the routes across the ocean. Use of the north-east trades is represented by Cabral's trajectory of 1500. He was also the first to complete the study of the wind-system by rounding the Cape of Good Hope with the westerlies, although Vicente Yañez Pinzón had admittedly preceded him as far as the coast of Brazil. The more southerly crossing, following the coast of Africa as far as Sierra Leone before heading west, was pioneered by Vasco da Gama and was followed by Magellan and Schouten and Le Maire. Vespucci's inscrutable records make it impossible to vindicate his claims to have penetrated deep into southerly latitudes. He and Pinzón take their due place in the second group: explorers of the coast of Brazil. The trail-blazing third group – explorers of the South Atlantic routes to the Pacific – is represented by Magellan, and Schouten and Le Maire.

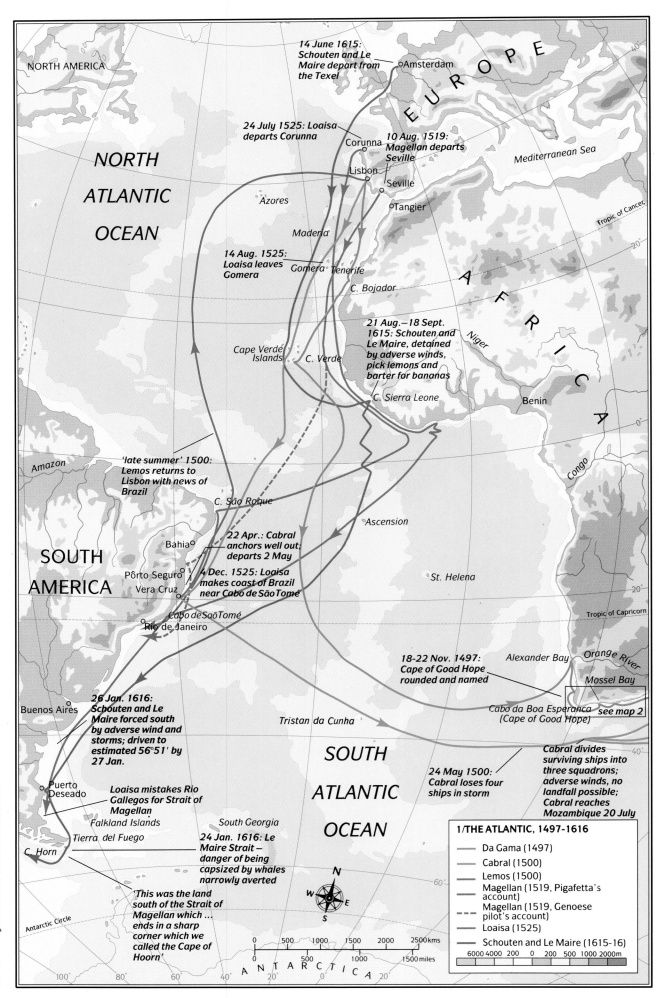

14 June 1615: Schouten and Le Maire depart from the Texel

24 July 1525: Loaisa departs Corunna

10 Aug. 1519: Magellan departs Seville

14 Aug. 1525: Loaisa leaves Gomera

21 Aug.–18 Sept. 1615: Schouten and Le Maire, detained by adverse winds, pick lemons and barter for bananas

NORTH AMERICA

EUROPE

Amsterdam

Corunna

Lisbon

Seville

Tangier

Mediterranean Sea

Azores

Madeira

Gomera · Tenerife

C. Bojador

A F R I C A

Cape Verde Islands

C. Verde

C. Sierra Leone

Niger

Benin

Congo

Tropic of Cancer

NORTH ATLANTIC OCEAN

Amazon

'late summer' 1500: Lemos returns to Lisbon with news of Brazil

C. São Roque

Ascension

22 Apr.: Cabral anchors well out; departs 2 May

Bahia

4 Dec. 1525: Loaisa makes coast of Brazil near Cabo de São Tomé

Pôrto Seguro
Vera Cruz

Cabo de São Tomé
Rio de Janeiro

SOUTH AMERICA

St. Helena

Tropic of Capricorn

18-22 Nov. 1497: Cape of Good Hope rounded and named

Alexander Bay

Orange River

Mossel Bay

Cabo da Boa Esperança (Cape of Good Hope)   see map 2

26 Jan. 1616: Schouten and Le Maire forced south by adverse wind and storms; driven to estimated 56°51' by 27 Jan.

Buenos Aires

Tristan da Cunha

Cabral divides surviving ships into three squadrons; adverse winds, no landfall possible; Cabral reaches Mozambique 20 July

24 May 1500: Cabral loses four ships in storm

Puerto Deseado

Loaisa mistakes Rio Gallegos for Strait of Magellan

Falkland Islands

South Georgia

SOUTH ATLANTIC OCEAN

Tierra del Fuego

C. Horn

24 Jan. 1616: Le Maire Strait – danger of being capsized by whales narrowly averted

'This was the land south of the Strait of Magellan which ... ends in a sharp corner which we called the Cape of Hoorn'

N W E S

Antarctic Circle

ANTARCTICA

1/THE ATLANTIC, 1497-1616

- Da Gama (1497)
- Cabral (1500)
- Lemos (1500)
- Magellan (1519, Pigafetta's account)
- Magellan (1519, Genoese pilot's account)
- Loaisa (1525)
- Schouten and Le Maire (1615-16)

0   500   1000   1500   2000   2500kms
0   500   1000   1500 miles

6000 4000 200   0   200 500 1000 2000m

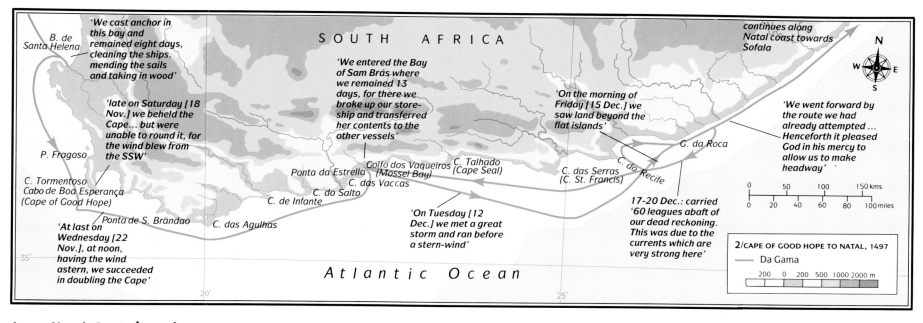

2/CAPE OF GOOD HOPE TO NATAL, 1497
— Da Gama

Map labels (clockwise):

'We cast anchor in this bay and remained eight days, cleaning the ships, mending the sails and taking in wood'

B. de Santa Helena

SOUTH AFRICA

'We entered the Bay of Sam Brás where we remained 13 days, for there we broke up our store-ship and transferred her contents to the other vessels'

continues along Natal coast towards Sofala

'late on Saturday [18 Nov.] we beheld the Cape... but were unable to round it, for the wind blew from the SSW'

'On the morning of Friday [15 Dec.] we saw land beyond the flat islands'

'We went forward by the route we had already attempted ... Henceforth it pleased God in his mercy to allow us to make headway'

P. Fragoso

C. Tormentoso Cabo de Boa Esperança (Cape of Good Hope)

Ponta da Estrella

Golfo dos Vaqueiros (Mossel Bay)

C. Talhado (Cape Seal)

C. das Serras (C. St. Francis)

G. da Roca

C. do Recife

Ponta de S. Brandao

C. do Salto

C. das Vaccas

C. de Infante

'At last on Wednesday [22 Nov.], at noon, having the wind astern, we succeeded in doubling the Cape'

C. das Agulhas

'On Tuesday [12 Dec.] we met a great storm and ran before a stern-wind'

17-20 Dec.: carried '60 leagues abaft of our dead reckoning. This was due to the currents which are very strong here'

Atlantic Ocean

0 50 100 150 kms
0 20 40 60 80 100 miles

200 0 200 500 1000 2000 m

---

1 LEFT *Vasco da Gama's wide sweep into the South Atlantic may have reflected the experience of Bartolomeu Dias in seeking the westerlies that would enable a fleet to round the Cape. That he still landed too far north and had a long inshore haul to Natal (**2** ABOVE) may have inspired his advice to Cabral, whose even more generous arc intersected with the coast of Brazil.*

THE voyages which can be said to have exposed the nature of the global access-routes of the South Atlantic were those of Vasco da Gama in 1497, and Pedro Alvares Cabral in 1500. Da Gama was a servant of the crown, executing an étatiste project inspired by royal policy; financial backing was raised by the crown, largely from Florentine merchant-houses in Lisbon, on the strength of commercial returns which, by the standards of exploratory voyages, must have seemed pretty secure. Da Gama sailed with four square-rigged ships: the caravels were left behind.

This shows that he expected to make his way on the high seas, without enduring the coastwise crawling of earlier Portuguese explorers (*see* ch. 12). His initial course from Lisbon was to the Cape Verde Islands and from there, with the south equatorial current, to the latitude of Sierra Leone. There he turned his prow to the open ocean in search of the westerlies of the South Atlantic. The plan was evidently to be carried round the southern extremity of Africa, like Dias before him. Da Gama could fairly have expected his detour across 6,200 miles of sea to have carried him far enough south: it was by far the longest unbroken journey yet made. In fact he made his landfall on the western side of the Cape of Good Hope, at Bahia de Santa Helena, on 8 November 1497, nearly three months out from his last port of call. From there he had to tack around the Cape before picking up the westerlies again in the 'good hope' of reaching the lands of spices.

Da Gama's voyage revealed the dominance of south-east trades in the central South Atlantic. It was presumably in order to find the shortest route across these cross-winds that the next voyage, Cabral's in 1500, attempted a different approach, leaving the Old World directly from the Cape Verde Islands and using the north-east trades, instead of the south equatorial current, to make as much southing as possible. This route, followed on the basis of da Gama's own reports and advice, led directly to Brazil. The fleet which made the journey represented a reversion to the chivalric mode of the days of the Navigator (*see* ch. 12). Cabral, its commander, was a gentleman of the court, as were most of the captains of the individual vessels. It was a prestigious assembly of 1,200 men in 13 ships, whose lavish caparisons decked the Tagus 'like a spring garden in bloom', one designed to impress and to intimidate the eastern potentates with whom it was expected to trade. The assurance of huge profits, which da Gama had brought back from India, made recruitment and finance easy. The mood of buoyant confidence aboard can be judged from the fact that, once out of Lisbon on 8 March, Cabral stopped neither for victuals nor water, until, on 22 April, he sighted Brazil.

This was almost certainly a fortuitous event. Though islands and mainlands in the South Atlantic had been rumoured at least since the 1440s, and Columbus had demonstrated the existence of a large landmass inland of the Orinoco delta (*see* ch. 10), no recorded voyage to Brazil occurred until Vicente Pinzón's arrival, on a course similar to Cabral's, in January 1500. By the time of Cabral's landfall, Pinzón was still working his way north along the coast of South America; his achievement cannot have influenced Cabral. The next leg of Cabral's journey exposed the hazards as well as the advantages of the South Atlantic wind-system. The expedition was now beyond the root area of the westerly winds and the season, by the time of Cabral's departure on 2 May, was unpropitious. The plan was to make for Mossel Bay, identified by Dias and da Gama as a suitable anchorage on the southern shore of Africa. Probably in the dangerous high-pressure zone north of Tristan da Cunha, they were struck by a tempest which sank four ships and scattered the rest (*see* **A**). The sundered squadrons were not re-united until they had rounded

A RIGHT *Cabral's tragic experience of the perils of the South Atlantic is captured in this depiction of his beleaguered fleet from a late 16th-century compilation of Portugal's East Indian fleets. **B** FAR RIGHT Vespucci's claims to pre-eminence in South Atlantic navigation are reflected in the proprietorial image of Waldseemüller's printed wall map of 1507, in which the navigator presides over a New World characterised by a long southward extent of coastline.*

B

DESPITE ITS auspicious name and the enthusiasm with which it was greeted by humanists and cosmographers, the New World was a disappointing find – an obstacle-course on the way to the Orient. Its vast southward extent pro-

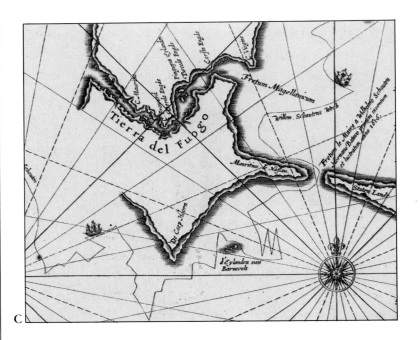

tracted the route by way of cold dangerous seas, and offered almost nothing exploitable. Nonetheless, it did offer several 'curiosities', the most intriguing of which were human. Patagonia was the last refuge of the monstrous races of the medieval imagination which explorers had been disappointed not to find elsewhere. The natives, though not particularly big, were perceived by Magellan's men as giants and continued to be depicted as such on maps for more than a hundred years. On the shores of the Strait of Magellan and in Tierra del Fuego, peoples were found of such extreme savagery, and in such hostile environments, as to pose radical questions about the relationship between man and the

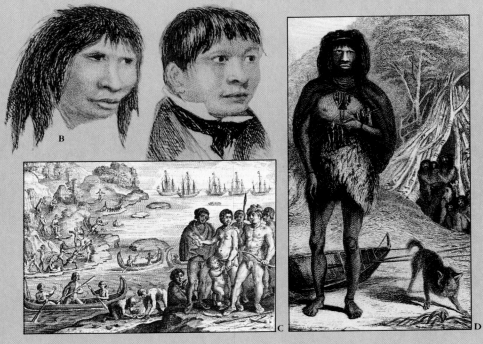

rest of creation. At first, these examples of 'natural man' were idealised. In 1615, Joris van Spilbergen could appear holding a civilised Renaissance *conversazione* with handsome natives of classical physique in southern Patagonia (C). In 1624 Jakob l'Ermite saw the Fuegians in much the same light (E). But by then the reality of life in a state of nature that was 'nasty, brutish and short' was already becoming apparent. Sir John Narborough, for example, in 1670 depicted the inhabitants with sympathetic realism (A).

Darwin, who arrived off Tierra del Fuego in the *Beagle* in December, 1832, posed the question best. 'Could our progenitors have been men like these?'. How could they survive virtually unclad in a climate where icebergs never thaw? The difference between 'savage and civilised man', greater 'than that between a wild and domesticated animal', was captured by the *Beagle*'s official artist (D). Captain Fitzroy of the *Beagle* brought home some Fuegians to be instructed in the arts and religion of western civilisation and then returned to their islands as the kernel of a mission. Drawn from the wildest of the native peoples, the Yaghans of the south, guinea-pigs like Fuegia Basket and Jemmy Button (B) became the darlings of London society. Restored to Tierra del Fuego with high hopes, they fell out among themselves and reverted rapidly to the wild. Jemmy Button led a massacre of missionaries in 1859; when Fuegia Basket died in 1883, she had forgotten all she had learned of Christianity. Though the experiment was discouraging, Darwin's observations of Fuegian indifference to the cold contributed to the formation of his theory of evolution by convincing him that they had adapted naturally to their hostile environments.

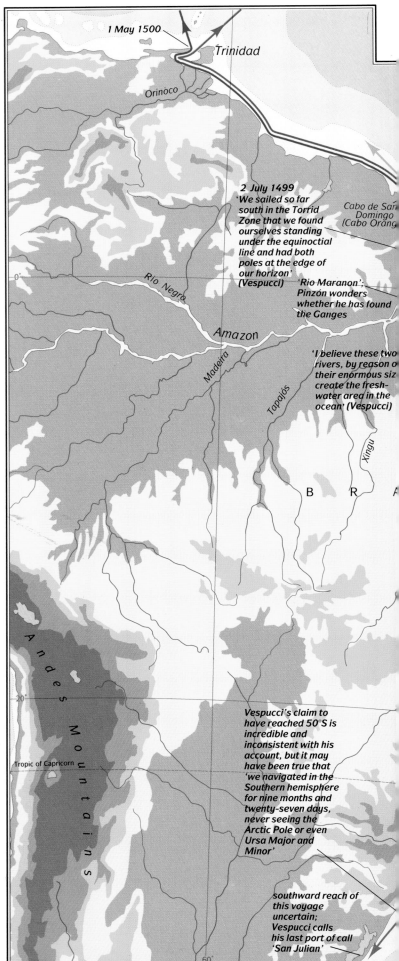

1 May 1500

Trinidad

Orinoco

2 July 1499
'We sailed so far south in the Torrid Zone that we found ourselves standing under the equinoctial line and had both poles at the edge of our horizon' (Vespucci)

Cabo de San Domingo (Cabo Orange)

Río Negro

'Río Marañon': Pinzón wonders whether he has found the Ganges

Amazon

Madeira

'I believe these two rivers, by reason of their enormous size, create the fresh-water area in the ocean' (Vespucci)

Tapajós

Xingu

B   R   A

Andes Mountains

Vespucci's claim to have reached 50°S is incredible and inconsistent with his account, but it may have been true that 'we navigated in the Southern hemisphere for nine months and twenty-seven days, never seeing the Arctic Pole or even Ursa Major and Minor'

Tropic of Capricorn

southward reach of this voyage uncertain; Vespucci calls his last port of call 'San Julian'

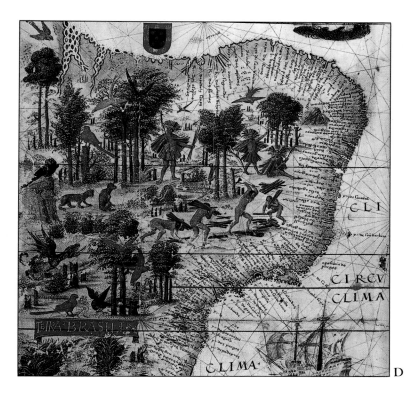

C FAR LEFT *The route through Le Maire's Strait and around Cape Horn, plotted in Schouten's 1619 account of the voyage, does not tally with their written accounts, which imply a course farther south, probably to about 57°S.*
D LEFT *This vivid view of the Brazilian coast, from the Portuguese Lopo Homem Atlas of 1519 depicts an exotic land peopled by proud natives and abundant animal and plant life.*

the Cape and reached Mozambique.

Pinzón's was the first of a number of privately financed voyages launched at about the same time as the Portuguese royal undertaking. Three of these were Spanish, made by crews which had got their experience with Columbus or during privateering voyages to West Africa. Pinzón's four caravels sailed from Palos on 18 November 1499 and skirted the Cape Verde Islands on the southern edge of the trades. Fortunate to be carried at speed by 'a terrible high sea', they arrived off 'Cabo de Consolación' on 26 January 1500, only 20 days out from the Cape Verde Islands. If Pinzón hoped to get round Columbus's presumed mainland to the south, he was deterred by the inauspicious trend of the coast, for he turned west to reconnoitre the mouth of the Amazon. He got back to Spain, via Hispaniola, in September 1500. By then a similar enterprise had been undertaken by Alonso Vélez de Mendoza, an impecunious hidalgo, who may have sailed farther south than Pinzón, probably discovering the mouth of the present Rio de São Francisco. The third voyage, by Diego de Lepe, made its landfall south of Pinzón's but added nothing further.

Vélez de Mendoza's expedition illustrates how such voyages were financed. It was conceived in a chivalric and romantic spirit; its objectives included a search for the earthly paradise. Yet Mendoza needed hard-headed backing. Antón and Luis Guerra, ships' victuallers who specialised in provisioning squadrons for Hispaniola, provided two caravels; Mendoza obtained another on credit. The Guerra brothers safeguarded their stake by seizing slaves and dyewood on the Brazilian coast. The originator of the enterprise was left penniless.

Other Atlantic navigators were eclipsed by the fame of two voyages to Brazil made shortly afterwards by Amerigo Vespucci, under Portuguese colours and command. (Vespucci had already detoured along the Brazilian coast in 1499, in the course of his Caribbean voyage with Ojeda, *see* ch. 10). Vespucci was an unreliable witness: he entered a false claim to be the discoverer of the mainland of the New World, omitted all mention of colleagues and superiors, and shuttled with dubious loyalty between Spanish and Portuguese service. He was, however, an investor and chronicler for voyages of genuine achievement. Unhappily, his descriptions are so vague, his sailing directions so amateurish and his calculations so wild that it is impossible to be sure by what routes he sailed or how far south he got. Nonetheless, he and his commander, Gonçalo de Coelho, reached a harbour they

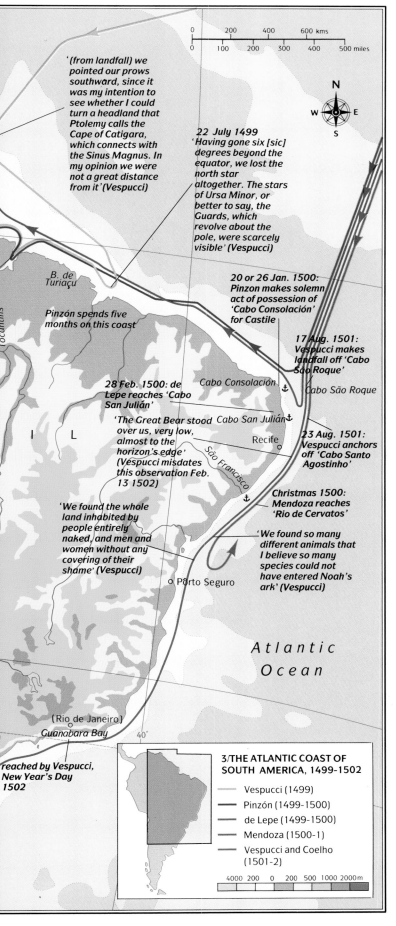

'(from landfall) we pointed our prows southward, since it was my intention to see whether I could turn a headland that Ptolemy calls the Cape of Catigara, which connects with the Sinus Magnus. In my opinion we were not a great distance from it' (Vespucci)

22 July 1499 'Having gone six [sic] degrees beyond the equator, we lost the north star altogether. The stars of Ursa Minor, or better to say, the Guards, which revolve about the pole, were scarcely visible' (Vespucci)

20 or 26 Jan. 1500: Pinzon makes solemn act of possession of 'Cabo Consolación' for Castile

17 Aug. 1501: Vespucci makes landfall off 'Cabo São Roque'

B. de Turiaçu

Tocantins

Pinzón spends five months on this coast

28 Feb. 1500: de Lepe reaches 'Cabo San Julián'

Cabo Consolación

Cabo São Roque

'The Great Bear stood over us, very low, almost to the horizon's edge' (Vespucci misdates this observation Feb. 13 1502)

Cabo San Julián

Recife

23 Aug. 1501: Vespucci anchors off 'Cabo Santo Agostinho'

São Francisco

'We found the whole land inhabited by people entirely naked, and men and women without any covering of their shame' (Vespucci)

Christmas 1500: Mendoza reaches 'Rio de Cervatos'

'We found so many different animals that I believe so many species could not have entered Noah's ark' (Vespucci)

o Pôrto Seguro

Atlantic Ocean

(Rio de Janeiro) Guanabara Bay

40°

reached by Vespucci, New Year's Day 1502

0   200   400   600 kms
0 100 200 300 400 500 miles

N
W   E
S

3/THE ATLANTIC COAST OF SOUTH AMERICA, 1499-1502

Vespucci (1499)
Pinzón (1499-1500)
de Lepe (1499-1500)
Mendoza (1500-1)
Vespucci and Coelho (1501-2)

4000 200 0 200 500 1000 2000m

3 LEFT *Knowledge of the Atlantic coast of South America developed rapidly from 1499. Vespucci's route can only be guessed at, a reflection of the vagaries and unreliability of his accounts.* E RIGHT *The 1516 edition of Waldseemüller's world wall-chart may reflect the contribution of an obscure voyage by Portuguese mariners, unknown except for a German account of 1514.*

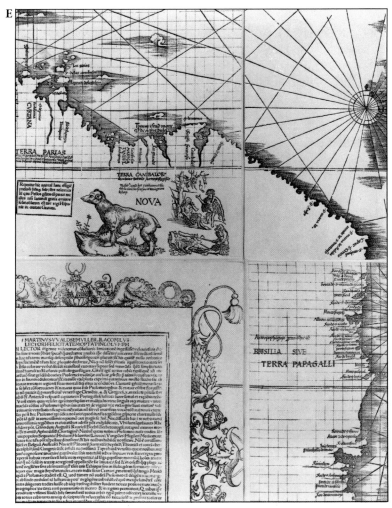

called Rio de Janeiro on their voyage of 1501-2.

None of these privately financed ventures solved the riddles of the nature of South America and of its relationship to Asia. Pinzón was convinced that he was on a gigantic promontory of Asia, as was Vespucci, despite his use of the phrase 'Mundus Novus', who also evidently shared Columbus's view that the globe was small. In the following decade, Portuguese logwood-concessionaires and the Spanish pilot Juan Díaz de Solís extended knowledge of the region of the River Plate (*see* ch.26) but the essence of the mystery remained unsolved.

Ferdinand Magellan, too, shared Columbus's picture of a small world in which the new discoveries were close to the known or reported riches of eastern Asia. The novelty of his enterprise was to push the search for a westward passage to the south. He declared with fanatical obduracy that he would sail to 75°S, adding, when pressed, that if he found no strait he would go to the Spice Islands by the 'Portuguese' route. As a companion of Abreu's voyage of 1511, (*see* ch.29) he had relevant experience, but, like Mendoza, was a gentleman-adventurer, disadvantaged, moreover, by an unprepossessing appearance. Like Columbus, he was shunned in Portugal, where the authorities had no interest in a new route. In October 1517, he abandoned his suit in his native country and transferred his allegiance. His partner, the cosmographer Rui Faleiro, calculated, wrongly, that the Spice Islands lay within the zone of expansion allotted by the Treaty of Tordesillas to Castile; this made Spanish patronage essential.

The most important backer was Juan de Aranda of the Casa de Contratación, or Board of New World Trade, at Seville, who lobbied at court in exchange for a fifth of any profits. Aranda had the enterprise adopted by the crown: ships and supplies were advanced, and the partners commissioned and paid by the king. They were granted a fifth of the profits of any trade they opened for 10 years and the governorship of any pagan lands they conquered. By encouraging him to attempt impracticable conquests, these terms doomed Magellan.

The expedition of five ships and 250 men, which sailed from Sanlúcar de Barrameda on 20 September 1519, was exceptionally well provisioned: Portuguese charts and pilots were carried, as were Portuguese water-casks that conserved their contents better than those of Spanish design. This reflects the uncertainties of conscious exploration and Magellan's expectation of a long sea

F LEFT *John Rotz's* Book of Hydrography *(1542), is one of the finest products of the Dieppe school's characteristic concern to incorporate the information of practical navigators, and perhaps includes the information on the river Plate region collected by Sebastian Cabot.*

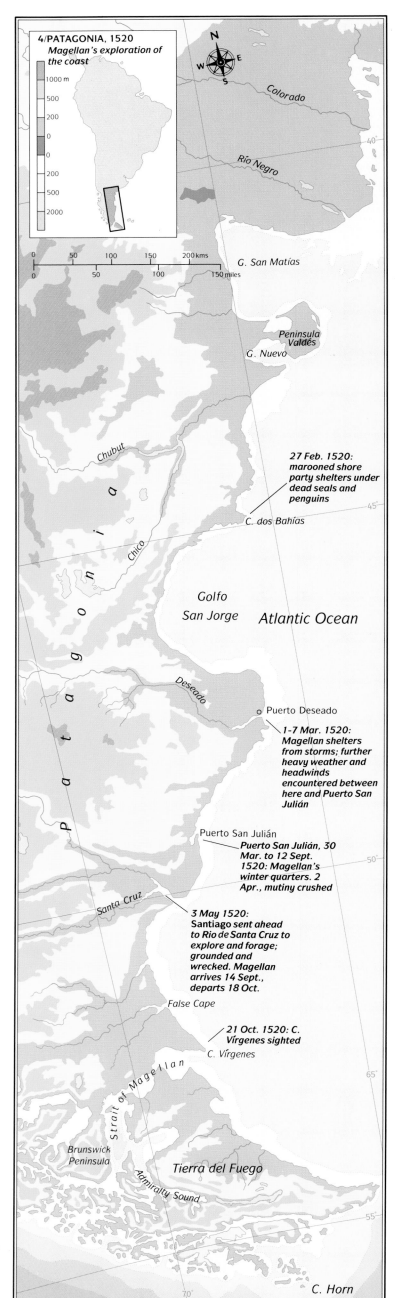

4 RIGHT *and* **5** BELOW RIGHT *Magellan's passage to and through the Straits seemed laborious enough, but the conditions he encountered were in fact relatively friendly. Loaisa's attempt to retrace Magellan's route in 1526 proved so arduous that the Strait was abandoned as a passage for Spanish shipping.*

4/PATAGONIA, 1520
Magellan's exploration of the coast

1000 m
500
0
200
500
2000

0   50   100   150   200 kms
0   50   100   150 miles

G. San Matías

Colorado

Río Negro

40

Peninsula Valdés

G. Nuevo

Chubut

Chico

Patagonia

C. dos Bahías

45

27 Feb. 1520: marooned shore party shelters under dead seals and penguins

Golfo San Jorge

Atlantic Ocean

Deseado

o Puerto Deseado

1-7 Mar. 1520: Magellan shelters from storms; further heavy weather and headwinds encountered between here and Puerto San Julián

Puerto San Julián

Puerto San Julián, 30 Mar. to 12 Sept. 1520: Magellan's winter quarters. 2 Apr., mutiny crushed

50

Santa Cruz

3 May 1520: Santiago sent ahead to Rio de Santa Cruz to explore and forage; grounded and wrecked. Magellan arrives 14 Sept., departs 18 Oct.

False Cape

21 Oct. 1520: C. Vírgenes sighted

C. Vírgenes

65

Strait of Magellan

Brunswick Peninsula

Tierra del Fuego

Admiralty Sound

55

C. Horn

70

voyage. Hitherto, Castilians had no experience of the long crossings typical of the India run, and Portuguese recruits joined the muster-lists, with a consequent strain on morale and unity.

Magellan's preference for a southerly Atlantic crossing – through storms off Sierra Leone in October and calms in the Doldrums – provoked an unsuccessful mutiny. On 29 November, the explorers reached the Brazilian coast off Recife, a useful point for southward-bound voyagers since the bulge of Brazil is hard to round from the north. After recuperation at Rio de Janeiro, they passed the height of the southern summer in a relatively agreeable search for a westward passage, but by the time they got to about 45°S at the end of February 1520 they were troubled by the cold and battered by squalls. By late March, with the rigours of winter only just beginning, they were at Puerto San Julián, where Magellan decided to await the turn of the season. The prospect provoked renewed mutiny. An attempted sortie from San Julián on 24 August proved premature and Magellan holed up for the rest of the winter at Rio de Santa Cruz, just beyond 50°S, renewing the voyage in earnest on 18 October. The longed-for strait proved to be only three days' sail away, at 52°30′S. As a result of the winter apparently wasted on the comfortless coast of Patagonia, the explorers arrived in the Pacific at the right season for the south-east trades; but for this, starvation or dehydration, which ultimately claimed so many of them, would surely have despatched the lot.

The outcome was judged encouraging. The great banking house of Fugger invested 10,000 ducats in a follow-up expedition. But as an avenue to the Pacific, the Strait of Magellan was flawed. The mouth was elusive, the exit remote, the passage troublesome. Magellan took seven weeks to navigate it; the 1525 expedition took four and a half months, subsequently recommending that the route be abandoned. No serious attempt to find an alternative south-west passage was launched for the remainder of the century, and when the emulous companions, the merchant Jakob Le Maire and the pilot Willem van Schouten, launched their effort from Holland in 1615, they had few illusions about the practicability of a westward route to the spice lands; rather they sought Terra Australis Incognita (*see* ch. 33) or fabled Pacific islands. By discovering Cape Horn and demonstrating the insularity of Tierra del Fuego, their voyage completed the mapping of the outlines of the South Atlantic.

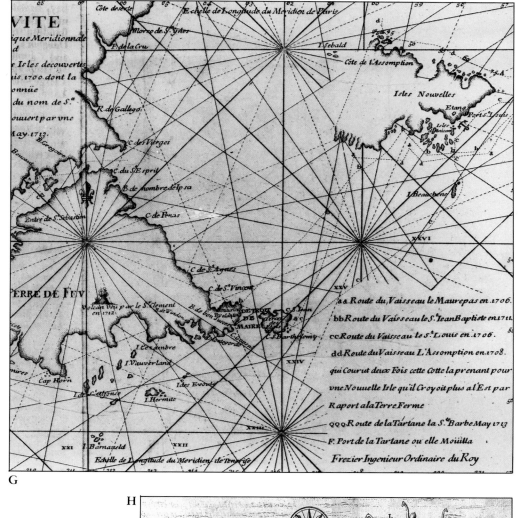

G **ABOVE** *Evidence to support the discovery of the Falkland Islands by 16th-century explorers is dubious. Their first unequivocal appearance is on Frézier's 18th-century map.* H **RIGHT** *The environment of the southern extremities of America excited the curiosity of early explorers. This view is from Schouten's account of his and Le Maire's voyage.*

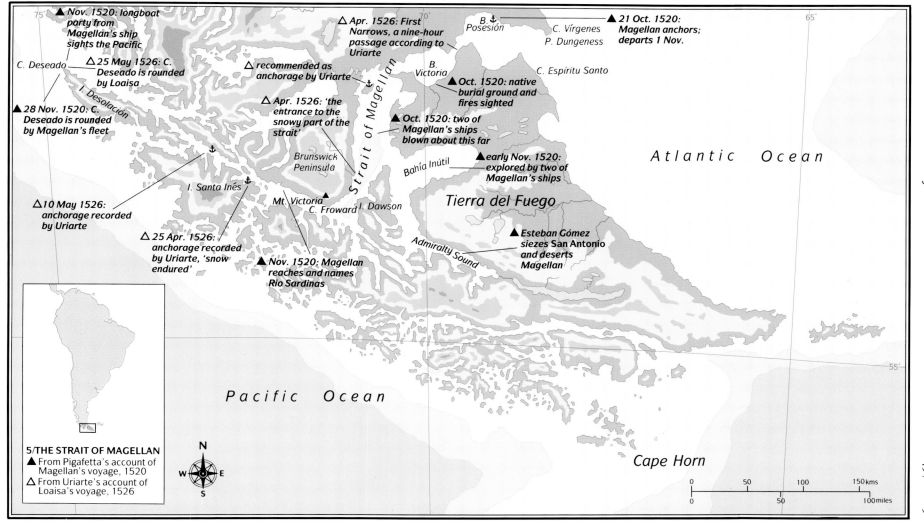

5/THE STRAIT OF MAGELLAN
▲ From Pigafetta's account of Magellan's voyage, 1520
△ From Uriarte's account of Loaisa's voyage, 1526

▲ Nov. 1520: longboat party from Magellan's ship sights the Pacific

C. Deseado

△ 25 May 1526: C. Deseado is rounded by Loaisa

I. Desolación

▲ 28 Nov. 1520: C. Deseado is rounded by Magellan's fleet

△ 10 May 1526: anchorage recorded by Uriarte

I. Santa Inés

△ 25 Apr. 1526: anchorage recorded by Uriarte, 'snow endured'

Brunswick Peninsula

Mt. Victoria
C. Froward I. Dawson

▲ Nov. 1520: Magellan reaches and names Rio Sardinas

△ Apr. 1526: First Narrows, a nine-hour passage according to Uriarte

△ recommended as anchorage by Uriarte

△ Apr. 1526: 'the entrance to the snowy part of the strait'

Strait of Magellan

B. Posesión
C. Vírgenes
P. Dungeness

▲ 21 Oct. 1520: Magellan anchors; departs 1 Nov.

B. Victoria

C. Espiritu Santo

▲ Oct. 1520: native burial ground and fires sighted

▲ Oct. 1520: two of Magellan's ships blown about this far

Bahía Inútil

▲ early Nov. 1520: explored by two of Magellan's ships

Tierra del Fuego

Atlantic Ocean

▲ Esteban Gómez siezes San Antonio and deserts Magellan

Admiralty Sound

Pacific Ocean

Cape Horn

N
W E
S

0   50   100   150kms
0   50   100miles

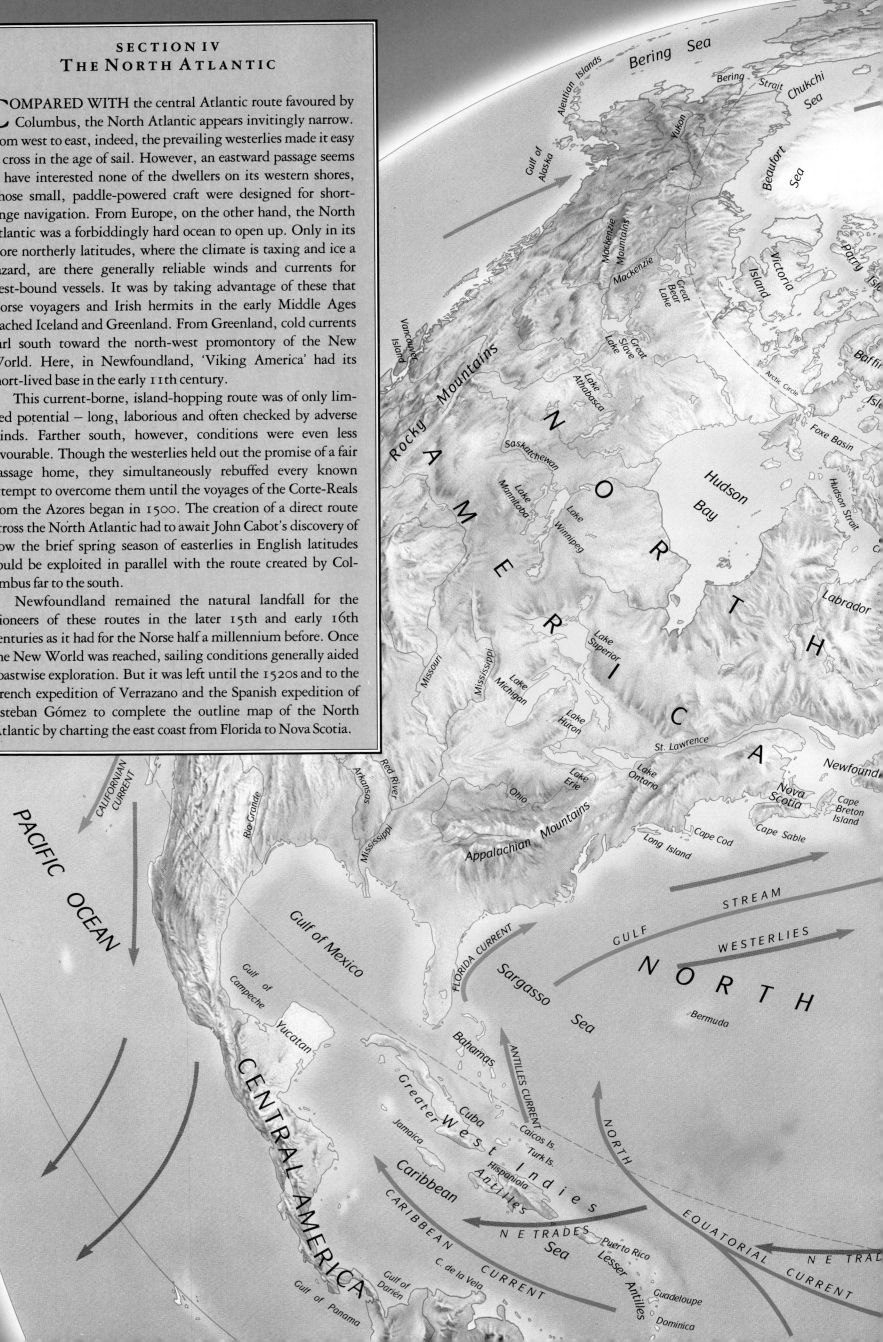

SECTION IV
THE NORTH ATLANTIC

COMPARED WITH the central Atlantic route favoured by Columbus, the North Atlantic appears invitingly narrow. From west to east, indeed, the prevailing westerlies made it easy to cross in the age of sail. However, an eastward passage seems to have interested none of the dwellers on its western shores, whose small, paddle-powered craft were designed for short-range navigation. From Europe, on the other hand, the North Atlantic was a forbiddingly hard ocean to open up. Only in its more northerly latitudes, where the climate is taxing and ice a hazard, are there generally reliable winds and currents for west-bound vessels. It was by taking advantage of these that Norse voyagers and Irish hermits in the early Middle Ages reached Iceland and Greenland. From Greenland, cold currents curl south toward the north-west promontory of the New World. Here, in Newfoundland, 'Viking America' had its short-lived base in the early 11th century.

This current-borne, island-hopping route was of only limited potential – long, laborious and often checked by adverse winds. Farther south, however, conditions were even less favourable. Though the westerlies held out the promise of a fair passage home, they simultaneously rebuffed every known attempt to overcome them until the voyages of the Corte-Reals from the Azores began in 1500. The creation of a direct route across the North Atlantic had to await John Cabot's discovery of how the brief spring season of easterlies in English latitudes could be exploited in parallel with the route created by Columbus far to the south.

Newfoundland remained the natural landfall for the pioneers of these routes in the later 15th and early 16th centuries as it had for the Norse half a millennium before. Once the New World was reached, sailing conditions generally aided coastwise exploration. But it was left until the 1520s and to the French expedition of Verrazano and the Spanish expedition of Esteban Gómez to complete the outline map of the North Atlantic by charting the east coast from Florida to Nova Scotia.

ARCTIC

OCEAN

New Siberian
Islands

Arctic Circle

Severnaya
Zemlya
(Nicholas II Land)

Novaya
Zemlya

A S I A

Ellesmere
Island

Queen
Elizabeth
Islands

Svalbard
(Spitsbergen)

Baffin Bay

Ural Mountains

Greenland

NORWEGIAN
CURRENT

Strait

Norwegian
Sea

Caspian
Sea

Labrador
Sea

Denmark

Iceland

Faeroe
Islands

LABRADOR

Shetland

Black Sea

CURRENT

Cape
Farewell

North
Sea

Elbe

E U R O P E

British

Rhine

Black
Sea

WESTERLIES

Isles

NORTH ATLANTIC DRIFT

WESTERLIES

Loire

Alps

Grand Banks

Race

field

WESTERLIES

WESTERLIES

Mediterranean

Sea

WESTERLIES

Nile

Tropic of Cancer

WESTERLIES

Azores

Strait of Gibraltar

-LANTIC OCEAN

Atlas Mountains

S a h a r a

Madeira

Hoggar

Tibesti

CANARIES CURRENT

Canary
Is.

N E TRADES

A F R I C A

N E TRADES

Lake Chad

N E TRADES

Niger

14
ROUTES OF THE NORTH ATLANTIC
C.825-1509

MUCH *uncertainty surrounds almost all European contacts with North America until well into the 16th century. The Norwegians between the 9th and 15th centuries were the first to cross the northern reaches of the Atlantic, occupying Iceland and then Greenland, from where limited contacts were made with some coastal regions of North America. Soon abandoned, and never reported in western Europe, these can scarcely be regarded as more than long-lost preliminaries to the discovery of the continent by the Portuguese and the English at the end of the 15th century.*

Extended Portuguese Atlantic voyaging began with the gradual exploration of the Azores and the Canaries (see ch.8). The key to the Portuguese success was understanding of the wind-systems of the Atlantic, specifically of the easterlies that blow in the spring and early summer, allowing westward voyages to be made, and of the westerlies that blow for much of the rest of the year, which, together with the eastward-flowing currents of the North Atlantic, made the return to Europe possible. By the mid-15th century, the Portuguese had progressed 1,000 miles into the Atlantic, from which point their eventual discovery of North America can be said to have been inevitable.

The Portuguese were aided by improvements in ship-construction, which enabled vessels to undertake more distant voyages, and in navigation, which enabled oceanic waters to be traversed with some likelihood of a landfall at least close to the intended spot. They had, too, the advantage of the lessons in seamanship acquired in their slow progress along the west African coast (see ch.12).

English ship-building skills also developed in the 15th century, in part the result of successful pioneering visits by east coast fishing vessels to the cod-rich waters of Iceland at the end of the 14th century, in part of regular contact with Portuguese traders and sailors. By the 1420s, frequent fishing and trading ventures to Iceland from Bristol had been initiated, making use of the easterlies between March and May and the northerly reach of the westerlies in August and September to bring them home.

These technical prerequisites, allied to increasing initiative on the part of individual mariners, who recognized considerable, if speculative, opportunities for personal enrichment in the discovery of new lands, frequently financed by substantial trading concerns, established the conditions that made the European discovery of North America a reality.

A BELOW *Though published only in 1668, Sigurddar Stefánsson's Skalholt map of 1590, copied from a lost original of 1570, is the earliest extant map to show the discoveries of the Norsemen. (The so-called Vinland map, first published in 1965 and purporting to date from the mid-14th century, is generally considered a forgery.)*

THE NORSE voyages to North America were a minor and final offshoot of the colonization of northern lands from Scandinavia. Iceland was colonized in the 9th century, Greenland towards the end of the 10th, and North America at the end of the 11th, probably as a result of ships bound for Greenland being swept too far to the north and west. Eric the Red colonized south-west Greenland towards the end of the 10th century, making his base at Brattahlid in the Eastern Settlement. Around 1000, Leif Eiriksson, Eric's son, on a return voyage from Norway, appears to have been driven off course up Davis Strait and well to the west. As he made his way southward, he sighted land of varying character, giving names to the more distinctive parts: Helluland ('Rockland', present-day Baffin Island); Markland ('Woodland', Labrador); and, finally, Newfoundland, which he named Vinland, apparently in the belief that grapes grew there. From there he returned north-east to Greenland.

Leif described the lands he found as being rich in salmon,

B ABOVE Norse ships proved astonishingly seaworthy. Those used for exploration and trade, known as knorrs, *were larger than the warship depicted in this 10th-century Anglo-Saxon manuscript, though were constructed following similar principles. The steering-oars are typical.*
1 BELOW Leif Eiriksson reached Vinland, the northern tip of Newfoundland, in around AD 1000, after being blown off course when making for Greenland.

grassland and, as noted, grapes, from which many writers have concluded that he sailed much farther south than Newfoundland, since the northern limit of grape cultivation is approximately the far north of what is now the United States. However, evidence either way is slim, with the only accounts of Leif's voyage coming from sagas passed orally from generation to generation and written down only in about 1300.

Leif is said to have established a homestead in Vinland and to have exploited it through members of his family for perhaps a dozen years. According to the sagas, a relation of Leif's by marriage, Thorfinn Karlsefni, brought colonists to Vinland but was later forced by hostile natives to return to Greenland after two or three winters. The sagas relate, too, tales of settlers returning to Greenland with grapes and vines and of expeditions to points along the American coast, though these have never been pinned down to specific locations. However, by 1010, possibly as late as 1025, the voyages to Vinland seem to have ended, never to be renewed – except for those to Labrador, which was a rich source of timber for tree-less Greenland. The Greenland colony itself died out in the early 15th century.

Until the 1960s, no genuine traces of a Norse settlement in North America had been found. But between 1961 and 1968 excavations were made at what was finally authenticated as a Norse site at L'Anse-aux-Meadows in Newfoundland, in the Strait of Belle Isle. Fifteen occupied dwelling sites were revealed, as well as a forge and smeltery for bog iron. However, few contemporary artefacts were found as the site had been clearly plundered over the centuries by Inuit. Further excavations have exposed some ships' timbers, with carving indicating that vessels were repaired there. The absence of remains of cattle-byres, graves and a substantial midden (a refuse heap, and normally found at sites occupied over long periods) indicates that it was not a colony, but a short-term base for exploring and trading. This conclusion remains contested, as does the question of whether or not this was the site of Leif's homestead.

If Vinland was as attractive as some passages in the sagas indicate, why was it abandoned? The answer seems to be because it was uneconomic for the Greenland colonists, themselves dependent on only occasional contact with Norway or Iceland, to maintain. Nonetheless, though the Vinland episode remains essentially mysterious, it should be viewed not as the 'discovery' of America so much as an isolated, if exciting, moment in Atlantic history.

The Portuguese, with their gradual westward advance from early in the 15th century and, more especially, from their colonization of the Azores (*see* ch.8), enjoyed a significant advantage in the exploration of the western Atlantic. Much of the

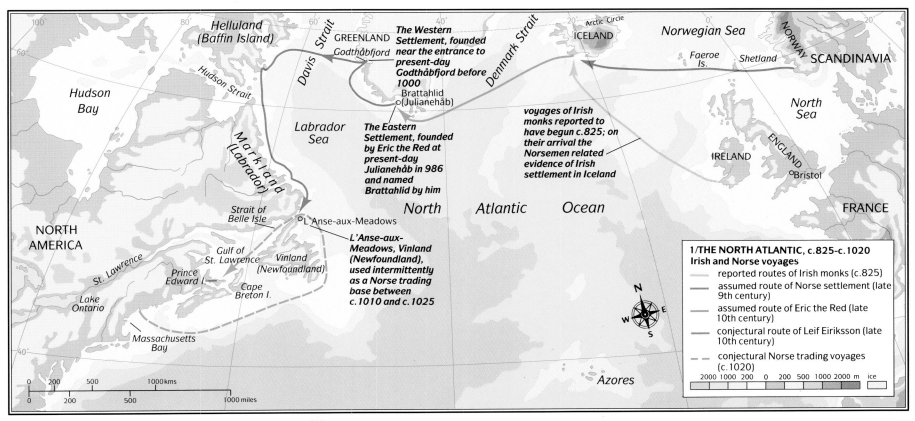

1/THE NORTH ATLANTIC, c.825–c.1020
Irish and Norse voyages
— reported routes of Irish monks (c.825)
— assumed route of Norse settlement (late 9th century)
— assumed route of Eric the Red (late 10th century)
— conjectural route of Leif Eiriksson (late 10th century)
-- conjectural Norse trading voyages (c.1020)

IV *The North Atlantic*

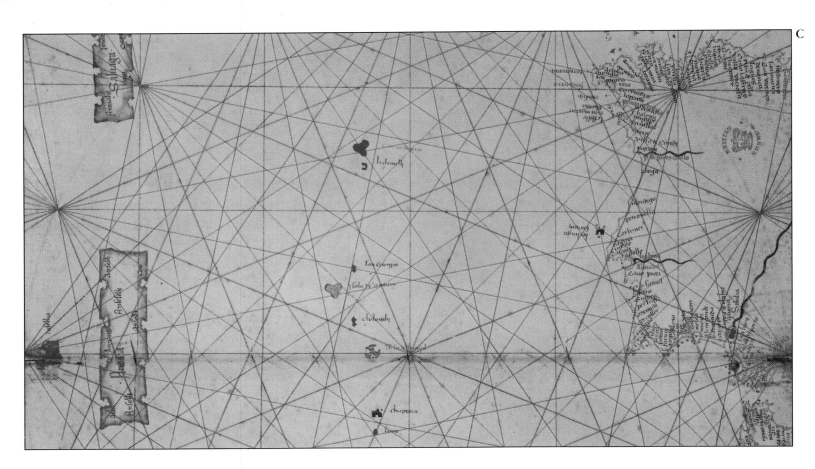

C LEFT *Portolan charts of the eastern Atlantic became increasingly common following the Portuguese exploration of the Azores in the 15th century. Part speculative and part the result of experience, they both reflected and promoted exploration.*

Azores archipelago was explored in 1427; colonization began in 1439; the outlying group (Corvo and Flores) was found in 1452. It was from an island in the central group, Terceira, that most of the initiative in North Atlantic exploration subsequently came. João Vaz Corte-Real, who was granted the hereditary captaincy of the island in 1474, is claimed by some Portuguese historians, though with little evidence, to have made or sponsored westward voyages, even to have discovered North America himself. Two of his sons, however, Miguel and Gaspar, genuinely contributed greatly to the exploration of its coasts, both losing their lives in the course of their efforts. A third son, Gaspar Annes, was granted rights over the fruits of his brothers' expeditions in 1506, but he seems never to have voyaged to North America to take advantage of this.

In 1500, Gaspar Corte-Real, with the backing of King Manuel of Portugal, set out northward from Terceira, making a landfall on the icy tip of Greenland at or near Cape Farewell. Greenland appeared barren and unprofitable so he turned west and sailed to what is now known as Labrador. From there he headed south along the coast before apparently sailing back to Lisbon, where he received royal authority to make a second voyage. Leaving Lisbon in May 1501 with two ships, Gaspar returned to his new coast. He may have gone north to Hudson

2 BELOW *Much of the impetus for Portugal's Atlantic voyaging came from the Azores, specifically Terceira. The most important long-term result of the Portuguese discoveries was the establishment of the lucrative fishery on the Newfoundland Grand Banks; the new lands themselves were not regarded as offering potential for settlement.*

Strait before turning south to Newfoundland – 'Terra Verde', he called it – landing somewhere along the Maritimes. Here he discovered many natives, about 50 of whom he enticed on board one of his ships and enslaved. His own ship was subsequently lost at sea, but the other, with its human cargo, caused a great stir when it reached Portugal.

Meanwhile, in 1499, a grant to explore in the west was also given to João Fernandes, a gentleman of Terceira. He made some discoveries of his own in North America, but when Gaspar Corte-Real returned from his first voyage in 1500, Fernandes decided not to compete. He left for Bristol, where he had already established trading connections, to offer his services on voyages to follow up the Cabot discoveries of 1497 and 1498 (*see* below). He was duly accepted to lead an expedition in 1501, from which it appears he did not return.

In May 1502, Miguel Corte-Real, having resolved to follow his lost brother, was granted royal permission to sail west. No narrative of his voyage has survived, though it is speculated that he followed the shoreline of part of Labrador and Newfoundland. His second vessel returned to relate that Miguel, too, had been lost at sea. The third brother, Gaspar Annes Corte-Real, did not attempt to follow his siblings in person but it was probably due to him that the Portuguese participated in

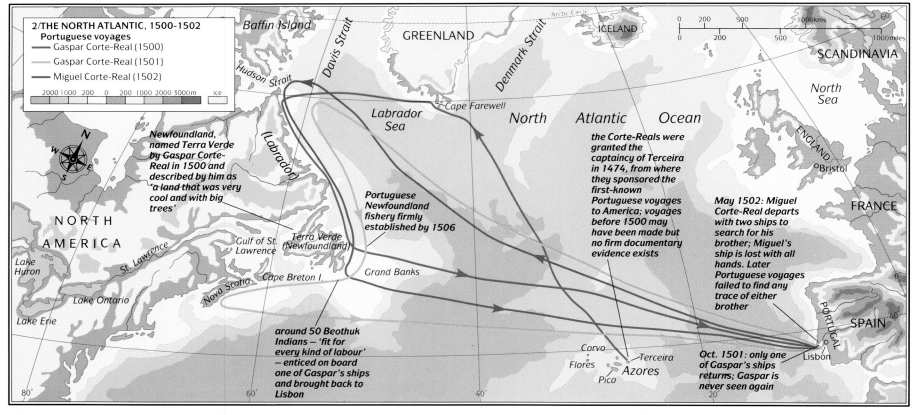

2/THE NORTH ATLANTIC, 1500-1502
Portuguese voyages
— Gaspar Corte-Real (1500)
— Gaspar Corte-Real (1501)
— Miguel Corte-Real (1502)

2000 1000 200 0 200 1000 2000 3000m   ice

Baffin Island   GREENLAND   ICELAND   SCANDINAVIA

Davis Strait   Denmark Strait   North Sea

Hudson Strait   Cape Farewell   North Atlantic Ocean   ENGLAND   Bristol

Labrador Sea

Newfoundland, named Terra Verde by Gaspar Corte-Real in 1500 and described by him as 'a land that was very cool and with big trees'

NORTH AMERICA

Lake Huron   Lake Ontario   Lake Erie

Portuguese Newfoundland fishery firmly established by 1506

Gulf of St. Lawrence   Terra Verde (Newfoundland)   Grand Banks

St. Lawrence   Nova Scotia   Cape Breton I.

around 50 Beothuk Indians – 'fit for every kind of labour' – enticed on board one of Gaspar's ships and brought back to Lisbon

the Corte-Reals were granted the captaincy of Terceira in 1474, from where they sponsored the first-known Portuguese voyages to America; voyages before 1500 may have been made but no firm documentary evidence exists

May 1502: Miguel Corte-Real departs with two ships to search for his brother; Miguel's ship is lost with all hands. Later Portuguese voyages failed to find any trace of either brother

FRANCE

PORTUGAL   SPAIN   Lisbon

Corvo   Flores   Terceira   Pico   Azores

Oct. 1501: only one of Gaspar's ships returns; Gaspar is never seen again

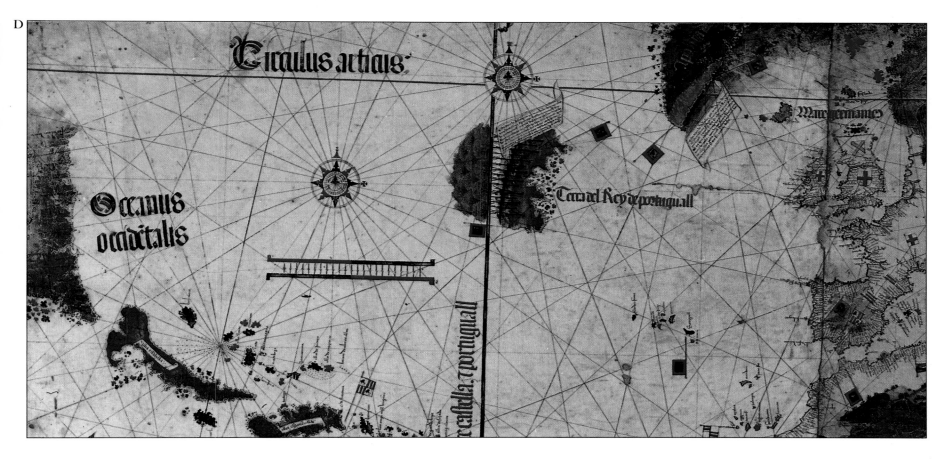

the Newfoundland fishery under the title to the lands discovered by his brothers between 1500 and 1502.

This is almost all that is known about the Portuguese contribution to North American exploration of this period other than what can be deduced from contemporary maps. The most notable is the Reinel map (*see* map **E**). It contains a generous number of Portuguese names on the eastern shore of Newfoundland, including some clearly linked with current names.

The Portuguese achievements of 1500-2 were substantial. Any attempt to sum them up must recognize that the Portuguese revealed land of continental proportions; that they helped familiarize Europeans with a substantial part of it, particularly through the circulation of manuscript maps such as Reinel's; and that they obtained a stake in the fishing grounds of the Grand Banks, which they were to exploit fully, while retaining rights to explore and annex for Portugal any further lands which they might discover and colonize.

England, especially the west country port of Bristol, was well placed for western exploration. Bristol not only had Iberian contacts which kept its merchants informed of Spanish and Portuguese discoveries, but considerable experience in penetrating the northern reaches of the Atlantic. The Iceland trade, developed from the 1420s onwards, was the main source of

D ABOVE *The Cantino map of 1502 shows the discovery of the Corte-Reals as an island east of the 1494 Tordesillas division of the Atlantic and accordingly signed as belonging to Portugal.*

Bristol's experience of Atlantic Ocean sailing. An initial voyage in 1480 in search of the mythical mid-Atlantic island of Brasil – an island often pictured on charts which the Bristol men received from their Iberian trading partners (*see* map **F**) – was followed by another in 1481. It was recorded in 1498 that between about 1490 and 1496 Bristolians had been sending two to four ships a year to search for land in the western Atlantic. No confirmation exists of this, however, and it seems unlikely that Bristol could afford to send more than one to two small ships, and then only intermittently, on purely exploratory voyages.

Not until after Columbus's first Atlantic crossing in 1492 did Atlantic voyaging from England take on a significant role. This was largely the work of the Italian-born John Cabot, who moved with his family to Bristol sometime after 1493. Cabot had unsuccessfully sought backing in Spain and Portugal for a westward voyage to Asia. His conviction that such a voyage would be shorter in higher latitudes was undoubtedly what attracted support, first in Bristol and then in London. His first voyage was unsuccessful for reasons unknown, but in March 1496 Henry VII granted him and his three sons rights to rule lands discovered in the west in the name of the crown. His famous voyage in the *Mathew*, between 20 May and 6 August

E RIGHT *Reinel's 1503 (or later) map of the North Atlantic reflects the Portuguese pre-eminence in the exploration of Newfoundland, with many Portuguese place names shown on the eastern shore. The strait to the south of Newfoundland has been speculatively identified as Cabot Strait. Farther south, a mainland culminates in what could be Cape Breton.*

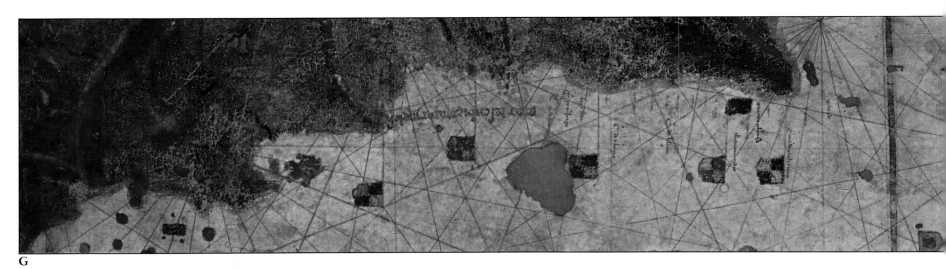

1497, disclosed 400 miles of coastline, which he identified as the Asia of the Great Khan – despite the fact that the Mongol dynasty in China had ended in 1368. The north-south limits of his voyage were described as lying between the latitudes of Dursey Head in Ireland and the mouth of the Garonne on the west coast of France (approximately between 51° and 46°N). He also reported the presence of many cod and expressed the view that tropical flora, such as the dyewood, brasil, would grow there.

In May 1498, with support from the king, Cabot set out with five vessels on a second voyage to trade with the Orientals whom he fully expected to find. The details of what happened to the expedition remain unknown. However, one of Cabot's

ships returned to Ireland badly damaged, suggesting that the fleet must have been hit by a severe storm. Cabot himself never returned and by September 1499 had been given up for dead.

Henry VII, excited by the new discoveries, attempted to persuade other Bristol merchants to search for what Cabot had found. Though Cabot had evidently left too few directions for others to follow his routes, in 1501, João Fernandes and two Terceirian associates, João Gonsales and Francisco Fernandes, appeared in Bristol ready to lead a group of merchants to the area they had previously discovered (*see above*). Their expedition of 1501 reached America, but nothing is known of its findings except that Fernandes was apparently lost.

Gonsales and Francisco Fernandes, however, together with

F BELOW *The so-called Paris map of c.1490 shows the mythical island of Brasil at the top of the map and the 'Islands of the Seven Cities' below the compass rose on the left. Both are farther north and west than their positions on earlier charts, probably to encourage English voyages to the west.*

F

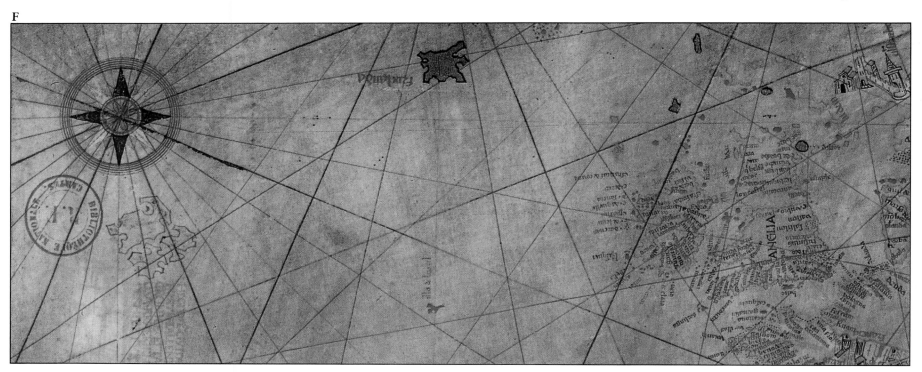

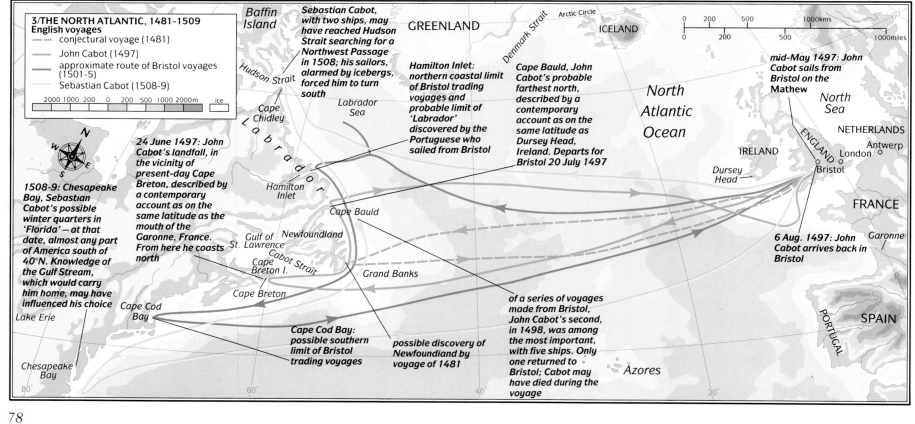

3/THE NORTH ATLANTIC, 1481–1509
English voyages
— conjectural voyage (1481)
— John Cabot (1497)
— approximate route of Bristol voyages (1501–5)
— Sebastian Cabot (1508–9)

2000 1000 200 0 200 500 1000 2000m   ice

Sebastian Cabot, with two ships, may have reached Hudson Strait searching for a Northwest Passage in 1508; his sailors, alarmed by icebergs, forced him to turn south

Hamilton Inlet: northern coastal limit of Bristol trading voyages and probable limit of 'Labrador' discovered by the Portuguese who sailed from Bristol

Cape Bauld, John Cabot's probable farthest north, described by a contemporary account as on the same latitude as Dursey Head, Ireland. Departs for Bristol 20 July 1497

mid-May 1497: John Cabot sails from Bristol on the Mathew

Baffin Island

GREENLAND   Arctic Circle   Denmark Strait   ICELAND

Hudson Strait   Cape Chidley   Labrador Sea

1508-9: Chesapeake Bay, Sebastian Cabot's possible winter quarters in 'Florida' – at that date, almost any part of America south of 40°N. Knowledge of the Gulf Stream, which would carry him home, may have influenced his choice

24 June 1497: John Cabot's landfall, in the vicinity of present-day Cape Breton, described by a contemporary account as on the same latitude as the mouth of the Garonne, France. From here he coasts north

Hamilton Inlet

Cape Bauld

Gulf of St. Lawrence   Newfoundland

Cabot Strait

Cape Breton I.   Grand Banks

Cape Breton

Lake Erie

Cape Cod Bay

Chesapeake Bay

Cape Cod Bay: possible southern limit of Bristol trading voyages

possible discovery of Newfoundland by voyage of 1481

of a series of voyages made from Bristol, John Cabot's second, in 1498, was among the most important, with five ships. Only one returned to Bristol; Cabot may have died during the voyage

North Atlantic Ocean

North Sea

NETHERLANDS   Antwerp   London

IRELAND   ENGLAND   Bristol

Dursey Head

FRANCE

6 Aug. 1497: John Cabot arrives back in Bristol

Garonne

PORTUGAL   SPAIN

Azores

0 200 500 1000kms
0 200 500 1000miles

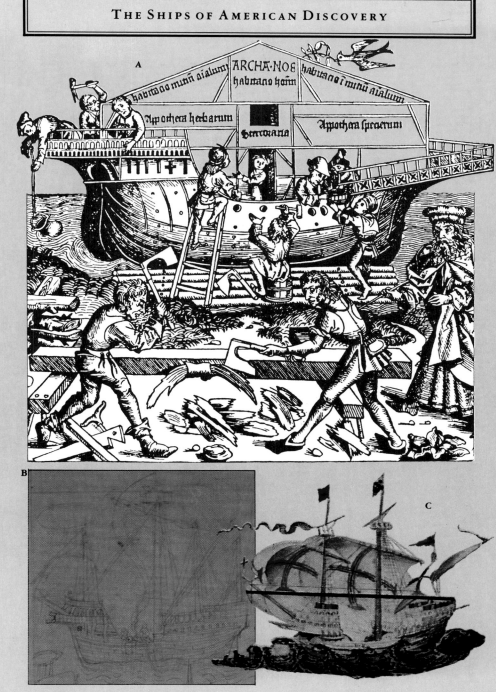

3 BOTTOM LEFT
Bristol merchants led by Robert Thorne and helped by João Fernandes continued the tradition of Atlantic voyaging begun by Cabot at the end of the 15th century. The chief benefit was involvement in the Newfoundland fishery; the hoped-for benefits of trade faded with the reality that a new continent had been discovered.

G ABOVE *Part of the early 16th-century Juan de la Cosa map shows a great continental shore in the western Atlantic. Though intended to represent Asia, it includes an area marked as discovered by the English and which may have been based on a sketch made during Cabot's 1497 voyage.*

Hugh Eliot and Robert Thorne, old associates of the Cabots, and Sebastian Cabot, John's son, made a series of further voyages. These were intended partly to establish the Newfoundland fishery on a regular basis; partly to explore, it is thought, from Labrador south to Cape Cod Bay. The voyages of 1502, 1503, 1504 and 1505 brought confirmation that the land found was not Asia, but a new continent. The new land was a disappointment, however, yielding none of the hoped-for opportunities for trade.

Sebastian Cabot was not satisfied with this outcome. He believed that if North America stood in the way of Asia, the next step was to go far enough north to find a passage around it. The Portuguese discoveries may have encouraged him in this belief. In 1506, he began to seek finance for two ships for this purpose and may have found backing in the Netherlands from Antwerp merchants. However, when he set out in 1508 it was apparently from Bristol. His exact route and destination are clouded by the conflicting stories which he subsequently told of his achievement. He may have reached Hudson Strait; if so, the great summer outpourings of melting ice and numerous icebergs would have forced him to return southwards. It was now too late, he considered, to return to England, so he continued south, doubtless inspecting the territory to which he was heir under the patent of 1496 while also looking for a passage to the Orient in lower latitudes. He wintered on the mainland coast, then sailed to approximately 35°N and made his way back to England on the westerlies. He reached Bristol at the beginning of May to find that Henry VII was dead. Though his pension was paid to him for the time he was away, this was revoked by unsympathetic officials and he was forced to return it by instalments. He had almost done so when, in 1511, he was sent with an English force to south-west France to make a map of Gascony and Guienne, for which he was given a small reward. Seeing no future for himself in England, Cabot made overtures to Spain and at Burgos agreed to enter the Spanish service, an arrangement that would last until 1548. He always hankered after a further attempt on the Northwest Passage but Spain would never back a venture into its icy waters. The English effort so long sustained was now largely abandoned – though the fishery continued – to be revived only in 1576 when Martin Frobisher began again the attempt to find the Northwest Passage (*see* ch. 16).

THE SHIPS of the European transatlantic voyages of discovery of the late 15th and early 16th centuries had all benefited from improvements in ship design over the previous 100 years or so. These originated principally in the Mediterranean, but it is clear that shipbuilders in northern Europe contributed at least partly to the overall process. Certainly northern European materials – Stockholm tar, for example, and masts from Riga – were much in demand, while the yards of the Hanseatic League, as illustrated in (A) of 1493, were among the busiest in Europe.

The principal changes were to hull shapes, which became longer in relation to ships' beams with more pronounced fore and aft castles, and to sail plans. A gradual increase in size also occurred. Though this naturally increased the space available for cargo, it did not necessarily improve either speed or safety. The *Mathew*, the vessel used by Cabot in 1497 on his first transatlantic voyage, and in all probability very similar to (B) of c.1485, though no more than 60 tons, was evidently a weatherly ship with excellent sea-keeping qualities and capable of considerable speed. Her return voyage may have been made in as little as 15 days, an excellent rate of sailing even for a modern racing yacht. Few ships of the period were likely to have been of more than 200 tons, however. Sebastian Cabot's claim to have carried a crew of 300 on his 1508 voyage seems wildly exaggerated.

The Portuguese were the first to make use of the triangular lateen sail, long known to the Arabs. Though less efficient for downwind sailing than the traditional European square sail, it had the immense advantage of allowing ships to sail to windward. With a lateen sail on the mizzen [rear] mast and square sails on the main and, as it came increasingly to be adopted, the foremast, ships such as (C) of c.1520 and the larger and more sophisticated (D) of the same date had excellent pulling power and considerable manoeuvrability.

15
THE EAST COAST OF NORTH AMERICA
1513-1620

THE EXPLORATION *of the east coast of North America made a halting start. Following the discoveries of the late 15th century of Columbus in the Caribbean and of Cabot and the Corte-Reals in Newfoundland (see chs. 10 and 14), the next explorers of these new lands to the west persisted in the belief that they were exploring not a new continent but unknown Asian coasts. The prevailing European world view in the early 16th century differed only marginally from that established by Ptolemy and other ancient Greek and Roman geographers. To Europeans, the lands and islands reported by voyagers to the west of Europe could only be on the dimly known coasts of eastern Asia: landmasses outside the known tripartite world of Europe, Asia and Africa existed in the realms of fable or philosophical speculation, not fact. Not until the 1520s was it generally accepted that the land was a new continent – America.*

Thereafter, despite extensive voyages along the south and north-eastern coasts of North America in the early years of the 16th century – by Spaniards in the south and by Portuguese, English and French in the north – a willingness to believe in the proximity of Asia and an easily sailed westward sea-passage to it proved tenacious. Only with the south–north navigation by Giovanni Verrazano in 1524 of the coast between Florida and Newfoundland did it become clear that Columbus's, the Corte-Reals' and Cabot's discoveries were merely parts of a nearly continuous landmass. But with its landward extent still unknown, the belief that a navigable strait existed dominated much later exploration. Even Verrazano was convinced that parts of his new-found coast were no more than an isthmus, narrower even than that discovered by Balboa at Panama (see ch. 10), across which a mare oriental *was easily reached.*

The realization that these new lands might prove valuable in themselves came very gradually. For many, they were still an obstacle on the way to the East. Colonization accordingly followed slowly, and with little success. Early Portuguese and French attempts at settlement came to nothing; later English efforts proved equally impermanent. Only the Spanish enjoyed much success, and then only with an isolated settlement. By the beginning of the 17th century, however, the picture altered radically as the French, the Dutch and the English all established settlements. Europe was poised to open up the new continent (see chs. 18 and 19).

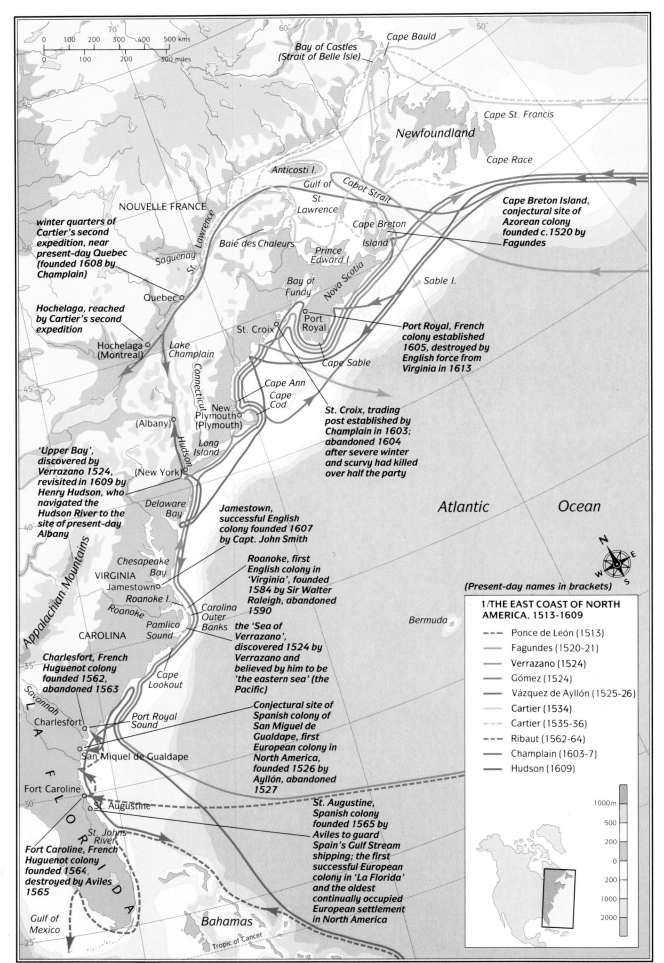

winter quarters of Cartier's second expedition, near present-day Quebec (founded 1608 by Champlain)

Hochelaga, reached by Cartier's second expedition

Cape Breton Island, conjectural site of Azorean colony founded c. 1520 by Fagundes

Port Royal, French colony established 1605, destroyed by English force from Virginia in 1613

St. Croix, trading post established by Champlain in 1603; abandoned 1604 after severe winter and scurvy had killed over half the party

'Upper Bay', discovered by Verrazano 1524, revisited in 1609 by Henry Hudson, who navigated the Hudson River to the site of present-day Albany

Jamestown, successful English colony founded 1607 by Capt. John Smith

Roanoke, first English colony in 'Virginia', founded 1584 by Sir Walter Raleigh, abandoned 1590

the 'Sea of Verrazano', discovered 1524 by Verrazano and believed by him to be 'the eastern sea' (the Pacific)

Charlesfort, French Huguenot colony founded 1562, abandoned 1563

Conjectural site of Spanish colony of San Miguel de Gualdape, first European colony in North America, founded 1526 by Ayllón, abandoned 1527

St. Augustine, Spanish colony founded 1565 by Aviles to guard Spain's Gulf Stream shipping; the first successful European colony in 'La Florida' and the oldest continually occupied European settlement in North America

Fort Caroline, French Huguenot colony founded 1564, destroyed by Aviles 1565

(Present-day names in brackets)

1/THE EAST COAST OF NORTH AMERICA, 1513-1609

- – – – Ponce de León (1513)
- ——— Fagundes (1520-21)
- ——— Verrazano (1524)
- ——— Gómez (1524)
- ——— Vázquez de Ayllón (1525-26)
- ——— Cartier (1534)
- ——— Cartier (1535-36)
- – – – Ribaut (1562-64)
- ——— Champlain (1603-7)
- ——— Hudson (1609)

PORTUGUESE domination in the exploration of the north-eastern coasts of America ended with the attempt at colonization made by João Fagundes around 1520. Fagundes appears to have established a colony of Azoreans on or near today's Cape Breton Island, but the colony disappeared sometime before 1526. With Portugal's withdrawal from the scene, it was the French king, Francis I, who challenged Spain's claim to control of the new discoveries in the west. The most important explorer sponsored by Francis was the Florentine, Giovanni Verrazano, who sailed in 1524 looking for a strait to Asia. In the process, he sailed the length of the American coast from south to north. Though Verrazano established the existence of a continuous coastline, he also propagated a significant geographical myth, when, rounding present-day Cape Lookout, he saw an 'isthmus a mile in width and about 200 long'. This was the ribbon of sandy islands now known as the Carolina Outer Banks. The waters on the far side of them Verrazano took to be the Pacific. On his return to Europe, Verrazano's 'isthmus' was widely accepted, chiefly through the medium of a map drawn by his brother Girolamo in 1529 (see map **B**).

Spain meanwhile was preoccupied with the colonization of the Indies and exploration of the Caribbean rimlands (see ch. 10). One of the leading figures in both enterprises was Juan Ponce de León, conqueror and first colonizer of Puerto Rico. The name of 'La Florida', bestowed on his accidental discovery of March 1513, eventually came to designate the whole of the south-eastern and southern portions of the present United States. Local Indians told the unbelieving Spaniards that their land was a mainland and named its provinces. Nonetheless, it was only with the voyages of Verrazano and Gómez more than a decade later that Florida came to be accepted as part of the continental mainland.

The Spanish were also preoccupied by the search for a sea-passage to the Orient. In March 1524, Esteban Gómez, a Portuguese-born pilot, was commissioned by Charles V of Spain to 'go and explore eastern Cathay … as far as our island of Maluco [the Spice Islands]'. According to the chronicler Peter Martyr, Gómez returned after a ten-month voyage during which he traced the Atlantic coast in the opposite direction to that sailed by Verrazano. In an attempt to capitalize on these discoveries, in 1525-26 Luis Vázquez de Ayllón established a short-lived colony at San Miguel de Gualdape on the coast of present-day Georgia or South Carolina.

More than a decade after Verrazano's momentous voyage, the French crown again backed an official expedition to North America. In 1534, Jacques Cartier was commissioned to sail to 'the New Lands and to pass the Bay of Castles [Strait of Belle Isle]' to find a route to Asia. He spent the summer exploring the Gulf of St. Lawrence. He returned the following year and sailed up the St. Lawrence to the site of present-day Quebec City. Leaving his ships there, he continued upstream to Hochelaga, an Indian town on the site of what is now Montreal. Cartier's party spent the winter at Quebec, discovering to its cost the ferocity of Canadian winters and the devastating effects of scurvy.

Further French attempts at settlement were accordingly made much farther south. In 1562, a party of French protestants sailed to America under the leadership of Jean Ribaut with the hope of establishing a colony. They made their landfall in Florida, from where they sailed north looking for a suitable location. They found it at Port Royal Sound, in present-day South Carolina; they called the settlement Charlesfort. Continuing religious conflict in France made the resupply of the base impossible, however, and the colony was abandoned. A further attempt to establish an American colony was made two years later under Ribaut's lieutenant, Laudonnière, who constructed a small settlement, Fort Caroline, a few miles upstream of the mouth of the St. Johns River. Alarmed at these incursions, the Spanish took drastic action. In 1565, Pedro Menendez de Aviles attacked Fort Caroline, killing most of the

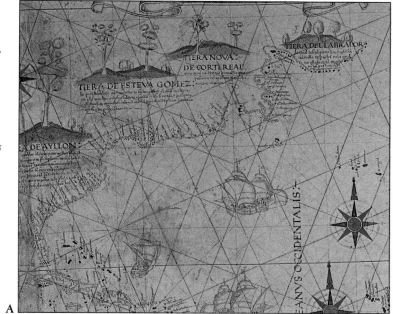

1 FAR LEFT *The revelation of a continuous coastline was made by Verrazano in 1524. In the rest of the century, Europeans explored the coast in depth; by 1565, the first successful colony had been established.*
A RIGHT *Diogo Ribeiro's world map of 1529 reflected the official Spanish view of North America's east coast. Ribero was responsible for Spain's official world map, the* Padron Real, *updating it as new discoveries were made.*

A

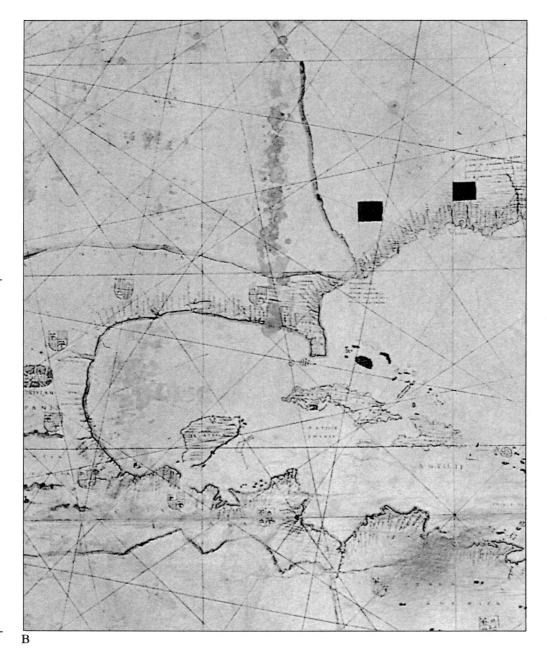

B

C

B ABOVE *Though accurate in its depiction of a continuous coastline from Florida to Newfoundland, the Verrazano map of 1529 promulgated the explorer's belief that a narrow isthmus separated the Atlantic from the Pacific.* **C RIGHT** *Sebastian Munster's 1540 map of America was the first widely circulated European map to show the New World clearly separated from the Old World. However, it, too, reflects the belief in a narrow North America.*

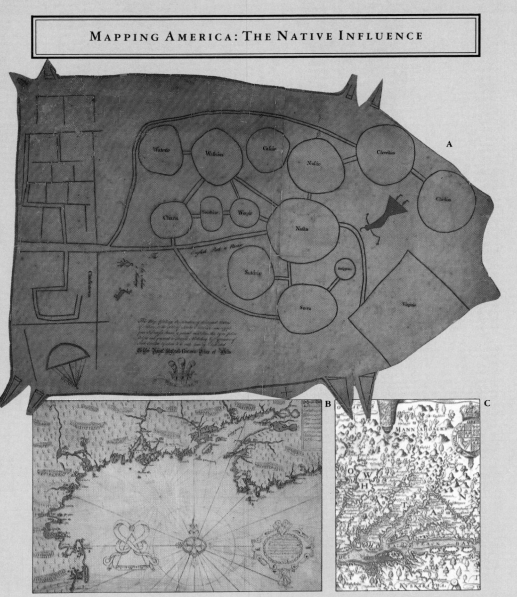

A

D

B

C

A T CAPE Ann, Massachusetts, in 1605, Samuel de Champlain went ashore to parley with the local Indians. In response to his sketching the coast, one of them 'pictured for me ... another bay which they represented as very large'. On it, were located the Indians' settlements and the principal rivers of the surrounding region. Champlain used this Indian map in producing his chart of 1607 (B). He was by no means unusual: every successful New World explorer relied on Indian wayfinding and cartography. The Velasco map (D) was prepared by an anonymous cartographer-spy in London working for the Spanish ambassador. Sent in 1611 with a coded letter to Philip III, it summarized East Coast exploration to date. A caption explains that the portions of the map coloured blue were 'drawn by the relations of the Indians' – from information 'related', by the Indians. In Captain John Smith's 1612 map of Virginia (C), those areas not explored by Smith are marked by crosses. The legend states that 'to the crosses hath bin discovered ... what [is] beyond is by relation'. Most Indian maps themselves were ephemeral, drawn in the sand or on bark, or chalked on a ship's deck. A few were more permanent, however, such as the map drawn on deer hide in around 1730 by a Catawba Indian for the governor of South Carolina (A). The maze-like pattern to the left is the Indian's impression of Charleston's city plan; the parachute-like object below is a ship. To the right is a schematic representation of the tribes of the interior.

D

settlers. He then attempted to cement the Spanish presence, establishing the colony of St. Augustine. It was to prove the first permanent European colony on the continent.

By the middle of the century, a new European player entered the game: England. Between 1584 and 1590, three separate attempts were made to establish a colony at Roanoke in 'Virginia', the name given to the new land by Walter Raleigh in honour of England's virgin queen. The settlement, in today's North Carolina, never prospered. When supply ships reached it, after a delay of two years, they found it deserted. Its fate has never been satisfactorily explained.

French, English and Dutch colonies in America were, however, established successfully in the early years of the new century. The French drive was spear-headed by Samuel de

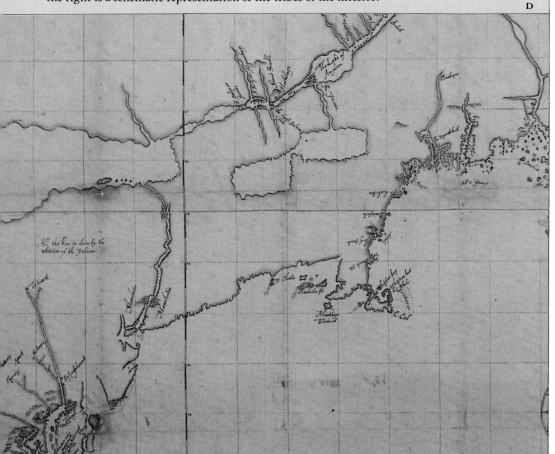

E

D FAR LEFT *Jacques la Moyne's* A recent and Most Exact draft of Florida (1562).
E LEFT 'The Arrival of the Englishmen in Virginia', *1590, by de Bry. Prints such as this created a vivid impression of the New World in Europe.* F ABOVE RIGHT *John Smith's map of New England (1616). Smith was a vigorous proponent of English overseas colonization. He coined the name 'New England'.* G BELOW *The extent of French exploration of the northeast coast of North America in the 17th century is highlighted by the improved detail in Sanson's 1656 map over that produced half a century earlier by Champlain (see ch.18, map A).*

F

Champlain who in 1603 followed the route pioneered by Cartier to Quebec and Montreal. His motive was less the search for a sea-passage to the Orient than a realization that the new lands could yield substantial dividends in the form of furs. Champlain's subsequent wide-ranging exploration of Canada ushered in a new era of European, specifically French, settlement and exploitation in and of North America (*see* ch.18). English attempts at settlement were renewed in 1607 with the establishment of Jamestown in the Chesapeake Bay by Captain John Smith and in 1620 with the arrival of the Pilgrim Fathers at New Plymouth in present-day Massachusetts. Neither settlement achieved much in the way of exploration of the vast interior to the west (*see* ch.19); the immediate aim was survival.

The Dutch, meanwhile, had also established themselves on

the coast, mid-way between the two English outposts. They had done so in 1609, principally through the efforts of the English explorer Henry Hudson (*see* ch.16). Reaching America on the latitude of Maine on behalf of the Dutch East India Company, Hudson coasted south to the Delaware River. Turning north, he entered what is now New York harbour, discovered but not explored by Verrazano in 1524. He sailed up the Hudson River to the site of present-day Albany, at which point he concluded that what he was seeing was simply a river, not a passage through the continent. His voyage nonetheless established the Dutch claim to much of the land Hudson discovered, most famously the island of Manhattan, later the Dutch settlement of New Amsterdam, from 1664 the English city of New York.

G

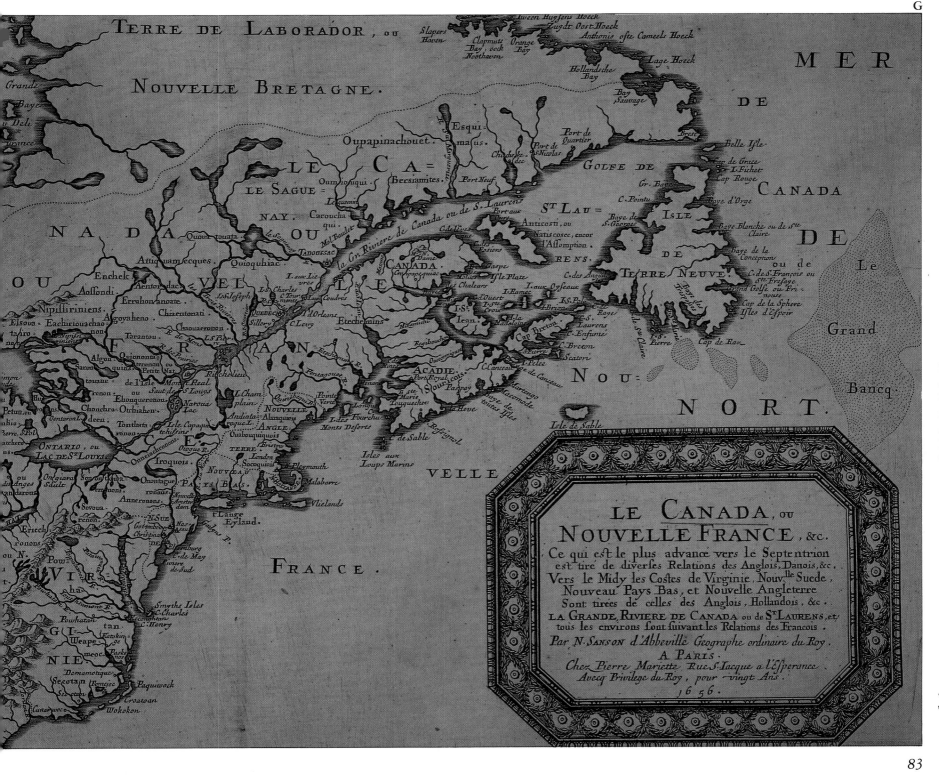

16
THE NORTHWEST PASSAGE 1576-1632

BY THE *early 16th century, European geographers were aware that the lands discovered across the Atlantic were part not of Asia, but of a great landmass that barred the way to the countries of spices, precious stones and fine silks. Explorers of the new continent sought long and hard for a way through to the Pacific, but the only strait found was that far to the south named after its discoverer, Magellan (see ch.13). For ships from Europe, this was both distant and dangerous, and French expeditions commanded by Verrazano and Cartier probed along the eastern seaboard of North America in a vain quest for a shorter and more convenient route. Farther north still lay unknown and desolate regions of ice.*

A ABOVE *Sir Humphrey Gilbert's heart-shaped map of 1576 is the earliest world map printed in England. It illustrates Frobisher's argument that a short Northwest Passage existed in temperate latitudes.* 1 LEFT *Europeans who encountered 'Eskimoes' in the 16th century had reached only the fringes of an expanding culture, one which had adapted with conspicuous success to one of the harshest environments on earth.*

It was there that English navigators sought the sea-route that they called the Northwest Passage. There is some evidence that Sebastian Cabot made a northern voyage in 1508 and 1509, possibly even reaching Hudson Strait, but English efforts to find a route to the Pacific were soon diverted to the search for a Northeast Passage (see ch.32). Not until the last quarter of the 16th century did attention return to the unknown area north of Newfoundland and Labrador. Then, for 60 years, English navigators explored the bleak and labyrinthine coastline of north-east America beyond 60°N. Support for these ventures came from government, nobles and merchants. As Sir Humphrey Gilbert argued in his Discourse, *the discovery of a Northwest Passage would revolutionize England's foreign trade. The* Discourse *was published in 1576, the year in which Martin Frobisher set out on the first of his three voyages.*

1/CENTRAL AND EASTERN CANADA, C.1500
Distribution of the Inuit
- Norse settlements 1000-1600
- main areas of Inuit settlement
- limits of Inuit expansion
- routes of Inuit expansion with dates

IN 1576, in a single small vessel, Martin Frobisher struggled through tempestuous seas off Greenland to reach the south-east coast of Baffin Island (*see* map 2). There he found an opening in 63°45′N, out of which surged a powerful tide. Because of this, 'they judged the open water beyond the headlands to be the West Sea, whereby to pass to Cathay'. Frobisher named the opening after himself: 'Frobishers Streytes, lyke as Magellanus at the Southwest ende of the Worlde, havying discovered the passage to the South Sea … called the same straites Magellanes streightes'.

In England, interest in this discovery was submerged by excitement over reports that mineral ore picked up by Frobisher's men contained gold, and the expeditions of 1577 and 1578 (the latter with 15 ships) were mining ventures rather than voyages of discovery. It was on this third voyage, in 1578, that Frobisher found his way into Hudson Strait, 'Mistaken Strait' as he called it, that great and difficult entrance to the heart of the Canadian north. Making his way to Frobisher Bay, as his 'strait' is now called, he became lost and entered an opening farther south that led directly west. He turned back after 20 days, though were it not 'for the charge and care he had of the Fleete and fraughted ships, he both would and could have gone through to the South Sea'. Frobisher was a better

2 BELOW *Explorers who entered Davis and Hudson Straits looking for a short route to the Pacific found a series of land-locked bays that offered no obvious outlet to the west.*

explorer than he was prospector, for the mineral ore laboriously mined and laden at Frobisher Bay turned out to be iron pyrites, 'fool's gold' (*see* map 3). The Company of Cathay, which had financed the ventures, collapsed amid derision.

The following decade saw three more northern voyages. They were led by John Davis. In 1585, Davis discovered Cumberland Sound, on the coast of Baffin Island north of Frobisher Bay: 'a very faire entrance or passage … and the water of the very colour, nature and quality of the marine ocean, which gave us the greater hopes of our passage'. Even so, Davis turned back after about 180 miles. The next year saw Davis making further explorations of the waters between Greenland and Baffin Island, but his most ambitious voyage was his final one, that of 1587. He sailed along the west coast of Greenland to 73°N, before turning west across the strait soon to be named after him. He explored Cumberland Sound to its head, entered Frobisher Bay, and to the south crossed 'a very great gulf'. It was Hudson Strait, once again ignored.

Despite the difficulties, the English voyages of the 1570s and 1580s placed the great opening of Davis Strait on the map, and brought back the first descriptions of Baffin Island and north-west Greenland and their Inuit inhabitants. Relations with the Inuit varied. The disappearance of five of Frobisher's

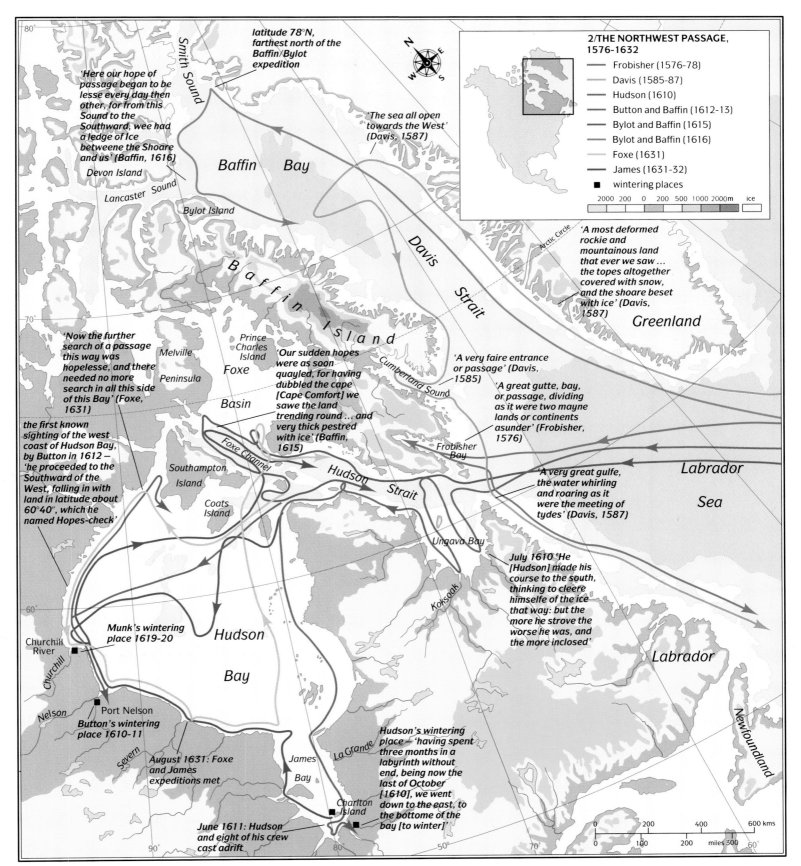

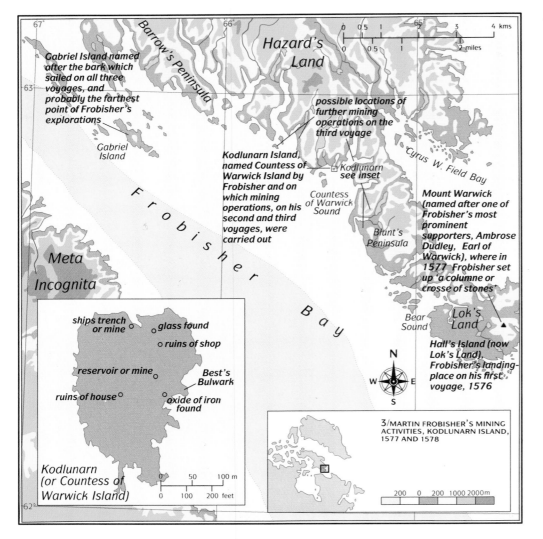

Gabriel Island named after the bark which sailed on all three voyages, and probably the farthest point of Frobisher's explorations

possible locations of further mining operations on the third voyage

Kodlunarn Island, named Countess of Warwick Island by Frobisher and on which mining operations, on his second and third voyages, were carried out

Mount Warwick (named after one of Frobisher's most prominent supporters, Ambrose Dudley, Earl of Warwick), where in 1577 Frobisher set up 'a columne or crosse of stones'

Hall's Island (now Lok's Land), Frobisher's landing-place on his first voyage, 1576

ships trench or mine
glass found
ruins of shop
reservoir or mine
Best's Bulwark
ruins of house
oxide of iron found

Kodlunarn (or Countess of Warwick Island)

3/MARTIN FROBISHER'S MINING ACTIVITIES, KODLUNARN ISLAND, 1577 AND 1578

oceanic strait. The emphasis of the search moved north, and in 1616 Bylot and Baffin sailed through Davis Strait, pushed through heavy ice, and found open water. At their farthest north – 78°N – they reached Smith Sound, though this was not finally penetrated until 1853. On the west side of Baffin Bay another large opening appeared, named Lancaster Sound by Baffin. It was, in the end, to prove the entrance to the Northwest Passage, but in 1616 it was blocked by ice. Baffin wrote that 'there is no passage in the north of Davis Straights'.

By 1616 the search for a navigable, ice-free passage suitable for merchant shipping was, to all intents and purposes, over. Illusions persisted, however, and a Danish expedition commanded by Jens Munk (1619-20) and English ventures by Luke Foxe (1631) and Thomas James (1631-32) all explored Hudson Bay in an attempt to find the elusive strait. These final voyages were richer in human drama than in geographical discovery: Munk's dreadful wintering at Churchill, which left only three survivors; the spirited account written by Foxe, who was the best explorer of the three; and the hardships described – and embellished – by James (which later found their way into *The Rime of the Ancient Mariner*). No passage may have been found, but for the English a tradition of Arctic navigation had been established, and a body of knowledge obtained that brought a professional approach to the problems of sailing in northern waters. Before long this experience would be turned to profit as the great trades of the north – in cod, whales and fur – began to exploit the natural resources of the region where the early explorers had suffered privation and death.

men into Inuit hands, for example, must be set against those occasions when the Englishmen traded amicably, and even wrestled and played football, with the local Inuit. 'Our men did cast them down as soone as they did come to strike the ball', recorded the chronicle of Davis's second voyage.

With peace signed with Spain in 1604, the search for a passage renewed early in the new century, though no major discovery was made until Henry Hudson, discoverer of the Hudson River, set sail in 1610. At the end of June, he entered Hudson Strait, and, unlike Frobisher and Davis, worked his way against its ice and tidal rips to reach the huge bay which was soon to bear his name. He wintered in the south-east corner of the bay, only to be cast adrift with eight others – all perished – by his mutinous crew the following summer. But the reports that the mutineers took home of this great inland sea soon brought other expeditions to the area. In 1612 and 1613, Thomas Button explored 600 miles of the unknown west and north shores of Hudson Bay and charted the estuaries of the Churchill and Port Nelson Rivers, later important arteries of the fur trade. But he found no passage. Nor did the expedition of Bylot and Baffin in 1615; they observed too much ice and too little tide in the Foxe Channel to encourage hopes of an

3 ABOVE *The site of Frobisher's mining activities in 1577-78 was identified by the American explorer Charles F. Hall in the 1860s. Signs of the diggings and the foundations of buildings erected by Frobisher's men are still visible.*

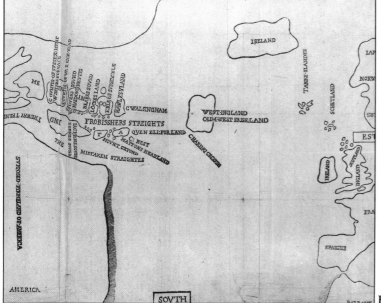

B LEFT *A crude woodcut map illustrating Frobisher's voyages, published in George Best's* A true discourse of the later voyages of discoverie *(1578). Best believed both Frobisher Bay and Hudson Strait ('Mistaken Straightes') led west to the Pacific and Cathay.*

C RIGHT *Section of Richard Haklyut's 1598 world map showing the discoveries of John Davis's voyages of 1585, 1586 and 1587.*

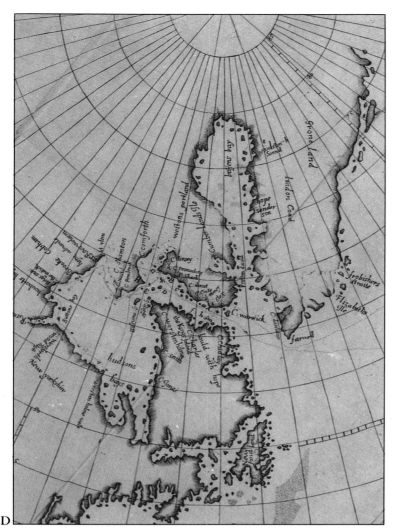

D

D ABOVE *The track of Captain Luke Foxe's voyage of 1631 to Hudson Bay, published in his account* North-West Fox *(1635). The map shows Foxe's place-names on the south and west shores of Hudson Bay, and suggests the possibility of an opening in its north-west corner.*

E

E RIGHT *Water-colour sketches by John White, who accompanied Frobisher's 1577 voyage, of three Inuit. The two lower sketches are of an Inuit man and woman who were forcibly brought back to England by Frobisher and died within a month of reaching it. These meticulous drawings are a unique record of the Inuit of Baffin Bay of the period.*

ICE NAVIGATION

Some 16th-Century Descriptions of the Problem

VESSELS STRUGGLING to find a way through the maze of North America's Arctic archipelago had to contend, even in the short navigable summer of two or three months, with ever-present hazards from ice. The ice blurred the distinction between land and sea; the shifts of floe-ice meant that a clear channel one day might be blocked the next and wooden ships, so resistant to cannon balls, might be crushed, overset, or pierced by ice. The whalers, fur traders and explorers of northern waters soon learnt to recognise the different forms of ice. The four icebergs below (A) illustrate Thomas Ellis's *A True Report*, published in 1578. Early sailing accounts often included an introductory page listing dangers – from the majestic iceberg, '*an insulated mountain of ice*', down to the insignificant sludge ice, '*having the appearance of snow just thrown in the water, which scarcely impedes the ship*'. Even the dispassionate terms of a glossary could not disguise the problems and dangers involved – from the definition of '*beset ... surrounded with ice so as to be obliged to remain immovable*' as in the 16th-century illustration of a ship (B), lifted by pressure ice, to the more eloquent '*nipt ... caught and jammed between two pieces of ice*'.

Seamen mastered the techniques of Arctic navigation: spotting leads from the mast-head and thrusting through them, laboriously winching or towing ships free, cutting a way through with ice-saws, fending off loose ice with boat-hooks and poles. Baffin in 1615, off the north-west coast of Hudson Bay, found '*the ice came drivinge with the tyde of floud from the south east with such swiftnesse, that ... unless the Lord himselfe had been on our side we had surely perished; for sometymes the ship was hoys{t}ed aloft; and at other tymes shee havinge,*

A

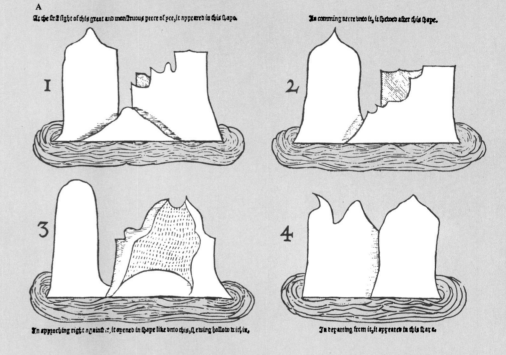

as it were, got the upper hand, would force great mighty peeces of ice to sinke downe on the other side of hir, and rise on the other'.

The experienced William Coats of the Hudson's Bay Company stressed the importance of getting the annual Company ships in and out of Hudson Bay and Straits in less than three months, for '*as it is very hazardous to enter the Straights before the beginning of July, for ice, so it is dangerous to be in that Bay after the middle of September; the gales of wind and snow setts in ... the severe frosts are such that you cannot work a ship; possibly as the frost prevails the winds decrease, but to what purpose? When blocks are locks, and ropes are bolts, and sails can neither be taken in nor left out, is surely the last extremity; the new ice near the shores and rivers, and the wash of the sea, stick to your ship and ropes like birdlime. and in your sails, like pitch, and so all opperations by water ceais*'.

B

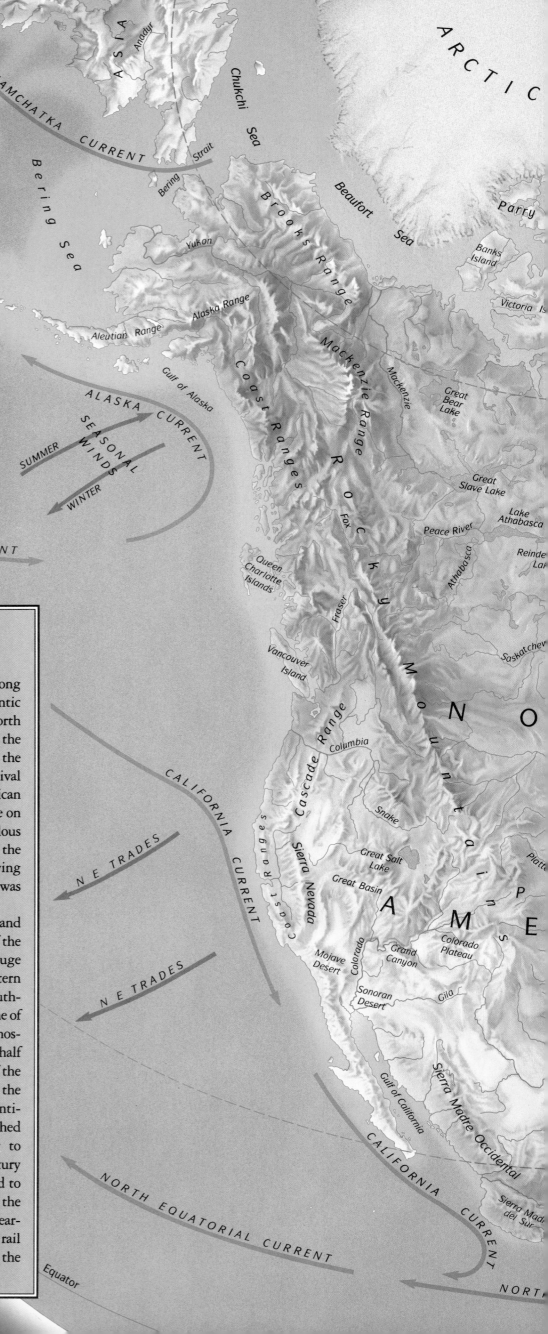

ASIA

Anadyr

ARCTIC

KAMCHATKA CURRENT

Chukchi Sea

Bering Strait

Beaufort Sea

Parry

Bering Sea

Brooks Range

Banks Island

Victoria Is

Yukon

Aleutian Islands

Alaska Range

Mackenzie Range

Great Bear Lake

NORTH PACIFIC CURRENT

Aleutian Range

Gulf of Alaska

Mackenzie

NORTH

ALASKA CURRENT

Coast Ranges

Great Slave Lake

PACIFIC

SEASONAL WINDS

SUMMER

Fox

Peace River

Lake Athabasca

Reindeer La

OCEAN

WINTER

R

o

c

k

Athabasca

Hawaii

NORTH PACIFIC CURRENT

Queen Charlotte Islands

y

Saskatchew

Vancouver Island

Fraser

M

o

u

n

N

O

t

Cascade Range

Columbia

a

i

Snake

Great Salt Lake

n

P

CALIFORNIA CURRENT

Coast Ranges

Sierra Nevada

s

Great Basin

Platt

A

NE TRADES

Colorado

Grand Canyon

Colorado Plateau

M

E

Mojave Desert

Gila

NE TRADES

Sonoran Desert

Gulf of California

Sierra Madre Occidental

CALIFORNIA CURRENT

Sierra Madi del Sur

NORTH EQUATORIAL CURRENT

NORTH

Equator

SECTION V
NORTH AMERICA

THE EXPLORATIONS of the 16th century mapped long stretches of the coastline of North America: the Atlantic seaboard, the Gulf of Mexico, and the Pacific coast as far north as California. It was to take another 300 years to complete the continental outline and to reveal the main features of the interior. The achievement was a multi-national one, as the rival imperialisms of Europe sought to control and exploit American soil. Even so, a common denominator was their dependence on native Indians as guides, carriers and allies. Myths of fabulous cities, illusions of a short sea-route to the Pacific and the demand for furs and land kept the course of exploration moving westward, though rarely systematically: the Indian trader was more typical of the forces of expansion than official agencies.

Topography was the main determinant of the direction and pace of exploration. The French used the great waterways of the St. Lawrence and the Mississippi to move swiftly though huge areas of territory. By contrast, the English on the eastern seaboard were hemmed in by the Appalachians. In the Southwest, the Spanish advance, already at the end of a tenuous line of communication, slowed and halted as it encountered an inhospitable region of desert and mountain. Not until the second half of the 18th century was there any inkling of the existence of the most dominant feature of North American geography: the Rocky Mountains. By 1800, the coastal outlines of the continent had been determined and overland expeditions had reached both the Pacific and Arctic coasts. It was left mainly to American traders, explorers and surveyors in the 19th century to complete the mapping of the trans-Mississippi West and to find passes through the mountains for the wagon-trains of the settlers. By mid-century new techniques of travel were appearing. The surveyors of the American West began looking for rail routes, while far to the north steam-vessels were charting the maze of the Arctic archipelago.

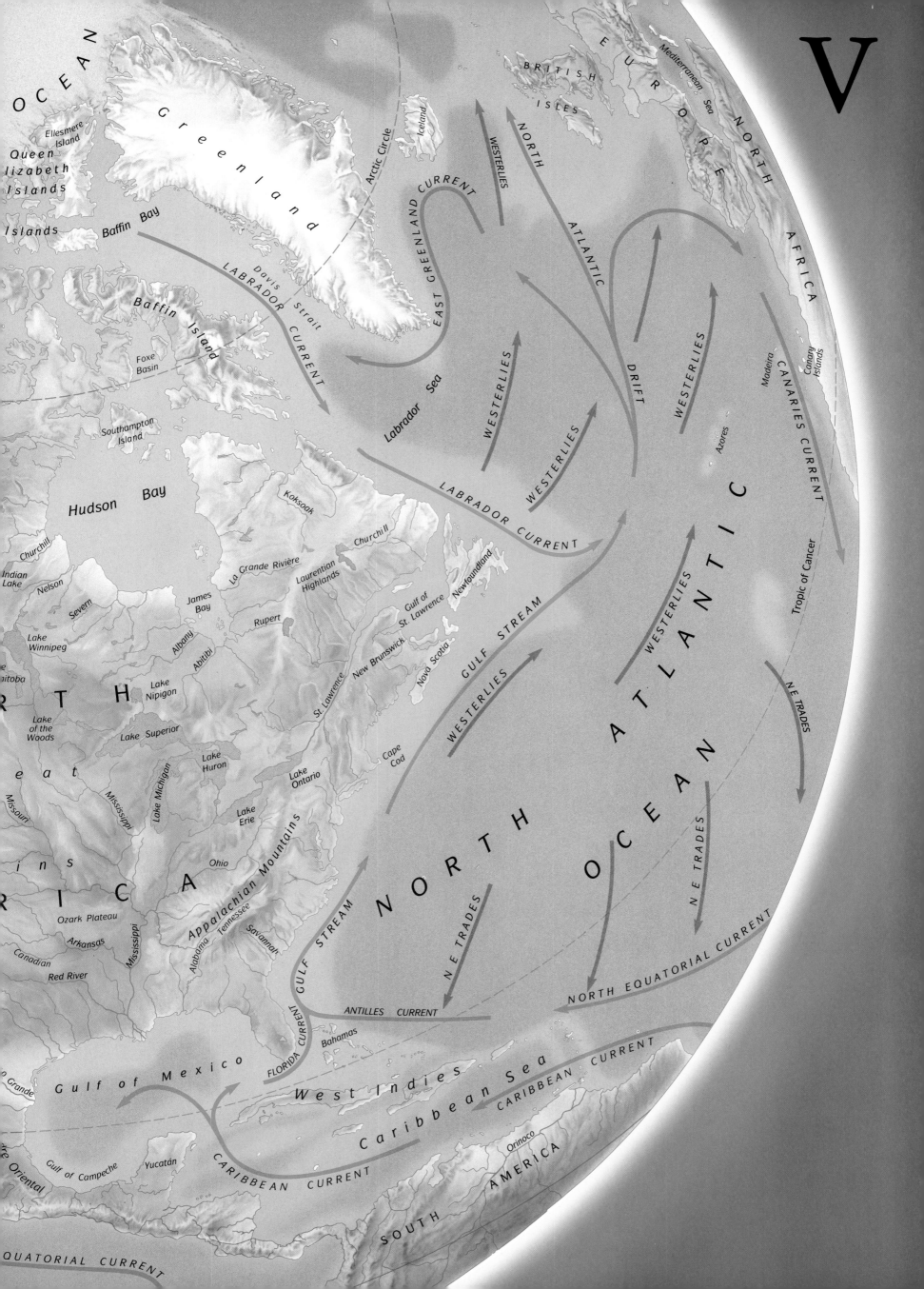

New Spain: The Spanish in North America

1513-1793

1 BELOW *Spanish exploration began in the south-east. Surviving shipwreck, de Vaca made the first crossing of the continent, de Soto and Coronado followed. The colonizing expedition of Oñate to New Mexico in 1598 cemented the Spanish presence in central North America.*

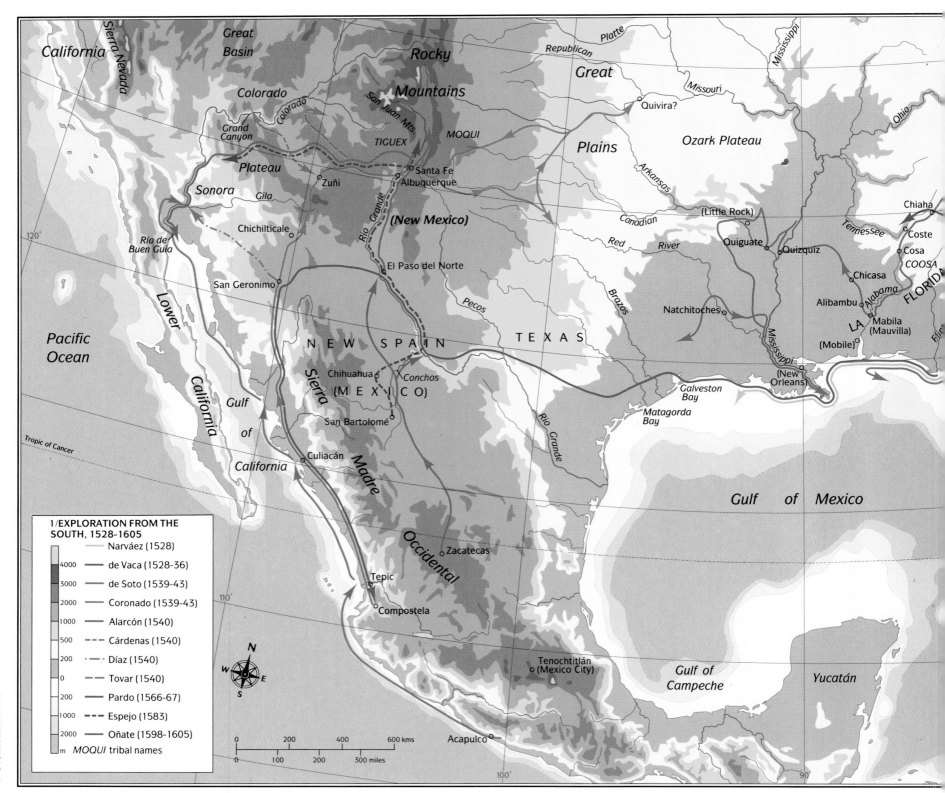

1/EXPLORATION FROM THE SOUTH, 1528-1605

- Narváez (1528)
- de Vaca (1528-36)
- de Soto (1539-43)
- Coronado (1539-43)
- Alarcón (1540)
- Cárdenas (1540)
- Díaz (1540)
- Tovar (1540)
- Pardo (1566-67)
- Espejo (1583)
- Oñate (1598-1605)

MOQUI tribal names

SPAIN WAS *the undisputed champion of exploration in North America in the 16th century, her dominant role ensured by the primacy in exploration established by Columbus and by her political strength in Europe, itself in part the fruit of successes in the New World. Yet though the exploration of New Spain was in many ways an epic undertaking, New Spain itself, despite the declamatory promise of its name, never became more than a minor northern extension of the vast Spanish empire in Central and South America. Further, the natural hazards of its terrain and climate combined with the hostility of its Indians, lengthening lines of communication and lack of manpower to make Spain's hold on these northern provinces tenuous at best.*

The first Spanish explorations, in the early 16th century, were more of an extended reconnaissance, frequently heroic, almost always arduous, than a systematic attempt at settlement. They were fuelled by a series of lingering geographical myths: the existence of a western sea-passage to the Orient; the search for the Seven Cities of Cíbola, a transplant to the New World of the Seven Cities of Antillia (imagined Atlantic islands that had driven much European expansion to the west) (see ch.20, map A); and the gold-rich land of Quivira described by an Indian to Coronado's expedition, eager for tales of riches, in 1540. As the Spanish moved north and west, so these phantom goals retreated before them.

The first permanent inland Spanish settlements were established by the early 17th century in present-day New Mexico. Starved of resources, they were little more than isolated outposts. The 17th century was a period of relative quiescence, as Spain tried to consolidate its hold on these new lands. Only toward the end of the century was there renewed Spanish activity, largely in response to the French incursions along the Mississippi. Missionaries and map-makers sparked a further burst of exploration in the 18th century, but by the 1760s, despite attempts to ward off the threat of renewed foreign incursions — by the British and the Russians as much as the French — it was clear that New Spain was more a name on a map than a political reality.

As Spain declined in Europe, so she declined in the New World. Unrest and rebellion in her American empire, coupled with the rise of an expansionist Yankee nation in the north, conspired in the early 19th century to ensure the demise not merely of New Spain but of the Spanish presence elsewhere in the New World.

THE BEGINNINGS of Spanish continental exploration in North America were more accidental than intentional.

Hernán Cortés learned of Tenochtitlán, Mexico, in 1519 from natives of Cempoala who were anxious to speed him on his way. His bloody conquest of the Aztecs (*see* ch.10) enticed and enabled him to press on in search of the northern sea-passage to Cipangu, Marco Polo's fabled island on the eastern shores of Asia. His expedition of 1533 got no farther than the tip of Lower California. Ponce de León's failure in western Florida in 1513 only triggered more ambitious efforts. Pánfilo de Narváez headed a tragic attempt to colonize the northern coasts of the Gulf of Mexico in 1528. His expedition, broken by storms and internal dissention, failed, but four survivors (Alvar Núñez Cabeza de Vaca, Alonso del Castillo Maldonado, Andres Dorantes and Estebanico, the 'Black Moor') survived and trekked from Galveston Bay through western Texas and across the mountainous continental divide to the deltas along the Gulf of California (*see* ch.10). Cabeza de Vaca's unintended eight-year exploration, returning with reports of large towns to the north, sparked new hopes of finding the elusive Seven Cities.

In 1538, Fr. Marcos de Niza was accordingly charged by Viceroy António de Mendoza to probe the unknown trails to the north. With Estebanico in the vanguard he followed Indian trading routes up the western flanks of the Sierra Madre. Passing the now-vanished Indian city of Chichilticale, he learned of the murder of Estebanico and many of his

A BELOW Universale alla Parte del Mundo Novamenta Ritrovata – *the first published map of the western hemisphere to show places visited by the 1540-41 expedition of Coronado. It was drawn by Giacomo Gastaldi, probably in 1553.*

B RIGHT *Richard Hakluyt's* Novus Orbis *(1587) was the first map to show Nuevo Mexico. Though up to date, too, in its depiction of Drake's* Nova Albion *(see ch.20), the map perpetuated the myth of the 'golden' lake reported by António de Espejo in 1580.*

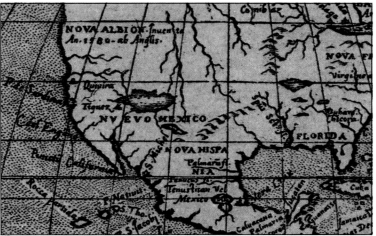

A

CONQVISTA
EN LOS BAÑOS ESTAVA
ATAGVALPAINGA

CONQVISTA
CAPITÁLVISDEAVA
LOS DE AIALA

B
ᵍᵉʳⁿᵃⁿᵈᵒ C el capitan

EVEN IN mountainous country, the adaptability of the horse enormously impressed Indian observers. In the Guatemalan highlands, depicted in the mid-16th century by Tlaxcalan artists (D), or in traditional pictures of the conquests of Mexico – by the illustrator of Diego Duran's history, (A) – and of Peru – by the native wise-man Felipe Guamán Poma de Ayala, (B) and (C) – horses were shown in a central role. Once into the flatlands of northern Mexico and the plains of North America, horses gave Spanish explorers incomparable range. Between June and October in 1542, for example, Coronado was able to cover 1,800 miles. French and English exploration of North America by contrast had to proceed on foot. The use of the horse and the nature of the terrain over which they approached helped the Spaniards to register spectacular achievements with modest resources and simple technology.

Quauhtemallā.

Indian companions. How far north he went is disputed, but he returned with 'confirmed' stories of golden cities – the 'Seven Cities of Cíbola'.

With rumours of wealth that surpassed Mexico's reinforced by Niza's claims, Francisco Vázquez de Coronado's huge and elaborate expedition of 1540-41 pressed ahead into the lands of the Zuni Indians. Niza's 'Seven Cities' turned out to be no more than elaborate earthen towns, or *pueblos*. Undaunted, Coronado sent exploratory parties in all directions. García López de Cárdenas thus became the first European known to have seen the Grand Canyon of the Colorado. In the spring of 1541 Coronado penetrated the plains that stretched east from the Rockies; following the Arkansas River, the party reached the presumed location of 'Quivira' near present-day Wichita, Kansas. In reaching a point close to the westward advance of Hernando de Soto (*see* below), Coronado had almost completed the reach of Spanish exploration across the North American continent.

Hernando de Soto, like Narváez before him, had set out in search of wealth and legendary kingdoms. His well-equipped force landed near Tampa Bay in 1539 and threaded its way through swampland into the country of the Apalachee. After wintering in present-day Florida, his columns worked their way into the mountains of Georgia, South Carolina and Tennessee, following river drainages into northern Alabama. There de Soto fought a bloody battle against Chief Tascalusa at Mabila (Mauvilla), to the north of present-day Mobile. The expeditionary force then turned north and west again until it reached the broad waters of the Mississippi. Crossing on four rafts, de Soto went up the Arkansas where he wintered, near present-day Little Rock, in 1542. After de Soto's death from malaria, the surviving explorers under Luis de Moscoso tried to return to Mexico overland across the Texas plains. Indian hostility forced them to return to the Mississippi which they followed to the Gulf of Mexico, from where they coasted along the Gulf shore westward to return to Mexico.

Spanish exploration in the Southeast revived with the establishment of forts along the Atlantic coast of Florida in the 1560s and probes across the southern Appalachians by Juan Pardo. The Southwest, by contrast, remained unexplored for nearly half a century, the result chiefly of a lack of resources to sustain wide-scale exploration along the thinly held borders of New Spain. Not until the 1580s were Spaniards once again in search of routes into pueblo country, where the myth of the Seven Cities had crumbled in the face of reality. António de Espejo retraced the routes of Coronado and went deeper into Moqui country; his reports of a golden lake (*see* map **B** on p.91) added the last touch of legend to the cartography of the *Terra Incognita*. Juan de Oñate's exploration of river trails westward to the Pacific in 1598 and eastward into the buffalo plains were the most ambitious undertakings of the late 16th and early 17th centuries.

By now, with New Spain's frontiers still shifting and uncertain, its frontiersmen a volatile amalgam of missionaries, soldiers and traders (often in fact slavers), pressure was increasingly exerted by the French to the east. The French explorers La Salle and Tonty had paddled the length of the Mississippi to the Gulf of Mexico by 1682 (*see* ch.18). Two years later, La Salle attempted to found a settlement at the mouth of the great river, though his colonizing efforts went awry after he landed by mistake at Matagorda Bay. Nonetheless, the French presence was rapidly consolidated, with the colony of Louisiana established by the end of the century and the city of New Orleans in 1718. The French naturally looked west to the vast regions between the Mississippi and New Mexico, hoping to open up trade with its Indian nations. Spain, alarmed, attempted to defend its exposed frontiers. It was never very successful in this, and the culmination of French penetration came in 1739 with the arrival in

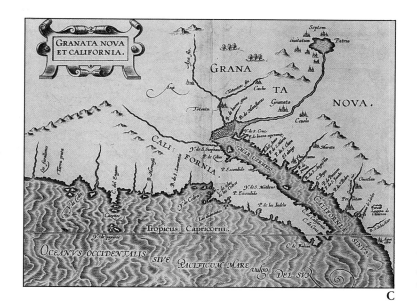

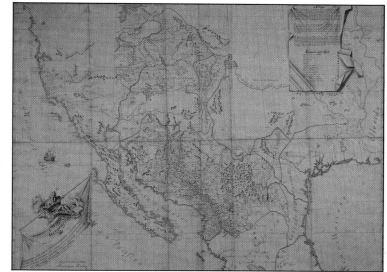

C

D

Santa Fe of the Mallet brothers, the first successful attempt to open direct trade links between Louisiana and New Mexico. Spanish officialdom may have disapproved, but it was powerless to prevent it. (In 1793 Pedro Vial became the first Spaniard to make the journey in the opposite direction.)

To the west and north of New Spain, the same period saw more successful Spanish attempts to come to grips with their huge, loosely held territories. Eusebio Francisco Kino in the 1690s and early 1700s re-opened serious exploration when he looked for a land route around the head of the Gulf of California to supply the missions along the coast of Lower California. In so doing, he settled for good the dispute as to whether or not California was an island (*see* ch.20). In a process of consolidation, the whole northern frontier was inspected by Brigadier Pedro de Rivera on a remarkable and systematic five-year reconnaissance beginning in 1724. The frontier regions were carefully mapped on this ambitious surveying venture by Francisco Álvarez Barreiro, who produced the most complete set of maps of northern New Spain of the early 18th century.

Shorter but equally strenuous expeditions criss-crossed mountains and deserts in further attempts to establish routes for trade and supply. By the second half of the 18th century, the need for further consolidation of the northern frontier brought about the extensive surveys of Rubí and La Fora in

1766-68, who covered the region from Texas to Sonora.

The old need for a land route from Sonora to California was given new urgency by the establishment in the 1760s and 1770s of Spanish settlements along the Upper Californian coast from San Diego to San Francisco. Their presence was to lead to expeditions across the Colorado desert in search of such a route by the experienced frontiersman Juan Bautista de Anza, accompanied by the Franciscan, Francisco Garcés. The ostensibly peaceful meanderings across the desert of Spanish groups, often with missionaries to the fore, were acceptable to the otherwise hostile Indians. Garcés was able to cross the Mojave Desert to the Camino Real in California and to return via Moqui country. The same urge to link New Mexico and California sparked the expedition of Friars Silvestre Escalante and Anastasio Domínguez, who became hopelessly lost on the desert *mesas* of Utah and trapped in the precipitous canyons of the Colorado, though in the process they crossed country never before seen by Europeans.

But ambitions to link the interior of northern New Spain and Upper California were shattered by the rebellion of the Yuma Indians of the lower Colorado in 1781. By now, however, a new player was about to enter the scene: the United States. Her dynamism and drive to the south and west of the North American continent would rapidly push back the frontiers of an enfeebled New Spain (*see* ch.22).

2 BELOW *Exploration gave way to defensive reconnaissance in the 18th century as Spain protected her interests against French and English incursions along the northern border of New Spain. Later, overland expeditions by Kino, Garcés, Anza and Domínguez incorporated the north-western frontier with the regions of northern New Spain.*

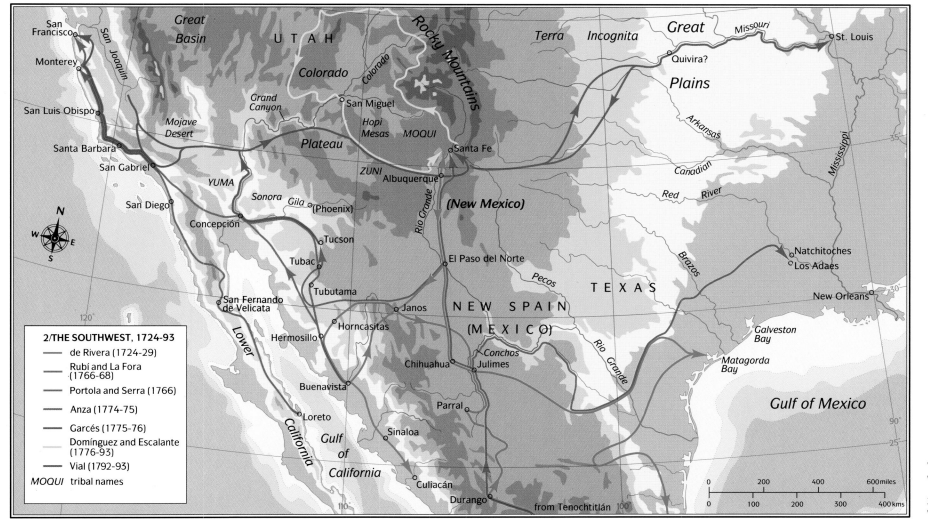

2/THE SOUTHWEST, 1724-93
— de Rivera (1724-29)
— Rubí and La Fora (1766-68)
— Portola and Serra (1766)
— Anza (1774-75)
— Garcés (1775-76)
— Domínguez and Escalante (1776-93)
— Vial (1792-93)
MOQUI tribal names

18

America: The Approach from the North
1603-1709

JACQUES CARTIER's voyages of 1534-42 and his discovery of the Gulf and river of St. Lawrence (see ch.15) paved the way for extensive French penetration of North America. In the following century Frenchmen thrust deep into the heart of the new-found continent.

The most impressive feature of French activity lay not in settlement, however, which remained sparse and scattered, so much as in the feats of individual explorers – fur traders, missionaries and soldiers. Moved by commercial enterprise, spiritual zeal and imperial ambition, French explorers revealed the full extent of the Great Lakes by the early 1670s and by 1682 had traced the course of the Mississippi River to its outlet on the sub-tropical shores of the Gulf of Mexico. Before the end of the century the prospect of a French American empire extending from Hudson Bay to the Caribbean had become real.

In the end, however, Spanish and British ambitions in North America – the former in the south and west, the latter in the north and east – were to thwart French hopes. The English Hudson's Bay Company, in particular, for all that its early attempts at extended exploration were unsystematic, indeed often feeble, represented a sphere of influence that could not be ignored by its more flamboyant French rivals.

A BELOW *Champlain's last and most comprehensive map of Nouvelle France (1632) incorporates his own explorations as well as information from other traders and from Indians. Though distorted, the Great Lakes appear as far as Lake Superior for the first time.*

A

THE first permanent French establishments – in Canada at Port Royal (1605) and, more significantly, at Québec (1608) – were followed by wide-ranging explorations by their founder, Samuel de Champlain. Hoping to exploit new fur areas, and possibly to discover a short route to China, Champlain explored much of modern Nova Scotia and New Brunswick; investigated the route southward from the St. Lawrence through Lake Champlain towards the Hudson; opened up the rugged terrain north of the St. Lawrence by way of the Saguenay and St. Maurice Rivers; and pushed west through the land of the Hurons towards the Great Lakes. Champlain's death in 1635, combined with Iroquois hostility to the French and their Huron allies, slowed the pace of the French advance, though Jean Nicollet, an associate of Champlain, made an important journey at about this time. He reached Lake Michigan, its first sighting by a European, and heard reports of the mighty Sioux nation to the west and of a great river (the Mississippi) leading to a sea, assumed by the French to be the Pacific. But there was as yet little realization of the extent of the North American continent in high latitudes and optimistic Frenchmen would have been appalled had they known when they reached Lake Superior that they were only one-third of the way across the continent.

Although speculation about the western sea continued, the more immediate French efforts concentrated on exploring the Great Lakes in the hope of both material and spiritual gain. By the early 1640s, the Jesuits had reached, in one direction, the vital strategic point of Sault Ste.Marie between Lake Huron and Lake Superior, and in another the confluence of the St. Lawrence and Ottawa rivers, where they founded Montréal. The reports sent back by the Jesuits, selections from which were published annually for 40 years as the *Jesuit Relations*, are an invaluable source of information about the Indians among whom the Jesuits lived and worked, and about the travels and explorations both of the Jesuits and their secular compatriots. These were traders and adventurers often unable to put down in writing their discoveries of the land and its people. It is usually in the Jesuit accounts that a glimpse of the rough *coureurs de bois*

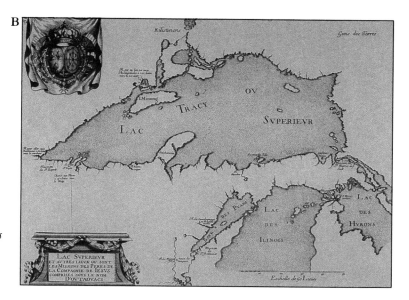

B RIGHT *This meticulous Jesuit map of 1672 of the Great Lakes is a tribute to the work of Jesuit and other French explorers.*

1 BELOW *The expansionist thrust of French traders and missionaries on the St. Lawrence in the 17th century took them west to the Great Lakes, north to Hudson Bay, and south to the Mississippi and the Gulf of Mexico.*

(literally, 'wood runners'), the true pioneers of discovery, is available, pushing far ahead of French officialdom in their never-ending quest for furs.

Further expansion was interrupted by war with the Iroquois but resumed in the 1650s when dozens of *coureurs de bois* ventured west. Among them were Radisson and Groseilliers, who made a number of important if ill-defined journeys which for the first time drew attention to the importance of the northern fur trade among the Cree Indians. In a different direction, Jesuit missionaries took advantage of a lull in the fighting to report on the Iroquois homeland, stretching away south of Lake Ontario into present-day New York State. By the early 1670s, after the final subduing of the Iroquois by French regular forces, Jesuit and other missionaries had mapped all the Great Lakes, and had followed Nicollet's old route to Lake Michigan and onto the Fox River. This river, one Jesuit wrote, 'leads by a six days' Voyage to the great river named Messi-Sipi'.

The task of tracing the river itself was entrusted to Louis Jolliet and the Jesuit Jacques Marquette who, in 1673, crossed the Fox-Wisconsin portage to reach the wide and sluggish waters of the Upper Mississippi. On their voyage downstream they saw a large river thundering in from the west (the Mis-

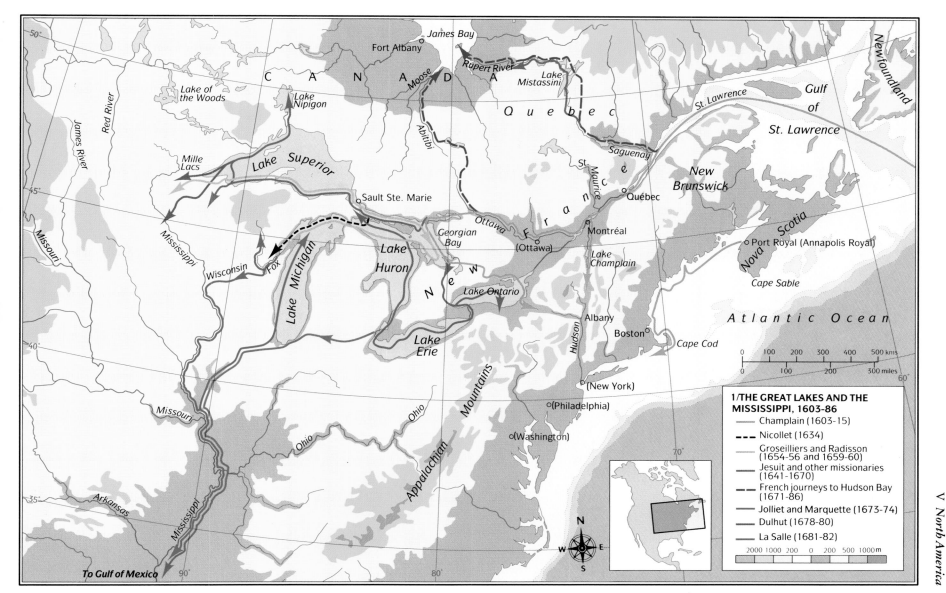

1/THE GREAT LAKES AND THE MISSISSIPPI, 1603-86
— Champlain (1603-15)
- - - Nicollet (1634)
— Groseilliers and Radisson (1654-56 and 1659-60)
— Jesuit and other missionaries (1641-1670)
- - - French journeys to Hudson Bay (1671-86)
— Jolliet and Marquette (1673-74)
— Dulhut (1678-80)
— La Salle (1681-82)

V North America

FRENCH and English involvement in the fur trade followed different patterns. The French traders from the St. Lawrence accompanied the Indians on their trapping expeditions far inland, and traded furs from them on the spot. In the process, many French trappers and traders adopted Indian hunting techniques. By contrast the Hudson's Bay Company awaited the Indians at Bayside posts such as York Factory (C) and Churchill (D). The two areas of activity operated in distant rivalry in the period between the founding of the Hudson's Bay Company (1670) and the British conquest of Canada (1759-60). Gradually the Indians became dependent on European weapons (A), traps (B) and implements; and the impact of the European fur trade was felt deep in the interior, affecting the way of life of many Indian peoples.

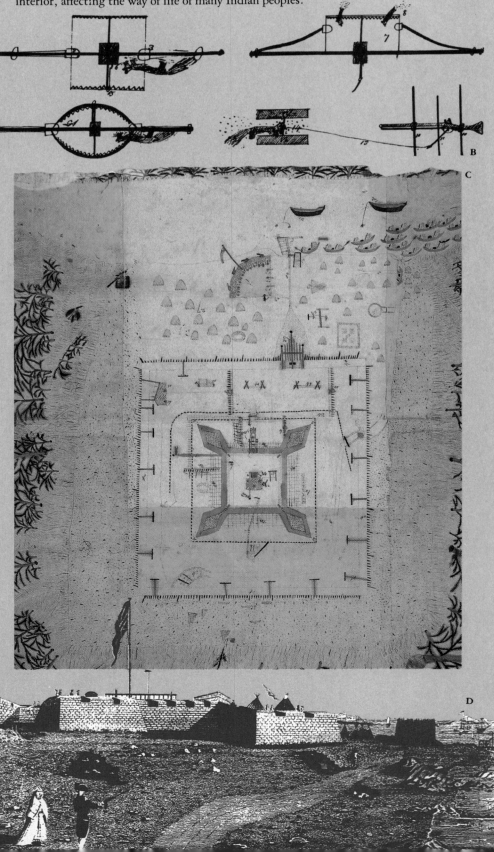

souri in flood), and another (the Ohio) from the east. Near the latter they met Indians, probably Cherokee, who had guns and powder obtained from 'Europeans on the eastern side', English traders. Fear of the Spaniards finally turned the explorers back, somewhere near the confluence of the Mississippi and the Arkansas Rivers, about 400 miles from the sea. In one sense, the discovery was an anti-climax: not only did they discover no gold or wealthy Indian nations, but the river clearly led not to the Pacific but to the Gulf of Mexico. The final step was taken nine years later by La Salle, whose determination to reach the mouth of the Mississippi was part of his grand design for a French commercial empire from the Great Lakes to the Gulf of Mexico. La Salle sighted the Gulf in early 1682, but his long-term hopes of establishing a French colony on its shores ended in failure and his own death in 1687.

If French ambitions in the south were thwarted by a combination of practical difficulties and Spanish opposition, equally their hopes of dominating the northern fur trade and the western routes were hindered by the English. It was the London-based Hudson's Bay Company which exploited the revelation by Radisson and Groseilliers that the finest beaver traded by the Hurons of the Great Lakes came from farther north, in Cree territory. The most direct access for those furs was not by the long and tortuous canoe route to the St. Lawrence, but by the shorter carry to the shores of Hudson Bay. With Groseilliers on board, an English vessel, the *Nonsuch*, wintered at Rupert House in James Bay (the southern extremity of Hudson Bay) in 1668-69 before returning with a good cargo of beaver. The following year the sponsors of the venture were incorporated as the Hudson's Bay Company. The Company soon built additional posts at Moose Factory and Fort Albany, and in 1682 moved outside the James Bay catchment area when it built a northerly post at York Factory to tap the rich fur trade of the west.

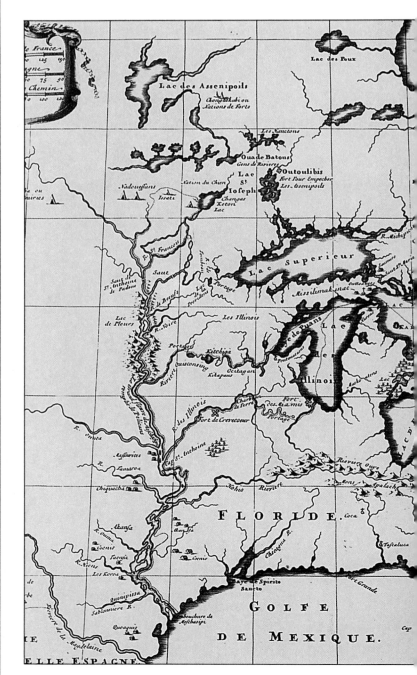

Alarmed by this new threat, the French in Canada reacted vigorously. In 1679, Dulhut reached Mille Lacs to the south-west of Lake Superior, while 200 miles to the north de Noyon in the next decade probably got as far as Lake of the Woods in New France's final westward thrust of the century. In a more direct response to the English presence during the 1670s the French sent three separate expeditions from the St. Lawrence to James Bay by way of the Saguenay River and Lake Mistassini; but interrupted as it was by more than 200 portages this canoe trail could not compete in commercial terms with the bulk-cargo capacity of the ship route running through Hudson Strait and into Hudson Bay.

During the Anglo-French hostilities of the late 17th century, the French several times attempted to seize the English posts, though with no permanent success. In this period of tension and uncertainty the Hudson's Bay Company attempted little inland exploration. The only venture of note was made by a young Company servant at York, Henry Kelsey, who in 1690 accompanied a party of Cree Indians on their return journey inland. During his two years of wandering, always in the company of Indians, Kelsey crossed the Saskatchewan and Red Deer Rivers and became the first white man to reach the plains of western Canada. There he saw the Assiniboine and Blackfoot Indians of the plains, the grizzly bear and the buffalo. His remarkable journey was a solitary and soon-forgotten feat. With the English traders remaining fast at their Bayside posts, it was the French in the next century who were the first to follow Kelsey's path.

C BELOW LEFT *Lahontan's engraving from his* New Voyages *(1703) shows four methods of hunting beaver.*

2 BELOW RIGHT *The Hudson's Bay Company established a line of Bayside posts in the late 17th century to tap the fur trade of the interior.*

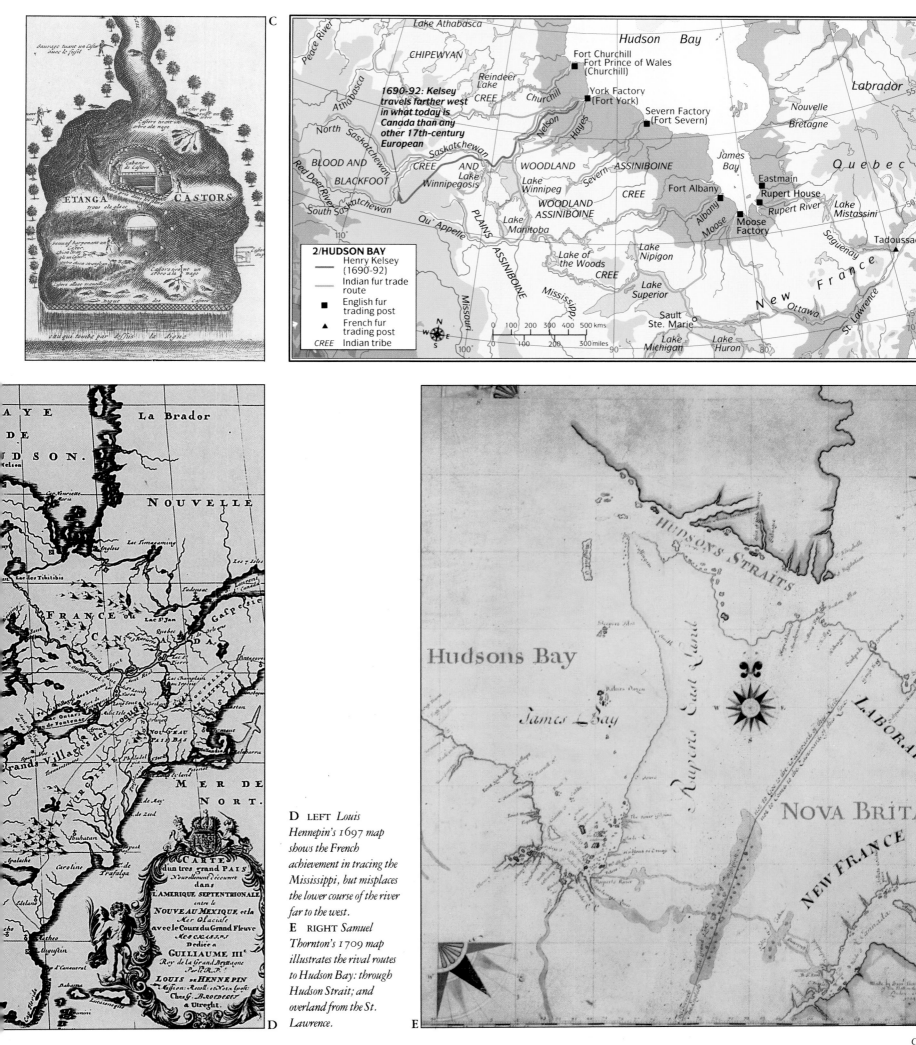

D LEFT *Louis Hennepin's 1697 map shows the French achievement in tracing the Mississippi, but misplaces the lower course of the river far to the west.*

E RIGHT *Samuel Thornton's 1709 map illustrates the rival routes to Hudson Bay: through Hudson Strait; and overland from the St. Lawrence.*

19
NORTH AMERICA: INLAND FROM THE EAST COAST
1607-1769

ENGLISH SETTLERS *along the east coast of North America in the 17th and 18th centuries were as curious about the New World as their French and Spanish rivals. Barred from easy access to the interior by the 1,500-mile-long range of the Appalachian Mountains, however, they produced few explorers to rival the Spanish in the south (see chs. 10 and 17) or the French in the north (see chs. 18 and 21). In addition, with colonial settlements isolated from one another and straggling practically the length of the continent's eastern seaboard – from Plymouth and Albany in New England to Charleston in the south – much exploration was little more than a series of isolated and only partially successful probes into the immense interior.*

Nonetheless, between 1607 and 1700, Englishmen discovered half a dozen routes through the Appalachians and explored virtually all the major river systems between Maine and the Mississippi. They paddled northward on Lakes Ontario, Erie and Huron, and southward along the Ohio, Alabama and Mississippi Rivers. In the following century, English traders and speculators pushed farther westwards and traversed much of the vast region between the Appalachians and the Mississippi.

The pace of English exploration was primarily determined by economic lures: animal skins, rich agricultural lands and the search for a navigable sea-passage to the Pacific. Profit rather than geographical knowledge was the spur. But though the direction of exploration was accordingly determined by financiers and politicians, for the most part the business of exploration itself was the province of frontiersmen as likely to come from Germany, Holland or Scandinavia as from Britain. Little is known about either the names or the routes of many of these early pioneers. A number, however, kept journals which have survived; some recounted their adventures to others who recorded them.

These early explorers blazed few new trails. Most relied on native guides, who led them along paths and river routes long known to the Indians. This was already well-populated territory, and most explorers found the Indians more hospitable than hostile. For their part, the Indians found that their desire for European tools and weapons almost always outweighed their fears of foreign intrusion. Though many Europeans lost their lives, the relative ease with which they moved inland was as much a testament to native assistance as to European initiative.

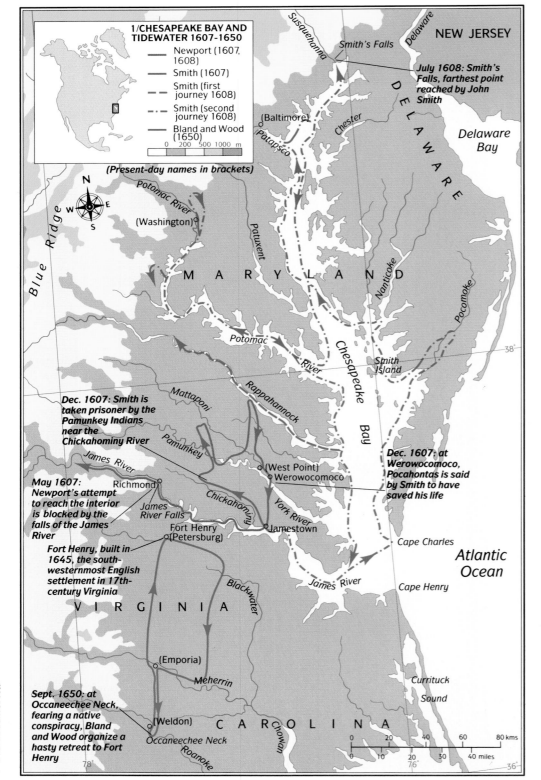

1 LEFT *America's first English frontier, Chesapeake Bay and its tributary rivers, was extensively explored by John Smith and Christopher Newport in the two years following the establishment of Jamestown in 1607. Almost half a century passed, however, before an English party, led by Edward Bland and Abraham Wood, examined the interior between the James and Roanoke Rivers.*

WITHIN a week of the establishment in 1607 of the first English colony in the Chesapeake – the Virginia Company's settlement at Jamestown – Christopher Newport, who had brought the English settlers to the New World, set forth into the interior. His goals seem to have been a search for gold and other precious metals and a passage to the Southern Sea – the Pacific – generally assumed to lie close at hand. Reaching present-day Richmond, he learned from the natives that the Quirauk Mountains – the Appalachians – could be reached in a few days' walk. These supposedly lay at the centre of the continent and were the source of the headwaters of rivers flowing west into a great sea. This apparent confirmation of a sea-passage to the Orient exerted a powerful influence on later English exploration.

With Newport's return to England, responsibility for exploring Chesapeake Bay passed to Captain John Smith. In December 1607, reconnoitring the Chickahominy River, Smith was captured by 200 Pamunkey Indians. During his month in captivity, he was taken along more than 100 miles of native paths. While in captivity, Smith also heard that a route existed connecting Chesapeake Bay to the South Sea. The following summer, he set out in a 14-man barge to explore the bay's

A BELOW LEFT John Farrer's A mapp of Virginia discovered to ye Falls appeared in several mid-17th century publications, including Edward Bland's The Discovery of New Brittaine (1651) and Edward Williams' Virgo Truimphans (1650). With west to the top, its depiction of a narrow North American continent appears to have been a factor stimulating Virginians to search for a route to the South Sea.

B RIGHT John Ogilby's A New Discription of Carolina (c.1672), oriented with west at the top, demonstrates the interest of map-makers in new discoveries. Although Lederer is not mentioned his 1670 route is shown by a fine line in the top right-hand corner.

A
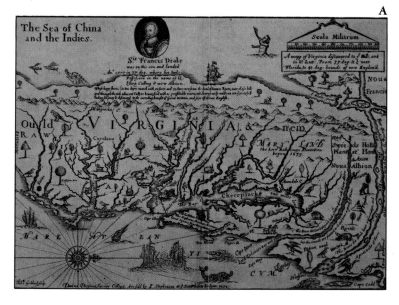

B
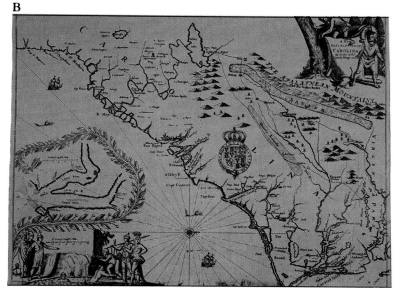

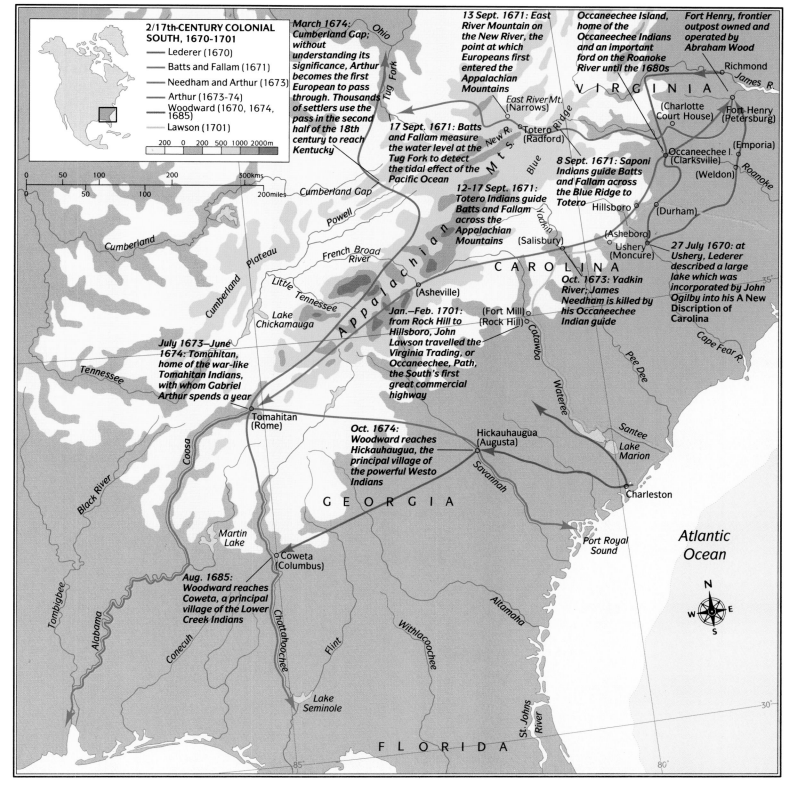

2 RIGHT Between 1670 and 1701 English knowledge of the Colonial South was greatly expanded by explorers and traders operating from settlements at present-day Petersburg, Virginia, and Charleston, South Carolina. Royal Governor Sir William Berkeley and frontier entrepreneur Abraham Wood initiated the Virginia-sponsored explorations. Henry Woodward, acting for the Carolina proprietors, pioneered the opening of the South Carolina and Georgia interiors.

2/17th-CENTURY COLONIAL SOUTH, 1670-1701
— Lederer (1670)
— Batts and Fallam (1671)
— Needham and Arthur (1673)
— Arthur (1673-74)
— Woodward (1670, 1674, 1685)
— Lawson (1701)

March 1674: Cumberland Gap; without understanding its significance, Arthur becomes the first European to pass through. Thousands of settlers use the pass in the second half of the 18th century to reach Kentucky

13 Sept. 1671: East River Mountain on the New River, the point at which Europeans first entered the Appalachian Mountains

Occaneechee Island, home of the Occaneechee Indians and an important ford on the Roanoke River until the 1680s

Fort Henry, frontier outpost owned and operated by Abraham Wood

17 Sept. 1671: Batts and Fallam measure the water level at the Tug Fork to detect the tidal effect of the Pacific Ocean

12-17 Sept. 1671: Totero Indians guide Batts and Fallam across the Appalachian Mountains

8 Sept. 1671: Saponi Indians guide Batts and Fallam across the Blue Ridge to Totero

27 July 1670: at Ushery, Lederer described a large lake which was incorporated by John Ogilby into his A New Discription of Carolina

Oct. 1673: Yadkin River; James Needham is killed by his Occaneechee Indian guide

July 1673–June 1674: Tomahitan, home of the war-like Tomahitan Indians, with whom Gabriel Arthur spends a year

Jan.–Feb. 1701: from Rock Hill to Hillsboro, John Lawson travelled the Virginia Trading, or Occaneechee, Path, the South's first great commercial highway

Oct. 1674: Woodward reaches Hickauhaugua, the principal village of the powerful Westo Indians

Aug. 1685: Woodward reaches Coweta, a principal village of the Lower Creek Indians

Ohio
Tug Fork
East River Mt. (Narrows)
VIRGINIA
Richmond
James R.
(Charlotte Court House)
Fort Henry (Petersburg)
Occaneechee I. [Clarksville]
(Emporia)
Roanoke
(Weldon)
New R.
Totero (Radford)
Blue Ridge
Hillsboro
(Durham)
Cumberland Gap
Powell
Appalachian Mts.
Yadkin
(Asheboro)
CAROLINA
Cumberland Plateau
French Broad River
(Salisbury)
Ushery (Moncure)
Little Tennessee
(Asheville)
Lake Chickamauga
(Fort Mill) (Rock Hill)
Catawba
35°
Cape Fear R.
Tennessee
Tomahitan (Rome)
Hickauhaugua (Augusta)
Wateree
Pee Dee
Coosa
Santee
Lake Marion
Charleston
Black River
GEORGIA
Savannah
Atlantic Ocean
Martin Lake
Coweta (Columbus)
Port Royal Sound
Tombigbee
Alabama
Conecuh
Chattahoochee
Flint
Withlacoochee
Altamaha
N
W E
S
Lake Seminole
St. Johns River
FLORIDA
30°
85°
80°

The Sea of China and the Indies.
Sr Francis Drake
Scala Miliarum
VIRGINIA
MARY LAND
MARE VIRGINIVM

V North America

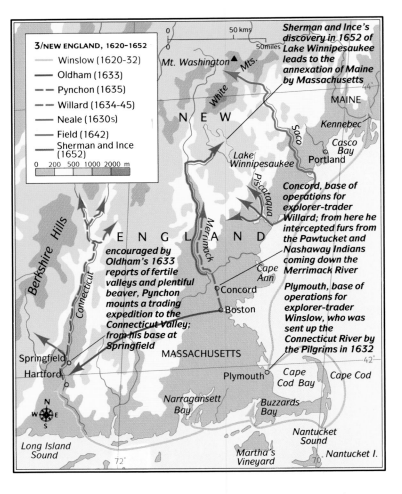

3 LEFT From trading posts at Plymouth, Concord and Springfield, the Puritan entrepreneurs Winslow, Oldham, Pynchon and Willard explored the river valleys of New England in their early 17th-century quest for native fur-trading partners and a route to the imagined wealth of the west.

friended by the Tomahitan king, spent almost a year travelling with the Indians, covering about 3,300 miles. On his return to Virginia in June 1674, Arthur had become the most widely travelled Englishman in 17th-century America. Of more lasting significance, he reinforced the growing realization of the hitherto unsuspected immensity of the new land.

After 1674, the impetus for southern exploration shifted to South Carolina. Henry Woodward, the individual primarily responsible, had already explored the interior along the Wateree River in 1670, a route John Lawson would later follow into North Carolina. Directed by the Carolina proprietors to open trade with the natives of the piedmont, in 1674 Woodward accompanied a party of Westo Indians to present-day Augusta, Georgia. A decade later, with the Westo monopoly on trade broken, Woodward led a dozen Charleston traders to the towns of the Lower Creek Indians. With a practicable route now open for them, Charleston-based traders pushed rapidly westwards, entering the mountainous territory of the Cherokees by the early 1690s. In 1698, Thomas Welch became the first known Englishman to cross the Mississippi to the Arkansas side.

To the north, in New England, exploration proved similarly hesitant, with mountainous and wooded terrain presenting major obstacles. The success of French fur-traders in Canada, however, prompted a number of Plymouth merchants as early as 1621 to penetrate the region's rivers in search of valuable pelts. Their principal explorer, Edward Winslow, entered Maine's Kennebec River in 1625, and Narragansett Bay and the Connecticut River in 1632. In 1633, John Oldham pioneered the 90-mile overland crossing from Boston to Hartford. Shortly thereafter, another Boston merchant, William Pynchon, established a trading post at present-day Springfield. From here, he dispatched traders throughout the upper Connecticut Valley. Similarly, Simon Willard, from his post at Concord, Massachusetts, pioneered the exploration of New Hampshire's Merrimack River. In the 1630s and 1640s, a few optimistic New Englanders attempted to discover a water passage to the vicinity of Lake Champlain. Walter Neale undertook several expeditions up the Piscataqua River. In 1642, Darby Field explored 70 miles along the Saco River to become the first European to penetrate the White Mountains.

When, in 1664, the English overthrew the Dutch in New Amsterdam, later New York, they found themselves the inheritors of a 50-year-old Dutch fur-trade based at Albany.

western and northern tributaries. At the head of the bay he interrogated five Susquehanna chiefs who had European implements. Hoping that these had been obtained from Spanish settlers in the west, which would confirm the proximity of the South Sea, Smith discovered that they came from French settlers to the north. The Chesapeake, it was clear, would yield no easy passage to the Orient.

Further efforts to survey the interior languished until 1650. In that year, Edward Bland and Abraham Wood, with the encouragement of the governor of the Virginia settlement, Sir William Berkeley, organized a small expedition. They explored as far south as the Roanoke River. A brush with the natives, however, persuaded them to beat a hasty retreat to Fort Henry, at present-day Petersburg, after only nine days. Between 1669 and 1674, Governor Berkeley, again with the assistance of Wood, organized the first English attempt to cross the Appalachian Mountains. In this burst of exploration, once more aimed at 'the discovery of the South Sea', much of the Virginia and North Carolina piedmont was explored, and the Appalachian barrier was twice traversed successfully.

In the spring of 1670, Berkeley sent John Lederer to probe the mountains further. Lederer's route is a matter of controversy. A recent analysis places the terminus of his 60-day, 400-mile journey just south of Durham, North Carolina. Lederer claimed to have encountered 'a continued marsh', which took him three days to cross; 'the Lake of Ushery', so wide that he could barely see its southern shore; and 'a barren Sandy desert', where he feared dying of thirst. Nonetheless, Lederer demonstrated that large expeditions were not needed for survival among the Indians. Thus the following year Wood dispatched Thomas Batts and Robert Fallam on a further mission to find the South Sea. On the Tug Fork River they convinced themselves that they had witnessed an ebbing South Sea tide. Despite their promising report, however, their route proved impractical for commercial use.

With a potential northern route blocked, in 1673 Wood sent James Needham to discover a more southerly avenue to 'the south or west sea'. Needham, accompanied by his servant, Gabriel Arthur, proceeded across central North Carolina. East of present-day Asheville, they encountered a party of Tomahitan Indians who guided them through the mountains to the Tomahitans' village at present-day Rome, Georgia. Here Needham left Arthur to return to Fort Henry, only to be killed by his Occaneechee guide during the journey. Arthur, be-

4 BELOW Determined to compete with the French for the lucrative fur trade of Lake Huron, in 1685 Governor Dongan of New York dispatched Albany trader Roseboom on a three-month, 800-mile expedition. The earliest European exploration of the Ohio River valley, which departed from Albany seven years later, was led by Viele, who had journeyed to Michili-mackinac with Roseboom.

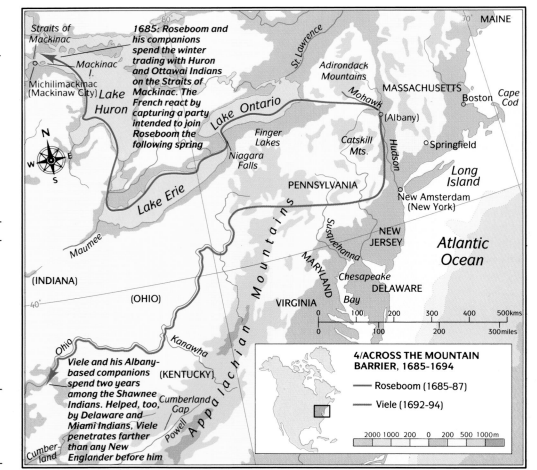

5 BELOW *The opening of the Ohio Valley to trade and English settlement was accomplished principally by Croghan, a Pennsylvanian Indian trader, and Gist and Walker, scouts for Virginia land companies. The earliest British attempt to explore the upper Mississippi River was sponsored by Major Robert Rogers.*

Much of this trade was fed by renegade French trappers bringing furs south from the Great Lakes. Eager to control the trade, in 1683 Thomas Dongan, Governor of New York, persuaded a French deserter to lead a British party under Johannes Roseboom on a three-month, 800-mile journey to Mackinac Island at the head of Lake Huron. Though a potential avenue of access had been established, the hostility of the French proved insuperable. Thwarted, the British turned their attentions westward. Between 1692-94, a party of Albany traders led by Arnout Viele explored the upper Ohio River and much of present-day Ohio, Indiana and Kentucky. But though Viele established the long-term possibilities of these territories, their remoteness rendered them no more than a future prospect.

The result of this expansion was conflict with the French over control of the fur-trade. War with them increased in scale and ferocity between 1744 and 1760, ending with British domination of all the region south of the Great Lakes. By now, British penetration of Ohio and the lands to the south in Virginia and what was to become western Kentucky was extensive. Much of the exploration was the work of trappers and traders. Among the most prominent were George Croghan and Christopher Gist, who in 1750 made an extended journey through Ohio and Kentucky, and Thomas Walker, who in the same year stumbled on the Warriors' Path from Virginia, which he followed through the Cumberland Gap into Kentucky.

It was not until 1760-61 that the British occupied what had formerly been French posts in Michigan, Indiana and Wisconsin. Major Robert Rogers, commander of Fort Michilimackinac, developed a scheme to direct the fur-trade of the upper Mississippi Valley into his own pocket. Rogers also revived the dream of a practical Northwest Passage through British America. To stimulate government backing, Rogers sent Jonathan Carver, William Bruce, James Tute and James Goddard to map the upper Mississippi and to win the loyalty of the Indians. In the autumn of 1766, having crossed Wisconsin, they ascended the Mississippi to present-day Minneapolis, Minnesota. The explorers returned by way of Grand Portage and Lake Superior, having made no major advance on the fur-trade but recording (though never seeing) the mountains which lay as a barrier to the Pacific, the Rockies.

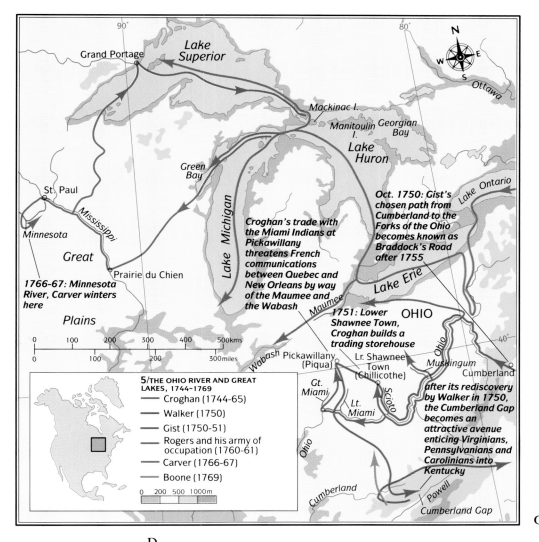

5/THE OHIO RIVER AND GREAT LAKES, 1744-1769
— Croghan (1744-65)
— Walker (1750)
— Gist (1750-51)
— Rogers and his army of occupation (1760-61)
— Carver (1766-67)
— Boone (1769)

Croghan's trade with the Miami Indians at Pickawillany threatens French communications between Quebec and New Orleans by way of the Maumee and the Wabash

Oct. 1750: Gist's chosen path from Cumberland to the Forks of the Ohio becomes known as Braddock's Road after 1755

1751: Lower Shawnee Town, Croghan builds a trading storehouse

1766-67: Minnesota River, Carver winters here

after its rediscovery by Walker in 1750, the Cumberland Gap becomes an attractive avenue enticing Virginians, Pennsylvanians and Carolinians into Kentucky

C

C ABOVE RIGHT *Henry Popple's* Map of the Northern Colonies *(1733) shows how little the British knew about the region west of the Appalachian Mountains. The Finger Lakes west of Albany are accurately drawn, but the nearby and much larger Lake Ontario, and the more distant Lake Huron, lying in French-held territory, are misaligned.* **D** RIGHT *Lewis Evans's* A General map of the Middle British Colonies in America *of 1755, the product of four years of travel and surveying, is considered one of the great maps of the Colonial period. Note the dramatic advances in British knowledge of the trans-Appalachian region as compared to Popple's map.*

D

20

THE PACIFIC COAST OF NORTH AMERICA
1539-1791

A BELOW *Part of the 1578 map of the western hemisphere by the Spanish or Catalan mapmaker, Juan Martínez. Its most notable feature is the representation of the mythical Seven Cities of 'Civola', or Cíbola, in present-day Arizona.*

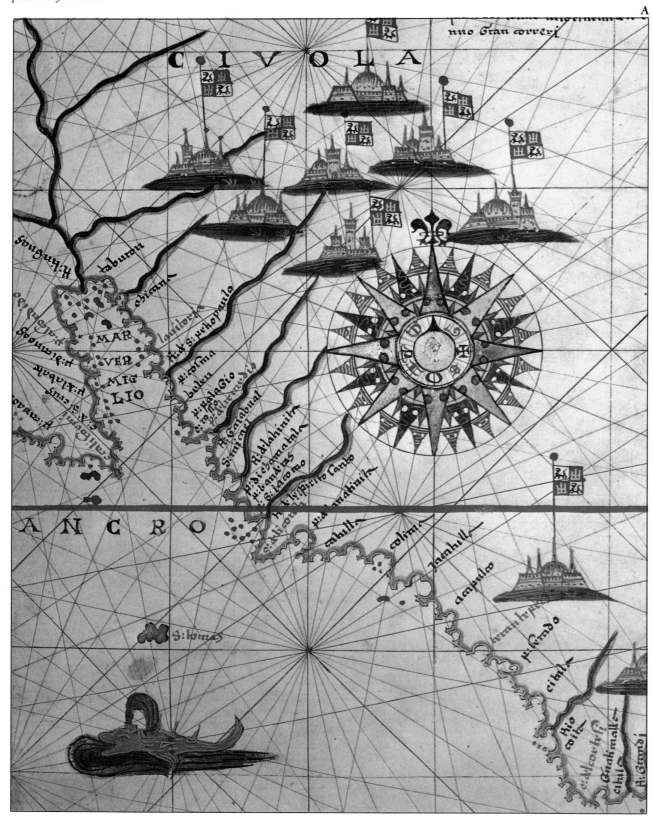

UNTIL *well into the 18th century, the north Pacific remained among the least-known areas of the inhabited globe. It was a region that presented baffling problems to geographers, in particular whether America and Asia were separated by sea or joined by a land-bridge.*

In the 16th century the initiative lay with the Spaniards. By the 1520s, they had established themselves in Mexico, and by the 1530s had reached lower, or peninsular, California. Though hindered by mountains and deserts on one side and a forbidding coastline on the other, exploration farther north was nonetheless driven forward by rumours of great riches. Here, it was thought, lay the Seven Cities of Cíbola, a vision conjured from medieval legend and Indian reports; Quivira, a city where boats had prows of gold; and the Strait of Anian, that phantom waterway between the Pacific and the Atlantic.

Although by the early 17th century Spanish survey expeditions from Mexican ports had coasted as far as 43°N they had found no sign of these fabulous realms. To the north stretched one of the longest unexplored coastlines in the world. In these empty spaces, speculative cartographers showed a great inland sea, and straits and rivers that seemed to connect the Pacific coast of north-west America with Hudson Bay or Baffin Bay to the east. The myths of Cíbola and Quivira had been replaced by the narratives of apocryphal voyages – by Juan de Fuca, Bartholomew de Fonte and Lorenzo Maldonado – which strengthened the conviction that a Northwest Passage existed.

On the opposite brinks of this great void in Europe's knowledge of the northern hemisphere stood two peninsulas 5,000 miles apart – California and Kamchatka, the one hot and arid, the other snow-covered for much of the year. The physical contrast was indication enough of the immensity of the task attempted in the 18th century, as the Russians in the far north and the Spaniards from their bases in New Spain groped their way towards each other. The final leap across the gap was made by the celebrated English explorer, James Cook, in the 1770s. His voyage brought both knowledge of the north-west coast and publicity, for his account drew attention to the region's wealth in furs. Before the end of the century, expeditions from six nations were trading along a coast which 20 years earlier had never seen a European vessel, and a fierce international struggle was being fought over possession of this remote region.

SPANISH exploration of the Pacific coast north of its new Mexican empire began in earnest with the voyages of Francisco de Ulloa (1539) and Hernando de Alarcón (1540) into the Gulf of California. These showed that California was a peninsula, not an island as earlier speculation had suggested. A more ambitious venture was the three-ship expedition of Rodríguez Cabrillo (1542-43) which pushed against the prevailing headwinds to reach the coastline of Upper California and discovered the harbour of San Diego. After Cabrillo's death one vessel continued north to about latitude 42°30′N, and was probably only just short of Cape Blanco when it turned back. It was a notable feat of exploration along 900 miles of unknown coast, but the expedition had found neither cities, riches nor any great strait; and because of the offshore winds it had missed the harbours of Monterey and San Francisco. Its findings seemed to confirm the disappointments of Coronado's elaborate interior foray of this period, and further northern exploration had to wait until the end of the century. This was prompted by the unexpected descent of the English seaman, Francis Drake, on the north-west coast in 1579, though the Spanish response was a leisurely one. Not until 1595 did a Spanish ship (the Manila galleon commanded by Sebastián Rodríguez Cermeño which had been diverted from its most direct track to Acapulco) reach the area of northern California where Drake had been. This diversion, a costly and unsuccessful one for the galleon was wrecked, was followed in 1602 by the final episode in this early European exploration of the north-west coast when Sebastián Vizcaino sailed north from Acapulco with three ships and orders to survey the coast as far as Cape Blanco. He entered San Diego Bay (as Cabrillo had done 60 years earlier), Monterey Bay and Drakes Bay. One of his ships reached Cape Blanco near latitude 43°N, where it was forced back by cold 'so great that they thought they should be frozen'. Apart from the pearl fishery of the Gulf of California, successive expeditions had found little of immediate value. In one sense, there had even been a diminution of knowledge, for

B RIGHT *Part of Henry Briggs's 1625 Map of North America. It shows California as an island and hints that the mainland coast turns east towards the inlets of Hudson Bay (here named Buttons Bay).*

B

1 BELOW *Spanish seaborne expeditions of the 16th century established the trend of the coastline of most of California and Oregon. Not until the 18th century did land expeditions confirm that Baja California was a peninsula and reveal the great bay of San Francisco.*

misinterpretation of one of the accounts of Vizcaino's voyage led to the presumption that California was, after all, an island. This error was not corrected until the explorations of the Jesuit missionary, Fr. Eusebio Francisco Kino, at the end of the 17th century when, during a series of arduous journeys which crisscrossed northern Sonora and southern Arizona, he sighted the land passage at the head of the Gulf of California.

Later Spanish coastal exploration was motivated more by fear than by hope, for rumours of Russian activity far to the north sent tremors of alarm reaching down to New Spain. By the early 18th century, Russian overland expansion across Asia had reached Kamchatka, and preparations began to continue the eastward movement by sea. Clearly such exploration should determine the reality or otherwise of those reports which hinted at the existence of land across the sea to the east. In 1728, a Russian expedition commanded by the Dane, Vitus Bering, sailed north-east from Kamchatka to reach the eastern tip of Asia; and although he saw no land across the water, in 1732 Mikhail Gwosdev, in Bering's old ship, did. He marked it on the map as '*bolshaya zemlya*', or 'great land' – a term full of continental implications. After 10 years of preparation which show something of the logistical problems which hindered expeditions in this distant part of the Russian empire, Bering, in 1741, sailed again from Kamchatka. Separated from each other, his two ships both sighted the Alaskan mainland coast. Bering's second-in-command, Chirikov, reached the American coast in latitude 55°21′N, near Sitka, but because of the loss of his boats was unable to land. Farther west, Bering landed at Kayak Island, though his stay of only a few hours revealed little of the region. For the first time the coastal outlines of north-west America can be dimly discerned on maps, though the fragmentary nature of the Russian discoveries led to conflicting interpretations as to whether the Russians had reached a continental landmass or had sighted only islands. The uncertainty was heightened by the attempt of geographers such as Philippe Buache to incorporate Bering's explorations onto maps based on the imaginative geography of the apocryphal accounts.

On the north-west coast itself, Russian exploration was followed by Russian trade as the rough *promyshlenniki* or maritime fur traders probed along the islands of the Aleutian chain in search of the prized sea-otter skins. By the 1760s, reports – much exaggerated – of Russian activities along the Alaskan coast convinced Spanish officials that New Spain's northern

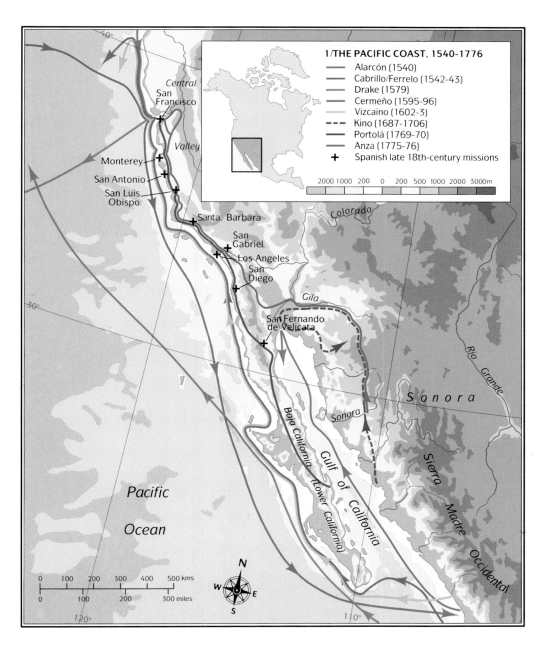

1/THE PACIFIC COAST, 1540-1776
— Alarcón (1540)
— Cabrillo/Ferrelo (1542-43)
— Drake (1579)
— Cermeño (1595-96)
— Vizcaino (1602-3)
--- Kino (1687-1706)
— Portolá (1769-70)
— Anza (1775-76)
+ Spanish late 18th-century missions

2000 1000 200 0 200 500 1000 2000 3000m

C LEFT *Phillipe Buache's map of 1752 shows north-west America divided by an inland sea and by the straits and rivers described in de Fonte's apocryphal voyage of 1640.* D BELOW *Cook's ships at Ship Cover, Nootka Sound, 1778 by John Webber.* E RIGHT *Pedro Font's 1776 map is one of the best early representations of San Francisco Bay.*

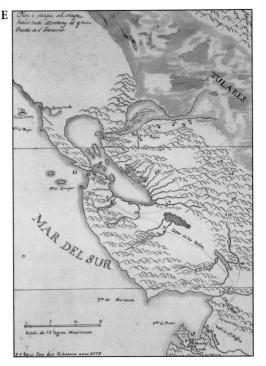

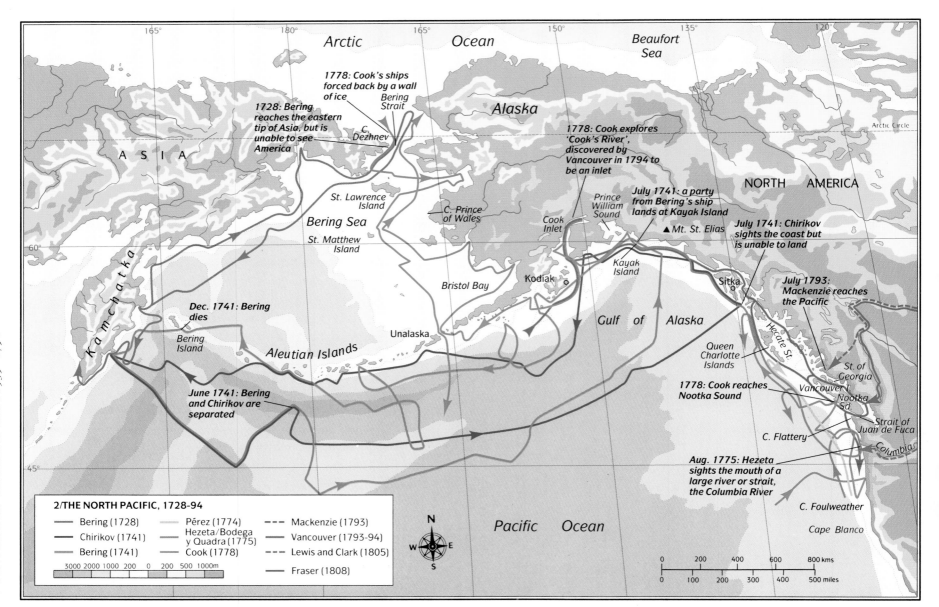

frontier must be advanced to meet this threat. The first stage aimed to complete the exploration of Upper California by sea and land, and to support it with the establishment of military posts and mission stations. In 1769, an overland party led by Gaspar de Portolá reached Monterey and the great bay of San Francisco, though the reality of its magnificent harbour was not grasped until 1775 when Juan de Ayala made the first recorded sailing through the Golden Gate. The harbour was, Fr. Pedro Font wrote in 1776, 'a marvel of nature … the harbour of harbours … it has the best advantages for founding in it a most beautiful city'. Although San Diego and Monterey had been garrisoned, and in 1771 a mission established at San Gabriel (Los Angeles) the Spanish position in Upper California was far from secure. All supplies had to be brought by sea from San Blas on the Mexican coast, and against headwinds the journey could take three or four months. One solution to the communications problem would be a land route from Sonora by

2 BELOW *The exploration of the north-west coast was a multi-national enterprise. It established the separation of America and Asia, demolished hopes of a Northwest Passage in temperate latitudes, and linked with overland explorers from the east.*

way of the Colorado and Gila rivers. In the 1770s Spanish army officers and missionaries explored along them and also entered for the first time the Great Basin, stretching from the Sierra Nevadas of California to central Utah. At the same time, Spanish vessels pushed farther north along the coast to check on the Russian presence. In 1774, Juan Pérez reached the Queen Charlotte Islands in 55°N, where he traded offshore with the local (Haida) Indians. The following year Francisco de la Bodega y Quadra in the *Sonora* reached 58°N, and for the first time Spaniards landed on the north-west coast. Far to the south Bruno de Hezeta in a consort vessel, the *Santiago*, sighted, though he did not enter, what seemed to be the mouth of a large river in 46°N. It might be, Hezeta thought, the entrance of De Fuca's strait. In reality it was the estuary of one of North America's major waterways, the Columbia River, sighted by Hezeta 17 years before the American trader, Robert Gray, claimed possession of it for the United States – by virtue of prior discovery.

While the Russians and Spaniards were still approaching each other in a giant pincer movement, the ships of James Cook reached the north-west coast in 1778. Inaccurate Russian reports and maps had led to the belief that Alaska was an island, separated from the American mainland by a wide strait; and it was this strait, which it was hoped might be the western entrance to a Northwest Passage, that Britain's most celebrated explorer had been sent to find. Cook sailed north from Vancouver Island along the great arc of the northern coast, and although he found no navigable passage he traced hundreds of miles of intricate coastline, outlined the shape of the Alaskan peninsula, and showed that the water reached by Bering 50 years earlier indeed separated Asia and America. That narrow stretch of water would soon be known as Bering Strait. Cook's account described the north-west coast from the densely forested shores of Vancouver Island to the startling volcanic peaks of Alaska. It also contained the fullest account yet of the native peoples of the north-west coast – from the Nootka Indians of Vancouver Island to the Aleuts of the islands off Alaska – and of the sea-otter skins which his crews had traded at high prices in Canton on the return voyage.

The posthumous publication of Cook's account was followed by a scramble in Europe and the newly-independent United States to fit out fur-trading expeditions to the north-west coast. As they traded, they also explored, and their commanders, several of whom had sailed with Cook, realised that what in 1778 had been assumed to be a continuous mainland coast was in fact a screen of islands. Behind this shelter might well lie the inland sea and the straits reputed to have been discovered in earlier times. In 1787 George Dixon, who had been with Cook, entered Hecate Strait and thought it was that followed into the interior by De Fonte in 1640. In the same year William Barkley sighted an opening south of Nootka (known ever since as the Strait of Juan de Fuca) which he was convinced was 'the long lost strait of Juan de Fuca'. At the same time as geographical speculation intensified, the region became a scene of international confrontation as Britain and Spain clashed in 1790 over the possession of Nootka Sound. The twin impulses of discovery and annexation prompted the contending powers to send expeditions to the coast. Between 1790 and 1792 Spanish vessels carried out painstaking surveys of the waterways inside Barkley's opening; but three summers of exploration ended in anti-climax when the Spaniards found that the intricate waterways they were tracing led back into the Pacific through the Strait of Georgia. In 1791 ships from the Malaspina circumnavigation were diverted north to the Alaskan coast to search for yet another reputed strait (the one claimed to have been discovered by Maldonado in 1588), while in 1792 Caamaño probed the coast around 53°N, in a vain search for De Fonte's strait. By the time that a British naval expedition commanded by George Vancouver (another of Cook's men) reached the coast in 1792, the Spaniards, after five seasons of meticulous exploration, had satisfied themselves that the straits of the ancient accounts did not exist.

This did not deter Vancouver from completing his own comprehensive survey of the coast. In three summers of exploration he confirmed the Spanish conclusion that there was no strait through the North American continent in temperate latitudes. The only transcontinental route would be similar to that laborious track of rivers, portages and mountain passes which had brought Alexander Mackenzie onto the Pacific coast in 1793. If there was a Northwest Passage, it could only exist in high latitudes, where ice made it unlikely that it would ever be used for commercial purposes. Vancouver's account and charts were published in 1798, whereas in Spain bureaucratic sloth and political upheaval meant that most of the fine surveys of his Spanish contemporaries remained buried in the archives. Vancouver's survey became the standard one, and his nomenclature is reflected on the present maps of the north-west coast.

FRANCIS DRAKE AND NEW ALBION

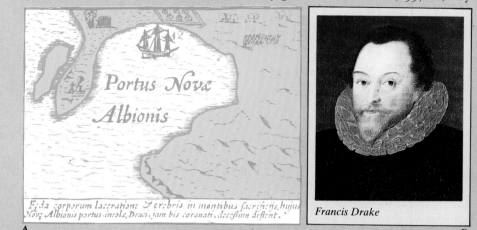

A

Francis Drake

B

LONG-STANDING Spanish assumptions that the north Pacific was immune to any foreign threat were roughly jolted by the appearance in the area of Francis Drake (B) on his celebrated voyage round the world (1557-80). By April 1579 Drake had plundered Spanish coastal settlements from Chile to Mexico, and, with the *Golden Hind* laden with bullion, was ready to head for home. For reasons which are not altogether clear, but which may have included the hope of discovering and returning by the fabled Strait of Anian, Drake sailed north. After keeping well out to sea he approached the coast near the present California-Oregon boundary before cold weather forced him south again. Somewhere on the coast of northern California he found a bay where he spent five weeks repairing his ship. He took possession of the country, which he named 'Nova Albion', because of its white cliffs, and so that 'it might have some affinity, even in name also, with our country, which was sometimes so called'. To mark the ceremony, a brass plate was engraved and nailed to a post.

The identity of this bay has been the subject of unending enquiry and disagreement (D). Among the claimants are Bodega Bay, San Francisco Bay and Drakes Bay inside Point Reyes, with the latter attracting most support. The discovery of what was thought to be Drake's plate of brass – first found, it seems, near one bay in 1933, discarded, then found again near another in 1936, and now in any case generally regarded as a forgery – has confused rather than clarified the issue. Nor does the crude representation of Drake's anchorage on a map of the early 1590s (A) much resemble any of the main contenders. More significant than the precise location of Drake's landing place was his act of possession, allegedly carried out with the consent of the local (Coast Miwok) Indians. New Albion began to appear on maps of North America (C) on equal terms with the huge expanses of New Spain to the south and New France to the east. Although Drake's incursion remained an isolated event, more than 200 years later at the time of the Nootka Sound controversy in 1790 between Britain and Spain it formed part of the British claim to the north-west coast.

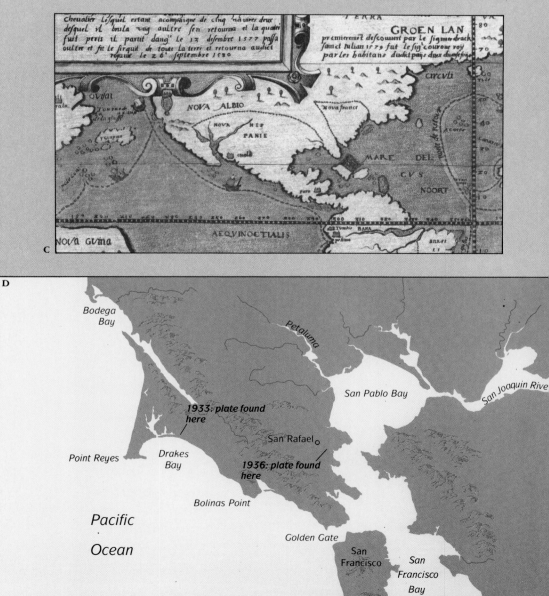

C

D

21
TO THE ROCKY MOUNTAINS AND THE ARCTIC 1686-1812

WHILE *the task of exploration and settlement on the eastern seaboard of the North American continent proceeded at a steady pace, to the north and north-west Europeans were making far-ranging surveys of continental dimensions. As in Champlain's day, these explorations were closely associated both with the fur trade and with the continuing hope that a passage might yet be found to the western ocean. Indeed, the process of expansion beyond the Great Lakes was dominated by the conviction that not far to the west lay a great interior sea, the* mer de l'ouest *of the French geographers. This mythical waterway was usually envisaged as a sort of North American Mediterranean, linked to the Pacific on the west and to some part of the river and lake network on the east. The equivalent and equally enduring British fantasy was of an easily navigable Northwest Passage. These twin phantoms proved potent distractions. It was not until the second half of the 18th century that any indication of the geographical reality of a massive north-south range of mountains, the Rockies, appeared on maps.*

1 BELOW *Driven by the search for the mythical western ocean and new fur-trapping areas, French, British and American 18th-century explorers crossed the Great Plains to reach the Rockies and, eventually, the Pacific.*

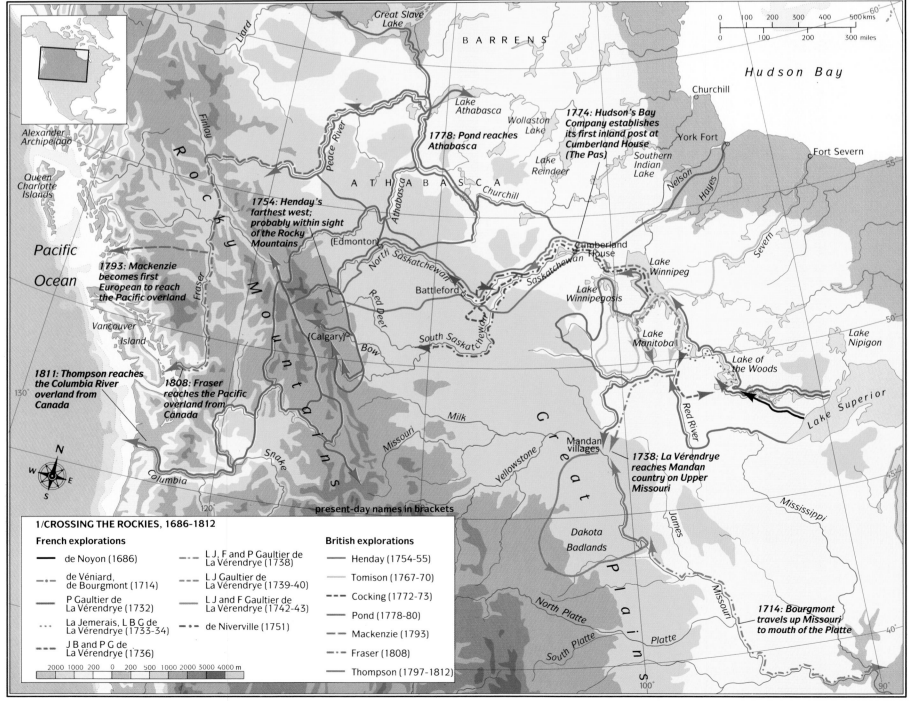

1774: Hudson's Bay Company establishes its first inland post at Cumberland House (The Pas)

1778: Pond reaches Athabasca

1754: Henday's farthest west; probably within sight of the Rocky Mountains

1793: Mackenzie becomes first European to reach the Pacific overland

1811: Thompson reaches the Columbia River overland from Canada

1808: Fraser reaches the Pacific overland from Canada

1738: La Vérendrye reaches Mandan country on Upper Missouri

1714: Bourgmont travels up Missouri to mouth of the Platte

present-day names in brackets

1/CROSSING THE ROCKIES, 1686-1812

French explorations
- de Noyon (1686)
- de Véniard, de Bourgmont (1714)
- P Gaultier de La Vérendrye (1732)
- La Jemerais, L B G de La Vérendrye (1733-34)
- J B and P G de La Vérendrye (1736)
- L J, F and P Gaultier de La Vérendrye (1738)
- L J Gaultier de La Vérendrye (1739-40)
- L J and F Gaultier de La Vérendrye (1742-43)
- de Niverville (1751)

British explorations
- Henday (1754-55)
- Tomison (1767-70)
- Cocking (1772-73)
- Pond (1778-80)
- Mackenzie (1793)
- Fraser (1808)
- Thompson (1797-1812)

2000 1000 200 0 200 500 1000 2000 3000 4000 m

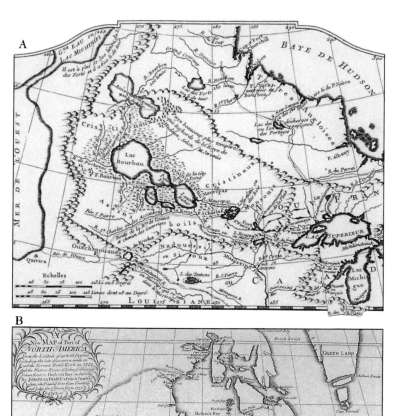

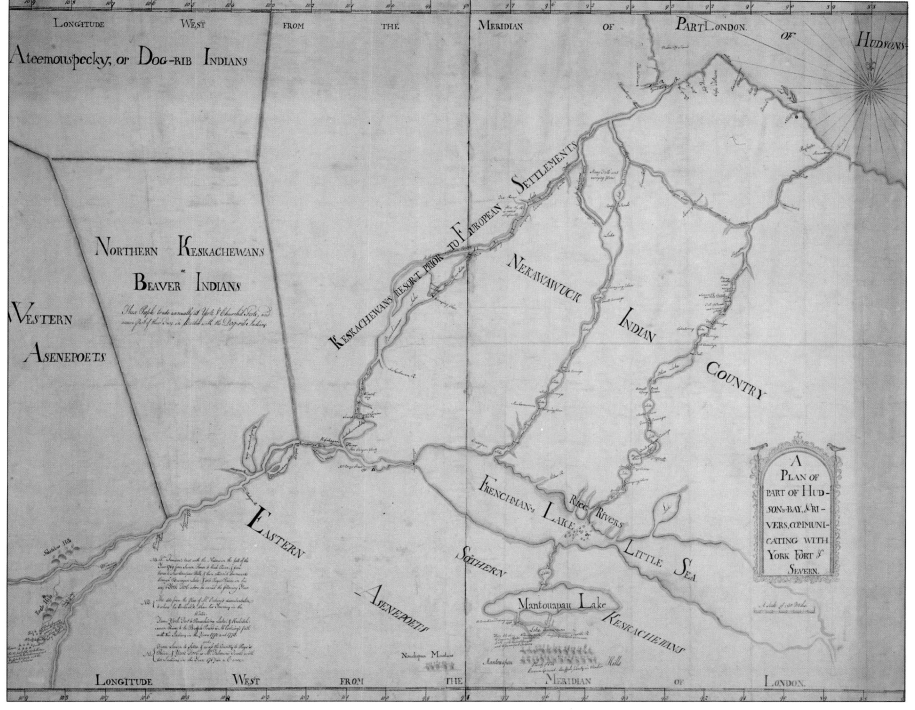

WHEN the long Anglo-French wars ended in 1713, the French once more began to move westward beyond Lake Superior. From the late 1720s this expansion was led by the last of the great French explorers of North America, La Vérendrye. At first the demands of the fur trade were paramount. La Vérendrye built depots at the Lake of the Woods and on the Red River south of Lake Winnipeg. As the French reached the edge of the plains, so they cut across the river routes which took furs north to the English posts on Hudson Bay.

From the south came persistent reports of an advanced, light-skinned people who lived along the banks of the 'River of the West', and were called 'Mantannes'. In the winter of 1738-39 La Vérendrye reached the Mandan villages on the Missouri, but found that their inhabitants were unmistakably Indian, though of different culture and appearance from the familiar Cree to the north. Of greater significance, hopes that this region might yield a westward-flowing river or great inland sea offering an easy passage to the Pacific were disappointed.

In 1742 two of the explorer's sons accordingly returned to the Missouri from where, in what was to prove an increasingly forlorn attempt to find the western sea, they reached the Badlands of North Dakota. La Vérendrye himself had turned back to the north and to another great waterway, the 'Rivière Blanche' or the Saskatchewan, and one of the most important arteries of the fur trade. In 1739, one of his sons reached the Forks of the Saskatchewan, and in 1751 Boucher de Niverville followed one of its branches far enough west to meet Indians from the Rockies. Of more immediate importance, however, was the fact that by the middle years of the century the French had come to dominate the Indian trade routes of the interior. Their

A LEFT *Buache's 1754 map illustrates how the French underestimated the westward scope of North America. La Vérendrye's 1738 route to the Mandans ('Ouachipouanes') is shown in the lower left-hand corner.* **B** LEFT *This English map of 1744 was based on Joseph la France's journey from Lake Superior to York Fort in 1742. The persistent English belief in a Northwest Passage is evident.* **C** BELOW *Despite obvious distortions, Andrew Graham's map of c. 1772 demonstrates that explorers of the Hudson's Bay Company had penetrated the interior beyond Lake Manitoba and the Forks of Saskatchewan.*

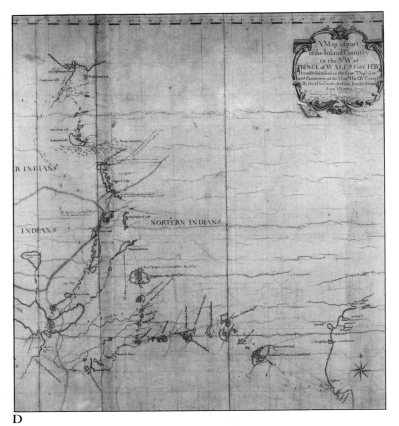

D

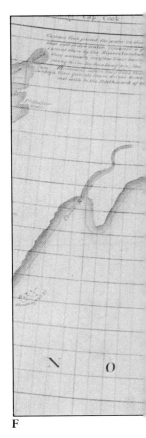

F

The Company was slow to react to the danger. Its only serious explorations were mounted by James Knight at York Fort, who had been convinced by Indian reports that a land of gold lay somewhere to the north-west. In 1715 he sent William Stuart inland with Indians, but Stuart's report on where he had been was confused. Nonetheless, he was certainly the first European to cross the Barrens of the northern tundra; that he reached Great Slave Lake, as some have claimed, seems unlikely, however. After establishing what was to be the most northerly of the Company's major posts, at the mouth of the Churchill River, Knight turned his attentions to a sea approach, the Northwest Passage. He was to prove no more successful in this endeavour than his predecessors in the 16th and 17th centuries (*see* ch.16). In 1719-20 his two vessels and their crews were lost off the west coast of Hudson Bay.

The disaster confirmed the reluctance of the Company and its servants to venture away from the posts, and it was left to outsiders to renew the search in Hudson Bay for a Northwest Passage. Prompted by the arguments, both geographical and commercial, of the Irish MP Arthur Dobbs, a naval expedition in 1741-42, and a private one in 1746-47, carried out useful surveys of the west coast of Hudson Bay, but these, too, failed to find a sea-passage.

Falling trade returns then forced the Company into a more vigorous policy of exploration, and in 1754 Anthony Henday left York Fort for the interior to report on the extent of the French threat. Like Kelsey, Henday travelled with Cree Indians, accompanying them to the North Saskatchewan, past the French posts, and onto the plains. There he saw great herds of buffalo and Indians on horseback, the Atsina or Blackfoot. At his farthest west, near present-day Calgary, according to his own estimates of his position, Henday should have been within sight of the Rockies, but made no mention of them.

But if his geography was vague, Henday's revelation of the true extent of the French encirclement was not. Before his employers could decide on action, however, war broke out between Britain and France, and Canada was conquered by Britain. The hopes of the Hudson's Bay Company that it could take over the western fur trade were short-lived, for the old French routes out of Montreal were soon in use again – now run

D ABOVE *Hearne's 1772 map shows the vast extent of his 1770-72 journey, made with Chipewyan Indian guides, from Hudson Bay to the Arctic Ocean.*

E BELOW *The frozen surface of Great Slave Lake as it appeared to Hearne in December 1771 on his return from the Coppermine River to Hudson Bay.*

F ABOVE *Part of Peter Pond's 1787 map of north-west America. Great Slave Lake is shown about 700 miles west of its true position, with a suggested communication between it and 'Cook's River'.*

E

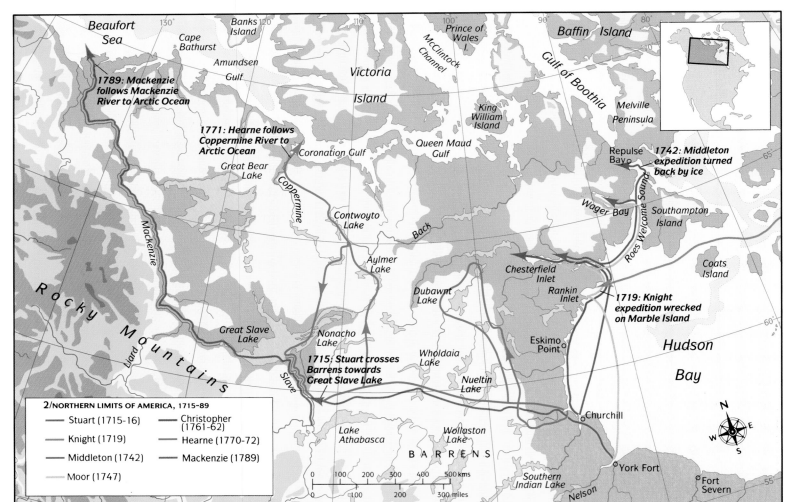

2/NORTHERN LIMITS OF AMERICA, 1715–89
- Stuart (1715-16)
- Knight (1719)
- Middleton (1742)
- Moor (1747)
- Christopher (1761-62)
- Hearne (1770-72)
- Mackenzie (1789)

2 LEFT *After the failure of mid-18th-century attempts to find a Northwest Passage through Hudson Bay, Hearne reached the shores of the Arctic Ocean overland in 1771; in 1789, he was followed, farther to the west, by Mackenzie. The northern limits of America were revealed.*

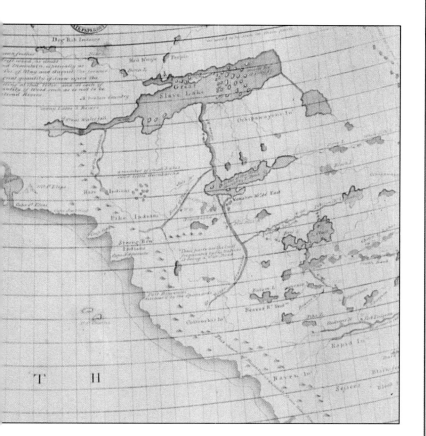

by a formidable combination of French *voyageurs* and Anglo/American capital and direction, which, in 1783, was incorporated as the North West Company.

The Hudson's Bay Company accordingly concluded that it had no alternative but to resume the policy first seen in Henday's journey of despatching probes into the interior. Reports subsequently brought back by William Tomison from the Lake Winnipeg region and by Matthew Cocking from the Forks of the Saskatchewan reinforced this fundamental change of policy. As a result, in 1774 the Company's first interior post was established. It was at Cumberland House, 400 miles inland from Hudson Bay.

The inland venture was commanded by Samuel Hearne, just back from a remarkable northern journey. Since the 1750s the Company had sent its sloops north from Churchill to exploit the Inuit trade and to search for the copper mines which had been reported since Knight's day. Coastal exploration failed to find either the mines or a sea-passage to the west, but escorted by Chipewyan Indians in 1770-72 Hearne crossed the Barrens and followed the Coppermine River to the polar sea.

He had reached the northern edge of the American continent, though he placed it almost four degrees too far north at 71°54′N – a common error among fur-trade explorers handicapped by a lack of surveying instruments and rudimentary skills. Inaccurate though it was, Hearne's single latitude was nonetheless enough to shatter contemporary hopes that an easily navigable Northwest Passage might soon be found through the continent; a few years later it was decisive in directing far to the north Captain James Cook's Pacific coast search for a sea-passage (*see* ch. 20).

The move inland marked the beginning of a half-century of competition and expansion in the fur trade which was to take the rival companies westward into Athabasca and across the Rockies. In 1778 Peter Pond ventured into Athabasca to open up a new fur-trading region. In the mid-1780s he returned to the north-west, and convinced himself that a water route ran from Great Slave Lake to Cook Inlet on the Pacific coast. It was left to another Nor'Wester, Alexander Mackenzie, to discover that the river from Great Slave Lake led, not to the Pacific, but to the ice-bound shores of the Arctic Ocean. In a second attempt, Mackenzie reached the Pacific in 1793 to make the first overland journey of the continent along perilous streams and difficult portages.

In fact, it was to be 500 miles farther to the south, on the Columbia River, that fur traders found a more practical route to the Pacific coast early in the next century, and were able to exploit the magnificent inland surveys of David Thompson.

INDIAN TRAVEL METHODS

FROM THEIR first arrival in North America, Europeans observed and imitated indigenous methods of travel. In Canada, the birchbark canoe, the snowshoe and toboggan became the indispensable means by which white men moved across the roadless terrain.

In winter, snowshoes, as in (A) and (B), were essential. As worn by the Indians, they might be up to six feet long. '… in walking the body is always lifted off the ground with the spring', wrote one European. Toboggans, hauled by men and dogs, were perhaps 12 feet long and 16 inches wide. Together, they made travel in all but the most severe winter conditions possible. The carriage of bulk goods, however, had to wait for the summer and the break-up of the lakes and rivers. It was then that that most remarkable form of transport – the birchbark canoe, (C) and (D) – came into its own.

'In the canoes of the savages one can go without restraint', wrote Champlain in 1603. Light and tough, with shallow draught and high manoeuvrability, the birchbark canoe could be used on most waters. Where it could not float, it was carried. Smaller canoes

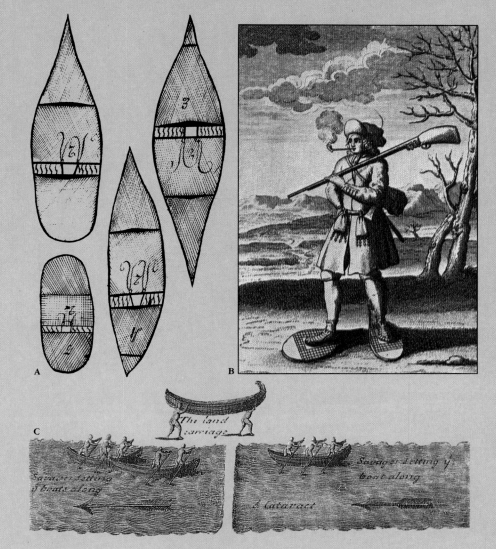

could be carried by one man; larger canoes up to 25 feet could be carried by two men. Easily damaged, they were equally easy to repair. The crews carried bark, twine and gum for what was often the nightly task of patching their craft.

From the St. Lawrence to Grand Portage at the western end of Lake Superior, the Montreal fur-traders used the great *canots du maitre*. Up to 40 feet in length, they carried a crew of ten men and four tons of goods. One trader wrote that a stranger, 'on seeing one of these slender vessels thus laden, heaped up and sunk with her gunwale within six inches of the water, would think his fate inevitable'. Farther west, the smaller *canots du nord* were used. At 25-feet long, they could carry one-and-a-half tons of cargo and a crew of six.

THE AMERICAN WEST
1804-1879

1 BELOW *Early 19th-century exploration of the West was shared between government-sponsored expeditions, whose aims were scientific, and private endeavours, fuelled by the prospects of discovering new fur-trapping regions and other commercial opportunities.*

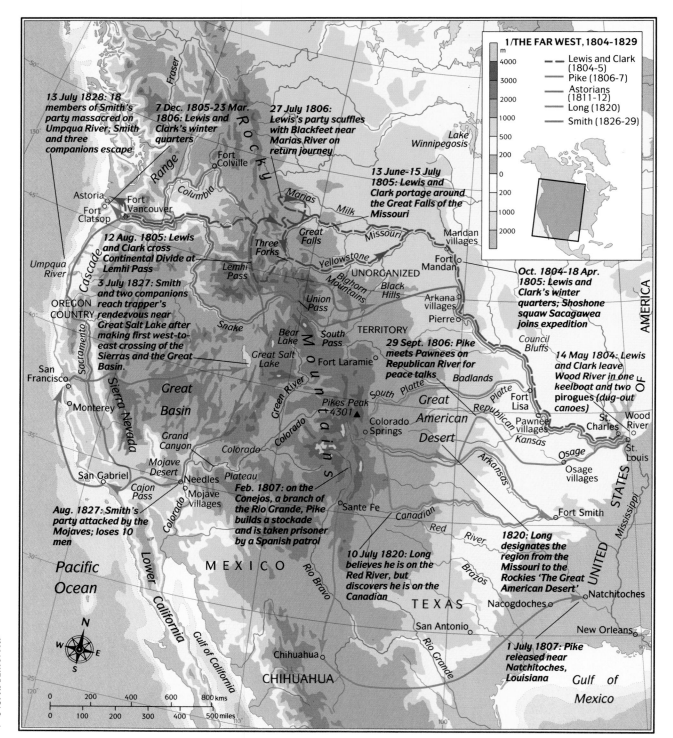

1/THE FAR WEST, 1804-1829

m
4000
3000
2000
1000
500
200
0
200
1000
2000

– – – Lewis and Clark (1804-5)
——— Pike (1806-7)
——— Astorians (1811-12)
——— Long (1820)
——— Smith (1826-29)

13 July 1828: 18 members of Smith's party massacred on Umpqua River; Smith and three companions escape

7 Dec. 1805-23 Mar. 1806: Lewis and Clark's winter quarters

27 July 1806: Lewis's party scuffles with Blackfeet near Marias River on return journey

13 June-15 July 1805: Lewis and Clark portage around the Great Falls of the Missouri

12 Aug. 1805: Lewis and Clark cross Continental Divide at Lemhi Pass

3 July 1827: Smith and two companions reach trapper's rendezvous near Great Salt Lake after making first west-to-east crossing of the Sierras and the Great Basin

Oct. 1804-18 Apr. 1805: Lewis and Clark's winter quarters; Shoshone squaw Sacagawea joins expedition

29 Sept. 1806: Pike meets Pawnees on Republican River for peace talks

14 May 1804: Lewis and Clark leave Wood River in one keelboat and two pirogues (dug-out canoes)

Aug. 1827: Smith's party attacked by the Mojaves; loses 10 men

Feb. 1807: on the Conejos, a branch of the Rio Grande, Pike builds a stockade and is taken prisoner by a Spanish patrol

10 July 1820: Long believes he is on the Red River, but discovers he is on the Canadian

1820: Long designates the region from the Missouri to the Rockies 'The Great American Desert'

1 July 1807: Pike released near Natchitoches, Louisiana

Fraser
Rocky Range
Columbia
Fort Colville
Astoria
Fort Vancouver
Fort Clatsop
Marias
Milk
Missouri
Great Falls
Yellowstone
Three Forks
Lemhi Pass
Bighorn Mountains
Black Hills
Mandan villages
Fort Mandan
Lake Winnipegosis
Umpqua River
OREGON COUNTRY
Cascade
Snake
Union Pass
Bear Lake
South Pass
Great Salt Lake
Fort Laramie
UNORGANIZED TERRITORY
Arkana villages
Pierre
Council Bluffs
San Francisco
Monterey
Sierra Nevada
Great Basin
Green River
Pikes Peak 4301
Colorado Springs
Badlands
South Platte
Platte
Republican
Fort Lisa
Pawnee villages
Kansas
St Charles
Wood River
St. Louis
Grand Canyon
Colorado
Great American Desert
Osage
Osage villages
AMERICA
UNITED STATES OF
Mojave Desert
San Gabriel
Needles
Mojave villages
Plateau
Colorado
Santa Fe
Arkansas
Canadian
Red River
Fort Smith
Cajon Pass
Lower California
MEXICO
Rio Bravo
Brazos
TEXAS
Natchitoches
Nacogdoches
New Orleans
Pacific Ocean
San Antonio
Rio Grande
Gulf of California
Chihuahua
CHIHUAHUA
Gulf of Mexico

N
W E
S

0 200 400 600 800 kms
0 100 200 300 400 500 miles

V North America

WHEN THOMAS *Jefferson became President in 1801, Americans were already acutely aware of the enticing, mysterious lands that lay west of their borders. 'Men of the Western Waters', flat-boating down the Mississippi to New Orleans, scanned the tree-shrouded western banks and dreamed of someday plunging into the wilderness. Jefferson was intensely curious: he was convinced that the nation's destiny lay west all the way to the 'South Sea'. For the fledgling nation, the elusive dream of an exploitable western passage to Asia proved as enticing as it had to their European forefathers. Now, however, it was the vision of trade with Asia, releasing Americans from their economic dependence on the Old World, which provided a fresh impetus to westward exploration.*

The vast region was not exactly Terra Incognita. Spanish knowledge began with Cabeza de Vaca and his journey across present-day Texas, New Mexico and Arizona in 1528-36 (see chs. 10 and 17). After almost two centuries of Spanish exploration, loosely linked, vaguely marked trails connected Spanish settlements from Nacogdoches in east Texas all the way across the Southwest and up to northern California. The French had also been west (see ch. 18). Jacques d'Eglise, a Frenchman encouraged by the Spanish, had made his way to the Mandan villages of the upper Missouri by 1790. Baron Louis-Armand de Lahontan claimed to have been up a 'Long River', the Mississippi, in the 1680s, and to have heard of a salt lake to the west. In 1742 the two Vérendrye brothers explored at least to Pierre, South Dakota, and may have been as far west as the Bighorn Mountains of Wyoming. Frenchmen had also made their way in an arc from north-west to south-west out of St. Louis, with the Mallet brothers reaching Santa Fe in 1739. A Frenchman named Menard was living at the Mandan villages in 1790. British trader-explorers were active in the West in the 18th century. The Welshmen David Thompson and John Evans and the Scot James Mackay were at the Mandan villages in the 1790s. By 1800, traders were forging up the Missouri, the Platte, the Osage and other rivers, returning with unverified stories of the wonders of the land.

In the 1780s and 1790s Thomas Jefferson had been frustrated in attempts to send explorers into the West. As President, he could now proceed. He offered a fellow Virginian, Captain Meriwether Lewis, leadership of an expedition to the 'South Sea' in 1804.

AMERICANS at the beginning of the 19th century had finally realized that it was thousands of miles across the deserts, mountains and plains to the South Sea. It was rumoured that in the extreme Northwest was a region called The Highlands from where the rivers that would become the Missouri-Mississippi, the Colorado and the Columbia emerged. Another stream possibly flowed north to the Arctic. To visionaries like Thomas Jefferson, the Pacific Ocean – if a practical route could be found to it – bore promise of lucrative trade with Asia for the new nation. Was there, he wondered, an all-water passage from St. Louis via the Missouri River to the Pacific?

To answer this question President Jefferson sent an expedition led by Captain Meriwether Lewis and Lieutenant William Clark to advance up the Missouri River to its headwaters, then across the Highlands, if they existed (they did not), to float down west-running streams to the Pacific Ocean. Their orders included complex instructions for scientific investigation. Lewis and Clark and their Corps of Discovery, numbering about 40 men, took two-and-a-half years (1804-6) to make the journey to the Columbia River estuary and return. They travelled almost 8,000 miles across unexplored territory (*see* panel on p.113).

Before they returned, Jefferson sent out other exploratory parties. The most notable was that conducted by Lieutenant Zebulon Montgomery Pike. Ostensibly sent to discover the headwaters of the Red River, in 1806 Pike advanced west from near St. Louis, first visiting villages of the Osage and Pawnee Indians. He then proceeded to the Arkansas River, which he followed upstream to the Rockies. He discovered and named the peak that bears his name, before advancing deep into the mountains and establishing a winter camp on a headwater stream of the Rio Grande. Here, he was captured by Spanish soldiers, who took him to the Mexican state of Chihuahua, from where he was released and returned to the United States at Natchitoches, Louisiana. His widely read *Journal* described the American Southwest as a desert in which no white people's civilization could thrive.

In 1820, Major Stephen H. Long led an exploration across the Great Plains. His expedition followed the Platte River and then its tributary, the South Platte, to the Front Range of the central Rockies. He then advanced southward to what he believed was the Red River, which he followed eastward to the settlements. To his chagrin he discovered that he had not followed the Red River, but the Canadian River, a tributary of the Arkansas. Long's report was assembled by a subordinate, the geologist Dr Edwin James. His detailed description of the flora and fauna of the Great Plains highlights the shift from pure exploration to the increasing importance of science in cataloguing the West.

By 1823, the reports of the Lewis and Clark and of the Pike and the Long expeditions were available. In addition, unofficial information continued to appear in newspapers and periodicals, culled from fur traders and trappers, among the most celebrated of whom were Jedediah Smith, Jim Bridger, Old Bill Williams and Osborne Russell. Among other independent explorers, the artist-naturalist John James Audubon and adventurous European nobility hunted, explored and sketched their way across huge areas of the West. In the 1840s, John Charles Frémont's explorations, admirably described in

2 BELOW *Although popularly known as 'the Pathfinder', Frémont's major contribution lay in spreading knowledge of the American West; the great trails he described were discovered by others.*

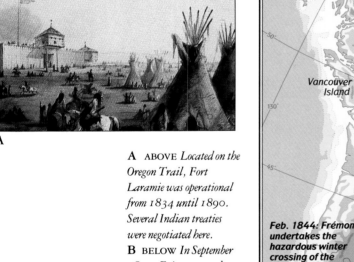

A

A ABOVE *Located on the Oregon Trail, Fort Laramie was operational from 1834 until 1890. Several Indian treaties were negotiated here.*
B BELOW *In September 1843, Frémont rowed a 'frail linen boat' across the Great Salt Lake to Frémont Island, where Preuss made this map.*

B

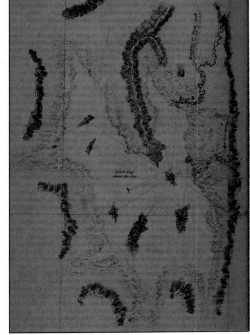

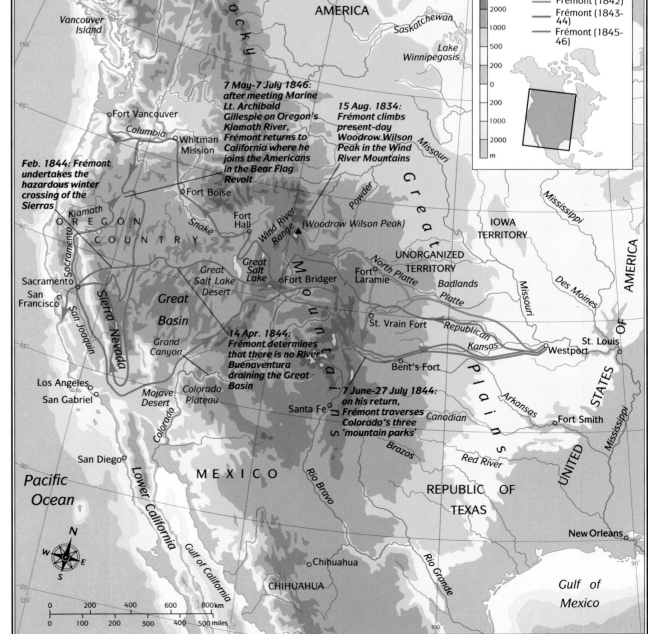

2/FRÉMONT'S GOVERNMENT-SPONSORED EXPEDITIONS, 1842-1846

— Frémont (1842)
— Frémont (1843-44)
— Frémont (1845-46)

7 May-7 July 1846: after meeting Marine Lt. Archibald Gillespie on Oregon's Klamath River, Frémont returns to California where he joins the Americans in the Bear Flag Revolt

15 Aug. 1834: Frémont climbs present-day Woodrow Wilson Peak in the Wind River Mountains

Feb. 1844: Frémont undertakes the hazardous winter crossing of the Sierras

14 Apr. 1844: Frémont determines that there is no River Buenaventura draining the Great Basin

7 June-27 July 1844: on his return, Frémont traverses Colorado's three 'mountain parks'

his reports, added to the nation's knowledge. As significantly, they helped encourage the first waves of western settlers that were beginning to cross the Missouri. By the 1850s, thousands of emigrants had reached Oregon and California. Still others had settled in Texas, while members of the Church of Jesus Christ of Latter Day Saints (the Mormons) had settled in the Salt Lake Valley. Yet communications between these far western settlements and the eastern population remained only as fast as a horse could gallop. The demand for faster and more reliable communications followed naturally.

In 1853 Congress appropriated funds for a series of surveys of the American West to determine feasible routes for a transcontinental railroad. Each survey party was to be accompanied by scientists to collect and classify flora and fauna; on a number of expeditions artists also accompanied the parties. The northern route between 47° and 49°N was surveyed by Isaac I. Stevens and Captain George B. McClellan. Captain John W. Gunnison, surveying a central route, was killed by Indians while working near Sevier Lake in Utah. Lieutenant Amiel Weeks Whipple headed the survey of the 35th parallel and Lieutenant John Parke and Captain John Pope surveyed the route along the 32nd parallel. Surveys of smaller areas, such as that for a route between Oregon and California, were also conducted. Seventeen massive volumes of scientific and geographic information were the result. The tensions of the period before the Civil War (1861-65) and the turmoil of the war itself prevented the railroads from being built, but after the war the Northern Pacific, the Union Pacific-Central Pacific, the Atchison, Topeka and Santa Fe, and the Southern Pacific railroads were built along at least parts of the routes surveyed.

C RIGHT *Hayden's odometer, pictured here in Yellowstone in 1871, was typical of the crude technology available to the topographers of the Great Surveys.* D BELOW *William Henry Holmes, who travelled with Hayden, was the greatest artist-topographer to work for the Surveys. This view of the La Plata Mountains, Colorado, reveals his painstaking approach.*

The Civil War similarly put a temporary end to further government-sponsored exploration. The end of hostilities, however, saw a frenzy of activity westward. The first transcontinental railroad, completed in 1869, was followed by four more by 1893. Settlement was so rapid that in 1890 the Director of the Bureau of the Census declared that the American frontier was at an end. The Wounded Knee massacre (29 December 1890) effectively ended the Indian Wars, removing the

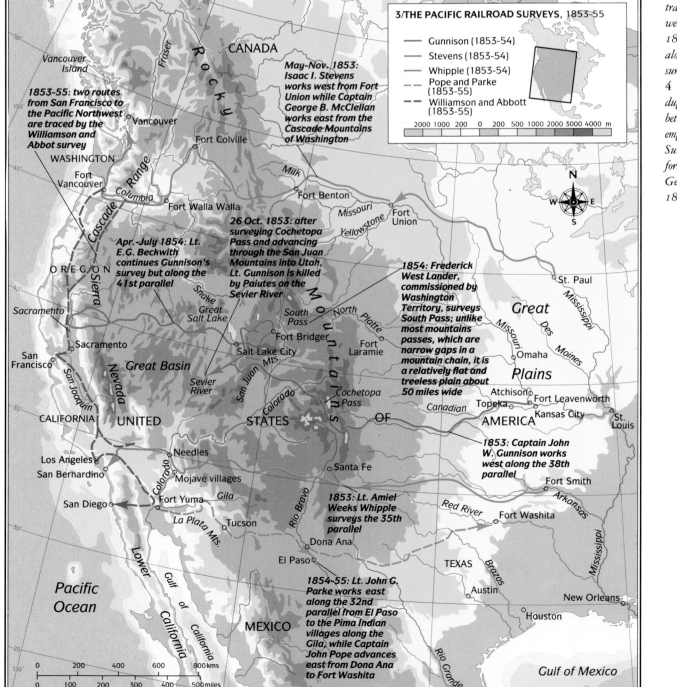

3/THE PACIFIC RAILROAD SURVEYS, 1853-55

- Gunnison (1853-54)
- Stevens (1853-54)
- Whipple (1853-54)
- Pope and Parke (1853-55)
- Williamson and Abbott (1853-55)

2000 1000 200 0 200 500 1000 2000 3000 4000 m

CANADA

Vancouver Island

Fraser

ROCKY

1853-55: two routes from San Francisco to the Pacific Northwest are traced by the Williamson and Abbot survey

Vancouver

Fort Colville

May-Nov. 1853: Isaac I. Stevens works west from Fort Union while Captain George B. McClellan works east from the Cascade Mountains of Washington

WASHINGTON

Fort Vancouver

Cascade Range

Columbia

Fort Walla Walla

Milk

Fort Benton

Missouri

Yellowstone

Fort Union

Apr.-July 1854: Lt. E.G. Beckwith continues Gunnison's survey but along the 41st parallel

26 Oct. 1853: after surveying Cochetopa Pass and advancing through the San Juan Mountains into Utah, Lt. Gunnison is killed by Paiutes on the Sevier River

OREGON

Sierra

Snake

Great Salt Lake

South Pass

North Platte

Mountains

Fort Bridger

Fort Laramie

1854: Frederick West Lander, commissioned by Washington Territory, surveys South Pass; unlike most mountains passes, which are narrow gaps in a mountain chain, it is a relatively flat and treeless plain about 50 miles wide

Great Plains

Mississippi

St. Paul

Des Moines

Missouri

Omaha

Sacramento

Sacramento

Great Basin

Nevada

Salt Lake City

Sevier River

San Juan Mts.

Colorado

Cochetopa Pass

OF

AMERICA

Atchison

Fort Leavenworth

Topeka

Kansas City

St. Louis

San Francisco

San Joaquin

CALIFORNIA

UNITED

STATES

Canadian

1853: Captain John W. Gunnison works west along the 38th parallel

Needles

Los Angeles

San Bernardino

Mojave villages

Colorado

Santa Fe

Fort Smith

Arkansas

Red River

Fort Washita

1853: Lt. Amiel Weeks Whipple surveys the 35th parallel

San Diego

Fort Yuma

Gila

La Plata Mts.

Tucson

Rio Bravo

Dona Ana

El Paso

1854-55: Lt. John G. Parke works east along the 32nd parallel from El Paso to the Pima Indian villages along the Gila, while Captain John Pope advances east from Dona Ana to Fort Washita

TEXAS

Brazos

Austin

Mississippi

New Orleans

Houston

Pacific Ocean

Gulf of California

Lower

MEXICO

Rio Grande

Gulf of Mexico

0 200 400 600 800 kms
0 100 200 300 400 500 miles

3 LEFT *Although no transcontinental railroads were built until the late 1860s, at least four ran along routes partially surveyed in 1853-55.*
4 RIGHT *Increasing duplication and conflict between the work of those employed by the Great Surveys lead to the formation of the U.S. Geological Survey in 1879.*

Vancouver Island

WASHINGTON TERRITORY

Portland

OREGON

San Francisco

NEVADA

Aug.-Sept. 1869: Powell loses three men to Shivwits Indians

CALIFORNIA

Los Angeles

San Diego

1869-79: Powell studies the geology of the canyon country and the Colorado Plateau

Pacific Ocean

0 200 400 kms
0 100 200 300 kms

threats to European settlement posed by the Indians.

To scientists, the American West was a challenging region. In a surge of scientific activity, four government-sponsored expeditions – the Great Surveys – explored the American West between 1867 and 1878. When they were merged into the single United States Geological Survey, they had already solved many of the mysteries of the region.

The first of these surveys was the United States Geological Survey of the 40th parallel, commonly known as the King Survey. Its Director, Clarence King, conceived the idea of making a thorough scientific survey of a 100-mile-wide strip through which the Union Pacific-Central Pacific Railroads passed from Cheyenne in south-east Wyoming to the California-Nevada boundary. Begun in 1867, its field work was essentially completed by 1872, but several more years were necessary to produce the seven volumes of scientific reports and an atlas.

The most productive of the Great Surveys was Dr Ferdinand Vandiveer Hayden's United States Geological and Geographical Survey of the Territories. Between 1867 and 1878 Hayden's organization explored the Yellowstone region; first reported the cliff dwellings in the Southwest; and produced an atlas of Colorado. Major John Wesley Powell's United States Geological Survey of the Rocky Mountain Region likewise did remarkable geological work. Powell descended the Colorado River canyons and wrote up the geology of the region, while a subordinate, Grove Karl Gilbert, produced a landmark study of the Henry Mountains in south-east Utah. The fourth survey, Lieutenant George M. Wheeler's United States Geographical Survey West of the 100th Meridian, proved less significant, although major geological work was conducted under its aegis.

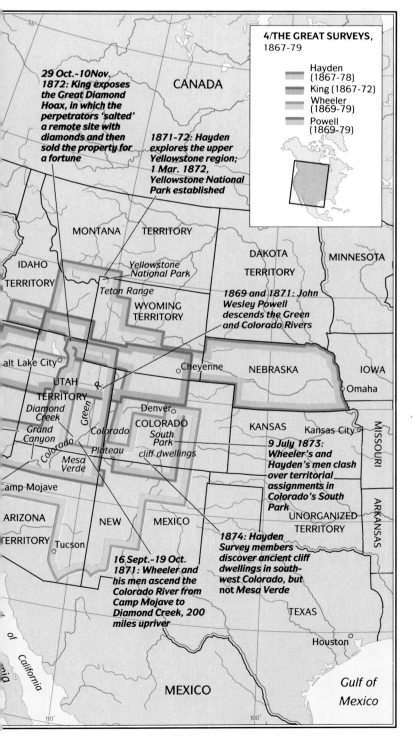

4/THE GREAT SURVEYS, 1867-79

Hayden (1867-78)
King (1867-72)
Wheeler (1869-79)
Powell (1869-79)

29 Oct.-10Nov. 1872: King exposes the Great Diamond Hoax, in which the perpetrators 'salted' a remote site with diamonds and then sold the property for a fortune

1871-72: Hayden explores the upper Yellowstone region; 1 Mar. 1872, Yellowstone National Park established

1869 and 1871: John Wesley Powell descends the Green and Colorado Rivers

9 July 1873: Wheeler's and Hayden's men clash over territorial assignments in Colorado's South Park

1874: Hayden Survey members discover ancient cliff dwellings in south-west Colorado, but not Mesa Verde

16.Sept.-19 Oct. 1871: Wheeler and his men ascend the Colorado River from Camp Mojave to Diamond Creek, 200 miles upriver

LEWIS AND CLARK

THE LEWIS and Clark Expedition lasted from May 1804 until September 1806. During it, the 'Corps of Discovery' ascended the Missouri River to its origin, crossed the Rocky Mountains and floated down the Columbia River to the Pacific. The expedition had a variety of aims: the search for a Northwest Passage; the opening of commercial possibilities; the recording of the animal and plant life of the Northwest; the establishment of good relations with the Indians. But its most lasting success could not have been anticipated at its outset: the revelation of the richness, diversity and scale of the region. Lewis and Clark reinforced the belief of many that the destiny of the United States would be forged in the vast spaces of the West. Although not conventionally well educated, Meriwether Lewis and William Clark were intelligent and resourceful. They returned with more information – compiled more systematically – then any previous explorers of North America. Clark, for example, though he had received no formal cartographic training, diligently mapped the expedition's course. (E) is his map of the portage around the Great Falls of the Missouri; (C) is his similarly careful map of the 'Great Shoote', or rapids, of the Columbia River. (A) is the bird since called Lewis's woodpecker, stuffed by the explorer and possibly the last surviving zoological specimen of the expedition. (D) is Lewis's sketch of a eulachon, or candlefish, whose fatty flesh, as Lewis reported, will burn like candle wax. The engraving of Lewis (B) shows him wearing the tippet (a long, scarf-like hat) presented to him by Chief Cameahwait of the Shoshones.

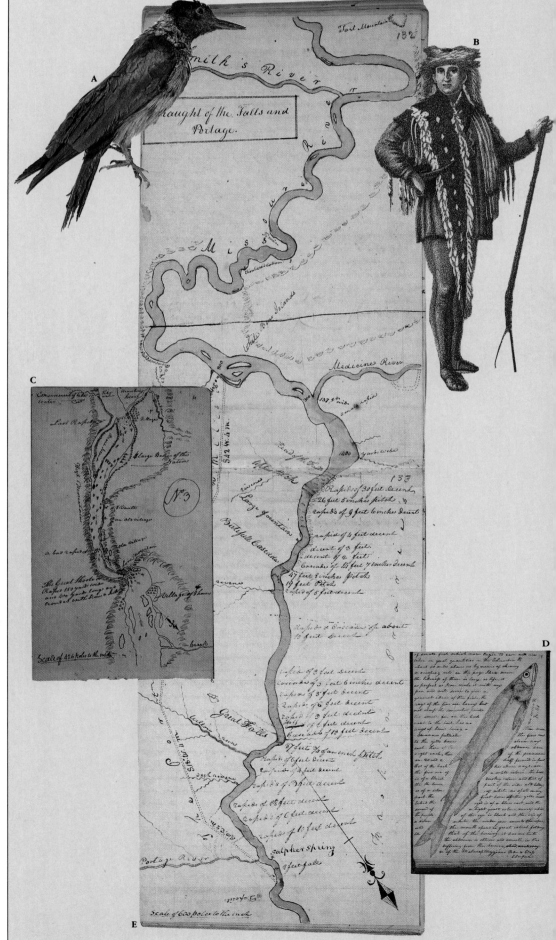

23
THE NORTHWEST PASSAGE REVEALED
1818-1906

ON 25 OCTOBER 1850 Commander McClure and a party of British sailors, from their vantage point on Banks Island at 73°30'N, sighted the frozen waters of Viscount Melville Sound to the east. McClure's ships had come through Bering Strait from the Pacific; Viscount Melville Sound had been discovered 30 years earlier by Parry's expedition forcing its way westward from Baffin Bay. A Northwest Passage had at last been found. It was not the short-cut between the oceans sought by earlier explorers. The passage laboriously traced by British expeditions in the first half of the 19th century was a labyrinth of narrow channels, choked by ice for much of the year. The search was marked by a clash of opposing methods between the Royal Navy and the Hudson's Bay Company. The Navy used heavy ships designed to smash a way through the ice; land journeys were made with unwieldy sledges hauled by gangs of sailors. In contrast, the Company explorers travelled singly or in small groups, living off the land and using light sleds pulled by dogs. They copied Inuit methods of travel, clothing and diet. The charting of the Arctic archipelago in the 19th century was the result of a marriage, not always harmonious, between the two methods.

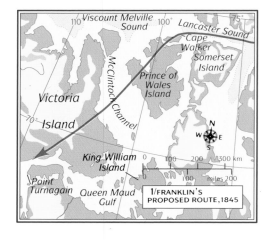

1 LEFT *Franklin in 1845 was instructed to sail across the unmapped area south-west of Cape Walker. It turned out to be land. The expedition left its iced-in ships off King William Island.*
2 BELOW *Expeditions in the 19th century revealed the intricate geography of the northernmost regions of America.*

1/FRANKLIN'S PROPOSED ROUTE, 1845

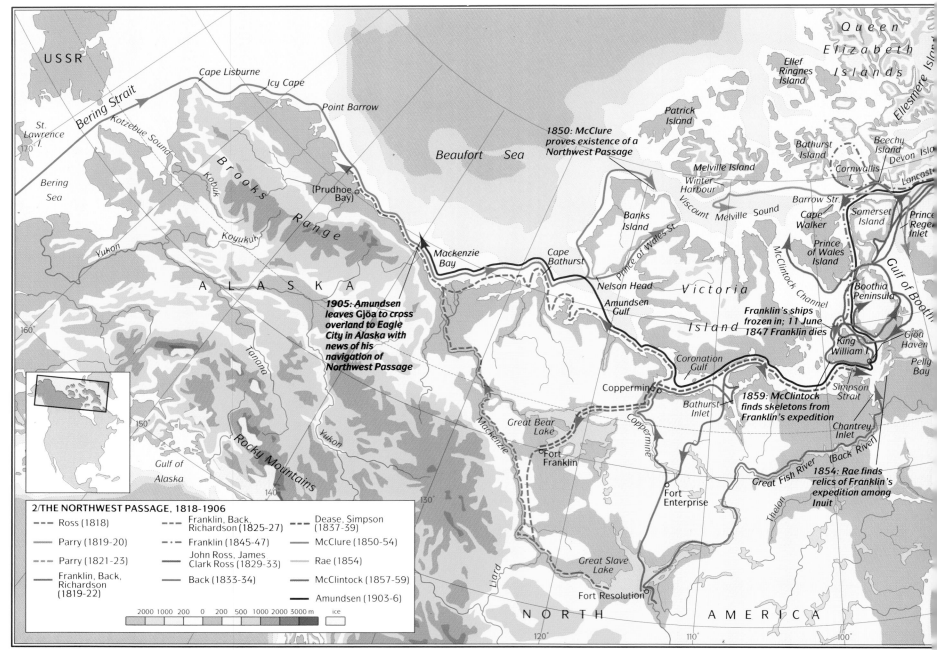

1850: McClure proves existence of a Northwest Passage

1905: Amundsen leaves Gjöa to cross overland to Eagle City in Alaska with news of his navigation of Northwest Passage

Franklin's ships frozen in; 11 June 1847 Franklin dies

1859: McClintock finds skeletons from Franklin's expedition

1854: Rae finds relics of Franklin's expedition among Inuit

2/THE NORTHWEST PASSAGE, 1818-1906

- - - - Ross (1818)
──── Parry (1819-20)
- - - - Parry (1821-23)
──── Franklin, Back, Richardson (1819-22)
- - - - Franklin, Back, Richardson (1825-27)
─·─·─ Franklin (1845-47)
──── John Ross, James Clark Ross (1829-33)
──── Back (1833-34)
──── Dease, Simpson (1837-39)
──── McClure (1850-54)
──── Rae (1854)
──── McClintock (1857-59)
──── Amundsen (1903-6)

2000 1000 200 0 200 500 1000 2000 3000 m   ice

IN 1818 the British Admiralty, with men and ships to spare following the end of the Napoleonic Wars, and encouraged by whalers' reports that Davis Strait was ice-free, sent James Ross and William Parry north to find a way through to the Pacific. They rediscovered Baffin Bay, which had faded from the maps since Baffin's voyage in the early 17th century (see ch. 16), and entered Lancaster Sound. The next year Parry returned to the Arctic and pushed 500 miles farther west, into Viscount Melville Sound, where he wintered. His progress was blocked by polar ice squeezing down from the Beaufort Sea into Viscount Melville Sound and farther south. The Admiralty turned its attentions to the possibility of a passage along the continental shore. Another naval officer, John Franklin, traced long stretches of the coast in overland expeditions in 1821 and 1826 before private and commercial expeditions took up the search. Most notably, James Ross carried out further exploration of Parry's Prince Regent Inlet (where his ship was frozen in for three winters, and eventually abandoned), located the magnetic pole on the west coast of Boothia Peninsula, and crossed King William Island. When an overland expedition under George Back looking for Ross followed the Great Fish River down to the coast most of the continental shoreline had been explored, and the remaining stretches were mapped by Peter Dease and Thomas Simpson of the Hudson's Bay Company in a series of journeys between 1837 and 1839.

It was still uncertain whether Boothia and King William Island were peninsulas – and thus obstacles to a sea-passage along the mainland coast – or islands. More worrying was the lack of knowledge about the region south-west of Cape Walker at the entrance of Viscount Melville Sound. In 1845 the Admiralty sent Franklin there with two ships, 134 men and instructions to sail across that uncharted area to the channels discovered by Dease and Franklin off the American mainland. The expedition became frozen in near the northern tip of King

William Island. Franklin died in 1847, and his ships were abandoned the following year by the remaining 104 men, all of whom died in attempting to cross King William Island to the mainland coast at the mouth of the Great Fish River. Before long there were a dozen ships in the Arctic looking for Franklin, part of a massive search operation which, though it failed to find the lost explorer, in the process charted most of the remaining unexplored areas of the Arctic archipelago. It was during the search that McClure made his discovery of a passage in 1850. Not until 1854 was there definite news of Franklin, when the Hudson's Bay Company explorer, John Rae, heard reports from the Inuit of Boothia about a large party of white men who had starved to death farther west some years earlier. Relics among the Inuit confirmed that these were Franklin's men. Five years later on King William Island, a party led by McClintock found a sad trail of skeletons, sledges and other objects from Franklin's ships. Further relics have continued to turn up, and examination of some of the human remains has shown that the main causes of death were scurvy, starvation and possibly lead poisoning (from the primitive soldered cans containing tinned meat). 'Franklin's crew took their environment with them', wrote the 20th-century Arctic traveller, William Stefansson, and they died in the process.

If the searches for Franklin had found a Northwest Passage, it was not one of commercial significance. Not until the first decade of the 20th century was one of the several possible routes successfully navigated. In a superb feat of endurance and seamanship, the Norwegian Roald Amundsen in the tiny ship *Gjöa* threaded his way through the Arctic maze south and then west from Lancaster Sound and along the mainland coast to Bering Strait. The voyage took four seasons, from 1903 to 1906. Not until 1943 was there another navigation of the passage, when an expedition on board the motor vessel *St. Roch* followed McClure's more northerly route.

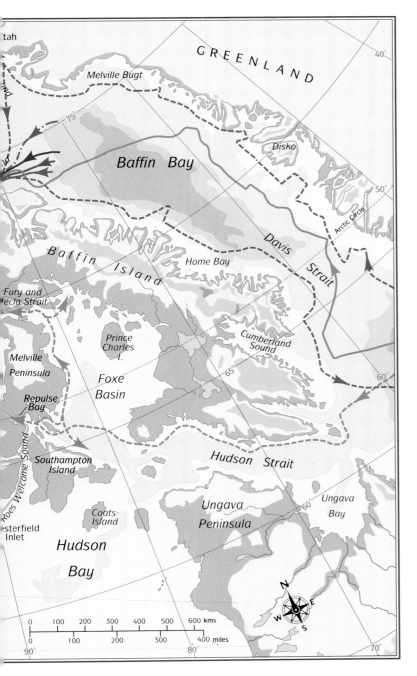

A

B

C

A ABOVE RIGHT *A drawing by John Sacheuse, the Inuit interpreter on Ross's Arctic voyage in 1818, shows the meeting between Captain Ross and Lieutenant Parry, in full naval uniform, and the Inuit of North Greenland.*
B CENTRE *A scene from Parry's second Arctic voyage (1819-20) showing the crews engaged in the laborious task of cutting a passage through the ice for the ships.*
C BELOW RIGHT *Two ships of Sir Edward Belcher's 1852-54 voyage in search of Franklin frozen in for the long, dark Arctic winter.*

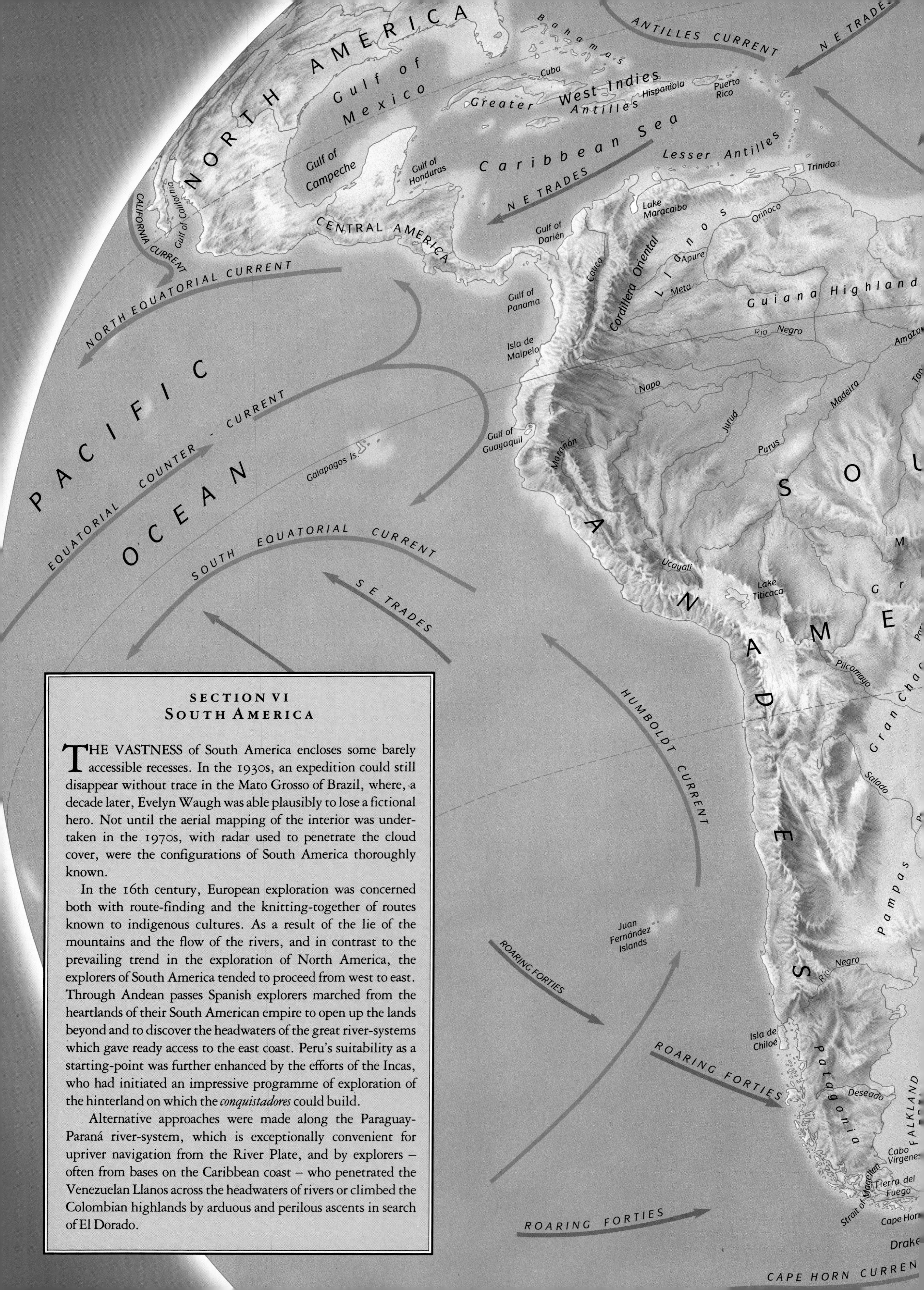

NORTH AMERICA

Gulf of Mexico

Gulf of Campeche

Gulf of Honduras

Bahamas

Cuba

Greater West Indies Antilles

Hispaniola

Puerto Rico

ANTILLES CURRENT

N E TRADES

Caribbean Sea

Lesser Antilles

Trinidad

N E TRADES

CENTRAL AMERICA

Gulf of Darién

Lake Maracaibo

Orinoco

L l a n o s

Apure

Meta

Guiana Highland

CALIFORNIA CURRENT

Gulf of California

Cauca

Cordillera Oriental

NORTH EQUATORIAL CURRENT

Gulf of Panama

Isla de Malpelo

Rio Negro

Amazo

PACIFIC

EQUATORIAL COUNTER - CURRENT

Napo

Juruá

Madeira

S O U

Gulf of Guayaquil

Galapagos Is.

Marañón

Purus

OCEAN

SOUTH EQUATORIAL CURRENT

S E TRADES

Ucayali

A N

Lake Titicaca

M

N A M E

Pilcomayo

Gran Chaco

HUMBOLDT CURRENT

Pampas

ROARING FORTIES

Juan Fernández Islands

Negro

Rio Negro

Salado

D

ROARING FORTIES

Isla de Chiloé

Patagonia

Deseado

FALKLAND

ROARING FORTIES

Cabo Vírgenes

Tierra del Fuego

Strait of Magellan

Cape Hor

CAPE HORN CURREN

Drake

SECTION VI
SOUTH AMERICA

THE VASTNESS of South America encloses some barely accessible recesses. In the 1930s, an expedition could still disappear without trace in the Mato Grosso of Brazil, where, a decade later, Evelyn Waugh was able plausibly to lose a fictional hero. Not until the aerial mapping of the interior was undertaken in the 1970s, with radar used to penetrate the cloud cover, were the configurations of South America thoroughly known.

In the 16th century, European exploration was concerned both with route-finding and the knitting-together of routes known to indigenous cultures. As a result of the lie of the mountains and the flow of the rivers, and in contrast to the prevailing trend in the exploration of North America, the explorers of South America tended to proceed from west to east. Through Andean passes Spanish explorers marched from the heartlands of their South American empire to open up the lands beyond and to discover the headwaters of the great river-systems which gave ready access to the east coast. Peru's suitability as a starting-point was further enhanced by the efforts of the Incas, who had initiated an impressive programme of exploration of the hinterland on which the *conquistadores* could build.

Alternative approaches were made along the Paraguay-Paraná river-system, which is exceptionally convenient for upriver navigation from the River Plate, and by explorers – often from bases on the Caribbean coast – who penetrated the Venezuelan Llanos across the headwaters of rivers or climbed the Colombian highlands by arduous and perilous ascents in search of El Dorado.

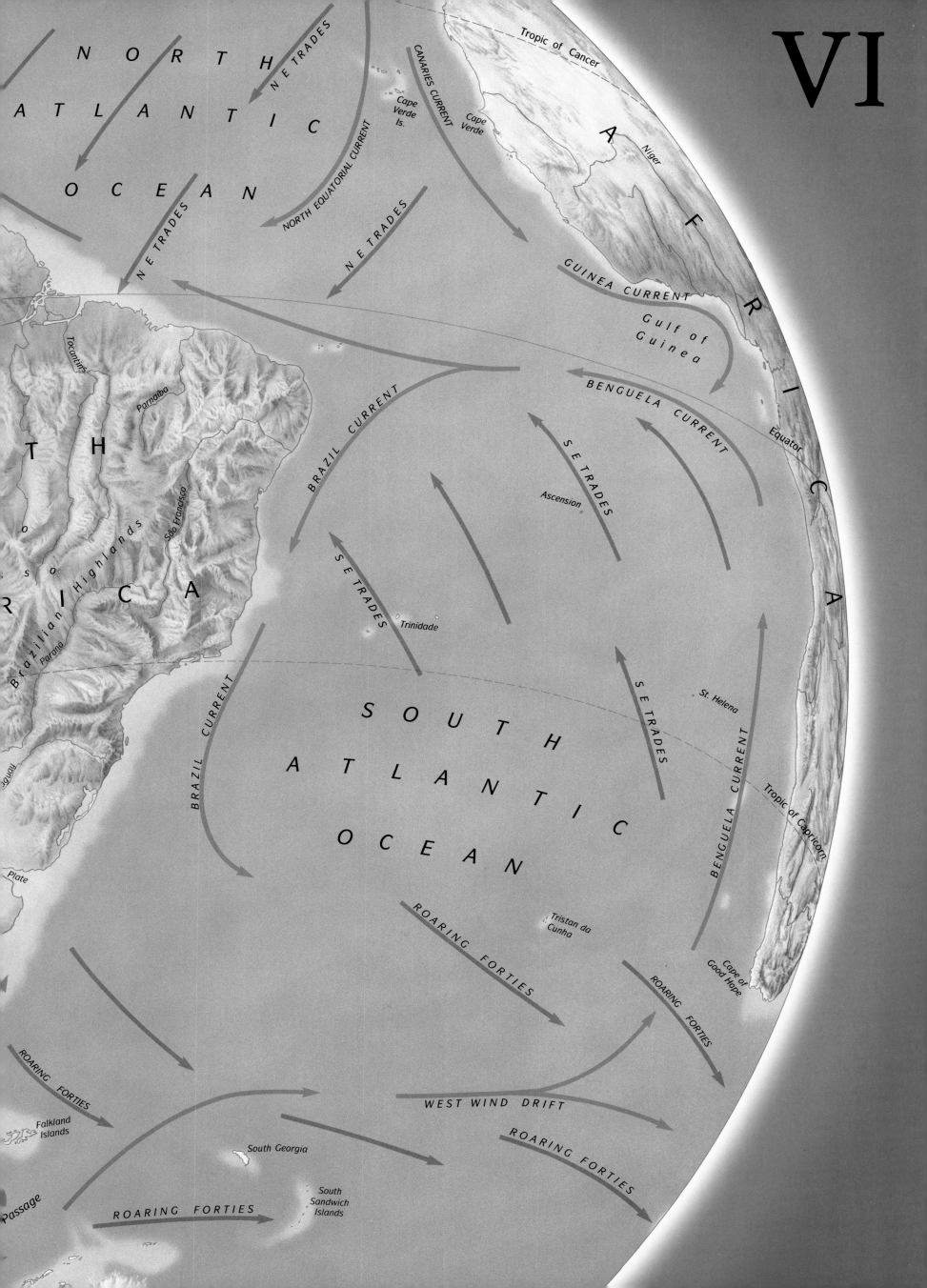

NORTH

ATLANTIC

OCEAN

N E TRADES

N E TRADES

N E TRADES

N E TRADES

CANARIES CURRENT

NORTH EQUATORIAL CURRENT

Tropic of Cancer

Cape Verde Is.

Cape Verde

A F R I C A

Niger

GUINEA CURRENT

Gulf of Guinea

Equator

BENGUELA CURRENT

Tocantins

Parnaíba

São Francisco

Brazilian Highlands

Paraná

BRAZIL CURRENT

BRAZIL CURRENT

BRAZIL CURRENT

S E TRADES

S E TRADES

S E TRADES

S E TRADES

Trinidade

Ascension

St. Helena

BENGUELA CURRENT

Tropic of Capricorn

SOUTH

ATLANTIC

OCEAN

SOUTH

AMERICA

Plate

Tristan da Cunha

ROARING FORTIES

ROARING FORTIES

Cape of Good Hope

ROARING FORTIES

Falkland Islands

WEST WIND DRIFT

ROARING FORTIES

South Georgia

Passage

ROARING FORTIES

South Sandwich Islands

24
OUTWARDS FROM PERU
1519-1744

A BELOW *Mid-16th-century maps such as this, taken from the* Mappemonde Dieppoise, *and made before the fanning out of exploration from Peru passed into cartographic tradition, showed few place names on the Pacific coast and an interior only vaguely embellished.*

A

LA MER DV SV

MER PACIFIQUE OV DE MAGELLAN

TROPIC

SPANISH *penetration of South America in the 16th century made little use of Atlantic bases. Some explorers were inhibited by the ill-defined zone of Portuguese sovereignty; others were deterred by the inhospitable climes and the paucity of exploitable assets. Apart from a few expeditions which began on the Caribbean coast, it was only from around the River Plate that much progress in exploration was made via the Atlantic (see ch.26).*

Thus, despite its remoteness from Spain, the Pacific became the Spanish highway to most of the South American interior. Peru, with its vast wealth and its dense concentration of native manpower, became Spain's vital bridgehead. It had to be approached from the Caribbean or New Spain, overland across the Isthmus and then by ship, but, once reached, provided promising routes towards 'unknown' lands.

First, there were the Inca roads into Colombia, Bolivia and southern Peru. From their remoter points, Spaniards could pick up ways already known to the inhabitants into territories beyond the reach of Inca hegemony: in the north, the Orinoco and Amazon river-systems; in the south, the trails followed by some of the most adventurous conquistadores into Chile and Tucumán. By the first of these trails Diego de Almagro struggled south from Lake Titicaca in 1535; by the second Pedro de Valdivia began the conquest of Chile in 1541; by the last Diego de Rojas crossed the Chaco to begin the conquest of Tucumán in 1543. Until well into the next century, explorers and missionaries gradually established a system of communications, between routes such as these and the avenues of access created by great rivers (see ch.26), which encompassed most of the continent. The European role involved little original path-finding, for it depended on guidance from the indigenous inhabitants, but it did meld native routes and natural causeways into a single system.

The last explorers' route from Peru on the other hand was a genuinely Spanish creation, linking Peru and Chile by sea. In some ways this was the most remarkable achievement of all; registered against wind and current, along inhospitable coasts or out into the Pacific. It, too, was motivated by cupidity: the gold Valdivia found in Chile made the opening of communications seem worthwhile, while the landward routes were beaten in the search for fabulous, wealthy lands in the image of Mexico and Peru.

E XPLORATION of the Pacific coast of the Isthmus of Panama made slow progress in the decade after Balboa's discovery (see ch.10). The farthest-reaching expedition — that of Gaspar de Espinosa, who explored by land and sea as far as Punta Burica in 1519 — went north; and though there were expeditions southward into the 'Mar del Sur', on Balboa's orders, in 1514, 1515 and 1517, these achieved so little that Pascual de Andagoya was able to claim in 1522 that 'this land has never been revealed, either by land or sea, from the Gulf of San Miguel southward'. Andagoya was a henchman of Pedrarias Dávila, who replaced Balboa and put him to death. He therefore had a vested interest in suppressing the achievements of his predecessors and arrogating to himself the distinction of garnering the first news of the existence of Peru. The terms in which he later recalled his commission from Pedrarias in 1522 — 'to discover the chief of Peru and the coast beyond the Gulf of San Miguel' — may, however, merely betray the influence of hindsight. By his own account, Andagoya's 1522 voyage was first to report 'a province called Birú', and directly inspired Pizarro's conquest. It seems improbable that his Birú was the great empire of Tahuantinsuyo to which the name 'Peru' became transferred. It is possible, however, that Andagoya's expedition ventured deep into what is now Colombia (see map 1).

The long story of the assimilation of Birú and Tahuantinsuyo, and of the transformation of both into Peru, really begins

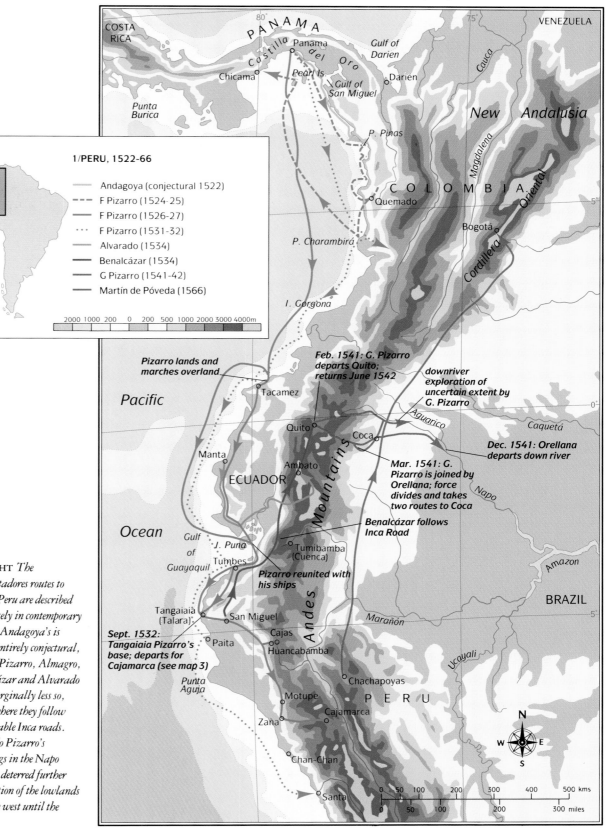

1 RIGHT *The conquistadores routes to and in Peru are described imprecisely in contemporary sources: Andagoya's is almost entirely conjectural, those of Pizarro, Almagro, Benalcázar and Alvarado only marginally less so, except where they follow identifiable Inca roads. Gonzalo Pizarro's sufferings in the Napo Valley, deterred further exploration of the lowlands from the west until the 1560s.*

1/PERU, 1522-66

— Andagoya (conjectural 1522)
--- F Pizarro (1524-25)
— F Pizarro (1526-27)
··· F Pizarro (1531-32)
— Alvarado (1534)
— Benalcázar (1534)
— G Pizarro (1541-42)
— Martín de Póveda (1566)

2000 1000 200 0 200 500 1000 2000 3000 4000m

COSTA RICA
PANAMA
VENEZUELA
Panama
Castilla del Oro
Gulf of Darien
Chicama
Pearl Is.
Gulf of San Miguel
Darien
Punta Burica
P. Pinas
New Andalusia
Cauca
Magdalena
COLOMBIA
Cordillera Oriental
Quemado
Bógota
P. Charambirá
I. Gorgona

Feb. 1541: G. Pizarro departs Quito; returns June 1542
downriver exploration of uncertain extent by G. Pizarro

Pizarro lands and marches overland
Tacamez
Pacific
Quito
Aguarico
Coca
Caquetá
Dec. 1541: Orellana departs down river
Manta
Ambato
ECUADOR
Andes Mountains
Mar. 1541: G. Pizarro is joined by Orellana; force divides and takes two routes to Coca
Napo
Ocean
Gulf of Guayaquil
J. Puná
Tumibamba (Cuenca)
Benalcázar follows Inca Road
Pizarro reunited with his ships
Amazon
Tumbes
BRAZIL
Tangaiaia (Talara)
San Miguel
Cajas
Sept. 1532: Tangaiaia Pizarro's base; departs for Cajamarca (see map 3)
Paita
Huancabamba
Marañón
Punta Aguja
Chachapoyas
Ucayali
PERU
Motupe
Cajamarca
Zana
Chan-Chan
Santa

N S E W

0 50 100 200 300 400 500 kms
0 50 100 200 300 miles

with the formation of a company in Panama in October 1524 to follow up Andagoya's information. The finance was subscribed in secret by Gaspar de Espinosa, using a priest, Hernando de Luque, as his nominee. The active partners were Diego de Almagro and Francisco Pizarro. Both were bastards: the first a misfit who became a runaway soldier at 15; the second a veteran of Balboa's band, who had the advantage of a clannish viper's brood of resolute, desperate brothers. The partners' self-perception is captured in the terms of the commission they eventually received from the crown for the conquest of Peru. Luque was to be a bishop, Almagro a governor and 'nobleman of some recognised seat', and the illiterate Pizarro a 'governor, captain-general and *adelantado*'.

Before obtaining these gratifying promises, Pizarro and Almagro had to endure appalling hardship and privation during three years of preparatory exploratory voyages from December 1524. When their companions' resolution flagged in 1527, Pizarro is said to have drawn a line with his sword in the sand and invited those willing to continue to cross it with him: the 13 'immortals' saved the enterprise, as, on another occasion (in March 1526), did 20,000 gold pesos subscribed by Espinosa 'to win or lose, as it shall please God'. Despite the loss of various fingers and an eye in combat with Indians, Almagro was tireless in recruiting manpower. Nevertheless, when Pizarro set out to conquer the Incas in January 1531, he had only 185 men. He was lucky to face an empire crumbling from rebellion at the edges and civil war at its heart. His strategy was copied from the example of Cortés: to capture the supreme ruler and exploit the empire through him. Though ill judged in Mexico, this method proved more serviceable in Tahuantinsuyo, which was much more like a unitary state with effective centres of command.

The state of civil war allowed Pizarro to establish a coastal base before venturing inland to meet the victor in the conflict. His own route followed the Inca road; a detachment led by his brother climbed across country to try the higher road through Huancabamba. When they met the victorious Atahualpa for a conference at Cajamarca in November 1532, they relied on surprise and cold steel to overcome odds of over 15-to-one, and on their capture of Atahualpa himself to deter vengeance by the huge armies he still commanded in the environs. Shortly afterwards, Atahualpa's men defeated and killed his rival and half-brother, Huascar. The captive Inca drank from his brother's gold-mounted skull, while a palace room was filled to a depth of nine feet with the ransom, which he promised Pizarro as the price of his life.

In the manner of kidnappers, Pizarro kept the gold and killed the victim, taking advantage of the disarray of Tahuantinsuyo to seize Cuzco, the main city of the southern Inca empire, where he attempted to centre his puppet state. It fell to the latecomers to the conquest – Sebastián Benalcázar, Diego de Almagro and Pedro de Alvarado – to dispute the honour of capturing the northern 'capital' at Quito. Almagro and Benal-

cázar maintained reasonably fraternal relations and combined to buy off Alvarado with 120,000 gold ducats. The treasure of Peru was already beginning to yield dividends.

Benalcázar was a man of similar stamp to Almagro and Pizarro – he had come to the Indies as a poor escapee from a family feud, and, after service with Pedrarias Dávila, had managed to recruit a ship and 30 men to aid the conquerors of Peru. He contributed more to the history of exploration than either of the other captains, sending reconnaissance parties in every direction once the Spanish hold on Quito was secure and undertaking a major expedition of his own into the Colombian highlands (*see* ch.25).

The role of Benalcázar beyond the limits of the Inca empire in the north was to be echoed in the south, though with less success, by Almagro. He had arrived in Peru only after the capture of Atahualpa; he had been beaten to the conquest of Quito; and the terms of the crown's rewards to the conquerors, negotiated in Spain by Hernando Pizarro, who carried Atahual-

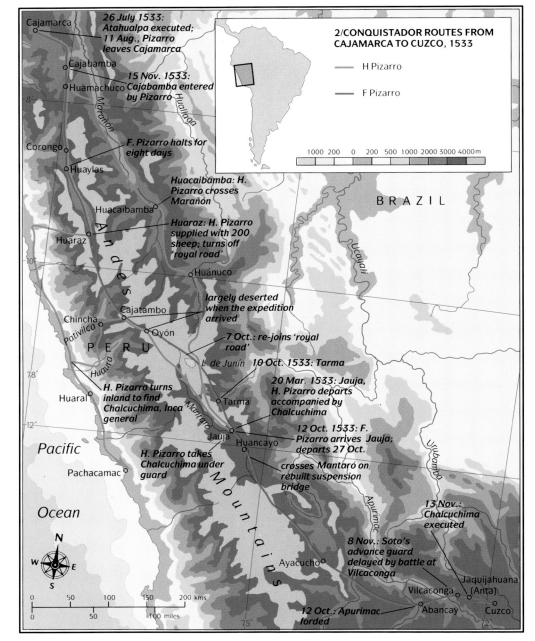

2 ABOVE *and* 3 BELOW *The conquerors of Peru were crossing a fairly unitary state traversed by impressive roads. A detachment from Francisco Pizarro's party, commanded by his brother Hernando, made a diversion to potential allies on the coast and to reconnoitre the high road to Cuzco.*

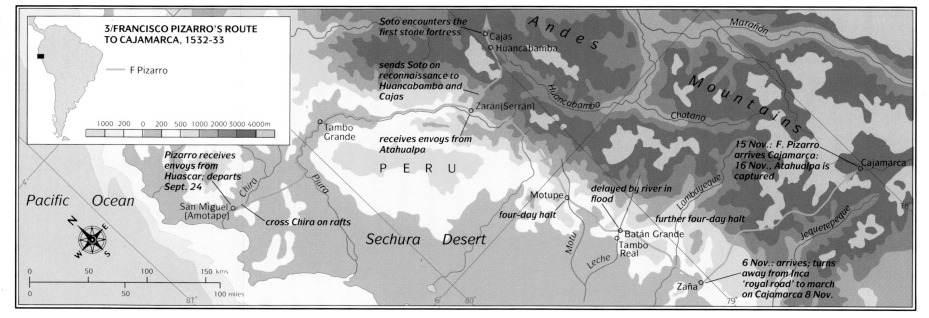

pa's ransom to his sovereign, assigned him an apparently remote governorship in 'New Toledo' south of the Inca domains. He was minded to fight the Pizarro brothers for a more equitable distribution of the spoils, but allowed himself to be persuaded to venture the conquest of Chile with capital subscribed by the brothers from Inca booty. The land was not utterly unknown. The Incas retained vestigial claims to sovereignty, calling the inhabitants 'rebels', and recalled, with possibly legendary embellishments, the campaigns of the fabulously well-travelled Tupa Inca Yupanqui as far south as the River Bíobío. They knew two routes to Chile, both hazardous: one across the Atacama desert; one across the badlands from Lake Titicaca. Almagro chose the latter because he intended to take a vast army of conquest, 12,000-Indians strong. The scale of the expedition reflected his fantasy of finding a second Peru, not the realities of the inhospitable terrain to be crossed beyond reach of supply. But by reaching fertile country in the Aconcagua valley, Almagro did establish the viability of a future, more manageable expedition.

Almagro returned to Peru to launch the series of internecine wars between his followers and Pizarro's, which led to the deaths of both protagonists. His successors in the south were men of quality, who stamped the conquest and colonization of this remotest province of Spain's American empire with a curiously aristocratic character. The first was Pedro de Valdivia, appointed by the crown to be Pizarro's royal standard-bearer. Almagro's self-inflicted disgrace gave Valdivia a chance to supplicate for a conquest of his own. In 1540 he revealed a talent for organisation and leadership of a high order. He took a force of 150 Spaniards and 3,000 Indians by Almagro's return route across the Atacama desert, avoiding disaster by ensuring precarious and laborious seaborne supplies. In 1544 he returned to Peru, where he became entangled in the civil wars; but the 80,000 pesos of gold he had brought with him ensured that he would be able to go back to Chile with plenty of new recruits. On his second expedition, he crossed the River Bíobío, the presumed limit of Inca exploration, and began in earnest the reduction of the 'Araucanos', the indomitable Indians of southern Chile.

His indefatigable efforts included the founding of 'cities' as far south as Concepción; the despatch of expeditions across the Sierra under Juan de Villagra; the sending of Francisco de Aguirre to found a permanent colony at Tucumán, Santiago del Estero; and the exploration of the coast to the Strait of Magellan under Francisco de Ulloa. But his unremitting drive exceeded his slender resources. The Araucanos were an almost unconquerable foe and Valdivia fell fighting them in December 1553. The conquest of Chile, disputed by his lieutenants, hung in the balance. But a felicitous appointment by the newly arrived viceroy in Peru assigned the job to García Hurtado de Mendoza, and assured that the Spanish presence would be confirmed and extended.

The routes followed by Mendoza's campaigns south of the

4 RIGHT *Diego de Almagro's attempt to conquer Chile opened up two new routes into lands outside the Inca empire: across the Atacama desert into Chile; and south from Lake Titicaca towards Tucumán.* B BELOW *By the time Braun and Hogenberg portrayed the cities of the New World in 1572, an idealised image of the Inca, as a pontiff-like figure, borne by classical-looking followers, had asserted itself.*

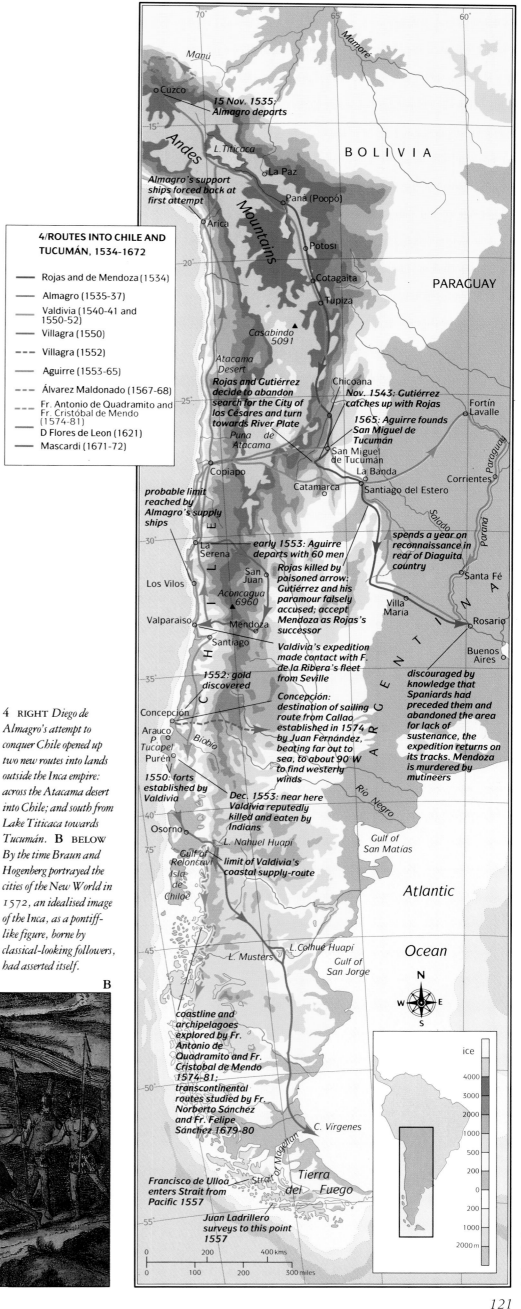

4/ROUTES INTO CHILE AND TUCUMÁN, 1534-1672

— Rojas and de Mendoza (1534)
— Almagro (1535-37)
— Valdivia (1540-41 and 1550-52)
— Villagra (1550)
--- Villagra (1552)
— Aguirre (1553-65)
--- Álvarez Maldonado (1567-68)
--- Fr. Antonio de Quadramito and Fr. Cristóbal de Mendo (1574-81)
— D Flores de Leon (1621)
— Mascardi (1671-72)

B

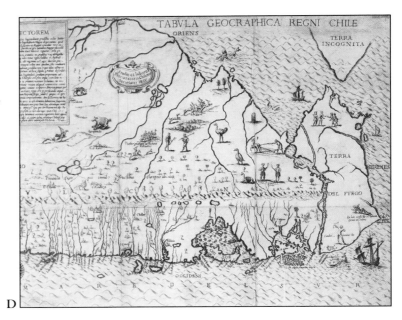

C LEFT *One of the earliest engravings of the Spanish encounters with the Incas displays a world combining savagery with majesty.* D RIGHT *The mapping of the cone of Chile was the work of Franciscan and Jesuit missionaries of the 17th-century. The Jesuits' scientific interests are represented by men and beasts, the civilizing mission by the figure ploughing.*

C

D

Bíobío can no longer be reconstructed, but he reached the Gulf of Reloncaví and patronised explorations which mapped Chiloé and the mass of islands to the south, beginning with the expedition of Juan Ladrillero in 1557-58 and continuing with those of the Franciscans Quadramito and Mendo in 1574-81. In one respect, the effects were counter-productive, tending to confirm Ladrillero's opinion that the 'cone' of South America contained nothing worth exploiting. Future exploration was left to the patient efforts of missionaries, mainly Franciscans and Jesuits, in the 17th century, of whom Nicolò Mascardi was the most conspicuous, but who included many almost anonymous figures whose routes are dubious but whose maps remain as evidence of their work (*see map* D).

5 FAR RIGHT *Adverse sailing conditions impeded exploration of the southern Chilean coast until the development of a route deep into the Pacific. Sarmiento de Gamboa surveyed the area in detail in 1579 and between 1581-85.*
E BELOW *A 17th-century map of the port of Tumbes, the anchorage at which Pizarro began the conquest of Peru.*

Almagro had opened the way not only to Chile but also – by broaching the hinterland of Lake Titicaca – towards Tucumán. His initiative was followed up, shortly after Valdivia's first expedition, by Diego de Rojas, apparently in search of the fabled 'City of los Césares'. Heroic and tragic (*see map* 4), the escapade found no great riches, but did reveal the fertile land of Tucumán and opened a potential route between the Pacific colonies and those on the River Paraguay. Farther north, the extraordinary talent for exploration of the Spaniards of Peru in the early 1540s also inspired Gonzalo Pizarro's search for the 'Cinnamon Land' – groves bearing a cinnamon-like condiment – in the jungles of the Napo valley. The gruelling nature of this expedition, and that of Rojas, and the small rewards

E

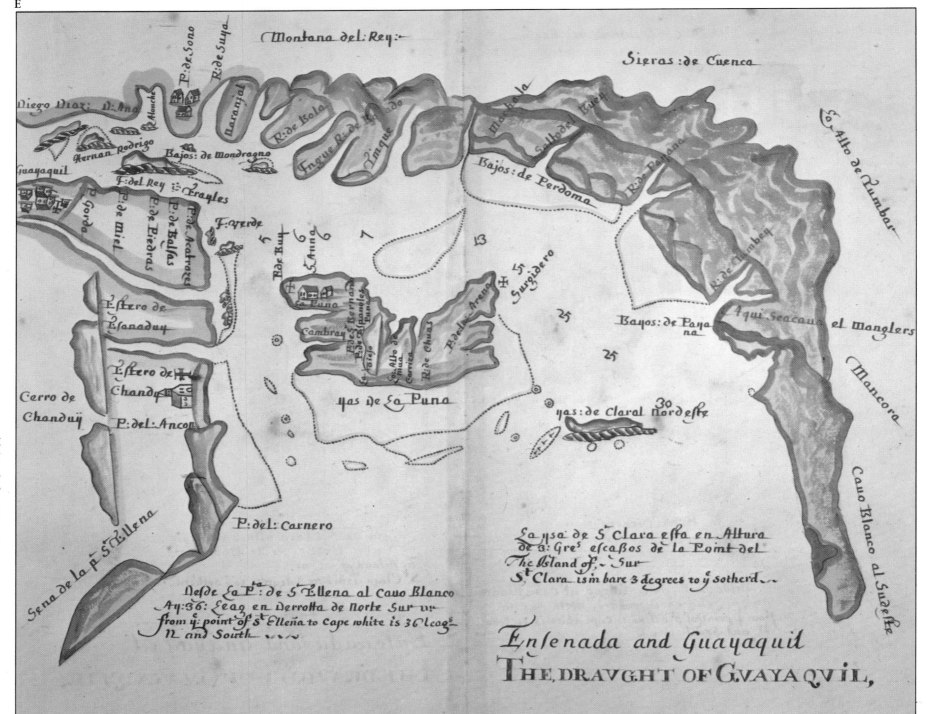

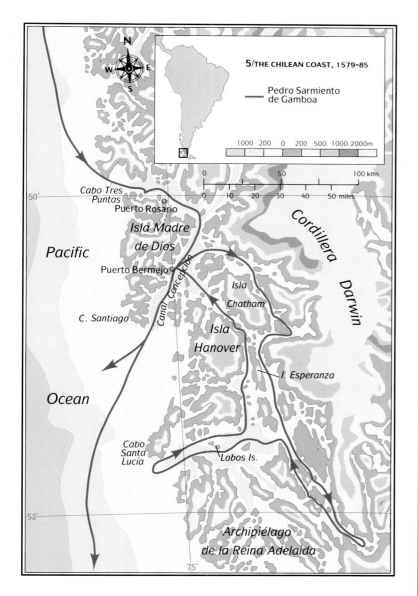

Pedro Sarmiento de Gamboa

obtained, deterred further exploration of the lowlands from the Andean bases until the 1560s. Martín de Póveda's epic march across the lowlands from south to north in 1566 would beggar belief had his departure from Chachapoyas and arrival in Bogotá not been incontrovertibly recorded. By tracing part of the Manú Valley in 1567-69, in search of a fabulous land called 'Patiti', Juan Álvarez Maldonado began the process by which the Andean highland routes were linked to the river-routes of the Amazon Valley (*see* ch. 26).

The last route created by exploration from Peru was that to Chile by sea. Valdivia's suppliers had struggled against the elements with commendable fortitude. One of them, the Genoese pilot Giovanni Battista Pastene, had explored as far south as Chiloé. Mendoza's explorers had made the ragged southward trend of the coast roughly known to pilots and cartographers, though Ladrillero lost half his men in the process. But though the riches of Chile ensured that sailings continued, the toil exacted was terrible. The run to Valparaiso from Callao took 90 days. The establishment of a viable route, which cut the sailing time by two-thirds, is traditionally ascribed to Juan Fernández, who picked up a sketchy knowledge of the Pacific wind-system from the pilot of Mendaña's voyage across the South Sea in 1567-69 and realised that by going well out to sea one could return to Chile with the westerlies.

Most of what remained unknown in the southern coastal region was revealed by the meticulous Pedro Sarmiento de Gamboa, one of the most remarkable intellects of late 16th-century Spanish America. He was an astrologer, twice tried by the Inquisition; an Inca expert, who rewrote Inca history for Spanish propaganda; a fortune-hunter, whose researches in Inca lore inspired Mendaña's voyages; and an excellent pilot who explored the region, first in 1579 in an attempt to thwart Drake's inruption into the Pacific, then in 1581-85 in an attempt to colonize and fortify the South American cone. All that came of his efforts was his own insuperable 'Description and Sailing Directions' and what he called his 'crown of triumph': impoverishment and personal disaster in the service of his king.

THE SPHERICITY OF THE EARTH

THE ENVIRONS of Quito, with high mountains in an equatorial setting, proved ideal for the largest-scale scientific experiment of the 18th century: the attempt to test the hypothesis of the sphericity of the earth by verifying the length of a degree along the surface of the world at the equator. Departing in 1735 under Charles-Marie de La Condamine, the expedition was complemented by another to the Arctic to carry out similar measurements. By comparing the two results, it would be possible to settle the debate on the shape of the world: Huyghens and Newton, who drew their conclusions from variations in the behaviour of pendulums, believed the globe must be distended at the equator, whereas observations made during the Survey of France suggested that if the sphericity of the world was modified at all it was by 'bulging' at the poles. Like Eratosthenes 2,000 years before, La Condamine aimed to calculate by trigonometry the angle subtended at the centre of the earth by a measured line between two fixed points. 18th-century technology, however, enormously enhanced the prospects of accuracy: La Condamine's quadrant stands prominently on the shore at the head of his account of his findings (**A**); the map of the measurement of the meridian of Quito in 1744 by his Spanish assistants, Jorge Juan and Juan de Ulloa, shows their use of triangulation techniques (**D**). From the same work, the bewigged figure bent over the Rococo table (**C**) completes calculations of the world's circumference. The result was inaccurate by about two per cent but convinced the world that Huyghens and Newton were right. The spirit in which the Spaniards undertook the expedition is shown by the frontispiece of their account, in which a figure representative of the useful sciences reveals Faith to the Indians (**B**). The French, however, were motivated partly by national pride, and the expedition broke up when the Spaniards felt excluded from their share of glory.

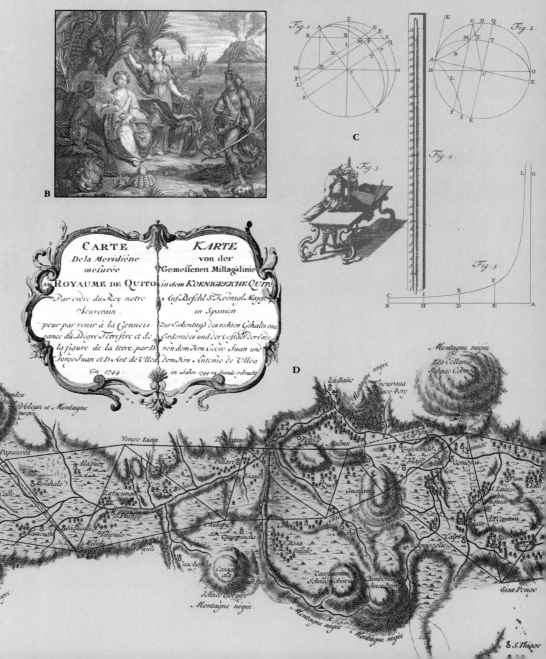

25
THE SEARCH FOR
EL DORADO
1512-1546

A **BELOW** *De Bry's engraving of the ritual gilding of the fabled 'El Dorado' dates from the end of the 16th century, when the search for him was at its most feverish.*
1 **RIGHT** *After Balboa's penetration along the river San Juan in 1514, explorers in the 1530s, following rumours of gold, tended to be led into the highlands. In the 1540s, the search moved eastwards, towards the Llanos.*

A

DESPITE the accessibility of much of the South American interior by river, to an astonishing degree early European explorers followed laborious cross-river routes. The struggles of Federmann and von Hutten across the Llanos Plains of Colombia and Venezuela, skirting the Andes to the east, where the headwaters of innumerable rivers scored the sodden terrain, or of the mutineers of Dortal's expedition of 1536, working their way across the northern tributaries of the Orinoco from east to west, were typical of this apparent willingness to defy the environment.

The cross-river routes had a common focus, tending to converge on the northern Andean highlands. Three river-valley routes from the Caribbean, along the Rivers Magdalena, Sinú and San Juan, led broadly towards the same goal. The unifying objective was the search for a land of fabulous wealth, which persistent rumours seemed to locate in that region, and which came to be associated with the name of El Dorado.

The first record of a legend of this kind inspired the earliest inland exploration of South America by Europeans: Balboa's search for the rich realm of Dabeiba along the San Juan valley in 1512. Indian informants tended naturally to tell their Spanish interlocutors whatever the visitors wanted to know. Expectations of rich lands were fed by imaginative reportage, designed both to please the newcomers and to speed them on their way. The fact that in the cases of Mexico and Peru the reports of gold-rich civilizations proved true was a further stimulus to the powerful El Dorado myth. It was first recorded in Latacungi by one of Sebastián de Benalcázar's captains, Luis de Daza, who had heard of a chief who was ritually dusted with powdered gold and then washed in a lake, into which many rich artefacts would then be plunged. This 'gilded man' – dorado in Spanish – gradually gave his name to this elusive country.

Scarcely an expedition in the second half of the century in the northern part of the continent did not find this legend, or something like it, confirmed by native reports. Most scholars – perhaps exhibiting a credulity similar to that of the conquistadores – have assumed that the legend has some factual basis. Certainly, it is true that pigmentation in suspension is a widely used form of personal adornment in this part of the world and that lakes make excellent sacrificial vessels: a company to dredge the treasures from the bottom of Lake Guatavita was in existence at intervals until the 1970s.

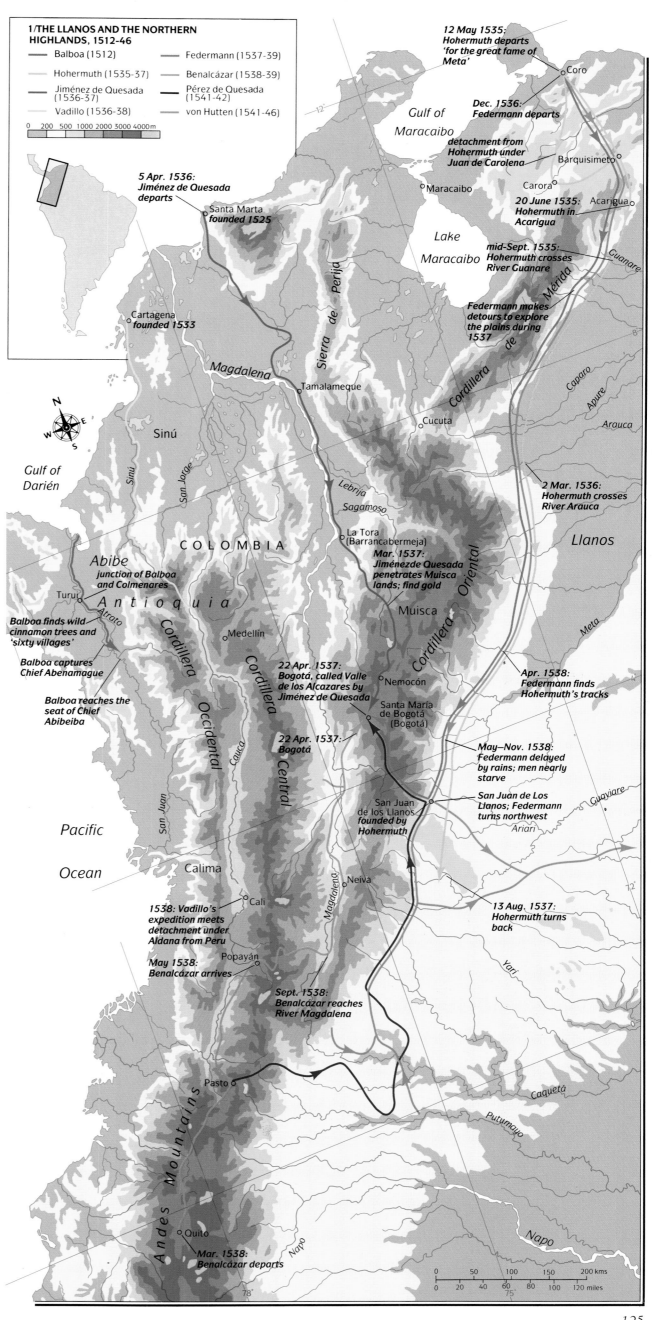

1/THE LLANOS AND THE NORTHERN HIGHLANDS, 1512-46

- Balboa (1512)
- Hohermuth (1535-37)
- Jiménez de Quesada (1536-37)
- Vadillo (1536-38)
- Federmann (1537-39)
- Benalcázar (1538-39)
- Pérez de Quesada (1541-42)
- von Hutten (1541-46)

0 200 500 1000 2000 3000 4000m

12 May 1535: Hohermuth departs 'for the great fame of Meta'

Coro

Dec. 1536: Federmann departs

Gulf of Maracaibo

detachment from Hohermuth under Juan de Carolena

Barquisimeto

Maracaibo

Carora

Acarigua

20 June 1535: Hohermuth in Acarigua

Lake Maracaibo

mid-Sept. 1535: Hohermuth crosses River Guanare

Federmann makes detours to explore the plains during 1537

5 Apr. 1536: Jiménez de Quesada departs

Santa Marta founded 1525

Cartagena founded 1533

Sierra de Perija

Magdalena

Tamalameque

Cucuta

Cordillera de Mérida

Caparo

Apure

Arauca

2 Mar. 1536: Hohermuth crosses River Arauca

Sinú

Gulf of Darién

Sinú

San Jorge

Lebrija

Sagamoso

La Tora (Barrancabermeja)

Mar. 1537: Jiménez de Quesada penetrates Muisca lands; find gold

Llanos

C O L O M B I A

Abibe junction of Balboa and Colmenares

Turur

Atrato

Antioquia

Balboa finds wild cinnamon trees and 'sixty villages'

Balboa captures Chief Abenamague

Balboa reaches the seat of Chief Abibeiba

Cordillera Occidental

Medellín

Cauca

Cordillera Central

Muisca

Nemocón

Santa María de Bogotá (Bogotá)

Cordillera Oriental

Meta

22 Apr. 1537: Bogotá, called Valle de los Alcazares by Jiménez de Quesada

22 Apr. 1537: Bogotá

Apr. 1538: Federmann finds Hohermuth's tracks

May–Nov. 1538: Federmann delayed by rains; men nearly starve

San Juan de Los Llanos; Federmann turns northwest

San Juan de los Llanos founded by Hohermuth

Guaviare

Ariari

San Juan

Pacific Ocean

Calima

Cali

1538: Vadillo's expedition meets detachment under Aldana from Peru

May 1538: Benalcázar arrives

Popayán

Magdalena

Neiva

13 Aug. 1537: Hohermuth turns back

Sept. 1538: Benalcázar reaches River Magdalena

Yari

Pasto

Caquetá

Putumayo

Andes Mountains

Quito

Mar. 1538: Benalcázar departs

Napo

Napo

0 50 100 150 200 kms
0 20 40 60 80 100 120 miles

BALBOA'S expedition of 1512 led in a promising direction. Beyond Abibe, lay Antioquia, rich in gold, which Francisco César would reach in 1537. In the meantime, however, Balboa's initiative had no successors. It took the discovery of Peru to re-awaken the search for other rich civilizations in the South American interior. Rumours of the existence of Peru were already rife when the process began in 1530, near the shores of Lake Maracaibo. Charles V had granted Venezuela in virtual pawn to his German bankers, the Welzer, and it was German servants of the financial house who undertook the first explorations. Ambrose Alfinger, who may have been related to partners of the Welzers and had been managing their business in Santo Domingo for three years, arrived as governor at Coro in February 1529 and immediately began to explore the banks of the lake.

Another of the Germans, Nicholas Federmann, was to play a major role as an explorer. Left in command at Coro during Alfinger's next expedition in September 1530, he was unable to contain his wanderlust. His excuse for setting off on an exploration of his own helps to explain the rapid progress of discovery on the mainland of South America in the 1530s. He had, he said, 'so many men, inactive and under-occupied, that I determined to undertake a voyage towards the South or Southern Sea'. The need to employ these large numbers of footloose would-be *conquistadores*, combined with the prevailing ignorance of South American geography, which made the South Sea seem accessible from Coro, was an enormous incentive to explore. Federmann also 'hoped to do something profitable'. Alfinger's first reconnaissance had probably gathered evi-

B BELOW *Fabulous native goldwork attracted Spanish explorers into the Atrato and Cauca valleys, and perhaps provided them with an epitype of El Dorado, in the form of golden figurines seated in attitudes of apparent majesty. This Quimbaya lime-flask shows such a figure making an offering of golden birds, dangling pectoral ornaments from their tails, similar to those worn by the Muisca. She wears a simple but enormous nose-ornament.*

B

dence of gold-yielding lands in the interior. Within a few days of Alfinger's departure, Federmann had set off on his unauthorised adventure.

Heading respectively west and east of Lake Maracaibo, between them Alfinger and Federmann explored both flanks of the northernmost range of the Andes, the Cordillera de Mérida. Alfinger's expedition turned into a vast Odyssey, which lasted for three years, reached the Rivers Magdalena and Sagamoso, and returned through the delta lands just west of the lake. In the course of it, Alfinger lost his life to an Indian dart.

Despite its more limited range, Federmann's expedition was in a sense the more important, for it descended the uplands through the Barquisimeto valley to reach the Llanos of Venezuela. This line of approach determined the future direction of exploration from Coro, and from the late 1530s the search for El Dorado would increasingly edge farther east into and across the vast plains of mud which Federmann had mistaken for the 'South Sea'.

El Dorado did not exist. There was, however, a relatively sophisticated polity, a sedentary and partly urban civilization, still to be found in the Colombian tableland, where trade had led to a concentration of gold which was worked into marvellously intricate artefacts. This area, the land of the Muisca, a branch of the widespread Chibcha language-group, became the focus of the ambitions of conquistadores in the second half of the 1530s. It was unknown to the Spaniards, save by the vaguest of rumours, and its discovery can fairly be said to have been accidental. But slowly, and with climactic effect, three Spanish expeditions converged upon it independently – and very much to each other's surprise – from different directions between 1536 and 1539.

First in the field was a party from Santa Marta, which had set out to explore the course of the River Magdalena. The colonists of Santa Marta had been feeling their way up the river since the expansion of their settlement in 1529 and already knew of Tamalameque and much of the course of the Lebrija and the Cauca. Evidence of a gold-source farther on was encouraging. It was assumed, moreover, that the river would provide quick access to Peru: by cutting out the long route via the Isthmus, the inhabitants of Santa Marta could make themselves wealthy.

The man who led the expedition that set out in pursuit of this chimera was an unlikely conquistador. Jiménez de Quesada was a professional lawyer, newly arrived in Santa Marta as a magistrate; he had none of the experience, either of war or of the Indies, which distinguished other great conquistadores. It may therefore have been a quick grasp of the commercial possibilities of a new route to Peru that won him a greenhorn-command. He set off in April 1536 with 800 men and a flotilla of rafts, but the difficulties of upriver navigation condemned most of the party to tortuous footslogging across the mouths of tributaries and through swamps, clearing jungle as it went. Extraordinary fortitude and indifference to heavy losses took them as far as the Opón valley, where the availability of products of trade – salt and textiles – from a superior civilization gave them a hint of the proximity of the Muisca. Abandoning the search for Peru, they headed up the course of the Opón and reached the tableland in March 1537. By now, deaths, desertions and strategic detachments had left the expedition less than 200 men strong. They advanced through the salt-pans of Nemocón, defeating the Muisca chief Tisquesusa, to enter the 'capital' at Bacatá, which they re-named Santa María de Bogotá, in the last week of April. Jiménez de Quesada had the run of the tableland for nearly two years before any of his rivals arrived. He employed his time in amassing an enormous treasure of gold and emeralds and re-clothing his force in the native textiles that were the industrial basis of Muisca wealth.

Meanwhile, excited perhaps by the example of Peru, the settlers of Coro had also nourished rumours of a rich land in the interior, which they called 'Xerira'. The first, disastrous, expedition in search of it was led by a well-born Welzer appoin-

C ABOVE *The El Dorado legend was fed by artefacts such as this golden raft of Muisca workmanship, apparently depicting a ritual sacrifice. It was among votive offerings recovered from the bed of Lake Siecha.*
D BELOW *The ceremonial departure of the Welzer expedition from Seville in 1534 depicted in a contemporary manuscript.*

D

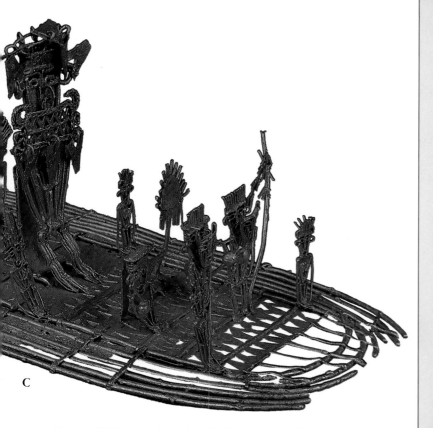

C

tee, Georg Hohermuth, who had superseded Federmann as governor of Coro, to the latter's understandable chagrin. Hohermuth left in May 1535, with 400 men in two columns, making for Los Llanos by mountain and valley routes respectively. The rains which tormented the expedition almost throughout its three years of wanderings began at once, and, by the time they had reached the Portuguesa valley, prevented further progress. In an interval of negotiable weather, they reached the Llanos at the beginning of 1536 and struggled across the tributaries of the Meta and the main stream itself before deciding to pursue rumours of a rich civilization in the mountains. They were on the point of reaching the Muisca lands, but Captain Juan de Villegas, deputed to reconnoitre, was unable to find a route of ascent. In August 1537 Hohermuth camped on a site near the river Ariari, where the future city of San Juan de los Llanos would be founded, before turning back in the face of the hostility of the Choque Indians. When the expedition got back to Coro in May 1538, only 90 survivors were left.

Before leaving Coro, Hohermuth had ordered Federmann to make a parallel expedition to the west of Lake Maracaibo. With characteristic insubordination, Federmann dallied until his superior could be supposed to be well out of the way. At the end of 1537, he then followed his chief into Los Llanos, a

MOST EARLY European explorers in America ignored the landscape. Columbus, writing what was effectively promotional literature, indulged in vague superlatives; Vespucci, who had a genuine observer's eye, included some

A

B   C

rhapsodical descriptions. Sensitivity to the beauties of nature was, however, a rare quality among early 16th-century laymen. Gradually, the Franciscan idea of the beauty of creation, supplemented by realistic Renaissance aesthetics, began to influence perceptions of the New World. The first attempt to depict American landscape realistically, but with an accent on the appeal of the grandeur of the wilderness, was made by Jan Mostaert, Margaret of Austria's court painter. Beginning in the 1520s, on the basis of reports from Mexico, and continuing into the 1540s, when he may have worked on eye-witness accounts of Coronado's expedition (see ch. 17), he filtered his hearsay sources through the typical colour-screen of Flemish landscape-painting of the day and added much that was fantastic and incongruous.

Not until the emergence of the 18th-century cult of sensibility did the landscape of the New World come to occupy a permanent place in the romantic imagination. The tradition began with the beautiful and exciting drawings made during their scientific explorations in the region of Quito by Jorge Juan (1713–73) and Antonio de Ulloa (1716–95) first published in 1752. As in (B), which shows the eruption of Cotopaxi, with the phenomenon of arcs of light observed in the sky, and on the mountain-slopes at Panambarca and elsewhere, their representations often took the ostensible form of scientific diagrams. The Andean settings they recorded remained the source of the most powerful romantic images of America. Cotopaxi became American landscape-painters' favourite subject. The high point of the tradition was marked by the illustrations from their journeys in mountain regions, especially of the Andes, by Humboldt and Bonpland in *Vues des Cordillères* (1806–14) (see ch.26). Shown here are Lake Guatavita, the alleged location of the El Dorado ritual (D), and the dramatic Quindiu Pass (C). Views like these defined a romantic image of South America for subsequent painters. Thomas Cole (1801–48), the founder of the Hudson River school, started a vogue for South American settings for scenes of cosmic high drama, typified by his vision of Eden with the expulsion of Adam and Eve (1828) (A), painted after a long sketching tour in the West Indies. Because 'preserved untouched since the creation', America's mountains were 'hallowed to his soul' in a continent where 'all nature is new to art'.

D

THE EXPLORATION of the New World was succeeded by 'scientific' exploration which ransacked the secrets of the sub-soil and the environment. No discoveries were more useful than those in botany, which can be grouped in three classes: foodstuffs, medicines and contributions to taxonomy. The first new foods to appeal to Europeans were fruits. Columbus was the first European to describe a pineapple, shown here on John White's late 16th-century drawing (A), as 'shaped like a pine cone and cut like a turnip'. Most modern varieties of strawberry are descended from a type discovered and drawn by Frézier in Chile in the early 18th century (background). The roots and tubers which formed staple foods in the Caribbean never appealed to colonists, but maize (D and E) was to become a world-wide cereal because of its enormous superiority, in terms of efficiency, over Old World grains. The cacao plant yielded a health-giving liquor which became a luxury beverage in 18th-century Europe and, thanks to industrial production in solid form in the 19th century, came to supply one of the world's favourite foods in the form of chocolate. Some medicinal plants proved equivocal in their effects: tobacco (F), which has had advocates and critics since it was first

identified by Columbus as 'some leaves which seem to be highly valued' by the Indians, has been prescribed over the years for conditions ranging from renal trouble to constipation, but is now out of favour with physicians. Coca (B) once esteemed as a source of pain-killers, is now only cultivated for the narcotics trade. These drugs were 'borrowed' from indigenous cultures, but quinine, perhaps the most beneficent of all which enabled man to conquer malaria, was discovered by accident, allegedly by a 17th-century viceroy of Peru for the treatment of his wife.

The systematic exploration, recording and classification of the flora of the New World can be said to have begun with the expedition of Francisco Hernández, sent to Mexico by Philip II to investigate the medicinal potential of previously unknown plants. In only six years, Hernández compiled an amazingly comprehensive account of the flora of New Spain. His principles were not, however, extended to other Spanish possessions until the 'enlightened' Bourbon monarchs of the late 18th century began a lavish programme of investment. Resident scientists like J C Mutis, who arrived in Peru in 1760, collected data which expeditions like that of Ruiz and Pavón (1777) transmitted. Gardens of acclimatisation were established in Orotava and Madrid. By the time Sidney Parkinson recorded the flora of Tierra del Fuego (C) on his way to the Pacific in illustrations that were as accurate as they were elegant, botanical illustrators and specimen-hunters had penetrated every type of environment which Spanish America had to offer.

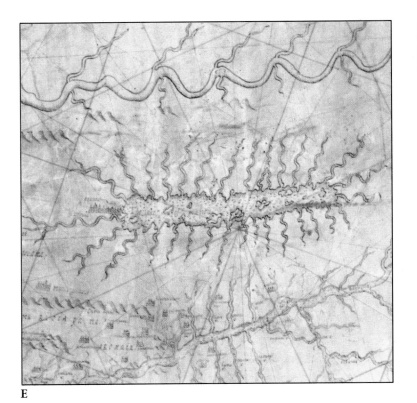

E

territory to which he perhaps felt his previous expedition had established a proprietory right. On his way he picked up the mutineers from Jerónimo Dortal's attempt to find an overland route from San Miguel de Neverí to the Orinoco. Abandoned by his men for his fanaticism (which would be rewarded on a second, successful expedition in 1540), Dortal had been left to return home alone, while the mutineers, led by Juan Fernández de Alderete, pursued rumours of rich lands to the east. Federmann led the combined force, some 300 strong, parallel to the mountains, allegedly in a search for Hohermuth, whom, however, he seems to have taken pains to avoid. In the Ariari valley, he encountered gold ornaments worked by the highlanders and decided to climb the Sierra to investigate. Losing nearly half his men in the ascent, he arrived in Bogotá, clad only in skins, to find Jiménez de Quesada already in possession.

Quesada bought peace from Federmann for 10,000 gold pesos. But his position was delicate, as a third force was approaching his territory of 'New Granada' from Peru. Sebastián de Benalcázar, the conqueror of Quito (*see* ch.24) had evaluated the exploratory probes made by his subordinates in every direction from his capital and had decided personally to follow up the promising road to the north. While detachments pressed on to the Cauca valley (where, in 1538, they met exploratory parties sent south via the Sinú river by Governor Juan

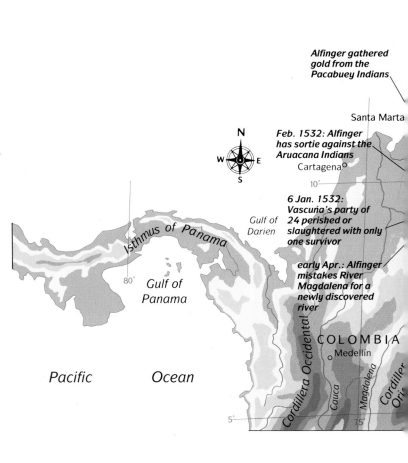

Alfinger gathered gold from the Pacabuey Indians

Santa Marta

Feb. 1532: Alfinger has sortie against the Aruacana Indians
Cartagena

10°

6 Jan. 1532: Vascuña's party of 24 perished or slaughtered with only one survivor

Gulf of Darien

early Apr.: Alfinger mistakes River Magdalena for a newly discovered river

Isthmus of Panama

Gulf of Panama

80°

Pacific   Ocean

COLOMBIA
Medellín

Cordillera Occidental

Cauca

Magdalena

Cordiller
Ori

5°

75

de Vadillo of Cartagena), Benalcázar marched from Popayán along the Magdalena. It proved a relatively easy route and his party arrived with equipment and armour intact, in contrast to Quesada's and Federmann's ragamuffins. Rather than force conclusions, however, the three leaders agreed on a joint re-foundation of Santa Fé de Bogotá, and to submit their rival claims to the arbitration of the crown.

None of them was satisfied by the procedures of the royal court. Federmann, for his pains, was disgraced and accused of heresy. Benalcázar was denied jurisdiction over Bogotá and sent back to the New World to look for cinnamon in Popayán. Jiménez de Quesada, whose claims to priority were finally vindicated, had to face nearly seven years of costly legal delays. Meanwhile, however, the legend of 'El Dorado' grew up in, and spread from, the camps of the conquerors of Bogotá.

The discoveries of three gold-rich civilizations of the Indies – Aztec, Inca and Muisca – naturally excited expectations of more in the offing. In the early 1540s, the search shifted beyond the sierra east into the Llanos and south of the area fruitlessly combed by Hohermuth and Federmann. Of Hernán Pérez de Quesada's exploration of the area between the Putu-mayo and Guaviare valleys – as of so many expeditions – the immediate inspiration was disappointed ambition. He had hoped to succeed his brother, Jiménez de Quesada, in the governorship of New Granada, and invested his thwarted hopes in a projected conquest of his own, one that was explicitly directed to 'El Dorado'.

It may seem odd that explorers should persistently have scoured lowland regions for lost civilizations, when the greatest finds so far – the Aztec, Inca and Muisca realms – had been highland civilizations. It is worth recalling, however, that it was Maya remains in the lowlands of Yucatán that first alerted Spaniards to the possibilities of spectacular cultures on the American mainland. Impressive sites near the foot of the eastern slopes of the Andes, at Gran Patajén and Trenchera, for example, with cunningly-wrought monumental buildings, may have contributed to the atmosphere of promise associated with the lowlands. Inca rumours, based on esteem for trading partners deep in the tropical forest, may also have helped. It is probable, despite the apparently unconducive environment, that the lowland regions really did enclose impressive sedentary cultures, capable of farming intensively and producing an economic surplus for trade. Turtle-farming in the Amazon basin and the large-scale production of bitter manioc (a cassava-like plant) gave the lowlands the potential to support populations

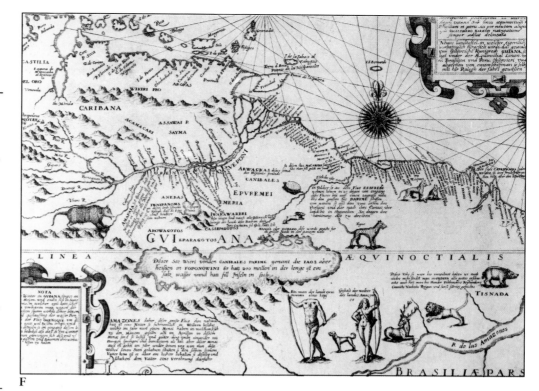

F

E ABOVE LEFT *and*
F ABOVE *Fruitless explorations farther west forced the mise-en-scène of El Dorado into the Guyana highlands. Sir Walter Raleigh's map of the region (E) associated the sacrificial lake with Lake Manoa. De Bry's map of the region (F) filled it with cannibals and Amazons.* 2 BELOW *Federmann and Alfinger explored east and west respectively from the Maracaibo region in search of the 'Southern Sea'. Federmann encountered Dortal's expedition, deflected from the attempt to reach the Orinoco by rumours of gold.*

unattainable by the forest Indians of today, and justified the reputation for wealth which attracted explorers to seek the realms of 'Omagua' and 'Machiparo'.

Shortly after Pérez de Quesada's effort, the same area was invaded from Coro by an apparently more auspicious expedition, also bound for 'El Dorado', led by Philip von Hutten, a survivor of Hohermuth's long march. This learned knight – cousin of the humanist Ulrich von Hutten and brother of a bishop – was the last of the great German explorers of South America of the Habsburg era; he died fighting to defend the Welzers' interests against the irredentism of native Spaniards.

His interim role in the search for El Dorado started in fine style, accompanied by 100 horsemen, with a son of the head of the Welzer firm in attendance. It ended ingloriously after five years of ill-reported wanderings. The result was neither to scotch nor to kill the legend of El Dorado, merely to shift the quest yet farther to the east; for, perhaps in attempted self-justification, the survivors of the journey brought back rumours of the wealth of the distant Omagua. By the last quarter of the 16th century, there was scarcely a Spanish report written east of Coro that did not include references to the ritually gilded chieftain – relegated now to the mysterious tableland of Guiana, where 17th-century fortune-hunters continued to seek him.

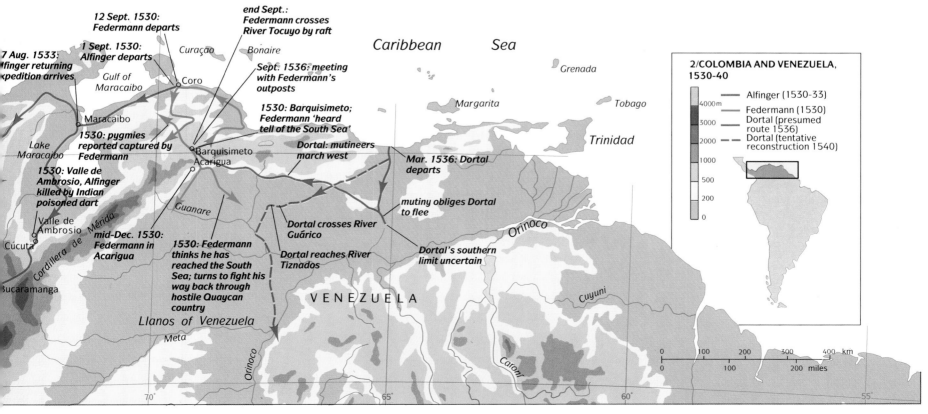

Caribbean Sea

12 Sept. 1530:
Federmann departs

7 Aug. 1533:
Alfinger returning expedition arrives

1 Sept. 1530:
Alfinger departs

Curaçao
Bonaire

end Sept.:
Federmann crosses River Tocuyo by raft

Grenada

Gulf of Maracaibo

Coro

Sept. 1536: meeting with Federmann's outposts

Margarita

Tobago

Maracaibo

1530: pygmies reported captured by Federmann

1530: Barquisimeto; Federmann 'heard tell of the South Sea'

Trinidad

Lake Maracaibo

Barquisimeto
Acarigua

Dortal: mutineers march west

Mar. 1536: Dortal departs

1530: Valle de Ambrosio, Alfinger killed by Indian poisoned dart

Guanare

mutiny obliges Dortal to flee

Orinoco

Valle de Ambrosio

Cúcuta

mid-Dec. 1530: Federmann in Acarigua

Dortal crosses River Guárico

Cordillera de Mérida

Bucaramanga

1530: Federmann thinks he has reached the South Sea; turns to fight his way back through hostile Quaycan country

Dortal reaches River Tiznados

Dortal's southern limit uncertain

Cuyuni

VENEZUELA

Llanos of Venezuela

Meta

Orinoco

Caroní

2/COLOMBIA AND VENEZUELA, 1530–40

Alfinger (1530–33)
Federmann (1530)
Dortal (presumed route 1536)
Dortal (tentative reconstruction 1540)

4000m
3000
2000
1000
500
200
0

0   100   200   300   400 km
0   100   200 miles

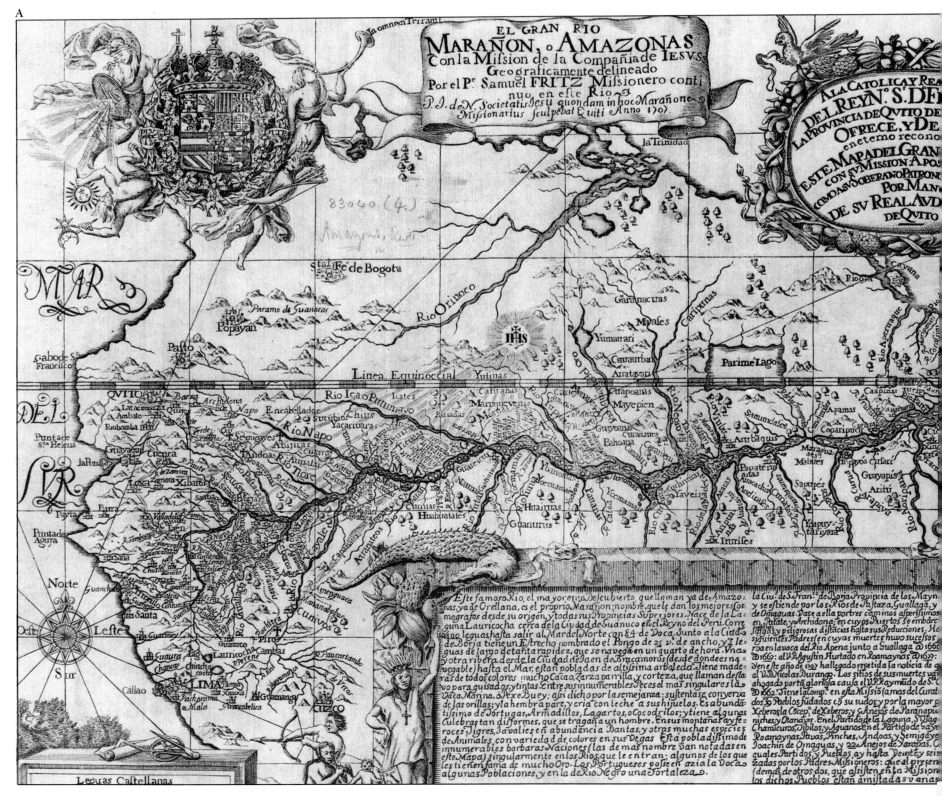

APART from the relatively isolated 'cone' of its southern extremity, the vast bulk of South America east of the Andes is drained by the three great river systems of the Orinoco, the Amazon and the Paraná-Paraguay. The main courses of all three form more or less navigable routes across the width of the continent from the Andes to the Atlantic. Yet despite the potential of these highways, and of the abundance of byways which lead from them in the form of tributaries and distributaries, they were little exploited by early explorers compared with the more difficult highland and cross-river routes (see chs. 24 and 25).

Their exploration was a long, slow process. In the second half of the 16th century and throughout the 17th, it was largely the work of missionaries, supplemented towards the end of the period by Portuguese fortune-hunters and slavers in the Amazon valley. The discovery of mineral wealth deep in the interior, particularly in Matto Grosso and Minas Gerais, was needed as an additional stimulus before the rhythm of exploration could recover the vitality of the 16th century.

Knowledge of the detailed configurations of the river-systems was barely complete when the era of disinterestedly 'scientific' exploration was inaugurated by La Condamine's expedition to test the sphericity of the earth in 1735 (see ch. 24) and von Humboldt's navigation between the valleys of the Amazon and Orinoco in 1800. The exploration of the rivers illustrates what seems to be almost a general law of the history of exploration: the prospect of material reward is a more potent incentive than missionary zeal or scientific curiosity.

The role played by the El Dorado legend in the Orinoco Valley was paralleled in the Amazon by rumours of the riches of 'Omagua' and of the 'Cinammon Land'. In the region of the Paraná-Paraguay and, by extension, in Tucumán and Patagonia, a similar function was served by two shadowy quests for the 'White King' – a fabulously rich potentate perhaps conjured by rumours of the Inca – and for 'the City of Los Césares', reported, in an uncertain location, by the survivors of an expedition from the River Plate in 1529. Unlike the explorers of the highlands, however, early penetrators of the river valleys found no wealth that could be easily exploited, only souls to be laboriously saved. The vigorous and rapid work of lay explorers, generating extensive but sketchy knowledge, yielded to the slower but equally heroic and vastly more methodical explorations of the missionaries.

1 RIGHT The navigability of the Paraná-Paraguay made the River Plate the first river route to be explored for access deep into the interior of South America. The country south of the Paraná basin was not systematically explored until the early 17th century.

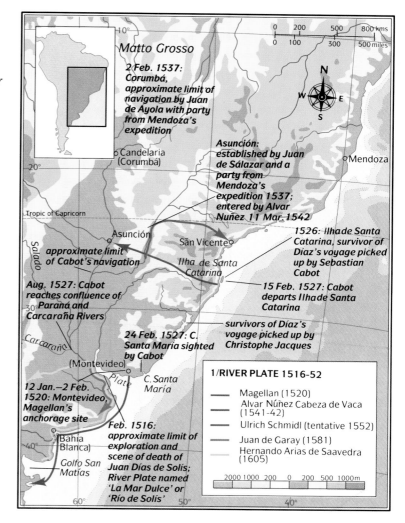

PRIORITY in the discovery of the River Plate is disputed. Possibly reached by Vespucci in 1502 (see ch. 13), and probably known to Portuguese dyewood-cutters in the first decade of the century, the river itself, according to an isolated source, was found by a Portuguese voyage of 1514. It became permanently known in 1516 when Juan Díaz de Solís (see ch. 10) turned into it searching for an opening towards Asia. Castaways from his fleet told of their Portuguese fellow-crewman, Alejo Garcia, who departed inland tracing rumours of a 'White King' in 'Mountains of Silver'.

Garcia, having penetrated almost to Peru, amassed a huge treasure before being killed by Indians in the Chaco region during his return. His exploit was not repeated until Alvar Núñez Cabeza de Vaca retraced Garcia's steps to the Chaco, and Domingo Martínez de Irala opened communications with Peru via Potosí in 1548.

Rumours of Garcia may have made Sebastian Cabot turn into the River Plate, guided by an old cabin-boy of Solis, during his intended voyage of 1526 to the Moluccas. He entered the Paraná in May 1527, reconnoitred the mouth of the River Uruguay and built the fort of Sancti Spiritus at the confluence of the Carcarañá and Paraná. He spent two years along the river: detachments explored the Paraguay and the Bermejo, while Francisco César led an ill-fated party south, originating the legend of Los Césares. But Cabot, dilatory and pusillanimous, though reinforced in May 1528 by Diego García de Moguer, could neither befriend nor intimidate the Carios Indians. Disheartened by the subsequent massacre of the garrison of Sancti Spiritus in September 1529, he returned to Spain.

Two expeditions followed: one to Patagonia; one to the River Plate itself. The first was led by Simón de Alcazaba, a Portuguese in Spanish service. In 1534, he ventured up a river which he named the Guadalquivir, but the unpromising environment broke up the expedition. The second, led and financed by the august Pedro de Mendoza in August 1535, was more impressive, with 14 ships, 2,000 men and backing from German bankers. The consequences of so large an expedition in a virgin land were inevitable. By June 1536 'so great was our pain and disaster from hunger that rats and mice did not suffice'. Mendoza fell hors de combat. He appointed a deputy of resource in Juan de Ayolas, who obtained supplies from the Timbu Indians upriver and saved the remains of the colony.

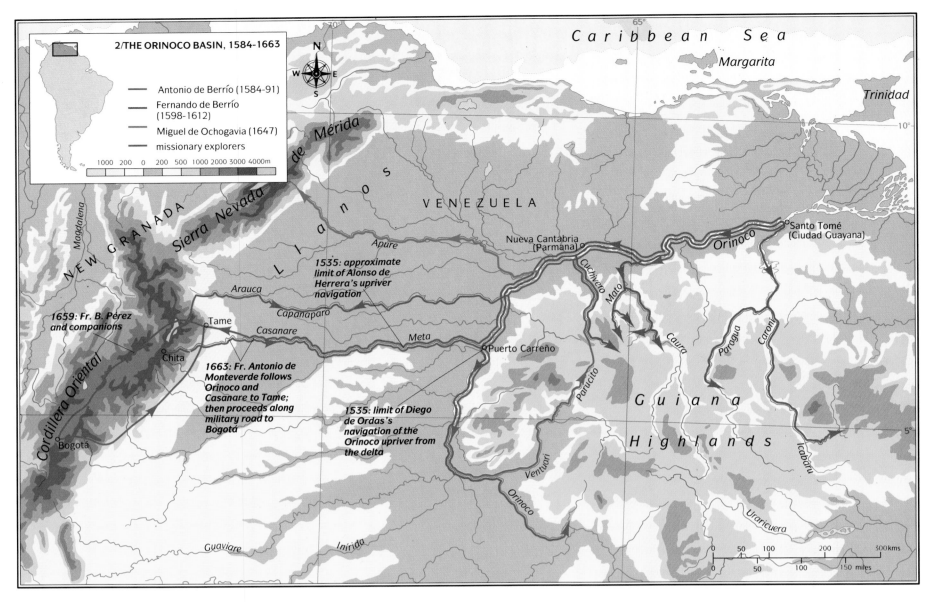

——— Antonio de Berrío (1584-91)

——— Fernando de Berrío (1598-1612)

——— Miguel de Ochogavia (1647)

——— missionary explorers

1000 200 0 200 500 1000 2000 3000 4000m

Caribbean Sea

Margarita

Trinidad

VENEZUELA

de Mérida

Sierra Nevada

NEW GRANADA

Llanos

Magdalena

Apure

Nueva Cantabria (Parmana)

Santo Tomé (Ciudad Guayana)

Orinoco

1535: approximate limit of Alonso de Herrera's upriver navigation

Arauca

Capanaparo

1659: Fr. B. Pérez and companions

Casanare

Tame

Meta

Puerto Carreño

Chita

1663: Fr. Antonio de Monteverde follows Orinoco and Casanare to Tame; then proceeds along military road to Bogotá

1535: limit of Diego de Ordas's navigation of the Orinoco upriver from the delta

Cuchivero

Mato

Parucito

Caura

Paragua

Caroní

Bogotá

Cordillera Oriental

Ventuari

Orinoco

G u i a n a

H i g h l a n d s

Icabarú

Guaviare

Inírida

Uraricuera

0 50 100 200 300kms

0 50 100 150 miles

Hoping perhaps for a more amenable site, perhaps for the 'Mountains of Silver', Ayolas pressed upstream to Corumbá, which he called Candelaria. His exact route then passes into oblivion. He turned west into the Chaco, perhaps drawn by shades of Garcia. His fate, if not his fortune, was the same as his precursor's and the party was massacred by Payaguas Indians. When his deputy, Domingo Martínez de Irala, heard of the debacle in 1541, he abandoned the expedition's base at Buenos Aires to concentrate his strength at Asunción.

Meanwhile, a strong relief force had left Spain under the heroic Alvar Núñez Cabeza de Vaca (*see* ch. 10). At Santa Catarina, he decided to emulate Garcia and march overland to Asunción. He left on 18 October 1541. Crossing the Serras do Mar and Espigão, he reached the Iguaçu on 3 December. At the confluence with the Paraná the party divided, one half travelling by canoe, the other cross-country. Asunción was reached on 11 March 1542. The following year, Cabeza de Vaca estab-

2 ABOVE *Of the main river systems of South America, the Orinoco presented the worst obstacles to navigation. Exploration upstream was abandoned in the 1540s and the Orinoco remained undeveloped as a channel of communications for another 100 years.* **B** BELOW LEFT *The feathered warriors armed with bows and clubs in* La France Antartique *are typical of 16th-century images of Brazilian Indians, whose lawlessness and cannibalism struck Europeans.*

C RIGHT *Fernández de Oviedo's map of the Orinoco includes material reported by the very earliest explorations, under Ordas and Dortal.*

lished a base at Puerto de los Reyes for the exploration of the upper Paraguay. From here he sent scouting parties perhaps as far as the Serranía de Santiago for clues to Garcia's treasure, but the climate compelled a return to Asunción in April 1544. Cabeza de Vaca's charisma, which continued to charm the Indians, now ceased to work on the Spaniards. Two years of anarchy followed 'such that the devil himself could not have ruled us', ended by Irala's proposal 'to go inland, to see if they could find gold or silver'. The force struck west into Guaicurú country, where Cabeza de Vaca had tried to pick up Garcia's trail. After 43 days, they drew lots whether to go on. 'Chance determined we should proceed' through hunger and hostile Indians for 42 days more, until they reached a river, possibly the Guaporé. Although only a deputation was allowed to continue to Lima, they had traced a route between the Paraná and Peru.

The abandonment of Buenos Aires, however, put a stop to new initiatives in the region. Not until the re-foundation of the

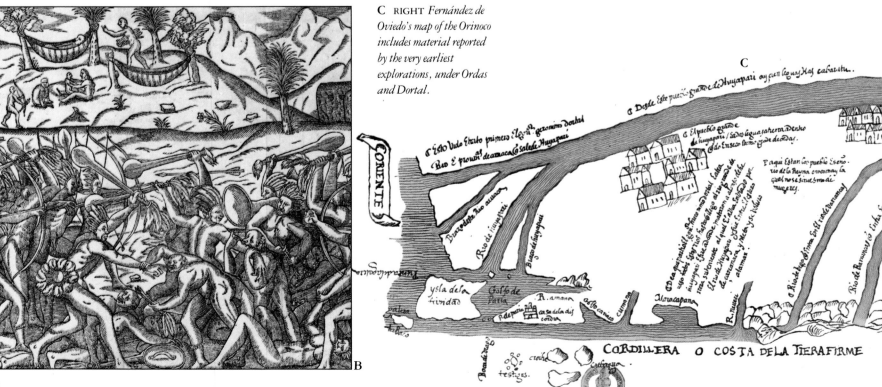

city did the search for Los Césares, and the energy of governors like Juan de Garay and Hernando Arias de Saavedra, extend the range of exploration from the River Plate to the south. The Uruguay was largely neglected, except by Portuguese slavers, until the early 17th century, when the Jesuit Roque González de Santa Cruz established the first of his missions.

The navigability of the Paraguay upriver could not be matched by the Orinoco or the Amazon. The Orinoco was first tackled by Diego de Ordás, a veteran of Cuba and Mexico. In 1530, he was commissioned to conquer from Venezuela to the River 'Marañón', probably the Paria. First entering the Orinoco in June 1531, he became possessed by tales of wealth and struggled to beyond the Meta. The treasurer of his fleet, Jerónimo Dortal, inherited his ambitions. Dortal used his governorship of Paria from 1531 to seek a route south to the river from the Cumaná coast (*see* ch. 25). His subordinate, Alonso de Herrera, went upriver in 1535, on an expedition few participants survived, reaching the Meta rapids. Beyond that point, the explorers declared the river impassable.

The question was re-opened in the second half of the century. The establishment of colonies in Venezuela and New Granada, which excited interest in the Orinoco as an avenue of access, and the frustration of the search for El Dorado in the north-west, caused the quest to shift to the Orinoco basin. In 1570, Diego Fernández de Serpa, governor of 'New Andalusia', died on the river. An attempt in 1575 to open a route from Los Llanos to the east cost the life of Pedro Malaver de Silva, governor of 'New Extremadura'.

The Orinoco defied further exploration until the intervention of Antonio de Berrío, nephew and heir of the conqueror of Bogotá, whose rich encomienda at Chita gave him the means to seek El Dorado. In 1584 he reached the Orinoco along the Casanare and Meta, and in 1591 repeated the feat along the marshy Capanaparo. He seems to have followed a huge loop through the Cuchivero and Parucito Rivers. From his foundation of Santo Tomé at the confluence with the Caroní, his son, Fernando, explored the vast tableland where the southern tributaries of the Orinoco rise. But these efforts did nothing to dispel the mystery of the region where Conan Doyle was to place his 'Lost World'.

Berrío's routes were impracticable for commerce. The need for an avenue across the northern segment of the continent was not met until 1647, when Miguel de Ochogavia, 'the Columbus of the Apure', opened communications between the Maracaibo region and the middle Orinoco. Ironically, he seems to have been deluded by floods into turning off the Apure and to have joined the Orinoco via the lower Arauca; but his achievement deserved the rapture with which it was hailed. Between the Atlantic and New Granada, Jesuits like Fr. Anton-

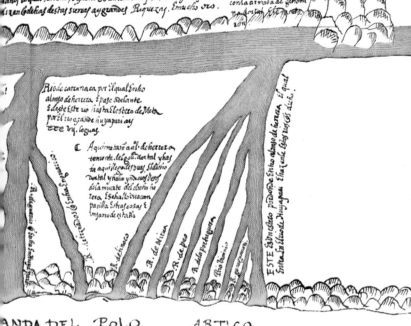

NATURAL MAN IN BRAZIL

THE VASTNESS and impenetrability of Brazil stimulated ethnographic discovery and speculation and contributed enormously to the 16th-century revolution in perceptions of 'natural' man. The earliest image (A) of 1505, illustrating Vespucci's account, is exotic and horrific, as plumed Caribs feed on severed flesh. The discovery of primitive forest tribes, however, seemed to confirm stereotypes of man's natural goodness, depicted by cartographers like Reinel (B). 'Savages' were paraded as curiosities in court festivities like the mock battle that marked Henri II's *joyeuse entrée* to Rouen in 1550 (C) and even cannibalism could be accommodated by the theory of cultural relativism, formulated in the 1550s by Montaigne in France and Las Casas in Spain. Yet as experience disappointed hopes of the discovery of some new civilization or exciting social anomaly, like the Amazons speculatively depicted in Sebastian Cabot's map of 1544 (E), 'unaccommodated man' seemed increasingly to be no more than 'a bare, fork'd animal'. Even as Miranda imagined man's potential, Caliban's snuffles could be heard in the background. Yet a further twist remained. Late 16th-century pastoral literature created a new medium for the idealisation of the primitive. The title page of Markgraf and Piso's compendium on Brazil of 1648 (D) shows the romantic image which could result – but this was in part a work of propaganda, intended to stimulate Dutch investment. Though admired in some quarters, most efforts from the outside have been devoted to transforming or exterminating the cultures of the interior.

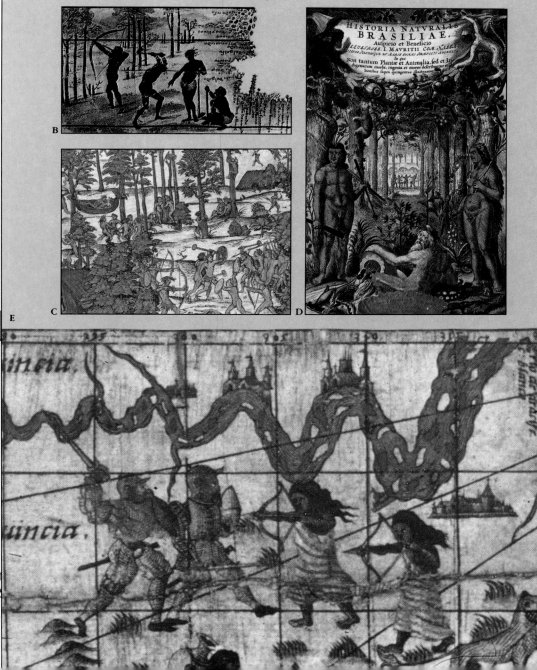

io de Monteverde in 1663, navigated up the Orinoco and Casanare, re-tracing the Jesuits' mountain trail via their remote mission at Tame.

The Amazon provided the best highway between the Andes and the Atlantic. The first long-range navigation of the river demonstrated its possibilities accidentally, when, during Gonzalo Pizarro's search for the 'Cinammon Land' (*see* ch.24), Francisco de Orellana took a detachment down the Napo to find food. Driven by hunger and rumours of gold, doubtful of his ability to return, he abandoned his allegiance to Pizarro and sailed on, emerging from the river's mouth with a conviction of riches narrowly missed. His attempt to conquer the region by the upstream route in 1545 ended with his death.

Though no one attempted the upstream navigation for nearly 100 years, Orellana had an inglorious successor in 1560 when an expedition of under-employed tiros from Peru attempted the conquest. Finding only mosquitos, mutineers massacred the commanders and set out to return to conquer Peru via the river-mouth and Venezuela. The 'tyranny' of the rebel leader, Lope de Aguirre, generated an enormous literary tradition but little else.

Early accounts of the Amazon evince accuracy and awe. The chroniclers of Aguirre's escapade, who found it 'great and powerful beyond comparison', were well informed about its relationship to the Ucayali and the Huallaga, favouring the theory that it rose in the environs of Cuzco. Aguirre himself captured its 'great and terrible' personality. Its vast breadth, its scattered archipelagoes, gave it a sea-like character. The ease of navigability over vast distances excited explorers of a transcontinental route. 'The grandeur of this river is admirable', reported an early 17th-century explorer, 'for, like a king over all others, it guards its gravity with measured steps'. Want of easy wealth, however, left its middle reaches neglected until the very route Orellana had discovered was revived, again by accident, in 1637. Two Franciscan lay brothers, Domingo de Brieva and Andrés de Toledo, who had joined an expedition along the Napo from Quito, became detached from their companions and sailed on 'borne by divine inspiration and driven

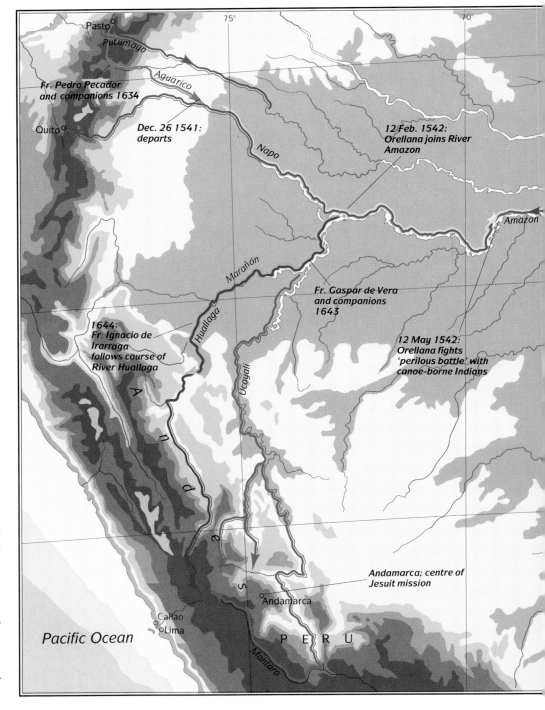

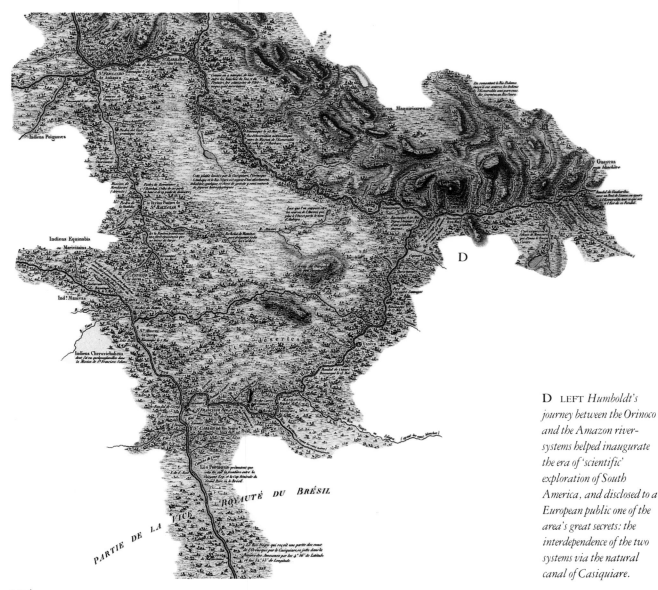

D LEFT *Humboldt's journey between the Orinoco and the Amazon river-systems helped inaugurate the era of 'scientific' exploration of South America, and disclosed to a European public one of the area's great secrets: the interdependence of the two systems via the natural canal of Casiquiare.*

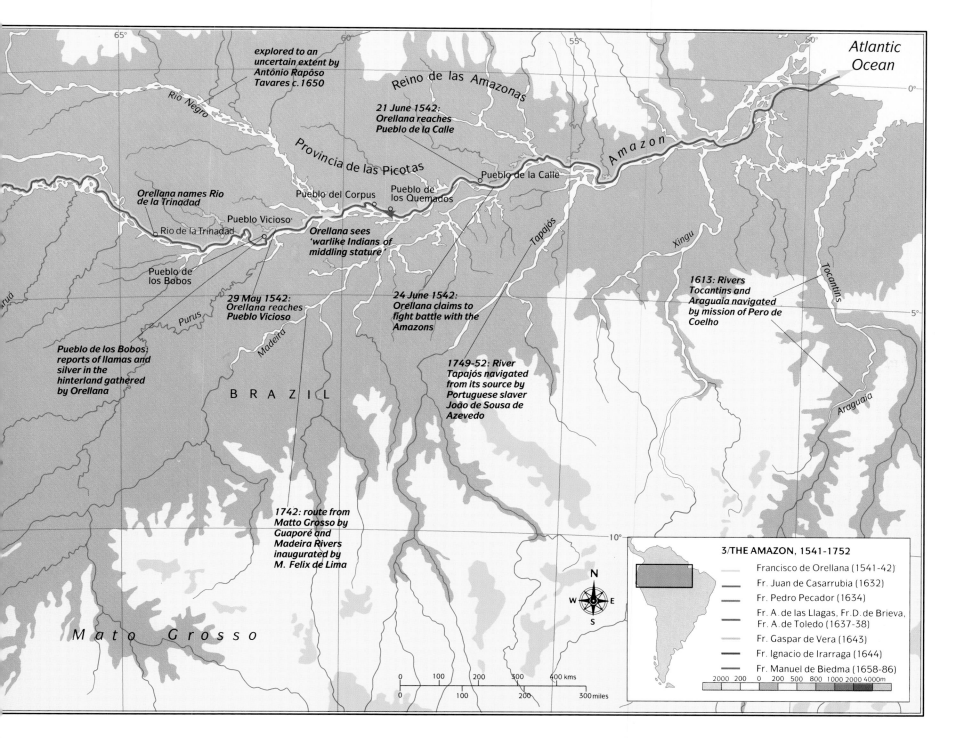

explored to an uncertain extent by Antônio Rapôso Tavares c.1650

Reino de las Amazonas

21 June 1542: Orellana reaches Pueblo de la Calle

Provincia de las Picotas

Rio Negro

Orellana names Rio de la Trinadad

Pueblo del Corpus

Pueblo de los Quemados

Pueblo de la Calle

Amazon

Pueblo Vicioso

Rio de la Trinadad

Orellana sees 'warlike Indians of middling stature'

Pueblo de los Bobos

29 May 1542: Orellana reaches Pueblo Vicioso

24 June 1542: Orellana claims to fight battle with the Amazons

Tapajós

Xingu

Tocantins

1613: Rivers Tocantins and Araguaia navigated by mission of Pero de Coelho

Purus

Madeira

Pueblo de los Bobos; reports of llamas and silver in the hinterland gathered by Orellana

1749-52: River Tapajós navigated from its source by Portuguese slaver João de Sousa de Azevedo

Araguaia

B R A Z I L

1742: route from Matto Grosso by Guaporé and Madeira Rivers inaugurated by M. Felix de Lima

M a t o   G r o s s o

N W E S

3/THE AMAZON, 1541-1752

Francisco de Orellana (1541-42)
Fr. Juan de Casarrubia (1632)
Fr. Pedro Pecador (1634)
Fr. A. de las Llagas, Fr. D. de Brieva, Fr. A. de Toledo (1637-38)
Fr. Gaspar de Vera (1643)
Fr. Ignacio de Irarraga (1644)
Fr. Manuel de Biedma (1658-86)

0   100   200   300   400 kms
0   100   200   300 miles

2000 200 0 200 500 800 1000 2000 4000m

E

3 ABOVE *Although most of the course of the Amazon was navigated downriver in 1541-42, the exploration of its headwaters and tributaries was a slow process, effected mainly by missionaries in the 17th century and mining prospectors in the 18th.* E LEFT *Santo Tomé, the town founded by Berrío on the lower Orinoco, was the base for Fernando de Berrío's river explorations into the highlands of Guiana and for English attempts to infiltrate the region, as in the attack depicted in this view of the 1630s.*

by want of food' to the Portuguese zone and the river's mouth. The Portuguese responded by sending them back to guide a major expedition under Pedro de Teixeira. The ascent took a year, but they arrived safely.

But for the revolution which sundered the crowns of Spain and Portugal in 1640, the Amazon might have become a trans-American highway at once. Rapid progress followed in the spread of missions at the foot of the equatorial Andes. Missionaries were vulnerable: Ramón de Santa Cruz died mapping the Archidona in 1662; Francisco de Figueroa was killed by slavers on the Ucayali in 1685. Yet as explorers and evangelists they were undeterred. Fr. Samuel Fritz conducted an heroic mission on the middle Amazon in the face of Portuguese slavers from 1686 (see map A).

The missionaries' foes, the slaving *bandeirantes* of São Paolo, were talented pathfinders. In 1650 Antônio Rapôso Tavares, led an expedition across Paraguay to the eastern flank of the Andes and down the Amazon, perhaps adding to knowledge of the River Negro. The discovery of mining wealth in the Mato Grosso revived secular interest. In 1742, for instance, a new route from the Mato Grosso via the Madeira to the Amazon was opened, and the prospector João de Sousa de Azevedo traced the Tapajós from its source near his mine. Yet the Amazon basin remained little known throughout the 18th century. When Humboldt sailed from the Orinoco to the Amazon via the Casiquiare in 1800, he was tracing locally known routes which had not been fully divulged. The exploration of South America had completed a cycle: the colonists who over the centuries had pieced together native knowledge in a roughly comprehensive map of the continent were now themselves subjected to a process of 'exploration' by scientific outsiders.

Map labels

Mediterranean Sea

Zagros Mountains

Tigris
Euphrates

Gulf of Suez
Gulf of Aqaba

Persian Gulf
Gulf of Oman

Indus

Thar Des[ert]

Nile

Red Sea

Arabia

Nubian Desert

Empty Quarter (Rub' al Khali)

Arabian Sea

SOU[TH]

SUMMER   WINTER   SEASONAL

MONSOON   WINTER

WINDS   SU[MMER]

Gulf of Aden

Blue Nile

Shabeelle

A F R I C A

I N D I

I N D I A N

Seychelles

Lake Nyasa

Comoro Is.

MOZAMBIQUE CURRENT

Mozambique Channel

S E TRADES

Mauritius

Reunion

Zambezi

S E TRADES

Limpopo

Vaal

Orange River

Drakensberg

BENGUELA CURRENT

Cape of Good Hope

Cape Recife

WEST WIND DRIFT

ROARING FORTIES

Crozet Is.

Prince Edward I.

SECTION VII
THE INDIAN OCEAN

THERE WAS a certain poetic truth in the ancient legend that the Indian Ocean was landlocked. Shipping from the west can enter only by way of an arduous detour through the South Atlantic and around Africa. Its southern approaches, which then have to be crossed, are guarded in the southern summer by fierce northerly storms. Access from the east, though easy in winter, is barely possible under sail in summer when storms tear into lee shores. Beyond the zone of easy access, the vast, sparsely populated expanse of the Pacific preserved the ocean from approaches from farther east until the 16th century. Thus for most of its history, this ocean remained the preserve of peoples whose homes bordered on it. Even within this fairly tight arc of exchange, sailing could be hazardous: the well-frequented route across the ocean's two great gulfs – the Bay of Bengal and the Arabian Sea – are wracked by storms throughout the year.

The Indian Ocean nonetheless provides the world's most favourable environment for long-range navigation. From remote antiquity, seafarers exploited this to open routes that extended the full breath of the ocean. The reason lies in the unremitting regularity of the monsoonal wind-system. North of the equator, north-east winds prevail in the winter; from the equator to about 10°S, they curl from the north-west. For most of the rest of the year, they blow steadily from the south and west. By timing voyages to take advantage of the monsoons, navigators could set out confident of a fair wind out and a fair wind home. As a bonus, the currents follow the winds faithfully.

But if the Indian Ocean was probably the world's first cradle of long-distance maritime exploration, its internal navigators found little incentive to extend their knowledge beyond its shores or, in the south, across the belt of storms. Access to and from the Atlantic and from the far Pacific was undeveloped until the arrival of the Portuguese inaugurated an era of increasing maritime contact with the wider world.

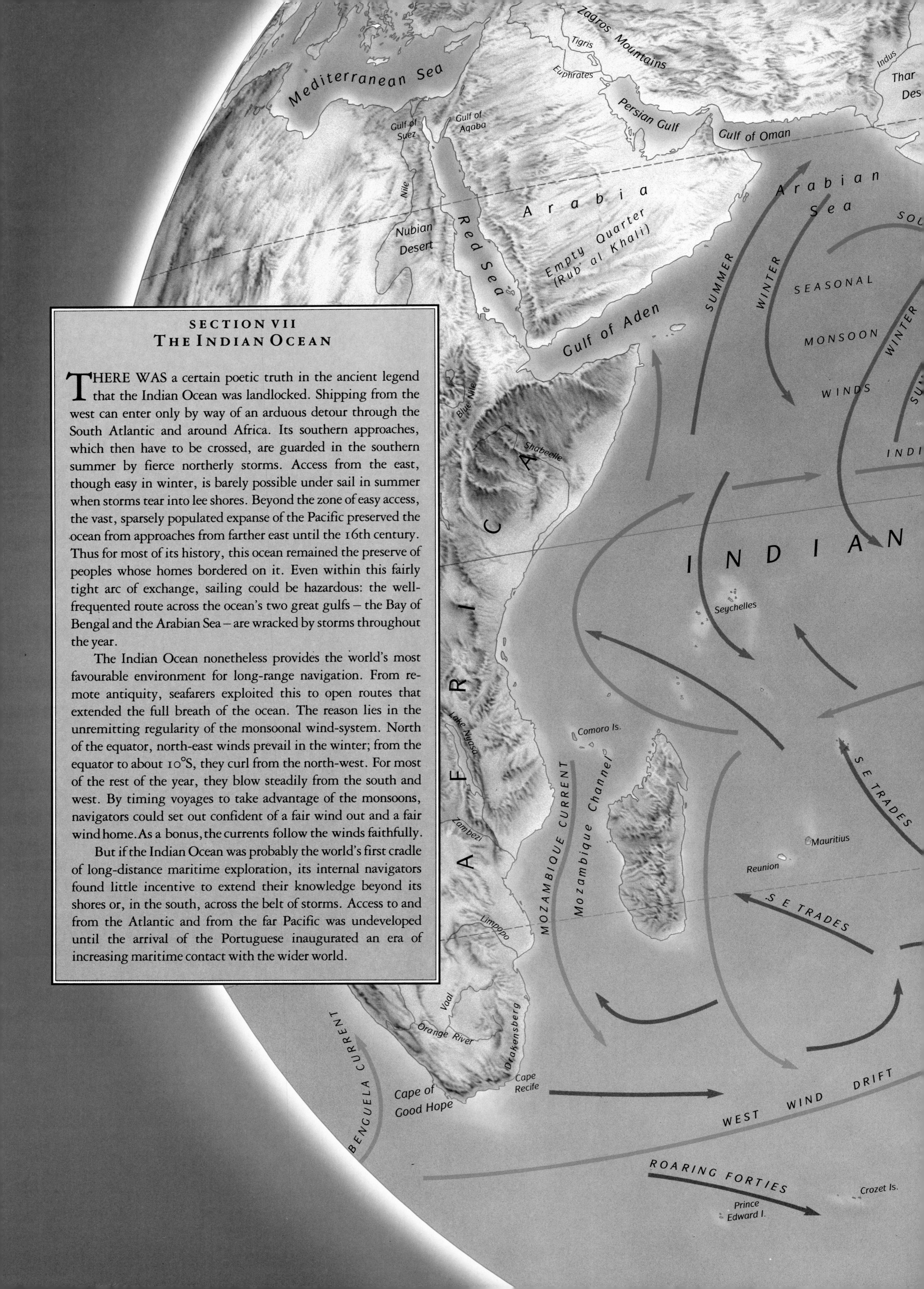

TIBET

Himalayas

Ganges

CHINA

Tropic of Cancer

Red River

*South
China
Sea*

Pacific Ocean

INDIA

Godavari

Krishna

Eastern Ghats

D e c c a n

Western Ghats

*Bay
of
Bengal*

Irrawaddy

WINTER

SUMMER

Andaman Is.

*Andaman
Sea*

SIAM

Mekong

INDO-CHINA

Gulf
of
Siam

WINTER

SUMMER

Philippine Islands

ccadive Is.

Ceylon

SEASONAL
MONSOON
WINDS

Nicobar Is.

Malay
Peninsula

SEASONAL
MONSOON
WINDS

Celebes
Sea

Maldive Is.

Borneo

Equator

ST MONSOON DRIFT

COUNTER - CURRENT

O C E A N

E a s t   I n d i e s

WINTER

SUMMER

Timor
Sea

Chagos
Archipelago

SEASONAL
MONSOON
WINDS

EQUATORIAL   CURRENT

S E TRADES

S E TRADES

WEST   AUSTRALIAN

Tropic of Capricorn

Gascoyne

AUSTRALIA

Murchison

CURRENT

Nullarbor Plain

Great
Australian
Bight

WEST   WIND   DRIFT

ROARING FORTIES

Kerguelen
Is.

EASTWARDS INTO AFRICA
1450-1770

THOUGH ITS *boundaries in the east and south are hard to define, the western limit of the Indian Ocean is fixed by the coast of East Africa. The strip of Africa which forms part of the basin of the ocean is, by comparison with the drainage areas washed on its other coasts, relatively large. It forms a tapering triangle, with its apex near the southernmost point of Africa and its base on the northern coast of the Horn, along the Gulf of Aden. It is divided from the rest of Africa by the Ethiopian plateau and highlands, the great lakes, the Zimbabwean plateau and the Drakensberg. Some formidable river-systems drain it, including those of the Juba, the Tana, the Rufiji, the Ruvuma and the lower Zambezi.*

By the 13th century, the East African coast and the cultures of the interior were becoming integrated into the trade routes of the Indian Ocean as these were pushed south by Arab and Indian merchants. Late-medieval Arab sailing directions include the coast as far as Sofala; it can be presumed that Arab, Indian and Chinese exploration had been extended much farther south by the second quarter of the 15th century when Admiral Cheng Ho surveyed at least to Kilwa. No attempt was made, however, to explore the interior until the Portuguese arrived in the Indian Ocean at the end of the 15th century. Aiming to link the new sea-route they had created around the Cape of Good Hope with the traditional transoceanic routes to India and the Far East, they established coastal staging-posts at Sofala, Kilwa, Moçambique, Malindi and Mombasa.

They were soon drawn inland by the allure of the two most conspicuous civilizations of East Africa: Ethiopia and the gold-rich empire of Monomotapa. Ethiopia yielded no prospects of material gain: its attraction was the romance of a beleaguered Christian state in Islam's rear. Monomotapa on the other hand appealed to greed, not zeal. These mixed motives inspired efforts of amazing intrepidity. The old Dom who guided Rider Haggard's heroes to King Solomon's Mines was a fictional character, but his spirit was genuinely that of the Portuguese pioneers, some of whom, by the second quarter of the 17th century, could be found deep in the African interior, ruling chiefdoms in and around the former lands of the enfeebled empire of Monomotapa. Meanwhile, farther south, a by-product of Portuguese navigation of the Indian Ocean was overland exploration by shipwreck victims of the coast from Natal to Sofala.

1 BELOW *Monomotapa became known to the Portuguese first as a result of the journeys of António Fernandes in the early 16th century, then in consequence of the military expeditions and commercial relations and individual adventurism which followed the abortive mission of Fr. Gonçalo da Silveira in 1560-61.*

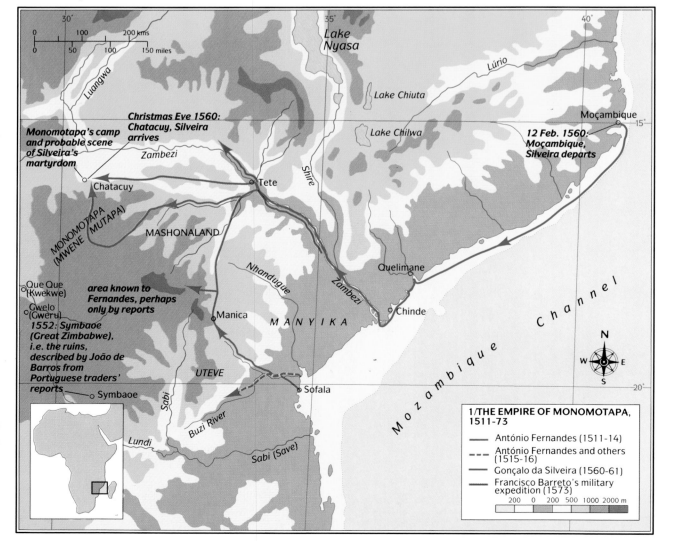

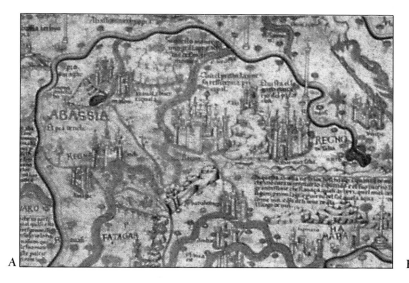

A

B

C

MONOMOTAPA and its ivory, silver and gold had an ancient reputation. Known to Ptolemy and located roughly in the area associated by cartographical tradition with the 'Mountains of the Moon', it lent itself to legends which associated it with the realm of Sheba and the Ophir of Solomon. The empire discovered by the Portuguese was, however, of relatively recent creation, the work of the dominant Rozwi clan of the Karanga people and, more particularly, of two chiefs, Mutota and his son Matope, in the second quarter of the 15th century. Interpreted by the Portuguese as 'lord of the mines' the ruler's title (also Monomotapa) really meant 'lord of the plundered lands'. Though waveringly located by early European cartography, the hegemony of the Monomotapa at its height seems to have been confined within an area defined by the 16th and 19th parallels South and the 30th and 35th meridians East. It was a loosely structured empire – more a confederacy of disparate chieftancies – but proved resilient and enduring.

News of the empire, transmitted to Portugal after the occupation of Sofala in 1506, aroused predictable cupidity. In about 1511, António Fernandes was commissioned to investigate. He was already an old African hand: he was in Kilwa (*see* ch.29, map 3) in 1501, and in 1505 assisted the first governor, Pero de Anaia, in the building of the fort of São Caetano. A carpenter by trade and a criminal by choice, he had been exiled from Portugal for an unknown crime. Fernandes exerted an extraordinary charismatic spell. 'The Blacks', according to a contemporary report, 'adore him like a God … If he goes to any place where there are wars, hostilities are suspended for love of him'. Two of his expeditions into the interior are known from reports home. They took him to the mines of Manica and deep into Mashonaland and, in 1515-16, some way along the River Buzi, yielding reports of places as far away as Que Que

A ABOVE LEFT *Fra Mauro's world map of the early 1450s reflects the knowledge of Ethiopia transmitted by 15th-century merchants, who approached it via the Nile.* **B** ABOVE *Livio Sanuto's 1588 map of southern Ethiopia is part of the first attempt to construct a specialized map of the kingdom.* **C** ABOVE RIGHT *Almeida's map of Ethiopia summarizes the explorations of the Jesuits until their expulsion in 1633. Almeida continued to chart the history and geography of the empire until his death in 1646.*

2 BELOW *Ethiopia was opened to direct access from the Indian Ocean by Pero de Covilhão and Rui da Lima, and by the military intervention of Christovão da Gama. The empire was mapped between 1603 and 1633 by Jesuit explorers, of whom Paez and Fernandes were the most remarkable.*

and Gwelo. Fruitless trading relations followed. In 1530, Portugal issued regulations for merchants visiting Monomotapa's fairs. In 1542, ambassadors were exchanged.

A new era was inaugurated in 1560 with the arrival of the Jesuit Gonçalo da Silveira, who converted the emperor known as Dom Sebastião, together with his consort and 100 Amazon bodyguards. When da Silveira fell victim to a court intrigue the Portuguese decided to combine a punitive expedition with the conquest of Monomotapa's wealth. A long and costly series of campaigns from 1571 to 1575 left Portuguese garrisons in control of some mining centres, but the effort of maintaining them could not be sustained for long. The Portuguese and the Rozwi settled into a productive relationship of mutual enrichment; it worked much better than more active and overt forms of imperialism. Commercial penetration and the writings of the Dominican missionary João dos Santos in the 1590s made Monomotapa, and its hinterland as far as the Limpopo, one of the best-known parts of Africa. Though increasingly fragmented, Monomotapa survived until conquered by the Ngoni of Natal in the 1830s (*see* ch.39).

Portuguese exploration of Ethiopia followed a similar pattern. Though known to European travellers in the 15th century, Ethiopia was hard to reach. The approach lay through Muslim country, along the Nile, then by caravan and ship to Massawa. Entering directly from the Red Sea via Zeyla in 1493-94 Pero de Covilhão opened a new era in communications with the outside world (*see* ch.28), but not until the return embassy of Matthew the Armenian arrived in Portugal in 1513 was interest stimulated sufficiently to ensure continuity of effort. In 1520 Rui da Lima was chosen to accompany Matthew home. Among his companions was the Franciscan Francisco Alvares, who compiled the first surviving European explorer's account of Ethiopia. The title-page of his book, *The*

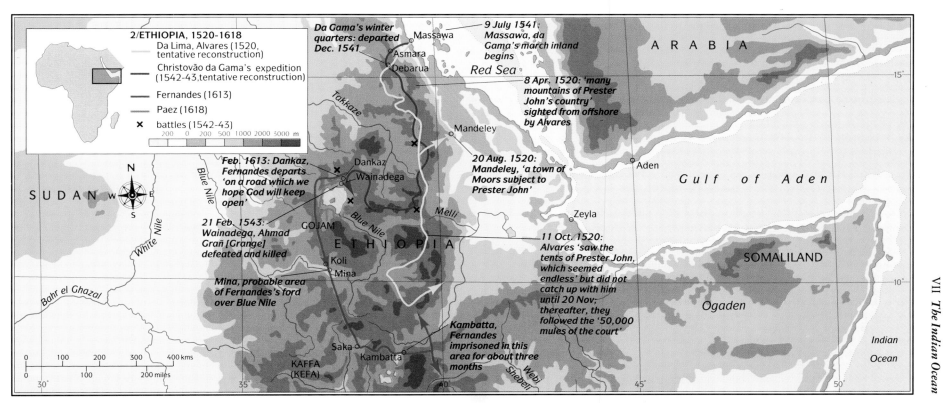

2/ETHIOPIA, 1520-1618
- Da Lima, Alvares (1520, tentative reconstruction)
- Christovão da Gama's expedition (1542-43, tentative reconstruction)
- Fernandes (1613)
- Paez (1618)
- × battles (1542-43)

200 0 200 500 1000 2000 5000 m

Da Gama's winter quarters: departed Dec. 1541

9 July 1541: Massawa, da Gama's march inland begins

8 Apr. 1520: 'many mountains of Prester John's country' sighted from offshore by Alvares

20 Aug. 1520: Mandeley, 'a town of Moors subject to Prester John'

Feb. 1613: Dankaz, Fernandes departs 'on a road which we hope God will keep open'

21 Feb. 1543: Wainadega, Ahmad Gran [Grange] defeated and killed

Mina, probable area of Fernandes's ford over Blue Nile

11 Oct. 1520: Alvares 'saw the tents of Prester John, which seemed endless' but did not catch up with him until 20 Nov; thereafter, they followed the '50,000 mules of the court'

Kambatta, Fernandes imprisoned in this area for about three months

Massawa · Asmara · Debarua · Mandeley · Dankaz · Wainadega · Koli · Mina · Saka · Kambatta

SUDAN · ARABIA · Red Sea · Aden · Gulf of Aden · Zeyla · SOMALILAND · Ogaden · Indian Ocean · ETHIOPIA · GOJAM · KAFFA (KEFA)

Takkaze · Blue Nile · White Nile · Bahr el Ghazal · Melli · Webi Shebeli

0 100 200 300 400 kms
0 100 200 miles

30° · 35° · 40° · 45° · 50° · 15° · 10°

Prester John of the Indies, discloses the alluring image he sought to project of the backward and beleaguered kingdom. He saw it as an exotic and quasi-Oriental land, whose ruler fulfilled medieval expectations of 'Prester John', a mythical Christian ruler in otherwise Islamic Africa. His description of the Negus's shabby court was calculated to impress: the 'endless tents' borne by 50,000 mules; the crowd of 2,000 at an audience; the clergy with mitre-shaped *coiffures*; the silks and scarlet; the plumed horses, caparisoned in fine brocade. The letters the Negus despatched under Alvares's instruction played shamelessly on the Prester John legend, vaunting 'men and gold and provisions like the sands of the sea and the stars of the sky'. They also claimed falsely that Ethiopia was anxious to join the Roman communion, at the expense of its Coptic liturgy and Monophysite creed, and would make territorial concessions to Portugal for help against Muslim assailants.

By the time the help materialized, the plight of the kingdom appeared irrecoverable. Nor was aid officially inspired. During the Portuguese expedition to the Red Sea in 1541, news of the apparent imminence of Muslim conquest moved some Portuguese gentlemen to take service with the Negus as a chivalric gesture. Christovão da Gama led the quixotic force – 400 Portuguese with 130 slaves, well-armed with arquebuses and artillery – claiming that 'to help Prester John was to serve God and the king of Portugal'. He faced a daunting task: to link up with the demoralized forces of the Negus Claudius in the south of the country across intimidating mountains, while the army of the Muslim chief, Grange, bestrode the way.

After wintering at Debarua (*see* map 2), he began his campaign in earnest in December 1541. Brushing aside Grange's garrisons he fought his way along the edge of the plateau, to the area around the source of the Melli, where, after exploring tentatively to locate Muslim garrisons and seek the Negus, he dug in to resist the growing pressure of an enemy concentration. In a battle at the end of August he was killed, along with most of his captains, and 'the heads piled high in his tent'. His intervention, however, had contributed to the reversal of the fortunes of the war. The 130 Portuguese survivors combined with the Negus and in February 1543 had their revenge when Grange fell to a Portuguese bullet.

Da Gama joined the host of Coptic saints and the fame of his exploits attracted missionaries to Ethiopia, especially from the fledgling Society of Jesus. During their period of supreme influence at court, between 1603 and 1633, Jesuit travellers effected a thorough reconnaissance of Ethiopia, although most of their discoveries were to remain unpublished for centuries. The most remarkable contributions to exploration were made by Fr. Pedro Paez, who discovered the source of the Blue Nile in 1618, and Fr. António Fernandes, whose attempt to find a route from Gojam to Mogadishu in 1613 (*see* map 2) was among the great exploring endeavours of the order, undertaken in the service of a Negus who was desperate to improve access to his realm from the rest of Christendom. Fernandes ventured into country barely known to the Ethiopians themselves, and not seen again by European eyes until the 19th century. His chosen route would have taken him south into Kaffa, but in the little Christian kingdom of Enyara he was directed east, with the idea of finding and following the Webi Shebeli. He crossed intervening pagan lands in safety, but the Muslim ruler of Alaba, after keeping him in fear of his life, returned him to the Negus. His offer to return to 'the road which we hope God will keep open' was dismissed as unrealistic and he spent the rest of his life in fasting and scholarship. He told the order's historian, Almeida, that on his epic journey 'in the depths of that vast and savage wilderness he thought of himself as an ant in a great meadow ... going along with the grain of wheat or millet he carried without fear of being trodden on or crushed, and without regarding the purposes of other travellers ... I think that the Father had this attitude not only on that journey, but throughout his life'.

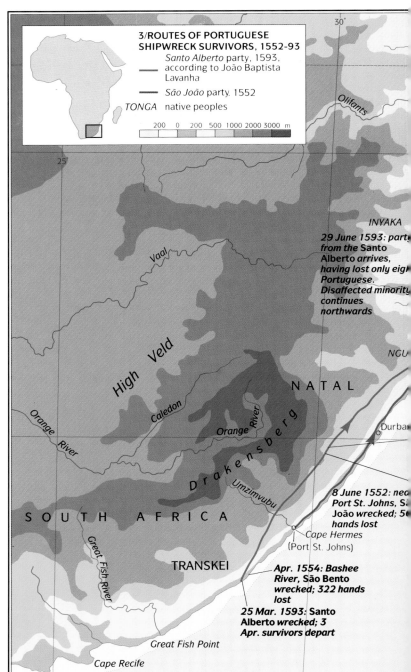

3 RIGHT *Exploration of the coast north towards Sofala by shipwrecked sailors yielded considerable information about the region's harsh terrain. Dense bush reached to the shore in many places and seasonal fluctuations turned rivers from dry to impassable.*

3/ROUTES OF PORTUGUESE SHIPWRECK SURVIVORS, 1552-93

Santo Alberto party, 1593, according to João Baptista Lavanha

São João party, 1552

TONGA native peoples

200 0 200 500 1000 2000 3000 m

Olifants

INYAKA

29 June 1593: part from the *Santo Alberto* arrives, having lost only eig[ht] Portuguese. Disaffected minority continues northwards

Vaal

High Veld

NATAL

NGU[...]

Orange River

Caledon

Orange River

Durba[n]

Drakensberg

Umzimvubu

SOUTH AFRICA

8 June 1552: nea[r] Port St. Johns, S[ão] João wrecked; 5[..] hands lost

Cape Hermes (Port St. Johns)

Great Fish River

TRANSKEI

Apr. 1554: Bashee River, São Bento wrecked; 322 hands lost

25 Mar. 1593: Santo Alberto wrecked; 3 Apr. survivors depart

Great Fish Point

Cape Recife

In the far south, the coast from Natal to Sofala was trekked by castaways, victims of the 'tragic history of the sea' celebrated by a long Portuguese literary tradition. Sailings home from Goa had to be launched, for safety, in late December or early January, but commercial and bureaucratic delays frequently postponed departure and ships found themselves exposed to the springtime perils of a stormy lee shore by the time they reached Natal. The pilots tried to vary the route between the Mozambique Channel and the 'outer route' around Madagascar, but both presented hazards. Greedy overloading of excessively big and top-heavy ships exacerbated the dangers, and the shore of Natal probably claimed over 100 ships in the first century of Portuguese navigation in the area.

Map 3 relates three representative cases of more than a dozen of which some account has been left. The crews' journeys

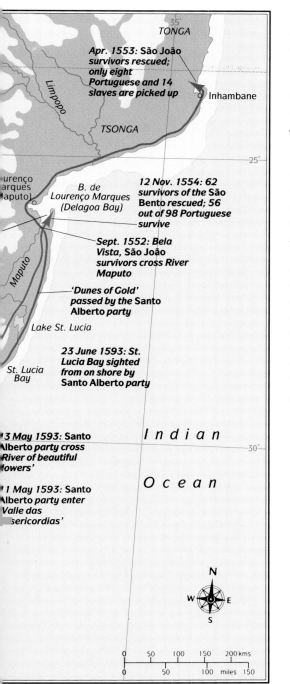

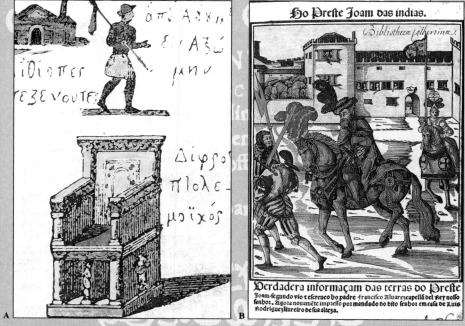

D ABOVE FAR LEFT *Almeida's map of the sources of the Blue Nile was made on the basis of Pedro Paez's information, which also inspired the route taken by the Jesuit Jeronimo Lobo (1629).*

E ABOVE CENTRE LEFT *Vossius's 1666 map of the Blue Nile reflects Jesuit discoveries in the region, including the belief that the source of the river had been found.* **F** ABOVE NEAR LEFT *Bruce's 1770 map of the sources of the Blue Nile is more detailed than those derived from Fr. Paez's account. Bruce disputed the Jesuit discoveries and claimed that they had been elaborated by 17th-century geographers.*

UNTIL THE the 15th century, Ethiopia was virtually an unknown land to European scholars. The 6th-century writer, Cosmas Indicopleustes, summarizing the knowledge bequeathed by Classical antiquity, claimed to have been there. He left sketches (A) of the port of 'Adule' (Zula), of Ethiopians on the road to Aksum and of a marble throne. But no significant advance was made in the study of the country until 1440, when Ethiopian delegates at the Council of Florence were interviewed by humanists and geographers: the detailed information in the maps of Jacopo d'Angiolo (before 1456) and Fra Mauro (1459) (map A) was the result. In about 1480 a permanent centre of Abyssinian studies was, in effect, established at Rome, when Pope Sixtus V founded a church for Ethiopian visitors, with a resident community of up to a dozen monks, at the Church of San Stefano dei Mori. A great deal of work was stimulated by travel. Tasfa Seyon, an Ethiopian monk who resided at San Stefano between 1538 and 1571, was indefatigable in the promotion of study of his native land. The Ethiopian embassy to Portugal of 1514 inspired Damião de Góes's *Fides, Religio Moresque Æthiopum* of 1544 and the return Portuguese embassy produced Alvares's *Ho Preste Joam das Indias* of 1540 (B).

Cartographical information continued to be refined until Livio Sanuto's work of 1578 (map B); humanists continued to show interest in the language. But little new was contributed until the intensive work undertaken by Jesuit missionaries in the early 17th century. Only part of their material was published, even after their expulsion in 1633. The Franciscans who succeeded them made little impression on the country. The polemical purposes which affected even some of the best work of the period which followed is suggested by the title page of Fr. Sandoval's Jesuit history of 1647, where scenes of baptisms by Jesuits flank a scene identifying the Negus with one of the Magi of the gospel above the text from the psalms: 'Ethiopia will stretch out her hands to God' (D).

Few travellers' accounts were available. The most redoubtable contribution was made by Job Ludolf, a Lutheran who published some 20 works on the subject between 1661 and 1704. As well as studies of Ethiopian history and theology, he produced an improved grammar of the liturgical language and the first printed lexicon and grammar of the vernacular Amharic. But the light he cast on the country was extinguished with his death. The renewed dominance of polemics is illustrated by the frontispiece of Veyssière la Croze's *Histoire du Christianisme d'Ethiopie et d'Arménie* of 1739 (C) which shows Imposture inspiring the forging of early Monophysite writings. The brief visit of the Franciscan Fr. Remedio Prutky in 1752-53 was soon forgotten and the researches undertaken by James Bruce of Kinnaird from 1768 to 1772 were not published until the 1790s. Virtually unvisited, Ethiopia became a fantasy-land, a playground for exotic fancies, even, in Voltaire's *Princesse de Babylone* of 1778, a setting for erotic mischief.

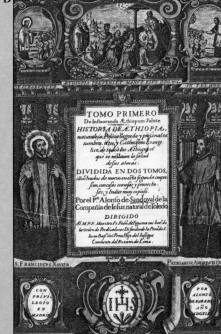

encompassed conscious exploration: the account of the survivors of the *Santo Alberto*, for instance, was made expressly for the benefit of future castaways. Its author, the famous humanist João Baptista Lavanha, based it on the pilot's journal and interviews with the men. His picture of the ship going down, its pumps clogged with pepper, makes a splendid cautionary vignette which betrays his ancillary moral purpose. Other descriptions were by participants, like Manoel Perestrelo, who wrote a moving but geographically vague account of the disaster of the *São Bento*. Some survivors continued their overland journeys to Sofala – those of the *São João Baptista* of 1622, for instance, and of the miserable *São Thomé* (which sank with 375 hands in 1589). But it was an undertaking fraught with hazard, illustrated by the massacre of a disaffected party from the *Santo Alberto*, who tried it in 1593 (*see* map 3).

28

THE INDIAN OCEAN: RED SEA ROUTES

1414-1541

'THIS *sea presents more hazards to navigation than the whole of the Great Ocean*', concluded João de Castro of the Red Sea in 1541. *His Arab predecessor, Ibn Majid, agreed in his* Fawa'id *of c. 1490 that it concealed 'many unknown places and things'. Despite the antiquity of travel along it, the Red Sea remained hazardous to shipping throughout the era of sail. Yet this apparently barren cul-de-sac has long been one of the world's great avenues of trade. Despite the persistence of 'unknown places', there was little original exploring left for the Portuguese interlopers of the 16th century: their role was the detailed hydrographic survey of the area. The motive was military rather than commercial. When Afonso de Albuquerque entered the Red Sea in April 1513, he intended to reach Suez to destroy the Sultan's fleet. After 1517, when the Ottomans extended their hegemony into the Yemen, Portuguese strategic concerns increased. In that year, Lopo Soares's expedition reached Jedda; in the decade after 1520 Portuguese fleets entered the sea five times. Little more was learned until the arrival of João de Castro in Estevão da Gama's punitive expedition in 1541. Castro's erudition produced the most comprehensive guide for the Red Sea until the 1830s.*

1 LEFT *Though Portuguese interlopers in the Red Sea relied on indigenous knowledge and Arab routes already established, the heavy ocean-going war fleets they introduced were unprecedented, while the hydrographic survey of João de Castro improved enormously on the existing tradition.*

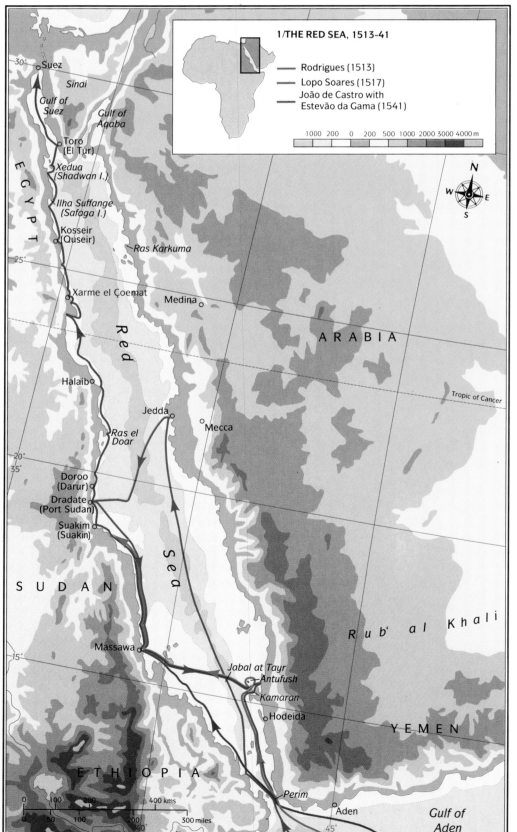

1/THE RED SEA, 1513-41

— Rodrigues (1513)
— Lopo Soares (1517)
— João de Castro with Estevão da Gama (1541)

1000 200 0 200 500 1000 2000 3000 4000 m

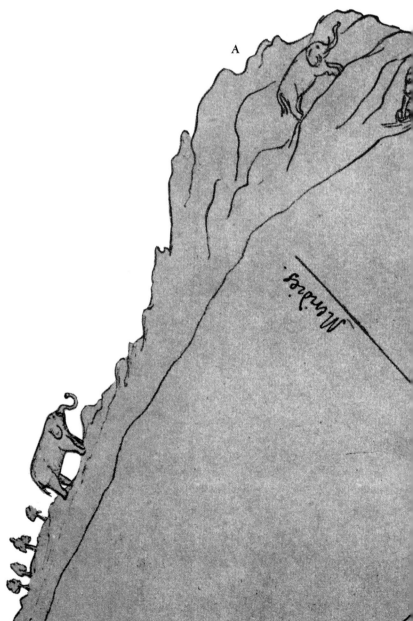

THE Red Sea has always been a 'route of spices'. The frank-incense and myrrh so prized in the ancient Levant came from around its southern tip. Sumerian inscriptions referring to Omani shipwrights suggest the trade may go back to the third millennium BC. The Red Sea was the Egyptian road to the land of Punt (*see* map 2) – never securely located but perhaps in or near Somaliland – to which Queen Hatsheput's expedition was recorded on the walls of her mortuary temple in c. 1500 BC. Among the Greeks of the 2nd century BC, southern Arabia had the reputation of a land where men 'burned cinnamon and cassia for their everyday needs'.

Yet between the exploration by Alexander's captain Anaxicrates in the 4th century BC and the arrival of the Portuguese in the 16th century AD, the exploitation of this difficult but lucrative thoroughfare was left to navigators from the lands along and near its shores. The adverse sailing conditions limited access to small craft carrying high-value cargoes, and left the sea with a daunting reputation among Indian and east Arabian merchants who preferred the Persian Gulf route from India. Ibn Majid, however, did much to systematize traditional knowledge and make it available to a wider world, synthesizing – he claimed – the lore passed on from his father and grandfather with his own unequalled experience. In 1538 Suleiman I was able to lead a fleet down the Red Sea from Egypt that was heavy enough to challenge the Portuguese in the Indian Ocean. His return route, hugging the east coast to Ras Karkuma, then crossing to Safaga Island before turning towards Suez, was recorded by a Venetian captive who accompanied the expedition.

The main function of the Red Sea was not, however, as a bolt-hole for Egyptian and Ottoman raiders of the Portuguese spice-routes, but as an avenue of commerce between Egypt and the lands of the Indian Ocean basin. In the 15th century, before the opening of the route around the Cape of Good Hope, it might have become an axis of communication between Latin Christendom and the Orient. Europeans knew of the vibrant world of commerce in the Indian Ocean from Marco Polo at the end of the 13th century, and, in the mid-14th century, from John of Marignolli, the last Franciscan bishop in Peking in the Mongol era, both of whom had made the return journey from China to Persia by sea. Merchants and missionaries naturally attempted to make the journey in reverse. After the collapse of Mongol rule in China in 1368, the Red Sea seemed to offer the best avenue of approach to the Far East. Red Sea travellers can be detected with surprising frequency in the early 15th century, bound for India and Ethiopia, sometimes making part of the journey upriver along the Nile and joining the Red Sea by overland caravan; indeed, almost throughout the century this seems to have been the favoured approach, rather than that from Suez. But if the numbers of Europeans trading in the Indian Ocean can never have been very high, and for all that they had little contact with their metropolitan bases, the extent of their penetration was remarkable. When Girolamo di San Stefano of Genoa was faced with confiscation of all his goods in Sumatra in the mid-1490s, he was saved by an official who could speak Italian.

Apart from itineraries for Abyssinia, however, little evidence of the routes followed by European Red Sea travellers of the period has survived. The most spectacular exception is the account of the Oriental odyssey of Niccolò Conti, which became the subject of a famous book by Poggio Bracciolini of 1439. The commonplace business of a Venetian merchant took him to Damascus, where, in 1414, he seems to have decided to attempt to investigate the sources of the spice trade of the Persian Gulf. Taking the generally favoured route out, via Hormuz, he covered most of the established shipping lanes of the Indian Ocean as far as Java and perhaps Saigon, though omitting the links between India and East Africa.

The change of fortune which led, indirectly, to his fame occurred when he returned to Cairo via the Red Sea in 1437.

A BELOW *Only a few of João de Castro's meticulous drawings of the Red Sea have survived. This panoramic view of Massawa, 'port of Prester John', as late-medieval travellers called it, shows the 'humble town' on the island marked 'A'.*

During a two-year wait for a passport, he was obliged to abjure his faith, and was to see his wife and children die in an epidemic. When he finally got back to Italy he went to Florence, where the Pope was presiding over a General Council, to seek absolution for his abnegation of Christianity. The occasion of the Council had brought together humanists and cosmographers from Italy and the Greek world, and Conti's story found a ready audience. Poggio represented it as a moral tale 'of the fickleness of fortune' yet it was a success as an example of the traditional genre of travel books. Twenty-eight 15th-century manuscripts of the work have survived. Conti's accounts of the Ganges and the Irrawaddy influenced Fra Mauro's world map of 1454 (*see* ch.27) and Pope Pius II relied heavily on Poggio's book, especially for reports of China and Burma, in writing a cosmographical treatise of his own.

The sobriety which makes Conti's story credible is backed up by two further accounts of Indian Ocean travels of the 1490s, both of which used the Red Sea as a route of access. The first, that of the journeys of Pedro de Covilhão, was based on a hurriedly made record of an old man's memories, and may be subject to distortion and embellishment, though the basic facts are amply corroborated. Covilhão had joined the service of Afonso V of Portugal from that of the duke of Medina Sidonia at a time of war between Portugal and Castile. He conducted diplomacy at Maghribian courts on behalf of João II before being sent, in 1487, with a companion called Afonso de Paiva, on a triple mission: to find the route to the lands of spices; to verify the navigability of a passage from the Atlantic to the Indian Ocean; and to make contact with Prester John, the legendary Christian potentate then generally identified with the Negus of Abyssinia. As Ptolemy's influential *Geography* had given the impression that the Indian Ocean was landlocked, Covilhão's mission had a specific scientific objective.

Florentine backers who were financing Portugal's exploration of an Atlantic route also provided the investment for Covilhão's and Paiva's attempt. The travellers made for Alexandria and Rhodes, disguising themselves as honey merchants. From Cairo, they joined the Red Sea at Toro and sailed its

length, via Suakim, to Aden. There they parted, Covilhão heading east in search of the spice lands, Paiva south for Prester John. The account of the former's exploits contains romantic episodes which may be doubted, and complexities which may arise from confusion. It seems unlikely, for instance, that he really travelled up and down the Red Sea four times, or that he visited Mecca and Medina in disguise, making his way from there to Cairo via St. Catherine's monastery in Sinai. On the other hand, it seems probable that he reached Hormuz and Calicut and investigated the route from southern India to East Africa as far south as Sofala. At some point in his travels – reportedly but implausibly in Cairo – he heard of Paiva's death and decided to continue the mission to Prester John in person, first despatching to Portugal a favourable report on the trading prospects. Unlike most travellers to Abyssinia, who normally went via Massawa, he was fortunate to be able to reach the country from Zeyla. Arriving before May 1494, he was welcomed with much honour and settled as the honoured guest – and virtual captive – of the Negus, enjoying the services of 'many vassals'. Here he was found by the next Portuguese embassy, which arrived in December 1520. It was a member of this mission, Fr. Francisco Alvares, who wrote the admiring account by which Covilhão's achievements are known.

Covilhão's route almost crossed with that of the Genoese merchants Girolamo de San Stefano and Girolamo Adorno who, in the spring of 1494, set off up the Nile to Keneh, turning aside to make a seven-day caravan journey to the Red Sea at Kosseir. They experienced the infamous character of navigation on that sea, taking 35 days to get to Massawah, which they recognised as 'the port of Prester John'. The remotest points on their Indian Ocean itineraries were Sumatra and Pegu, in Burma, where Adorno died. Despite shipwreck at Cambay, San Stefano made it home via Hormuz by taking service with some Syrian traders. Like their precursors, they stopped short of the Spice Islands, and had limited their efforts to well-known routes of indigenous shipping. Nonetheless, their experiences stimulated the search for new routes to the Orient via the Atlantic.

B

B ABOVE *The Red Sea turtle was among the flora drawn by James Bruce, the early 18th-century explorer of the Horn of Africa.*
2 BELOW *The possible routes of Niccolò Conti and Pedro de Covilhão are plotted over the traditional indigenous routes of the Indian Ocean, which had been gradually explored since remote antiquity.*

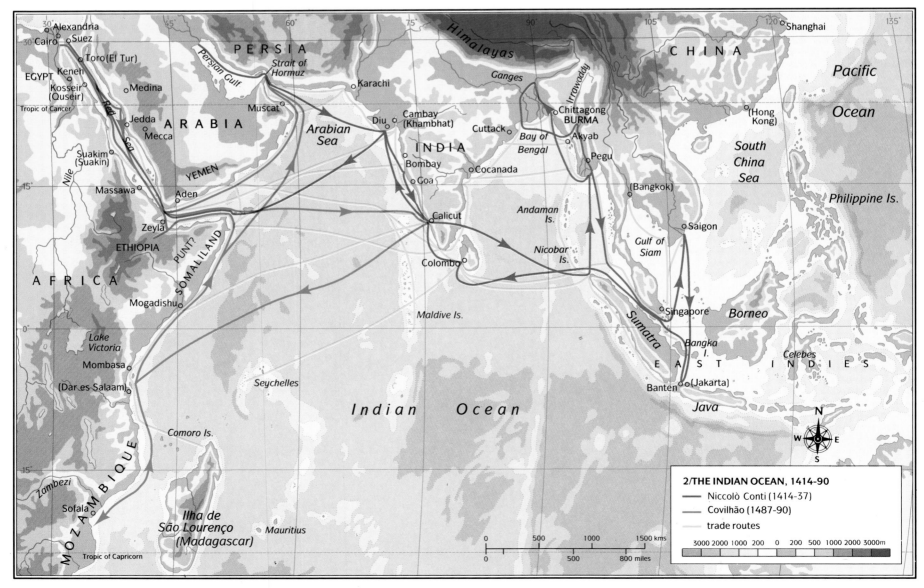

2/THE INDIAN OCEAN, 1414–90
— Niccolò Conti (1414–37)
— Covilhão (1487–90)
— trade routes

29

THE INDIAN OCEAN: TRANSOCEANIC ROUTES 1498-1611

IN 1498 Vasco da Gama entered the Indian Ocean by a route never, so far as is known, sailed before (see ch.13). He crossed it, under local guidance, by a route known for centuries. The sailing routes of the northern and central parts of the Indian Ocean are determined by the monsoons and by the distribution of trading civilizations from East Africa to the East Indies. The origins of their exploration are irrecoverably remote, as are those of the techniques by which it was done. Ibn Majid ascribed the discovery of the first lodestone to David, who had used it to defeat Goliath. According to an Indian text of the 1st century AD, Buddha was so skilful a navigator that 'knowing the course of the heavenly lights, he was never uncertain of the whereabouts of a ship'.

Trade routes across the Indian Ocean can be reconstructed from the provenance of goods in ancient times. From the mid-9th century they can be documented from surviving Arabic manuals of navigation. Ibn Majid handled works of the 11th century on the coasts and coastal routes 'under the wind' – that is, in the Bay of Bengal – and 'on from the land of China'. In late-Abbasid times, the chain of routes was extended down the eastern coast of Africa as far as Sofala. Evidence of the transference of cultural influences, and knowledge of the overall shape of the continent revealed by medieval Chinese maps, have led some scholars to speculate that navigation might have been pursued farther round the coast. However that may be, the route around the Cape pioneered by the Portuguese intersected a well-established network of sea-lanes.

The commercial world of the Indian Ocean was changed more, perhaps, by the spread of Islam than by the arrival of the Portuguese. Increased global trade in spices expanded the volume of traffic by traditional routes despite the importance of the new route around the Cape. Perhaps more significant in volume terms was the growth of the carrying trade on the pilgrimage routes to Mecca. Already when Ibn Majid wrote his compendious sailing directions towards the end of the 15th century he was able to represent the demands of the haj – the ritual pilgrimage to Mecca – as the sole justification for his labour. 'For how long', he exclaimed, 'have we sailed in ships from India and Syria, the coasts of Africa and Persia, the Hejaz and the Yemen and other places, with the fixed intent of not being turned aside from the direct route to the desired land, either by worldly possessions or by human agency!'

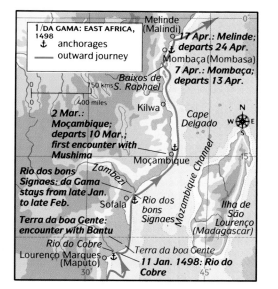

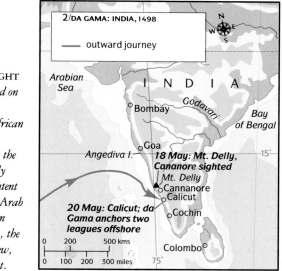

1 LEFT and 2 RIGHT Vasco da Gama relied on local knowledge in exploring the East African and Indian coasts.
3 BELOW Whereas the Portuguese in the early 16th century were content to follow the existing Arab shipping-lanes between Sofala and the Indies, the Dutch later opened new, direct routes to the east.

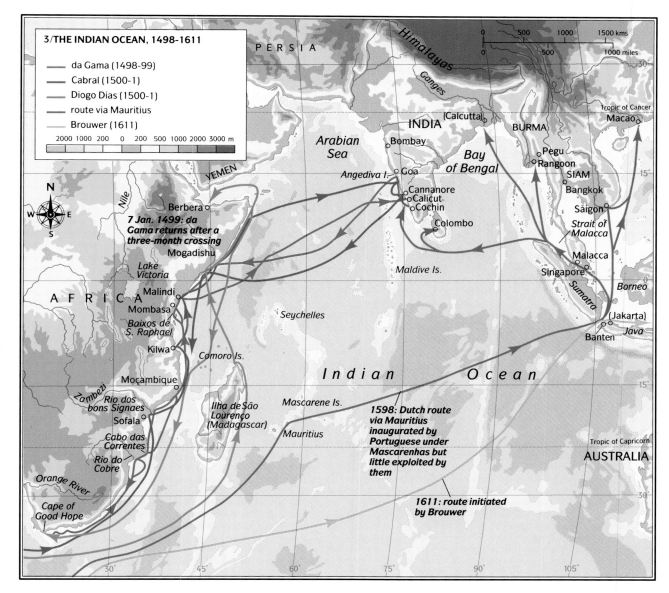

VASCO da Gama was guided across the Indian Ocean by a pilot generally identified in early accounts as a Gujerati Muslim. The Portuguese called him Molemo Canaqua, a corrupt form of the Arabic for 'pilot-astrologer'. This suggests that they were dealing with an erudite individual, capable of sophisticated celestial navigation. A rumour current in the mid-16th century identified him – most improbably – as Ibn Majid himself. Though the story should probably not be taken literally, it suggests the enormous influence of Ibn Majid's writings as a guide to the ocean's routes. The stature of his work barely diminished with time: as Sheikh Majid, he was venerated by the fishermen who ferried Sir Richard Burton from Aden in 1854.

The Portuguese dependence on Arab routes had a restrictive effect on their trade, committing them to a long passage via East African ports and attendance on the monsoon. Even the discovery of Mauritius and the Mascarene Islands in the early 16th century, which would have allowed a more southerly route across the Indian Ocean, was not followed up. Perhaps as a result, the Portuguese relied on coercive rather than competitive methods to break into the spice trade. Instead of cutting costs, they invested heavily in an aggressive naval policy of intimidating suppliers, bombarding competitors and shunting their wares between fortified posts.

Not until the Dutch began to probe the Indian Ocean in the late 1590s was Mauritius fully exploited as a staging-post. The Dutch lacked resources to back their commercial initiative with naval muscle and could make an impact on the trade only by under-cutting the Portuguese. But the Mauritius run, though it represented a short-cut direct to the sources of spices, was arduous and dangerous, involving a long struggle with variable winds across open sea. Nor could it operate outside the seasonal constraints of the monsoon.

In 1611 this problem was circumvented when Hendrik Brouwer initiated a more southerly route to Banten. By passing well to the south from the Cape of Good Hope, Dutch ships could ride on the 'roaring forties' and the southern ocean drift to a point beyond about 80°E, where the connecting current would help them make their northing. It was a passage that demanded heroic seamanship, with a huge oceanic detour necessary in the South Atlantic to get beyond the Cape followed by another vast journey, across the Indian Ocean. It was, however, serviceable throughout the year.

The richest prizes of the Indian Ocean trade lay beyond the Straits of Banda and Malacca in the fabled Spice Islands. Portu-

A RIGHT *Captured by the Portuguese in 1510, Goa became the capital of Portugal's eastern seaborne empire. This drawing illustrated the* Itinerario *of Jan van Linschoten, whose intelligence about the Indian Ocean was the basis of Dutch efforts.*

guese determination to pursue the spice trade to its sources was evinced by a series of enterprising viceroys who gradually drove the range of Portuguese navigation eastwards. Afonso de Albuquerque seized Malacca in 1511. His intelligence-gathering on the subject of access to the Spice Islands is revealed in letters of 1512, in which for the first time the name of Francisco Rodrigues appears: in April, the latter was mentioned as having obtained a large fragment of a Javanese pilot's map; in August, he had been appointed as pilot of the fleet António de Abreu was to lead to the islands, because 'he possesses excellent knowledge with which to make maps'.

The viceroy's tribute was amply justified by Rodrigues. The three vessels departed towards the end of 1512 with 120 men. 'No more ships or men went to discover New Spain with Christopher Columbus', wrote the expedition's first chronicler, 'nor with Vasco da Gama to India, because the Moluccas are no less wealthy than these, nor ought they to be held in less

4 BELOW *The routes followed by Abreu, Rodrigues and Serrão to Ceram and the Moluccas, and by Pires to China, owed much to the work of Rodrigues himself in compiling information about the coasts.*

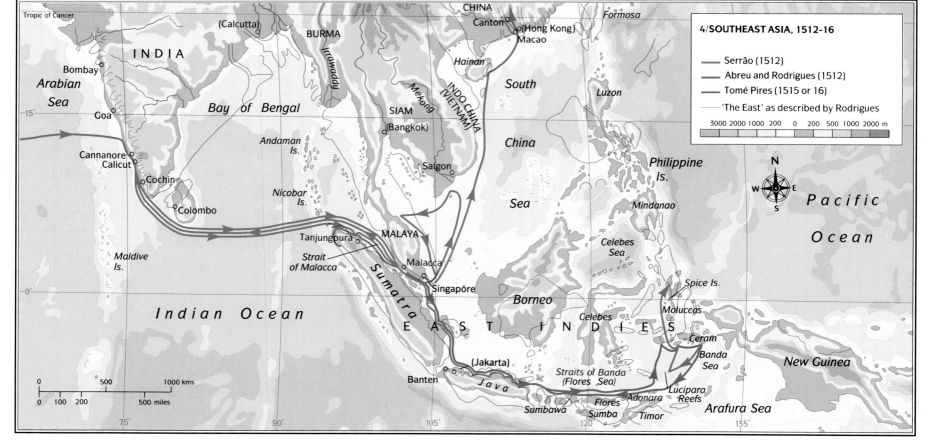

4/SOUTHEAST ASIA, 1512-16

— Serrão (1512)
— Abreu and Rodrigues (1512)
— Tomé Pires (1515 or 16)
····· 'The East' as described by Rodrigues

3000 2000 1000 200   0   200 500 1000 2000 m

B LEFT *Madagascar first appeared on a western map in 1492. The legend on this Portuguese map of c. 1519 proclaims it 'the most cultivated and populated of all the islands in the sea'.*
C RIGHT *Rodrigues's reputation as a chartmaker was based on the virtuosity of draughtsmanship, such as in this view, probably of Adonara. His style seems to have been influenced by his Oriental – especially Javanese – sources.*

esteem'. In one sense the expedition was a failure, turning back from Banda before the Moluccas were reached, but fate intervened to supply an unexpected success. One of the ships, commanded by Francisco Serrão, had been abandoned and replaced with a junk, in turn wrecked on the way back on the reefs of Lucipara. Serrão was able to make his way from there by native shipping to the Moluccas, establishing the first known European presence and initiating a Portuguese monopoly which was challenged but feebly for the rest of the century.

The information Rodrigues brought back from the voyage was vital for the promotion of further Portuguese efforts, combining maps made from his own observations in the eastern archipelago with others synthesising intelligence gained from native sources, and providing a guide to navigation from the Bay of Bengal to China. His panoramic drawings reveal his skill as an observer and a draughtsman (*see* illustration C).

Rodrigues's information was followed up in the second half of the decade when the Portuguese mounted their first attempt to open direct relations with China. The protagonist of this effort was Tomé Pires, an apothecary of the royal household who had arrived in the Indies in September 1511, probably in order to advise on the purchase and shipping of medicinal drugs. After a year in the job he found himself, as he wrote to his brother, 'more rich than you can imagine'. Apparently un-

satisfied with mere material wealth, he made a voyage to Java in March 1513 as 'overseer of cargo' – almost entirely of cloves – and took the opportunity to assemble a great deal of information about the island. Early in 1515 he sailed from Malacca for the South China Sea 'to bring all things duly explained' and report on a reputed diamond-mine in 'Tanjungpura'.

When the new viceroy, Lopo Soares de Albergaria, sought an envoy to the Court of China in February 1516, Pires, despite his background as an apothecary, was by no means as surprising a choice as is commonly said. The fleet which carried him was driven back off the Vietnamese coast in September, but a new attempt on a larger scale in June the following year reached Canton without misadventure on 15 August. Despite delays from Chinese officials, Pires was at last put ashore 'with thunder of artillery and trumpets' as the Chinese were seen to be 'very particular about protocol'.

The problems of communicating successfully with the 'Court of Heaven' defeated him, as they defeated most western ambassadors who followed him for the next three centuries, and his writings on China have been lost. His achievement, however, deserves some tribute from historians of exploration for it represents the unification of previously ill-connected chains of communication that linked the fringes of the northern Pacific, across the Indian Ocean, to the Atlantic.

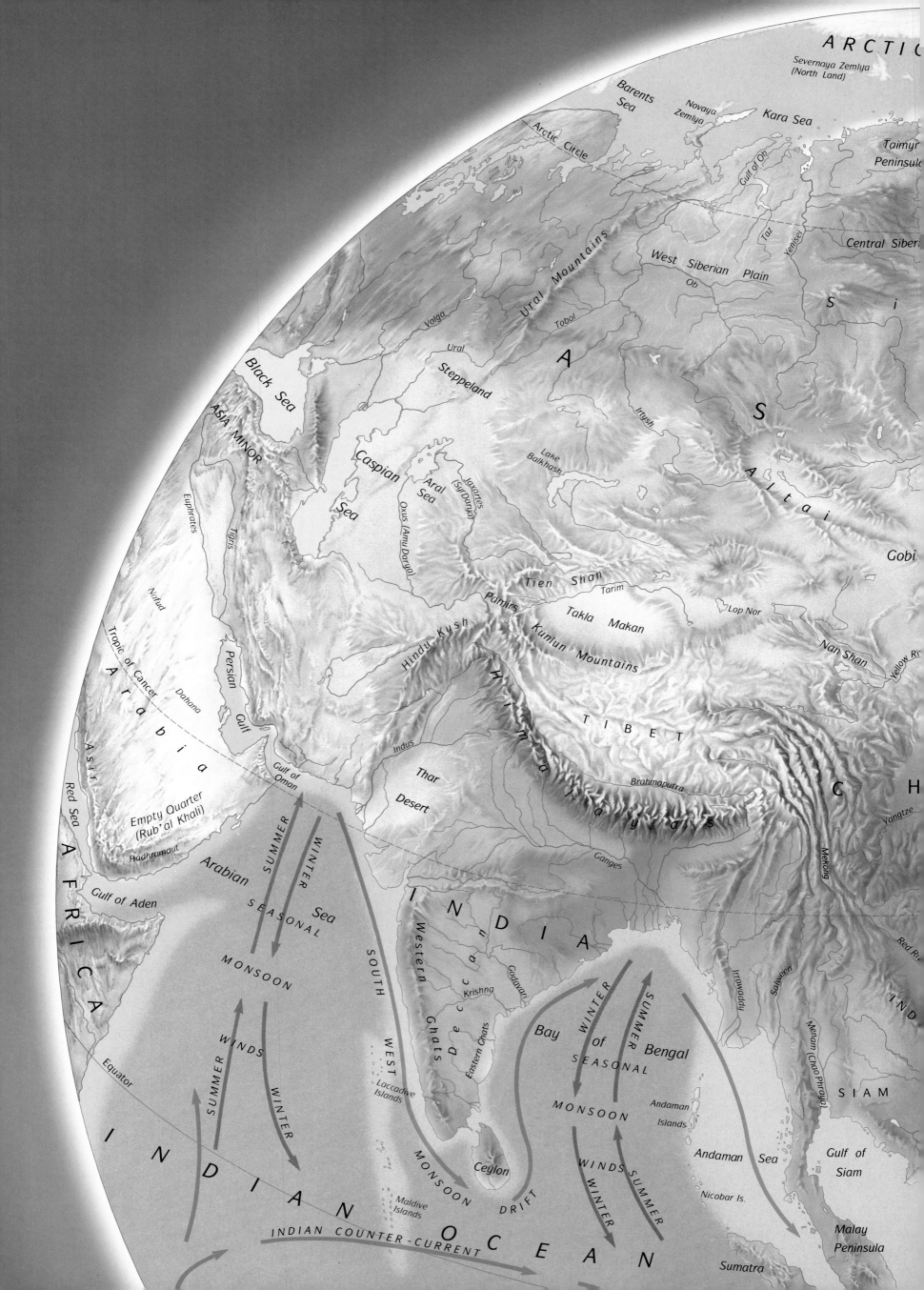

OCEAN

Laptev Sea

New Siberian Islands
(Novosibirkiye Ostrova)

East Siberian Sea

Bering
Chukchi
Peninsula Strait

teau

Lena

Indigirka

Kolyma

KAMCHATKA CURRENT

Bering Sea

Aleutian Islands

S i b e r i a

b e r i a

I A

Lake Baikal

SUMMER

WINTER

Sea of
Okhotsk

SEASONAL WINDS

Sakhalin

Kurile Islands

Manchuria

Amur

Desert

PACIFIC OCEAN

Hokkaido

WINTER

SUMMER

SEASONAL WINDS

Sea of Japan

WINTER

SUMMER

Korea

Yellow River

Yellow Sea

J A P A N

Honshu

Shikoku

CURRENT

Yangtze

I N A

Kyushu

East China Sea

Ryukyu Islands

KUROSHIO OR JAPAN

Formosa Strait

Formosa

WINTER NE TRADES

ulf of
ngking

SEASONAL

South

China

Sea

Luzon

NORTH EQUATORIAL CURRENT

Philippine

HINA

WINTER

SUMMER

MONSOON

SUMMER SE MONSOONAL WINDS

Sulu Sea

WINTER

Islands

Mindanao

SUMMER

WINTER NE TRADE WINDS

WINDS

Borneo

Celebes Sea

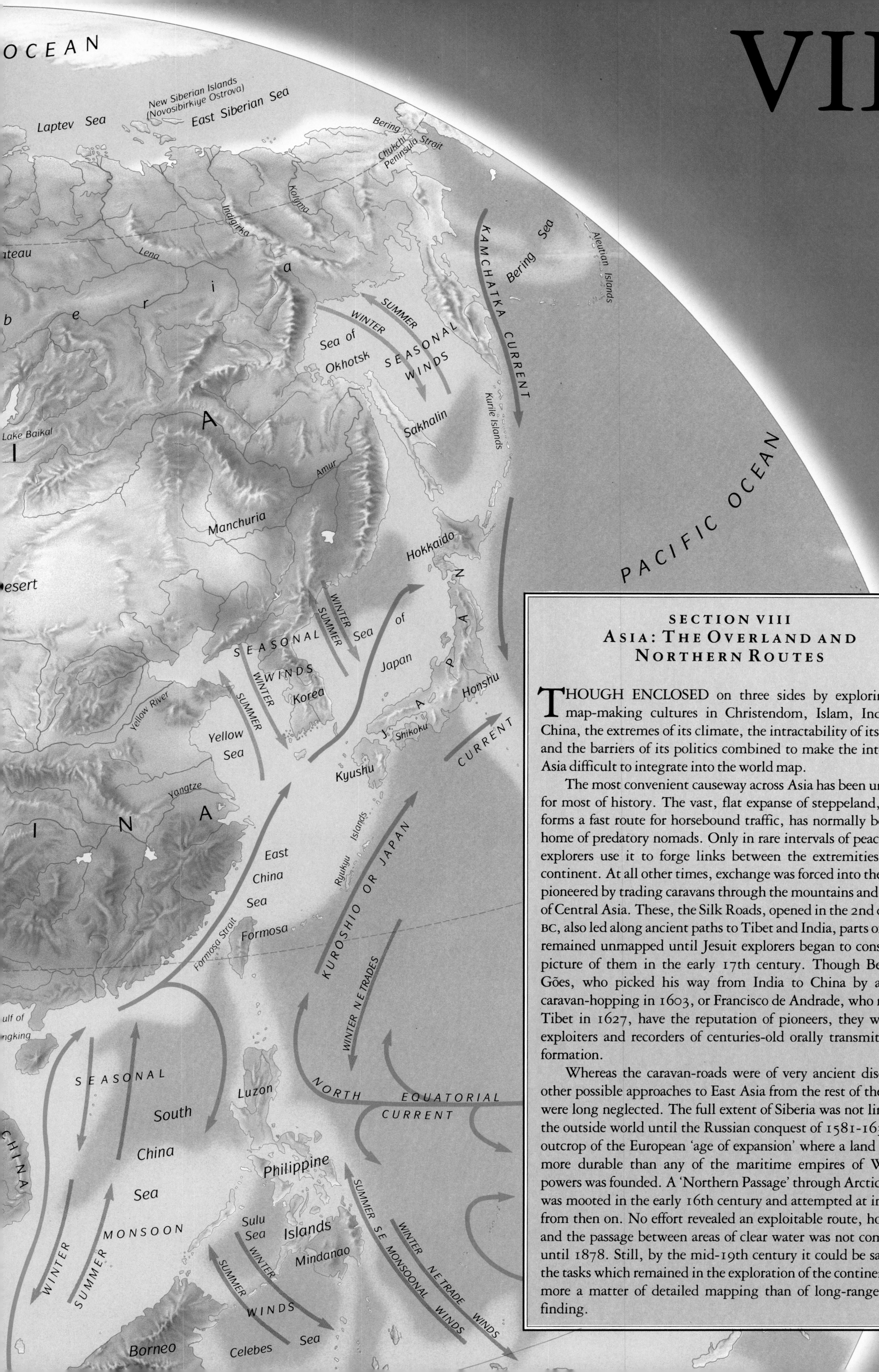

SECTION VIII
ASIA: THE OVERLAND AND NORTHERN ROUTES

THOUGH ENCLOSED on three sides by exploring and map-making cultures in Christendom, Islam, India and China, the extremes of its climate, the intractability of its terrain and the barriers of its politics combined to make the interior of Asia difficult to integrate into the world map.

The most convenient causeway across Asia has been unusable for most of history. The vast, flat expanse of steppeland, which forms a fast route for horsebound traffic, has normally been the home of predatory nomads. Only in rare intervals of peace could explorers use it to forge links between the extremities of the continent. At all other times, exchange was forced into the routes pioneered by trading caravans through the mountains and deserts of Central Asia. These, the Silk Roads, opened in the 2nd century BC, also led along ancient paths to Tibet and India, parts of which remained unmapped until Jesuit explorers began to construct a picture of them in the early 17th century. Though Bento de Gões, who picked his way from India to China by arduous caravan-hopping in 1603, or Francisco de Andrade, who reached Tibet in 1627, have the reputation of pioneers, they were the exploiters and recorders of centuries-old orally transmitted information.

Whereas the caravan-roads were of very ancient discovery, other possible approaches to East Asia from the rest of the world were long neglected. The full extent of Siberia was not linked to the outside world until the Russian conquest of 1581-1639 – an outcrop of the European 'age of expansion' where a land empire more durable than any of the maritime empires of Western powers was founded. A 'Northern Passage' through Arctic waters was mooted in the early 16th century and attempted at intervals from then on. No effort revealed an exploitable route, however, and the passage between areas of clear water was not completed until 1878. Still, by the mid-19th century it could be said that the tasks which remained in the exploration of the continent were more a matter of detailed mapping than of long-range route-finding.

30

SILK ROADS FROM ASIA
138 BC - C. AD 1650

A LEFT *The value and range of goods transmitted along the Silk Roads was demonstrated by the remarkable finds of a Belgian expedition at Begram in 1938. Though one of the lesser towns of the trans-Asian trade routes, Begram was nonetheless evidently an important trading centre. The objects discovered were in two bricked-up storerooms and were apparently deposited between the 1st and 4th centuries AD. They came from as far apart as China, India and the Mediterranean. Those shown here are a bronze statue of Serapis-Hercules of the 1st–4th centuries AD and made in Alexandria, and a painted glass vase with a scene of Europa and the Bull of the 1st–2nd centuries AD, also from Alexandria.*

A

B

VIII *Asia: Overland and Northern Routes*

THE MORE famous European explorations of the Silk Roads, the routes across Central Asia from the Middle East to China in the 13th and 14th centuries (see ch.31), should not be permitted to overshadow the earlier travels and accounts of these routes by Asian merchants, missionaries and ambassadors. Centuries before Marco Polo, Chinese, Arab, Persian, Jewish and Turkish traders ventured along the Silk Roads between China and the West. As early as the 1st century AD, the Romans had developed a craving for Chinese silks, and caravans traversed the deserts, steppes and mountain ranges on a perilous trek through Central Asia to satisfy this demand. Notwithstanding that the largely anonymous merchants who pioneered and developed these routes left few records of their travels, knowledge of the trade routes was remarkably detailed.

Nor should the fame of the long-distance Silk Roads overshadow the trade conducted on the shorter-distance routes between China and its neighbours in the steppes and deserts of its west. Not only did these short-distance routes endure into the 19th century, long after the demise of the long-distance Silk Roads, but, as the goods transported along them were for the most part essentials, the trade was much more active than that carrying the luxuries of the Silk Roads.

The pastoral nomads and oasis dwellers along China's frontiers who took part in this less exotic commerce were rarely able to carry more than basic household goods during their migrations, and their dependence on trade goods was considerable. Furthermore, since many of these pastoral peoples did not develop an artisan class, they also needed craft goods. Thus a lively trade, at any rate in times of peace, was conducted between them and the Chinese. The Chinese in turn, for all their assertions that trade with these neighbouring people was of no benefit to them, nevertheless valued the horses, camels, furs and jade the nomads possessed.

Despite the relatively shorter distances over which this trade was conducted in comparison with those of the Silk Roads proper, and despite the complex infrastructure that supported it, its travellers nevertheless faced significant hazards. Reports of corpses of both men and animals along the routes underline the ever-present perils from looters and bandits as much as from the frequently harsh and inhospitable terrain to be traversed. The survival of the trade was testimony to the hardiness of those who conducted it.

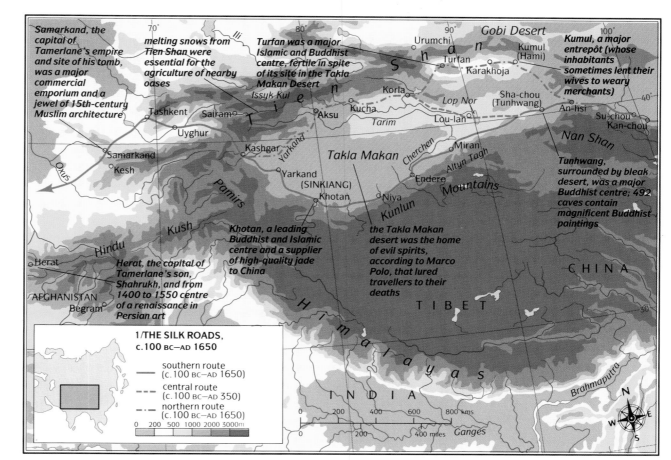

(see ch.31)

Samarkand, the capital of Tamerlane's empire and site of his tomb, was a major commercial emporium and a jewel of 15th-century Muslim architecture

melting snows from Tien Shan were essential for the agriculture of nearby oases

Turfan was a major Islamic and Buddhist centre, fertile in spite of its site in the Takla Makan Desert

Kumul, a major entrepôt (whose inhabitants sometimes lent their wives to weary merchants)

Herat, the capital of Tamerlane's son, Shahrukh, and from 1400 to 1550 centre of a renaissance in Persian art

Khotan, a leading Buddhist and Islamic centre and a supplier of high-quality jade to China

the Takla Makan desert was the home of evil spirits, according to Marco Polo, that lured travellers to their deaths

Tunhwang, surrounded by bleak desert, was a major Buddhist centre; 492 caves contain magnificent Buddhist paintings

1/THE SILK ROADS, c.100 BC–AD 1650

southern route (c.100 BC–AD 1650)
central route (c.100 BC–AD 350)
northern route (c.100 BC–AD 1650)

1 ABOVE The Silk Roads from China were the main east–west caravan routes from the 1st century BC to approximately 1650. The oases and towns in modern Sinkiang, Soviet Central Asia and Afghanistan could not have flourished without the economic stimulus provided by Silk Road traders, who also played a vital role in transmitting Buddhism and Islam throughout Asia.

COMMERCE between China and its neighbours had developed as early as the Scythian period in Central Asia (7th to 9th centuries BC), but the first recorded accounts of relations stem from the mission of Chang Ch'ien in the 2nd century BC. The Emperor Wu sent Chang to Central Asia to seek allies against the Hsiung-nu, nomadic Huns who raided across the Chinese frontiers. Though Chang was unable to secure an alliance, his account of his travels stimulated a demand for trade. This short-distance trade continued intermittently until the 19th century, with successive Chinese dynasties keeping the routes relatively safe.

The courses of the routes from China to Central Asia traced a variety of paths across the inhospitable Takla Makan desert. All followed the same route from Ch'ang-an to beyond Sha-chou, which eventually emerged as a centre of Buddhist learning and art. At An-hsi they divided. The southern route from Sha-chou entered the Tarim River basin before skirting the

B LEFT Mongol ponies, such as that on the left being presented as tribute to the Ming court, opened a fast highway across the Asiatic steppelands which 13th- and 14th-century travellers could ride with some security. C RIGHT This bronze captures the T'ang image of a Persian merchant brought to China on the Silk Roads: a barbarian of freakish appearance on an outlandish but serviceable beast. Similar images of unfamiliar visitors were common in T'ang China and underline the frequency of early travel along the Silk Roads. C

VIII Asia: Overland and Northern Routes

151

TURFAN and Tunhwang were typical of the vital oases along the Silk Roads. Both were on the fringes of the desert, while Turfan was 'below sea level and so hot the people have to live underground in summer'. Carefully constructed irrigation works permitted the inhabitants to cultivate wheat and millet, to grow melons, grapes and pomegranates, and to keep horses and sheep.

Central Asian states and kingdoms sought to control Tunhwang and Turfan to obtain commercial advantages. They found themselves competing with the more powerful Chinese dynasties who attempted to rule and to station garrisons in the towns to control trade and to bolster defence of their frontiers. In the 1st century AD, a Chinese army of the Han dynasty occupied the region, facilitating trade between China and Central Asia, Persia and the Middle East. As the dynasty declined and lost control of Tunhwang and Turfan, so trade on the Silk Roads diminished, to be revived only when the T'ang dynasty

(618-907) conquered the area in the 7th century. T'ang domination promoted commerce from which Persians, Turks, Arabs and Chinese all benefited. When the T'ang weakened in the 9th century, trade declined until the 'Mongol Peace' of the 13th century, when travel across Eurasia increased dramatically (*see* ch. 31). Commerce persisted until the early 17th century, when the sea route from Europe to Asia began to eclipse the overland Silk Roads.

The art of Turfan reflects the diverse influences represented in its multi-ethnic population. The wall-painting of Uighur princesses (D) found in the Bezeklik caves, now in the outskirts of present-day Turfan, are meant to depict 9th-century Turkish women. But their facial features, stiff poses and robes are Chinese in origin. Similarly, another wall-painting from the same caves, of a dragon leaping out of water (A), offers a combination of Chinese influence (the dragon) and Persian motifs (the rippling water).

These cave paintings underline the importance of Tunhwang in the transmission of Buddhism; indeed, Tunhwang and other Central Asian towns were as significant for cultural diffusion as for facilitating trade. The wall painting of the Boddhisattva Avalokitesvara (B), with a recently deceased nun to his right holding an incense burner and a dead official to his left carrying a plate with a lotus flower, are typical of the Buddhist paintings in the caves. The inscription is a prayer for the souls of the two deceased to be re-born in the Pure Land, or Buddhist Paradise. Another frequent motif is that of the Guardian King of the North (C). He is seen riding across the waters with his warriors before doing battle with the forces opposed to the Buddhist Law.

northern flanks of the Kunlun Mountains. One of the first important stops was Miran, from where the caravans followed the Cherchen River to Endere and Niya. They completed this 500-mile segment of the journey at the oasis of Khotan, from where they continued along the Kunlun Mountains to rejoin the two other routes across the Takla Makan at Kashgar.

The central route traversed the Lop Nor depression, until recently considered impassable. However, in the late 19th century the Swedish explorer Sven Hedin discovered the bed of a lake fed from the Tien Shan mountains and which had permitted the establishment of the town of Lou-lan in the middle of the desert. After crossing the Lop Nor, travellers reached the town of Korla and there joined the northern trade route. They then followed the southern foothills of the Tien Shan through the fabled oases of Kucha and Aksu and along the Yarkand River to Kashgar.

The longer and more circuitous northern route supplanted the central one by early T'ang times in the 7th century AD. Skirting all but one stretch of the desert areas it was less perilous than the Lop Nor route. Its course was the same as that of the southern route until the town of An-hsi. Here it took a sharp detour to the north to cross a section of the Gobi Desert. Once Kumul was reached, the most arduous part of the journey was completed. The route then followed the foothills of the Tien Shan to Turfan and Korla, and from there traversed the same road as the Lop Nor route to Kashgar.

A detailed 15th-century description of this northern route was provided by Ch'en Ch'eng, Chinese ambassador to the court of Shahrukh, Tamerlane's son. Ch'en started in the conventional way, skirting the Takla Makan desert and taking the northern detour through Kumul. He passed through Karakhoja and Turfan, but from there veered north instead of heading for the customary juncture of Kashgar. He skirted the lake of Issyk Kul and stopped in Sairam for two days. Within a month, he visited Tashkent, Samarkand and Kesh, the birthplace of Tamerlane. His travels ended in Herat, the capital of the Timurid empire.

The average journey between Samarkand and Peking may have been as long as six months. Though travelling relatively short distances the caravans were therefore costly. In addition to supplies for men and animals, considerable resources were necessary to keep bandits at bay and to maintain the oases en route. The trade routes themselves required substantial physical protection. The Chinese, for example, erected watch towers three-quarters of a mile to five miles apart depending on topography, with communications between them by means of smoke and flag signals. Postal stations were also built. Though the principal objective was the speedy conveyance of government documents, they also benefited commerce: each station had a specified number of horses, mules, ox-drawn carts or sedan chairs, and merchants could usually be accommodated.

Caravans faced numerous difficulties. Desert travel was always hazardous; vivid descriptions of sandstorms appear in the accounts of nearly all travellers in these areas. The intense heat was still another peril, while extreme cold in winter and in the mountains, where altitude sickness was an additional problem, was commonplace. Away from the oases water was a permanent concern. A good supply of camels was also essential. The camel could carry more weight, approximately 400–500 pounds, than any other pack animal. It also required less water and pasture, and its hooves did not sink into the sand.

Man-made barriers were as critical to this trade as the sometimes inhospitable natural environment. Tribes or the ruling elites in oases often demanded so-called protection costs or tariffs. Bandits roamed the steppelands and the fringes of the desert regions of Central Asia. When China or the rulers of Central Asian tribes, kingdoms or states failed to maintain the watch towers, garrisons and postal stations, caravans faced even more perilous journeys.

D LEFT *In the early 15th century, Tamerlane, whose tomb in Samarkand presides over a great emporium, promised to re-unite the lands of the Silk Roads by conquest, stimulating a new wave of European travel into southern Central Asia.*
E RIGHT *Popes and emperors depicted in an illuminated copy of Rashid al-Din's* World History. *This 14th-century work reflects the mutual knowledge exchanged across the length of the Silk Road.*
F BELOW *The Mongol Peace kept the road to Peking 'safe by day and night' in the early 14th century, and guaranteed the security of camel caravans bivouacked in the open.*

E

F

SILK ROADS AND STEPPELANDS: LATE-MEDIEVAL ROUTES TO ASIA 1246-1295

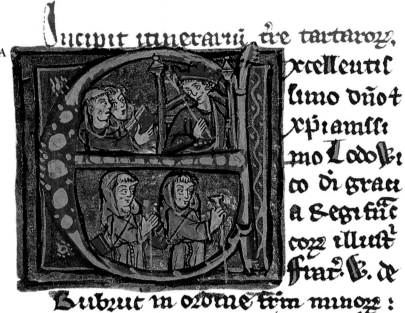

A LEFT *William of Rubruck takes his leave of Louis IX in an illumination from one of the few surviving manuscript copies of his work. The Mongols insisted on treating his mission as an official embassy, though he saw himself as a simple evangelist.* **1** BELOW *In the 13th century a northern steppeland highway to Asia was added to the traditional Silk Road and sea-lanes. All three types of route were used by Franciscan missions to the Mongol khans and by the Polo family in their travels to and from China.*

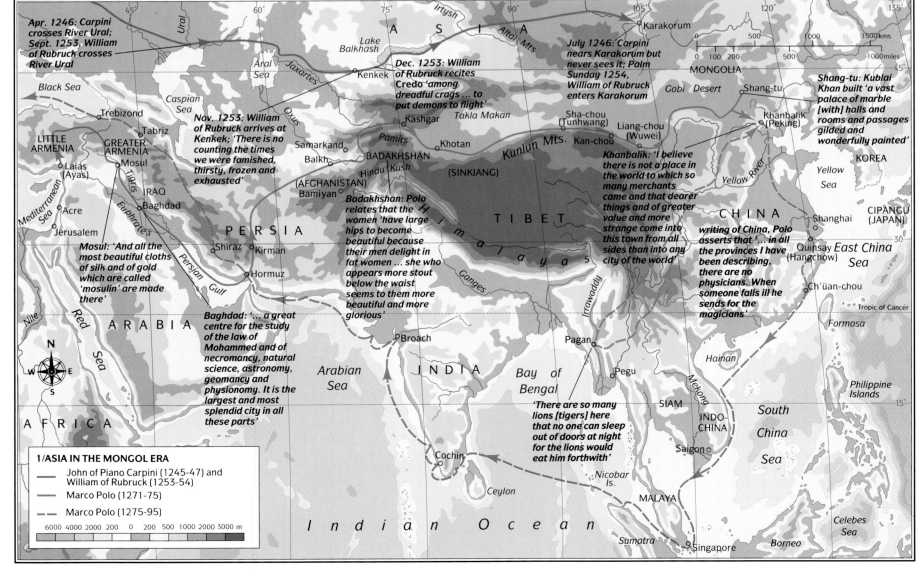

Apr. 1246: Carpini crosses River Ural; **Sept. 1253,** William of Rubruck crosses River Ural

Dec. 1253: William of Rubruck recites Credo 'among dreadful crags ... to put demons to flight'

July 1246: Carpini nears Karakorum but never sees it; Palm Sunday 1254, William of Rubruck enters Karakorum

Shang-tu: Kublai Khan built 'a vast palace of marble [with] halls and rooms and passages gilded and wonderfully painted'

Nov. 1253: William of Rubruck arrives at Kenkek; 'There is no counting the times we were famished, thirsty, frozen and exhausted'

Khanbalik: 'I believe there is not a place in the world to which so many merchants came and that dearer things and of greater value and more strange come into this town from all sides than into any city of the world'

Mosul: 'And all the most beautiful cloths of silk and of gold which are called 'mosulin' are made there'

Badakhshan: Polo relates that the women 'have large hips to become beautiful because their men delight in fat women ... she who appears more stout below the waist seems to them more beautiful and more glorious'

writing of China, Polo asserts that '... in all the provinces I have been describing, there are no physicians. When someone falls ill he sends for the magicians'

Baghdad: '... a great centre for the study of the law of Mohammed and of necromancy, natural science, astronomy, geomancy and physionomy. It is the largest and most splendid city in all these parts'

'There are so many lions [tigers] here that no one can sleep out of doors at night for the lions would eat him forthwith'

1/ASIA IN THE MONGOL ERA

— John of Piano Carpini (1245-47) and William of Rubruck (1253-54)
— Marco Polo (1271-75)
-- Marco Polo (1275-95)

6000 4000 2000 200 0 200 500 1000 2000 3000 m

THE MONGOL conquest of China, Persia, Central Asia and much of Russia and the Middle East in the 13th and 14th centuries directly linked Europe and eastern Asia for the first time in history. A Pax Mongolica (which was, on occasion, shattered by conflicts among the various regional Mongol khanates) permitted merchants, missionaries and envoys to travel relatively unhindered across Eurasia. The diaries of a few of these travellers provide precise descriptions of the routes and travel conditions between East and West along the fabled Silk Road. Marco Polo's account is by far the most renowned, but the records of the Franciscan missionaries who preceded him on the road to the central Mongol domains in eastern Asia also often yield valuable descriptions of the towns, deserts and mountains on the way to the capitals of the great khans.

From the Mediterranean, European travellers of the overland route journeyed across Persia or southern Russia and through Central Asia before arriving either in the original Mongol capital at Karakorum or in the second capital at Khanbalik (modern Peking). Some came seeking to convert the Mongols to Christianity; others to propose alliances with them; most came hoping to trade for Chinese goods. Foreign merchants, it is reported, 'never ceased to visit China', drawn by the anticipation of vast fortunes that would justify the risks, hardships and expense of the Silk Road.

It was as a direct consequence of this trade that the first Europeans reached China in the 13th century; so far as is known no inhabitant of China arrived in Europe before 1287. Marco Polo himself, the son of a Venetian merchant, accompanied his father and his uncle on a combined trade and political mission, though Kublai Khan eventually recruited him as an adviser and envoy for the Mongol court.

Paradoxically, however, it was, at least in part, the very success of the travellers and chroniclers of these overland routes in stimulating demand in Europe for Asian silks and spices and other luxury goods, and in describing the wealth of the East, whether real or imagined, that led to the eventual demise of the Silk Road. Anxious to avoid the laborious sometimes several-year-long journey, from the mid-15th century Europeans pioneered new sea routes to the Orient, in the process discovering the most valuable and practical of all, that around the Cape of Good Hope and across the Indian Ocean (see chs. 12 and 29).

B

B ABOVE *The Catalan Atlas, probably of c. 1375-85, shows camel caravans and mounted travellers on the Silk Road. The steppeland route was severed by the Ming Revolution in China in 1368, just before the map was made.* C BELOW *Silk Roads overlapped for much of their length with Buddhist pilgrim routes from China to India; the shrine at Bamiyan, shown here, was among the most celebrated.*

THE MONGOL contribution to the opening of trans-Asiatic routes in the late Middle Ages was vividly summarized by John of Marignolli, who, sent by the Pope to the see of Peking, first saw the Altai Mountains in 1341. 'Before the days of the Tartars [Mongols] nobody believed that the earth was habitable beyond these … but the Tartars by God's permission, and with wonderful exertion, did cross them, and … so did I, and that twice'. It was then exactly a century since the westward expansion of the Mongols had forged a unified highway across the Central Asian steppes. The Mongol phenomenon evoked an immediate response in Latin Europe, anxious for allies against Islam and converts to Rome. No mission got far, however, until that of John of Piano Carpini's intelligence-gathering expedition. Using Mongol horse-teams, Carpini covered 3,000 miles in 106 days to the environs of Karakorum in 1246. Carpini dismissed the Mongols as savage, dangerous and intractable to Western purposes. His fellow

C

TRAVELLERS who undertook the arduous caravan journey from Europe to the East fostered both trade and cultural links. Since most were merchants, it was, necessarily, commerce that was boosted most significantly. Yet these same travellers contributed to cultural diffusion and transmission, too. Flourishing Eurasian trade permitted an uninterrupted flow of ideas, art and literature.

During the 13th and 14th centuries, astronomical instruments from Persia reached China; Chinese ceramics influenced the patterns and decorations of Middle Eastern ceramics; European craftsmen lived and worked in China; and Chinese motifs and designs influenced Persian painting. This intermingling of cultures permeated some of the most important historical, literary and artistic works of the time.

The *World History* of Rashid al-Din reflects the manifold influences on a great history written early in the 14th century. Rashid al-Din, probably of Jewish heritage, served successively as physician, court historian and vizier (senior minister) in the Mongol Khanate of Persia. Commissioned by the khan to produce a chronicle, Rashid al-Din wrote a true world history. Having access to Western, Persian and Mongol sources, he included, for example, such western conceptions as the stories of Adam and the Patriarchs. But he also wrote histories of the Turks and the Mongols and narratives of pre-Islamic and Islamic Persia, and accounts of Indians, Jews and Franks.

The illustrations in manuscripts of his work reveal the extent of the artistic borrowings and inter-relationships that the Mongol Peace encouraged. (A), for example, of *The Magnificent City of Iram in Southern Arabia*, shows a melange of influences from the arts of diverse cultures. The building in the centre of the illustration is a palace apparently modelled on Chinese lines. The horseman is Mongol, however, though wearing a Seljuk Turkish crown. The tree to the right of the building, with drooping and feathery leaves, is clearly Chinese in style, while the trees to the left have the more substantial leaves associated with Iraqi art.

Yunus {Jonah} and the Whale in (B) is the product of a similar interweaving of cultural traditions. The subject matter comes from the Judeo-Christian tradition, though it also has echoes in the Islamic world. The figure of Yunus and the gourd plant behind which he shelters are typical of early Christian models. The waves in which the immense fish disports, however, reflect both Chinese and Iraqi traditions.

Franciscan, William of Rubruck, following in 1253 as the ambassador of Louis IX, was more sympathetic and compiled a report, unsurpassed in some respects until the 19th century. The Mongols, it seemed to him, inhabited 'a kind of other world', but were receptive to ideas from outside. Had he been able 'to work miracles, like Moses', he thought he might have converted Möngke Khan.

By the second half of the 13th century, Mongol hegemony in Asia had both fostered stability and promoted commerce. Unlike the Chinese emperors and other rulers they overthrew, the Mongol khans actively encouraged trade. They supported merchant associations, provided loans to traders, issued paper money and were hospitable to foreign merchants. When the Polo brothers reached China in 1260, for example, Kublai Khan greeted them warmly and entrusted them with commercial and diplomatic missions in the West.

Having attempted to fulfil these tasks on their return to Europe, they set forth for China again in 1271 accompanied by the young Marco Polo. Marco Polo's account of his voyage, published in 1301 and titled, simply, *Description of the World*, though initially disbelieved, was later widely circulated in Europe and became a principal source of European knowledge of the land routes to the Orient. His description of Japan – Cipangu – which he never visited, was the first to reach the West. His erroneous faith in its 'measureless quantities' of gold had a deep influence on Europeans.

From Acre in the Holy Land, then an eastern outpost of European civilization, where they received a blessing from Pope Gregory X, who also entrusted them with letters for Kublai, the Polos travelled to Laias, the present-day town of Ayas on the Turkish coast, then part of Little Armenia and the centre of an extensive trade in cotton and spices. From Little Armenia the Polos headed to Greater Armenia via modern Anatolia, a region Marco referred to as 'Turcomania'. It was here that Marco Polo encountered Muslims for the first time. His listing of the native products, a regular feature of his account, included carpets, horses, mules, gold and silk. These were traded throughout 'Turcomania' by Greek and Armenian Christians, who seem to have been able to roam freely across the region.

From here the Polos travelled through the Mongol Ilkhanate of Persia. Marco Polo's description emphasizes not only the spectacular cities encountered but the striking absence of obstacles to travel, whether bandits, extortionary officials or treacherous terrain, evidence that the route was well travelled and well established. The first city on the caravan trail was Mosul, on the banks of the Tigris, and known for both its sizeable Nestorian Christian community and its fine textiles (which came to be known as 'muslin', after the city). Reaching

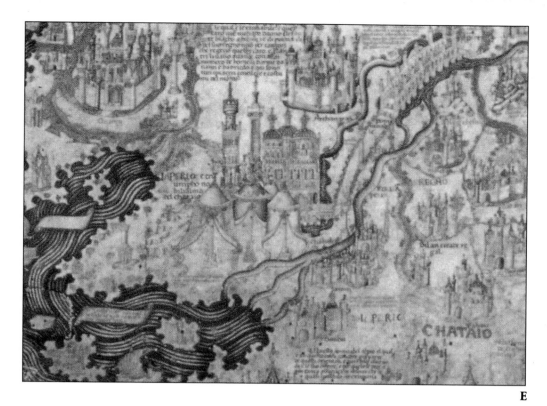

E

D ABOVE LEFT *An early 15th-century French illumination of the Chinese city of Quinsay, from an early edition of Marco Polo's account, its bridges 'so lofty that a great fleet could pass beneath them'.*

E ABOVE RIGHT *Though Marco Polo's accounts were widely dismissed as fantastic in late-medieval Europe, Fra Mauro's mid-15th-century world map used them extensively for its gilded picture of Cathay.*

F BELOW *The 'Mongol Peace' was brought at the price of terrible devastation, as in the destruction of the Caliph's capital at Baghdad in 1258.* G BELOW RIGHT *The illuminator of the French translation of Marco Polo depicted the world of Kublai Khan in entirely Western imagery. The Polo family kneeling before him are indistinguishable from the Chinese courtiers in feature and dress.*

Baghdad, which had been devastated by the Mongols in 1258 but which was beginning to recover its earlier significance on the trade routes, Marco was told that the Mongols allowed the last caliph to starve to death surrounded by his enormous cache of gold and silver; in Tabriz, north of Baghdad, he found a centre for commerce in pearls; in Kirman he observed the operation of a sophisticated trade in turquoise.

The Polos then embarked on the most dangerous section of the route, across the deserts and massive mountain ranges of Central Asia. From Hormuz, they travelled north-east for about a week through desert lands, from where a somewhat easier journey brought them to Balkh in modern Afghanistan. The Mongols had largely destroyed the city earlier in the century, but the surrounding regions had recovered sufficiently to provision caravans. The Polos again travelled north-east, to Badakhshan, just north of the Hindu Kush. Here they learned of the region's precious stones, particularly rubies and lapis lazuli. The route from Badakhshan to Kashgar, the next major halt, entailed enduring the freezing temperatures of the Pamirs, whose 'wild sheep of great size' were subsequently named after Marco, the *ovis poli*.

Descending from the Pamirs, the Polos reached the oases on the fringes of the Takla Makan desert. Surrounded by a bleak and inhospitable landscape, these oases had sufficiently plentiful water supplies from rivers fed from the mountains to the north and south to sustain self-sufficient agriculture. Kashgar, the first of the oases the Polos reached, was remarkable, too, for the production of cotton and as an important commercial crossroads. Like others of these oases, it was inhabited by a variety of ethnic groups who gave foreign merchants a cordial

reception. From Kashgar, the Polos had to choose between the route north of the Takla Makan desert or that skirting its southern fringes. They took the southern route, via Khotan, a well-known centre of jade which provided much of China's supply. The journey east from Khotan traversed hazardous desert regions, including the southern extremities of the Gobi, inhabited, according to Marco, by 'evil spirits' – mirages which lured incautious travellers to their deaths. Over a month of such desert travel elapsed before Marco and his companions reached the relative safety of Sha-chou, which lay within the boundaries of China. The remainder of the journey was less strenuous. The Polos travelled from north-west China via a well-protected and clearly delineated route to Kublai Khan's summer capital at Shang-tu in modern Inner Mongolia. En route, they passed through the largest cities they had visited since Persia: Kan-chou, Liang-chou, and others along the northern bend of the Yellow River.

Marco offers a vivid description of the marvels he saw in Shang-tu. He was impressed in particular by the palace, 'painted within with pictures and images of beasts and birds and trees and flowers and many kinds of things, so well and so cunningly that it is a delight and a wonder to see'. The hunting preserve in which were kept special breeds of white mares and cows, whose milk 'no one else in the world dares drink ... except only the great Khan and his descendants', also captured his attention.

The Polos travelled south with Kublai to the newly built capital at Khanbalik. The longest section of Marco's work is devoted to descriptions of life in the city and the imperial palace, including the lavish banquets reputedly organized for 40,000, at which lacquered bowls brimmed over with meat and rice and gold pitchers overflowed with *kumiss*, the fermented mare's milk favoured by the Mongols. Marco was also impressed by the wide circulation of paper money, by the postal relay system which transmitted important official mail at a rate of 250 miles a day, and by the use of coal as a heating fuel, enabling the Chinese to take several baths a week. He noted with particular interest the markets displaying wares from as far away as Samarkand and Baghdad, and Riazan in Russia.

Marco remained at the khan's court for 17 years before journeying back to Europe. According to his account, Kublai repeatedly entrusted him with important missions, which he undertook with great enthusiasm. By 1292, however, Marco was eager to return to the West and persuaded Kublai to allow him to escort a Mongol princess to Persia. Departing from the southern city of Ch'üan-chou, he travelled by ship to Hormuz on the Persian Gulf, touching en route at Indo-China, Malaya and India. From Hormuz, he took a northerly overland route, via Shiraz and Tabriz, to Trebizond on the Black Sea where he boarded a ship for the journey to Constantinople from where he continued to Italy.

F

G

32
THE NORTHEAST PASSAGE AND SIBERIA
1553-1932

THE IDEA OF *a sea route through the Arctic to the Pacific and Cathay was propagated by the Bristol merchant Robert Thorne in 1527, though whether to north-west or north-east, or indeed straight across, was not yet determined. The idea was taken up by Sebastian Cabot, who in 1553 became the first governor of the Muscovy, or Russia, Company. He had probably read an account of Muscovy published in 1549 by Sigismund von Herberstein, ambassador of the Holy Roman Empire in Moscow in 1516-18 and again in 1526. Von Herberstein reported that the sea route north of Scandinavia from the White Sea had been used by a returning Danish ambassador in 1496. Vardø, then a Danish outpost, was also well known, so one may assume that there was no mystery about access to the Barents and White Seas by the mid-16th century.*

It was the opening up of a major new trade route that interested Cabot, the overland route across Europe having been made too hazardous by the constant wars between Muscovy and its western neighbours. But there was a diplomatic side to the launching of the Muscovy Company's first venture to the north in 1553. Its ships were to carry a message from King Edward VI to the 'Kings, Princes, and other Potentates, inhabiting the Northeast partes of the world'. Thus the notion of Arctic voyaging seemed to fit well with the aim of trade to the north-east, and the first efforts were accordingly made in that direction. The search for a Northwest Passage was to be made a little later (see ch. 16).

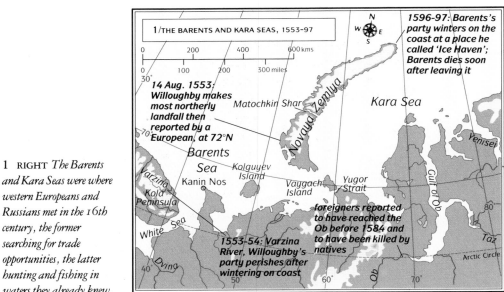

1/THE BARENTS AND KARA SEAS, 1553-97

1596-97: *Barents's party winters on the coast at a place he called 'Ice Haven'; Barents dies soon after leaving it*

14 Aug. 1553: *Willoughby makes most northerly landfall then reported by a European, at 72°N*

Kara Sea

Matochkin Shar

Novaya Zemlya

Barents Sea

Kolguyev Island

Kanin Nos

Vaygach Island

Yugor Strait

Yarzina

Kola Peninsula

White Sea

Dvina

Yenisei

Gulf of Ob

foreigners reported to have reached the Ob before 1584 and to have been killed by natives

1553-54: *Varzina River, Willoughby's party perishes after wintering on coast*

Ob

Taz

Arctic Circle

1 RIGHT *The Barents and Kara Seas were where western Europeans and Russians met in the 16th century, the former searching for trade opportunities, the latter hunting and fishing in waters they already knew.*

A BELOW LEFT *The Mangazeya Sea – the gulf of the Rivers Ob and Taz in the southern Kara Sea – was crossed by ships bound for Mangazeya. Taken from an unpublished Russian atlas of 1697, this map may date from 1603. It would have been used principally to follow waterways. As with most Russian maps of this period, north is at the bottom.*

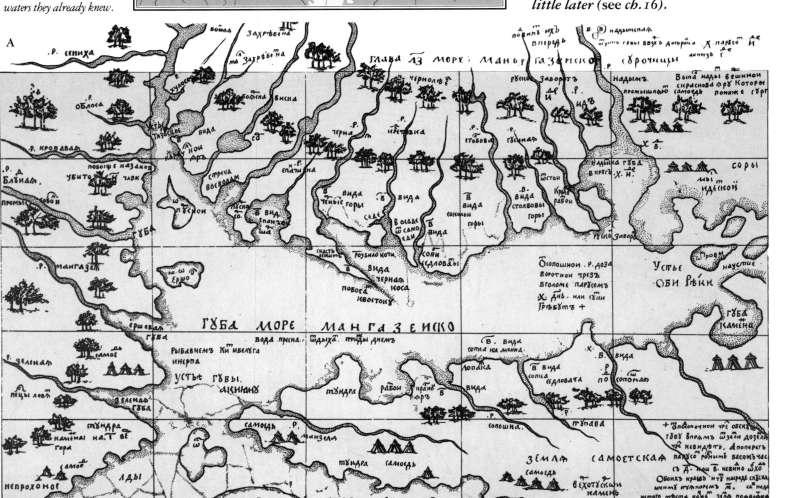

St. Petersburg

Archangel

Moscow

Volga

Ural

Arctic Circle

SIXTEENTH-CENTURY geographers and seamen in Europe knew that it was possible to sail north of Scandinavia, but it was Norsemen and Russians from the Kola Peninsula and the White Sea littoral who had personal experience of these waters. No first-hand Russian accounts survive, however, probably because those who might have written them were illiterate. Our present knowledge we owe to English and Dutch writers of the time, who naturally tended to give prominence to the exploits of their compatriots. Thus it is wrongly believed by many that the voyages of Sir Hugh Willoughby and Richard Chancellor for the Muscovy Company in 1553 were the pioneering ventures. They were important, however, since Chancellor reached the mouth of the Dvina in the White Sea, from where, continuing overland, he journeyed to Moscow to make official contact with Ivan IV. (Willoughby's venture ended in disaster, with all aboard dying after wintering in the Kola Peninsula.)

Chancellor returned to England the following year, and the company sent out follow-up expeditions in 1556, 1568 and 1580. These succeeded in strengthening trade links, but little progress was made in getting farther east. Only the 1580 expedition, under Arthur Pet and Charles Jackman, penetrated to the Kara Sea, and then only for a few miles. It seems, however, that some English, or at least non-Russian, seafarers reached the River Ob, only to be killed by the Samoyed inhabitants there. Who they may have been remains unknown.

In the next decade, three Dutch voyages were dispatched from Amsterdam with the same broad objectives as the Muscovy Company's. The 'chief pilot' of each was Willem Barents. On his third voyage, he managed to round the northern tip of Novaya Zemlya, thereby reaching a corner of the Kara Sea previously unvisited by western mariners. The expedition was forced to winter there, and Barents died on the return voyage.

This half-century of effort by the English and the Dutch was probably an overall success in economic terms, but it had done little to reveal the existence of a Northeast Passage. Further, the increase in foreign shipping in these northern waters caused anxiety in Muscovy, and in 1619 the route into the Kara Sea and the River Ob was closed by the Tsar's command.

While these voyages were being launched, a new overland thrust to the east was gaining strength, using the rivers as highways. The motivation was the search for fur. From forays over several centuries, Russians knew something of the great

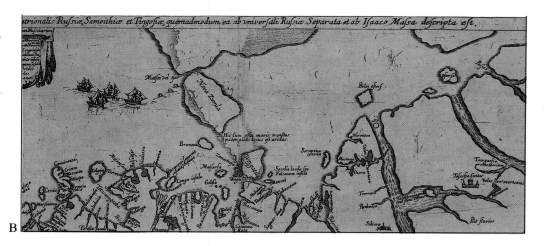

B ABOVE *Isaac Massa, a Dutch geographer, spent some years in Moscow in the early 17th century. He used Russian sources to compile this 1611 map of the present-day Barents and Kara Seas. Massa was to play a leading role in the compilation of western European maps of Russia.*

2 BELOW *The two main movements north and east by Russians were hunting parties in the 17th century and exploring and surveying parties in the 18th century. Whereas the former were motivated principally by the search for furs, the latter – the Great Northern Expedition – was a systematic attempt at exploration.*

land beyond the Urals, but the first enduring advance was made by the cossack Yermak in 1581 or 1582. Although Yermak himself was killed near present-day Tobol'sk, not very far into Siberia, the movement he started gathered momentum to the extent that the Pacific, at the Sea of Okhotsk, was reached by Ivan Moskvitin in 1639. The farthest tip of the continent was then reached by Semen Dezhnev, who sailed through the Bering Strait from north to south in 1648, though without realizing that it was a strait he was seeing.

The parties that carried out these pioneer travels were generally small, and composed chiefly of cossacks. They were not necessarily skilled hunters themselves, so found it easier to hunt natives, who were, and compel them to pay tribute in fur to the Russian ruler. The high speed of the advance was due in part to the enforced success of these native hunters. Many groups started out eastwards from Mangazeya, an outpost on the Taz River, and, because the major rivers in Siberia tend to run from south to north, some parties went down to the sea and followed the coast to the next river, from where they could head inland again. The most easterly of these rivers, the Kolyma, from where Dezhnev sailed in 1648, was reached by 1641. Thus, by mid-century the only substantial coast that seems not to have been traversed was that round the peninsula of Taimyr. None of the information gathered was recorded in any systematic way, however, so the knowledge gained was of little use in any wider context. Even the fact that Asia was not connected to another continent to the east did not become generally known. This failure in communication was a direct cause of the next stage in the exploration of the Northeast Passage.

At the end of his life, Peter the Great, influenced by adv-

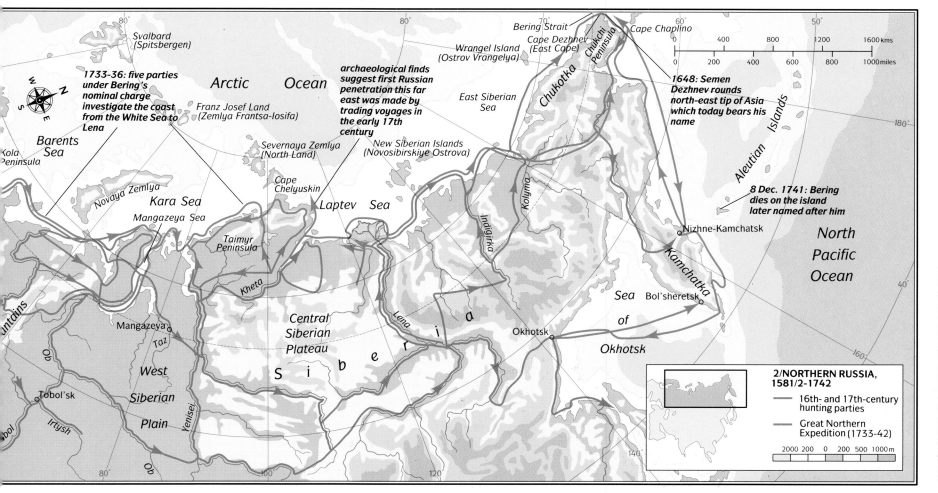

2/NORTHERN RUSSIA, 1581/2-1742

— 16th- and 17th-century hunting parties
— Great Northern Expedition (1733-42)

ances in western scientific thought, decided to investigate the distant north-east of his domains. He set in motion what was to be the first of the great exploring expeditions of the 18th century. He selected as leader Vitus Bering, a Danish officer in his newly created navy. Bering was instructed to go to Kamchatka, build a boat and sail north along the coast to discover where the land joined with America, the report of Dezhnev's voyage of 80 years earlier having been forgotten. In 1728 Bering did indeed sail round the tip of Asia, but never caught sight of the American coast (less than 50 miles away). He was accordingly sent out on a more ambitious voyage in 1733. Not only did Bering succeed in sighting North America (*see* ch.20), he also oversaw an epic survey of the north and east coasts of Russia, from the White Sea to Kamchatka: the Great Northern Expedition. Virtually the whole coast was mapped by 1742.

Subsequent highlights in the exploration of the Northeast Passage were the sighting and mapping of the offshore island groups; the New Siberian Islands (Novosibirskiye Ostrova) in 1770 and 1808-12; Wrangel Island (Ostrov Vrangelya) in 1821-24; and Novaya Zemlya also in 1821-24 and again in 1845. As they were revealed, the possibility of peninsulas jutting north from the mainland disappeared entirely. The way was clear for a voyage through the Northeast Passage.

The man who accomplished it was the scientist and scholar Baron A.E. Nordenskiöld, a Swedish Finn. In 1878 he sailed from Stockholm on the *Vega*, a strongly built and powered schooner. It was a favourable year for ice and good time was made across the Laptev and East Siberian Seas. If Nordenskiöld had not stopped at various points to carry out the scientific work that was one of his principal objectives, he would have completed the transit to the Bering Strait in one season. As it

D

was, he was obliged to winter on the north coast of Chukotka. He completed the passage the following summer.

At the beginning of the 20th century, the Russian government, perceiving the usefulness of the passage, built two small ice-breakers, *Taymyr* and *Vaygach*, which carried out a hydrographic survey of the route between 1910 and 1915. In 1913, they discovered the last significant island group along the route. They named it Nicholas II Land after the Tsar; its name was subsquently changed to Severnaya Zemlya (North Land). In 1914-15, they completed the first east-to-west transit, overwintering en route. The first one-season transit of the whole route, now called the Northern Sea Route, was made by the Soviet ice-breaker *Sibiryakov* in 1932. Today, the route is used extensively by Soviet shipping.

A parallel development to the probing of the Northeast Passage was the process of infiltration and absorption by which

C LEFT *A page from the Remezov Chronicle of c.1700. One of a number of accounts of Yermak's 16th-century campaign in Siberia, it was the only one to be illustrated.*
3 BELOW *The Northeast Passage is finally conquered. The first west-to-east traverse was made in 1878-79; the first east-to-west traverse in 1914-15; the first one-season traverse in 1932.*

D ABOVE *An illustration from Bulichev's 1856 account of his travels in Siberia. In a region where roads were all but unknown, winter travel was often easiest on frozen rivers. This shows a camp on the River Tauy.*
E BELOW RIGHT *Nordenskiöld's Vega at Cape Chelyuskin on 19 August 1878, the most northerly point of Eurasia. The crew is shown surveying.*

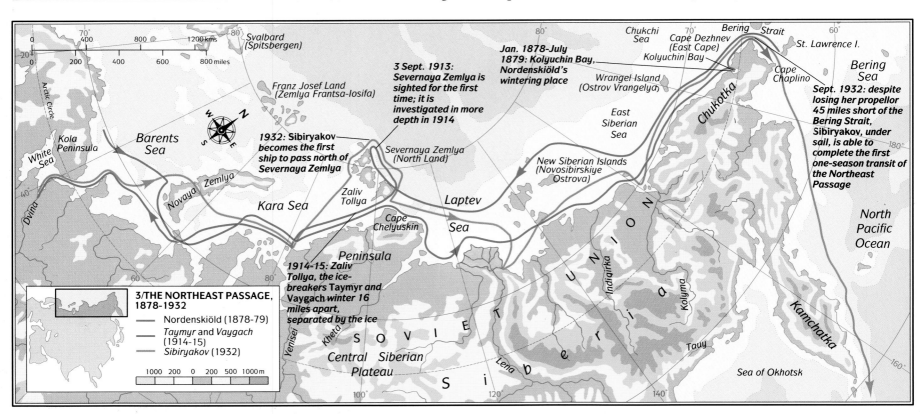

3/THE NORTHEAST PASSAGE, 1878-1932

— Nordenskiöld (1878-79)
— *Taymyr* and *Vaygach* (1914-15)
— *Sibiryakov* (1932)

Jan. 1878-July 1879: Kolyuchin Bay, Nordenskiöld's wintering place

3 Sept. 1913: Severnaya Zemlya is sighted for the first time; it is investigated in more depth in 1914

1932: Sibiryakov becomes the first ship to pass north of Severnaya Zemlya

1914-15: Zaliv Tollya, the ice-breakers Taymyr and Vaygach winter 16 miles apart, separated by the ice

Sept. 1932: despite losing her propellor 45 miles short of the Bering Strait, Sibiryakov, under sail, is able to complete the first one-season transit of the Northeast Passage

Russia conquered Siberia. Just as parties of fur hunters contributed to knowledge of the north coast in the 17th century, the same process took place inland, as rivers were ascended and descended and strong points (*ostrogi*) were established at key locations. None of this was conscious exploration, however. That might be said to have come about for the first time during Bering's second expedition, when the so-called academic detachment was deputed to fill exactly that role. The leading figure was the German polymath G.F. Müller, who became a member of the new Imperial Academy of Sciences in 1731. His responsibility was the social sciences. With him were the German botanist J.G. Gmelin, the French astronomer Louis Delisle de la Croyère, the German naturalist G. Steller, and a dozen or so Russians in more junior positions. Members of the detachment travelled through Siberia for many years, laying the basis for a scientific study of the region.

A

FLOATING ice is the most serious hazard facing a navigator in high latitudes. It is mostly sea ice, as in (C), which is the frozen surface of the sea, and it may reach a thickness, if undisturbed, of three to four metres. Hummocks, as in (A), and ridges, as in (D), both caused by fracturing, may increase thickness to 10 metres and more. Sea ice is quite different from the other type of floating ice found at sea: the iceberg. These, as in (B) in the foreground, derive from land ice which has slid down into the sea in the form of a glacier. Land ice and its derivatives are likely to be much bulkier and tougher than sea ice: an iceberg such as that illustrated in (E) may stand 100 metres out of the sea, and have a draught of several times that figure. But if land ice is therefore the greater threat to ships, it is also found much more rarely – and in the waters of the Northeast Passage hardly ever.

Whereas a ship approaching an iceberg will always try to avoid it, specially designed ships can force a way through sea ice. Most sea ice is in more or less continuous motion under the influence of wind and current, and this is the major problem. The earliest ice-going ships were made of wood, with thick, rounded hulls that forced them to be

B **C** **D**

squeezed upwards, out of the ice, when pressure came on. When mechanical power became available, the first icebreakers were designed to cut the ice with their stems, or bows. Later, the method was to crush it, using the weight of the ship, as it slid up over the edge of a floe. This method remains in use today. But sailing vessels may still have an advantage over powered ones: the greater likelihood of patience in the captain. Tide and wind can change a situation unrecognizably in a few days, even hours, but the captain of a ship costing £50,000 a day to run is not going to find it easy to do nothing. But though no ship has yet been built, or designed, which could go anywhere in ice at any time, today's biggest icebreakers can maintain steady movement in ice two metres thick.

E

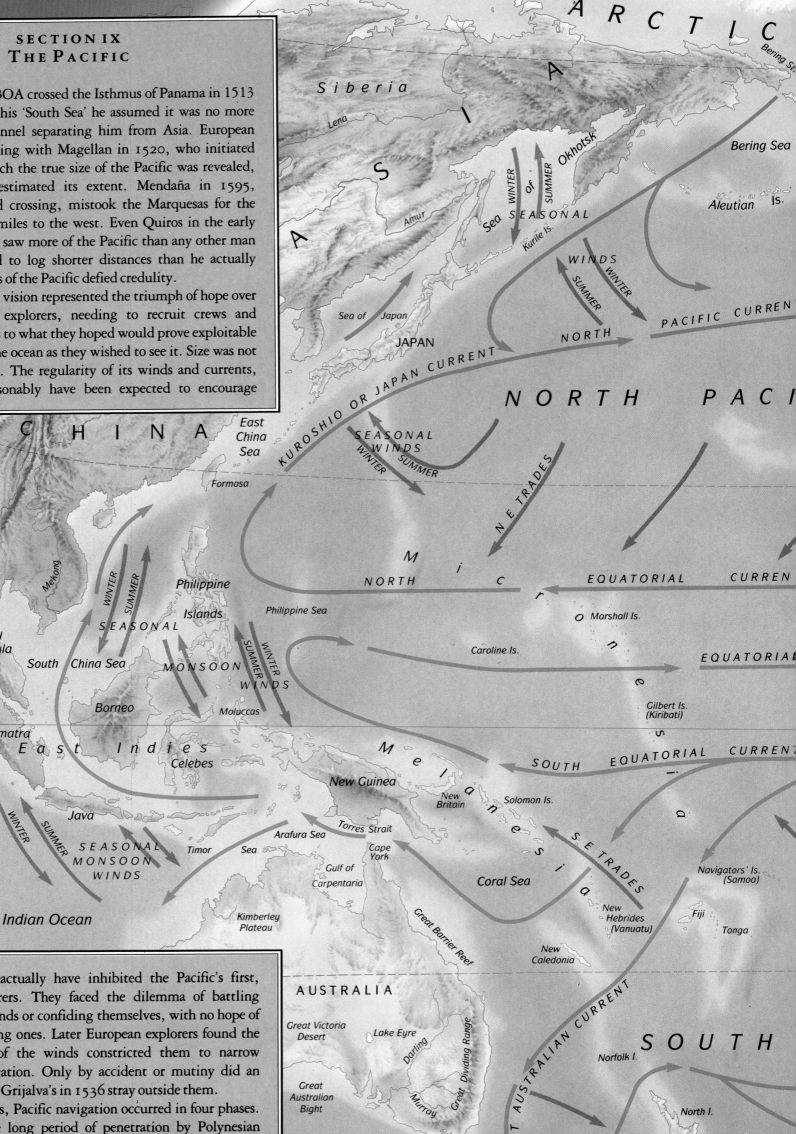

SECTION IX
THE PACIFIC

WHEN BALBOA crossed the Isthmus of Panama in 1513 and beheld his 'South Sea' he assumed it was no more than a narrow channel separating him from Asia. European navigators, beginning with Magellan in 1520, who initiated the process by which the true size of the Pacific was revealed, continually underestimated its extent. Mendaña in 1595, making his second crossing, mistook the Marquesas for the Solomons, 4,000 miles to the west. Even Quiros in the early 17th century, who saw more of the Pacific than any other man of his day, tended to log shorter distances than he actually sailed. The vastness of the Pacific defied credulity.

This blinkered vision represented the triumph of hope over experience. Early explorers, needing to recruit crews and backers for voyages to what they hoped would prove exploitable lands, portrayed the ocean as they wished to see it. Size was not the only difficulty. The regularity of its winds and currents, which might reasonably have been expected to encourage

navigation, may actually have inhibited the Pacific's first, indigenous explorers. They faced the dilemma of battling against adverse winds or confiding themselves, with no hope of return, to following ones. Later European explorers found the same regularity of the winds constricted them to narrow corridors of navigation. Only by accident or mutiny did an expedition such as Grijalva's in 1536 stray outside them.

In broad terms, Pacific navigation occurred in four phases. The first was the long period of penetration by Polynesian seafarers, which attained its greatest extent by about AD 400. The second, prompted by the need to find new routes to the Far East, and essentially the work of Spanish 16th-century explorers, was the discovery of the wind-borne cross-ocean routes. The third, in the 17th and 18th centuries, was dominated by the search for the 'unknown Southern Continent' postulated by academic geography. In the fourth, imperialistic ambitions came to dominate strictly scientific and commercial motives.

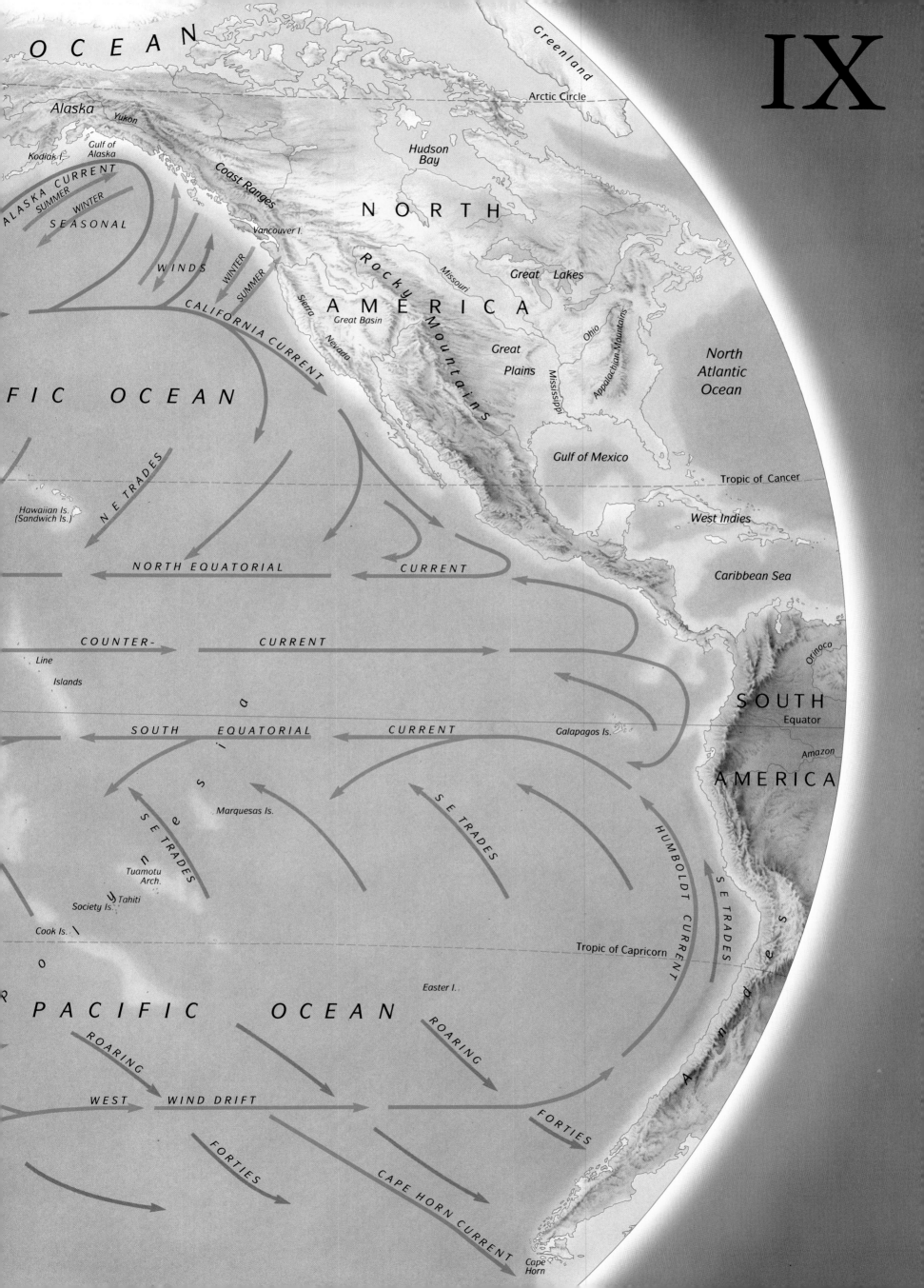

O C E A N

Greenland

Arctic Circle

Alaska

Yukon

Gulf of
Alaska

Kodiak I.

N O R T H

Hudson
Bay

ALASKA CURRENT

SUMMER

WINTER

SEASONAL

Coast Ranges

Vancouver I.

WINDS

WINTER

SUMMER

CALIFORNIA CURRENT

A M E R I C A

Rocky Mountains

Great Basin

Sierra

Nevada

Great
Plains

Missouri

Great   Lakes

Ohio

Mississippi

Appalachian Mountains

North
Atlantic
Ocean

FIC   OCEAN

N E TRADES

Hawaiian Is.
(Sandwich Is.)

N E TRADES

Tropic of Cancer

NORTH   EQUATORIAL

CURRENT

Gulf of Mexico

West Indies

Caribbean Sea

COUNTER-

CURRENT

Line

Islands

SOUTH   EQUATORIAL   CURRENT

Galapagos Is.

Orinoco

S O U T H

Equator

Amazon

A M E R I C A

a

SOUTH   EQUATORIAL   CURRENT

Marquesas Is.

S E TRADES

S E TRADES

S E TRADES

HUMBOLDT CURRENT

e

s

Tuamotu
Arch.

i

Tahiti

Society Is.

y

Cook Is.

n

Tropic of Capricorn

o

Easter I.

A
n
d
e
s

P A C I F I C   O C E A N

ROARING

ROARING

ROARING

WEST   WIND DRIFT

FORTIES

FORTIES

FORTIES

CAPE HORN CURRENT

Cape
Horn

THE PACIFIC: THE WESTWARD APPROACHES

1520-1606

1 BELOW *Magellan and Saavedra between them established the best route across the ocean from east to west, but it was not until 1565 that a viable return route to New Spain was established.*

early Aug. 1565: Urdaneta forced south by NE winds

1 Jan. 1528: Saavedra discovers Fais; departs 10 Jan.

mid-Dec. 1527: Saavedra alters course for Ladrone Is.

5 Sept. 1526: Loaisa makes landfall at Guam

17 Sept. 1526: Loaisa driven back by monsoon

31 Oct. 1527: Saavedra departs Navidad

22 Aug. 1526: Loaisa makes landfall at San Bartolome; tries unsuccessfully to find an anchorage

late Nov. 1527: Saavedra makes diversion on supposed signs of land

early Nov. 1565: Urdaneta makes landfall at Acapulco

late Feb. 1521: Magellan, believing he has passed Cipangu, alters course to WSW

9 Nov. 1527: Saavedra alters course to west

Apr. 1536: Grijalva departs Paita

late Feb. 1521: Magellan's crew suffering from scurvy and starvation

11 Dec. 1527: Saavedra alters course to NW on supposed signs of land

mutineers kill Grijalva and sail for Maluco

Grijalva attempts to return to New Spain; forced back by NE trades

Grijalva's mutineers shipwrecked: survivors reach Maluco two years later

mid-Dec. 1520: Magellan turns NW on reaching warmer latitudes

22 June 1526: Loaisa turns NW

28 Nov. 1520: Magellan emerges from Strait of Magellan

25 May 1526: Loaisa emerges from Strait of Magellan

Bering Sea

North Pacific Ocean

ASIA

CHINA

CIPANGU (JAPAN)

NORTH AMERICA

Santa Rosa I.

NEW SPAIN (MEXICO)

Atlantic Ocean

Navidad Acapulco

Gulf of Mexico

Tropic of Cancer

Ladrone Is. (Mariana Is.)

Guam Fais

San Bartolomé

Hawaiian Is.

Caribbean Sea

Philippine Is.

Marshall Is.

M I C R O N E S I A

Caroline Is.

Gilbert Is. (Kiribati)

Galapagos Is.

PERU

Malacca Borneo

Maluco (Spice Is.) (Moluccas)

Tiburones (Caroline I.)

Paita

EAST INDIES

see map 2

New Guinea

New Britain

Solomon Is.

M E L A N E S I A

Marquesas Is.

Callao

SOUTH AMERICA

Navigators' Is. (Samoa)

New Hebrides (Vanuatu)

Fiji

Society Is.

Tuamotu Archipelago

Tahiti

P O L Y N E S I A

Tonga

New Caledonia

TERRA AUSTRALIS (AUSTRALIA)

Tropic of Capricorn

South Pacific Ocean

CHILE

Tasman Sea

NEW ZEALAND

Strait of Magellan

1/THE PACIFIC, 1520-65

- Magellan (1520-21)
- Loaisa (1526)
- Saavedra (1527)
- Grijalva (1536, conjectural route)
- Urdaneta (1565)

0 500 1000 1500 2000 2500 kms
0   500   1000   1500 miles

3000 2000 1000 200 0 200 500 1000 m

THE PACIFIC, *although dauntingly vast on maps and, for a long time, almost impermeable to shipping from outside, is scored by navigable routes, defined by winds and currents. The extremities of the ocean, south of about 25°S and between 30° and 55°N, though stormy and dangerous, are dominated by fairly reliable westerlies. On either side of the wide belt of calms that lies north of the Equator, two central avenues of access from east to west are provided by trade winds and the North and South Equatorial Currents. The north-east trades, blowing between about 15° and 25°N, are among the world's most reliable winds; the south-east trades, blowing over a wider corridor from the Equator to about 20°S, are only slightly less so. Over the western margins of the ocean, conditions are monsoonal, with northerly winds in winter and southerly winds in summer. Along the eastern rim, navigation is governed by the Humboldt (or Peruvian) Current, which carries ships north from the ragged south-west coast of Chile almost to the Equator, and by the California Current, which flows south across the root area of the north-east trades, linking the American coast from southern Oregon to southern Mexico.*

This extensive but essentially simple system was not exploited to the full until the arrival of European explorers between the 16th and 18th centuries. Long before this, indigenous navigators had made extended voyages across parts of the Pacific, but with neither the means nor the incentive to find the routes that bound the ocean from coast to coast and linked it to the rest of the world. Their achievements remained limited, even though they sometimes spanned significant distances. In the far north, for example, unrecorded crossings from China to America have been postulated, dating back to at least 1200 BC. In the central and southern Pacific, the peopling of remote islands demanded astonishing feats of seamanship; the colonization of the Hawaiian Islands, probably unknown to Europeans until the 18th century, was a spectacular feat achieved by Polynesian navigators by c. AD 400.

The crucial stages in the revelation of the nature of the Pacific – the discovery of the east–west routes across the central Pacific and the way back via the westerlies in the north – were accomplished by small bands of Spanish and Portuguese in the 16th and 17th centuries. The decisive voyages were those of Magellan (1520-21); Saavedra (1527); Urdaneta (1565); and Mendaña (1567).

A RIGHT *Battista Agnese's Venetian portolan atlas of c. 1544 paid tribute to Magellan's expedition by showing the entire route of the circumnavigation completed by Magellan's flagship, Victoria, after his death.* **B** BELOW *One version of Pigafetta's manuscript features decorative maps of the islands encountered by Magellan; this depicts a clove tree beside the 'Sea of Maluco'.* **C** BELOW CENTRE *The* Codex Boxer *records late 16th-century impressions of Philippine natives. The Visayans of Cebu and Samar depicted recall Pigafetta's 'various patterns'.*

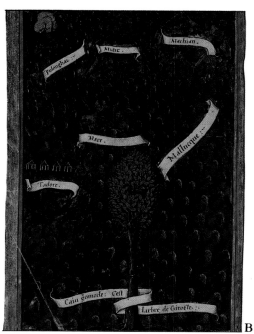

D BOTTOM LEFT *Nuño García de Toreño's chart of 1522 is the first to record Magellan's discoveries. The Spice Islands are shown on the Spanish side of the Tordesillas line.*

2 BELOW *Explorers from the Pacific could only approach Ternate and Tidore via the Philippines: this last leg was time-consuming, arduous and sometimes fatal.*

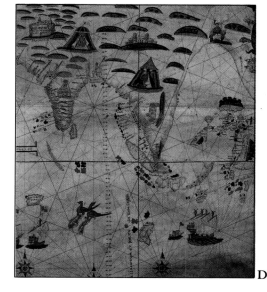

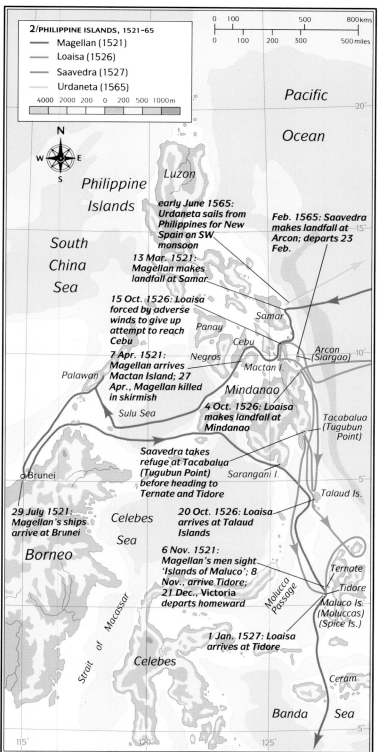

2/PHILIPPINE ISLANDS, 1521-65
- Magellan (1521)
- Loaisa (1526)
- Saavedra (1527)
- Urdaneta (1565)

4000 2000 200 0 200 500 1000m

Pacific Ocean

Philippine Islands

Luzon

South China Sea

early June 1565: Urdaneta sails from Philippines for New Spain on SW monsoon

Feb. 1565: Saavedra makes landfall at Arcon; departs 23 Feb.

13 Mar. 1521: Magellan makes landfall at Samar

Samar

15 Oct. 1526: Loaisa forced by adverse winds to give up attempt to reach Cebu

Panay

Cebu

Arcon (Siargao)

Negros

Mactan I.

7 Apr. 1521: Magellan arrives Mactan Island; 27 Apr., Magellan killed in skirmish

Palawan

Mindanao

4 Oct. 1526: Loaisa makes landfall at Mindanao

Tacabalua (Tugubun Point)

Sulu Sea

Saavedra takes refuge at Tacabalua (Tugubun Point) before heading to Ternate and Tidore

Sarangani I.

Talaud Is.

Brunei

29 July 1521: Magellan's ships arrive at Brunei

Celebes Sea

20 Oct. 1526: Loaisa arrives at Talaud Islands

Borneo

6 Nov. 1521: Magellan's men sight 'Islands of Maluco'; 8 Nov., arrive Tidore; 21 Dec., Victoria departs homeward

Ternate

Tidore

Molucca Passage

Maluco Is. (Moluccas) (Spice Is.)

Strait of Macassar

1 Jan. 1527: Loaisa arrives at Tidore

Celebes

Ceram

Banda Sea

IX *The Pacific*

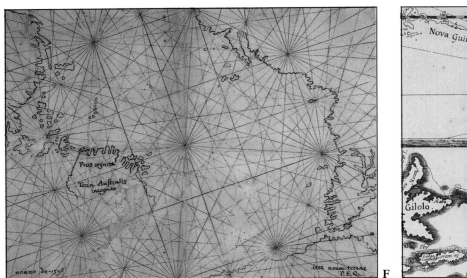

LIKE COLUMBUS'S crossing of the Atlantic, Magellan's of the Pacific was the outcome of luck and miscalculation: luck, because his winter at San Julián (*see* ch. 13) delayed his arrival in the Pacific until the southern summer, ensuring that he would cross the Equator when the north-east trades were broadest; miscalculation, because he appears to have believed that the Spice Islands (Moluccas), for which he was bound, lay not more than 80 days' sail across a sea broken by intermediate landfalls. Had he known that he faced 99 days of unrelieved navigation, he could hardly have accepted the risk of extinction from starvation and thirst.

Magellan's course was nearly disastrous. After rounding Cape Horn, he followed an oblique track through the doldrums and, in an ocean speckled with archipelagoes, missed land from

E ABOVE LEFT
Ortelius's 1595 map of the Pacific shows the Victoria *making her crossing, the 'Southern Continent not yet Discovered', the Solomon Islands, New Guinea and the 'Isle of Silver' north of Japan.* **F** ABOVE
Quiros's own map of the Pacific of 1598 suggests that he identified the southern continent with New Guinea, here shown stretching east and south from a point east of Gilolo.

the day he entered the Pacific, on 28 November 1520, until he sighted Guam, on 6 March 1521. For the first 20 days he sailed north, perhaps to escape from cold seas as quickly as possible. Then he altered his course gradually to the west, reaching the Equator on 13 February 1521. He sighted small islands on 24 January and again on 4 February, but was unable to land. At the Equator he made the surprising decision to continue north-west rather than due west for the supposed location of the Spice Islands. This has inspired conjectures that his main destination was the fabled island of Cipangu (*see* ch.9), but he may equally well have been motivated by a conviction that there was 'no food in Maluco', or by lack of wind. By the time Guam was sighted, the explorers were drinking putrid water and eating wormy biscuit, 'which stank strongly of rats'

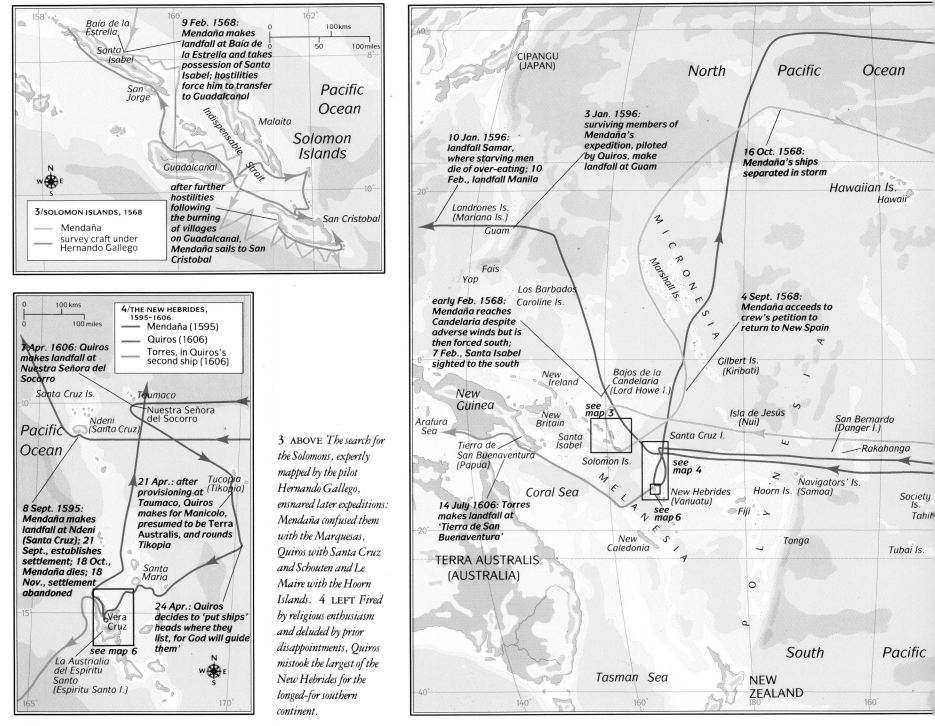

3/SOLOMON ISLANDS, 1568
— Mendaña
— survey craft under Hernando Gallego

Baía de la Estrella — Santa Isabel — San Jorge — Guadalcanal — Malaita — Indispensable Strait — San Cristobal — Pacific Ocean — Solomon Islands

9 Feb. 1568: Mendaña makes landfall at Baía de la Estrella and takes possession of Santa Isabel; hostilities force him to transfer to Guadalcanal

after further hostilities following the burning of villages on Guadalcanal, Mendaña sails to San Cristobal

4/THE NEW HEBRIDES, 1595–1606
— Mendaña (1595)
— Quiros (1606)
— Torres, in Quiros's second ship (1606)

7 Apr. 1606: Quiros makes landfall at Nuestra Señora del Socorro

Santa Cruz Is. — Taumaco — Nuestra Señora del Socorro — Ndeni (Santa Cruz) — Pacific Ocean — Tucopia (Tikopia) — Santa Maria — Vera Cruz — La Australia del Espiritu Santo (Espiritu Santo I.)

21 Apr.: after provisioning at Taumaco, Quiros makes for Manicolo, presumed to be Terra Australis, and rounds Tikopia

8 Sept. 1595: Mendaña makes landfall at Ndeni (Santa Cruz); 21 Sept., establishes settlement; 18 Oct., Mendaña dies; 18 Nov., settlement abandoned

24 Apr.: Quiros decides to 'put ships' heads where they list, for God will guide them'

see map 6

3 ABOVE *The search for the Solomons, expertly mapped by the pilot Hernando Gallego, ensnared later expeditions: Mendaña confused them with the Marquesas, Quiros with Santa Cruz and Schouten and Le Maire with the Hoorn Islands.* **4** LEFT *Fired by religious enthusiasm and deluded by prior disappointments, Quiros mistook the largest of the New Hebrides for the longed-for southern continent.*

CIPANGU (JAPAN) — North Pacific Ocean — Hawaiian Is. — Hawaii — MICRONESIA — Marshall Is. — Gilbert Is. (Kiribati) — Isla de Jesús (Nui) — San Bernardo (Danger I.) — Rakahanga — Navigators' Is. (Samoa) — Hoorn Is. — Society Is. — Tahiti — Tubai Is. — Tonga — Fiji — New Caledonia — NEW ZEALAND — Tasman Sea — South Pacific — TERRA AUSTRALIS (AUSTRALIA) — Coral Sea — New Hebrides (Vanuatu) — Santa Cruz I. — Solomon Is. — Santa Isabel — New Britain — New Ireland — New Guinea — Arafura Sea — Tierra de San Buenaventura (Papua) — Bajos de la Candelaria (Lord Howe I.) — Los Barbados — Caroline Is. — Fais — Yap — Landrones Is. (Mariana Is.) — Guam — MELANESIA — POLYNESIA

10 Jan. 1596: landfall Samar, where starving men die of over-eating; 10 Feb., landfall Manila

3 Jan. 1596: surviving members of Mendaña's expedition, piloted by Quiros, make landfall at Guam

16 Oct. 1568: Mendaña's ships separated in storm

early Feb. 1568: Mendaña reaches Candelaria despite adverse winds but is then forced south; 7 Feb., Santa Isabel sighted to the south

4 Sept. 1568: Mendaña accedes to crew's petition to return to New Spain

14 July 1606: Torres makes landfall at 'Tierra de San Buenaventura'

see map 3 — see map 4 — see map 6

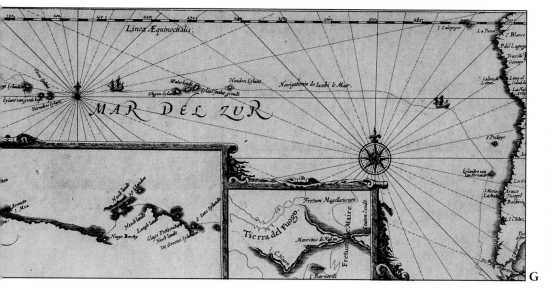

urine'. Confronted by 'robbers' on the island, Magellan set the tone of European behaviour in the Pacific by burning their villages before, on 9 March, departing refreshed.

A remark by one of his fellow travellers suggests that he expected his next landfall to be on the coast of China. After seven days, he sighted Samar, in the Philippines. He had chanced on the islands that were to form the focal point of Spanish Pacific navigation over the next 100 years. The expedition's subsequent and painful progress to the Spice Islands is shown in map 2. Though Magellan's death at the end of April, in an ill-judged intervention in local conflicts, impaired Spanish prestige, the solitary surviving ship out of the original fleet of five that left three years before was able to return home to Spain via the Cape of Good Hope. This, with its valuable cargo

G ABOVE *Schouten and Le Maire's 1616 Pacific crossing was the first Dutch voyage in search of the southern continent. Their major discovery was New Ireland.* 5 BELOW *With no reliable means of determining longitude, explorers had difficulty in distinguishing South Pacific Islands. The voyages of 1595 and 1605 were lost looking for the discoveries of 1567-69.*

of cloves, was deemed to justify the voyage.

Magellan had exposed the vastness of the Pacific and identified invaluable stepping-stones in the search for a viable east–west Pacific route to Asia. The long continuation of that search over many voyages is shown in maps 1 and 5. Explorers who followed Magellan from Cape Horn, like Loaisa in 1526 and Schouten and La Maire in 1616, made only marginal advances on knowledge of the ocean. The tracing of useful routes for the exploration and exploitation of the Pacific was mainly the work of voyages from New Spain, the first of which, Álvaro de Saavedra's in 1527-28, was decisive. Saavedra discovered the best outward route and reinforced Loaisa in the Philippines at a moment when the Portuguese threatened to eliminate the Spaniards. Magellan and his successors can be said to have found one major route of access: direct from the Atlantic with the south-east trades; Saavedra and his successors established a second, from New Spain straight across the North Pacific. The last viable east–west route, across the South Pacific from Peru, took much longer to explore (*see* map 5).

Pacific navigation along Magellan's route via Guam was directed from New Spain towards reliable commercial goals: the spices of the Moluccas; the silks of China; the bullion of Japan. Only with the growth of Spanish colonies in Peru did an incentive emerge to attempt discoveries of unknown lands in the South Pacific, where the colonists might hope for rewards as rich as those enjoyed by their counterparts farther north. Three distinct traditions stimulated such attempts: the Inca legend of rich islands deep in the Western Sea (*see* ch.6); the myth of a great 'unknown southern continent', Terra Australis; and rumours reported in Chile that the true location of the

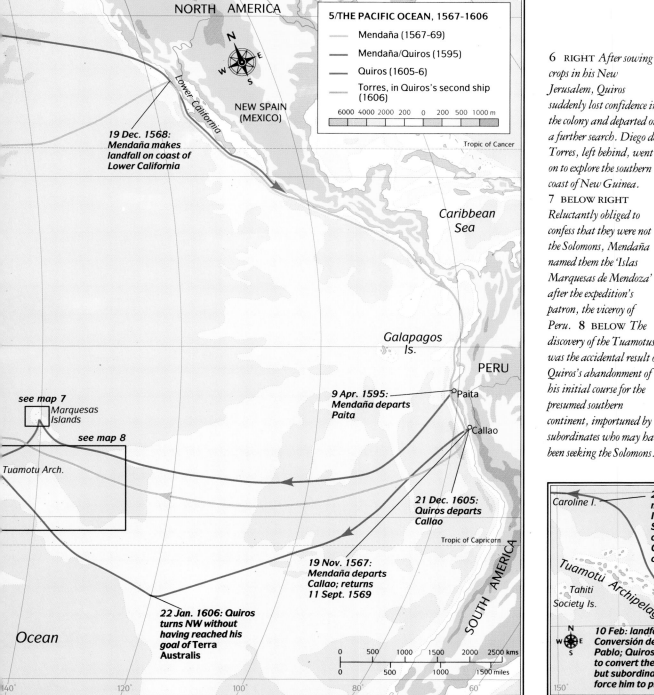

5/THE PACIFIC OCEAN, 1567-1606
- Mendaña (1567-69)
- Mendaña/Quiros (1595)
- Quiros (1605-6)
- Torres, in Quiros's second ship (1606)

6000 4000 2000 200 0 200 500 1000 m

19 Dec. 1568: Mendaña makes landfall on coast of Lower California

9 Apr. 1595: Mendaña departs Paita

21 Dec. 1605: Quiros departs Callao

19 Nov. 1567: Mendaña departs Callao; returns 11 Sept. 1569

22 Jan. 1606: Quiros turns NW without having reached his goal of Terra Australis

see map 7 — Marquesas Islands
see map 8

6 RIGHT *After sowing crops in his New Jerusalem, Quiros suddenly lost confidence in the colony and departed on a further search. Diego de Torres, left behind, went on to explore the southern coast of New Guinea.*
7 BELOW RIGHT *Reluctantly obliged to confess that they were not the Solomons, Mendaña named them the 'Islas Marquesas de Mendoza' after the expedition's patron, the viceroy of Peru.* 8 BELOW *The discovery of the Tuamotus was the accidental result of Quiros's abandonment of his initial course for the presumed southern continent, importuned by subordinates who may have been seeking the Solomons.*

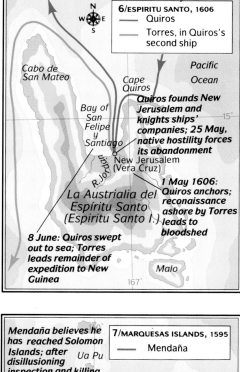

6/ESPIRITU SANTO, 1606
- Quiros
- Torres, in Quiros's second ship

Quiros founds New Jerusalem and knights ships' companies; 25 May, native hostility forces its abandonment

1 May 1606: Quiros anchors; reconaissance ashore by Torres leads to bloodshed

8 June: Quiros swept out to sea; Torres leads remainder of expedition to New Guinea

La Austrialia del Espíritu Santo (Espíritu Santo I.)

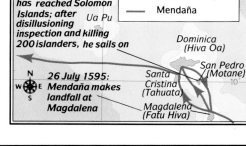

7/MARQUESAS ISLANDS, 1595
- Mendaña

Mendaña believes he has reached Solomon Islands; after disillusioning inspection and killing 200 islanders, he sails on

26 July 1595: Mendaña makes landfall at Magdalena

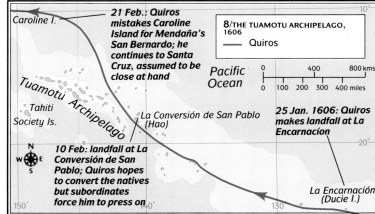

8/THE TUAMOTU ARCHIPELAGO, 1606
- Quiros

21 Feb.: Quiros mistakes Caroline Island for Mendaña's San Bernardo; he continues to Santa Cruz, assumed to be close at hand

25 Jan. 1606: Quiros makes landfall at La Encarnación

10 Feb: landfall at La Conversión de San Pablo; Quiros hopes to convert the natives but subordinates force him to press on

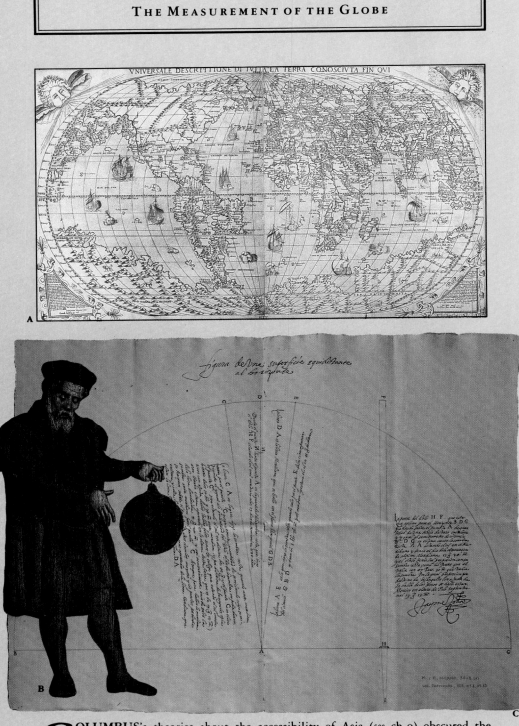

C OLUMBUS's theories about the accessibility of Asia (see ch.9) obscured the vastness of the globe. Even Pacific navigation, which alerted navigators to the distances involved, had only a gradual impact on enquiry into the size of the planet. Forlani's map of 1565 (A), though accurate in its configuration of the Pacific, seriously underestimated its size; Juan López de Velasco's careful investigation of 1575 (D) was similarly flawed. Spanish thinking was anyway clouded by political considerations: under the terms of the Treaty of Zaragoza of 1529 a contracted globe would secure Spain more of the East Indies disputed with Portugal. Nevertheless, under the influence of dispassionate students such as Pedro de Medina (B) scientific priorities gradually took over. The problems of fixing Spanish and Portuguese spheres of influence became inseparable from those of calculating the value of a degree in terms of distance, and of finding a reliable means of measuring longitude. Impressive, if unsuccessful, efforts were made, such as Jaime Juan's attempt to calculate the longitude of Mexico City by timing a lunar eclipse in 1584; his calculations are illustrated in (C). But if an accurate measurement of the planet eluded 16th-century geographers, the practical experience of Pacific navigation had at least revealed the scale of the problem, and in the process demonstrated the implausibility of Columbus's 'small world'.

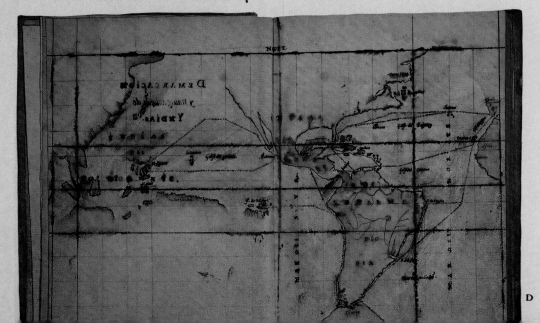

lands of the Amazons and of King Solomon's mines lay in the same direction.

The first voyage in pursuit of these objectives, under Hernando de Grijalva in 1536, ended in mutiny and disaster. The next, made on the orders of the Governor of Peru in 1567, was by Álvaro de Mendaña, whose inspiration was evangelical and whose goal was a new colony. He was assisted by the chief purveyor of Inca legends, Pedro Sarmiento de Gamboa (see ch.24). These divided aims were complicated further by the ambitions of Mendaña's chief pilot, Hernando Gallego, obsessed with his own quest for New Guinea, whose size and merits seem to have been exaggerated in his mind. The whole voyage was characterized by changes of purpose and of course. The expedition left Callao with two ships on 19 November (see map 5). By the end of December the explorers seem to have abandoned the search for the fabled islands and to have put themselves in Gallego's hands. By mid-January no land had been found and their drinking water was polluted. Sighting the Isla de Jesús, Gallego refused to allow them to investigate, much to Mendaña's regret. On 7 February, however, they were rewarded with the discovery of the optimistically named Isles of Solomon (see map 3). The exploration of the archipelago was thorough but futile: hostilities with the natives made exploitation impossible, while the problems of open-sea navigation without technical means of verifying longitude, and hence their exact position, made the islands effectively unrecoverable.

This was demonstrated when Mendaña's long-delayed attempt to follow up his discovery was launched a full generation later. The new expedition, departing in April 1595, was a

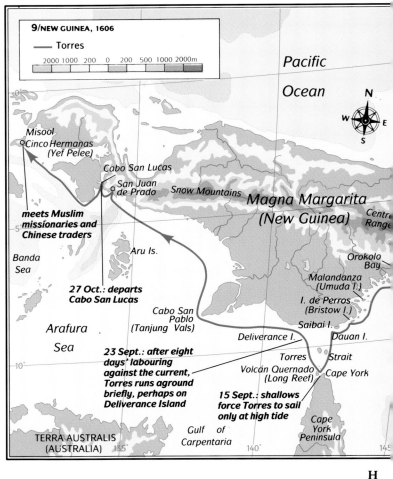

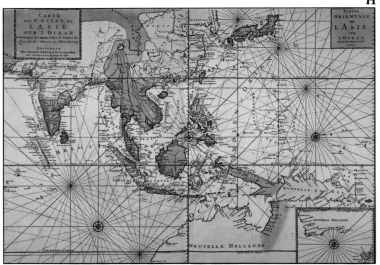

I TOP RIGHT *F. Vaz Dourado's map of 1573 shows the image of Japan in European cartography before the reception of information compiled by the Jesuits, who began to transmit annual reports to Rome in 1579.*

J CENTRE RIGHT *St. Francis Xavier's mission to Japan, which ended shortly before his death in 1552, inaugurated the conversion of perhaps as many as 150,000 Japanese by the mid-1580s, when members of the order compiled this map from indigenous sources.*

K BOTTOM RIGHT *Nagasaki was granted as a base for Christian traders by the Christian daimyo Omura Sumitada; by the 1640s it had become the only outlet for foreign commerce, as shown in this plan of the harbour in the 1660s.*

9 ABOVE *Torres, piloting the abandoned members of Quiros's party along the coast of New Guinea, undertook detailed surveying work, but the results remained in manuscript until the late 17th century.* H LEFT *The 1700 edition of d'Ablancourt's Neptune Français was the first printed atlas to do justice to Torres's findings, although the orientation of New Guinea is curiously reversed.*

costly undertaking, with 378 colonists aboard two galleons plus supporting vessels. As the pilot, Pedro Fernández de Quiros, said, 'expeditions without [a] royal purse cannot set off without mischief'. By the time of their first landfall, on 26 July, when the Marquesas Islands were discovered (*see* map 7), the auspicious mood had brought about 15 shipboard marriages. Mendaña indeed thought he had already reached the Solomons; his unjustified optimism marked the beginning of the decline of morale.

After a disappointing reconnaissance of the Marquesas the explorers sailed without relief until they reached the large and fertile island of Santa Cruz on 8 September. 'If God had not given us this island, we should all have perished', said Quiros. The attempt to found a colony was accompanied with indiscriminate massacres, brutal dissensions among the Spaniards, the wreck of one galleon and the death of Mendaña, his ideals shattered, on 18 October. Under the nominal command of Mendaña's widow, Doña Isabel, who was accused of withholding her private livestock from the sick and dying, Quiros piloted the remains of the expedition to the Philippines; the supporting ships were lost or deserted but the galleon made port on 10 January with only 100 survivors.

The Spanish crown was still disinclined to abandon hope in the South Pacific, and his survival through suffering left Quiros with an ardent sense of mission to return to those seas and discover another New World. He became convinced that the islands Mendaña had found were the outliers of the great southern continent and proclaimed himself a 'second Columbus', divinely selected to find it. Although he was a skilful pilot, he still tended to under-estimate Pacific distances and to disbelieve in the unremitting consistency of the wind-system. His expedition, leaving Callao on 21 December 1605 in two galleons equipped with water-condensers, was soon as bafflingly lost as that of 1595 (*see* map 5). Quiros's sense of purpose began to go awry on 22 January 1606, when he abandoned his course for the suspected continent and headed for the safety of a region where islands were known to lie. After a series of disillusioning landfalls (*see* maps 4 and 8), on 24 April he abandoned his fleet to the guidance of God.

In a mood of religious exaltation, Quiros convinced himself that the island he called La Austrialia del Espíritu Santo, discovered on 3 May, was the longed-for continent. He founded a municipality of 'New Jerusalem', and distributed sonorous but vacuous knighthoods to his men, right down to his Black cooks. But where Quiros had promised gold and hatfuls of pearls, his crew found only 'devils with poisoned arrows'. After less than a month, the commander lost his nerve and decided to look further. When he emerged from port on 8 June to make a reconnaissance he was swept away by the force of the south-east trades. Unable to return he rallied sufficiently to pilot the ship to Mexico; thereafter the 'second Columbus' was destined to eke out the remainder of his life like the first, nursing his bitterness and lobbying unsuccessfully for more commissions and rewards.

The voyages of Mendaña and Quiros, for all their failures and frustrations, had opened the southern corridor across the Pacific from east to west. The return route across the North Pacific was used by the navigators of northern and southern corridors alike. Without it, Pacific avenues were useless to the European world, yet it proved cruelly hard to find. Saavedra, in 1529, and the *San Juan* of Villalobos under Iñigo Órtiz de Retes, in 1545, searched south of the Equator without success; quests northwards up to 30° by Saavedra and Bernardo de la Torre proved equally frustrating. By the mid-1540s it was generally acknowledged that, if there was a return route, it must lie even farther north. The honour of discovery is generally accorded to the Augustinian priest, Andrés de Urdaneta, recalled from the cloister to his former vocation as a navigator in the 1560s. He realized that the key to a successful round trip between New Spain and the Philippines lay in timing: to

exploit both the broadest extent of the north-east trades outward and the southerly monsoons to speed a fleet north on its return, the entire voyage had to be completed in a single summer. Departing in June 1565, he made the longest voyage so far recorded without a landfall – 11,600 miles – in five months and eight days (*see* map 1). He was beaten home by his consort vessel, the *San Lucas* under Alonso de Arellano, which had been separated from him on the outward voyage, by two months. But Arellano's voyage was regarded as virtually an act of desertion and the chart Urdaneta made became the basis for all Pacific sailing directions for the rest of the age of sail.

On the western margins of the ocean, exploration from the Pacific met that from the Indian Ocean. The first Spaniards to reach Yap found evidence that Portuguese missionaries had preceded them. New Guinea – much of the southern coast of which was surveyed by Luis de Torres after Quiros's sudden departure had left him in La Austrialia del Espíritu Santo (*see* map 9) – had been discovered from the opposite direction as early as 1526, when Jorge de Meneses was borne off course on a voyage from Malacca to the Spice Islands. Portuguese commercial and missionary expansion into the China Seas opened the first European contacts with Japan in the 1540s. 'Cipangu' had been coveted by Pacific explorers since Magellan, and Arellano's journey of 1565 (if his account can be trusted) must have been aided by the Kuroshio Current and so have passed close to Japan. The northward extension of European knowledge of the Pacific, however, like that of the remoter recesses of the South Pacific, belongs to a later phase of exploration, which flowered almost two centuries later (*see* chs. 34 and 35).

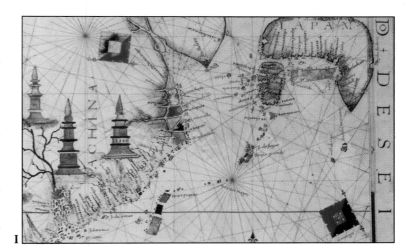

I

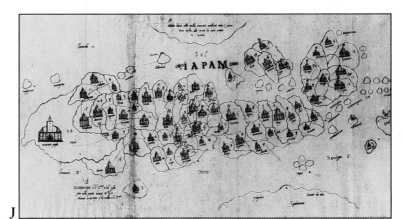

J

K

THE PACIFIC: MYTH AND REALITY
1605-1768

A

LONG BEFORE *Magellan's ships entered the Pacific in 1520, the ocean's 25,000 or so islands had experienced a steady process of discovery and settlement. The chart drawn for Cook in 1769 by Tupaia, a priest or* arii *from Raiatea in the Society Islands (see map* C), *gives some indication of the range of geographical knowledge acquired by the inhabitants of the Pacific before the European arrival. Centred on Tahiti, the chart marked 74 islands, scattered over an area 3,000 miles across and 1,000 miles from north to south. The type of craft used in Pacific voyaging ranged from the small single-hulled outriggers of Micronesia to giant double-hulled outriggers in Polynesia, some of which were longer than the European discovery vessels and could make voyages of several thousand miles. Navigation was by empirical observation of stars, currents, wave and wind patterns, and the shape or loom of the islands, rather than by instrument. To think in terms of a process of planned exploration on an oceanic scale would be misleading, however. Many voyages and landfalls were accidental; island-hopping was the most usual form of progress.*

For European navigators, the immensity of the ocean, problems in determining longitude, the menace of scurvy and the constraints of wind and current posed intimidating obstacles. Despite early ventures into the great ocean by Spaniards, Portuguese and English (see chs.20 and 33), European knowledge of the Pacific in the early 17th century remained patchy. To the north stretched the one regular European trade route across the ocean, that of the annual Spanish galleon between Acapulco and Manila. Japan had been roughly charted, but the ocean to the north and east remained unexplored. How far east Asia extended was uncertain, as was its relationship to North America, whose Pacific coast was firmly mapped only as far north as California. In the south Pacific, a few of the island groups lying on the diagonal sailing track between the tip of South America and New Guinea had been discovered (see map 4), but their location on maps tended to shift from voyage to voyage. Dominating the world maps was a gigantic presumed southern continent, covering almost the whole of the temperate zone of the Pacific. Terra Australis Incognita *was a concept sustained by the lingering influence of Ptolemaic geography, by misreadings of Marco Polo and by the pseudo-scientific notion that a southern landmass was needed to 'balance' the continents of the northern hemisphere.*

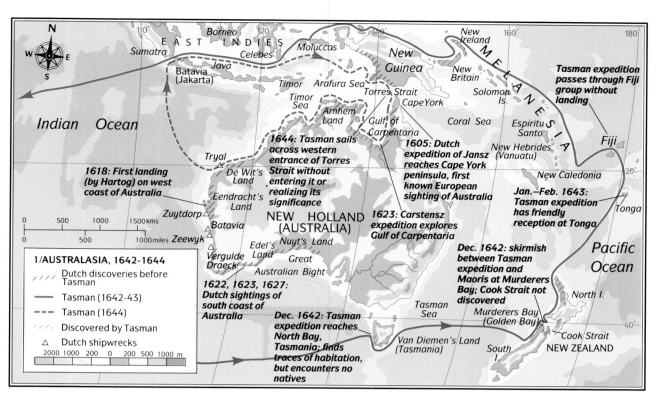

1/AUSTRALASIA, 1642-1644
//// Dutch discoveries before Tasman
— Tasman (1642-43)
- - - Tasman (1644)
—— Discovered by Tasman
△ Dutch shipwrecks

1618: First landing (by Hartog) on west coast of Australia

1644: Tasman sails across western entrance of Torres Strait without entering it or realizing its significance

1605: Dutch expedition of Jansz reaches Cape York peninsula, first known European sighting of Australia

1623: Carstensz expedition explores Gulf of Carpentaria

Tasman expedition passes through Fiji group without landing

Jan.–Feb. 1643: Tasman expedition has friendly reception at Tonga

1622, 1623, 1627: Dutch sightings of south coast of Australia

Dec. 1642: skirmish between Tasman expedition and Maoris at Murderers Bay; Cook Strait not discovered

Dec. 1642: Tasman expedition reaches North Bay, Tasmania; finds traces of habitation, but encounters no natives

1 ABOVE *The achievement of the Dutch in southern waters during the first half of the 17th century was considerable, but uncertainties remained: whether Van Diemen's Land was insular; the relationship of New Zealand to a possible landmass to the east; whether New Guinea and Australia were connected; and the location of the east coast of Australia.*

B RIGHT *Tasman's Voyages by F. J. Visscher, who sailed with him, from the Van der Hem Atlas (1670). The map shows the cumulative increase of Dutch knowledge of the coastline of the western half of Australia, and above all the great circular sweep of Tasman's voyages of 1642-43 which touched at Van Diemen's Land, New Zealand, Tonga and Fiji.*

C BELOW *A copy by Cook of the chart of the Society Islands drawn for him by Tupaia in 1769. Although impressive in extent, the map is difficult to interpret – partly because of name changes, partly because the islands are arranged in concentric circles according to their sailing time from Tahiti.*

D BOTTOM *An anonymous manuscript chart illustrating Maartin de Vries's voyage to the north of Japan in 1643. 'Companies Land', much inflated, has a strong hint ot continental dimensions; this misrepresentation influenced geographers until Bering's voyage in the next century (see ch.20).*

E BELOW RIGHT *A section of the John Senex map of Asia (1711). Senex perpetuated the belief that the seas north of Japan contained large landmasses – 'Land of Yedso' and 'Land of Compagnia' – the latter perhaps part of America.*

IN THE 17th century, more purposeful exploration began to erode the hazy outlines of the southern continent from the map, replacing them with the real South Land, the island continent of Australia. The Dutch took over from the Spaniards as the leading explorers of the Pacific, and their voyages south from Java revealed the real rather than the fanciful geography of the border area between the Indian Ocean and the Pacific. In 1605, a year before Quiros reached Espiritu Santo on one of the last of the Spanish voyages (see ch.33), the

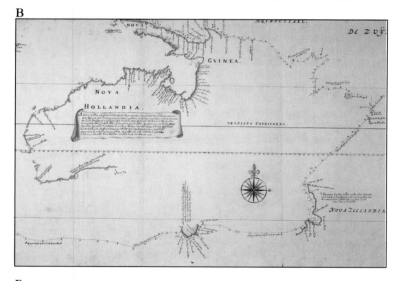

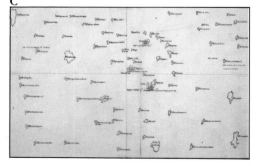

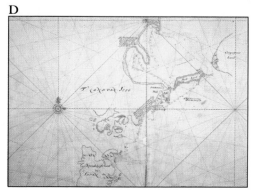

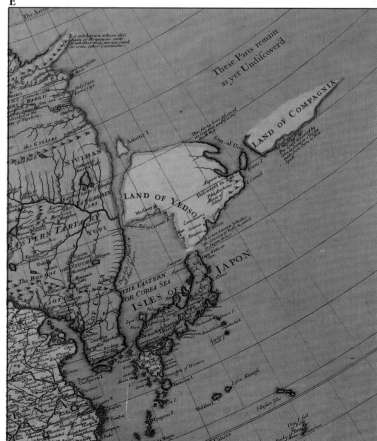

Dutch sailed into the Gulf of Carpentaria to make the first known European landing in Australia. This was followed by a series of reconnaissance probes by the Dutch East India Company which culminated in the voyages of Tasman. Planned exploration was supplemented by accidental (and sometimes disastrous) encounters with the west coast of Australia. These resulted from Company instructions to its seamen to sail east in high latitudes from the Cape of Good Hope before swinging north to Java. Archaeological evidence from the wreck in 1629 of the Dutch East Indiaman *Batavia* shows that survivors formed a makeshift settlement there, a century and a half before the first colonists arrived in Botany Bay. Even before Tasman's voyages the Dutch had a good idea of much of the west and southern coastline of Australia (named New Holland by the Dutch) from 21°S, as well as of the Gulf of Carpentaria.

Tasman's first exploring venture in the Company's service had been in the North Pacific, where the Dutch mounted expeditions to search for the islands of gold and silver – Rica de Oro and Rica de Plata – reputed to lie east of Japan. In 1639 Tasman and Quast explored the Bonin and Volcano island groups to the south of Japan, and struck across the ocean east of Japan as far as 175°W. A more important northern venture was that of Maartin Fries (or De Vries) in 1643, who also probed the empty ocean far to the east of Japan before turning north to sail past Sakhalin and the westernmost islands of the Kurile chain to enter the Sea of Okhotsk (*see map* D). His sightings of various islands were to be conflated by his own misinterpretations and by later cartographers into landmasses – Jeso (present-day Hokkaido), Staten Land (Iturup) and Compagnie Land (Urup), the last of which appeared on some maps as the westernmost protrusion of America. Not until Bering in the next century was the confusion resolved (*see ch.20*).

Tasman's greatest achievements lay elsewhere. His voyage of 1642-43 from Mauritius took him into far southern latitudes, until he landed on the shores of Van Diemen's Land (Tasmania). From there he continued east until he reached further unknown coasts – a land which he named New Zealand. From the west coast of South Island, and after a skirmish with Maoris at Murderers Bay (Golden Bay), Tasman headed along the coast of North Island before sailing to Batavia by way of the further new discoveries of Tonga and Fiji. Yet for all the importance of the voyage, Tasman had caught no glimpse of the mainland coast of Australia. On a further voyage in 1644 he sailed from New Guinea along Australia's northern shores and past the western end of Torres Strait, which he assumed was a bay. The achievement of the Dutch voyages was revealed by the maps which showed the distinctive, if unfinished, shape of Australia. What the maps could not convey was the Dutch reaction to New Holland, for its proud name flattered to deceive. Hopes of the wealth faded before the reality of a region where Tasman had 'found nothing profitable, only poor naked people'.

Geographers recognised that New Holland could not be the legendary *Terra Australis* since the new landmass had been circumnavigated by the Dutch. But some hoped that the great continent lay to the south-east, with New Zealand its western tip. As far as New Holland was concerned, much of the coastline had been sketched, though in places with a shaky hand. Puzzles remained: about whether Van Diemen's Land was the southernmost extremity of New Holland; whether New Guinea was joined to New Holland; and whether the Espíritu Santo of Quiros was part of the mainland, though only an approach from the east was likely to solve this last conundrum. In short, the Australian problem was defined but not solved. Within the area bounded by Tasman's great sweep there remained more doubt than certainty.

If the geography of the Pacific was uncertain and often fanciful, so was knowledge of its inhabitants. Successive waves of migration across the ocean had produced a complex racial and cultural pattern which mystified European explorers. Mod-

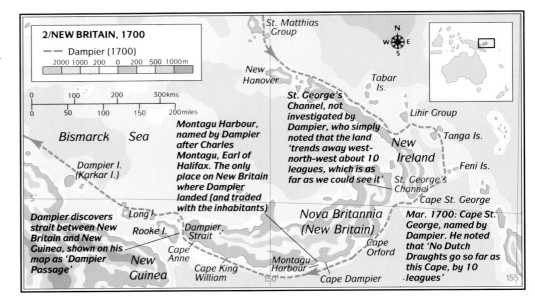

2/NEW BRITAIN, 1700
- - - Dampier (1700)

2000 1000 200 0 200 500 1000m

St. Matthias Group

New Hanover

Tabar Is.

St. George's Channel, not investigated by Dampier, who simply noted that the land 'trends away west-north-west about 10 leagues, which is as far as we could see it'

Lihir Group

Tanga Is.

New Ireland

Feni Is.

Bismarck Sea

Dampier I. (Karkar I.)

Montagu Harbour, named by Dampier after Charles Montagu, Earl of Halifax. The only place on New Britain where Dampier landed (and traded with the inhabitants)

St. George's Channel

Cape St. George

Dampier discovers strait between New Britain and New Guinea, shown on his map as 'Dampier Passage'

Long I.
Rooke I.
Dampier Strait

Nova Britannia (New Britain)

Cape Orford

Mar. 1700: Cape St. George, named by Dampier. He noted that 'No Dutch Draughts go so far as this Cape, by 10 leagues'

New Guinea

Cape Anne
Cape King William

Montagu Harbour

Cape Dampier

ern scholars point out that the three main groupings of the Pacific islands into Melanesia, Micronesia and Polynesia are capable of further division and sub-division. Explorers were entering a region where societies were organized in a series of baffling, overlapping layers, for there had been a mingling of peoples after migration, and a seeping of cultural influences from one island group to another. Running counter to the European belief that physical appearance was conditioned by climatic zone was the difference of colour between inhabitants of the same region. This had puzzled the explorers from the beginning. Mendaña had written of the Solomon Islanders in 1568 that although most of them were black, others were red, or fair, or even white. Linguistically deficient, the explorers were ill-equipped to present any systematic account of the peo-

2 ABOVE *Dampier, discoverer of New Britain in 1700, assumed that, with New Ireland and New Hanover, New Britain formed one large island.* F BELOW *From William Hack's Wagoner of the Great South Sea (1682). The marooning of Alexander Selkirk on Juan Fernández from 1704 to 1709 served as the basis for Defoe's Robinson Crusoe.*

F

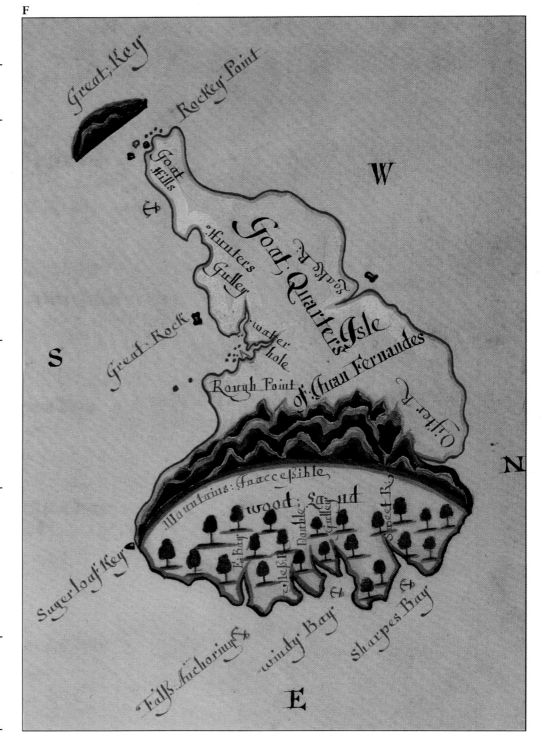

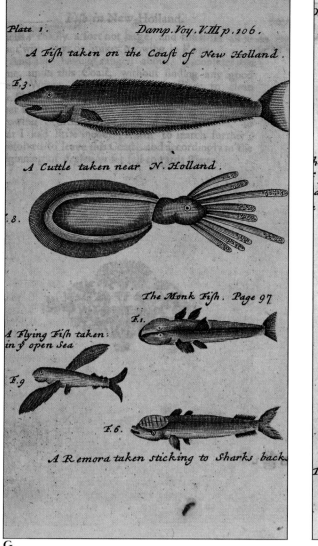

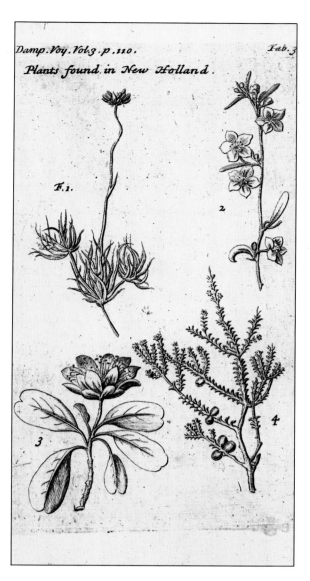

G

ples they encountered. Many of the discoverers were, by the standards of the time, moderate and humane men. Even so, to the islanders they seemed apparitions, *atua* or men from the sky, appearing and disappearing without warning. Encounters varied from friendly to violent, but all too often ended with a blast of gunfire on one side and a shower of stones and spears on the other.

By the late 17th century the Pacific had caught the imagination of English voyagers and writers – though their 'South Sea' was in reality little more than the waters which lapped the Pacific shore of Spain's vast American empire. Among the buccaneers who pillaged along those coasts was William Dampier, a perceptive observer whose books became classics of travel and adventure. Although most of his time was spent in Spanish America and the East Indies, he also ventured into more remote areas. In 1688 he reached the western shores of Australia, where his reaction to those arid shores and its Aboriginal inhabitants – 'the miserablest People in the World' – only confirmed the dismal impression given by his Dutch predecessors. These impressions, and much else from Dampier's peregrinations, were transmitted to generations of readers, for Dampier's *New Voyages* of 1697 became a best-seller. It attracted the attention of the government, and in 1699 Dampier was given command of a naval discovery expedition (in itself a rarity) to carry out further exploration along the coasts of New Holland. Dampier's original intention to sail by way of Cape Horn to the unknown eastern side of New Holland, possibly coasting along the shoreline of the great southern continent, was abandoned.

In the event his explorations along the west and north-west coasts of New Holland revealed little that the Dutch had not seen; Dampier in fact had one of Tasman's maps on board for guidance. His most significant discovery was of the 'island' (in fact, three islands) of New Britain just east of New Guinea. But Dampier's main importance was as a publicist rather than as an explorer. Further indication of the contemporary interest in the Pacific came in the writings of Jonathan Swift and Daniel Defoe. Gulliver's travels took him to Lilliput in the South Pacific and to Brobdingnag in the North, while the is-

G ABOVE *Australian flora and fauna, drawn on Dampier's voyage to New Holland in 1699 by an unknown artist, mentioned by Dampier only as 'a Person skill'd in Drawing'. The drawings were first published in 1703 in Dampier's* Voyage to New Holland.

3 BELOW *After an arduous crossing of the north Pacific and refitting at Macao, Anson in the* Centurion *captured the treasure-laden Manila-bound galleon off Cape Espiritu Santo in June 1743.*

land adventures of Robinson Crusoe were based on the marooning on Juan Fernández of the privateer Alexander Selkirk. In general, the narratives of Dampier and other privateers such as Rogers and Shelvocke provided more in the way of literary entertainment than geographical knowledge. As commerical ventures their expeditions were insignificant compared to the numerous French trading voyages to the Pacific coasts of Spanish America and across to China in the early 18th century. In terms of exploration they were surpassed by the Dutch expedition of Roggeveen in 1722, which discovered Samoa, touched on the fringes of the Society Islands, and brought back the first reports of Easter Island.

Official English interest in the Pacific quickened with the outbreak of war with Spain in 1739 and the decision to send a naval squadron under Anson to raid the coasts of Spanish America. In the end, despite losing all but one of his ships and most of his men, Anson captured the Acapulco treasure galleon off the Philippines, and after refitting at Canton completed a dramatic circumnavigation. The publicity surrounding the voyage led to a more purposeful surge of activity as considerations of geography, commerce and strategy pointed to the exploration of the Pacific as one of the most important global objectives left for the rival imperial powers of Europe. The geographer Alexander Dalrymple suggested that the southern

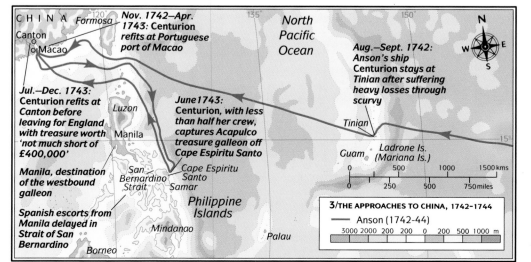

EVER SINCE the discovery of the New World, questions had arisen in Europe as to whether the early stages of man's existence might not in some ways have been superior to his current state. Had man degenerated rather than advanced? To students of primitive peoples, the newly discovered Pacific islands seemed an ideal laboratory in which to test their theories. Unlike the natives of America and Africa, those of the Pacific had not been contaminated and ravaged by centuries of European contact. William Hodges's *Tahiti Revisited* (C) was a characteristic image of a pristine land peopled by voluptuous innocents. In the unspoilt surroundings of the South Seas would surely be found the evidence to test the presumptions of those who believed in the 'noble savage'.

The first accounts of Tahiti did little to clarify the issue. In an idyllic setting where, at first, all men seemed free and happy, Wallis's crew discovered in 1767 that ferocious inter-island raiding took place, and that private property, rulers, priests and a hereditary aristocracy all existed. Bougainville, too, lost his early enchantment with Tahiti as he sailed home, learning from his shipboard companion, Ahu-toru, brother of a Tahitian chief, that 'the distinction of ranks is very great at Tahiti and the disproportion very tyrannical'. Omai, another Pacific islander brought back to Europe, this time by Cook's second expedition, became a minor celebrity in London society. Joshua Reynolds painted him in Classical pose, the epitome of uncorrupted dignity (B). In the end, however, Omai found himself trapped between different cultures. Back in the Pacific, complete with armour and firearms, he became a forlorn figure who survived for only two or three years.

Scepticism about the alleged perfection of the Pacific islands, and concern about the effect on them of the European intrusion, were strengthened by events on the later discovery voyages. The killing of two dozen men from a French expedition in New Zealand in 1772, the massacre of one of Cook's boat-crews not far away the following year, and the revelation of human sacrifice, as in (A), painted during Cook's third voyage, produced feelings of revulsion in Europe. The death of Cook at Hawaii in 1779 brought the conflict of attitudes into sharp focus. There were still those who looked to the islands for traces of the golden age of man's past; others could see only ignorance and backwardness.

continent, when discovered, would prove to be 5,000 miles across and to be populated with 50 million inhabitants. The 'scraps' from its economy, he insisted, 'would be sufficient to maintain the power, dominion and sovereignty of Britain, by employing all its manufactures and ships'. In France, Charles de Brosses had proclaimed the discovery of the continent a nobler objective for French ambitions than the endless European wars. 'What comparison can be made between the execution of a project such as this, and the conquest of some little ravaged province?' After the ending of the Seven Years War in 1763 both Britain and France experienced a 'Pacific craze' in which a new type of national hero emerged in the shape of naval explorers: Bougainville, Cook, La Pérouse. Expeditions set off into the unknown, to return three years later laden with specimens from the South Seas, eager to publish accounts, maps and views of the wondrous places they had visited.

The first voyage in the new era of state-sponsored Pacific discovery was that of Commodore John Byron in 1764. It was an unconvincing start. After claiming possession of the Falkland Islands in the South Atlantic, Byron followed the customary sailing route north-west across the Pacific from the Strait of Magellan, and made no discoveries of note. In 1766 the Admiralty sent out another expedition, under Captain Wallis and Lieutenant Carteret, with instructions to sail into high latitudes in search of the southern continent. After becoming accidentally separated from his consort vessel, Carteret crossed the Pacific farther south than any of his predecessors to slice a segment off the supposed continent. He also sighted, though he did not identify, the Solomon Islands, almost two centuries after their discovery by the Spaniards (*see* ch.33), and carried out some useful surveys around New Britain.

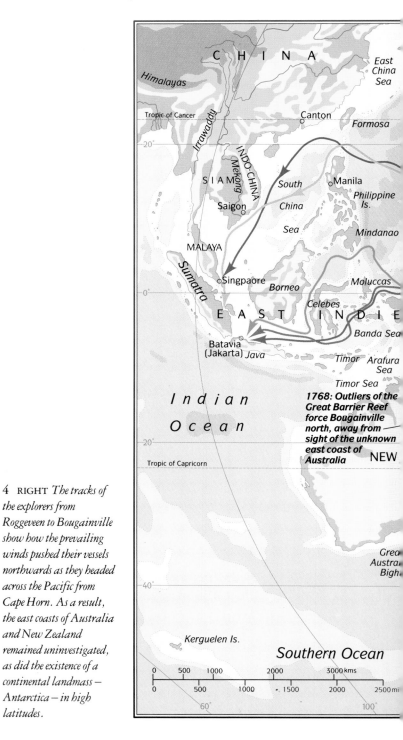

4 RIGHT *The tracks of the explorers from Roggeveen to Bougainville show how the prevailing winds pushed their vessels northwards as they headed across the Pacific from Cape Horn. As a result, the east coasts of Australia and New Zealand remained uninvestigated, as did the existence of a continental landmass – Antarctica – in high latitudes.*

Wallis took a more cautious route, but made a discovery which was to have enormous impact on Europe's impressions of the Pacific and its islands. In June 1767 he sighted Tahiti, an island of idyllic beauty, which for generations was to conjure up voluptuous images of the South Seas. To the men of the discovery vessels after months at sea, the islands of Polynesia seemed an earthly paradise. The climate was balmy, the food was fresh and plentiful and the inhabitants, if thievish, were usually friendly. Expurgated though they were, the printed journals from the expeditions revealed to their readers scenes of sexual licence which, in the words of one of Wallis's officers, 'made all our men madly fond of the shore, even the sick who had been on the doctor's list for some weeks'. Images both exotic and erotic were given even more extravagant definition the following year when a French expedition under the command of the celebrated soldier and diplomat, the Chevalier Louis Antoine de Bougainville, reached Tahiti. Bougainville named the island New Cythera after Aphrodite's fabled realm, though his naturalist wanted to go the whole way and name it Utopia. From Tahiti, Bougainville sailed through the Samoan group and on to the Espíritu Santo of Quiros. He found it insular (the New Hebrides or Vanuatu) not continental, as the Spaniard had imagined and as many of the maps showed. The expedition continued westward in quest of the east coast of New Holland before the outliers of the Great Barrier Reef forced it away north.

For all the flurry of activity and publicity which these voyages represented, and the adding of more Pacific islands to the map, little progress had been made towards solving the central issue of the existence of a great southern continent. The continent had simply receded farther south. New Holland re-

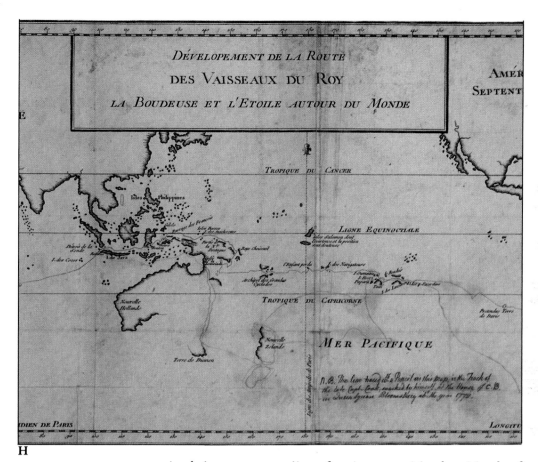

H

H ABOVE
*Bougainville's 1768
Pacific crossing from his*
Voyage autour du
Monde. *Cook added the
pencil lines to show his
1769-70 route.*

mained the western outline of an immense island or islands of unknown extent; New Zealand was an intriguing squiggle on the map, perhaps insular, possibly part of a great land-mass. Yet within a few years there was no longer any doubt. The Pacific appeared on the maps in much the same form as it does today; and the man responsible for this leap in knowledge was the greatest of 18th-century explorers, James Cook (*see* ch. 35).

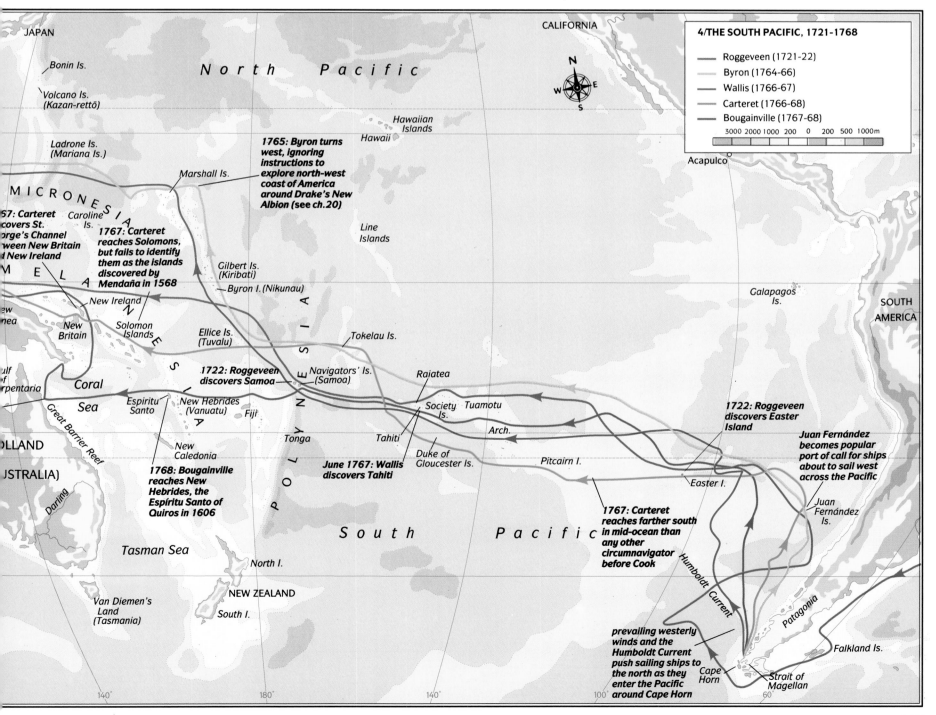

4/THE SOUTH PACIFIC, 1721-1768

- Roggeveen (1721-22)
- Byron (1764-66)
- Wallis (1766-67)
- Carteret (1766-68)
- Bougainville (1767-68)

3000 2000 1000 200 0 200 500 1000m

JAPAN

Bonin Is.

Volcano Is.
(Kazan-rettō)

Ladrone Is.
(Mariana Is.)

Marshall Is.

MICRONESIA

Caroline Is.

57: Carteret covers St. orge's Channel d New Ireland

1767: Carteret reaches Solomons, but fails to identify them as the islands discovered by Mendaña in 1568

New Ireland

New Britain

Solomon Islands

Gilbert Is. (Kiribati)

Byron I. (Nikunau)

Ellice Is. (Tuvalu)

North Pacific

Hawaiian Islands

Hawaii

1765: Byron turns west, ignoring instructions to explore north-west coast of America around Drake's New Albion (see ch.20)

Line Islands

CALIFORNIA

Acapulco

Galapagos Is.

SOUTH AMERICA

Tokelau Is.

Coral Sea

Espíritu Santo

New Hebrides (Vanuatu)

Fiji

1722: Roggeveen discovers Samoa

Navigators' Is. (Samoa)

Raiatea

New Caledonia

Tonga

Great Barrier Reef

OLLAND

(USTRALIA)

Darling

Tasman Sea

Van Diemen's Land (Tasmania)

North I.

NEW ZEALAND

South I.

POLYNESIA

Society Is.

Tahiti

Duke of Gloucester Is.

Tuamotu Arch.

June 1767: Wallis discovers Tahiti

1768: Bougainville reaches New Hebrides, the Espíritu Santo of Quiros in 1606

South Pacific

Pitcairn I.

1722: Roggeveen discovers Easter Island

Easter I.

Juan Fernández becomes popular port of call for ships about to sail west across the Pacific

Juan Fernández Is.

1767: Carteret reaches farther south in mid-ocean than any other circumnavigator before Cook

Humbolt Current

Patagonia

prevailing westerly winds and the Humboldt Current push sailing ships to the north as they enter the Pacific around Cape Horn

Cape Horn

Strait of Magellan

Falkland Is.

140°   180°   140°   100°   60°

THE PACIFIC IN THE AGE OF COOK
1768-1803

A LEFT *A recently rediscovered portrait of Captain Cook, by William Hodges, c.1775.* **1** BELOW *The tracks of Cook's first two voyages trace his explorations of the Pacific islands, Australia and New Zealand; he also sailed far enough south to demolish hopes of finding a great southern continent in temperate latitudes.*

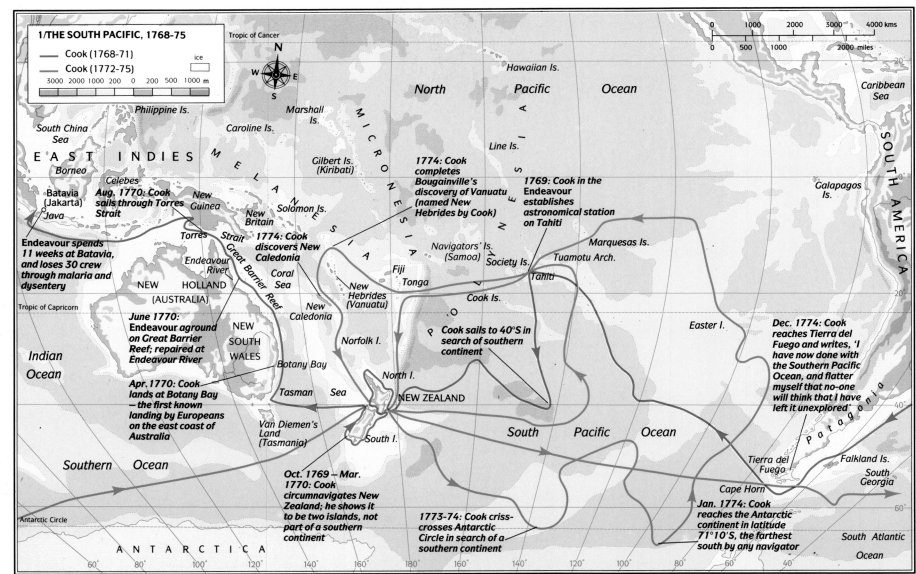

1/THE SOUTH PACIFIC, 1768-75

Cook (1768-71)
Cook (1772-75)
ice
3000 2000 1000 200 0 200 500 1000 m

0 1000 2000 3000 4000 kms
0 500 1000 2000 miles

Tropic of Cancer

Hawaiian Is.

North **Pacific** **Ocean**

Caribbean Sea

Philippine Is.

Marshall Is.

South China Sea

Caroline Is.

Line Is.

EAST INDIES

Gilbert Is. (Kiribati)

1774: Cook completes Bougainville's discovery of Vanuatu (named New Hebrides by Cook)

1769: Cook in the Endeavour establishes astronomical station on Tahiti

Galapagos Is.

Borneo

Celebes

Aug. 1770: Cook sails through Torres Strait

New Guinea

Solomon Is.

Batavia (Jakarta)

Java

New Britain

Torres Strait

1774: Cook discovers New Caledonia

Navigators' Is. (Samoa)

Society Is.

Marquesas Is.

Tuamotu Arch.

Endeavour spends 11 weeks at Batavia, and loses 30 crew through malaria and dysentery

Endeavour River

Great Barrier Reef

Coral Sea

Fiji

Tonga

Tahiti

NEW HOLLAND (AUSTRALIA)

New Caledonia

New Hebrides (Vanuatu)

Cook Is.

SOUTH AMERICA

Tropic of Capricorn

June 1770: Endeavour aground on Great Barrier Reef; repaired at Endeavour River

NEW SOUTH WALES

Norfolk I.

Cook sails to 40°S in search of southern continent

Easter I.

Dec. 1774: Cook reaches Tierra del Fuego and writes, 'I have now done with the Southern Pacific Ocean, and flatter myself that no-one will think that I have left it unexplored'

Apr. 1770: Cook lands at Botany Bay — the first known landing by Europeans on the east coast of Australia

Botany Bay

North I.

NEW ZEALAND

Tasman Sea

Indian Ocean

Van Diemen's Land (Tasmania)

South I.

South **Pacific** **Ocean**

Patagonia

Tierra del Fuego

Falkland Is.

South Georgia

Southern Ocean

Oct. 1769 – Mar. 1770: Cook circumnavigates New Zealand; he shows it to be two islands, not part of a southern continent

Cape Horn

Jan. 1774: Cook reaches the Antarctic continent in latitude 71°10'S, the farthest south by any navigator

1773-74: Cook criss-crosses Antarctic Circle in search of a southern continent

South Atlantic Ocean

Antarctic Circle

ANTARCTICA

EVEN BEFORE *the return of Wallis's expedition from the Pacific, the British government had decided to send out another. In 1769 the planet Venus was due to pass across the face of the sun, and astronomers suggested that among the worldwide observations of the transit should be a set from the South Pacific. The Admiralty agreed to the Royal Society's representations on the subject, and Tahiti was chosen as the most suitable spot for an observatory. Command of the expedition was given to James Cook, a naval lieutenant who had helped to survey the St. Lawrence during Wolfe's Quebec campaign of 1759, and after the war had spent five years making meticulous charts of the difficult coastline of Newfoundland. He had all the technical skills necessary to make an effective explorer, and the next few years were to show that he also possessed remarkable qualities of leadership and determination. His ambition, as he put it, was 'not only to go farther than any man has ever been before but as far as it was possible for man to go'.*

Cook's instructions show that the establishment of an observatory at Tahiti was only one objective of the voyage. From Tahiti, Cook was to sail south as far as 40°, since 'there is great reason to imagine that a continent, or land of great extent, may be found to the southward of the track lately made by Captain Wallis'. If he discovered the continent, Cook was to survey its coasts, bring back specimens of its produce, negotiate alliances with its inhabitants, and, with their consent, take possession of the region for Britain. Despite the collaboration of the Royal Society, and the presence on Cook's expeditions of scientists and artists, there were reasons other than those of scientific investigation behind the voyages. The editor of one of Cook's journals showed a clear awareness of their commercial and competitive aspect: 'Every nation that sends a ship to sea will partake of the benefit {of the published accounts}; but Great Britain herself, whose commerce is boundless, must take the lead in reaping the full advantage of her own discoveries'.

As the accounts, maps and views came off the presses – not only in England but on the Continent, too – Cook became a figure of European renown. His observations, and those of his contemporaries – scientists and artists as well as navigators – combined to give a fuller picture of the Pacific within a dozen years than had emerged during the previous two centuries of sporadic, often secretive, exploration.

B BELOW *A kangaroo, painted between 1771-72 by George Stubbs. First seen by Cook's men at Endeavour River in June 1770, the kangaroo was described by Cook as like a greyhound 'but for its walking or running in which it jumped like a hare or a deer'. Stubbs produced his painting using a kangaroo skin brought home on the* Endeavour *and from pencil sketches made on the voyage by Sydney Parkinson.*
C BELOW RIGHT *Cook's magnificent chart of New Zealand was the result of six months' exploration between October 1769 and March 1770, during which he mapped 2,400 miles of coastline.*

B

D BELOW *Australian red honeysuckle (*Banksia serrata*), painted by J.F. Miller in 1773 from a dried specimen brought back from Botany Bay on Cook's first voyage and from an unfinished sketch by Sydney Parkinson.*

D

COOK LEFT England in August 1768 in the *Endeavour*, not the usual naval frigate but a bluff-bowed Whitby collier of shallow draught and ample storage capacity. He sailed in a similar vessel, the *Resolution*, on his second and third voyages. The expedition sailed first to Tahiti, where it carried out the astronomical observations which were the ostensible purpose of the voyage, before turning south. Cook reached 40°S as ordered, but sighted no continent; and the long ocean swell coming from the south made him doubtful whether 'any such thing exists unless in a high latitude'. The *Endeavour* then turned west to New Zealand, whose coasts Cook mapped with a magnificent running survey which revealed the outlines of both North and South Island (*see* C). If New Zealand was not part of a continental landmass, Cook's landings nonetheless showed that it was a fertile land with a temperate climate – useful as a base for future Pacific explorers and, beyond that, a possible colony of European settlement. From New Zealand, Cook sailed towards Van Diemen's Land (Tasmania) in search of the unknown east coast of New Holland. He reached it just north of Van Diemen's Land, and turned north to run along its full extent. After landing at several places along the coast, including Botany Bay, and narrowly escaping shipwreck on the Great Barrier Reef, Cook settled a vexed geographical issue by sailing through the strait Torres had passed along in 1606 (*see* ch. 33).

Unlike his French contemporary, Surville, who was also exploring along the New Zealand coast in 1769 – but with an expedition afflicted by sickness – Cook suffered no losses from scurvy. Ironically, the only serious illness came from a stay ashore, when many of the crew picked up malaria and dysentery at Batavia. Nor were there to be any deaths from scurvy on his second and third voyages. Cook was by no means certain of the causes of scurvy, and paid no particular attention to the evidence produced by James Lind's research on the antiscorbutic properties of lemon juice. Not until 1795 did the Admiralty make the issuing of lemon juice on board naval vessels compulsory. What Cook and his surgeons did was to combine all the suggested remedies – lemon and orange juice, sauerkraut,

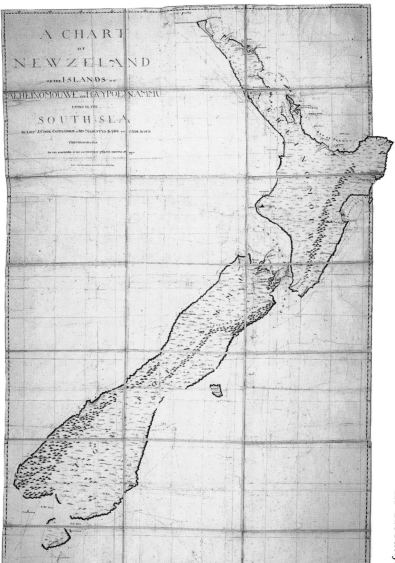
C

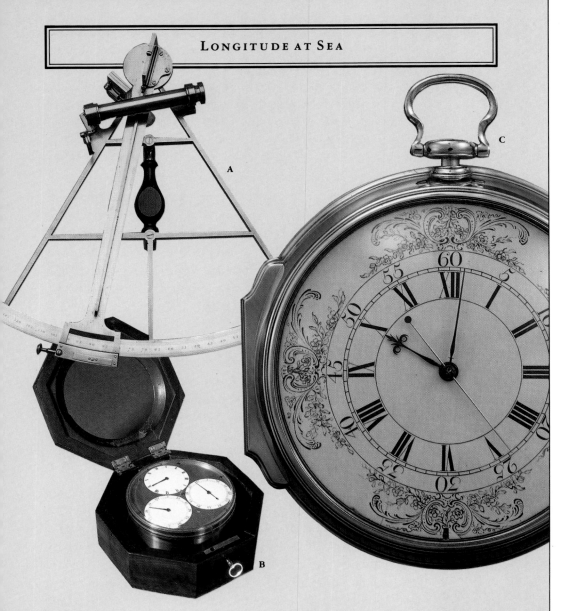

I N THE mid-18th century the map of the Pacific was one of confusion. Islands and coasts had been sighted and resighted, identified and then lost again, with names and locations which varied from explorer to explorer. Establishing latitude by meridian altitudes of the sun taken with the improved quadrants or sextants of the period was not a problem. (A) shows the Hadley quadrant used on Cook's third voyage. Finding longitude was a more intractable business. The Astronomer Royal, Nevil Maskelyne, complained that 'by the common methods of keeping a reckoning, five, ten or even fifteen degrees, are errors into which no one can be sure that he may not fall in the course of long voyages'. In 1741 Anson's squadron almost ran aground on Tierra del Fuego at a moment when dead-reckoning put its track, shown by the dotted line on the contemporary map (D), more than 300 miles out to sea. Since 1714 an Act of Parliament had offered £20,000 for 'such method for the discovery of longitude as shall have been tried and found practicable and useful at sea'; and since the 1730s John Harrison had been working on the development of a marine chronometer or spring-driven clock which would keep accurate time in all conditions. By correlating local time with the time along a standard meridian as shown by a chronometer, the difference in hours and minutes could be converted into degrees and minutes. Harrison's chronometers were still at the testing stage when the Pacific voyages of the 1760s were mounted, and Cook on his first voyage found longitude by the new but laborious method of 'lunar distances'. The radical development came on his second voyage, when for the first time a chronometer was carried. The *Resolution* had on board K.1 – a precise copy made by the clockmaker Larcum Kendall of Harrison's celebrated fourth chronometer (C), the first in watch shape. K.1, 'our faithful guide', was with Cook again on the *Resolution* on his third voyage, while Kendall's third chronometer (B), was on his consort vessel, *Discovery*.

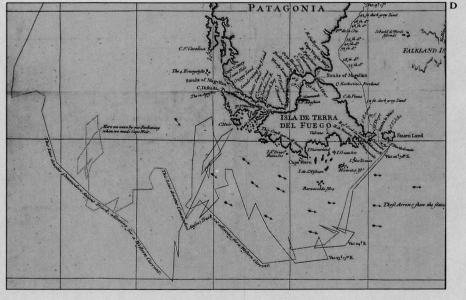

vinegar, malt wort, fresh meat and vegetables, dry clothes and bedding – and enforce them with unwavering strictness. Cook had men flogged for failing to follow their prescribed diet, but he eliminated scurvy from his ships.

Pressure for Cook to make a second voyage mounted with the lingering hopes that a continent might yet be found in high latitudes, and with the realization that France and Spain were also sending expeditions into the South Pacific. Four French expeditions went out between 1770 and 1773, searching for islands and continents, while the Spaniards sent ships to Easter Island and Tahiti. In 1772, Cook left once more to search for the southern continent on a voyage which vindicated wholly the application of cold logic to a problem which, as he wrote, had engrossed 'the geographers of all ages'. Crossing and recrossing the Antarctic Circle, Cook sailed through the heart of the continent sketched by the speculative cartographers. At his farthest south – farther than any man had been – he reached 71°10′S, where he encountered the ice-barrier that marks the edge of Antarctica. It was not the fertile continent of the theorists but, in Cook's words, 'a country doomed by nature never once to feel the warmth of the sun's rays, but to lie for ever buried under everlasting snow and ice'. On this voyage Cook did more than demolish continental myths. He located, identified and connected many of the landfalls of the earlier explorers: the Marquesas, Tonga, New Caledonia, the New Hebrides, Easter Island and, in the South Atlantic, the South Sandwich Group and South Georgia. On his two great voyages he had laid the foundations for an intelligible map of the South Pacific which now showed the island groups of Polynesia and southern Melanesia; New South Wales and Torres Strait; and the southern extremities of the great ocean.

One mystery of the Pacific had been solved; another remained, and in 1776 Cook left England to search for the western entrance of the elusive Northwest Passage (*see* ch.20). In taking the unfrequented route from the Society Islands to the north-west coast of America, Cook discovered the northernmost extension of Polynesia, the Hawaiian Islands. The presence of iron on the islands, and the shape of the crested feather 'helmets', raised in the minds of some of Cook's men a possibility which has since been intensely, if inconclusively, debated by scholars – that Spaniards had landed on the islands in the 16th century. If they had, it was more likely as castaways than as discoverers. In the 18th century the islands were indelibly associated with Cook, for it was there, in February 1779, that he met his death.

Although Cook's three voyages had defined the main outlines of the Pacific, much detailed work remained to be done; and there were further discovery voyages to the Pacific before the end of the century. Among them was the prestigious but ultimately tragic expedition of La Pérouse (1785-88); the D'Entrecasteaux expedition (1791-93) sent in search of La Pérouse; Vancouver's meticulous surveys of the north-west coast of America which corrected and completed Cook's charts; and the Spanish expedition under Malaspina (1789-94), the most elaborate of them all.

The sweep of these voyages was on a grand scale. La Pérouse's expedition spanned both the North and the South Pacific, from north of Japan to Botany Bay. His most significant explorations were off the Asian mainland where his surveys in the Gulf of Sakhalin and along the Kurile chain did something to clear up the confusion left after the Dutch voyage of de Vries in 1643 (*see* ch.34). The voyage ended in disaster: after leaving Botany Bay in early 1788, the expedition disappeared. It was almost 40 years later before relics were found on Vanikoro, north of New Caledonia, which showed that the French vessels had been wrecked there. D'Entrecasteaux failed to find any trace of La Pérouse, but carried out useful explorations along the south-west and southern coasts of Australia, and in the seas east and south of New Guinea where his quest took him to New Caledonia, the Solomons, New Ireland and the

Admiralty Islands. The Malaspina expedition, best equipped of all the ventures of the period, coasted the Pacific shores of America from Chile to Alaska before making for the Philippines, New Zealand, Australia and Tonga.

Exploration was followed by exploitation. The maritime fur traders reached the north-west coast of America in search of the sea-otters reported by Cook's men. Whalers followed up the reports from Cook's second voyage to hunt down the fur seals and the great sperm whales of the southern seas. Merchant

vessels moved among the islands, trading in pork, sandalwood and *bêche-de-mer*. In 1797 the first missionaries reached Tahiti, and they were followed by others in Tonga and the Marquesas. The most portentous development of all came in 1788 when the 'First Fleet' of convict settlers from Britain arrived at Botany Bay. Sufficient trust was placed in Cook's favourable reports of 1770 by the government for it to choose Botany Bay as the new destination for convicts who previously would have been transported to the American colonies. Less-publicized reasons may also have played a part: plans to produce naval stores; the establishment of a strategic base south of the Dutch East Indies; and a desire to stifle French initiatives in the area. As the settlers from the fleet and its successors established themselves around Sydney harbour, detailed exploration of the nearby coasts began, though inland the steep escarpment of the Blue Mountains blocked early attempts at expansion. In 1798 Flinders and Bass confirmed that Van Diemen's Land or Tasmania was an island, and Bass Strait became a useful short cut on the eastern haul from the Cape to Sydney. On a larger scale altogether, in the years 1801-3 the Baudin expedition from France and the Flinders expedition from Britain mapped long stretches of the Australian coastline. Thirteen-hundred miles distant, New Zealand had to wait longer for settlement despite the presence of whalers, missionaries and the occasional naval expedition. Not until the 1840s was there settlement on any scale in those islands which Cook had described as well suited to European colonization.

By the first decade of the 19th century, the complete coastal profile of the South Land, or New Holland of the Dutch discoverers, was outlined on the maps. Appropriately, the continent was to have a new name, though one associated with the old myths of Terra Australis. From 1817 Lachlan Macquarie, Governor of New South Wales, used the name 'Australia' as it appeared on Flinders' maps – in the hope that it would be 'the name given to this country in future'.

E ABOVE *Officers from La Pérouse's 1786 voyage to Easter Island measure the statues (while islanders pilfer their belongings).*
F BELOW LEFT *Sydney Cove in 1792. Settlement spread steadily since the foundation of the infant colony in 1788. Governor Arthur Phillip's house is on the left.* **2** BELOW *By 1775 the main features of the South Pacific were known. Thereafter explorers investigated the north Pacific, discovering Hawaii and surveying the north-west coast of America.*

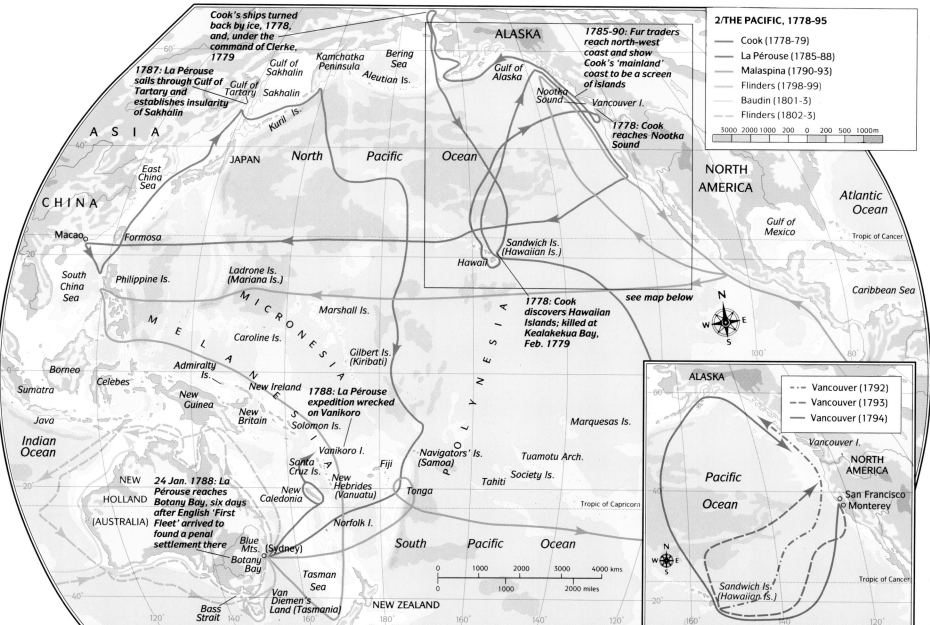

36
AUSTRALIA: THE INTERIOR REVEALED
1788-1900

A BELOW *Flinders's 1814 map highlights the magnitude of the Australia that lay to be explored. Though the outlines of the newly discovered continent had been established early in the century, the vast interior was almost entirely unknown. The European settlements were tiny enclaves on the fringes of a huge and empty landmass.*

A

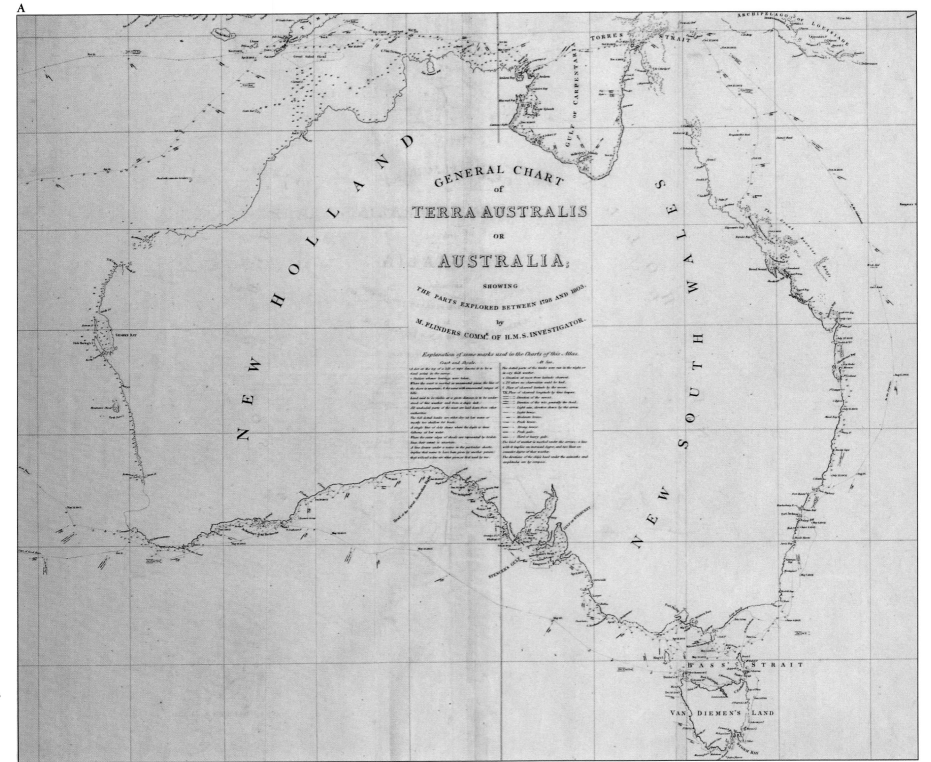

THE EUROPEAN exploration of Australia began at scattered spots along its eastern coastlines. Until 1810 settlement was confined to the Cumberland Plain, a bulbous lowland extending 40 miles to the north and south and 25 miles to the west of Sydney, founded in 1788 and the first European colony in Australia. Small settlements were established on Norfolk Island, 1,000 miles to the east in the Pacific Ocean in the same year; at Newcastle to the north in 1802; and on the estuaries of the Derwent River in south-east Tasmania in 1803 and of the Tamar River in the north of the island between 1804-6 (see map 2).

In these years, there were some slight beginnings at land exploration, with colonists seeking out fertile areas on the Cumberland Plain, and with a succession of attempts to cross the Blue Mountains to its west. Those abrupt escarpments proved too arduous for small-scale expeditions, however. But with the Cumberland Plain extensive enough to meet their major needs there was in any case little incentive for colonists to mount larger ones.

At the same time, the settlements at Hobart and Launceston in Tasmania were consolidated. While this island's river-valleys offered much easier access into the interior, the smaller number of settlers and animals, combined with resistance on the part of the Aborigines, meant that here, as on the mainland, the colonists were initially confined to coastal areas.

Accordingly, colonists in this period looked outwards over the ocean towards distant islands and destinations, rather than inwards to the reaches of the continent. The most important explorations of the period reflected this concern: all these were sea-based – Bass and Flinders's discovery of Bass Strait and circumnavigation of Tasmania, in 1797 and 1798-99 respectively, and Baudin's and Flinders's delineation of the continent's coastline in 1801-3 (see map A).

When significant inland exploration did begin, it came as a consequence of the colonists' need to find more extensive pastures for their multiplying herds and flocks. Throughout the 19th century, as other parts of the coastline were settled (Brisbane in 1824, Albany in 1826, Perth in 1829, Melbourne and Adelaide in 1836), pastoralism continued to be the fundamental determinant of inland exploration. But subsidiary motives existed, too: principally those of establishing overland routes between the settlements, of resolving geographical speculations and, for some explorers, of achieving personal fame.

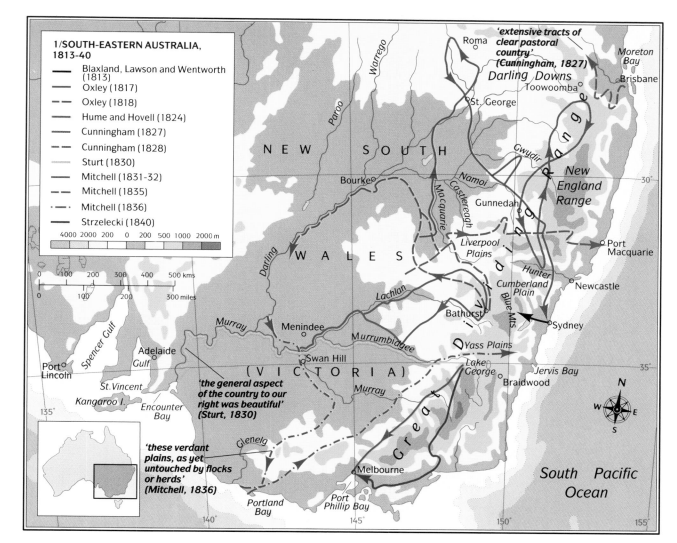

1/SOUTH-EASTERN AUSTRALIA, 1813-40

- Blaxland, Lawson and Wentworth (1813)
- Oxley (1817)
- Oxley (1818)
- Hume and Hovell (1824)
- Cunningham (1827)
- Cunningham (1828)
- Sturt (1830)
- Mitchell (1831-32)
- Mitchell (1835)
- Mitchell (1836)
- Strzelecki (1840)

'extensive tracts of clear pastoral country' (Cunningham, 1827)

'the general aspect of the country to our right was beautiful' (Sturt, 1830)

'these verdant plains, as yet untouched by flocks or herds' (Mitchell, 1836)

1 ABOVE The need to find new pastures for multiplying herds and flocks underlay the exploration of the south-east between 1813 and 1840. Although unspectacular, this phase of exploration was nonetheless vital, defining the axis along which European habitation spread and the core area of Australia's pastoral and agricultural production.

B BELOW Duncan Cooper's watercolours of Challicum Run, Victoria, echo Mitchell's 1836 observations on, 'A land so inviting, and still without inhabitants!'

IN MAY 1813, seeking fresh land for their animals away from the over-grazed Cumberland Plain, Gregory Blaxland, William Lawson and William Wentworth found a way over the Blue Mountains. Their crossing constituted the true beginning of European land exploration of Australia. Governor Lachlan Macquarie then commissioned George Evans and William Cox to survey and build a road to the Bathurst Plains, where, in 1815, he established a government settlement. A burst of exploration in the following ten years to the north, west and south (see map 1), revealed extensive pastoral lands. As governors rewarded the finders with grants, Europeans and their animals began to spread west of the Great Dividing Range. The situation was similar in Tasmania, where pastoralists followed explorers along the inland corridors, so that by 1820 the settlements of Hobart and Launceston were linked by a ribbon of holdings (see map 2).

Exploration and occupation received an enormous impetus in the 1820s both from increasing demand by British manufacturers for fine wool and Commissioner J.T. Bigge's attendant recommendation that the future of the colony should lie in its

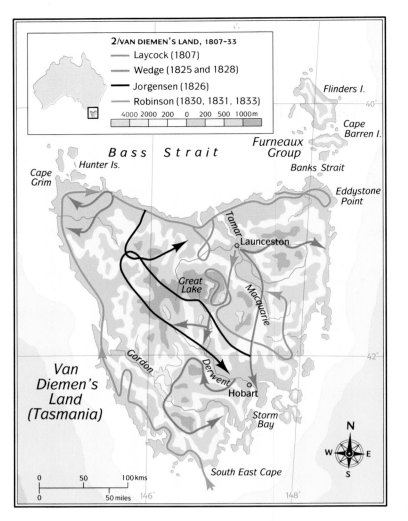

Laycock (1807)
Wedge (1825 and 1828)
Jorgensen (1826)
Robinson (1830, 1831, 1833)

4000 2000 200 0 200 500 1000m

Flinders I.

Cape Barren I.

Bass Strait

Furneaux Group

Hunter Is.

Banks Strait

Cape Grim

Eddystone Point

Tamar

Launceston

Macquarie

Great Lake

Van Diemen's Land (Tasmania)

Gordon

Derwent

Hobart

Storm Bay

South East Cape

N W E S

0 50 100 kms
0 50 miles

146° 148° 42° 40°

2 LEFT *Because river valleys offered easy access to the interior, early pastoral expansion in Tasmania went forward more rapidly than on the mainland. But by cutting across Aboriginal migration paths it led to great conflict, culminating in the 'Black War' of the 1820s. In the 1830s, when most grazing had been taken up, Tasmanians pioneered the settlement of the southern fringe of Victoria.*

pastoralists flooded into the new lands. By the end of the 1840s, Europeans had occupied a broad arc of the Australian continent extending from Brisbane on the east coast to Adelaide on the southern one and much of Tasmania. An enduring basis for economic prosperity had been laid.

Geographical curiosity mixed with commercial and personal ambition then gave rise to further exploration. All the other continents exhibit inland lakes, or 'seas', and great traversing waterways. Analogy told Europeans that this should also be the case in Australia. Oxley, Alan Cunningham and Charles Sturt each entertained visions of 'noble' transcontinental rivers and 'Mediterranean' seas. Pointing to the inland basin formed by the curve of the Great Divide, Mitchell observed, 'Supposing the course of the desired river to be analogous to that of the Amazons, we must believe its estuary to be amongst these unexplored inlets of the Sea, which Captain King saw on the North Western Coast of Australia'. It was the dream of finding this river that led Mitchell to explore northward. At the end of 1845, he pushed up into what is now Queensland. Investigating first the Belyando River, he then retraced his route before turning west to strike the Barcoo River. This he proclaimed to the world as the 'Desired Blessing'. His triumph was short-lived, however. In 1847 Edmund Kennedy established that the rivers flowed south-west into the arid heartland.

Others also explored north at this time. In 1844-45, starting from the Darling Downs, Ludwig Leichhardt moved along the Great Divide to the Gulf of Carpentaria, then, following

production. A steady expansion followed, as squatters sought out pastures for their flocks of Saxon-cross sheep. In an attempt to contain and to systemize the expansion, the government commissioned teams under John Oxley and Sir Thomas Mitchell to survey the regions already explored, with the result that 19 counties were declared in New South Wales in 1826. Similar steps were taken in Tasmania.

However, the demand for fine wool was such that the search for new grazing land was resumed almost at once. These explorations largely defined the Murray-Darling River system, and revealed extensive areas suited to grazing. With sheep numbers exceeding the resources of the 19 counties of New South Wales and the settled areas of Tasmania, in the 1830s

C BELOW *One motivation for the exploration of the centre and north was the hope of finding the inland sea or waterway predicted by speculative geographers such as on this 1827 map. These mirages animated Cunningham, Sturt and Mitchell in turn, only to disappear into the interior's desert sands.*

C

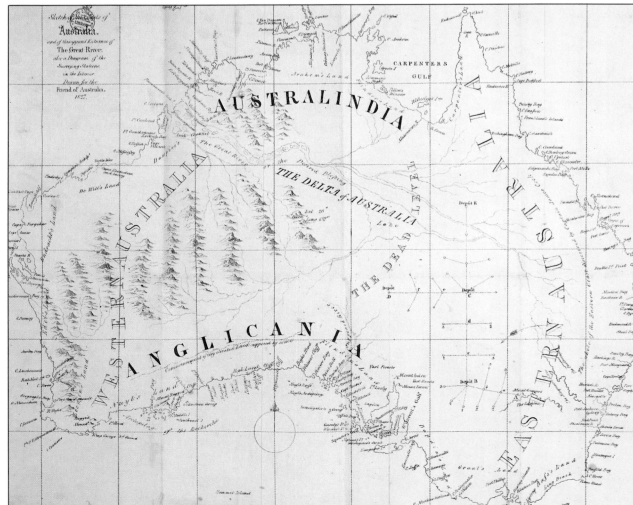

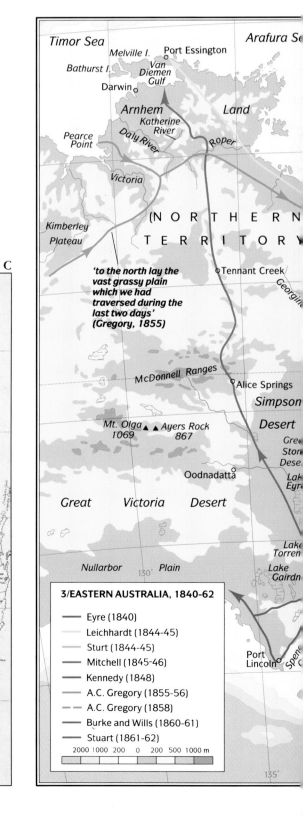

Timor Sea

Arafura Se

Melville I. Port Essington

Bathurst I.

Van Diemen Gulf

Darwin

Arnhem

Land

Katherine River

Daly River

Roper

Pearce Point

Victoria

Kimberley Plateau

(NORTHERN

TERRITORY

'to the north lay the vast grassy plain which we had traversed during the last two days' (Gregory, 1855)

Tennant Creek

Georgin

McDonnell Ranges

Alice Springs

Simpson

Mt. Olga 1069

Ayers Rock 867

Desert

Gre Sto Des

Oodnadatta

Lak Eyre

Great Victoria Desert

Lake Torren

Lake Gairdn

Nullarbor Plain

130°

3/EASTERN AUSTRALIA, 1840-62

Eyre (1840)
Leichhardt (1844-45)
Sturt (1844-45)
Mitchell (1845-46)
Kennedy (1848)
A.C. Gregory (1855-56)
A.C. Gregory (1858)
Burke and Wills (1860-61)
Stuart (1861-62)

2000 1000 200 0 200 500 1000 m

Port Lincoln

Spen

135°

the coast westwards, crossed Arnhem Land to reach Port Essington. At the end of 1846, he again went north, with the intention of crossing the continent from east to west, but illness and the hostile terrain forced him to abandon the attempt. Two years later, he tried again, to disappear forever.

In 1848, Kennedy followed the Great Divide from Rockingham Bay up to Cape York Peninsula; and in 1855-56, after examining the Victoria River basin, Augustus Gregory crossed the Northern Territory, skirted the edge of the Barkly Tableland, and crossed the Gulf Country to reach the east coast at Port Curtis (Gladstone).

In these same decades, explorers ventured into the continent's centre. In 1840 Edward Eyre proceeded inland from Spencer Gulf to the Flinders Range. His experience of the desolate fringes of Lake Torrens persuaded him that there was no inland sea. In 1844-45, Sturt struck north from the Darling River on a harrowing journey that took him to Cooper Creek and across the Stony Desert to the sandhills of the Simpson Desert. In 1858, starting from the Dawson River, Augustus Gregory followed the Barcoo River down to Cooper Creek before continuing past Lake Torrens to Adelaide.

In 1860, Robert Burke and Willam Wills left Melbourne at the head of the largest and most lavishly equipped of all colonial expeditions in an attempt to cross the continent from south to north, only to suffer those tragic consequences that Sturt so narrowly avoided. Burke was no bushman and no leader, and, as one section of the party moved north to its point of

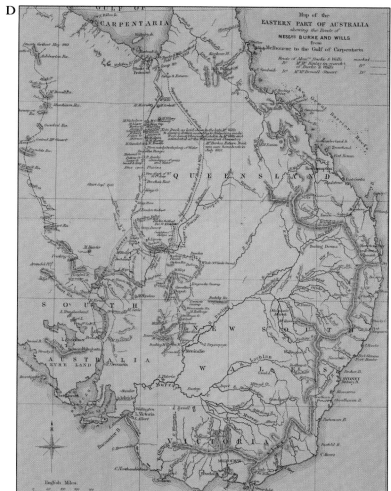

D RIGHT *Born from personal ambition and colonial rivalry, Burke and Wills's was one of the largest and most lavish of the inland expeditions, setting off in style, as depicted by Becker (***E*** BELOW RIGHT). It was also one of the most tragic. Determined to be the first to cross the continent from south to north, Burke led his party obstinately to disaster. Nonetheless, as did those that followed in search of the missing men, the journey did much to reveal the continent's eastern interior.*

E

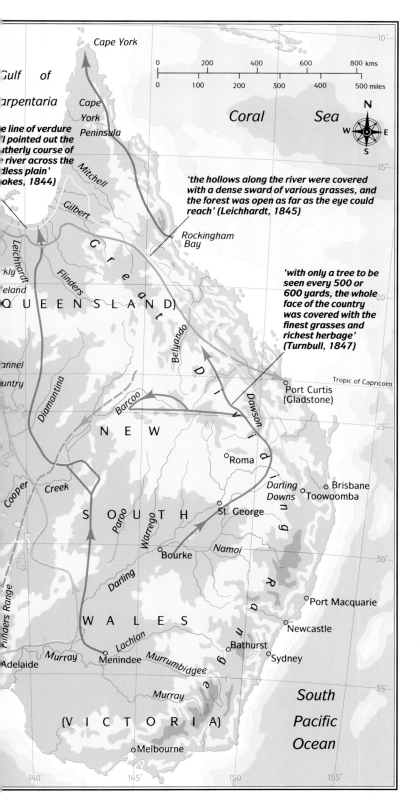

'the hollows along the river were covered with a dense sward of various grasses, and the forest was open as far as the eye could reach' (Leichhardt, 1845)

'with only a tree to be seen every 500 or 600 yards, the whole face of the country was covered with the finest grasses and richest herbage' (Turnbull, 1847)

3 LEFT *The revelation of the north and centre of Australia constituted the 'heroic' phase of the exploration of the continent, typified at first by conflict with the Aborigines and often desperate struggles for survival. Explorers, forced to make the best use of meagre local resources, came to depend heavily on Aboriginal help.*

real departure at Menindee, quarrels developed. When the other section failed to arrive there as planned, Burke impetuously pushed ahead with seven men. Leaving on 19 October they reached Cooper Creek on 11 November. There they established a depot. Taking three men with him, Burke set out for the Gulf of Carpentaria. In mid-February, he reached his northernmost point, only for coastal swamps to prevent his glimpsing the sea. He then returned down the Channel country, to find the depot deserted on his arrival on 21 April. (Ironically, the others had set off for Menindee only eight hours before, leaving food buried.) After resting for two days, Burke, Wills and King left for the south, deciding to follow a route down the Flinders Range. Encountering great hardships, Burke and Wills died; of the eight who had pushed ahead from Menindee, only King survived. In a series of expeditions between 1858 and 1862, John Stuart did achieve a south to north crossing, however, progressively reaching Alice Springs, Tennant Creek and the Roper and Katherine Rivers until he found the Indian Ocean at Van Diemen Gulf.

Together, these explorations revealed the main features of the continent's eastern half, with gaps being filled in by the expeditions that went in search of the missing Burke and Wills. They found extensive grasslands spread in a broad band along the inside of the Great Divide and across the tropical north. Equally, though, they showed how unyielding the Outback could be, and they foretold the inevitable risks of pastoral occupation. Most of the exploring parties suffered grievously from scurvy; the often arduous terrain exhausted men and

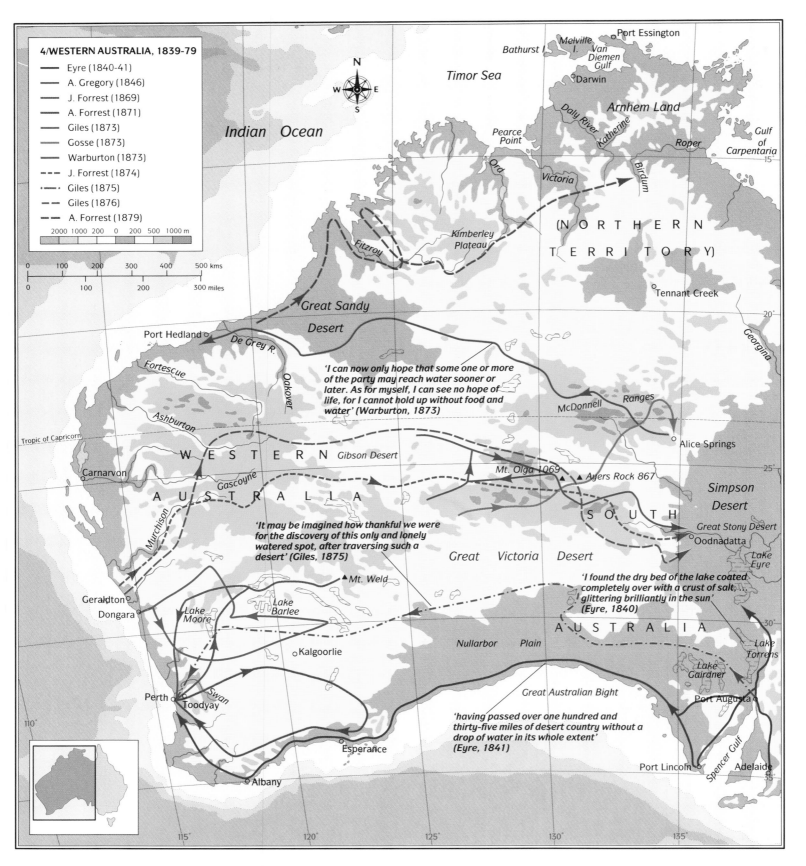

4/WESTERN AUSTRALIA, 1839-79

— Eyre (1840-41)
— A. Gregory (1846)
— J. Forrest (1869)
— A. Forrest (1871)
— Giles (1873)
— Gosse (1873)
— Warburton (1873)
--- J. Forrest (1874)
— Giles (1875)
--- Giles (1876)
--- A. Forrest (1879)

2000 1000 200 0 200 500 1000 m

0   100   200   300   400   500 kms
0   100   200   300 miles

'I can now only hope that some one or more of the party may reach water sooner or later. As for myself, I can see no hope of life, for I cannot hold up without food and water' (Warburton, 1873)

'It may be imagined how thankful we were for the discovery of this only and lonely watered spot, after traversing such a desert' (Giles, 1875)

'I found the dry bed of the lake coated completely over with a crust of salt, glittering brilliantly in the sun' (Eyre, 1840)

'having passed over one hundred and thirty-five miles of desert country without a drop of water in its whole extent' (Eyre, 1841)

4 LEFT *Expeditions of western Australia revealed mostly vast wastes of desert, marginal grazing lands and what have now become notable tourist destinations such as Ayers Rock and the MacDonnell and Olga Ranges. As they came to understand the forbidding nature of the terrain, explorers relied increasingly on camels, whose descendents now roam wild across the centre.*

animals; and all progress depended on access to water: 'I must go where the water leads me', Stuart poignantly observed.

After local exploration had revealed the geography of the continent's south-western corners, men pushed farther. In 1838-39, Sir George Grey explored the region behind Carnarvon, and the littoral south towards Perth. As subsequent explorers of the west and centre were to do, Grey's party experi-

enced hardship, but his explorations did bring some grazing areas to light. In 1840-41, seeking a stock route from South Australia to the Swan River settlement, Eyre travelled west from Port Lincoln across the Nullarbor Plain. This arduous journey produced the information that there was very little water, and no grazing lands, close to the coast of the Great Australian Bight. In 1846, the Gregory brothers pushed into the

F LEFT *Frome's 1843 First View of the Salt Desert was painted by the explorer on his expedition of the same year, one intended to resolve the puzzle concerning the extent of this salt depression, first discovered by Eyre in 1840. It makes clear the inhospitable aridity of much of central Australia.* **5** RIGHT *Planned to have pasture and water at regular intervals, these stockroutes saw many epic drives in the second half of the 19th century, with up to 20,000 head of cattle driven huge distances. Travelling more slowly than the explorers, and looking more closely, the drovers filled in many topographical details.*

interior behind Geraldton, to the large salt pan of Lake Moore, and then south towards the Hutt River; and in 1848 Augustus Gregory repeated and extended this survey, travelling inland from Toodyay to the north of the Murchison River. Dense scrub, rough terrain and lack of food and water variously hindered these attempts. In 1858, J.F. Gregory followed a large inland arc from the mouth of the Murchison to that of the Gascoyne River, and in 1861 explored the area between the Ashburton and De Grey Rivers. In 1869, following rumours of traces of Leichhardt's expedition, John Forrest went north-east from Perth, past Lake Barlee as far as Mount Weld. The next year, he travelled from Perth east along the coast of the Bight to Port Augusta, confirming Eyre's account. In 1871, his brother, Alexander, went inland from Perth past Kalgoorlie, then south to Esperance.

The building of the Overland Telegraph line from Darwin to Adelaide along Stuart's route in 1871-72, with depots placed at intervals to facilitate maintenance, created a line of destination and departure for those exploring the continent's arid western interior. They included William Gosse, who in 1873 revealed the Great Victoria Desert; Peter Warburton, who in the same year crossed the Great Sandy Desert; and John Forrest, who in 1874 crossed the centre of the continent to the telegraph line near Oodnadatta. The Gibson Desert, too, was traversed in this period, by Ernest Giles in 1873 and 1876.

Without exception, these were arduous journeys, with men, horses and camels suffering greatly from the intense heat and waterless terrain. As they struggled to reach the west coast, Warburton wrote: 'Our condition is so critical that I am determined, should it please God to give us once more water, so that we may not be compelled to go further back, to risk everything, and make a final push for the River Oakover. Some of us might reach it, if all could not'. The message these explorers returned with was that there was no fertile centre to the continent, but rather vast areas of desert, mitigated at long and uncertain intervals by waterholes, and fringed by areas of spinifex scrub that might support beef cattle.

In general, the explorers of the north, centre and west of Australia travelled in small parties, consisting typically of between five and eight people. The principal reason was the need for mobility: the desolate aridity of these huge wastes, where it might take days to locate the next waterhole or pasture, made the use of clumsy drays an unjustifiable risk. The growing tendency in the period to use horses and, later, camels reflected the priority accorded mobility.

As was the case in south-east Australia and in Tasmania, pastoralists soon followed the explorers into the centre and north. By 1890, most of the viable grasslands had been occupied by people raising cattle and sheep. The need to get animals to markets and processing factories then led to a good deal of informal explorations, as drovers established an extensive network of stockroutes (see map 5). By 1900, the southern continent was essentially revealed to European eyes.

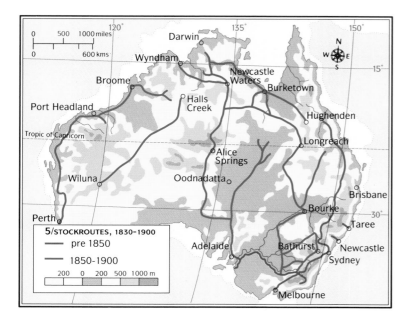

EUROPEAN explorers inevitably came in contact with the Aboriginal inhabitants of Australia. The most immediately striking aspect of this contact was hostility, with Aborigines stalking and attacking the exploring parties repeatedly. Though casualties were sometimes inflicted, more often European technology and resources proved superior. (A), by Thomas Baines, illustrates a confrontation between Aborigines and Baines and Bowman in 1855, in which the Aborigines were routed.

Yet by no means all contact was hostile. Aborigines of the Nullabor repeatedly pointed out waterholes and fodder to Eyre in 1840-41. In the inhospitable region such as that shown in Becker's painting of the *Mud Desert near Desolation Camp*, (B), Burke, Wills and King were succoured by inland Aborigines, who gave them food and shelter.

Aboriginal bush craft, hardiness and courage were often indispensible to European explorers. Giles's 1875 party went without fresh water for 17 days until Tommy, their guide, found a spring. In October 1845, another guide, Charley, found two members of Leichhardt's expedition after they had been lost for three days. Charley also proved himself more adept than his white companions at shooting animals for food. Some Aborigines identified themselves with the white employers to the extent of helping repel attacks by hostile Aborigines. Becker's painting of *Dick, the brave and gallant native guide* (C) is an eloquent example of a European's sympathy for his Aboriginal companion, and of how Australia's inhospitable reaches brought black and white together.

Portrait of Dick
the brave and gallant native guide.

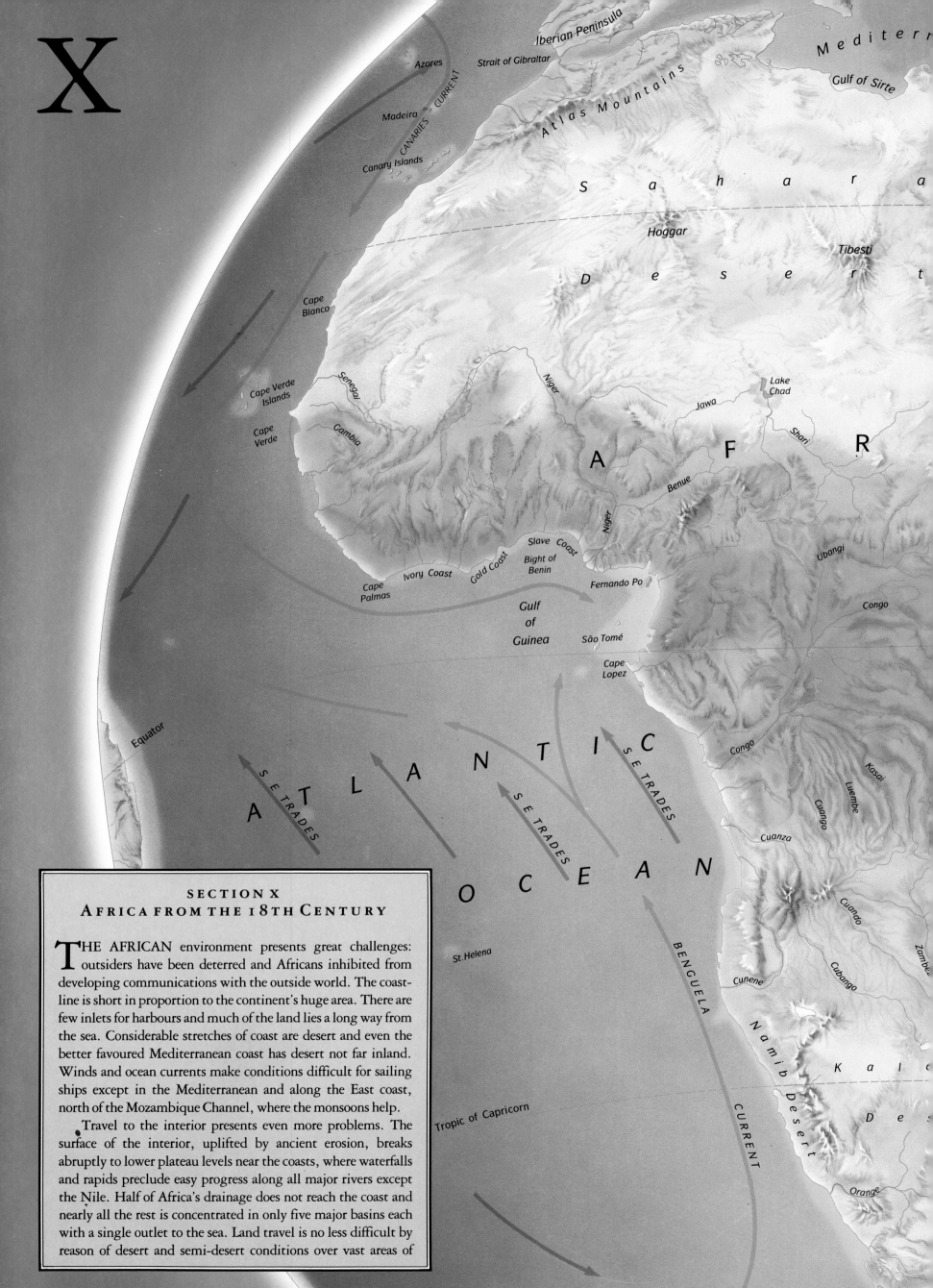

X

Iberian Peninsula

Strait of Gibraltar

Mediterr

Gulf of Sirte

Azores

Madeira

Atlas Mountains

CANARIES CURRENT

Canary Islands

S a h a r a

Hoggar

Tibesti

D   e   s   e   r   t

Cape
Blanco

Cape Verde
Islands

Senegal

Niger

Lake
Chad

Jawa

Cape
Verde

Gambia

A

F

R

Benue

Niger

Ubangi

Slave Coast

Bight of
Benin

Ivory Coast   Gold Coast

Fernando Po

Congo

Cape
Palmas

Gulf
of
Guinea

São Tomé

Cape
Lopez

Equator

Congo

Kasai

S E TRADES

Luembe

A T L A N T I C

S E TRADES

Cuango

Cuanza

S E TRADES

S E TRADES

O C E A N

Cuando

St.Helena

BENGUELA

Cuanza

Cunene

Zambe

SECTION X
AFRICA FROM THE 18TH CENTURY

THE AFRICAN environment presents great challenges:
outsiders have been deterred and Africans inhibited from
developing communications with the outside world. The coastline is short in proportion to the continent's huge area. There are
few inlets for harbours and much of the land lies a long way from
the sea. Considerable stretches of coast are desert and even the
better favoured Mediterranean coast has desert not far inland.
Winds and ocean currents make conditions difficult for sailing
ships except in the Mediterranean and along the East coast,
north of the Mozambique Channel, where the monsoons help.

Travel to the interior presents even more problems. The
surface of the interior, uplifted by ancient erosion, breaks
abruptly to lower plateau levels near the coasts, where waterfalls
and rapids preclude easy progress along all major rivers except
the Nile. Half of Africa's drainage does not reach the coast and
nearly all the rest is concentrated in only five major basins each
with a single outlet to the sea. Land travel is no less difficult by
reason of desert and semi-desert conditions over vast areas of

Tropic of Capricorn

Namib Desert

K a l a

D e s

CURRENT

Orange

Cape of Good Hope

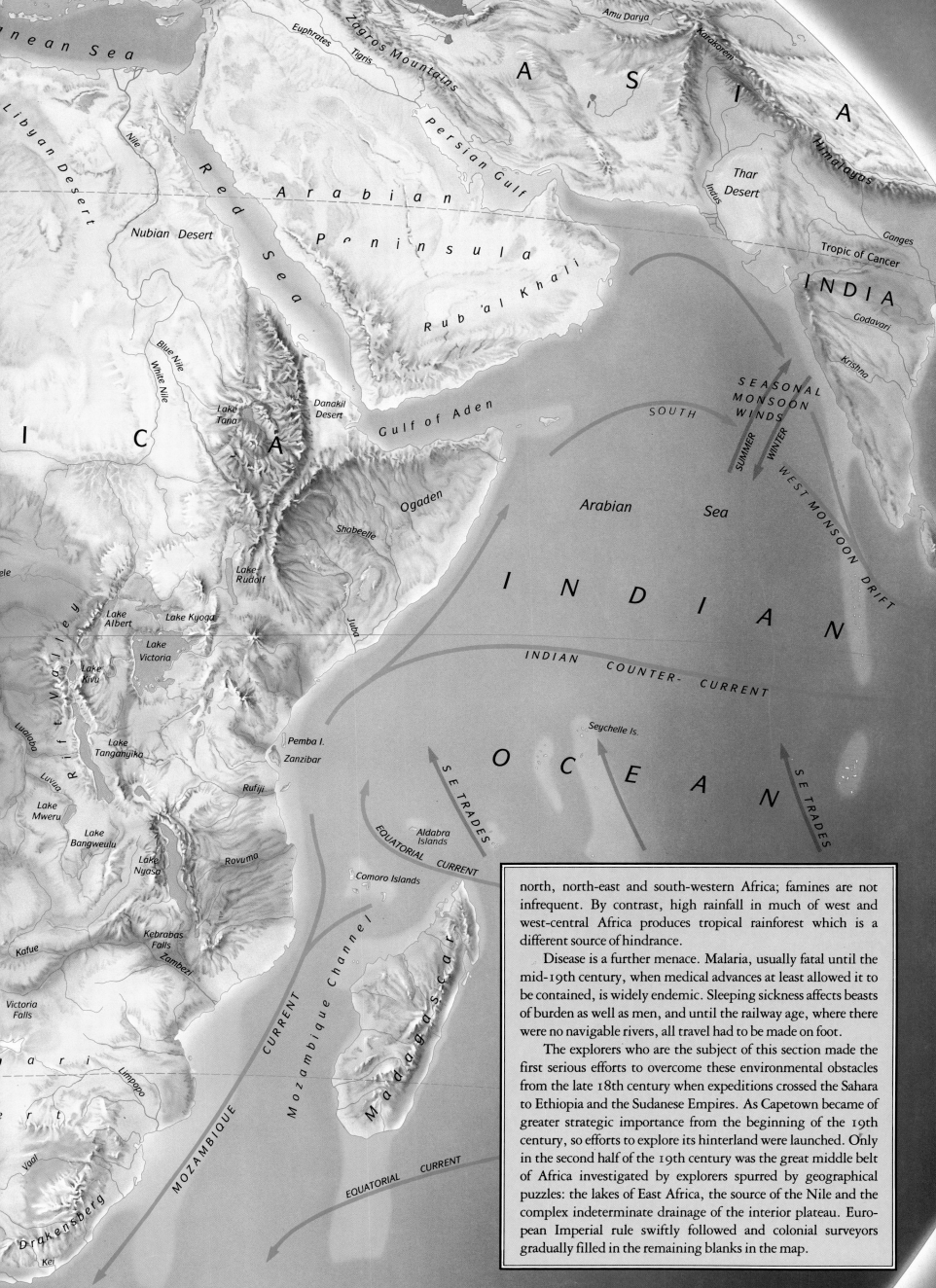

Labels on map

Amu Darya

Euphrates
Tigris

Zagros Mountains

Karakorem

...nean Sea

A S I A

Libyan Desert

Nile

Red Sea

Nubian Desert

Arabian

Peninsula

Persian Gulf

Himalayas

Thar Desert

Indus

Ganges

Tropic of Cancer

INDIA

Blue Nile
White Nile

Lake Tana

Danakil Desert

Rub 'al Khali

Godavari

Krishna

Gulf of Aden

I C A

Ogaden

Shabeelle

Lake Rudolf

SEASONAL MONSOON WINDS

SOUTH

SUMMER WINTER

WEST MONSOON DRIFT

Arabian   Sea

Juba

Rift Valley

Lake Albert

Lake Kyoga

Lake Victoria

Lake Kivu

INDIAN

INDIAN COUNTER- CURRENT

Lualaba

Lake Tanganyika

Pemba I.
Zanzibar

Seychelle Is.

O C E A N

Luvua

Rufiji

SE TRADES

SE TRADES

Lake Mweru

Lake Bangweulu

Lake Nyasa

Rovuma

EQUATORIAL CURRENT

Aldabra Islands

Comoro Islands

Kafue

Kebrabas Falls

Zambezi

Mozambique Channel

Madagascar

Victoria Falls

MOZAMBIQUE CURRENT

...ari

Limpopo

Vaal

EQUATORIAL   CURRENT

Drakensberg

Kei

Cape Recife

Text box

north, north-east and south-western Africa; famines are not infrequent. By contrast, high rainfall in much of west and west-central Africa produces tropical rainforest which is a different source of hindrance.

Disease is a further menace. Malaria, usually fatal until the mid-19th century, when medical advances at least allowed it to be contained, is widely endemic. Sleeping sickness affects beasts of burden as well as men, and until the railway age, where there were no navigable rivers, all travel had to be made on foot.

The explorers who are the subject of this section made the first serious efforts to overcome these environmental obstacles from the late 18th century when expeditions crossed the Sahara to Ethiopia and the Sudanese Empires. As Capetown became of greater strategic importance from the beginning of the 19th century, so efforts to explore its hinterland were launched. Only in the second half of the 19th century was the great middle belt of Africa investigated by explorers spurred by geographical puzzles: the lakes of East Africa, the source of the Nile and the complex indeterminate drainage of the interior plateau. European Imperial rule swiftly followed and colonial surveyors gradually filled in the remaining blanks in the map.

AFRICA: THE APPROACH FROM THE NORTH AND WEST 1768-1889

RENEWED European exploration of Africa north of the 5th parallel began around 1770. Though intellectual curiosity provided much of the impetus, explorers also hoped for new economic opportunities. By the 19th century, a new motive came into play: the desire to eradicate the slave trade.

The first attempts to penetrate the region were made from the north, via the trade routes of the Sahara to its southern fringe, where sophisticated Christian and Muslim societies were known to exist (see chs. 11 and 27). Hence the journeys of Bruce, Hornemann, Clapperton and Barth. Mungo Park, however, pioneered the approach from the Atlantic coast near Cape Verde. His chief goal was the solution to the problem of the River Niger. The question of which way the Niger flowed, and to where it flowed, was one of the great unknowns of African geography in the period, much as that of the source of the Nile would be later. The discovery in 1830 that it flowed south-east, emptying into the Atlantic Ocean in the Bight of Benin, was the prelude to the rapidly increasing European activity that climaxed in the 'scramble' for Africa at the end of the century and in the continent's partition among Europe's colonial powers.

A RIGHT *Bruce was a pioneering traveller, whose visit to Ethiopia and the source of the Blue Nile in 1770 inaugurated the modern exploration of Africa. This ostentatious image of him as a Roman emperor adorned his account of the journey.*

1 BELOW *The 18th-century European belief that the interior of North Africa was uninhabitable, though partly true, ignored the existence of trade routes linking the Mediterranean with the Sudanic region followed by the first scientific travellers.*

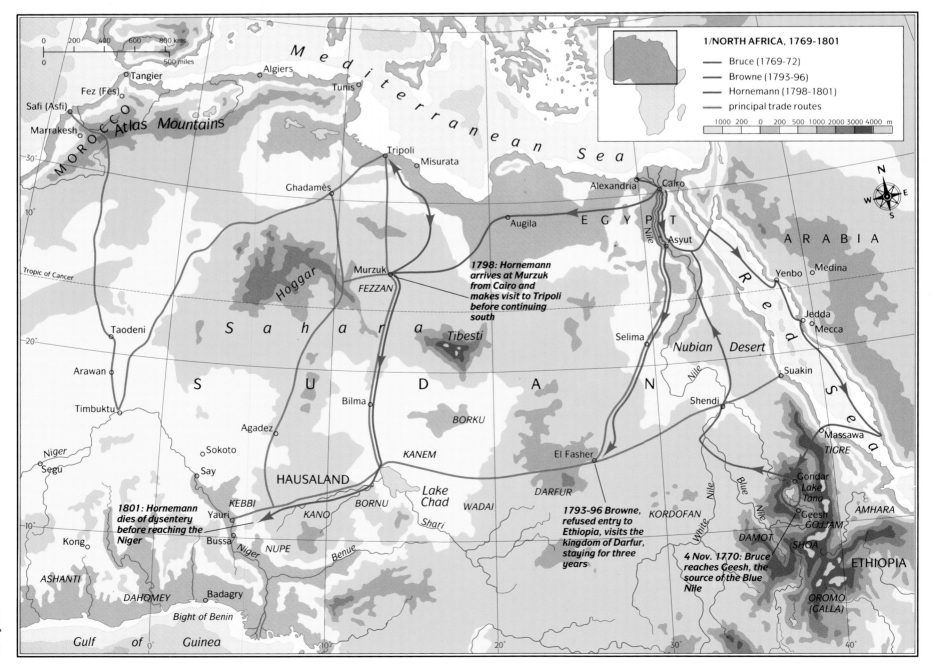

1/NORTH AFRICA, 1769-1801
— Bruce (1769-72)
— Browne (1793-96)
— Hornemann (1798-1801)
— principal trade routes

1000 200 0 200 500 1000 2000 3000 4000 m

1798: Hornemann arrives at Murzuk from Cairo and makes visit to Tripoli before continuing south

1801: Hornemann dies of dysentery before reaching the Niger

1793-96 Browne, refused entry to Ethiopia, visits the kingdom of Darfur, staying for three years

4 Nov. 1770: Bruce reaches Geesh, the source of the Blue Nile

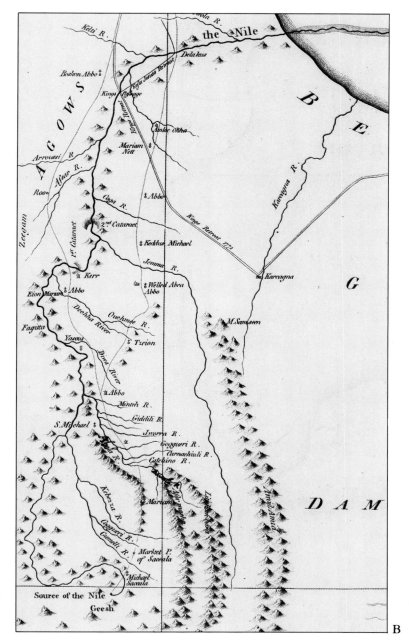

B LEFT *Bruce's map showing his route to the source of the Blue Nile (in the lower left-hand corner). The sceptical reaction to his discoveries began with his arrival in Paris when the cartographer d'Anville pointed out that Jesuit missionaries had preceded him by 152 years.*

C LEFT *Barbaric splendour and mystery are powerfully evoked by this 1844 depiction by W.C. Harris of Sahla Selassie, king of Shoa in Ethiopia. He was a shrewd politician and warrior who set his family on the path that made his descendants emperors of all Ethiopia.*

D LEFT *Murzuk, as depicted by Barth in the 1850s. The oasis town was the key to the route south to Bornu and the Hausa states. It was also a centre for slave trading, especially of women destined for harems.*

JAMES BRUCE was a Scottish laird made prosperous by the development of coal mines on his estate at Kinnaird. Though his education and early travels gave him an interest in the non-European world, it is not altogether clear why, in 1768, he resolved to journey to Ethiopia to seek the source of the Nile. Well equipped with intellect and determination, he reached his goal and brought back a wealth of information which ought to have given him a fame equal to that of his great contemporary Captain Cook. Yet even today he is not always treated as seriously as he deserves. The reasons are not hard to find. Bruce did not discover the ultimate source of the Nile, and even the source of the Blue Nile, which he did reach, had been visited before, by the Jesuit Pedro Paez in 1618. Further, his stories of life in Ethiopia were received sceptically in London. Bruce, treated unfairly, retreated angrily to Kinnaird. Yet his own vanity and pomposity were partly to blame. He was touchy, not always truthful and he treated his artist companion, Balugani, with gross ingratitude. Not until 1790 was Bruce mollified enough to publish an account of his travels. Although the book revived some of the derisive comments, Bruce's achievement became clear. He had put the source of the Blue Nile on the map more or less accurately and followed the river itself to its confluence with the White Nile. He had studied the languages, the cultures and some of the history of the peoples of Ethiopia. He had depicted plants, animals and buildings, had kept meteorological records and had fixed his positions by means of astronomical observations. He was a modern scientific explorer as well as a traveller.

Bruce reached Ethiopia, via Egypt and the Red Sea, and climbed from Massawa to Gondar in November 1768. He was immediately embroiled in the turbulent politics of the Ethiopian empire. The leading men of Ethiopia, especially church leaders, were inimical towards Europeans, as a result of earlier Portuguese activities, and absorbed in their own rivalries. The Emperor had little independent authority. Real power lay with Ras Michael of Tigre, who had recently murdered the two previous emperors. His rival, Fasil, warlord of Gojjam and Damot, controlled the region Bruce would need to visit to reach the source of the Blue Nile. The princes of Amhara and Shoa also had independent power, while the non-Christian Oromo (Galla) of the south further complicated politics.

Nonetheless, Bruce's facility with the language and his political acumen in winning the support of the Queen Mother and Michael's wife, Esther, won him permission to travel to the source of the Blue Nile. Having ingratiated himself with Fasil, he reached the springs at Geesh on 4 November 1770 and claimed he was, '… standing in that spot which had baffled the genius, industry and inquiry, of both ancients and moderns, for the course of near three thousand years'. After further adventures, including a crossing of the Nubian Desert, Bruce reached Egypt early in 1773 from where he returned to Europe for the 20-year anti-climax of the rest of his life.

Whatever other reactions it may have provoked, Bruce's book nevertheless inspired expeditions into Ethiopia in the early 19th century by men such as Henry Salt, William Cornwallis Harris and a new wave of both Protestant and Catholic missionaries including Ludwig Krapf (*see* ch. 39). Another independently financed scholar-traveller, W.G. Browne, aiming to check Bruce's information, was refused permission to enter Ethiopia. He therefore visited the Kingdom of Darfur in 1793, describing it in detail after an involuntary three-year stay.

By the mid-1790s, however, the Association for Promoting the Discovery of the Interior Parts of Africa (*see* panel on p. 191), was more interested in the kingdoms farther west through which the Niger might flow. The Association had already made two unsuccessful attempts to send travellers towards them from the north by following one or other of the Saharan trade routes. Another northern approach was to be made in 1798 by Friedrich Hornemann.

Hornemann was a good enough Arabist to pose as a merchant. He joined a caravan in Cairo and got himself to Murzuk in Fezzan. This was an important oasis town and staging point on the trade route from Tripoli to Bornu and the Hausa kingdoms. Hornemann set off south from Murzuk in 1800 and became the first European to cross the Sahara to Bornu. Unfortunately, he was to die of dysentery just short of the Niger and less than 500 miles from the Gulf of Guinea. None of his records survived and only confusing hearsay information from Murzuk was transmitted to the Association about the Niger.

To understand the Niger problem and the difficulties which confronted explorers, one has to take account of the profound changes which were occurring in the western Sudan around 1800. Reformism in the Islamic world had encouraged new attitudes in West Africa. Particularly affected were the Fula people, groups of whom had been migrating eastwards from the Senegambia region for several centuries. The charismatic Uthman dan Fodio was only the most notable of the Fulani reformers who believed that the comfortable compromises between Islam and African paganism must be ended. Uthman called a *jihad* in Hausaland in 1804 and set up a new political order – an empire – which he and later his son, Mohammed Bello, ruled from Sokoto. To the east, however, a new ruler of Bornu emerged who rejected Sokoto's claims to spiritual and political overlordship. Mohammed al-Kanemi's treatment of explorers who reached Bornu was accordingly determined by whether they wanted to go on to Sokoto. Like all Muslim rulers, he was in any case suspicious of white travellers who had no obvious economic objects, whose religion was anathema and who might well attempt to undermine the lucrative slave trade.

These changes in West African Islam meant a considerable redrawing of the political map, which rendered the information from earlier ages (used by scholars and mapmakers such as James Rennell, *see* ch.27) inappropriate and misleading. New or old, information about physical geography tended to be confused. So it was still possible credibly to state in 1790 that the Niger flowed west (*see* map E). Even when Mungo Park had shown it to flow east, it was supposed that the barrier of the

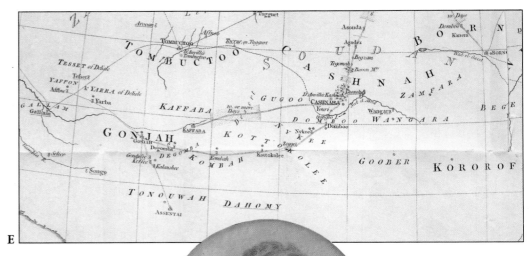

E

E ABOVE *James Rennell's 1790 map of west Africa reflects the poverty of European knowledge of the region. Timbuktu is too far north; more significant, the Niger is shown wrongly flowing to the west.* **F** BELOW *Rennell's 1799 map by contrast is much better informed, the result chiefly*

of the efforts of the Scot Mungo Park, **G** LEFT. *The mystery of the Niger outlet remained, however. Here, Rennell speculates that it may link with the Nile. His fallacious belief in the mythical Mountains of the Moon seems to have prevented his drawing the conclusion that it flowed south-east.*

G

F

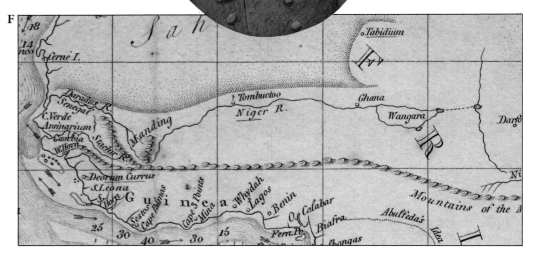

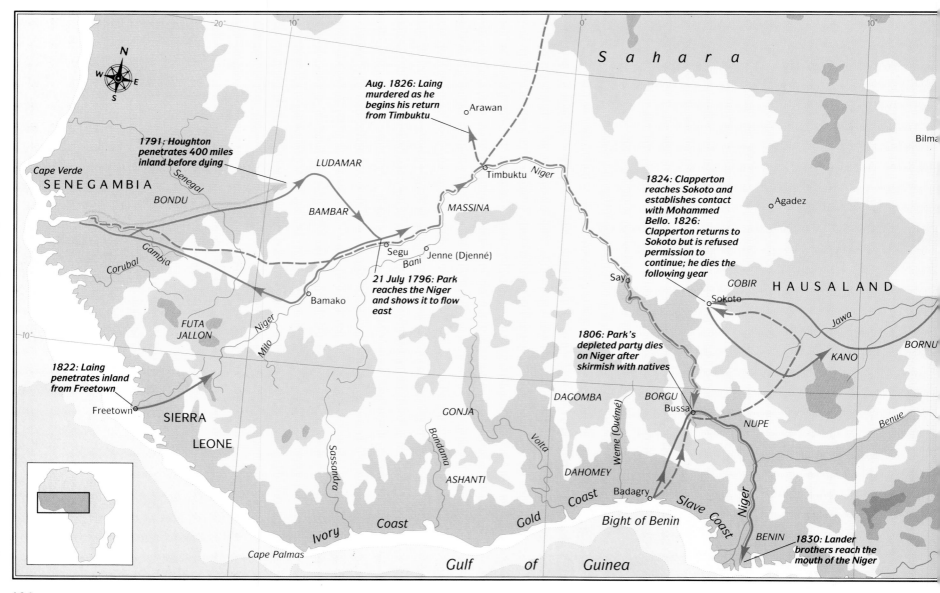

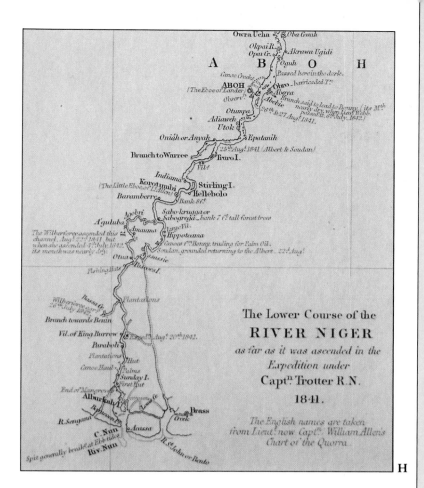

The Lower Course of the
RIVER NIGER
as far as it was ascended in the
Expedition under
Capt.ⁿ Trotter R.N.
1841.

The English names are taken
from Lieut.ⁿ now Capt.ⁿ William Allen's
Chart of the Quorra.

H

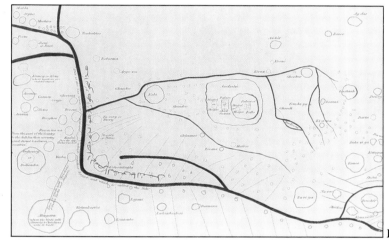

I

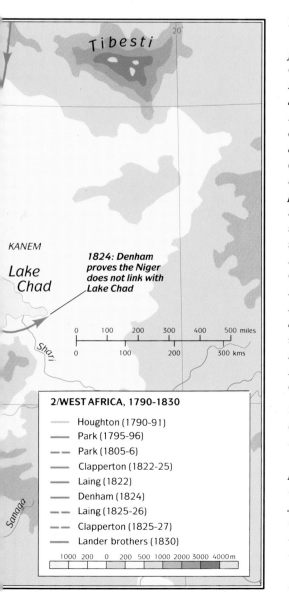

KANEM

Lake
Chad

1824: Denham
proves the Niger
does not link with
Lake Chad

| 0 | 100 | 200 | 300 | 400 | 500 miles |
| 0 | 100 | 200 | 300 kms |

2/WEST AFRICA, 1790-1830

Houghton (1790-91)
Park (1795-96)
Park (1805-6)
Clapperton (1822-25)
Laing (1822)
Denham (1824)
Laing (1825-26)
Clapperton (1825-27)
Lander brothers (1830)

| 1000 | 200 | 0 | 200 | 500 | 1000 | 2000 | 3000 | 4000m |

H TOP *The discovery in 1830 that the Niger flowed into the Gulf of Guinea suggested that steam vessels could use it as a route to the interior. The British Niger Expedition of 1841 highlighted the difficulties still to be overcome. Detailed knowledge was collected, permitting maps such as this, but many expedition members succumbed to malaria.* **I** ABOVE *Mohammed Bello's map of Central Africa shows the Niger flowing east to the Nile. The error seems deliberate: Clapperton reported that Bello had told him in 1826 that the Niger flowed to the Gulf of Guinea.*

2 LEFT *The great period of west African exploration lasted from 1790 to 1830. Though Park pioneered the approach from the west, the desert routes from Tripoli continued to be used in the 1820s. Nonetheless, it was from the west that Lander in 1830 solved the problem of the outlet of the Niger.*

IN LONDON, on 9 June 1788, a little group of aristocrats turned their dining club into an 'Association for Promoting the Discovery of the Interior Parts of Africa'. The leading figure was Sir Joseph Banks (**B**), who had been with Cook on his first voyage (*see* ch.35). As President of the Royal Society for over 30 years, Banks was the doyen of British scientists. James Bruce recognized his eminence by naming the Cusso tree (**A**) he had discovered *Banksia abyssinica*. This, now known as *Hagenia abyssinica*, is medicinal, its dried flowers a remedy for tapeworm. Banks wanted to extend practical and systematic exploration into the African interior to increase such valuable scientific knowledge. Indeed, the 'wide, extended blank' on the map was a 'reproach upon the present age'. Rational enquiry, the growth of knowledge and the triumph of the man of learning were championed enthusiastically. Thus, the major motive for the African Association to send travellers to Africa was the thirst for scientific knowledge. It was a tradition of intellectual enquiry carried on from 1830 by the Royal Geographical Society and similar bodies in Paris and Berlin.

In 1888 a German geographer, Supan, attempted to show just how much had been achieved by Banks and his successors. Using an 1888 base map (**D**) he demonstrated that in 1788 only at the southern tip of Africa and in the Ethiopian and Nile valley regions explored by Bruce were there areas beyond the coast known to science.

By the 1880s (**C**), the situation had changed radically: regions shown in dark red were known in detail; those in lighter red had been explored partly. Even the areas left white were, for the most part, indirectly known.

B

C

1880

1788

D

speculative Mountains of the Moon prevented its turning south. Reports of the existence of Lake Chad and the River Benue lent credibility to the idea that the Niger terminated somewhere towards the Nile. That so few expeditions had tried to solve the problem by penetrating the region from the Gulf of Guinea in this period reflects the real difficulties facing Europeans from malaria and other tropical diseases in the region, not to mention the hostility of the forest kingdoms and other slave-trading societies near the coast.

Despite these problems, from the end of the 18th century a succession of explorers began to visit the region. They were prompted, to various degrees, by curiosity about possible new markets, the campaign against the slave trade and strategic considerations. Governments became involved, too, with the British government taking over from the African Association the sponsorship of the major expeditions after 1802.

Mungo Park, even more than Bruce, was a child of the Scottish Enlightenment. Equipped with botanical and medical training from Edinburgh University, he attracted the African Association's favourable attention by research in Sumatra in 1793. Already impressed by the possibility of using the River Gambia valley as a route into the interior, the result of the work of their traveller Major Houghton, who had penetrated 400 miles before he died in 1791, the Association sent Park inland in May 1795. Travelling by horse and accompanied by only one servant, Park was robbed, ill-treated and at one stage imprisoned for three months by Muslims. His great achievement was to overcome all these tribulations by sheer determination allied to a propensity for friendship, even to those who persecuted him. Although he did not quite reach Timbuktu, on 21 July 1796, near Segu, 'I saw with infinite pleasure the great object of my mission – the long sought for majestic Niger, glittering to the morning sun, as broad as the Thames at Westminster, and flowing slowly *to the eastward*'. Park returned to London by Christmas 1797. His *Travels* became a best seller. Even if 'improved' by the African Association's editor, the book's description of his adventures and its sensible account of what he had learned has deservedly kept it in print since 1799.

As later with Livingstone (*see* chs.38 and 39), the individual achievement led to unsuccessful leadership of a much more ambitious expedition. Unable to settle to the life of a country doctor, Park accepted the British government's offer to lead a 40-man military expedition to the Niger to frustrate French ambitions in the region. Setting out again from the Gambia in April 1805, Park's party began to suffer from fevers as the wet season began. By the time Park reached the Niger and built a boat to sail down it, only four followers were left, and he himself seemed resigned to death when, before launching the boat, he wrote to the Colonial Secretary, '... if I could not succeed in the object of my journey, I would at least die on the Niger'. Die he did, at the Bussa rapids in 1806, presumably after a skirmish with local inhabitants. It seems that Park had unwisely tried to sail down the river ignoring or fighting off local people. For many years, however, Park's fate remained unknown and the course of the Niger a mystery.

Hostile climate and people, plus the return of Senegal to the French at the 1815 Treaty of Vienna, discouraged further initiatives from that region. The British government accordingly reverted to the northern approach from Tripoli. An expedition in 1818 got no further than Murzuk, but in January 1822, Walter Oudney and Hugh Clapperton, both of the Royal Navy, joined an army officer, Dixon Denham, to cross the desert to Lake Chad and the kingdom of Bornu. Denham was able to disprove the idea that the Niger flowed either into or out of the lake. Oudney then died but Clapperton continued west to the Empire ruled by Mohammed Bello – who would not allow him to go beyond Sokoto towards the real Niger. He had to be content with a map Bello provided (*see* map I). By January 1825 he and Denham were back in Tripoli.

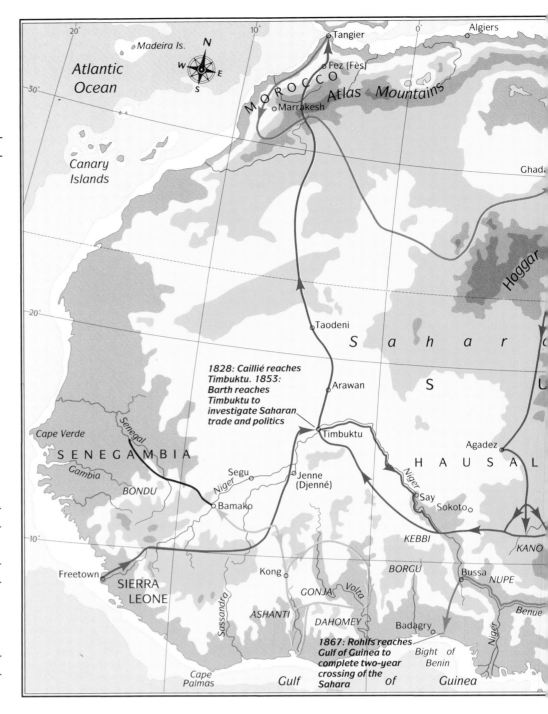

1828: Caillié reaches Timbuktu. 1853: Barth reaches Timbuktu to investigate Saharan trade and politics

1867: Rohlfs reaches Gulf of Guinea to complete two-year crossing of the Sahara

3 ABOVE *With Park never to return from his 1805 expedition, Timbuktu remained a mystery until Caillié's visit of 1828. The later expeditions of Barth were more important still, solving the problems of Lake Chad, the Benue and the middle Niger.*

J LEFT *The Islamic empires of the western Sudan were sustained by substantial military campaigns. Barth recorded this scene of a chief and his followers in Kanem in the 1850s.*

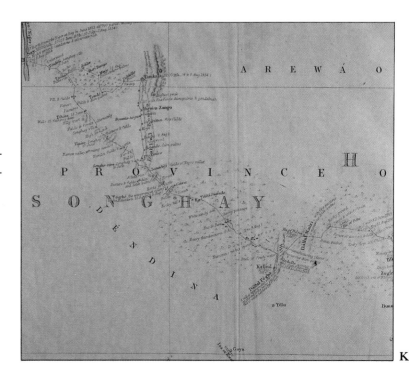

K LEFT *Barth's map of his 1852-53 route to the Niger at Say reveals his meticulous approach to cartography.* L RIGHT *Caillié found Timbuktu in 1828 smaller and less prosperous than medieval reports led Europeans to expect, though it was clean and well ordered. His drawing shows one-storey mud brick houses and rounded herdsmen's huts.*

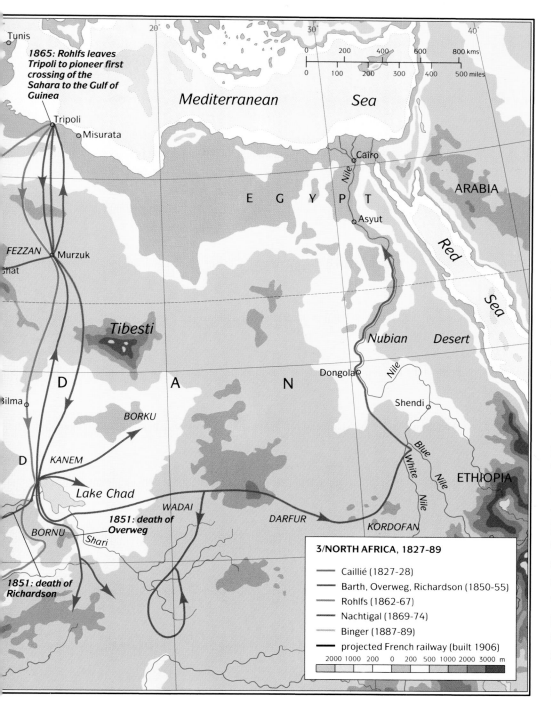

3/NORTH AFRICA, 1827-89

— Caillié (1827-28)
— Barth, Overweg, Richardson (1850-55)
— Rohlfs (1862-67)
— Nachtigal (1869-74)
— Binger (1887-89)
— projected French railway (built 1906)

2000 1000 200 0 200 500 1000 2000 3000 m

Map labels: Tunis; *1865: Rohlfs leaves Tripoli to pioneer first crossing of the Sahara to the Gulf of Guinea*; Tripoli; Misurata; Mediterranean Sea; Cairo; ARABIA; FEZZAN; Murzuk; hat; EGYPT; Asyut; Red Sea; Tibesti; Nubian Desert; Dongola; Nile; Shendi; Bilma; BORKU; D; A; N; D; KANEM; Lake Chad; White Nile; Blue Nile; ETHIOPIA; WADAI; DARFUR; KORDOFAN; *1851: death of Overweg*; BORNU; Shari; *1851: death of Richardson*

L

Despite their mutual dislike and their failure to solve the problem of the source of the Niger, the two men had been spectacularly successful in accumulating information and proving that there were sophisticated societies, under the rule of men like al-Kanemi and Bello, that wanted British goods and British support – even at the price of curtailing the slave trade.

Clapperton himself agreed to return to sign treaties in 1825, this time penetrating from the south. But at Sokoto, Bello seemed much less co-operative than in 1824: at war with al-Kanemi, he refused Clapperton permission to travel onwards. Clapperton died of dysentery in April 1827. Complete disaster was averted, however, when his servant, Richard Lander, managed to return home. Lander offered to take up the Niger task by returning to the Badagry-Bussa route and then sailing down the Niger. Accompanied by his brother, John, Lander did just this in 1830. Mungo Park's work had been completed and an age-old geographical problem solved. Surely steamboats on the river could now give better access to the interior than caravan routes across the Sahara? Lander himself was shortly to die in one of the attempts. Many more died of malaria on the ambitious Niger expedition of 1841. As elsewhere in Africa, European technology did not always triumph.

Even before Lander's triumph, a visit to Timbuktu had been managed. As part of the series of British expeditions from Tripoli, Alexander Gordon Laing, who had earlier explored near Sierra Leone, set out in 1824. Laing reached Timbuktu in August 1826 but was murdered at the outset of his return journey. His surviving letters gave little information about the city. In 1828, René Caillié also reached the city in the guise of an Egyptian Muslim escaping from French captivity. He continued across the desert to Tangier and from there to Paris, where he collected a 10,000-franc prize from the Paris Geographical Society. To this day some British chauvinists believe that Caillié was an impostor in a French plot to kill Laing and steal his notes. This nonsense made a better story than the rather dull one Caillié had to tell about Timbuktu, which he found far declined from its medieval splendour.

The next prominent explorer to visit Timbuktu was Heinrich Barth, in 1853. Barth, although a German, was recruited to join the British Central African Mission of 1849-55. The British government wished to investigate the slave trade, to persuade African rulers to replace it with 'legitimate trade' and to thwart any French moves in the region. The leader, James Richardson, had already investigated the desert slave trade for the Anti-Slavery Society. Barth's linguistic and geographical knowledge was complemented by the geological expertise of a third traveller, Adolf Overweg. Having different objectives the three men often quarrelled; yet they achieved much. They explored a new route across the desert south from Ghat. Beyond Agadez they parted and Richardson died in April 1851. Barth settled the puzzling drainage of the Lake Chad region and showed the Benue to be quite separate. His greater exploit, after Overweg's demise, was to travel westwards to Timbuktu making treaties with several rulers and recording a mass of information on history and ethnography. His journey constitutes one of the great examples of scholarly exploration.

Another German, Gerhard Rohlfs, was inspired by Barth to spend 20 years exploring the Sahara. His greatest feat was to cross Africa from the Mediterranean to the Gulf of Guinea in 1865-67. Rohlfs played a large part in creating interest among the newly united Germans in African ventures, as did Gustav Nachtigal, whose own achievement was to travel from Tripoli to Bornu and then eastwards to Darfur in 1869-74.

At the western end of the Sudan, by the 1870s French expeditions led to talk of a Senegal–Niger railway link and French overlordship. Yet unexplored territory remained south of the great bend of the Niger. In perhaps the last great exploratory journey in West Africa, Louis Binger made treaties as he examined the countries to the west of the Volta Basin in 1887-89. By this date, the 'scramble' was well underway.

AFRICA: THE APPROACH FROM THE SOUTH 1777-1856

A RIGHT *Kibangu Keleka, the fourth Cazembe (king) of the Lunda, shown here in court dress, ruled from 1805 to 1850. The Portuguese explorers Monteiro and Gamitto noted his 'great elegance and state'. Courteous to explorers, he resisted concessions that threatened his independence.*

1 BELOW *From the later 18th century, travellers were encouraged to push beyond the frontiers of the Cape Colony by the prospect of new plants and animals. In the following century, economic, political and religious developments also sparked expeditions northwards, with Livingstone reaching the Zambezi by 1851.*

THE EXPLORATION of southern Africa was conditioned both by physical and political considerations. The climax was reached with Livingstone's epic mid-century crossing of the continent.

The area of the Cape of Good Hope itself, with its relatively favourable Mediterranean climate, is bounded to the north by desert and to the east and north-east by the semi-desert Karroo. Beyond are the plateau lands of the high veldt, separated from the wetter eastern coastal plain of Transkei and Natal by the great mountain escarpment of the Drakensberg. Both Africans and Europeans, in competing for land and water, broke out on to the high veldt in this period.

In the broadest sense, black Africans, white settlers, Christian missionaries, metropolitan capitalists and government officials all found it necessary to explore. With the advance of the Europeans, for example, the San, or Bushmen, people had to retreat to more and more marginal land. The Khoikhoi, or Hottentots, were only slightly less vulnerable; some tried to find new land with the aid of missionary allies. The Bantu of the south-east, though more advanced and numerous, were similarly disrupted by the rise of the Zulu leader Shaka in the 1820s; they, too, had to look for new lands. Their bitter rivals in this search were the trekboers of the Afrikaner people, descendants of Dutch and Huguenot settlers. More recent British settlers, big-game hunters and mineral prospectors complicated the competition, as did evangelical missionaries whose contacts with British sponsors made them a powerful force in the search for some kind of promised land. Often unwillingly, the British Cape authority found itself trying to control the competition of these different groups; to do so, it, too, had to know the region. The presence of the Portuguese in Mozambique and in Angola added a further complication.

It is not surprising that the more purely scientific exploration which tended to interest scholars in Europe was subsumed by these other interests. Moreover, there was no one great geographical puzzle, such as the course of the Niger or the Nile, to generate excitement and controversy. When David Livingstone leapt to world fame in the 1850s it was because of the sheer magnitude of his achievements. Yet Livingstone's travels had been prompted by his reaction as a Christian missionary to the racial and the political situation in the Cape Colony and in the emerging Boer republics.

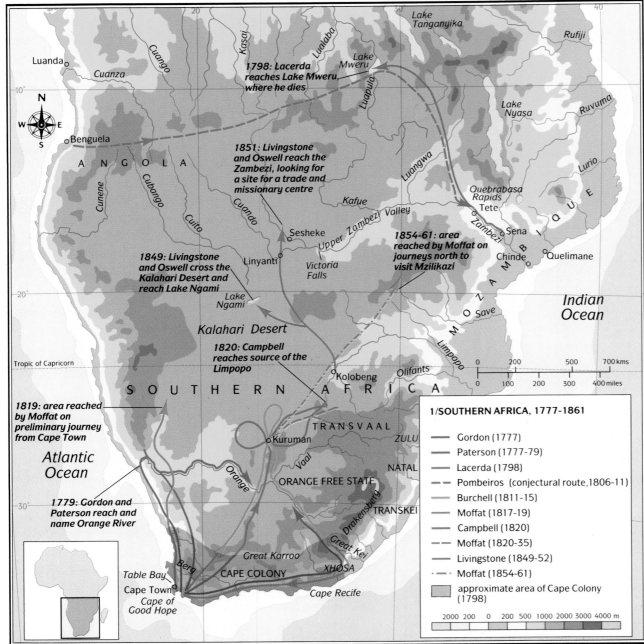

1798: Lacerda reaches Lake Mweru, where he dies

1851: Livingstone and Oswell reach the Zambezi, looking for a site for a trade and missionary centre

1849: Livingstone and Oswell cross the Kalahari Desert and reach Lake Ngami

1854-61: area reached by Moffat on journeys north to visit Mzilikazi

1820: Campbell reaches source of the Limpopo

1819: area reached by Moffat on preliminary journey from Cape Town

1779: Gordon and Paterson reach and name Orange River

1/SOUTHERN AFRICA, 1777-1861

- —— Gordon (1777)
- —— Paterson (1777-79)
- —— Lacerda (1798)
- – – – Pombeiros (conjectural route, 1806-11)
- —— Burchell (1811-15)
- —— Moffat (1817-19)
- —— Campbell (1820)
- – – – Moffat (1820-35)
- —— Livingstone (1849-52)
- –·–·– Moffat (1854-61)
- [shaded] approximate area of Cape Colony (1798)

2000 2000 0 200 500 1000 2000 3000 4000 m

B

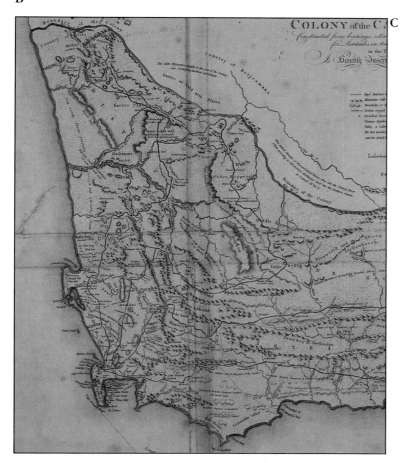

B ABOVE *Burchell's view of Cape Town and Table Bay in the early 19th century.* **C** LEFT *John Barrow's 1801 map of south-west Africa shows that detailed European knowledge extended no more than 250 miles from Cape Town.*

D BELOW *19th-century South Africa attracted hunters after exotic game. This gnu and zebra appeared in W.C. Harris's 1841* Wild Sports of Southern Africa. **2** BOTTOM *Reacting to the rise of the Zulu Empire, the Nguni and Sotho peoples migrated huge distances. They were joined – and challenged – by Boers seeking new lands away from British rule.*

Xhosa peoples continued, while the effect of the Great Trek was to introduce similar contests for land, labour and cattle to vast areas of Natal and the high veldt beyond the Orange River. In an attempt to retain control, Britain annexed Natal in 1845 and then the 'Orange River Sovereignty'. But in 1852 and 1854 two conventions were signed which, in deference to anti-colonial sentiment in Britain, recognized the Transvaal and Orange Free State as independent Boer republics. At the same time, Cape Colony itself was given a parliament.

The British had become disillusioned not only about controlling settlers, but about the possibility of stable relationships with black African people. This is not surprising given the effects of the rise of the Zulu kingdom under Shaka in the 1820s. Shaka was a military genius and iron disciplinarian whose conquests set off a chain reaction known as the *Mfecane*, or 'continuing wars', among the Sotho/Tswana and Nguni groups of Bantu. This complex series of wars, migrations, raids, conquests and state-building exercises had repercussions as far north as Lake Victoria. In Southern Africa itself the effects included the creation of the Sotho state and the migrations of another Sotho group, the Makololo, which led them eventually to the Upper Zambezi Valley where Livingstone was to find them overlords of the Lozi kingdom. Similarly, Nguni groups created several new kingdoms besides Zululand itself,

IN THE LATE 18th century the chief interest of South Africa to the scholarly world lay in its exotic plants and animals. The Swede Anders Sparrman, the Scot William Paterson and the Dutchman Colonel Robert Gordon all made extensive plant-collecting journeys through the Karroo, before making for the head waters of the Orange River, which Paterson and Gordon had named when they reached the mouth of the river in 1779. These and similar travels made the region south of the Orange reasonably well known by 1800, as John Barrow's map testifies (*see* map C).

Barrow's presence as secretary to a British governor reflects a major change in South Africa's history which had occurred in 1795, when, hoping to secure their sea route to the East against the French, the British occupied Cape Town. There was absolutely no desire for the rest of the Dutch East India Company's territory, which by now included a hostile and ill-defined boundary with Bantu peoples to the east. In the same year, the London Missionary Society was formed. Its first representatives arrived in South Africa in 1799. Not only did they minister to the African inhabitants of the colony, whose interests they championed against the Afrikaner settlers, they also tried to extend their work beyond the colony. In fact, settlers, missionaries and their Khoikhoi allies were constantly expanding the effective limits of the colony. The British authorities found it difficult either to control the frontiers or to ignore what was happening there, and practically everything they did exacerbated the problem. Partly under the influence of the London Missionary Society, the government gave legal standing to the Khoikhoi and in 1833 freed all slaves in the colony. Such measures exasperated many of the Afrikaner pastoralists – the Boers – who organized themselves to trek out of the colony and British control after 1836. In 1820 British settlers had been introduced to the south-east of the colony in the naive expectation that they might solve frontier problems by interposing themselves between the Boers and the Africans. But conflicts with

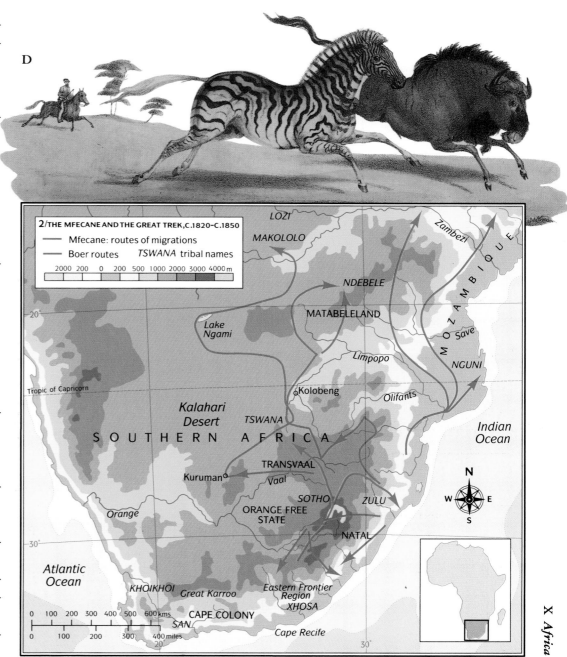

E**XPLORERS** of Africa in the 19th century could surprisingly rarely take advantage of Europe's technological superiority. Either the technology could not be deployed or it was inappropriate. Thus the constraints imposed by Africa's landscape, climate, vegetation and, especially, its diseases could never be ignored. Nor could the people. Explorers had to learn to co-operate with Africans since they rarely had the resources to ensure military superiority. But even if European technology was not always able to triumph immediately, the foundation for its eventual success could be laid.

Captain Speke (**B**) is shown symbolically at the source of the Nile as the efficient scientist with his usefully pocketed waistcoat, his sextant at his feet, his chronometer in his hand. But his Blisset rifle provided no military advantage. Many Africans, too, had firearms, albeit only flintlock muskets, as in (**C**). William Burchell's 'Faithful Hottentot', Juli, pictured in 1812, came from a people who were not averse to using firearms against whites. Moreover in 1879 a Zulu army with only assegais defeated the British Army. Not until the advent of the Maxim gun was Europe certain to prevail militarily.

Not even Europe's manifest superiority in transport could easily be deployed in Africa. The use of ox-wagons in South Africa conveyed an important advantage. (**E**) shows an ox-wagon being ferried across the Berg River in 1811. But the vulnerability of oxen and horses to sleeping sickness, spread by the tsetse fly, limited their uses significantly. Surely, though, lakes and rivers which the explorers discovered must be ideal for steamboats? Macgregor Laird built the *Quorra*, (**A**), to exploit Lander's 1830 discovery of the course of the Niger. But even paddle-boats could be stranded on sand bars, as here, or be impeded by waterfalls. The *Quorra* did eventually make its way up-river, but its crew was overcome by malaria. By the 1850s most explorers could combat the fever to some extent; Livingstone's 'rousers' (**D**) were pills with resin of jalap, calomel, rhubarb and the essential quinine. Yet until the way in which malaria was transmitted by the mosquito was understood in the 1890s, this, one of the great scourges of Africa, could not be entirely overcome.

notably the Ndebele overlordship of what is now Zimbabwe. A shifting series of alliances between African groups and trekkers increased the disorder on the high veldt.

Meanwhile, more formal exploration of the areas beyond the Cape Colony continued. William Burchell had maintained the tradition of botanical and zoological exploration in a series of journeys made in 1811-15 which took him into Tswana country and back via the Vaal-Orange confluence. In addition to producing a number of outstanding landscape pictures, he identified new plants and animals including the zebra (*Equus burchelli*), which was named after him. In the same period, the big game of the veldt became more and more attractive to British gentlemen-hunters, in whose interest it was to keep open the road to the north over the Orange River through Tswana country and west of the main Boer settlements. Later in the century, this route was to be important to Cecil Rhodes and local capitalists seeking mineral, railway and other investment possibilities to the north. In the 1840s and 1850s, however, before the great diamond and gold discoveries of 1867 and 1886, the London Missionary Society had the greatest interest in the way north. As early as 1812 Dr John Campbell tried to set up a mission station among the Tswana; he returned to the region in 1820 and reached the sources of the Limpopo, at around 24°S.

By this time Robert Moffat had arrived. Another Scot, he had made some preliminary forays in the south-west before, in 1820, finding his vocation as resident missionary at Kuruman among the Tswana. Though the success and prosperity of his mission was threatened by Ndebele marauders, Moffat struck up a friendship with their leader Mzilikazi. In his search for security from the Boers and others, Mzilikazi eventually led his followers to what is now Zimbabwe. Moffat made several major journeys north to visit him, in 1854, 1857 and 1861.

Even more significant journeys were made by David Livingstone. Livingstone rose from industrial wage slave to one of the 19th century's great heroes. Self-educated in the liberal and scientific tradition of the Scottish Enlightenment, and strongly Calvinistic, he had joined the LMS and arrived in South Africa in 1841. He took up work considerably beyond Kuruman with a Sotho group, the Kwena, whom he established at Kolobeng. Impatient with conventional missionary work, he believed it necessary for the missionary to leave African Christians to look after themselves and carry the gospel farther into the interior. Moreover, he did not hesitate to work for the right conditions in which Christianity could take root. If this meant opposing the Boers, who in turn opposed him violently, wrecking his house at Kolobeng, he would do so. If it meant keeping the road to the north open for legitimate trade and missionary work, he would travel north. If areas free of Boer settlers or slave traders were needed, he would seek them. If in turn these missionary aims necessitated his becoming an effective geographical explorer, equipped with all the appropriate scientific skills, he would become one. Through a potent mixture of faith, determination and intellect, Livingstone turned himself into a remarkable explorer.

Livingstone's first considerable journey was made in 1849 across the Kalahari to Lake Ngami. He was accompanied by William Cotton Oswell, a big-game hunter, who helped finance some of his subsequent journeys. For Livingstone was now determined to explore regions even farther north in the hope of finding the right location for a missionary and legitimate trade centre. Preliminary attempts were made in company with Oswell and Livingstone's own growing family in 1850 and 1851, in which latter year they actually reached the Zambezi. The discovery excited Livingstone. Geographers had not previously been sure that the river extended from this far west. Moreover, the valley might contain a suitable area for development while the river itself might furnish a means of contact with the coast shorter then the trek to the Cape and without the hindrance of the Boers. In addition, the Makololo

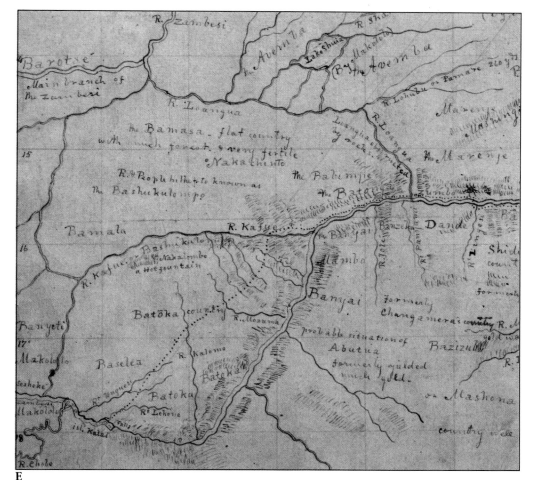

people who now lived in the valley might be appropriate African allies. To prepare for a thorough exploration, Livingstone took his wife and family back to the Cape and packed them off home to Scotland, returning to the Zambezi and the Makololo in May 1853. Two major factors affecting his travels now came into play. First, he was beyond the area where he could travel by ox-wagon because of the tsetse fly. Secondly, he was now entering a region affected by Portuguese activities and to which indeed they laid some claim.

In 1798, the Portuguese Dr Francisco Lacerda, reacting to the British occupation of the Cape, had foreseen British influence extending northwards. He thought Mozambique and Angola should therefore be linked and as a first step explored the route from Tete on the lower Zambezi to the Cazembe's kingdom near Lake Mweru, where he died. The Portuguese Monteiro and Gamitto were to make roughly the same journey in the 1830s, aiming to establish good relations with the monarch, while between 1806 and 1811 two half-caste traders, Baptista and Jose Pombeiro, had crossed from near Benguela to Tete. Nearer Livingstone's time, Silva Porto, a Portuguese trader from Benguela, had reached Linyanti on the Upper Zambezi. But Lacerda's ambition of Portuguese control from coast to coast was never realized. Two Zanzibar Arab traders, whom Livingstone met, had crossed the continent from east to west. A Hungarian traveller, Ladislaus Magyar, also deserves credit for his journeys from Benguela. If one of Livingstone's less attractive traits was his reluctance to give credit to rivals, he may have been right to discount them as scientific travellers.

Livingstone's achievement after May 1853 is simply described, however difficult it was to accomplish. Sometimes on ox back, sometimes by canoe, but mainly on foot, he covered almost 5,000 miles. Finding that the Upper Zambezi had drawbacks — including the encroachment of slave traders from the west — and that the route to and from Luanda which he now explored was not an easy one, he returned to Linyanti in September 1855 and then set out for the east coast. He discovered the Victoria Falls in November: 'scenes so lovely must have been gazed on by angels in their flight'. Keeping as close as he could to the Zambezi, Livingstone and his Makololo followers reached the coast in May 1856. He returned to Britain his fame assured.

E ABOVE *Livingstone's manuscript map of the middle reaches of the Zambezi, a region he hoped to make a centre for Christianity, Commerce and Civilization. Rivers shown with double lines are those he thought would prove navigable.*

F RIGHT *Livingstone reached the Victoria Falls — Mosioatunya, 'the smoke that sounds' to the Makololo — on 16 November 1855; he probably made this sketch at the time. The distances noted are reasonably accurate.* **3** RIGHT *Livingstone was neither the first man to cross Africa nor the only explorer of the Zambezi. It was the range of his scientific accomplishments that made him the greatest explorer of middle Africa.*

G BELOW *David Livingstone in the 1860s, by now one of the great heroes of Victorian Britain.*

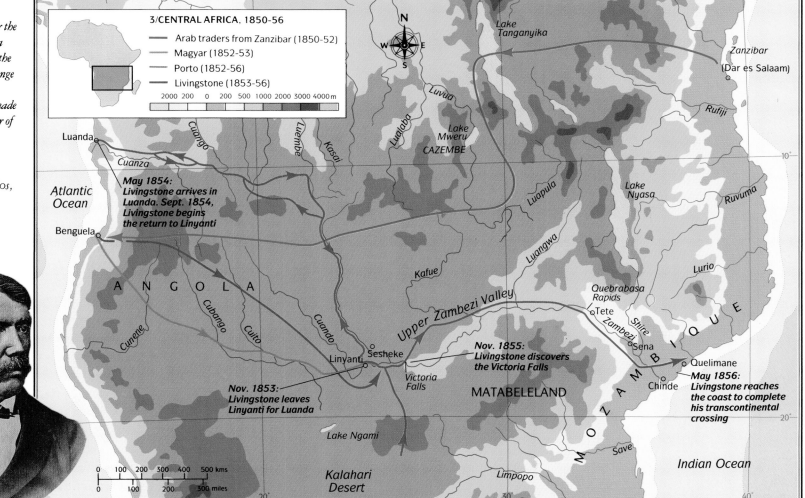

3/CENTRAL AFRICA, 1850-56
Arab traders from Zanzibar (1850-52)
Magyar (1852-53)
Porto (1852-56)
Livingstone (1853-56)

2000 200 0 200 500 1000 2000 3000 4000m

May 1854: Livingstone arrives in Luanda. Sept. 1854, Livingstone begins the return to Linyanti

Nov. 1853: Livingstone leaves Linyanti for Luanda

Nov. 1855: Livingstone discovers the Victoria Falls

May 1856: Livingstone reaches the coast to complete his transcontinental crossing

EAST AFRICA AND THE SOURCE OF THE NILE 1822-1888

WHEN LIVINGSTONE *returned to Britain after crossing Africa in 1856 (see ch. 38), the interest he helped kindle emphasized that the whole middle belt of the continent north of his route remained unknown. In the same year, the Royal Geographical Society in London, the RGS, accordingly determined to sponsor expeditions from the east coast to the reputed lakes and snow mountains of the interior, where the source of the Nile was also assumed to lie. The investigation of these problems generated immense interest, in which the lingering influence of Classical geography, fragments of information from half-forgotten Arab geographers and earlier Portuguese travellers vied with the more precise information European explorers were slowly accumulating. Dominating the debate, in fact rapidly transformed into one of the great causes célèbres of mid-Victorian Britain, was the question of where exactly the source of the Nile lay. Paradoxically, its discovery in 1862 by Speke only intensified the controversy. Livingstone found himself drawn into the argument, 11 years later effectively sacrificing his life on a new but futile search for it.*

For all that the 'problem of the Nile' dominated the exploration of East Africa, and indeed despite the RGS's being animated by purely scientific reasons, European exploration as a whole was fuelled by subsidiary motives. Livingstone's campaign against the slave trade that the Arabs of the coast controlled found many supporters in Europe determined to choke it out, a process that exploration alone could not achieve. Similarly, the British and Indian governments, both of which played some part in financing exploration, were conscious of the potential commerical and strategic benefits control of the region could bring.

East Africa itself, mostly high plateau broken by the two arms of the Great Rift Valley, has much indeterminate drainage which complicated the task of establishing its basic physical geography. But, as elsewhere in the continent, the main hurdles European explorers had to overcome were human. From about 1800 the peoples of the interior had made contacts with the Arabs on the coast, to whom they found they could sell slaves and ivory. From the 1840s, however, the Arabs moved inland to capture the sources of supply. Though it was their routes that explorers tended to follow, the conflicts the Arabs engendered between the Africans and themselves frequently hindered European explorers.

A RIGHT *'Aha Mr Nilus! So I've found you at last'. (Punch, 1863). Britannia may have found the source of the Nile but patriotic pride in Speke's achievement did not save him from attempts to discredit his discovery.*

1 BELOW *Penetration by Arab slave traders from the coast, the northward migration of the Ngoni and confrontations between the Bantu and other tribes was the background against which the European discovery of East Africa began in the mid-19th century.*

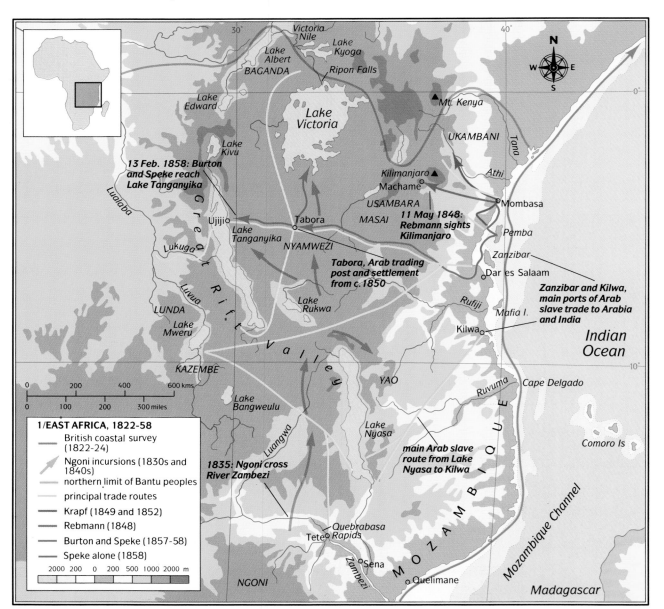

1/EAST AFRICA, 1822-58
- British coastal survey (1822-24)
- Ngoni incursions (1830s and 1840s)
- northern limit of Bantu peoples
- principal trade routes
- Krapf (1849 and 1852)
- Rebmann (1848)
- Burton and Speke (1857-58)
- Speke alone (1858)

0   200   400   600 kms
0   100   200   300 miles

2000 200 0 200 500 1000 2000 m

13 Feb. 1858: Burton and Speke reach Lake Tanganyika

Tabora, Arab trading post and settlement from c. 1850

11 May 1848: Rebmann sights Kilimanjaro

Zanzibar and Kilwa, main ports of Arab slave trade to Arabia and India

main Arab slave route from Lake Nyasa to Kilwa

1835: Ngoni cross River Zambezi

ON 11 MAY 1848, an obscure German missionary caught sight of the snow-covered summit of Kilimanjaro, Africa's highest mountain. The missionary was Johann Rebmann. With J. Ludwig Krapf, he was in the service of the English Church Missionary Society, based near Mombasa. The following year, Krapf, with minimal resources, also journeyed into the interior, to Ukambani, where he discovered a second snow-covered mountain, Kenya. Krapf went on to explore the kingdom of Usambara. He also sailed down the East African coast as far as Kilwa, in the process providing the first new information on the coast since the 1820s. The map Krapf produced of his travels (*see* map E) gives a reasonable picture of the extent of his explorations and the not wildly inaccurate information he gathered from coastal people about the lakes and mountains of the interior. But though Krapf's information was based on first-hand sources, most European geographers gave more credence to a map compiled by James Erhardt, briefly a companion of Krapf's. This, made from reports garnered from Swahili traders, postulated one huge lake in the interior in the shape of what came to be called a 'monster slug'.

Orthodox European geographical knowledge of East Africa in the period was exemplified by W.D. Cooley. In 1845, he had produced a geography of the region compiled from Classical sources and information from an Arab trader. However speculative, Cooley's authoritative pronouncements tended to be believed in the face of the missionaries' first-hand information. Cooley confidently dismissed Krapf's and Rebmann's claims to have seen snow on Kilimanjaro and Mount Kenya, for example. Not least in his faith in the authority of ancient sources, he was typical of the 'armchair geographers' of the period who were to provide a barrage of criticism and speculation through the great period of East African exploration.

It was partly to end this speculation that from the middle of the century the RGS, now emerging from a period of financial constraint, began to plan more systematic exploration of East Africa. As sponsor of most of the major expeditions to East Africa between the 1850s and the 1870s, the RGS effectively became the most important player in the drama, its medals the mark of success for explorers.

The RGS was a curious blend of the tradition of gentlemanly travel and amateur scholarship, which disavowed any connection with commerce, and of the developing science of the period, which also claimed to eschew commerce or imperialism. Yet these matters arose. The British Government, and its offshoot in India, were concerned with the strategic position in the northern Indian Ocean, and were drawn to Zanzibar as a result of its connections with the Persian Gulf Sultanate of Oman. The Bombay authorities especially saw East Africa as becoming ever more closely linked economically to India. And, of course, the promotion of legitimate commerce went hand in hand with

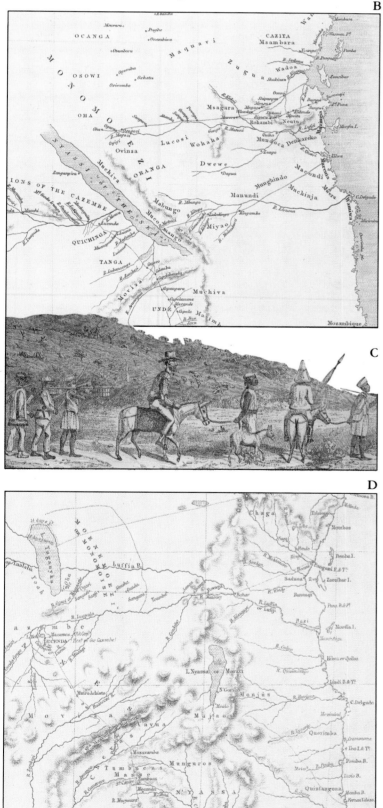

B

C

D

B LEFT *Cooley's 1845 map of East Africa was based on information from a Zanzibar Arab. Though inaccurate in many details, it was nonetheless accepted as authoritative. The links forged by Arabs between the coast and the lakes of the interior are shown clearly.*
C BELOW LEFT *Burton and Speke's 1857-59 expedition on the move. After the 1850s, sleeping sickness made all animal transport impossible; until railways were built at the end of the century, all later travel had to be made on foot.* **D** BOTTOM LEFT *James McQueen's 1855 map of East Africa was also based on Arab testimony. Lakes Tanganyika and Nyasa are shown as separate, but there is still no hint of Lake Victoria.*

E RIGHT *The practical results of Krapf's and Rebmann's explorations between 1845-52 are evident in the increased detail of Krapf's map, although distances are exaggerated. Lake Victoria appears only as part of the large lake speculated by Erhardt in 1855 (on the left) shaped 'like a monster slug'. The map also shows Krapf's earlier travels in Ethiopia.*

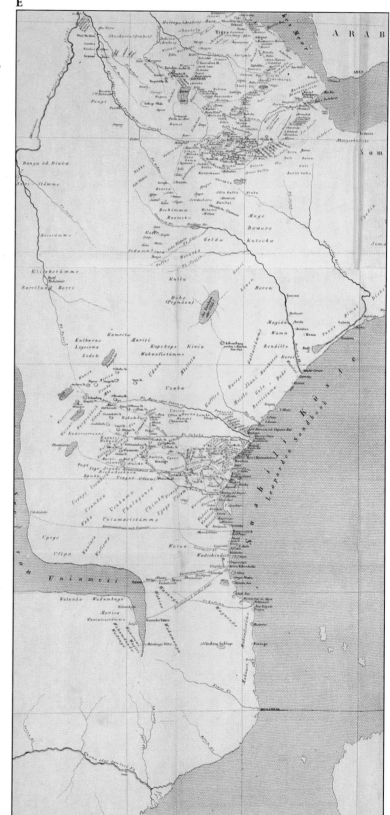

E

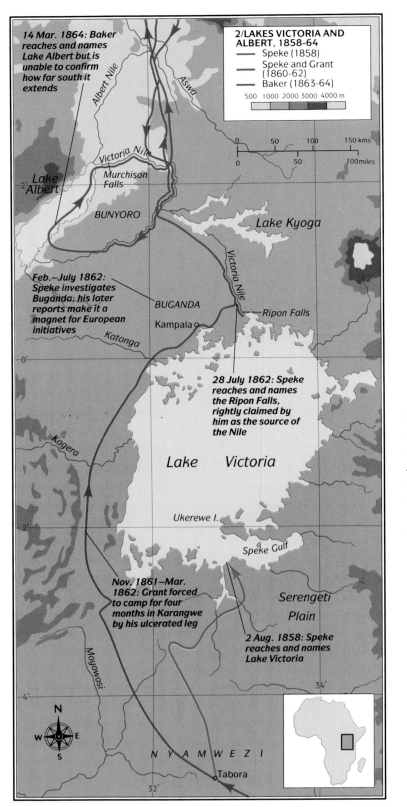

2/LAKES VICTORIA AND
ALBERT, 1858-64
— Speke (1858)
— Speke and Grant
(1860-62)
— Baker (1863-64)

500 1000 2000 3000 4000 m

14 Mar. 1864: Baker
reaches and names
Lake Albert but is
unable to confirm
how far south it
extends

Feb.–July 1862:
Speke investigates
Buganda; his later
reports make it a
magnet for European
initiatives

28 July 1862: Speke
reaches and names
the Ripon Falls,
rightly claimed by
him as the source of
the Nile

Nov. 1861–Mar.
1862: Grant forced
to camp for four
months in Karangwe
by his ulcerated leg

2 Aug. 1858: Speke
reaches and names
Lake Victoria

2 LEFT *The area around
Lakes Victoria and Albert
was of key importance, not
just because it contained the
source of the Nile at the
Ripon Falls but because of
the presence of the
sophisticated kingdom of
Buganda.* F BELOW
*Speke's own map of the
northern shores of Lake
Victoria and its Nile outlet
(on the far right). The
difficulty of mapping the
swampy land on the lake's
north-west shore is
apparent. Independent
travels entrusted to Speke's
chief porter, Bombay, are
shown, as is the site of the
camp (at the top of the map)
where the unfortunate
Grant had to wait while
Speke achieved his
triumph.*

anti-slave trade activities: there were already limitation treaties
with Oman and Zanzibar of 1822 and 1845, while Livingstone's
influence was to result in the attempt in 1873 to end the East
African slave trade altogether. Generally, it was in Britain's
interest to maintain an unofficial domination of Zanzibar and,
through Zanzibar's vague influence over the mainland, a sort of
watching brief on East Africa. Hence the government's willingness to give limited financial help to the RGS expeditions and
direct employment to Livingstone in 1858.

In East Africa itself, Seyyid Said, the ruler of Oman, was
drawn increasingly to Oman's dependency, Zanzibar. He encouraged Indian capitalists to finance clove plantations which
needed slave labour from the mainland and trading caravans to
fetch slaves and ivory in return for cloth and beads. The Arab and
Swahili traders from the coast then began to supplant African
traders. The conflicts that followed made many African tribes
increasingly warlike, with Mirambo, in what is now Western
Tanzania, the most notable of the warlords. European explorers
had to contend not just with the turmoil caused by these changes
but were forced to conduct delicate negotiations with local chiefs
over *hongo*, a sort of transit tax. The resultant haggling was
among the greatest problems they faced in East Africa. For
traders and explorers alike, the chiefdom of Unyanyembe was an
important nodal point, not simply because of its position, but
the fact that its Nyamwezi people were great traders and skilled
caravan porters. Further, the Arabs had established a settlement
there, Tabora (*see* map 1).

The man chosen by the RGS to enter this volatile region was
Richard Burton. A rebel against many Victorian values, Burton
was a brilliant linguist and noted Arabist. Having already penetrated to Mecca in disguise (*see* ch.42) he was financed by the
Bombay Government to explore Somaliland in the Horn of
Africa. Although he reached the 'forbidden city' of Harar, while
a fellow Indian Army officer, John Speke, made a minor expedition east of Berbera, it was clear that Somaliland, with its harsh
environment and mutually hostile clans, could not provide a
viable route into East Africa. Moreover, given the British Government's hold over Zanzibar and Burton's own sympathy with
the Arabs, it was more likely that Burton would be able to fulfil
the RGS instruction to 'ascertain the limits of the inland sea
known to exist' by imitating an Arab trade caravan making for
the interior from the coast opposite Zanzibar. Again accompanied by Speke, in June 1857 Burton set off.

F

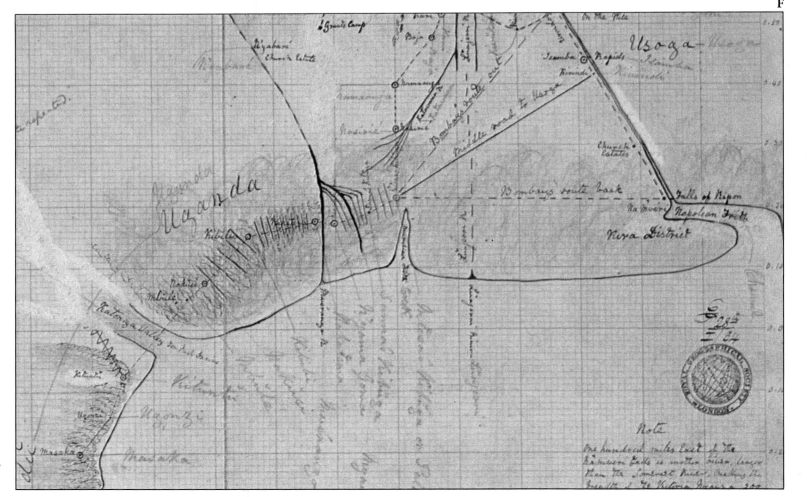

G TOP RIGHT *Kamrasi,
king of Bunyoro, has his
first Bible lesson; from a
watercolour sketch by
Grant. If European
explorers learnt much about
Africa, Africans, too,
were necessarily learning
much about Europe.*
3 ABOVE RIGHT
*Livingstone revisited the
Victoria Falls in 1860 on
the Zambezi Expedition.
But with the Quebrabasa
Rapids blocking the
possibility of steamboat
access to the middle
Zambezi, Livingstone then
investigated the Lake
Nyasa region. However,
both the Ruvuma and the
Shire Rivers proved
awkward as routes of
access.*

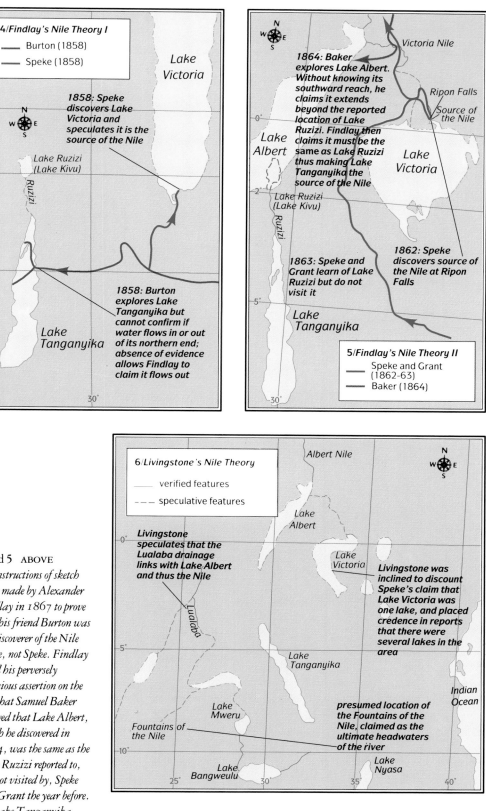

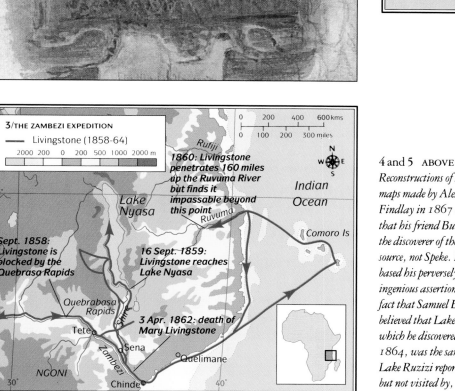

4 and 5 ABOVE
Reconstructions of sketch maps made by Alexander Findlay in 1867 to prove that his friend Burton was the discoverer of the Nile source, not Speke. Findlay based his perversely ingenious assertion on the fact that Samuel Baker believed that Lake Albert, which he discovered in 1864, was the same as the Lake Ruzizi reported to, but not visited by, Speke and Grant the year before. As Lake Tanganyika, which Burton had discovered in 1858, was known to link with Lake Ruzizi, and as Lake Albert was known to link with the Nile, if Lakes Albert and Ruzizi were the same, then Burton's Lake Tanganyika, lying farther south than Speke's Lake Victoria, must be the headwaters of the Nile.
6 ABOVE RIGHT *In the dispute that followed Speke's controversial claim in 1862 to have found the source of the Nile, Livingstone speculated that the River Lualaba (later shown to be the Congo) flowed north to Lake Albert from the 'Fountains of the Nile', the mythical ultimate source of the Nile described by the Greek geographer Herodotus in 457 BC. Livingstone's tenacious belief in Herodotus was shared by many in the 19th century.*

The expedition took until November to reach Tabora. To reorganize the porters in the caravan and go on to Ujiji on Lake Tanganyika took another four months. The lake was reached on 13 February 1858. It then proved difficult to find a suitable boat in which to explore it, with the result that Burton was unable to establish with certainty whether water flowed in or out at the northern end. It was to prove a significant failing, which left the lake's relationship to the Nile unverified. On the return trip Speke made a 'flying' journey northwards from Tabora to reach what proved to be the southern end of Lake Victoria. Without much evidence, he claimed that he had fulfilled a subsidiary RGS instruction, 'the determination of the head sources of the White Nile'. When the two men reached London in mid-1859, arguments over expenses and many petty matters fuelled Burton's resentment at the way Speke was claiming all the glory. Although given unprecedented opportunities to publicize his extensive geographical and ethnographical information, Burton was further upset by the RGS decision to send Speke back to East Africa to vindicate his Nile claim.

Speke set out in October 1860 with yet another Indian Army officer, James Grant. There were hold-ups near Tabora because of African-Arab trade disputes; then Grant's ulcerated leg delayed progress. Nonetheless, Speke reached Buganda in February 1862, spending much of the next four months in the kingdom. He was forced to become one of the many petitioners at court, intriguing and supplicating for royal favour – in his

case, permission to go on to the source of the Nile. On 28 July 1862 he reached what he named the Ripon Falls, where the Nile issues from Lake Victoria (*see* map 2). Grant, encamped some way off, was denied a direct share in the glory of the discovery. The two men then went north to Bunyoro, whose ruler, Kamrasi, already worried by Khartoum-based merchants allying with his dissident cousin, was suspicious of the explorers' desire to open up the route north. Consequent delays meant that Speke did not examine the Nile where it enters Lake Albert but continued directly to Gondokoro, Khartoum, Egypt and home. Nonetheless, he was received with adulation: the greatest geographical prize had been carried off by a British officer.

There had been hopes that a trader called Petherick would travel up the Nile to join Speke and Grant. In the event, it was Samuel Baker, a private traveller, whom they met, at Gondokoro. Speke suggested Baker inspect the lake which one year later, having explored its northern shores, Baker was to name Lake Albert. Although Baker confirmed that Speke's Nile stream did flow into, and then almost immediately out of, the lake, his sketchy exploration of the rest of the lake left a legacy of uncertainties (*see* maps 4 and 5).

Meanwhile, farther south, Livingstone was returning from the government-sponsored Zambezi Expedition. His attempts to navigate the Zambezi by steamboat had failed, principally because the Quebrabasa Rapids – which he had not seen in

A

B

C

D

PUBLISHING an account of his travels was the explorer's route to permanent fame. Jottings in a notebook, such as those in (D) by Livingstone, could be worked up for a journal, and then polished again for publication – if not always by the author himself. Either way, there was scope for distortion. The same was true of pictures, which publishers increasingly demanded. Livingstone was no artist, as his attempts to show these Lunda Africans and a slave caravan demonstrate, and an engraver in Britain was employed to work on his sketches. J.A. Grant, who produced the watercolour of musicians in Buganda in 1862 (A), was more accomplished. Even so, the artist/engraver who re-worked Grant's sketch for the *Illustrated London News* (B) made subtle changes. The player of the *hanga* on the right holds the instrument in what the engraver thinks is a natural way but not the way Grant saw him playing it; the feet of the chief drummer have been hidden; and all the players are given European or perhaps Indian facial features. Fewer liberties could be taken with the work of Thomas Baines, the best artist among the explorers of Africa (and Australia). Accompanying Livingstone on the Zambezi Expedition, he made the sketches which formed the basis for his magnificent painting of the *Elephant in the Shallows*, (E). Significantly, on the same expedition John Kirk used a camera to photograph the expedition's later steamboats, shown in (C) under construction. A new method of recording Africa was coming into use.

E

1856 – made the middle part of the valley inaccessible by boat. He was increasingly drawn to the Lake Nyasa area as his centre for Commerce, Christianity and Civilization. Livingstone actually reached the lake in 1859. Blocked by the Murchison cataracts to the south, he attempted and failed to find a water route from the east coast via the Ruvuma. By this time, Livingstone's European companions had been dismissed or had resigned and slave traders had wrecked attempts to set up a Christian mission. The Foreign Office brought the whole venture to an end in 1864. Despite the apparent disaster, Livingstone had nonetheless obtained immense amounts of new geographical and other scientific information.

By 1864, the major East African lakes and the Nile source were on the map and the main outlines of the region's physical and human geography had been established, all in the space of less than ten years. Yet this was not the end of the story. Because Baker's Lake Albert was ill-defined; because scholars expected Herodotus and other Classical authorities to know about the Nile; and because Burton and others were jealous of Speke's fame, Speke's solution to the Nile problem remained disputed. Speke, meanwhile, had accidentally shot himself dead just before a planned debate with Burton in front of British Association scientists in September 1864, an incident some took as an admission of error. The continuing controversy had major implications for Livingstone, with the RGS determining that he should resolve the problem. Livingstone, in fact, had his own theories about the Nile and its 'fountains', the latter derived from Classical authorities, in whom he placed much unjustified faith, as well as a great desire to return to Africa to find ways to defeat the slave trade and introduce Christianity.

Livingstone's last journey was an epic of saintly endurance, which revived the humanitarian cause in addition to yielding substantial amounts of geographical information. On the other hand, the expedition was poorly financed, which made it difficult for the now aging explorer to drive quickly towards his goals. His consequent increasing reliance on the support of the very men whom he was trying to defeat, the Arab and Swahili slave traders, put him in an ambiguous position, although the 'Manyuema Massacre' (*see* H), which he witnessed, was finally to disillusion him with their methods. But above all, his delusions about the Nile led him to persist in the arduous explorations which were to end in his death.

Experiments with camel and buffalo transport failed as Livingstone was forced to trek around Lake Nyasa and then northwards to Lakes Tanganyika, Mweru and Bangweulu. He entered the area as the Arab warlord, Tippu Tip, was establishing his hegemony. Livingstone retreated to Lake Tanganyika seeking supplies. It was at Ujiji that he was met by the journalist, Henry M. Stanley. This celebrated encounter, in October

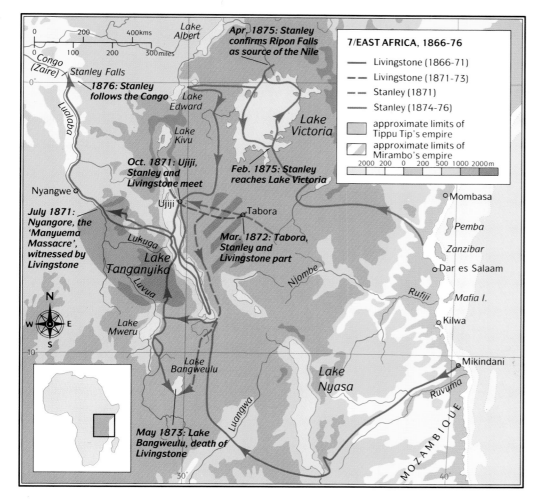

7/EAST AFRICA, 1866-76
- Livingstone (1866-71)
- Livingstone (1871-73)
- Stanley (1871)
- Stanley (1874-76)
- approximate limits of Tippu Tip's empire
- approximate limits of Mirambo's empire

Apr. 1875: Stanley confirms Ripon Falls as source of the Nile

1876: Stanley follows the Congo

Oct. 1871: Ujiji, Stanley and Livingstone meet

Feb. 1875: Stanley reaches Lake Victoria

July 1871: Nyangore, the 'Manyuema Massacre', witnessed by Livingstone

Mar. 1872: Tabora, Stanley and Livingstone part

May 1873: Lake Bangweulu, death of Livingstone

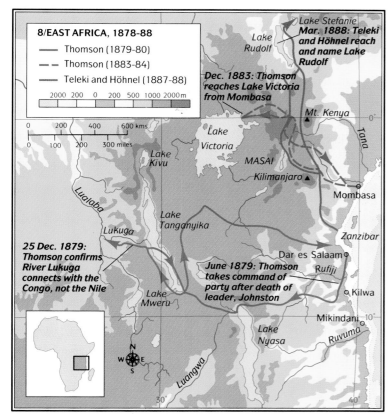

8/EAST AFRICA, 1878-88
- Thomson (1879-80)
- Thomson (1883-84)
- Teleki and Höhnel (1887-88)

Mar. 1888: Teleki and Höhnel reach and name Lake Rudolf

Dec. 1883: Thomson reaches Lake Victoria from Mombasa

25 Dec. 1879: Thomson confirms River Lukuga connects with the Congo, not the Nile

June 1879: Thomson takes command of party after death of leader, Johnston

7 ABOVE *Lack of resources, disruptions from warlords and an obsession with the Nile made Livingstone's last expedition ineffective. In contrast, Stanley in 1874-76 proved ruthlessly efficient.* 8 LEFT *Thomson's discoveries were important preludes to the development of East Africa.* H BELOW LEFT *Slave traders massacre hundreds of market women on the banks of the Lualaba in July 1871. 'It gave me the impression of being in Hell', wrote Livingstone.* I BELOW RIGHT *Livingstone's sketch map of the sources of the Nile. The 'Fountains of the Nile' are in the bottom left-hand corner.*

1871, resulted from the outside world's increasing anxiety for reliable news of Livingstone. Though the RGS had sent relief expeditions, the journalist Stanley, dispatched by his newspaper, thwarted them, much to the Society's chagrin.

Livingstone refused to go home with Stanley and returned to the Lualaba river-system west of Lake Tanganyika – actually the upper waters of the Congo (Zaire) River, not the Nile as he hoped. He intended to examine it in detail before seeking the 'fountains' of which Herodotus had written. But he died in May 1873 in the swamps of Lake Bangweulu. The carrying of his body back to Zanzibar by his remaining porters and his emotional funeral in Westminster Abbey passed into Victorian legend, and inspired attempts to follow up his work with scientific, missionary or imperialistic activity.

Verney Lovett Cameron, sent by the RGS in 1873 in another search for Livingstone, had met only the explorer's body. Undeterred, he decided to press on in his own right. He produced accurate maps of Lake Tanganyika and demonstrated that its outlet was the Lukuga on its western shore. He went on to make the first European east-to-west crossing of the continent (*see* ch.40). Of more significance for East African geography was Stanley's new expedition in 1874. Nothing could be a greater contrast with Livingstone's progress: Stanley was amply financed and drove his huge caravan ruthlessly through East Africa. His circumnavigation of Lake Victoria revealed it as one lake, and that the Nile did flow from it; he confirmed the importance of Buganda and its people; and, although he did not solve fully the Lake Albert problem, he went on to work on the Lualaba and was able to show that it was part of the Congo system, not the Nile.

The RGS had no control over Stanley and disliked his strong-arm methods. But in any event, the initiative was now passing out of its hands. King Leopold's Brussels Conference had initiated a sort of unofficial European scramble for the lake region (*see* ch.40). The RGS response was two important expeditions which brought fame to Joseph Thomson. Thomson explored the direct route from Dar es Salaam to Lake Nyasa and confirmed Cameron's Lukuga outlet before returning to the coast without, unusually, having lost a single porter. More important was Thomson's filling of the last major gap in East African exploration, in 1883-84: the route from Mombasa to Lake Victoria. The allegedly fearsome Masai, whom even Stanley was reluctant to encounter, Thomson diverted with his false tooth and the effervescence of Eno's Fruit Salts.

The last major East African lake, Rudolf, was reached and named by the Hungarian Count Samuel Teleki and the Austrian Ludwig von Höhnel in March 1888. But, by then, the European powers were laying political claim to what were seen as more desirable regions around the other lakes (*see* ch.40).

H

I

THE CONGO BASIN AND THE BEGINNINGS OF IMPERIALISM
1816-1889

THE EXPLORERS *Cameron and Stanley entered the Congo Basin from the east in the mid-1870s (see ch.39) just as the character of African exploration was beginning to change: 'pure' scientific enquiry was being superseded by more imperialistic activity. Europeans recognized the advantages of securing positions in the more desirable areas exploration had revealed, especially around the great lakes. Even if such activities would produce few immediate benefits, it was considered necessary to take out insurance on future needs. As these would include transport to the lakes, Stanley's revelation of the potential of the Congo River as a route to the interior was crucial.*

In the late 1870s it was generally unofficial groups who showed the greatest interest in these matters. European governments remained reluctant to be drawn in too far. King Leopold, who tapped, and to some extent manipulated, all this unofficial energy, was acting in a private capacity, not as king of the Belgians. His Brussels Geographical Conference of 1876 assembled explorers and geographers ostensibly to plan a co-operative way forward in Africa. But the resulting 'International Association' to direct further exploration in fact created much more overt rivalry among Europeans. Meanwhile, 'sub-imperial' powers such as Egypt and Zanzibar struggled to maintain their interests, while Africans themselves also undertook their own 'African Scramble for Africa'. In simple economic terms the issue was whether the ivory resources of the lakes area should be taken out northwards for the benefit of Egypt, eastwards for the benefit of the Arab warlord Tippu Tip, and possibly the African Mirambo (as well as Zanzibar), or westwards via the Congo for the benefit of Leopold and his European associates. Settlement of such questions was to involve increasing greed and violence.

The Congo Basin was the hub of these developments. The activities of Stanley dominate the story from 1876 to 1890, as the explorer revealed the river-basin, built a state for Leopold and then, in an attempt to expand it, undertook the astonishing Emin Pasha Relief Expedition. By this point European governments were heavily involved. The Berlin West Africa Conference of 1884-85 was held principally to deal with the Congo Basin area: the object was to maintain an open field for all. In this the Conference failed utterly. Having become the imperialist, the explorer would need to become the pro-consul.

A LEFT *Stanley's ingenious 40-foot sectioned boat,* Lady Alice. *It was carried 2,000 miles overland and sailed for 4,000 miles, most importantly on Stanley's pioneering 1877 descent of the Congo.* **1** BELOW *The Congo was the key to west central Africa. Once Stanley had established its course, Leopold II, the French and the Portuguese competed to control it.*

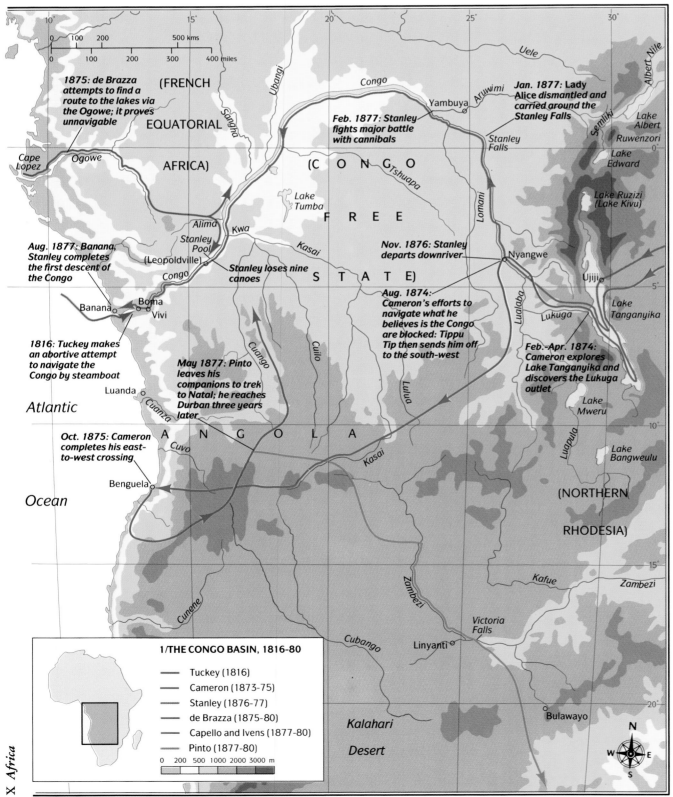

1875: de Brazza attempts to find a route to the lakes via the Ogowe; it proves unnavigable

Jan. 1877: Lady Alice dismantled and carried around the Stanley Falls

Feb. 1877: Stanley fights major battle with cannibals

Aug. 1877: Banana, Stanley completes the first descent of the Congo

Nov. 1876: Stanley departs downriver

Aug. 1874: Cameron's efforts to navigate what he believes is the Congo are blocked: Tippu Tip then sends him off to the south-west

1816: Tuckey makes an abortive attempt to navigate the Congo by steamboat

May 1877: Pinto leaves his companions to trek to Natal; he reaches Durban three years later

Feb.-Apr. 1874: Cameron explores Lake Tanganyika and discovers the Lukuga outlet

Oct. 1875: Cameron completes his east-to-west crossing

1/THE CONGO BASIN, 1816-80

— Tuckey (1816)
— Cameron (1873-75)
— Stanley (1876-77)
— de Brazza (1875-80)
— Capello and Ivens (1877-80)
— Pinto (1877-80)

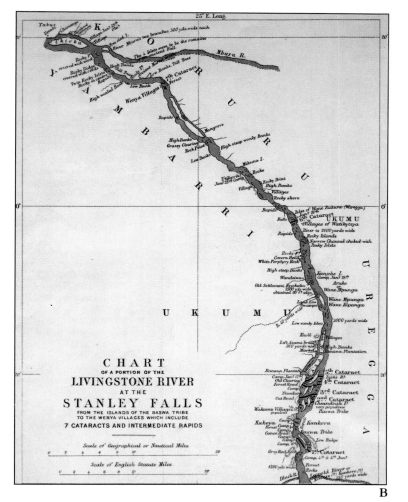

CHART
OF A PORTION OF THE
LIVINGSTONE RIVER
AT THE
STANLEY FALLS
FROM THE ISLANDS OF THE BASWA TRIBE
TO THE WENYA VILLAGES WHICH INCLUDE
7 CATARACTS AND INTERMEDIATE RAPIDS

Scale of Geographical or Nautical Miles

Scale of English Statute Miles

B

B LEFT *It took Stanley the whole of January 1877 to negotiate the seven major falls and rapids of the Congo that now bear his name. Whatever the hazards of leading his party of 143 men, dismantled boat and flotilla of canoes while defying hostile inhabitants, he nonetheless mapped his progress with care. His one failure was his campaign to re-name the river the Livingstone.*

Tippu Tip, who may possibly have obstructed Cameron's efforts to follow the river, then dispatched him to Benguela. When he reached it, in November 1875, he had crossed the continent but was almost dead from starvation.

Cameron recovered and returned to Europe in April 1876 to recount the appalling scenes of brutal slave-raiding he had witnessed and to state his conviction that slavery could be ended and riches won in the centre of Africa if European skills and technologies were applied. In fact, the general impression that Cameron and others gave was that the lakes region constituted an especially hopeful environment for European activity: it was high and therefore healthy; it had peoples who were relatively advanced; and it offered the possibility of using steamboats on the lakes themselves. The problem, however, was access from the coast. Much of what transpired in the next 15 years was concerned with this question.

Prominent among those who responded to the promise of the great lakes was the Egyptian government, who saw it as a means of solving its chronic debts. Samuel Baker was sent to Lake Albert as leader of the first Egyptian attempt in 1869-73. Then came General Charles Gordon who, though more circumspect, was not notably more successful. An aide, Eduard Schnitzer, a German Jew converted to Islam as Emin Pasha, then succeeded Gordon as Governor of the Upper Nile province of Egypt. A considerable explorer and naturalist, Emin also had an army at his command. Once established, he seemed a for-

THERE HAD been an unsuccessful attempt to enter west central Africa to seek Prester John, the legendary Christian ruler of Ethiopia, via the Congo River as early as the 1480s (*see* ch. 11). The first serious modern attempt was a Royal Navy effort in 1816, which also saw the first appearance of a steamboat on an African river. Commander James Tuckey hoped to penetrate far enough to discover if the Congo estuary was the mouth of the Niger. But the steamboat would not operate properly, and Tuckey and many of his men died before the expedition had done more than discover formidable cataracts not far inland. The proper exploration of the Congo Basin had to wait another 60 years, when it was accomplished from the east. After leaving Lake Tanganyika, which he had shown to be part of the Lualaba drainage (*see* ch.39), Cameron reached Nyangwe. By calculating the Lualaba's altitude there, and comparing it with known Nile altitudes, he proved that the stream could not be the Nile. Cameron in fact was certain the Lualaba was the Congo but, unable to hire boats or men to follow the river downstream, conclusive proof eluded him.

C

midable power in the Gondokoro-Lake Albert region.

No one, however, was more impressed with the explorers' accounts of the lakes region than Leopold II, king of the Belgians from 1865. Anxious to find a role for himself, and, perhaps, his country, in overseas enterprise, he was especially interested in Cameron's views when they met in May 1876. This meeting probably gave the king the idea of calling a conference of African explorers and geographical experts at Brussels in September to discuss what ought to be done next in Africa. The conference, in which governments were not involved, recommended setting up 'stations' in a line across the continent. These would serve as bases for further exploration and 'beacons of civilization'. An International Association was to manage the enterprise, and each participating group would set up its own 'national committee' to undertake actual projects for stations. The idea that national committees of geographers would cooperate effectively, or that governments need not be involved, seems so naive that there is some reason to believe that the scheme was simply a cloak for Leopold's own ambitions.

In Britain, the RGS hardly knew how to react to the International Association. Its claim for special rights, based on the fact that so much of Africa had been revealed by British explorers, had little effect. In the end it set up a special fund

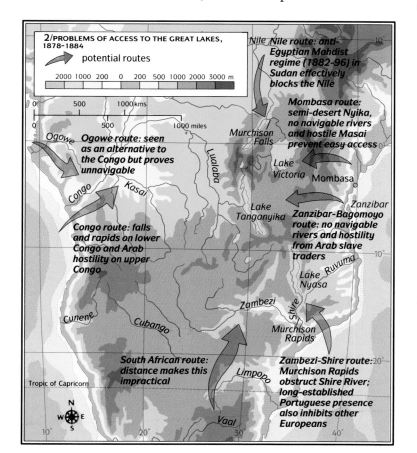

2/PROBLEMS OF ACCESS TO THE GREAT LAKES, 1878-1884

→ potential routes

2000 1000 200 0 200 500 1000 2000 3000 m

Nile route: anti-Egyptian Mahdist regime (1882-96) in Sudan effectively blocks the Nile

Mombasa route: semi-desert Nyika, no navigable rivers and hostile Masai prevent easy access

Ogowe route: seen as an alternative to the Congo but proves unnavigable

Congo route: falls and rapids on lower Congo and Arab hostility on upper Congo

Zanzibar-Bagomoyo route: no navigable rivers and hostility from Arab slave traders

South African route: distance makes this impractical

Zambezi-Shire route: Murchison Rapids obstruct Shire River; long-established Portuguese presence also inhibits other Europeans

C ABOVE *N' Dumba Tembo, an Angolan king, sketched by the Portuguese explorer Ivens in 1879. However imposing a figure locally, Tembo's sovereignty, like that of other African kings, was now threatened as exploration paved the way for the European political takeover.* **2** LEFT *The great lakes of Africa were the focus of European imperial ambitions. But the difficulties of reaching them necessitated further exploration to locate convenient routes from the coasts.*

WITH SLEEPING sickness in most of tropical Africa making the use of animals as beasts of burden impractical, the *pagazi* – the porters – were vital to the success of explorers. Indeed, the most effective African explorers were those who managed their 'caravans' of followers best. Porters were needed to carry essential equipment – tents, clothes, medicines, guns, navigational instruments, and so on – and the boxes of beads and bales of cotton cloth, as in (C), that were the effective currency of African explorers. These were used both to buy food and to pay *hongo*, the transit tax demanded by all chiefs, kings and warlords. With each man able to carry only about 70 lbs., large numbers of porters were essential. Servants, cooks and guards were also needed, many of whom, like the porters themselves, were accompanied by wives and other dependants. It was not unusual for an expedition to be several-hundred strong, or for the line of trudging figures to stretch for miles. Sometimes, as in the picture of Portuguese explorers Capello and Ivens, (B), the porters might find themselves carrying their employers, too (though usually because the explorer was too ill to walk).

Hardship and low wages were the twin poles of a porter's life. In response, the pagazi developed a distinct camaraderie and way of life. If this was upset and they refused to continue, an expedition stood no chance of success. Much depended on the porters' leader, the *kirangozi*, who organized the day-to-day life of the expedition. Perhaps the greatest was 'Bombay', shown in (D) flanked by two fellow porters. He was a Yao from near Lake Nyasa who was enslaved and taken to India as a boy (hence his name). Freed, he returned to Africa and served with Burton in 1857-59. As Speke's caravan leader in 1860-63, he deserves much of the credit for the discovery of the source of the Nile. In 1873-76 he crossed the continent with Cameron. The RGS recognized his worth by giving him a pension. Jacob Wainwright was rather different. Having joined Livingstone's party in 1871, he ensured that Livingstone's body was preserved after his death and carried to the east coast to be shipped home. His stilted letter to Cameron (A) broke the news of the death of Livingstone ('your father'). Wainwright, a Christian, journeyed to Britain with Livingstone's corpse. In Africa again, and caught between two cultures, the rest of his life passed in unhappiness.

independent of Leopold's schemes which made possible Thomson's explorations (*see* ch. 39). German geographers, however, did set up stations in East Africa, in the process sparking an interest which led to later annexations. In France, meanwhile, a group already impressed with the importance of finding a route to the lakes had sent Savorgnan de Brazza in 1875 to penetrate the region via the Ogowé. In response to Leopold's initiative, the French National Committee sent him back to the region. He set up two stations – one on the Congo at Stanley Pool – and then negotiated a treaty with an African leader, Makoko, under which France later claimed sovereignty in the area.

No Portuguese geographers had been invited to Brussels, a cause of bitter resentment in Portugal. Nonetheless, in 1877-79, Hermenigildo Capello and Roberto Ivens undertook useful surveys in the hinterland of Luanda and Benguela, especially along the Cuango Valley. Aleixandre Serpa Pinto had set out with them, but turned south to make a remarkable journey over the mountains to the Zambezi valley and the Victoria Falls before continuing south to emerge on the east coast in Natal. These endeavours did much to restore Portuguese pride.

Capello and Ivens had spent some time with Stanley, who had just emerged from his 999-day crossing of Africa, before they set off. Whatever reservations there might be about his methods, Stanley was an efficient and accurate explorer. Having solved many of the remaining East African geographical problems (*see* ch. 39), Stanley had gone on to Nyangwe. Unlike Cameron, he had been able to follow the Lualaba downstream, in November 1876, with some help from Tippu Tip for the first stages. The *Lady Alice*, which had sailed round Lake Victoria, now came into use again to head a flotilla of canoes. Stanley overcame the many obstacles thrown up by the river to complete the first navigation of the Congo in typically epic style in August 1877.

With the navigation of the river now shown to be possible, Leopold persuaded Stanley to return to the river with which his destiny now seemed linked. From 1879 to 1882 Stanley became 'Bula Mutari', the 'breaker of rocks', building a road around the cataracts on the Lower Congo to the navigable stretches. He also set up stations at Vivi and at what became Leopoldville. Though these were technically Belgian National Committee establishments, clearly Leopold was establishing some kind of political dominion. The king was thus extremely perturbed by Brazza's encroachment on what he saw as his

Ukhonongo october 1873

Sir
We have heared in the month of August that you have started from Zanzibar for Unyanyembe, and again and again lately we have heared your arrival. your father died by disease beyond the country of Bisa, but we have carried the corpse with us. 10 of our soldiers are lost and some have died. Our han-presses us to ask you some clothes to buy provision for our soldiers. and we should have an answer that when we shall enter there shall be firing guns or not, and if you permit us to fire guns then send some powder. We have wrote these few words in the place of Sultan or King Mbowra.
The writer Jacob Wainright
Dr. Livingstone Exp.

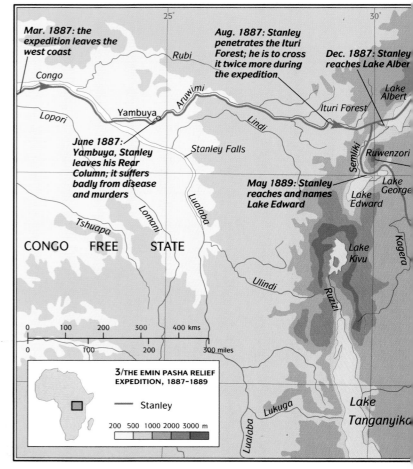

3/THE EMIN PASHA RELIEF
EXPEDITION, 1887-1889

Mar. 1887: the expedition leaves the west coast

Aug. 1887: Stanley penetrates the Ituri Forest; he is to cross it twice more during the expedition

Dec. 1887: Stanley reaches Lake Alber

June 1887: Yambuya, Stanley leaves his Rear Column; it suffers badly from disease and murders

May 1889: Stanley reaches and names Lake Edward

CONGO FREE STATE

Congo, Rubi, Lopori, Aruwimi, Yambuya, Lindi, Ituri Forest, Lake Albert, Stanley Falls, Semliki, Ruwenzori, Lualaba, Lomani, Tshuapa, Lake George, Lake Edward, Lake Kivu, Ulindi, Ruzizi, Kagera, Lukuga, Luaba, Lukuga, Lake Tanganyika

Stanley

0 100 200 300 400 kms
0 100 200 300 miles

200 500 1000 2000 3000 m

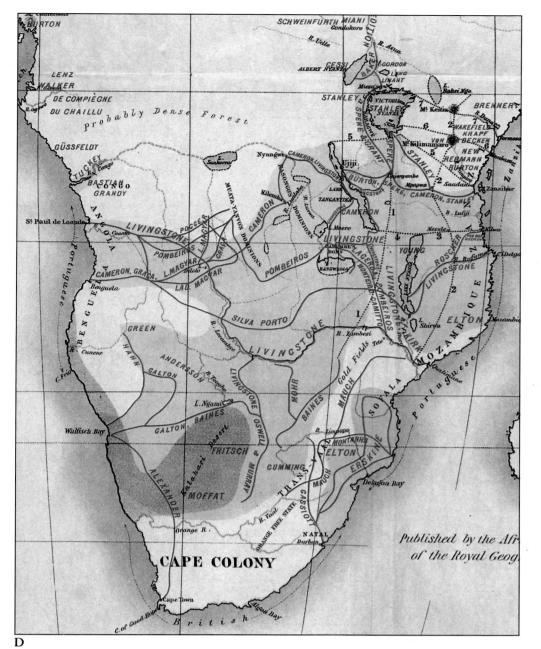

D

Apr. 1888: Stanley's party meets Emin Pasha

Murchison Falls

Lake Kyoga

GANDA

June 1889: Stanley's associates Parke and Jephson identify the Ruwenzori massif

Lake Victoria

ec. 1889: Stanley nd Emin Pasha each the east coast

ANGANYIKA

RRITORY)

N W E S

particular prize seemed to be Emin Pasha's Equatoria province. Since 1882 this had been cut off from Egypt by the Mahdist rising and Egypt itself had renounced responsibility. Emin with his army was believed to constitute a ready-made administration on the Upper Nile for whichever power could gain his adherence. Through the missionary Alexander Mackay in Buganda, the Imperial British East Africa Company tried to recruit him. Then in 1886, the Company's chairman, William Mackinnon, anxious to thwart German ambitions in the Nile region, called on Stanley to lead an expedition through East Africa to link up with Emin and relieve him by taking supplies. Mackinnon's business associate and friend, King Leopold, insisted, however, that as Stanley was *his* employee, the expedition must go via the Congo. In fact, Leopold was determined that Emin's province should be delivered to the Congo Free State.

Stanley, leading 10 Europeans and 600 Zanzibari porters, arranged for Tippu Tip to provide more porters and supplies in the area of his ivory empire on the Lualaba. When Yambuya was reached Stanley left the 'Rear Column' there to wait for Tippu Tip while he went forward through the unexplored Ituri Forest to Lake Albert. The journey took five months and 180 lives before the party reached the lake in December 1887. Stanley returned part of the way to get his boat and then met Emin, who proved much less in need of relief than the now grey-haired and haggard Stanley. Stanley retraced his steps to pick up the Rear Column only to find most of its members victims of murder or disease – a disaster for which he unfairly blamed Tippu Tip. Once more, Stanley returned to Lake Albert, having by January 1889 crossed the Ituri Forest three times.

This feat of exploration was followed by two others. Stanley's associates Thomas Parke and A. Mounteney Jephson identified the Ruwenzori massif of snow mountains, while Stanley finally identified the ultimate sources of the Albert Nile in Lakes George and Edward. The discoveries were the final pieces in the Nile puzzle and a considerable geographical exploit. On the other hand, as an imperialist exploit the Emin Pasha Relief Expedition was something of a flop. Stanley had gone on to the east coast with Emin making some rather unconvincing treaties for Mackinnon on the way. But statesmen in Berlin and London decided boundaries in 1890 without much reference to Stanley's work, although Leopold did get a temporary footing on the Nile. Emin himself threw in his lot with Germany, to the predictable annoyance of Leopold and Mackinnon.

3 BELOW *The Emin Pasha Relief Expedition was intended as an imperial venture; it also revealed the Ituri Forest, Lake Edward and the Ruwenzori massif and settled the limits of Lake Albert's Nile drainage.*

D ABOVE *The RGS response to Leopold's territorial claims was to assert British rights on the basis of priority of exploration, as in this map of 1877. The numbered routes are those the RGS saw as requiring further exploration.*

E BELOW RIGHT *Stanley's 1887 march to Lake Albert saw pygmies revealed in their national forest habitat for the first time. They are seen here with Sudanese soldiers of Emin Pasha and two of Stanley's companions.*

F BOTTOM RIGHT *A local ruler, Makoko, granted the French National Committee rights over a large area north of the Congo near Stanley Pool, much to Stanley's disgust. Thereafter, Makoko loyally defended French interests.*

sphere. Brazza and Stanley themselves had confrontations, both in Africa and in Paris, after which Brazza eventually removed his station to the north side of Stanley Pool. In effect, some sort of partition was underway.

Governments were brought in when the French recognized Brazza's Makoko Treaty as official in 1882. In a devious design to frustrate both the French and Leopold and to maintain openings for British merchants, the Foreign Office in February 1884 said it recognized Portugal as having political overlordship of the Congo estuary area. This in turn provided Germany with an excuse to react to what it claimed was a British slight to Bismarck over German claims in south-west Africa. The Berlin Conference was called. This set ground rules for annexations and agreed that a wide area around the Congo Basin should be a zone of free trade and free access for all. By the time the conference ended in February 1885, most powers had recognized Leopold as having political jurisdiction over much of this zone as the 'Congo Free State'. Leopold soon forgot free access. A series of political annexations followed, with Germany in particular claiming large areas of the south-west, and the east and the west African coasts.

Far from preventing partition, the Berlin Conference had encouraged it. Even so, there was a pause after mid-1885 as coastal annexations were digested. Further, the interior, including the lakes region, remained available for disposal. A

E

F

41
IMPERIAL EXPEDITIONS AND COLONIAL SURVEYING
1884-1954

THE PARTITION of Africa occurred between about 1884 and 1900. It was a period when exploration became subordinated to imperial purposes. The first task facing the European governments was to send expeditions to bring Africans under their control, sometimes by force, sometimes by agreement, sometimes by intervening in African struggles. Competing territorial claims between the European powers then needed to be reconciled. Though force, or the threat of force, might be used, politicians in Europe preferred to make peaceful agreements, especially over boundary questions. Demarcation on the ground then required new kinds of exploration. These were all processes that required detailed surveying, not just to establish the precise limits of the new colonies, but to ensure that they were then well enough known for efficient government to be possible.

For all the optimism that surrounded the colonies, however, the famines and diseases of the 'Ecological Catastrophe' in East and Central Africa in the 1890s underlined that coming to terms with the African environment would be a much more arduous process than many had anticipated. The additional exploration and scientific research that followed lasted until well into the 20th century.

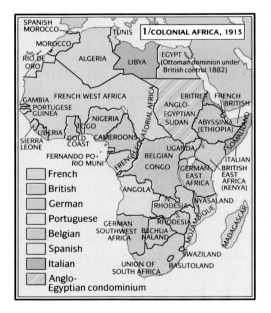

1 LEFT The European partition began with hesitant annexations of some coastal areas in 1884-85. It was resumed with more enthusiasm in 1889. By the outbreak of World War I, it was complete. **A** RIGHT The Anglo-German division of East Africa of 1886 was quite unrelated to realities on the ground. Detailed exploration was required to produce the more rational boundary, agreed in 1893, shown here.

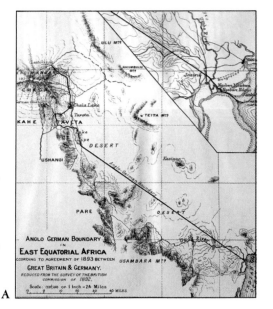

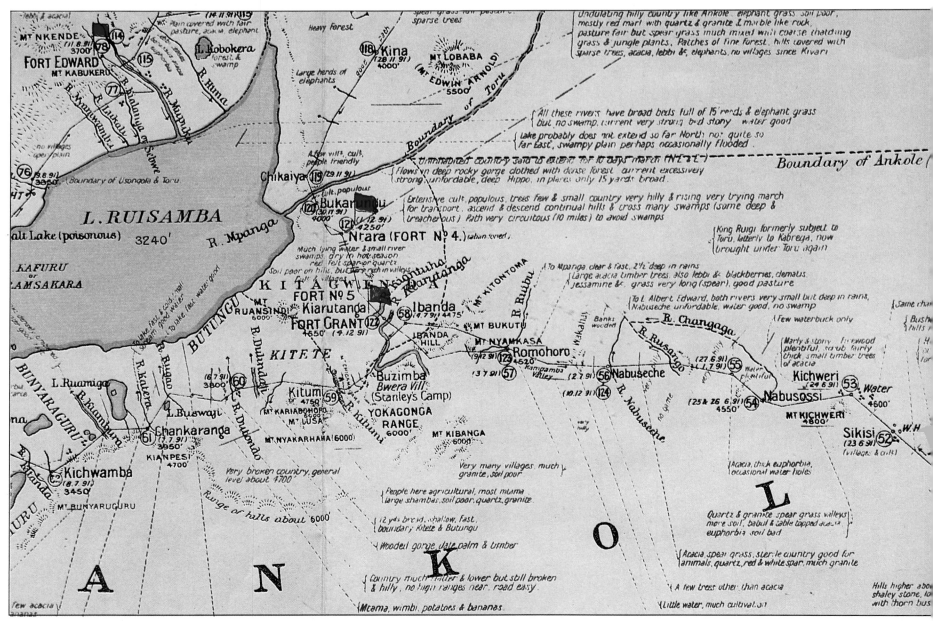

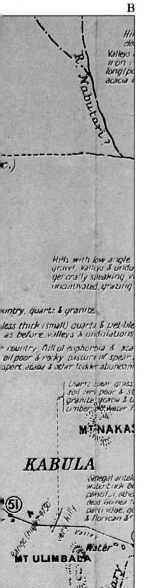

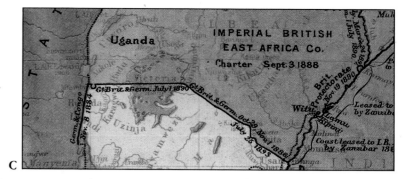

I N NORTHERN Africa, the European takeover involved chiefly France, which secured the north-west (despite some challenge from Germany in 1905 and 1911), and Britain, which had 'temporarily' occupied Egypt in 1882, basing its strategy on continued occupation of the country and its life-blood, the Nile. Italian ambitions in Ethiopia, however, were thwarted, a defeat which Mussolini was to avenge in 1935.

West Africa in 1885-1901 saw France's soldiers heavily engaged against old Muslim enemies, especially Ahmadu, while Dahomey was conquered in 1893. Britain similarly conquered the Sokoto Empire revealed by Clapperton (*see* ch.38) and campaigned against the Ashanti north of the Gold Coast. Establishing a boundary between French and British territories proved difficult, especially along the Niger, not least given the energies and ambitions of the soldier-imperialists involved.

The presence of settlers in southern Africa and the abundance of diamonds and gold created problems of their own. In Rhodesia, the explorer F.C. Selous was the 'scout' for the 'Pioneer Column' of settlers in 1890. They became powerful enough to defeat the Ndebele and Mashona without direct aid from Britain. The lure of the gold fields presented more intractable problems, with English settlers competing with the Afrikaners for control of them. In the end, Britain found itself drawn into the long and costly Boer War of 1899-1901 to resolve the dispute.

Though East Africa appeared to have no such great prizes, Arab and Swahili ivory and slave traders fought to maintain their positions against the British on Lake Nyasa and the Germans in Tanganyika, the latter the scene of the tragic Maji Maji revolt in 1905. Alienated by German attempts to force them to grow cash crops, many Africans accepted new leaders who, they believed, would make them immune to German bullets. The inevitable deaths of thousands exacerbated the already serious problems of drought and famine.

The Nile source area revealed by Speke 30 years before (*see* ch.39) was a particular magnet, the result of its supposed riches and its intelligent people. But the people of Buganda had already been divided by adherence to new religions: Muslim, Roman Catholic, Protestant and pagan factions squabbled for control of the throne and the major chiefships. It was to this volatile region that the Imperial British East Africa Company sent Frederick D. Lugard in 1890. Unable to dominate all the factions and forced to choose between them, he intervened in a Protestant-Catholic civil war in 1892 on the 'Inglezi', or Protestant, side. His maxim gun proved decisive. He then patched up a more permanent settlement. The previous year he had organized a major expedition westward of Buganda (*see* map B), to secure military control of all the areas in the British sphere agreed in the 1890 Anglo-German Treaty. Lugard went home in 1892 to report on his exploration and his political activities, and to persuade the British Government to take over control of the Uganda region from the Company. It agreed to do so in 1894. Almost immediately, Uganda's western boundary with Leopold's Belgian Congo became a problem.

In the Congo Free State, the 1890s had seen a savage war with the Arab traders of the Lualaba Valley. Leopold's ambition for more territory, meanwhile, remained voracious. A series of bizarre boundary arrangements with Britain accorded him access to Lake Albert and the west bank of the Nile for his lifetime. After his death, and in the light of knowledge of where 30°E actually was, the boundary was simplified by the 1910 agreement which also finally cleared up the Mufumbiro affair (*see* map C).

Despite such absurdities, the boundaries agreed among the colonial powers have, for better or worse – often worse – been preserved as one of modern Africa's principal inheritances of the partition. But however arbitrary many of the frontiers imposed by the colonial powers, the business of government demanded that they be mapped precisely. Similarly, military campaigning, railway building, tax collecting and judicial circuit work

were among the new colonial activities which required survey work of some kind on the ground. Lands and Survey Departments were likewise set up to manage surveys for legal and administrative purposes. By World War II most territories had some large-scale topographic maps. Yet these were mainly 'compilation maps' based on whatever earlier maps and other information happened to be available; there was comparatively little direct surveying for the sole purpose of constructing topographic maps. One difficulty was technical: before the age of wireless, establishing accurate positions was still difficult. As early as 1883 the Astronomer Royal at the Cape had begun to organize the accurate fixing of where exactly on the ground the 30°E meridian was. The object was to develop a basis for accurate ground survey by triangulation in the territories near this line. The project was not completed until 1954.

By the 1950s surveying on the ground was only a back-up to aerial surveys. As colonial powers and the successor independent states of Africa realized that maps were a necessity in development schemes, attempts were made to produce full coverage at scales varying from 1:50,000 to 1:250,000. Maps produced from aerial photography now available fulfil the same purpose of accurate cartographical delineation which Livingstone lost his life striving to achieve in 1873. Most important of all, Africans themselves have to live with the consequences of the encounters between their world and the developed world which began with exploration.

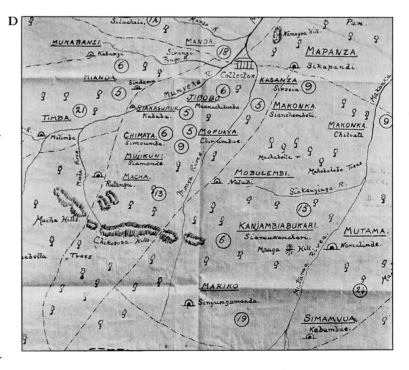

Ob

West Siberian Plain

Volga

Ural Mountains

Tobol

Ural

Yenisei

A

S

I

S
i

Altai

Irtush

Black Sea

Caspian Sea

Aral Sea

Jaxartes (Syr Darya)

Lake Balkhash

Gobi

Euphrates

Tigris

Zagros Mountains

Oxus (Amu Darya)

Pamirs

Tien Shan

Tarim

Lop Nor

Yellow River

Najud

Tropic of Cancer

Dahana

Persian Gulf

Hindu Kush

Takla Makan

Kunlun Mountains

H
i
m
a
l
a
y
a
s

T I B E T

C

H

A r a b i a

Gulf of Oman

Indus

Thar Desert

Empty Quarter
(Rub' al Khali)

Brahmaputra

Yangtze

Asir

Red Sea

Hadhramaut

Gulf of Aden

SUMMER

WINTER

S E A S O N A L

M O N S O O N

Arabian Sea

WINDS

SUMMER

WINTER

I N D I A

Ganges

Mekong

Red River

AFRICA

Equator

SOUTH

Western Ghats

D
e
c
c
a
n

WEST

Laccadive Is

Krishna

Godavari

Eastern Ghats

Bay of Bengal

WINTER

S E A S O N A L

SUMMER

M O N S O O N

Andaman Is.

Irrawaddy

Salween

Menam (Choo Phraya)

Mekong

INDO

SIAM

Ceylon

MONSOON

DRIFT

WINDS

SUMMER

WINTER

Andaman Sea

Andaman Is.

Nicobar Is.

Gulf of Siam

Malay Peninsula

Sumatra

Maldive Is.

INDIAN

COUNTER-

CURRENT

S E   T R A D E S

S E   T R A D E S

Strait of Malacca

EQUATORIAL

CURRENT

S E   T R A D E S

S E   T R A D E S

Sunda Strait

E

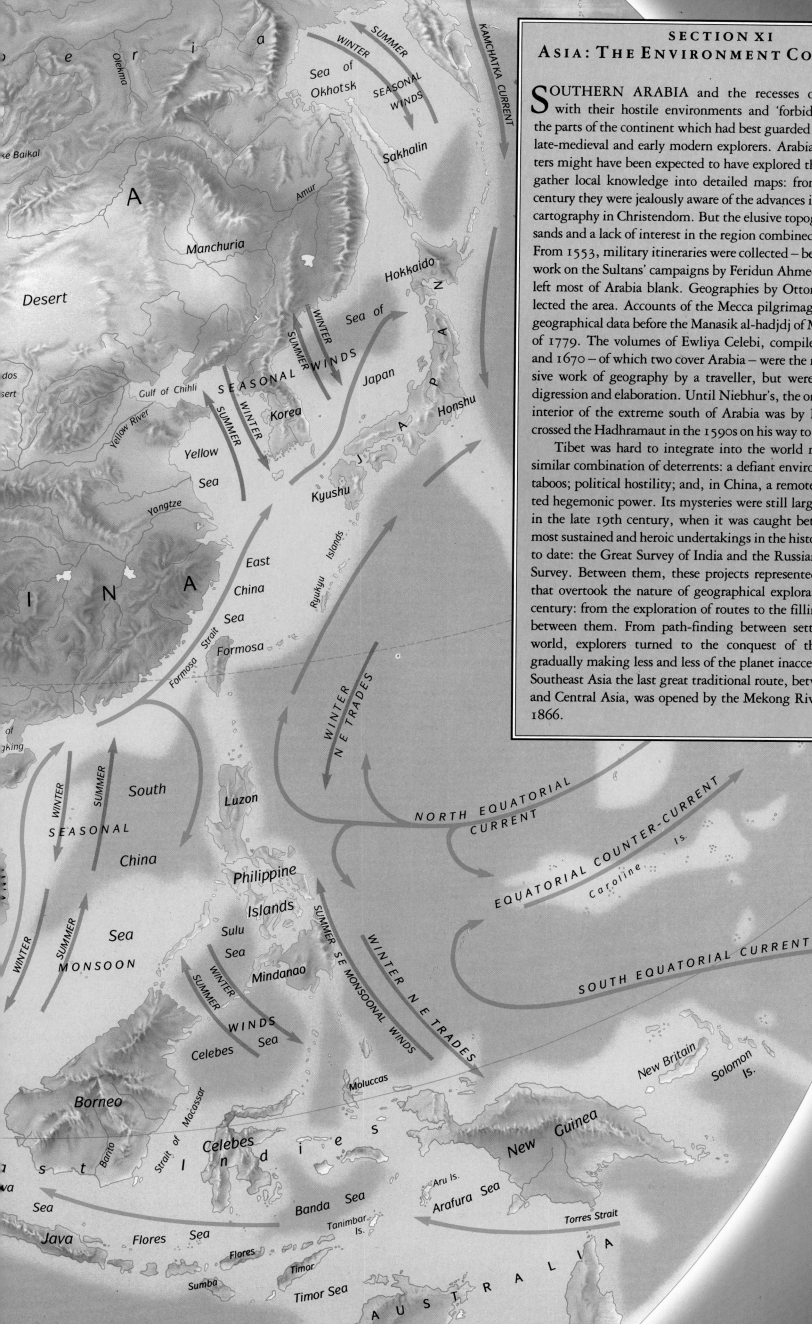

OUTHERN ARABIA and the recesses of Central Asia, with their hostile environments and 'forbidden cities', were the parts of the continent which had best guarded their secrets from late-medieval and early modern explorers. Arabia's Ottoman masters might have been expected to have explored the Middle East to gather local knowledge into detailed maps: from the early 16th century they were jealously aware of the advances in exploration and cartography in Christendom. But the elusive topography of shifting sands and a lack of interest in the region combined to inhibit them. From 1553, military itineraries were collected – beginning with the work on the Sultans' campaigns by Feridun Ahmed Beg – but these left most of Arabia blank. Geographies by Ottoman writers neglected the area. Accounts of the Mecca pilgrimage rarely included geographical data before the Manasik al-hadjdj of Mehemmed Edlib of 1779. The volumes of Ewliya Celebi, compiled between 1631 and 1670 – of which two cover Arabia – were the most comprehensive work of geography by a traveller, but were full of fantastic digression and elaboration. Until Niebhur's, the only account of the interior of the extreme south of Arabia was by Pedro Paez, who crossed the Hadhramaut in the 1590s on his way to Ethiopia.

Tibet was hard to integrate into the world map because of a similar combination of deterrents: a defiant environment; religious taboos; political hostility; and, in China, a remote and uncommitted hegemonic power. Its mysteries were still largely unpenetrated in the late 19th century, when it was caught between two of the most sustained and heroic undertakings in the history of exploration to date: the Great Survey of India and the Russian Central Asiatic Survey. Between them, these projects represented the sea-change that overtook the nature of geographical exploration in the 19th century: from the exploration of routes to the filling-in of the gaps between them. From path-finding between settled parts of the world, explorers turned to the conquest of the environment, gradually making less and less of the planet inaccessible to man. In Southeast Asia the last great traditional route, between Indo-China and Central Asia, was opened by the Mekong River Expedition of 1866.

42
THE MIDDLE EAST
1798-1948

DESPITE *its antiquity of human settlement, at the end of the 18th century the Middle East remained, in the wider world, among the least-known regions of the globe. The long history of conflict between Islam and Christian Europe, in partial consequence of which non-Muslims were banned from entering much of Arabia, had led Europeans to regard the region as the home of fanaticism and violence. First-hand observations were rare, although Ludovico Verthema of Rome reached Mecca in 1508 'for no better reason than ardent love of knowledge' and the Englishman Joseph Pitts reported his visit as a Haji's slave in the 1680s.*

Whereas from the 15th to the 17th centuries Islam was seen as posing a real threat to the stability of Europe, by the 18th century the evident decay of the Ottoman Empire, which ruled large areas of the Middle East, was taken as proof of its backwardness and corruption. As with the Wahhabi strongholds of much of the rest of central Arabia, the Ottoman Middle East, largely by-passed by European artistic and scientific achievements since the Renaissance, was thought immune to the civilizing influence of Christian Europe. The nomads and pastoralists of the deserts were dismissed as bestial or treated with the condescension due to the possessors of primitive virtues.

Exploration was inhibited both by the notoriously difficult navigation of the Red Sea and by the hostility of most of the desert regions. As late as the 1930s, most of the 'Empty Quarter' of southern Arabia had never been visited by Europeans. Much of the process by which the Middle East came to be explored and mapped in the 19th and early 20th centuries was underpinned by European assumptions of superiority. The imperial ambitions of the Great Powers, chiefly France and Britain, demanded that they assume control over ever larger areas of the Middle East. This stemmed not just from a belief in their own fitness to do so but from the need to limit the expansionist ambitions of Russia and, for Britain, above all to secure the commercial and military lifelines to India.

It was a policy that both led to and was reinforced by the opening of the Suez Canal in 1869. In consequence, huge areas of the Middle East were explored and mapped. The League of Nations mandate which entrusted direct rule of much of the Middle East to France and Britain after World War I and the discovery of huge oil reserves in the 1920s intensified the process.

1 RIGHT *Mecca and Medina, Islam's two holiest cities, though barred to non-Muslims, exerted a powerful hold on 19th-century European imaginations.*

2 BELOW *European penetration of the Middle East revealed a hitherto largely unknown region to the wider world.*

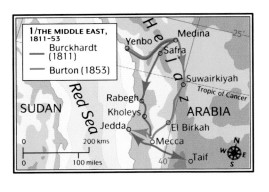

1/THE MIDDLE EAST, 1811-53
— Burckhardt (1811)
— Burton (1853)

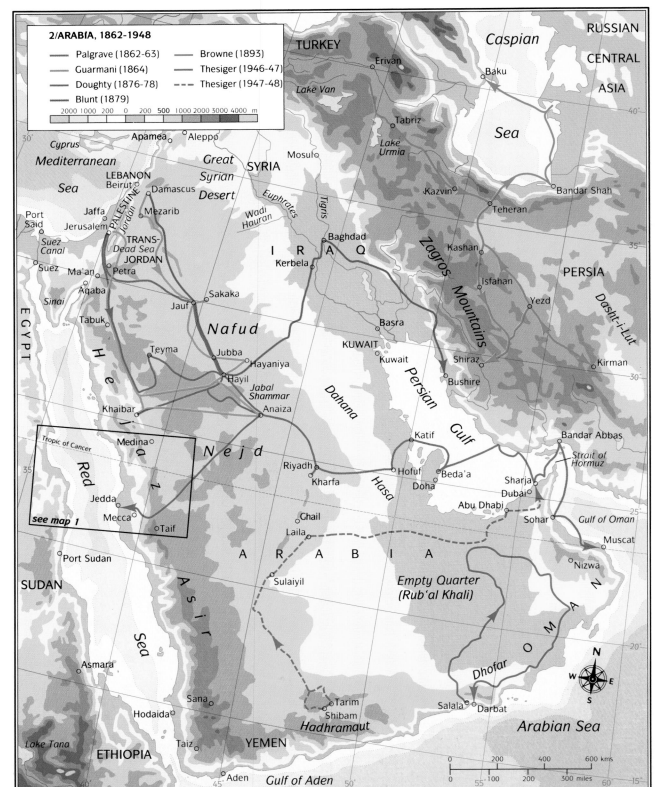

2/ARABIA, 1862-1948
— Palgrave (1862-63)
— Guarmani (1864)
— Doughty (1876-78)
— Blunt (1879)
— Browne (1893)
— Thesiger (1946-47)
-- Thesiger (1947-48)

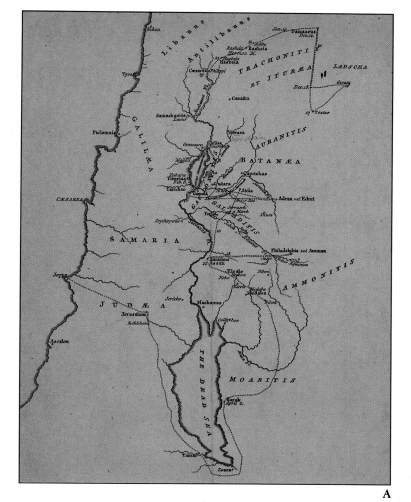

A

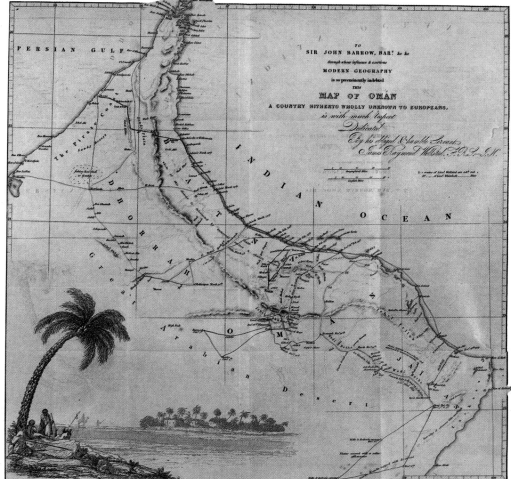

B

IN THE EARLY 19th century, maps of the Middle East were few and inaccurate. Carsten Niebuhr's Danish exploration of 1762-63 excited interest in Arabia but explored in detail no more than a small corner of the Yemen between Sana, Hodaida and Taiz. Napoleon's invasion of 1798 took geographers, artists and archaeologists to Egypt and Palestine. They produced, among much else, the first detailed maps of Egypt and the Palestine coast. It was an endeavour in marked contrast to many that followed, undertaken in a spirit of genuine inquiry, for all that Napoleon's claims to 'respect God, his prophet [Mohammed] and the Koran' were motivated at least as much by political expediency as by a genuine regard for Islam.

Nonetheless, at least something of the same spirit seems to have marked, in the following decade, the German explorer Ulrich Seetzen and the Swiss explorer Johann Burckhardt, both of whom had made extensive and generally sympathetic studies of Islamic customs and religious practices. Like many who followed them, both also adopted native dress for their travels, passing themselves off as natives. Though this was clearly in part an imperative if they were to visit central Arabia, then

A ABOVE LEFT *Seetzen's 1810 map of Palestine reflects the vagueness of European knowledge in the period. The size of the Dead Sea is exaggerated, as are the loops of the River Jordan to the north.*
B ABOVE RIGHT *The British naval lieutenant James Wellsted made this chart of the Omani coast and parts of the interior in 1838. He was surprised to encounter fertile valleys, in place of 'unvarying and desolate' desert.*
C BELOW *James Rennell's 1831 map of the Great Syrian Desert highlights the shortcomings of European knowledge, with huge areas of the interior unknown.*

forbidden to foreigners, it seems also to have stemmed from the fascination with the East shared by many Europeans, an image of Arabia as a tempting playground where fancy-dress was compulsory. Both visited Mecca – Seetzen in 1809 in the guise of a dervish, Burckhardt in 1815, almost uniquely, as the guest of the Ottoman Viceroy of Egypt – and both died in the Middle East. Seetzen was murdered at Taiz, where his diaries were also destroyed; Burckhardt died from dysentery in Cairo in 1817. The loss of Seetzen's diaries ensured that Burckhardt would prove the more influential, and his five published works detailed much new knowledge of the Bedouin and their lives in the harsh environments of Syria and northern Arabia. His travels excited considerable interest in Europe, especially his descriptions of Apamea in Syria and the Nabataean site of Petra, east of the Jordan Valley. He reported, too, the nature of the country between Aqaba and the Dead Sea, the structure of the Sinai Peninsula and the topography of the Hauran.

An even stronger taste for adventure, though little in the way of sympathy for the Arabs, prompted the visit of Richard Burton to Mecca in 1853. It was intended as only the prelude to a crossing of the Arabian Peninsula, a crossing which, in the

C

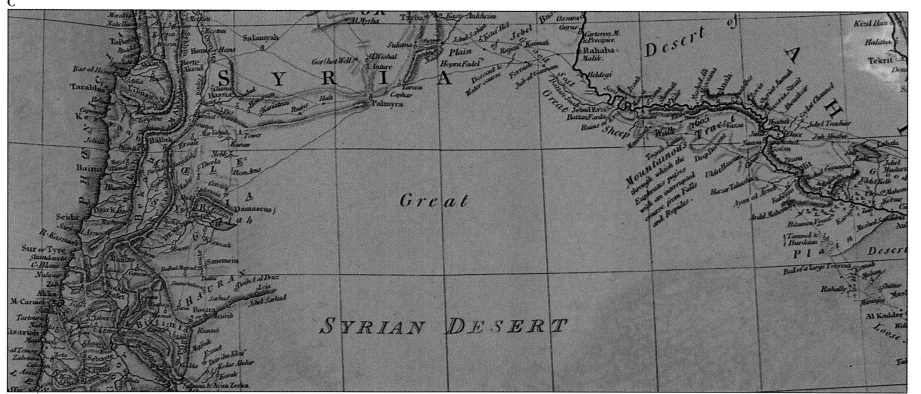

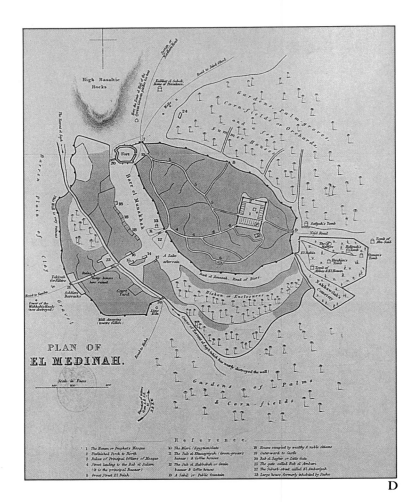

the region, he nonetheless produced a valuable account of early Wahhabi Arabia. His feat was partly reproduced by the Italian explorer Guarmani in 1864, who was also sponsored by Napoleon III, this time in the more innocent pursuit of buying horses for the French imperial stud. His account of his journey was substantially more detailed than Palgrave's: his map and list of settlements of the Jabal Shammar region was still a standard reference more than half a century later.

Valuable though these cartographic efforts were, they lacked precision and detail in comparison with those maps beginning to be produced by European military surveys, especially those of the coasts of Arabia and the eastern Mediterranean on behalf of the British Admiralty. In many cases, these were the first accurate hydrographic charts of the region available to Europeans. They were essential in establishing the viability of maritime routes along the Red Sea, enabling the long haul around the Cape of Good Hope to the Indian Ocean to be abandoned in favour of this much more direct route. With the completion of the Suez Canal and the resulting increase in European shipping in the Red Sea, they assumed greater significance still. The annexation of Aden, at the south-western tip of the Arabian peninsula, by Britain in 1839 was crucial to British strategic concerns in the Middle East, ensuring European control of both ends of the Red Sea.

The following decade saw two further intrepid travellers to Arabia: Lady Anne Blunt and Charles Doughty, both of whom contributed detailed accounts of the Arabs, though, as with other 'Orientalists' of the period, these seem to have been intended as much to reinforce European preconceptions of the Arabs and their picturesque ways as to reach a serious understanding of their culture. Anne Blunt, typical of a small number of energetic and enterprising upper-class women who made remarkable visits to Arabia in the 19th and 20th centuries, was the first European woman to penetrate the Arabian peninsula. She journeyed with her husband, who was, unusually, making the trip for his health, from Damascus to Bushire, in the process winning an audience with the Amir of Hayil, Ibn Rashid, a privilege denied her husband. Doughty travelled more extensively among the Arabs of central and western Arabia than any other 19th-century explorer, spending two years (1876-78) with the Bedouin. Though lauded for his finely observed accounts of desert life, which make obvious his appreciation of its violent beauty, and though professing veneration for Arab

event, illness, fatigue and 'the fatal fiery heat' ensured was never made. Burton added little to Burckhardt's discoveries but, as a shrewd and vivid observer of Arabia, his work reinforced the prevailing view of the romance and perils of the Arabian explorer. His readiness to adopt local guise (to the extent of submitting to circumcision), his command of Arabic and his later scholarly translations of *The Arabian Nights* and Oriental erotica were to link him with Arabia in the popular European imagination as firmly as T.E. Lawrence 70 years later.

More substantial exploration was undertaken by the Jesuit William Palgrave in central and eastern Arabia between 1862 and 1863. His journey was sponsored by Napoleon III in order to report on the lands near the Suez Canal, by then under construction, in which France had invested so much. Palgrave made the first crossing of Arabia, travelling from west to east, braving the hostility of the Wahhabis and disguised as a Syrian Christian. Though adding little to geographical knowledge of

D ABOVE LEFT
Disguised as a Muslim pilgrim, Richard Burton produced detailed plans of Medina following his clandestine visit of 1854.
E BELOW LEFT *The Jesuit William Palgrave's map of Arabia was the result of his two-year visit between 1862-63, during which he made the first west to east crossing of the peninsula.*

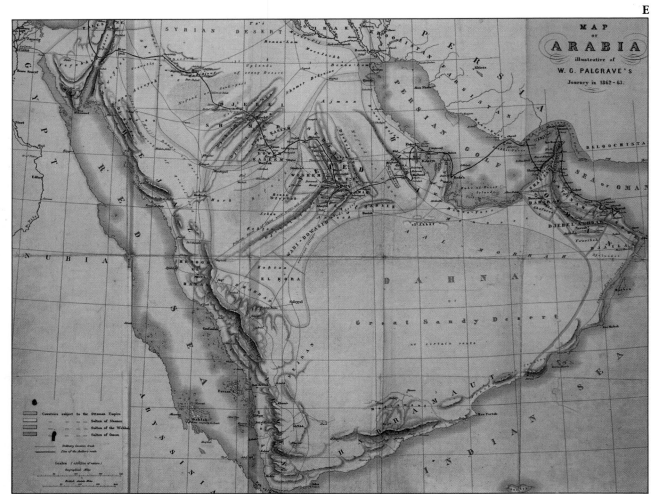

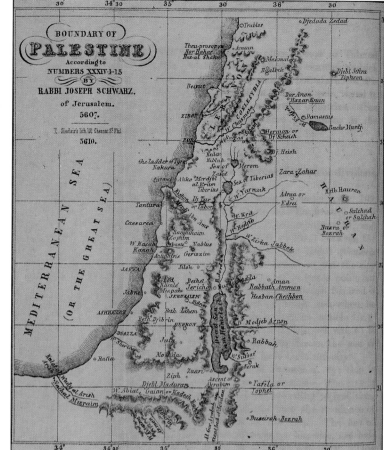

F   G

culture – which he saw as 'a great Semitic law, unwritten; namely the ancient faith of their illimitable, empty wastes' – he seems not to have been aware that the Bedouin on whom he imposed, and who fed and protected him, made him welcome with reluctance. Living in conditions of near-subsistence, they bore this burden on meagre resources with fortitude. The picturesque appeal of Arab life was spread still further in this period by the proliferation of landscape painters who descended on the region. Their compelling views of an exotic, distant land did little to aid a genuine understanding of the region, however, for all their popularity.

It was a view of the Middle East that found its most famous embodiment in T.E. Lawrence 'of Arabia'. He was unquestionably instrumental in helping direct, at least for a time, British policy toward the cause of Arab independence, in return for help in defeating the rump of the Ottoman Empire. But despite having travelled widely in the region, he undertook

F ABOVE LEFT *Idealized views of a romantic Middle East, such as this view of Jaffa painted by Carne in 1837, did much to confirm European preconceptions of the region's remote and exotic nature.* **G** ABOVE RIGHT *The Holy Land was a potent attraction for Europeans, whether Christian or Jewish. Rabbi Joseph Schwarz's 1829 map, compiled on the basis of his own pioneering travels, is among the earliest accurate representations of it.*

H

H LEFT *The hope that remoter regions of Arabia might yield minerals prompted European prospecting visits from the end of the 19th century that helped spread additional knowledge of it. This view of Ghail in southern Arabia was painted by H.B. Molesworth in 1893 during a search for coal. His journey anticipated the more systematic scientific exploration for oil in the 20th century.*

little that can be called exploration, being more eager to promote himself as poet, visionary, statesmen and man of action, chiefly through his remarkable account of his desert campaigns, *The Seven Pillars of Wisdom*. British policy was in any case soon compromised by the promise in 1917 to support the establishment of a Jewish homeland in Palestine and by the confirmation in 1920 by the League of Nations of the mandate under which France and Britain were awarded direct rule over much of the region, France governing Syria and Lebanon, Britain governing Palestine, Transjordan, Iraq and Kuwait. Control of the southern Arabian Peninsula fell to the dominant Saudi family, who in 1932 established the modern kingdom of Saudi Arabia. The occupying European powers instituted systematic and comprehensive surveys of the regions under their control. The maps that resulted were made more detailed still by surveys produced by oil companies from the late 1920s. Colonial administrators also played an important role in recording further the topography of the region and settling border disputes. The territorial entities they established have had a lasting influence on the turbulent politics of the Middle East.

The role of the individual traveller in exploring Arabia persisted into this period, however, and three of the most heroic feats were undertaken in the 1930s and 1940s. The goal of all three explorers was to cross the Rub' al Khali of southern Arabia, the Empty Quarter, or Abode of Emptiness, one of the few remaining genuinely unexplored regions of the world. The first to make the crossing, in 1930–31, was Bertram Thomas. His account of his journey, *Arabia Felix*, provided valuable data on the geology and geography and animal and plant life of the region. His achievement was matched two years later by Harry St. John Philby, a British administrator in the Indian government sent to Arabia to 'concert measures' against Ibn Rashid of Saudi Arabia, whose rule was thought to threaten Britain's mandated territories. Among much else, his journey helped discredit Palgrave's 19th-century reports of southern Arabia. The third explorer was Wilfred Thesiger, who made two desert crossings, in 1946–47 and 1947–48. He was also the most celebrated, the result chiefly of his sensitive account of the Arabs of southern Arabia, whose way of life had remained substantially unchanged for thousands of years. His insights into their fragile existence and his humility in the face of their accumulated store of desert lore, both shortly to be swept away by the irresistible tide of Western influence, are in stark contrast to the conceits of earlier European travellers.

43
SURVEYING INDIA
C.1500–C.1900

THOUGH scholars once thought India had no indigenous tradition of map-making, many varieties of Indian maps and plans have since been discovered. However, the great majority of these date from after 1500, and it remains uncertain how far European, Arab or Chinese models were important in their creation. In India, as in other societies, a strong tradition connected map-making with cosmography: the attempt to locate the sacred places of this world in an imagined universe. Some Indian maps also conveyed secular and administrative information. Similarly, detailed 17th- and 18th-century itineraries have survived, a few with map-like drawings.

Nevertheless, the Indian tradition of map-making had significant limitations. Few surviving maps were geographical in the sense that they were drawn to fixed scales and depicted space as well as distance. Nor, apparently, were maps and charts a central feature of administrative and commercial life. Why was this? One reason may be that Indians put great store by memorized information. Many travellers attest to Indian guides who could pinpoint routes and assess distances with accuracy. Yet Mughal officials also built up huge accumulations of written information connected with harvests, taxation and military affairs which was rarely expressed in map form.

A BELOW *Gentil's map of the Subah, or Province of Allahabad, from his* Atlas of India *of 1770. Gentil apparently combined his own information and that from British and French route maps with place names from a 16th-century Mughal administrative treatise,* The Institutes of [the Emperor] Akbar. *The margins are illustrated with zodiacal coins and exotic and mythological scenes.*

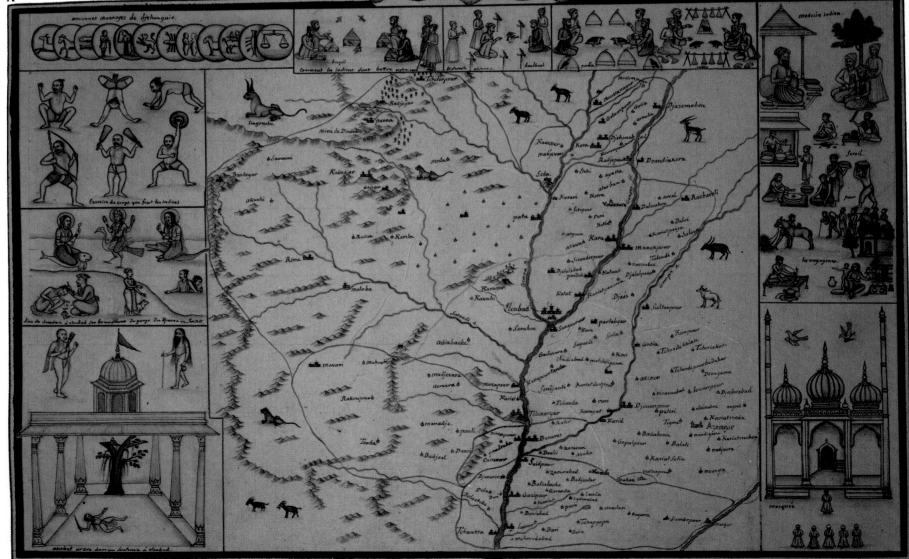

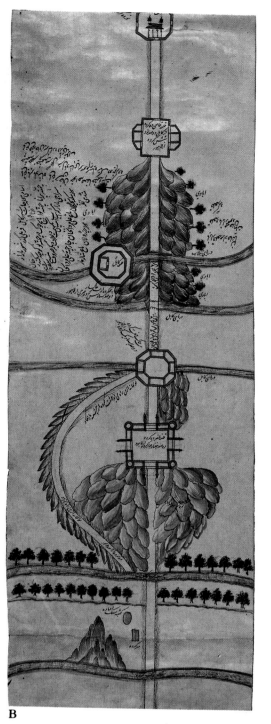

B

B LEFT *This 18th-century Mughal-style route map illustrated a written itinerary. Cities, trees and rivers act as markers on the road, which was conceived as a straight line. It is similar to medieval European route maps such as the Peutinger map (see ch.7, map B).*
C BELOW *A section of Rennell's Bengal Atlas of 1779 showing part of the mouths of the Ganges and its tributaries. Precise British map-making in India began with maps of inland waterways and coastal charts, a reflection of the importance of maritime trade to the East India Company.*
D BOTTOM *Mid-18th-century British knowledge of the Indian interior came partly from military route maps, such as this made by Major Adam, one of many East India Company soldiers to penetrate the interior as British influence grew. It shows the route from Patna in Bihar to Culcutta.*

C

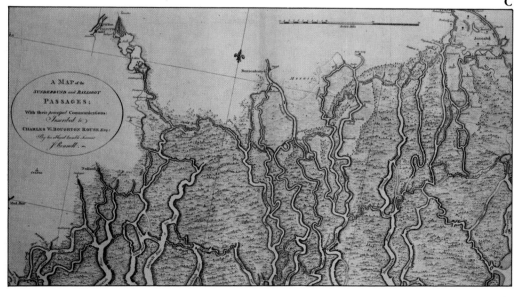

D

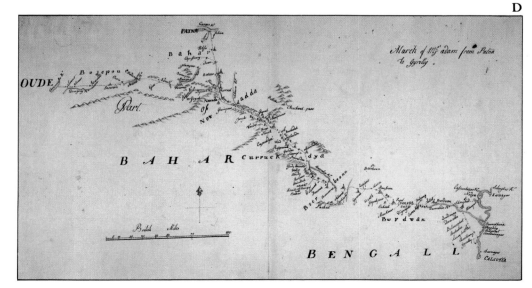

PERHAPS map-making did not take firmer root in Indian society because Indians did not conceive landholding as a simple, and saleable, dominion over measured space. Measures of land varied according to its productivity. Men held complex and interpenetrating rights to produce and labour rather than definitive plots. Arbitration was localized, relying on memory not text. In Europe it had been the legal haggling over the boundaries of plots, estates and kingdoms which helped diffuse geographical map-making throughout the whole society. Though Indian traders, like their Arab contemporaries, used compasses and possessed maritime itineraries, in Europe the closer interest in trade of competitive, centralized states helped to build up archives of maritime charts which the printing press later brought into the public domain.

When Europeans began to establish their military power in India in the 18th century, it was competition between them, allied with a clear sense of proprietary dominion over land area, which spurred on map-making. For the European conquerors, to rule was to be able to reduce the lives of the subject peoples to closely delineated and measured spaces. In this, information derived from Indian informants and Mughal itineraries or manuals was critical, but Indian maps as such played only a small part.

Of course, the Western mapping of India was not driven simply by military and commercial motives. Exploration was valued as a recovery of the knowledge of the Ancients. Even a supremely practical map-maker such as James Rennell was keen to locate the rivers and towns of India mentioned by Ptolemy and other Greek and Roman sources. Nevertheless, the development of Western mapping closely followed the expansion of European trading interests. Sixteenth-century Portuguese maps, charting holdings at Goa and elsewhere, were the first to add significantly to Classical and Arab knowledge and what had been gleaned from late-medieval travellers. The Dutch, who supplanted the Portuguese in the 17th century, made maps of areas where they had trading settlements, such as Gujerat on the west coast and Bengal on the east.

By the end of the 17th century, the centre of European map-making had passed from Amsterdam to Paris. French travellers to the Mughal Empire, notably François Bernier, had begun to fill in the details of the Indian interior. The French East India Company then began to make its late bid for trade and influence in India, while in 1752 d'Anville, official cartographer to the Compagnie des Indes, published his *Carte de l'Inde*, perhaps the first modern map of the subcontinent. French 'men-on-the-spot' such as Colonel Jean-Baptiste Gentil in Lucknow in the 1760s and '70s also contributed to the growth of geographical knowledge following increased competition between the two nations during the Anglo-French wars of the 1740s and '50s (*see* map A).

As befitted the nation with the greatest trading interests in the East, British cartography was most developed in the area of maritime charts. In the 1780s James Rennell could assert that 'soundings on the coast of Bengal are better known than those of the British [English] Channel'. Robert Clive's conquest of Bengal in 1757 and the subsequent capture of its land revenues in 1765 then imposed new priorities on British administrators and cartographers. In 1764 Rennell began to survey Bengal. Over the following 12 years he made survey journeys throughout Bengal and Bihar which filled out details from the Mughal sources and resulted in his *Bengal Atlas* of 1779 (*see* map C).

After his return to England, Rennell, the 'father of Indian Geography' to the British, continued to take an active interest in Indian cartography, building up an archive of route plans and descriptions which increased as Britain expanded its influence across the subcontinent. Political conflict in India was again the motive for Rennell's more general *Memoir of a Map of Hindoostan or the Mogul's Empire* of 1783, which was occasioned, he wrote, by the British 'wars, alliances and negociations, with all the principle powers of the [Mughal] Empire'. Rennell's

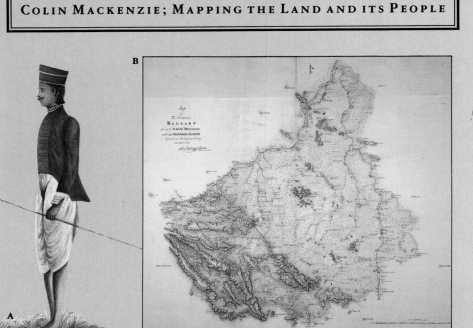

COLIN Mackenzie (**C**) represented the fusion of 18th-century antiquarian passion with the 19th-century vogue for scientific measurement. Mackenzie landed in India in 1782, serving originally as an Engineers officer. His training in mathematics and the humanities served him well. Wherever his duties as sapper and surveyor took him, he continued to accumulate a huge store of ethnographic materials. Mackenzie's first maps were drawn in the territories ceded by Tipu Sultan to Hyderabad in 1792. After the defeat and death of Tipu Sultan in 1799, he compiled a trigonometrical survey of the whole state; (**B**) is his map of the district of Bellary. Indian man-power was critical to the project, and training Indians in scientific work was among Mackenzie's most notable achievements. (**A**) shows an Indian with his survey pole. It was then that Mackenzie first worked with William Lambton, pioneer of the Trigonometrical Survey of India. The culmination of Mackenzie's career came in 1819, when he was appointed Surveyor-General of India. But by now Lambton and others were pushing forward the cause of trigonometrical mapping. The real contribution of Mackenzie's later years was the accumulation of hundreds of local histories, royal genealogies and sacred legends.

own work had been severely practical, though he was interested in ancient geography and was keen to pursue his rivalry with French geographers. But other travellers and officials now began to combine route mapping with ethnographic and economic description as the British became avid for data on the lives, customs and resources of their Indian subjects.

The next critical breakthrough was also inspired by political considerations. As the British penetrated deeper into the subcontinent, they became aware of the need for accurate representations not only of distance and place but of space. As systems of taxation were introduced which based assessment on the extent of holdings rather than on status or political clout, collectors of revenue needed to know the exact extent of a magnate's lands. Then, as the Company's army turned from offensive campaigns to defence of the territories conquered between 1798 and 1818, Engineers officers such as William Lambton and Colin Mackenzie began formal trigonometrical surveys (*see* panel). The full impact of the 'trigonometrical revolution' was delayed by the miserliness of the Government of India and, ironically, by the conservatism of the earlier generation of geographers (including Rennell), who were reluctant to see their work superceded. Lambton faced many setbacks in his attempts to set up a general trigonometrical survey that would bring mathematical precision to Indian mapping, and, by his death in 1823, had only been able to complete one stretch of the Great Arc of triangular measurements. This, a precisely mapped baseline for all further measurements, was to run up the spine of India from Cape Comorin to the Himalayas.

The achievement of Lambton's pupil Sir George Everest was made possible by the new spirit of administration introduced into India by Lord William Bentinck, the Whig grandee whose period as Governor-General (1828-35) has often been called the Company's 'Age of Reform'. Bentinck, believing that good government began with accurate information, wished to transform India through the application of Western science, capital and Christian humanitarianism. Though many of his projects foundered on the rocks of the Company's financial weakness or the resistance of Indian society, the Great Survey was carried through to a triumphant conclusion.

Everest was not a pioneer in the theory of land measurement, but he was a master of its practical application. He gave impetus to the Survey with innovations such as setting his triangulations in definite chains like the bars of a gridiron (see map E). Direct measurements of the land and subsequent triangulations were carefully checked by precise astronomical calculations. All this required an immense effort of human management and politics as well as technical virtuosity. Indian staff had to be trained to do the work and repair instruments. European staff who fell 'sacrifices to the climate', including Everest himself, had to be nursed through lethal diseases acquired in remote terrain. Observation towers had to be built (and protected from suspicious residents) throughout India's great plains. Indian rulers who feared that the appearance of a surveyor's pole signalled the end of their sovereignty had to be cajoled. In the territories of the Muslim Nizam of Hyderabad, surveying flags were re-made in Islamic green; in Orchha state the fort commander at first refused permission to hoist the survey flags because when a British flag had been raised before 'the whole Raj had been the prey of loot and desolation'.

The work of Everest and his successor Andrew Waugh stood as the benchmark of all later British efforts to map and define India and its people. The vogue for mapping extended to all aspects of Indian life. Revenue surveys mapped the country for taxation purposes down to individual fields (see map F). Economic and forest surveys were followed by Sir Alexander Cunningham's *Archaeological Survey of India* (1871-87) and Sir George Grierson's *Linguistic Survey of India* (see map G). Early anthropologists were even to measure the Indian body and its cranial capacity on a gridiron chart similar to Everest's original trigonometrical gridiron. European 'voyages of discovery' became precisely charted expeditions into social and moral space in vindication of the supremacy God and Science had given to the white man. In the longer run Indians were to adapt Western learning to their own priorities. By the 1870s revenue officials were reporting that peasant proprietors were beginning to use survey maps in legal battles over property rights with their rivals, landlords or administrators. Indians had begun to use the Raj's tools against it.

E BELOW LEFT *Sir George Everest planned his series of trigonometrical triangulations on a vast grid covering the subcontinent. Initial measurements had been made on William Lambton's Great Arc, which was to run from Cape Comorin in the south to the Himalayas. It was bisected by the Base Line, running east to west beneath the line of the Himalayas.*

F RIGHT *This village map of coastal Cuttack in Orissa was made by R. Smyth in 1838-39. It illustrates how mapping was increasingly used to record boundaries and properties. It would have been used both to assess land revenues and to decide legal disputes over rights to land.* **G** BELOW RIGHT *Mapping techniques found applications in the human sciences. Sir George Grierson's* Linguistic Survey of India, *completed in the early 20th century, gave precise boundaries to India's languages and dialects. This map shows the languages of the Indo-Aryan group, which includes the dominant language, Hindi.*

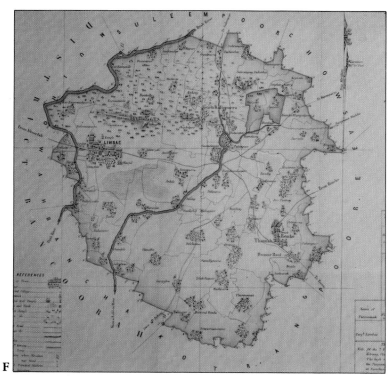

F

G

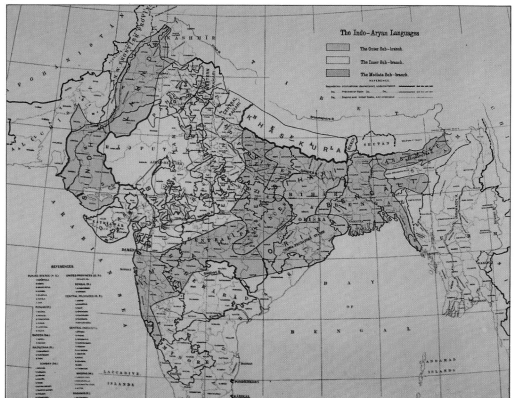

44
TIBET AND CENTRAL ASIA
1661-1928

A

REMOTE *and mountainous, Tibet remained among the least-known regions of the world until well into the 19th century. Though established as an independent kingdom by at least the 7th century, it was first reported in the West in the mid-13th century by John of Piano Carpini and William of Rubruck (see ch. 31). Though Jesuits from China and India reached outlying areas in the early 17th century, the capital was not visited by Europeans until 1661. In October that year the Jesuits Grueber and d'Orville, hoping to pioneer a new route from China to Europe, reached Lhasa. The hardships of their route, the cause of d'Orville's later death in northern India, ensured that few followed them. Prominent among those who did, however, were a series of Jesuits in the early 18th century. They hoped to establish missions in Tibet, as they had already done in China. Though unable to overcome the Tibetans' profound Buddhism, they meanwhile surveyed Tibet in sufficient detail to enable Jesuits in China to draw up a map of the country.*

Enough was known of Tibet by the end of the 18th century to make the prospect of further European exploration tempting. Britain in particular was excited by the country, seeing it as both a potential market, despite its remoteness, and as a buffer against Russian expansion into India. The needs of imperial security were to prove central to the gradual revelation of the country by Europeans, with Britain and Russia competing by the second half of the 19th century to bring Tibet within their spheres of influence. Both had to contend with the Chinese determination to keep foreigners out of Tibet, over which it had exercised suzerainty since the late 18th century.

Whatever the imperatives of colonial politics, however, the exploration of Tibet by Europeans eventually owed as much to scientific travellers as to imperial adventurers. In part, this was because the inaccessibility and poverty of Tibet made it clear that it was unlikely to yield great commercial dividends. Of more immediate significance, however, neither Britain or Russia could conquer Tibet without first knowing something of its geography. The fortitude and endeavour of those who penetrated Tibet in the 19th century to survey it, usually in the face of extreme Tibetan disapproval, were remarkable. Tibetan autonomy after 1912 did little to make the country more accessible to outside influences, though a number of outstanding scientific travellers continued to visit it.

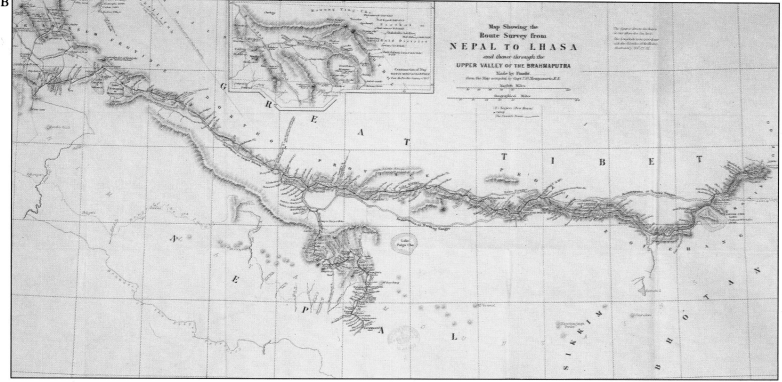

B RIGHT *An anonymous 'pundit' map of Tibet; it was subsequently published by the Royal Geographical Society in 1868. Though the detail revealed by the pundits was impressive, the constraints under which they were forced to work made it impossible for them to attempt accurate surveys of areas away from their immediate routes. Lhasa is shown on the far right.*

BY THE latter half of the 18th century Britain's presence in India was sufficiently well established for Warren Hastings, first Governor-General of India, to want to investigate the mountainous regions to the north-east. In 1774 he dispatched George Bogle and Alexander Hamilton as representatives of the East India Company to Tashi Lhunpo, the seat of the Panchen Lamas, the second most important of Tibet's rulers. This and a follow-up embassy under Samuel Turner in 1783 to establish relations with the new Panchen Lama, then 18 months old, were politely received but little more. The prospects of trading relations seemed all the more remote when, in 1792, China closed Tibet to foreigners.

This seems to have been no deterrent to Thomas Manning, who, having failed to obtain government backing for a visit, embarked on a private visit to Tibet in 1811, apparently for no better reason than that he was curious. Manning reached Lhasa in December, having travelled via Bhutan to Gyangtse. He was the first European to enter the Holy City since 1745, when the

1 BELOW *Guarded by mountains to the south and vast expanses of desert to the north, it was the geographical remoteness of Tibet – itself at an average altitude of 15,000 feet – as much as its political isolation that made its exploration so problematic.*

last Christian mission departed. Though adding little to geographical knowledge, Manning nonetheless left a vivid account of Lhasa, 'its habitations begrimed with smut and dirt', and its seven-year-old ruler, the ninth Dalai Lama.

Thirty-four years passed before the next successful European visit to Tibet. It was also the last attempt to establish a Christian mission in the country. Two French monks, Evarist Huc and Joseph Gabet, made an 18-month journey via Mongolia from China, arriving in Lhasa in January 1846 in a caravan of more than 2,000 people and 4,000 animals. In March, the Chinese *amban*, the representative of the emperor, had them expelled. They were the last Europeans to penetrate the country openly until the 20th century.

Chinese hostility remained the principal obstacle, with repeated British attempts to re-open relations rebuffed. By the 1860s, Tibet remained tantalisingly unknown, its principal geographical features, even the positions of its cities, known only vaguely, its political and economic character known

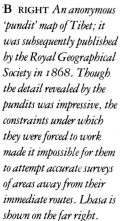

A LEFT *This late 18th-century view of the Dalai Lama's palace of Potala in Lhasa was typical of an indigenous tradition of Tibetan landscape painting. Similar views of the principal buildings of Tibet were executed.*

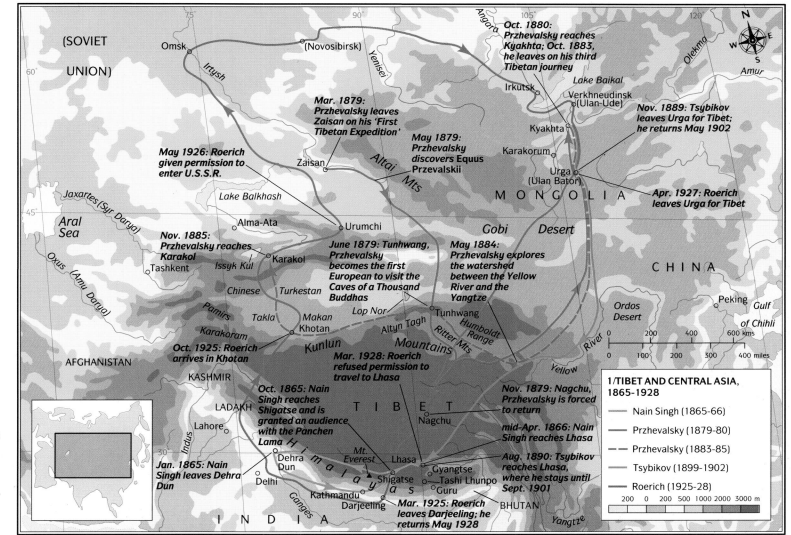

1/TIBET AND CENTRAL ASIA, 1865-1928

— Nain Singh (1865-66)
— Przhevalsky (1879-80)
--- Przhevalsky (1883-85)
— Tsybikov (1899-1902)
— Roerich (1925-28)

NICOLAS ROERICH: EXPLORER AND ARTIST

THE three-year, 16,000-mile expedition of Central Asia undertaken by the Russian explorer Nicolas Roerich between 1925 and 1928 provides a striking example of the way scientific and cultural exploration supplanted the largely geographical explorations of the previous century. Roerich's aim was to investigate what he asserted was the common cultural heritage of the nomadic peoples of a huge area of Central Asia, extending from the western Himalayas to the Russian steppes. Unusually, his was very much a family expedition. His wife Elena, a devotee of Agni Yoga, and his elder son George, a speaker of Chinese, Mongolian and Tibetan as well as several Indian languages, accompanied Roerich.

The most persuasive evidence unearthed by Roerich to support his theory was the similarity he identified between the Tibetan concept of *Shambala*, a mythical Kingdom of Righteousness, and the belief in the *Belovodye*, the White Water Lands, of the Russians of the Altai Mountains that run from Russia into Mongolia and China. Possibly of more lasting significance, however, was his investigation of the cultures of the region, still the bedrock of anthropological studies of Central Asia. His other principal accomplishment was as a painter, a talent his younger son Svetoslav inherited. From sketches made during his epic travels, Roerich subsequently worked up more than 500 finished canvasses, most at his home in the Kulu Valley of northern India. These aimed not so much to reproduce exactly the landscapes of Central Asia as what he felt to be their spirit. The harsh colours and bold outlines of (A) and (B), respectively of Ladak and Maitreya in Tibet, are typical of the intensity of his vision. (C) is a suitably patriarchal portrait of Nicolas himself painted by Svetoslav in 1937.

C

C

hardly at all. Britain in particular was enticed by this conundrum. It was a member of the Great Trigonometrical Survey, Captain Thomas Montgomerie, who devised a means of penetrating Tibet. In 1863, he proposed that Indian natives be trained as surveyors and, disguised as pilgrims or traders, sent to Tibet to map it. They were to be supplied with instruments that could be hidden in prayer wheels and walking staffs, and with prayer beads with 100 beads, rather than the normal 108, to allow them to measure distances by counting their steps. The information gathered by these 'pundits', from the Sanskrit for 'learned man', when worked up into maps, and their identities were to be kept secret.

However improbable the venture, it was extraordinarily successful. Between 1865 and 1881 a series of pundits visited Tibet and many of the surrounding regions, mapping and recording as they went. The first visit, made from January 1865 to April 1866, was undertaken by Nain Singh, accompanied by his cousin Mani Singh. Disguised as horse traders, they travelled from Kathmandu to Ladak in Tibet. By the end of October, by now travelling alone, Nain Singh reached Shigatse, Tibet's second city. In January he reached Lhasa, whose position and altitude he was the first to measure accurately. He also made surveys of the three largest monasteries around Lhasa: Sera, Drepung and Galdan.

Of the pundits who followed, the most remarkable were Krishna Singh, who made a four-year journey into Tibet and China from 1878 (and who is credited with having made a 230-mile journey on horseback in the course of it, counting his horse's steps to measure the distance) and Sarat Chandra Das, the only Bengali among the pundits. He made two visits to Tibet, in 1879 and 1881, afterwards becoming a noted Tibetan scholar.

The success of the pundits highlighted the relative failure of Russia in Tibet by this period. This was not for want of trying. Russian efforts to explore the country were spearheaded by Nikolai Przhevalsky, who, between 1870 and 1888, made no less than four attempts to reach Lhasa from Mongolia, then under Chinese rule. Though none was successful, the victim of extremes of terrain and temperature as much as of Chinese hostility, he nonetheless surveyed vast areas of Central Asia, as well as completing substantial botanical and zoological studies. His accounts of travels that were often made in the face of extraordinary obstacles are vividly revealing.

On his first Central Asian expedition (1870-74), during which he became the first recorded European to enter Tibet from the north as well as the first to survey its northern regions, he collected more than 3,000 animal specimens and 600 plants. On a further expedition in 1876, he became the first European to reach the lake of Lop Nor since Marco Polo. Przhevalsky reached Tibet for the second time in November 1879,

D

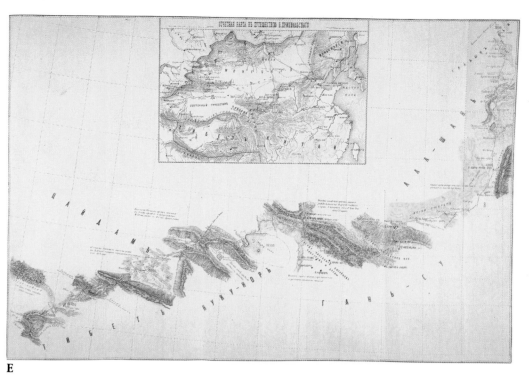

E

F

G

on what became known later as his 'First Tibetan Expedition', penetrating to within 170 miles of Lhasa before being forced to return by the Tibetans. On two further expeditions, he trekked across vast swathes of Central Asia, mapping the source of the Yellow River and the watershed between it and the Yangtse, and discovering and naming the Humboldt, the Marco Polo and the Ritter Mountains and the last known species of wild horse, *Equus Przevalskii*.

With Przhevalsky's death in 1888, Russian initiatives lapsed until the end of the century. When revived, they took two distinct forms. The first, a solo effort by a student from St. Petersburg University, Gombozhab Tsybikov, was almost wholly academic. In 1899, disguised as a Buddhist pilgrim, Tsybikov joined a Mongolian caravan at Urga. In August, his disguise intact, he reached Lhasa. He spent over a year in Tibet, visiting the monasteries at Tashi Lhunpo, Tsetan and Samye, and compiling detailed information on the country's history, religions and administration.

The second, though ultimately wholly political, remains a mystery. Agran Dorjiev, a Buddhist from Buryatia in Siberia, entered Tibet at around the same time. He did this openly and without restriction, indeed seems at first to have been no more than a high-ranking Buddhist scholar. As such, he was assigned as one of a number of teachers to the 13th Dalai Lama. Having gained his confidence, Dorjiev became the Dalai Lama's political advisor. Whether this had been his aim from the start, or whether he realised the potential of his position only later, is unclear. At all events, he proposed a Tibetan-Russian alliance, making three journeys to Russia to report to the Tsar. Alarmed by clear evidence of Russian designs on Tibet, Britain responded with a diplomatic mission. It was headed by Colonel Francis Younghusband and accompanied by 1,000 heavily armed troops. Reaching the village of Guru in March 1904, it was faced by 15,000 Tibetan soldiers. A four-minute battle saw the Tibetans routed, with over 700 dead. Younghusband continued unopposed to Lhasa, reaching it in August. The Anglo-Tibetan Treaty that resulted saw Tibet within Britain's sphere of influence.

Though by now firmly established on the map of the world, Tibet nonetheless remained, as to some extent it remains, a world apart, shielded by its geographical remoteness. It remained more or less within Britain's sphere of interest until 1947, when Britain withdrew from India. In 1951, after a brief independence, it reverted to Chinese rule, becoming, forcibly, a province of Communist China in 1959. Until swallowed by China it had been visited further by a series of Europeans, notably the Swede Sven Hedin and the Russian Nicolas Roerich (*see* panel). They fall within the category of scientific and scholarly travellers, whose interest was the further exploration of Tibetan culture rather than Tibetan geography.

45

SOUTHEAST ASIA
1854-1868

SOUTHEAST *Asia is the southern extremity of the Asian landmass. Mainland Southeast Asia is divided by the great plains created by the Irrawaddy, Menam, Mekong and Red Rivers, while the great archipelagos of maritime Southeast Asia are fragmented by the sea. But these seas have also provided the great lines of communication between the region and the wider world. For more than a millennium, they have brought trade, peoples and religions from the Middle East, India and China.*

Surviving records of exploration date from no earlier than the later Middle Ages, however: in Chinese maps and literature and in Javanese sources. The 14th-century Javanese king, Hayan Wuruk, for example, ordered a comprehensive survey of his country which seems to have generated detailed maps. When the Portuguese arrived in the early 16th century they made use of Javanese maps in exploring the East Indies. The spread of European colonialism through Southeast Asia from the 19th century vastly increased knowledge of the region in the wider world. Imperialism demanded geographical knowledge to facilitate administration and to increase trade. Though the mapping of the region was to continue well into the 20th century, the pioneering contributions made to the conquest of its environment are exemplified by the scientific work of Wallace in the 1850s and the French Mekong River expedition of 1866-68.

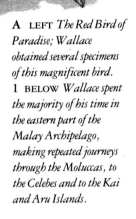

A LEFT *The Red Bird of Paradise; Wallace obtained several specimens of this magnificent bird.*
1 BELOW *Wallace spent the majority of his time in the eastern part of the Malay Archipelago, making repeated journeys through the Moluccas, to the Celebes and to the Kai and Aru Islands.*

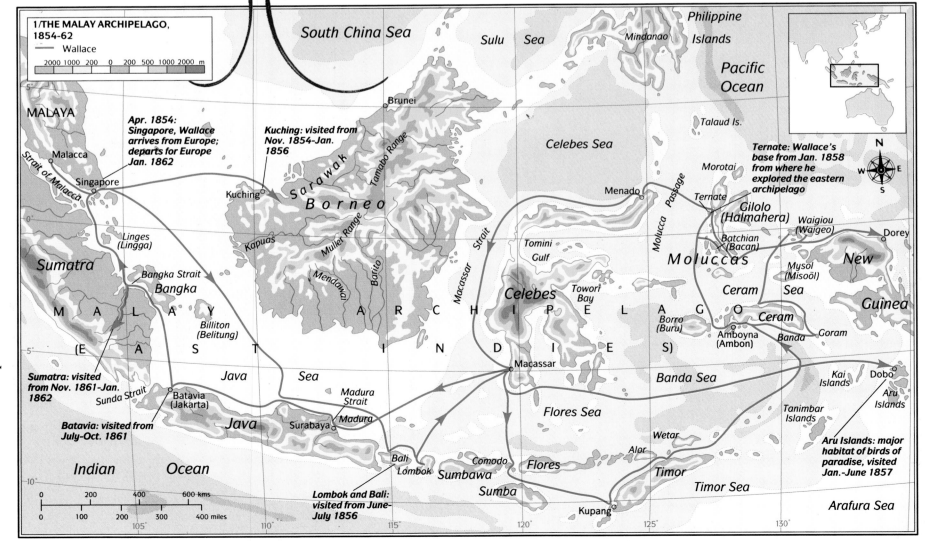

1/THE MALAY ARCHIPELAGO, 1854-62
— Wallace
2000 1000 200 0 200 500 1000 2000 m

South China Sea

Sulu Sea

Philippine Islands

Mindanao

Pacific Ocean

MALAYA

Apr. 1854: Singapore, Wallace arrives from Europe; departs for Europe Jan. 1862

Malacca

Strait of Malacca

Singapore

Brunei

Kuching: visited from Nov. 1854-Jan. 1856

Talaud Is.

Celebes Sea

Morotai

Ternate: Wallace's base from Jan. 1858 from where he explored the eastern archipelago

Kuching

Sarawak Range

Tamabo Range

Borneo

Menado

Molucca Passage

Ternate

Gilolo (Halmahera)

Waigiou (Waigeo)

Dorey

Linges (Lingga)

Muller Range

Kapuas

Macassar Strait

Tomini Gulf

Batchian (Bacan)

Mysol (Misoöl)

Moluccas

New Guinea

Sumatra

Bangka Strait

Bangka

Mendawai

Barito

Celebes

Towori Bay

Ceram Sea

Ceram

M A L A Y

Billiton (Belitung)

A R C H I P E L A G O

Borro (Buru)

Amboyna (Ambon)

Banda

Goram

Sumatra: visited from Nov. 1861-Jan. 1862

Java Sea

(E A S T

I N D I E S)

Macassar

Banda Sea

Kai Islands

Dobo

Batavia: visited from July-Oct. 1861

Batavia (Jakarta)

Madura Strait

Madura

Sunda Strait

Java

Surabaya

Flores Sea

Wetar

Tanimbar Islands

Aru Islands

Aru Islands: major habitat of birds of paradise, visited Jan.-June 1857

Indian Ocean

Bali

Lombok

Comodo

Sumbawa

Flores

Alor

Sumba

Timor

Timor Sea

Arafura Sea

Lombok and Bali: visited from June-July 1856

Kupang

0 200 400 600 kms
0 100 200 300 400 miles

WALLACE'S expeditions in the Malay Archipelago in the mid-19th century held no commercial or imperial ambition. Their importance lay, rather, in the great contribution they made to scientific advance. Alfred Russel Wallace ranks among the greatest scientific travellers of the 19th century. Having undertaken a major expedition to the Amazon region between 1848-52, in early 1854 he set off for the eastern seas, arriving in Singapore in April. He spent the following eight years travelling through and living in the islands of the Malay Archipelago – Borneo, Java and, most importantly, the islands of the eastern archipelago, including the Celebes, Ternate, Ceram, and the Kai and Aru Islands. During this time he amassed a collection of 125,000 insect and animal specimens, many of species then unknown. He also observed the magnificent birds of paradise in the eastern archipelago, and the orang-utan on Borneo. He returned to London in 1862, and his account of his travels was published in 1869. It remains a classic of natural history and travel.

The Malay Archipelago is dedicated to Charles Darwin. Indeed, quite independently of Darwin, Wallace, too, developed the concept of the evolution of species by natural selection, and his name deserves to rank with that of Darwin in this field. Important here was a scientific paper, 'On the Tendency of Varieties to Depart Indefinitely from the Original Type', written by Wallace during a stay on Ternate in February 1858 and sent to Darwin in England. This, together with papers by Darwin, was read at a meeting of the Linnean Society in London on 1 July 1858. Although poorly received at the time, the papers established the principle of natural selection.

A central element in Wallace's work in the Malay Archipelago – and in his discovery in 1858 of natural selection – was his observation that a dramatic change in fauna occurs in the middle of the archipelago. In the eastern archipelago, mammals, birds and insects were of Australian form; in the western part, Asian. Therefore the western part of the archipelago, Wallace argued, was a separated portion of the Asian landmass; the eastern part, the fragmentary continuation of a former Pacific continent. Thus separated in earlier ages, the fauna on these two component parts of the archipelago had evolved in quite distinctive ways. The line marking this division is called, in his honour, the Wallace Line. Wallace's views as to the precise location of the line within the archipelago changed with time; indeed the location and nature of the demarcation have remained matters of considerable conjecture among zoologists and, to a lesser extent, botanists, while they have accepted the central importance of Wallace's concept.

The Mekong River expedition, by contrast, was motivated largely by imperial ambitions. It left Saigon, the capital of the new French colony of Cochin China, on 5 June 1866. It was led by Commander Ernest-Marc-Louis de Gonzague Doudart de Lagrée, who had recently spent more than two years as the French representative at the Cambodian court, and included Francis Garnier, a young naval officer. The Mekong rises in Tibet, runs north–south through the western extremity of China, and then through Laos, Cambodia and Cochin China to discharge into the South China Sea, 2,800 miles from its source. The Mekong is a great river, not simply in its length but in its huge volume. For trading interests and administrators in French Cochin China, it offered the prospect of commercial access from French territory to China and its fabled markets.

For the expedition making its way up the great river from Pnom Penh in the middle of 1866, that prospect soon evaporated when fierce rapids and plunging falls were encountered. The expedition pressed on, however, sustained, unreasonably, by the hope that ways would be found to make the river navigable, and occupied by the tasks of mapping its course and recording their observations. The expedition reached Vientiane in March 1867, making its way to the royal capital of Laos, Luang Prabang, the following month. From there it headed for the border and into China. But the group had been much weakened by illness. On 12 March 1868, Doudart de Lagrée died at Hui-tse, while other members of the expedition were away to the west. They made their way out of China through I-pin, Hankow and Shanghai, and from there to Saigon which was reached on 29 June 1868. Though it had failed in its main objective, the Mekong River expedition had nonetheless opened up another prospect: commercial access to China by means of the Red River in Tongking. French imperial ambitions were now directed towards the extension of French rule north from Cochin China.

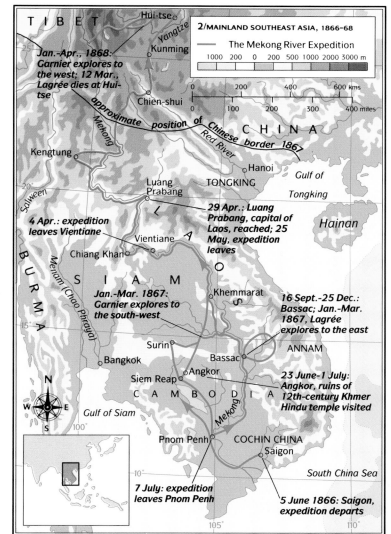

B LEFT *The rapids and sharp ravines of the Mekong River were encountered by the French Mekong River expedition only a short distance from the Cambodian capital, Pnom Penh. Hopes that the river would prove a practical trade route to China from French Cochin China were shortlived.*
2 RIGHT *The French expedition followed the Mekong from near its mouths in the Cochin China delta through Cambodia, into Laos and then into China. Members of the party also undertook a series of short exploratory excursions away from the main route.*

2/MAINLAND SOUTHEAST ASIA, 1866-68
The Mekong River Expedition

Jan.-Apr., 1868: Garnier explores to the west; 12 Mar., Lagrée dies at Hui-tse

29 Apr.: Luang Prabang, capital of Laos, reached; 25 May, expedition leaves

4 Apr.: expedition leaves Vientiane

Jan.-Mar. 1867: Garnier explores to the south-west

16 Sept.-25 Dec.: Bassac; Jan.-Mar. 1867, Lagrée explores to the east

23 June-1 July: Angkor, ruins of 12th-century Khmer Hindu temple visited

7 July: expedition leaves Pnom Penh

5 June 1866: Saigon, expedition departs

BEYOND THE reach of traditional technology and of un-aided human intrepidity lay the most challenging envir-onments explorers faced: the polar regions; the barely accessible heights and depths of the earth; and worlds dimly visible or speculatively inferred in space. With the penetration of these strongholds of nature, exploration has undergone four roughly simultaneous transformations of character.

First, it has become dependent on post-industrial technolo-gy. One of the remarkable lessons of this book so far has been that throughout almost the entire history of world exploration traditional technology sufficed for explorers' needs. For the first 100 years after the start of the industrial era, the main innovations in technology tended to make exploration easier without greatly extending its potential range. The arenas of exploration entered in the present century, however, have demanded new resources and new techniques.

Secondly, exploration has penetrated untrodden environ-ments for the first time in recorded history. The exploration of polar ice or of the ocean bed is qualitatively different from

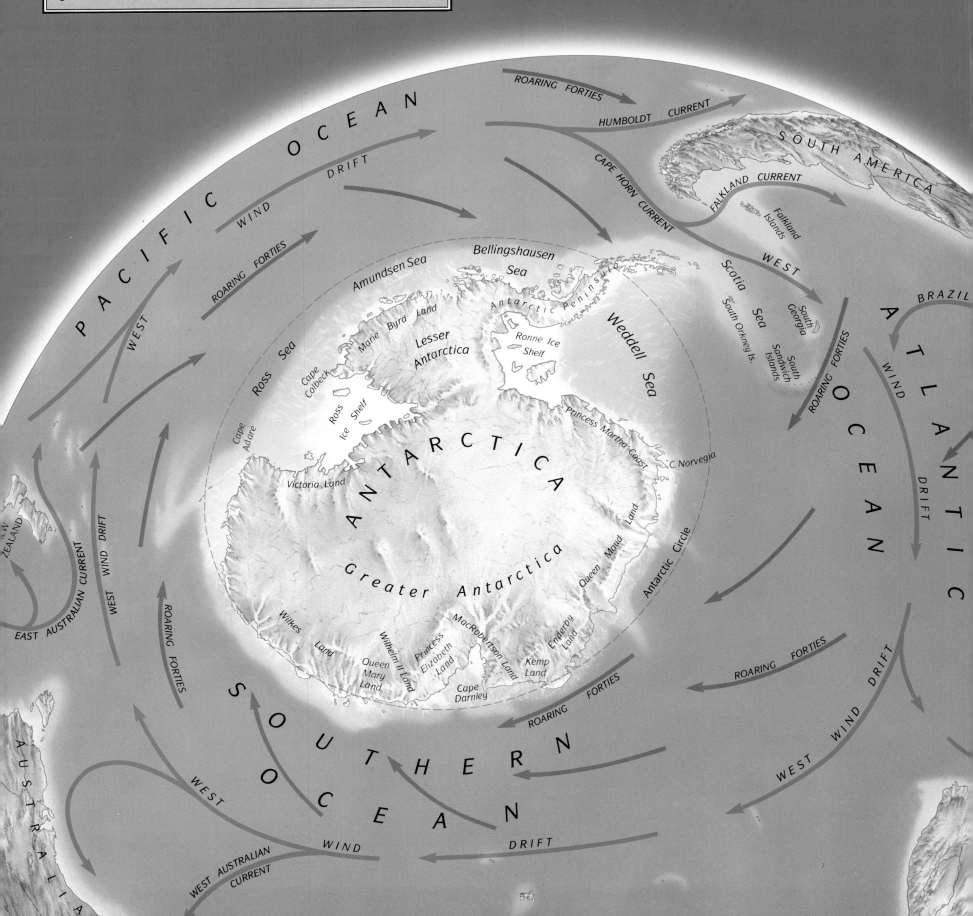

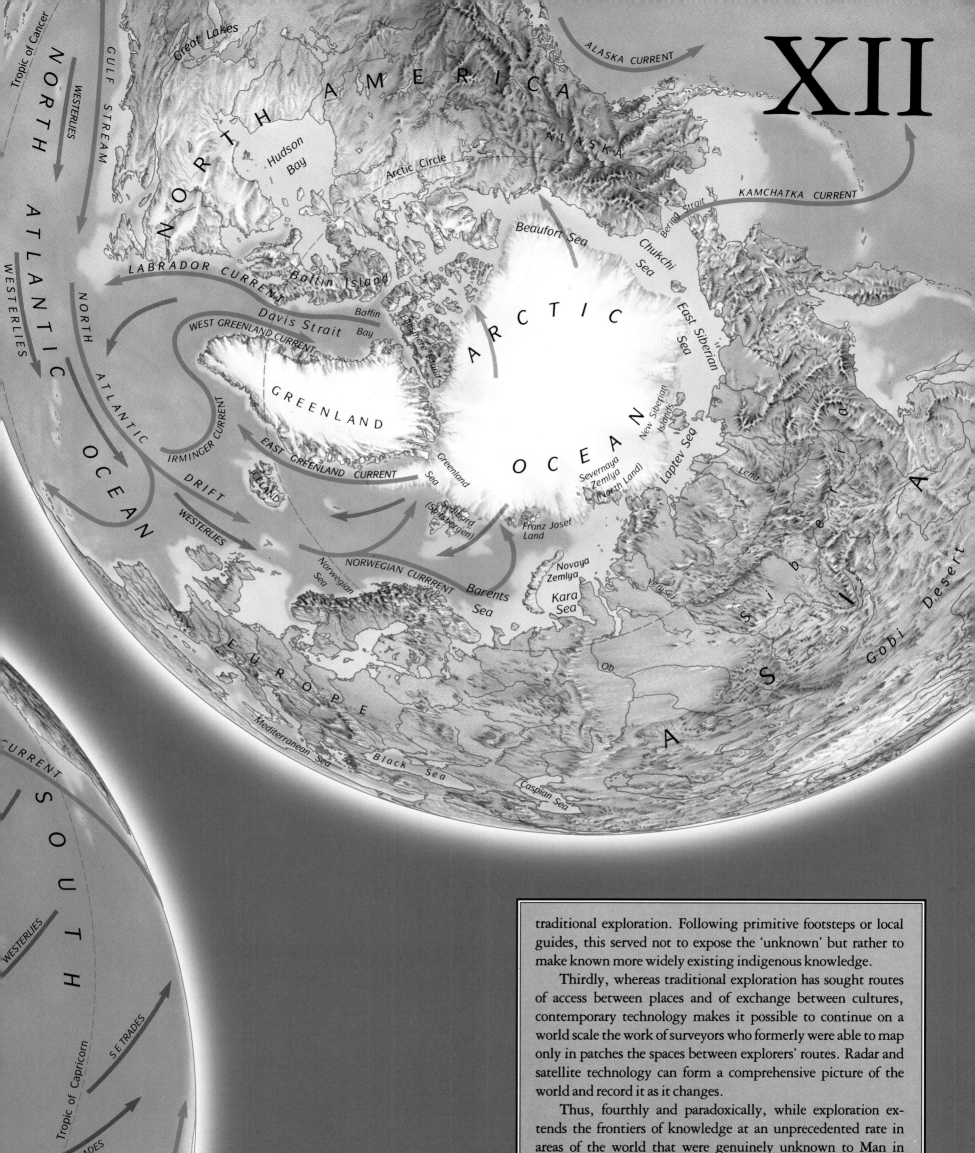

traditional exploration. Following primitive footsteps or local guides, this served not to expose the 'unknown' but rather to make known more widely existing indigenous knowledge.

Thirdly, whereas traditional exploration has sought routes of access between places and of exchange between cultures, contemporary technology makes it possible to continue on a world scale the work of surveyors who formerly were able to map only in patches the spaces between explorers' routes. Radar and satellite technology can form a comprehensive picture of the world and record it as it changes.

Thus, fourthly and paradoxically, while exploration extends the frontiers of knowledge at an unprecedented rate in areas of the world that were genuinely unknown to Man in previous eras, the use of remote-sensing and robot-craft has stripped exploration of its traditional sense of adventure, which derived, more than anything else, from the explorers' direct reliance on their own senses in 'discoveries' which could only be imagined until they were actually experienced. Challenges in exploration remain, but they will never again have to be faced with the uncertainty that daunted or inspired the explorers of the past.

46

THE POLAR REGIONS
FROM 1596

THE 'CENTRAL' ARCTIC comprises those regions lying to the north of about 75°N and includes the Arctic Ocean, the extreme north of Greenland, the Svalbard archipelago and the northernmost islands of the Russian and Canadian Arctic. It is one of the most hostile and inaccessible areas of the globe. Most of it has never had an indigenous population – although small groups of Inuit have occasionally settled in northernmost Greenland and the Canadian Arctic islands since the third millennium BC. Otherwise, the region's harsh climate and winter darkness deterred all potential settlers, while the dense drifting sea ice of the Arctic Ocean made both the seas and islands inaccessible to commercial hunters and to explorers seeking a navigable northern passage to the Orient. All these groups quickly learned to limit their activities to the more open waters of the continental margins, generally to the south of 75°N. It was not until the late 19th century, when new motives of scientific discovery and the symbolic conquest of the Pole began to supplant the primarily commercial motives of hunters and passage-seekers, and when steam-powered ships replaced sailing vessels, that the exploration of the central Arctic began in earnest.

ANTARCTICA is the most inhospitable and inaccessible of all continents. Its predominant feature is a vast and slowly moving ice sheet which covers nearly 99 per cent of the land area at an average depth of over 6,000 feet and which in places spills from the land into the sea to form huge floating ice shelves. Surrounding the continent is the Southern Ocean, which encircles the world in sub-Antarctic latitudes. Much of it is covered by pack ice, which presents a severe hazard to shipping in summer, and in winter thickens and extends northward to present an almost impenetrable barrier. All these circumstances combined to protect Antarctica from any incursion by man until very recent times, though Rarotongan legends suggest that Polynesian voyagers may have sailed as far south as the frozen ocean in the 7th century AD. Even the small groups of relatively temperate islands on the fringes of the Southern Ocean remained free from human occupation until the arrival of sealers and whalers in the 19th century. The continent of Antarctica itself, though often sighted, and sometimes landed on, during the 19th century, resisted exploration until this century. It still has no permanent population, though a shifting population of around 2,500 scientists occupy about 50 research stations.

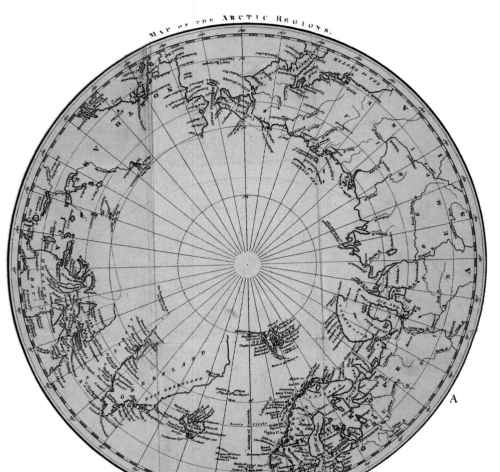

A LEFT *John Barrow's map of 1818, with an almost empty central Arctic region, highlights how little Arctic Ocean exploration had advanced before the 19th century. The main exception was the Svalbard archipelago.*
B BELOW *Gerard van Keulen's map of Svalbard, c.1707, demonstrates the already extensive knowledge of the archipelago, the result chiefly of visits by British and Dutch whalers.*

THE ARCTIC An important exception to the general inaccessibility of the central Arctic was Svalbard (Spitsbergen), where the sea is kept partially ice-free by the warm waters of the Gulf Stream. It was discovered by Dutchman Willem Barents in 1596, and became the main base for a new European whaling industry from 1611. By 1710, whalers had mapped most of its coasts.

Whalers in the 18th century occasionally reported reaching improbably high latitudes – typically 82° to 84°N – in open water north of Svalbard. These reports gave rise to theories of an 'open polar sea', suggesting a largely ice-free Arctic Ocean, which in turn led several British and Russian naval expeditions between 1765 and 1818 to seek a passage across the ocean to the Bering Strait. All were quickly stopped by ice close to

1 BELOW Most of the New Siberian Islands were discovered by the hunters Ivan Lyakhov and Ivan Sannikov between 1770 and 1806. Systematic exploration and mapping of the islands was undertaken by Gedenshtrom and Pshenitsin, 1808-11, and Anzhu, 1820-23.

Svalbard. In 1827, William Parry, suspecting a permanent ice cover, tried to reach the Pole from Svalbard using boats mounted on sledge runners. He reached only 82°45′N, but, as expected, he found mainly ice. After that, British explorers turned their attention to the more attainable goal of the Northwest Passage (*see* ch.23). In Russia, too, explorers were disillusioned with the prospect of Arctic Ocean navigation and began instead to investigate the islands on the fringes of the ocean (*see* ch.32). Russian hunters had been familiar with south-western Novaya Zemlya since at least the 14th century, and with some of the New Siberian Islands (Novosibirskiye Ostrova) since the 1770s. In the first half of the 19th century, scientific expeditions mapped the unexplored northern and eastern areas of both island groups.

When other nations entered the field of Arctic exploration after 1850, it was the strangely tenacious notion of the open polar sea which attracted them. The main proponent of the theory was the German geographer August Petermann, who urged navigators to explore the Arctic Ocean in previously untested areas. As a result, a series of American expeditions led by Elisha Kane (1853-55), Isaac Hayes (1860-61) and Charles Hall (1871-73) explored northward from Baffin Bay, and in so doing discovered the important Smith Sound route towards the ocean, through the channel separating Greenland and Ellesmere Island. The British Arctic Expedition of 1875-76 completed the exploration of the route as far as the Arctic Ocean, but predictably found the ocean covered with ice. During it, A.H. Markham sledged to a new record of 83°20′N.

Petermann's influence lay behind two other major expeditions. In 1872-74 the Austro-Hungarian expedition of Weyprecht and Payer sought a route between Svalbard and Novaya Zemlya, and discovered the remote islands of Franz Josef Land. In 1879-81 the American, George de Long, tried to cross the

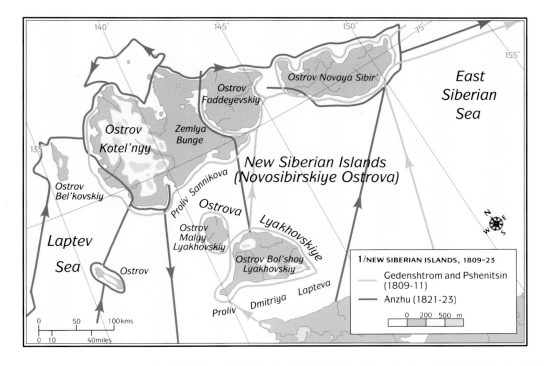

2 RIGHT Exploration of the Arctic has been by many different means. Parry (1827) used sledge-boats of his own invention; Nares (1876, see map 5) used man-hauled sledges. Nansen, Cagni and Peary all favoured dog-sledges. Amundsen (1926) used the airship Norge to make the first crossing of the ocean; Commander W.R. Anderson (1958) made the first crossing by nuclear-powered submarine (not shown); Wally Herbert reverted to dog-sledges to make the first surface crossing. Byrd (1926) pioneered the use of aircraft. Severnyy Polyus and T-3 (Bravo) were scientific stations built on drifting ice floes. Jeannette and Fram, one accidentally trapped in the ice and the other deliberately so, and the icebreaker Arktika proved in their different ways that even ships could explore where once they could not penetrate.

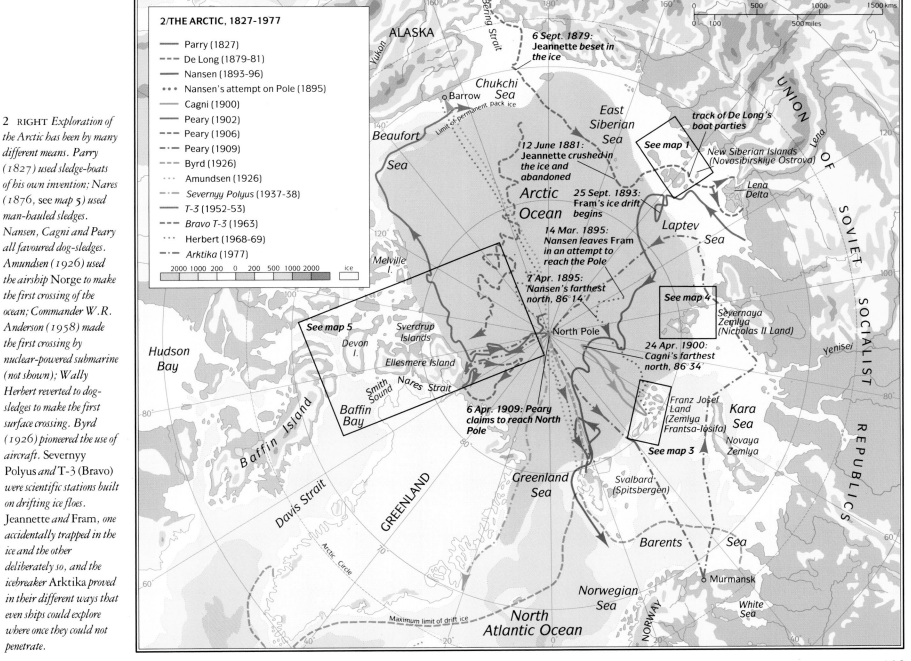

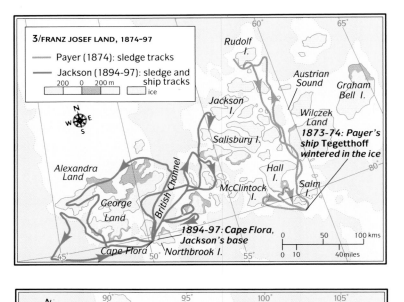

3/FRANZ JOSEF LAND, 1874-97
— Payer (1874): sledge tracks
— Jackson (1894-97): sledge and ship tracks

Rudolf I.

Austrian Sound

Graham Bell I.

Jackson I.

Wilczek Land

Salisbury I.

1873-74: Payer's ship Tegetthoff wintered in the ice

Alexandra Land

George Land

British Channel

Hall I.

McClintock I.

Salm I.

1894-97: Cape Flora, Jackson's base Northbrook I.

Cape Flora

4/SEVERNAYA ZEMLYA, 1910-32
— Ushakov (1930-32)

Ostrov Shmidta

Ostrov Komsomolets

Ostrov Pioner

Ostrov Domashniy

Ostrov Domashniy: Ushakov's base camp

1913: east coast explored from Russian icebreakers Taymyr and Vaygach

Ostrov Oktyabr'skoy Revolyutsii

Laptev Sea

Proliv Shokal'skogo

Kara Sea

Ostrov Bol'shevik

Proliv Vil'kitskogo

5/QUEEN ELIZABETH ISLANDS, 1875-1902
Nares (1875-76)
— ships' tracks
- - - sledge tracks
Sverdrup (1898-1902)
— ship's tracks
- - - sledge tracks

Arctic Ocean

12 May 1876: Markham's attempt on Pole; reaches 83°20'N

1875-76: winter quarters of HMS Alert

Lincoln Sea

Robeson Channel

GREENLAND

Kane Basin

Beaufort Sea

Queen Elizabeth Islands

Sverdrup Islands

Axel Heiberg Island

Ellef Ringnes I.

Amund Ringnes I.

Cornwall I.

Ellesmere Island

Smith Sound

Nares Strait

Parry Islands

Bathurst Island

Wellington Channel

Devon Island

1899-1900: Harbour Fiord, winter quarters of Fram

Lancaster Sound

Baffin Bay

Viscount Melville Sound

Somerset Island

Bylot Island

Baffin Island

3 LEFT The exploration of Franz Josef Land was an international accomplishment. The Austro-Hungarian expedition of Weyprecht and von Payer (1872-74) made the first discoveries; the Englishman F.G. Jackson explored the western part of the archipelago. Other islands were discovered by Nansen (Norwegian), 1893-97, the duke of Abruzzi (Italian), 1899-1900, and the American Walter Wellman (1898-99).
4 LEFT The exploration of Severnaya Zemlya was entirely Russian. Its eastern side was discovered by the Russian Hydrographic Expedition, 1910-15; G.A. Ushakov (1930-32) mapped the remainder of the archipelago. 5 RIGHT The exploration of Ellesmere Island and the Sverdrup Islands almost completed the discovery and mapping of the Canadian Arctic archipelago. The British Arctic Expedition (1875-76) explored the north coast of Ellesmere Island, from where it also tried to reach the North Pole. Otto Sverdrup's Norwegian Fram expedition, 1898-1902, explored the Sverdrup Islands.

Arctic Ocean from the Bering Strait. His ship, *Jeannette*, became beset by the ice, drifted and sank; the crew retreated by boat to the Lena delta, where many died. With that, all hope of an open polar sea finally vanished. However, de Long also unwittingly ushered in a new age of scientific investigation. Wreckage from the *Jeannette* drifted to Greenland, prompting the Norwegian scientist Fridtjof Nansen to conjecture that a suitably strengthened ship might safely do likewise. In 1893, he deliberately beset his ship *Fram* with the ice near the New Siberian Islands; in 1896 *Fram* was freed off Svalbard. The existence of a permanent ice cover was demonstrated.

As the scientific study of the Arctic developed, so the attainment of the Pole itself began to grasp the popular imagination. Sponsors in America, Sweden and elsewhere were encouraged to mount expeditions with no object other than the Pole. Most failed badly, though one of the more successful was the duke of Abruzzi's Italian expedition, during which Umberto Cagni sledged to 86°34'N from Franz Josef Land in 1900. The most persistent Pole-seeker was the American Robert Peary who, after many years' exploration in Greenland, spent a decade perfecting his sledging techniques with the sole aim of reaching the Pole. He made four attempts, reaching 83°50'N in 1900, 84°17'N in 1902, 87°06'N in 1906 and, he maintained, the Pole itself in 1909. But his triumph was clouded by the simultaneous claim of another American, Frederick Cook, to have reached the Pole in 1908. Cook's claim was disbelieved almost from the start, and rapidly came to be dismissed as a fraudulent one. The validity of Robert Peary's claim, meanwhile, remains controversial.

Whether he succeeded or not, the 'conquest' of the Pole did not end with Peary. With the coming of new developments in aviation, shipping and sledging, the 20th century has seen no shortage of new 'conquests': by airship and by airplane (Roald Amundsen and Robert Byrd) in 1926; by submarine

(USS *Nautilus*) in 1958; by snowmobile (Plaisted) in 1968; and by ship (the Soviet icebreaker *Arktika*) in 1977.

The real importance of 20th-century exploration lies not in the symbolic conquest of the Pole, but in the enormous advances made in scientific exploration and discovery. At the beginning of the century, there was still land to be discovered around the Arctic Ocean. The Norwegian Otto Sverdrup discovered several large islands (now the Sverdrup Islands) on the Canadian side in 1900-2, thus almost completing the discovery of the Canadian Arctic archipelago. Peary mapped the north coast of Greenland in 1900, and the Dane Mylius-Erichsen completed the outline mapping of the north-east coast of Greenland between 1906 and 1908. The last land in the Arctic Ocean to be discovered, the archipelago of Severnaya Zemlya, was explored in 1930-32 by G.A. Ushakov.

Also in the 1930s, Soviet scientists pioneered a new method of exploring the ocean itself by establishing manned stations on large, stable floes of drifting ice. The first ice station, *Severnyy Polyus 1* (North Pole 1) was established near the Pole in 1937; it was evacuated off East Greenland in 1938. World War II interrupted research, but the Soviets established a second ice station, *SP-2*, in 1950. So successful have these stations proved that the Soviet Union has continued to replace evacuated stations with new ones; the most recent, *SP-31*, was set up in 1988. America has also made frequent use of ice stations; its first, *T-3*, was established in 1952-53 and was re-occupied as ice station *Bravo* from 1957 to 1960 and from 1963 to 1971. With additional research being conducted by submarine, ship, aircraft and satellite, the Arctic Ocean and its thin, but once impregnable covering of ice, is being investigated more thoroughly than ever before. As the greenhouse effect threatens the very existence of that ice layer, the need for a comprehensive understanding of the Arctic Ocean is greater than it has ever been.

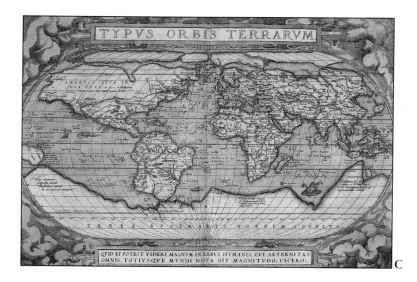

C

D

C ABOVE *Speculation about the southern polar regions varied from the huge landmass of Ortelius's Terra Australis in his 1570 world map to (**D** ABOVE RIGHT) the expanse of sea on Munster's 1545 world map.*

E

E LEFT *Whalers and sealers, such as these in this 1822 view of Crozet Is., played a leading role in the discovery of the Antarctic islands.* **F** BELOW *Bellingshausen's 1820 sketch map of Princess Martha Coast is the earliest map of the Antarctic continent.*

THE ANTARCTIC

THE ANTARCTIC The theory of a great frozen zone around the South Pole was proposed by Greek geographers in the 5th century BC. It was a notion that was accepted with little refinement for a further 2,000 years. By the Middle Ages there was speculation that the frozen southern zone might be occupied by a continental landmass, the 'Terra Australis' of some 16th-century world maps. It was not, however, until the 18th century that the first tentative approaches in search of the supposed southern continent were made. The Frenchman Bouvet de Lozier probed the fringes of the Antarctic pack ice in the South Atlantic in 1738-39, and may have discovered Bouvet Island. In 1771-72, two other Frenchmen, de Kerguelen-Trémarec and Captain Marion-Dufresne, discovered the small sub-Antarctic groups of the Kerguelen Islands, the Prince Edward Islands and the Crozet Islands. But the most important advance was made by James Cook in 1772-75 (*see* ch. 35). Circumnavigating the world at high southern latitudes, he discovered the South Sandwich Islands, but was unable to penetrate the pack ice. If a continental landmass existed, it must lie within the pack ice.

In the 1790s, American and British sealers and traders began to visit the sub-Antarctic islands. They discovered more small islands and groups (Macquarie Island in 1810; the South Shetland Islands in 1819) and reduced further the area where a continent might be found. The discovery of the landmass itself finally came in 1820 when three separate expeditions recorded sightings. Though Bransfield's British expedition and Palmer's American expedition both glimpsed parts of the Antarctic Peninsula, priority is usually accorded to Fabian Bellingshausen, whose Russian expedition sighted an ice-covered area of Princess Martha Coast in January 1820.

Though the years 1819-23 marked the peak of Antarctic sealing, whaling and other commercial vessels visited the region throughout the 19th century, in the process revealing the remaining sub-Antarctic islands (notably the South Orkneys in 1821) and parts of the continental coastline, including Enderby Land in 1831, Kemp Land in 1833 and additional stretches of the Antarctic Peninsula.

In the mid-19th century a further impetus was given to Antarctic exploration by advances in geomagnetic science and the need for magnetic data from the far south. Expeditions from France, America and Britain were accordingly despatched. All made important discoveries: the Frenchman Dumont d'Urville discovered Terre Adélie (1837-40); Charles Wilkes of the U.S. Navy discovered Wilkes Land (1838-42); and James Ross of the Royal Navy discovered Victoria Land and the Ross Ice Shelf (1839-43).

Few advances in Antarctic exploration followed for nearly 60 years: by the end of the century even the outline of the continent was still only vaguely known and no inland penetration had been attempted. The start of intensive exploration on the continent came in 1895 with the Sixth International Geographical Congress, which identified Antarctica as the last great challenge for explorers. The two decades that followed have rightly been labelled the 'heroic age' of Antarctic exploration; it was a period that witnessed extraordinary feats of endurance as well as a great leap forward in knowledge of the continent.

Between 1897 and 1917, 16 expeditions from nine countries were launched. The first, de Gerlache's Belgian expedition of 1897-99 explored around the Antarctic Peninsula; its ship,

F

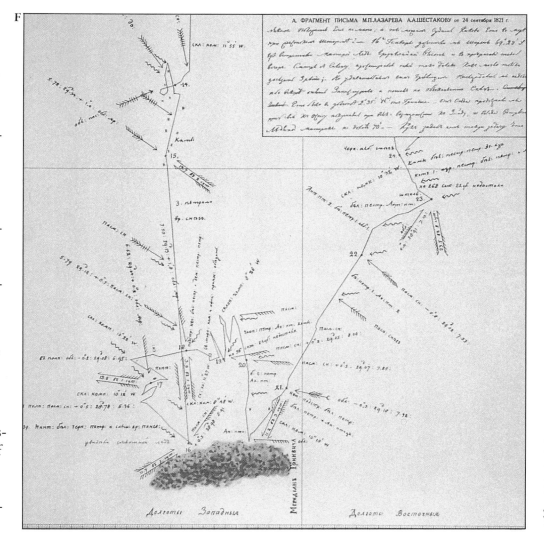

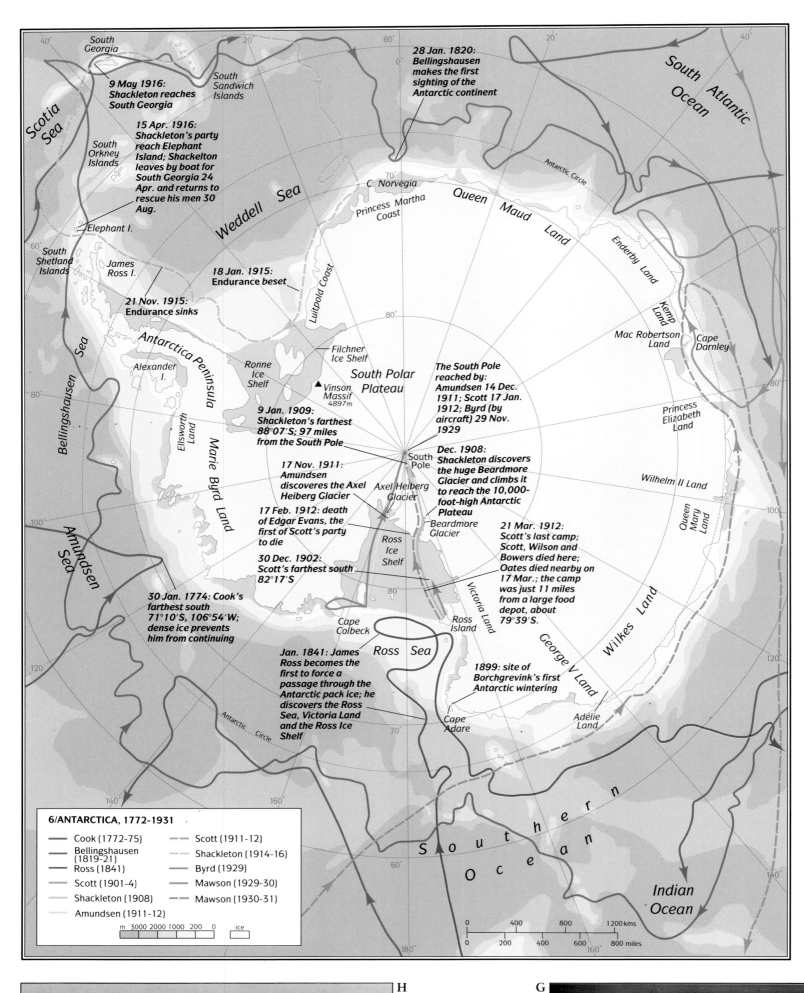

6/ANTARCTICA, 1772-1931

— Cook (1772-75)
— Bellingshausen (1819-21)
— Ross (1841)
— Scott (1901-4)
— Shackleton (1908)
— Amundsen (1911-12)
- - - Scott (1911-12)
- - - Shackleton (1914-16)
— Byrd (1929)
— Mawson (1929-30)
- - - Mawson (1930-31)

m 3000 2000 1000 200 0   ice

28 Jan. 1820: Bellingshausen makes the first sighting of the Antarctic continent

9 May 1916: Shackleton reaches South Georgia

15 Apr. 1916: Shackleton's party reach Elephant Island; Shackleton leaves by boat for South Georgia 24 Apr. and returns to rescue his men 30 Aug.

18 Jan. 1915: Endurance beset

21 Nov. 1915: Endurance sinks

9 Jan. 1909: Shackleton's farthest 88°07'S; 97 miles from the South Pole

17 Nov. 1911: Amundsen discoveres the Axel Heiberg Glacier

17 Feb. 1912: death of Edgar Evans, the first of Scott's party to die

30 Dec. 1902: Scott's farthest south 82°17'S

30 Jan. 1774: Cook's farthest south 71°10'S, 106°54'W; dense ice prevents him from continuing

Jan. 1841: James Ross becomes the first to force a passage through the Antarctic pack ice; he discovers the Ross Sea, Victoria Land and the Ross Ice Shelf

The South Pole reached by: Amundsen 14 Dec. 1911; Scott 17 Jan. 1912; Byrd (by aircraft) 29 Nov. 1929

Dec. 1908: Shackleton discovers the huge Beardmore Glacier and climbs it to reach the 10,000-foot-high Antarctic Plateau

21 Mar. 1912: Scott's last camp; Scott, Wilson and Bowers died here; Oates died nearby on 17 Mar.; the camp was just 11 miles from a large food depot, about 79°39'S.

1899: site of Borchgrevink's first Antarctic wintering

0 400 800 1200 kms
0 200 400 600 800 miles

6 LEFT *The coast of Antarctica was first sighted only in 1820. The first landing was in 1821 and the first major inland penetration (Shackleton's) in 1908. The last major coastal features of a continental scale were discovered only in 1976 and the bed rock beneath the ice mapped by 1980.*

H

G

G LEFT *Scott's dispirited party stand by a tent abandoned by Amundsen at the South Pole in January 1912. Though beaten to the Pole, Scott had at least the meagre consolation of confirming that both parties had reached it.* H RIGHT *The Vinson Massif, the highest peak in Antarctica, was climbed only in 1966.*

Belgica, was the first to winter in the Antarctic. Borchgrevink's British *Southern Cross* expedition of 1898 to 1900 made the first wintering ashore on the continent, in Victoria Land. Between 1901 and 1904, Robert Scott's British National Antarctic Expedition made the first extensive land explorations in Antarctica. Scott also made the first extended sledge journey towards the South Pole, reaching 82°17′S. In the same period, German, Swedish, French and Scottish expeditions explored Wilhelm II Land, the east and west coasts of the Antarctic Peninsula and the Weddell Sea respectively.

More single-minded attempts to reach the Pole itself began with Ernest Shackleton's *Nimrod* expedition of 1907-9. In an epic of polar exploration, made in the face of severe technical shortcomings, Shackleton crossed the Ross Ice Shelf, made the first ascent onto the vast ice sheet of the Polar Plateau and sledged to a point only 97 miles from the Pole. He was followed in 1910 by Scott and the Norwegian Roald Amundsen. Scott's expedition on *Terra Nova* went equipped for a wide-ranging scientific and exploratory programme, of which the Pole journey was only a part. Amundsen's *Fram* expedition had the Pole alone in its sights. After wintering at opposite ends of the Ross Ice Shelf, both parties set out on what had now become a race for the Pole: Amundsen's team of Arctic veterans skilfully using dogs to haul their sledges; Scott's team, far less experienced, laboriously man-hauling theirs. Predictably, experience triumphed: Amundsen reached the Pole on 14 December 1911; Scott arrived over a month later and his exhausted five-man party perished during the return journey, a journey, as revealed in Scott's diary, that nonetheless provided one of the enduring classics of exploration literature.

Other nations continued to make significant advances in exploration. W. Filchner's *Deutschland* expedition of 1911-12 discovered the Luitpold Coast and Filchner Ice Shelf, while Douglas Mawson's Australasian Antarctic Expedition of 1911-14 discovered George V Land and Queen Mary Land.

A fittingly heroic climax to the period was provided by Shackleton's Imperial Trans-Antarctic Expedition of 1914-17. The expedition was unable even to begin its proposed crossing of the continent after its ship, *Endurance*, was crushed in the ice of the Weddell Sea, but Shackleton's subsequent 800-mile open-boat journey to South Georgia to alert rescuers to the plight of his stricken crew (all of whom were saved) ranks among the most stirring episodes of exploration history.

Large-scale exploration resumed in 1928 when two expeditions sailed for Antarctica. Between them, they introduced a new element to polar exploration: aerial exploration. The Australian Hubert Wilkins made the first flights over the continent, surveying the Antarctic Peninsula. The American Robert Byrd took three aircraft and used them to explore the region east of the Ross Ice Shelf, where he discovered Marie Byrd Land. Byrd led three further expeditions to Antarctica, in 1933-35, 1939-41 and 1946-47, extending his explorations in and around Byrd Land. Other notable exploration in the same period was conducted by Mawson's British, Australian and New Zealand Antarctic Research Expedition of 1929-31, which discovered Mac Robertson Land and Princess Elizabeth Land, and by a long series of Norwegian expeditions promoted by Lars Christensen, which discovered and explored Queen Maud Land and other areas between 1927 and 1937.

After World War II there was a significant increase in international activity in Antarctica. A further stimulus to research and exploration was provided by the International Geophysical Year of 1957-58, during which 12 nations operated simultaneously from about 50 base stations. In 1961, these same nations came together as signatories of the Antarctic Treaty, which served to demilitarize Antarctica, set aside all territorial claims and preserve the continent for scientific research. Under the Treaty's regime of international collaboration, basic research and detailed geographical surveying have continued at a high level of activity.

POLAR SLEDGING

WHEN IN the mid-19th century explorers first reached high Arctic latitudes they turned to native sledges in designing their own. The most suitable was the *komatik*. Developed over 2,000 years ago by the Inuit, it consisted of two narrow wooden runners joined by cross-slats and lashed with leather thongs. Light and flexible, it could also be pulled by dogs, leaving the driver free to manoeuvre it.

The first to adapt the komatik were the British. But in 'improving' the native design, its virtues were discarded. Only the shape was retained. Their sledge was a heavy and rigid hardwood structure, with nailed joints and iron-shod runners which had no 'glide'. Dogs were replaced by teams of sailors, who found hauling their unwieldy sledges brutally exacting. Other novelties were added: sails assisted travel downwind as in (**D**); and each sledge bore its own name, motto and flag to encourage team spirit (**B**). This cont-

rived worthiness of shared hardship and *esprit de corps* gave rise to a proud British sledging tradition which was as perverse as it was long lasting. In 1911, while Amundsen was gliding to the South Pole with dog-sledges, Captain Scott's doomed party laboured in man-harnesses, brandishing sledge flags and defiant mottoes.

The sledge designed by the Norwegian Fridtjof Nansen for a crossing of the Greenland ice cap in 1888 (**C**), by contrast, reverted to the komatik principles. Nansen genuinely did improve it, however. His inspired innovation was to replace the narrow komatik runners with the broad ski-like runners of the traditional Norwegian sledge, the *skijælke*, which could cope with soft snow. The Nansen sledge remained in use in polar exploration for nearly 100 years, despite the development of motor sledges. V.E. Fuch's Commonwealth Trans-Antarctic Expedition, 1955-58, made free use of them (**A**), while the British Antarctic Survey did not discard them until the 1970s.

47
THE PRESENT
AND THE FUTURE

A LEFT *The 68,000-mile cruise of HMS* Challenger *in the 1870s largely initiated modern oceanography. Fifty volumes of scientific data resulted.* **B** BELOW *The ocean floor can be mapped from space by measuring its effect on the surface of the sea with radar. The mid-ocean ridges of the Atlantic and the gashes of the Pacific's trenches are conspicuous on this* Seasat *image.*

C TOP RIGHT *A chart of water temperatures in the Gulf of Mexico produced by a U.S. weather satellite. The warmest water is shown as red; cooler water is green and blue. The pool of warm water around Cuba (bottom right) is the source of the Gulf Stream.*

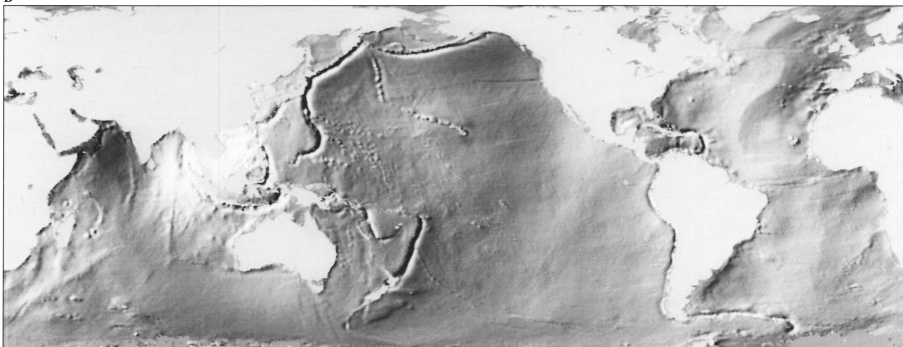

BY THE *late 20th century, the superficial exploration of the world could be said to be almost complete. The big unfinished agenda of recent times has been dominated by two tasks: monitoring of changes on the Earth's surface; and exploration of domains inpenetrable to earlier technology – the upper atmosphere, the deep oceans and the not-so-solid crust and core. Today, hourly variations in the weather, the unremitting impact of human activity, the contour-shaping processes that last for millions of years and even the almost infinitely ponderous phenomenon of continental drift can be mapped with earth-orbiting tools that observe the world continuously and comprehensively as a dynamic system.*

Yet satellite images have confirmed – not transformed – a world-map established for us by explorers and mapmakers who relied on traditional technologies. The explorers of the past were like artists executing a huge mural, unable to stand sufficiently far back to see it whole. By the late 18th century, with the aid of slowly developed techniques for finding longitude, measuring long distances and verifying the shape of the earth, a picture of the entire world other than the polar regions had been built up. When spacecraft held up a mirror to the earth and enabled human beings to see their planet for the first time, it looked exactly as they had formerly imagined.

In the late 20th century exploration has not only changed focus: its nature has changed. Exploration has become a high-technology business. Today's explorers, whatever hazards they face, know where they are going. As ventures out of this world take robot-craft to the farthest reaches of the Solar System, the romance of exploring in the age of Columbus will never be experienced again.

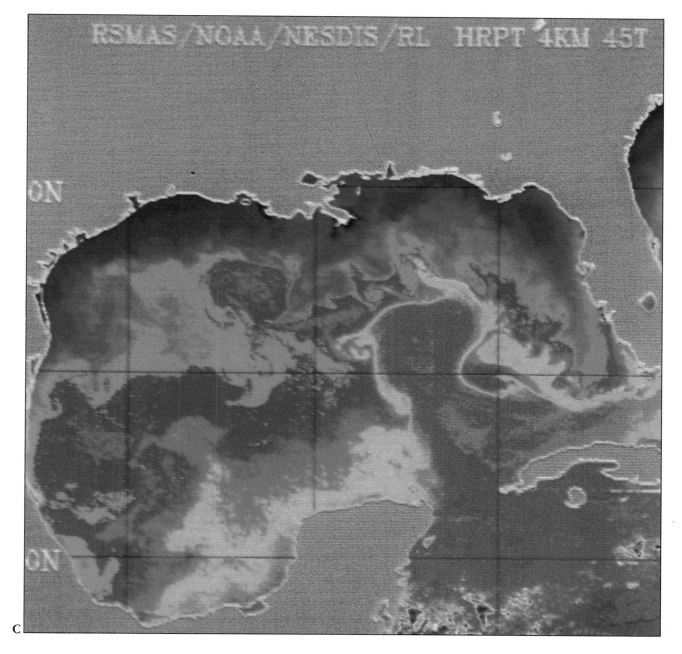

C

D

D ABOVE RIGHT *Giant tube worms, discovered in 1977 and typically six-feet long, are among the strangest inhabitants of the deep oceans. They feed on plant-like bacteria that grow not by sunlight but by geochemical energy released as hydrogen sulphide from vents in the ocean floor.* **E** RIGHT *Microscopic plants tinge the oceans' surface waters, enabling a Color Scanner to measure their growth from space. Coastal regions, coloured red and yellow, show the most life; the large purple expanses of the tropics are relatively barren.*

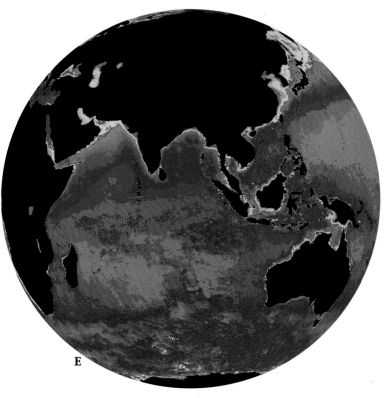

E

THOUGH much of the story of the world's exploration necessarily involves the navigation of its seas, until the middle of the 19th century the sea-bed itself was almost wholly unknown. Only the comparatively shallow waters of the continental shelf had been plumbed, by sounding leads, trawl nets and, from 1837, by divers in unwieldy suits.

Deep ocean basins cover most of the Earth's surface. They are filled with water with an average depth of two-and-a-half miles. Navigators who first crossed them knew only that their sounding leads reached 'no bottom'. With the laying of telegraph cables across the floor of the oceans in the mid-19th century, scientists became aware of the existence of huge undersea ridges in mid-ocean, and of life persisting at great depths. Deep-sea oceanography began in earnest with the world-wide cruise of the British research ship HMS *Challenger* in 1872-76. Discoveries by its scientists included the planet-wide layer of cold water that fills the ocean basins below its warmer surface, and strange nodules rich in metal ores.

Submersibles built to withstand enormous pressures have taken explorers to the ocean floor. Great scars known as trenches are the deepest features in the Earth's crust. In 1960 the bathyscaphe *Trieste*, piloted by the Swiss Jacques Piccard and Donald Walsh of the U.S. Navy, reached the ocean bed in the deepest of all, the Marianas Trench in the Pacific, more than seven-and-three-quarter miles beneath sea level. In the 1970s, the U.S. manned submersible *Alvin* discovered huge deposits of newly formed metal sulphide ores in the Pacific, as well as colonies of giant worms and other life forms, all nourished by the raw geochemical energy of the ocean floor. The development of advanced acoustic sounders (sonars) and complex lifting arms and grabs that can be operated from the surface via remote-controlled television cameras have since made human descents unnecessary for most purposes. It was technology of this kind that allowed a French and American team in 1985 to discover the wreck of the *Titanic* in the North Atlantic, lying

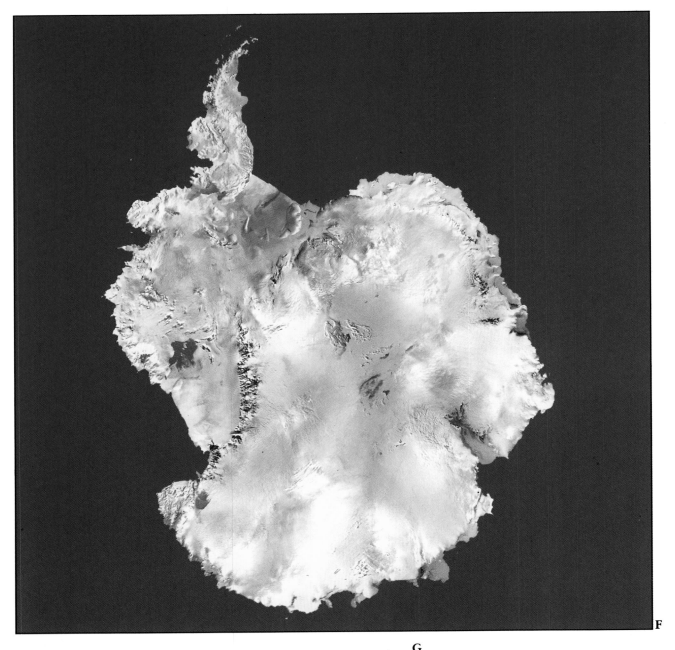

F LEFT *Antarctica was first laid bare by U.S. weather satellites. In this compilation of data from a number of satellite passes, the main ice-sheet covers the semi-circular region to the right. It is separated from the lesser ice-sheet that buries Western Antarctica (top left) by the Transantarctic Mountains.* **G** BELOW *This view of the U.S. Space Shuttle* Challenger *orbiting high above the Earth was taken by a camera in a remotely controlled pallet of instruments.* Challenger, *named after the 19th-century British survey vessel, exploded during a 1986 launch.*

two-and-a-half miles down.

Among the most significant discoveries of the nature of the ocean floor is that the continents are in perpetual motion about the face of the Earth. The sea-bed – the oceanic crust – renews itself at the mid-ocean ridges by pushing up from below, and destroys itself in the trenches, where it is forced back into the body of the Earth. The immense forces generated by this process push the continents around. It was magnetic surveys from surface ships and deep-sea drilling into the ocean floor that confirmed this cycle of renewal in the 1960s, but a graphic illustration of the process was provided by the American *Seasat* satellite in 1978 (see **B**), laying bare the topography of the deep sea-bed and the mechanisms of its ridges and trenches. Variations in local gravitational fields produce small humps and hollows in the surface of the sea that match the very much larger ridges and trenches below them. By taking a precise radar measurement of them, the *Seasat* produced, in effect, a picture of the sea-bed.

The problems associated with the study of the sea stem not just from its vastness and depth, but from the fact that, being a liquid, it is in a permanent state of flux. For example, oceanographers were slow to recognize the existence of powerful eddies in the oceans, the watery equivalent of storms. The abnormal temperatures they generate, however, make them conspicuous to satellites measuring sea temperatures (see **C**). Satellites can also produce continuously updated reports on weather over the oceans and on the pack-ice and icebergs of the polar seas. The pastures of the broad oceans, where small green plants grow in abundance, have long been sampled by research ships, but the first comprehensive seasonal charts of this living sea were produced by an orbiting Coastal Zone Color Scanner (see **E**).

While intense pressure – 960 times the weight of the atmosphere at sea level in the Marianas Trench, for example – was the danger in descents to the ocean floor, the thinness of the air and sub-zero temperatures were the principal hazards for

H

I

by revealing otherwise inaccessible terrain and by enabling photographs to be taken of it. High-precision airborne cameras, developed originally for taking pictures behind enemy lines during the First World War, initiated aerial photogrammetry as a valuable map-making aid, especially over remote regions. The first flight over the South Pole, made in 1929 by Richard Byrd (*see* ch.46), marked an early phase in the long-lasting aerial exploration of Antarctica. Even today, it is a continent better known from the air than from the ground. Airborne cameras and instruments of many kinds, applied worldwide, now observe visible light and other forms of radiation as well as the local gravity and magnetism of the Earth. Their applications are considerable, serving military, commercial and scientific aims alike.

Earth observation was also the first serious purpose of satellites in space. Even before the Soviet Union launched the first orbiting spacecraft, *Sputnik I*, in October 1957, the U.S. Air Force had planned an orbiting photo-reconnaissance system. As the military spacecraft of the Cold War drove the technology forward, civilian systems followed in their wake. Apart from recoverable cameras operated from manned spacecraft, civilian Earth-observing systems rely mainly on images and other data sent by radio from unmanned spacecraft. Typically, their orbits pass close to the Earth's poles, allowing them to see the whole world as it rotates beneath them. A number of important weather satellites orbit around the Equator, keeping pace with the Earth's rotation so that they watch the same regions continuously.

Satellites like these have transformed the study of the Earth's atmosphere, land surface and oceans, both locally and globally. The first weather satellite, used for observing clouds and other atmospheric phenomena from space, was *Tiros I*, launched in 1960. In 1972, *Landsat I* (or *ERTS*) pioneered the examination of geological structures, vegetation and land use

balloonists, whose flights, first made from the end of the 18th century, added an aerial dimension to exploration. Men fainted, in some cases died, from lack of oxygen and intense cold at great heights. But as the problems were understood, so the basic structure of the lower atmosphere, where temperatures decline until an abrupt warming at about 33,000 feet marks the base of the stratosphere, came to be charted. The first to penetrate the stratosphere were the Swiss balloonists August Piccard and Paul Kipler, who in 1931 ascended to 52,000 feet in a pressurized cabin.

Balloons and, later, powered aircraft made their own contributions to the exploration of the surface of the Earth, both

H and **I** ABOVE *The colours in these* Landsat *images of San Francisco were generated artificially to highlight particular features. The image on the left reveals algae in the waters of the Bay; that on the right shows urban areas as blue and vegetation as red. Both show the San Andreas fault slanting left from the bottom right-hand corners.*

J RIGHT *The living planet is portrayed as never before in a composite space image of plant activity on land and sea. It combines Color Scanner data of the oceans (where areas in red are the most fertile) with data from a U.S. weather satellite used to plot plant growth on land (where areas coloured green are the most fertile). The importance of such imagery is in monitoring seasonal changes.*

J

N FAR RIGHT *Neptune, pictured by* Voyager 2 *in 1989, can be considered the farthest point of human active exploration thus far.*

K RIGHT *Stationed over Africa, its orbit synchronized with the Earth's rotation,* Meteosat *generates images every half-hour from visible and infra-red light.* Meteosat *is Europe's contribution to the ring of geo-synchronous weather satellites that keeps the Earth under continuous observation.*

K

O FAR RIGHT BELOW *A composite image of Saturn and some of its moons as seen by* Voyager 1. *The remarkable diversity of the major planets' moons has been one of the surprises of interplanetary exploration.*

from space. In 1978, *Seasat* and *Nimbus* 7 initiated the oceanographic revolution mentioned earlier. These were all American developments, although the Soviet Union had similar but more secretive programmes. European, Japanese and Indian space agencies have launched Earth-observing satellites of their own. French *Spot* satellites give the most detailed civilian images available so far: they are capable of detecting objects 33 feet wide.

Oil companies employ satellite images in their search for new oil and gas fields. The U.N. Food and Agriculture Organization makes use of them in forecasting famine in Africa. Changes in river courses during floods can be mapped almost instantly by satellites. Similarly, the spread of urban development can be monitored. By the 1990s, concern that human activity might be overtaxing the Earth's environment gave added urgency to the observations from space, following, for example, the charting by *Nimbus* 7 of a hole in the ozone layer over Antarctica. Other satellites directly monitor pollution, the destruction of forests, the degradation of land and the effects of river mismanagement, of which the drying up of the Aral Sea in Soviet Central Asia is a graphic example.

Nonetheless, the most important payoff from Earth observation by satellites is likely to be of a more fundamental

L RIGHT *The U.S. landed six two-man parties on the Moon between 1969-72. Though intended partly to demonstrate the superiority of American technology, tangible scientific benefits also resulted. This picture is from the* Apollo 15 *mission in 1971, in which the first lunar buggy (far left) was used.*

L

M RIGHT *Two unmanned U.S.* Viking *spacecraft were landed on Mars in 1976. They showed the planet to be a barren desert. In this image, radioed to Earth by* Viking 1, *the conspicuous boulder – 'Big Joe' – is about 10-feet long. The rust-coloured sand that gives Mars its blood-stained look is obvious.*

M

kind. The combination of satellites and computers in weather forecasting allows the Earth to be treated successfully as a single system. Clouds, oceans, vegetation, polar ice and volcanic eruptions all affect the atmosphere in complex ways. Deep mysteries and uncertainties remain about how the Earth works as a coherent system, and satellites offer the best hope for advances. Especially encouraging is the work of space scientists in America who can map terrestrial vegetation worldwide, season by season, computing its interactions with the atmosphere and the climate.

Unlimited scope for exploration remains in outer space. Unmanned probes have pioneered the exploration of the entire Solar System. The Soviet Union achieved 'firsts' with probes that sent pictures of the far side of the Moon (*Luna 3*, 1959); crashed into Venus (*Venera 3*, 1965); and deposited simple instruments in a soft landing on Mars (*Mars 2*, 1971). Superior engineering soon gave America scientific mastery. A pair of *Viking* spacecraft, launched in 1975, landed complex instruments on Mars to test the soil for the presence of life. They found none, thereby disposing of an ancient speculation. The *Voyager* mission, launched in 1977, was arguably among the greatest engineering triumphs of all time, employing a pair of spacecraft for visits to the outer planets: Jupiter, Saturn, Uranus and Neptune. From a distance of nearly 3,000 million miles, radio signals from *Voyager 2* spent four hours travelling at the speed of light to carry back its pictures from Neptune in 1989.

The European Space Agency joined in the exploration of the Solar System in 1986 with the *Giotto* probe. This braved a cosmic dust-storm to fly close to the nucleus of Halley's Comet, which it unmasked as a mere snowball, very dirty and shaped like a lumpy potato. The fact that Japanese, Soviet and American probes were in the offing, and made co-ordinated observations during that encounter, augured well for future multinational ventures in deep space.

The mass and bulk of equipment required to keep human beings alive in space gives a large technical advantage to unmanned probes. Nevertheless, the exploits of cosmonauts and astronauts inevitably generate more interest. Manned capsules, space stations and the re-useable Space Shuttle have proved that survival in space is possible – even for months on end, as Soviet space stations have demonstrated. The first, brief, space flight, on 12 April 1961, once around the world in the Soviet capsule *Vostok 1*, was made by Yuri Gagarin. A mere eight years later, on 20 July 1969, Neil Armstrong and Edwin Aldrin landed the lunar module of the U.S. *Apollo 11* spacecraft on the Moon's surface. During the period up to December 1972, another five *Apollos* made successful visits to the Moon, and one mission was aborted without loss of life.

In the 1990s, the main manned project will be the international space station *Freedom*, masterminded by NASA. The European Space Agency is acquiring a capacity for manned spaceflight with a miniature space shuttle of French conception. Space enthusiasts will be disappointed if manned flights to Mars do not begin early in the 21st century. Will human beings set off one day to travel to other stars? At present interstellar travel looks technically far-fetched, but then so did a moon landing just a lifetime ago.

Reasons offered for space voyaging include military advantage, scientific curiosity, the quest for useful materials and the extension of the domain of life – 'the greening of the Galaxy'. Politically, the early exploration of space was tailored to television presentation and was motivated by the quest for superpower kudos during the Cold War. But why did world-wide prestige flow from the sight of space-suited astronauts loping in the low lunar gravity? Any answer must acknowledge a human urge to explore. Future historians may judge it more than a coincidence that, just as exploration of the Earth was being completed in the mid-20th century, the human breakout into space began.

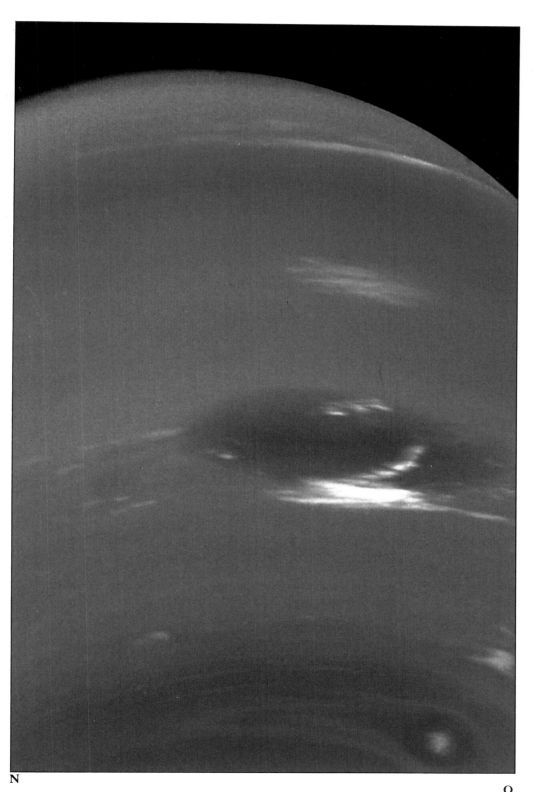

N

O

ANTIQUE MAPS *reproduced in the* Atlas

Acknowledgements

Chapter 1
18B Bibliothèque Nationale, Paris
B Fujita Art Museum, Osaka
19C Photo Dominique Darbois
20D The British Library, OIOC 15406.a.74/1
21E The British Library, 679.h.13
F The British Library, 15520.A.1
G By courtesy of Cambridge University Press
H The British Library, 15520.A.1
22I The Library of Congress, Washington
J The British Library, OIOC ST 476, vol.XX
23K By permission of the Syndics of Cambridge University Library
L The British Library, 455.f.1

Chapter 2
25A The New York Public Library, De Ricci 97

Chapter 3
27A Shōsō-in, Nara
B Ninna-ji, Nara
C Hōryū-ji, Nara

Chapter 4
28A By courtesy of Erwin Neumeyer
B Prince of Wales Museum of Western India, Bombay
29C The British Library, 434.e.8
D Museum of the History of Science, Oxford
E Prince of Wales Museum of Western India, Bombay
F National Museum, New Delhi. MS 82.263

Chapter 5
30A The British Library. Maps 856(6)
31B The British Museum, Department of Western Asiatic Antiquities
C Topkapi Sarayi Museum. MS H 452
D The British Library. Add. MS 23, 544
32E Bibliotheek der Rijksuniversiteit, Leiden. Cod. Or 3101
33F Bibliothèque Nationale, Paris Arabe MS 5847
G Bibliothèque Nationale, Paris Arabe MS 5847

Chapter 6
34A Courtesy of the Latin American Library, Tulane University Library, New Orleans, Louisiana
35B Princeton Collections of Western Americana, Princeton University Library
C Fotomas Index
D The British Library, 278.a.39

Chapter 7
36A Herzog August Bibliothek, Wolfenbüttel. MS Arcerianus
B Österreichische Nationalbibliothek, Vienna. Cod. 324
37C The British Library, Roy. MS 14.c.vii
D The Bodleian Library, Oxford. MS Gough Gen. Top. 16
38E Bayerische Staatsbibliothek, Munich. Cim.137
F Bibliothèque Nationale, Paris. MS Lat. 4939
39G Topkapi Sarayi Museum, Istanbul
H The British Library. Maps C.1.d.4
I Bibliothèque Nationale, Paris. Rés. Ge B 1118

Chapter 8
42A Mary Evans Picture Library
43B Bibliothèque Nationale, Paris. Rés. Ge. B. 696
C Biblioteca Ambrosiana, Milan. MS.260 inf.

Chapter 9
45A Bibliothèque Nationale, Paris. Rés. Ge A 276
48B The British Library. Maps 184.b.1
C Topkapi Sarayi Museum, R.1633 mük
D Österreichische Nationalbibliothek, Vienna
49E Museo Naval, Madrid. Photo MAS
F Biblioteca Estense, Modena. C.G.A.2
G National Archives of Canada, Ottawa. NMC118245
H The British Library. Maps C.2.cc.4

Chapter 10
50A Bibliothèque Nationale, Paris. S.H. Archives no.1
51B Biblioteca Universitaria, Bologna. Raro D.26
52C Biblioteca Apostolica, The Vatican. Borgiano III
53D Universiteitsbibliotheek, Amsterdam
E Archivo General de Indias, Seville. M. y P. Mexico 5
53 panel
A Bibliothèque Nationale, Paris. MS Fr. 150
B Private Collection
C National Maritime Museum, Greenwich
D The British Library. C.75.c.14
54F Archivo General de Indias, Seville. M. y P. Mexico 14
55G Private Collection

Chapter 11
58A Bibliothèque Nationale, Paris. MS Esp.30
60B Museu Nacional de Arte Antigua, Lisbon
C Museu Marítim, Barcelona. Inv. 3236
61 panel
A Biblioteca Apostolica, The Vatican. Borgiano VIII
B Bibliothèque Nationale, Paris. Rés. Ge B 696
C Photo MAS
D Bibliothèque Nationale, Paris. Rés. Ge AA 566

Chapter 12
62A Biblioteca Ambrosiana, Milan. MS 260 inf.
63B Biblioteca Estense, Modena. C.G.A.2
64C The British Library. MS Eg.73
65D The British Library. Add. MS 15760
65 panel
A Alhambra, Granada. Photo MAS
B Private Collection
C Fotomas Index
D Bibliothèque Nationale, Paris, Rés. Ge AA 562
E The British Library. C.20.e.3

Chapter 13
67A Academia des Ciências, Lisbon
B National Archives of Canada, Ottawa. NMC117792
68 panel
A The British Library. Maps K. Top.CXXIV.84
B The British Library. 798.bb.5
C Fotomas Index
D The British Library. 789.bb.5
E The British Library. 10028.df.17
68C The Bodleian Library, Oxford. VET.2.e.7
69D Bibliothèque Nationale, Paris. Rés. Ge DD 683 & Ge AA 640
E National Archives of Canada, Ottawa. NMC117948
70F The British Library. Roy MS 20.E.IX
71G Fotomas Index
H The Bodleian Library. VET.B2.e.7

Chapter 14
74A Det Kongelige Bibliotek, Copenhagen
75B The Hulton Picture Company. H15279
76C The British Library. Add. MS 18454
77D Biblioteca Estense, Modena. C.G.A.2
E Bayerische Staatsbibliothek, Munich. Cod. icon.132
78F Bibliothèque Nationale, Paris. Rés. Ge AA 562
G Museo Naval, Madrid. Photo MAS
79 panel
A The Mansell Collection
B The British Library. Cott. MS Jul.E.iv.6
C Bibliothèque Nationale, Paris. Rés. Ge DD 683 & AA 640
D National Maritime Museum, Greenwich

Chapter 15
81A Biblioteca Apostolica, The Vatican. Borgiano III
B Biblioteca Apostolica, the Vatican. Borgiano I
C National Archives of Canada, Ottawa. NMC21090
82 panel
A The British Library. MS Sloane 4732
B The Library of Congress, Washington
C Robert Douwma Ltd
D Archivo General de Simancas. Estado Leg.2588, f.22
82D The Bodleian Library, Oxford. Mason BB.2
83E The British Library. MS Sloane 1622
F The Library of Congress, Washington
G The British Library. Maps K. Top. 119.1

Chapter 16
84A Courtesy of The John Carter Brown Library at Brown University
86B The British Library. G6527
C National Archives of Canada, Ottawa
87D National Archives of Canada, Ottawa. NMC6172
E The British Museum, Department of Prints and Drawings
87 panel
A The Library of Congress, Washington
B Fotomas Index

Chapter 17
91A The Bodleian Library, Oxford. VET F.1.c.17
B The Bodleian Library, Oxford. Don f.34
92 panel
A The British Library. L.20.i.14
B Fotomas Index
C Fotomas Index
D American Museum of Natural History, New York
93C The British Library. Maps C.1.c.6
D The British Library. Add. MS 17652 A

Chapter 18
94A National Archives of Canada, Ottawa. NMC15661
95B National Archives of Canada, Ottawa
96 panel
A National Archives of Canada, Ottawa. C-1917
B Hudson's Bay Company Archives, Provincial Archives of Manitoba
C Hudson's Bay Company Archives, Provincial Archives of Manitoba
97C National Archives of Canada, Ottawa. C79241
D National Archives, of Canada, Ottawa. NMC6596
E Hudson's Bay Company Archives, Provincial Archives of Manitoba

Chapter 19
99A Courtesy of The John Carter Brown Library at Brown University
B Yale University Library Map Collection
101C The British Library. I TAB 45
D The British Library. C.32.h.12

Chapter 20
102A The British Library. MS Harl. 3450, f.10
103B The Bodleian Library, Oxford. I.1.3. Art Seld.
104C The British Library. Maps C.27.g.22
D National Maritime Museum, Greenwich
E The British Library. Add. MS 17651
105 panel
A The British Library. Maps T.6.a.2
B National Maritime Museum, Greenwich
C The British Library. Maps C.2.a.7.(1)

Chapter 21
107A National Archives of Canada, Ottawa
B National Archives of Canada, Ottawa
C Hudson's Bay Company Archives, Provincial Archives of Manitoba
108D Hudson's Bay Company Archives, Provincial Archives of Manitoba
E The British Library. 146.f.7
F The Public Record Office. C.O. 700 Am. N&S. no 49
109 panel
A Hudson's Bay Company Archives, Provincial Archives of Manitoba
B The British Library. 982.a.21-4
C The British Library. C.32.e.16
D Glenbow Museum, Calgary

Chapter 22
111A Bancroft Library, University of California, Berkeley
B The British Library. 14131.k.6
112C Smithsonian Institute, Washington
D Library of Congress, Washington
113 panel
A The Houghton Library, Harvard University
B The Library of Congress, Washington
C American Philosophical Society, New York. Codex H, p.4
D American Philosophical Society, New York. Codex E, p.132-3
E American Philosophical Society, New York. Codex J, p.93

Chapter 23
115A The British Library. 981.g.23
B The British Library. 569.f.12
C The British Library. 2370.g.2

Chapter 24
118A Bibliothèque Nationale, Paris
121B The Newberry Library, Chicago
122C The British Library. C.32.m.4
D The British Library. 454.c.13
E The British Library. MS 4034
123 panel
A The Bodleian Library, Oxford. 18422.d.11
B The British Library. 211.c.7,8
C The British Library. 211.c.7,8

Chapter 25
124A Fotomas Index
126B Museo del Oro, Bogotá
C Musco del Oro, Bogatá
D The British Library. Add. MS 15,217
127 panel
A The Karolik Collection of American Paintings, 1815-1865. Courtesy, Museum of Fine Arts, Boston
B The British Library. 211.c.7,8
C The British Library. 149.i.3,4
D The British Library. 149.i.3,4
128 panel
A The British Museum, Department of Prints and Drawings
B The Bodleian Library, Oxford. 19127.a.1
C By Courtesy of the Natural History Museum
D Universitätsbibliothek, Erlangen. MS2386, I
E The British Library. 648.c.2
128E The British Library. Add. MS 17,940
129F Fotomas Index

Chapter 26
130A The British Library. Maps 83040(4)
132B The British Library. G. 7101
C The British Library. 9773.w.6
133 panel
A Fotomas Index
B Bibliothèque Nationale, Paris. Rés. Ge DD 683 & GE AA 640
C The British Library. 9781.d.12
D The British Library. 443.k.7
E Bibliothèque Nationale, Paris.
134D The British Library. 149.i.2
135E Archivo General de Indias, Seville. Plano Venezuela, 21

Chapter 27
139A Biblioteca Nazionale Marcianas, Venice.
B The British Library. Maps C.21.c.6
C The British Library. Add. MS 9861
140D The British Library. Add. MS 9861
E The British Library. 234.i.37
141F The British Library. 10096.gg.9
141 panel
A The British Library. Ac.6172/76
B The British Library. C.32.1.5
C The British Library. 295.k.31
D The British Library. 583.i.11

Chapter 28
143A Bibliothèque Nationale, Paris. GE DD 2987/7953
144B The British Library. G.7391

Chapter 29
146A The British Library. 569.g.10.1,2
147B Bibliothèque Nationale, Paris. Rés. Ge DD 683 & Ge AA 640
C Assemblée National, Paris. MS 1248. ED,19

Chapter 30
150A Josephine Powell, Rome
B Musée Guimet (Réunion des Musées Nationaux)
151C Courtesy of the Freer Gallery of Art, Smithsonian Institution, Washington D.C. 15.16
152 panel
A Museum fuer Indische Kunst Berlin MIK III 8383. Staatliche Museen Preussischer Kulturbesitz
B The British Museum. Department of Oriental Antiquities 1919. 1-1.014
C The British Museum. Department of Oriental Antiquities 1919. 1-1.045
D Museum fuer Indische Kunst Berlin MIK III 6876b. Staatliche Museen Preussischer Kulturbesitz
152D Courtesy of the Royal Ontario Museum, Toronto. ROM 920.1.74
153E Picturepoint, London
F Topkapi Sarayi Museum, MS H.1654
G National Palace Museum, Taipei, Taiwan, Republic of China

Chapter 31
154A The Master and Fellows of Corpus Christi College, Cambridge. MS 66A
155B Bibliothèque Nationale, Paris. MS Esp. 30
C Picturepoint, London
156 panel
A Edinburgh University Library. Or MS 20
B Edinburgh University Library. Or MS 20
156D The Bodleian Library, Oxford, MS Bodl. 264
157E Bibliteca Nazionale Marciana, Venice
F Bibliothèque Nationale, Paris. MS Pers. Suppl.143
G The Bodleian Library, Oxford. MS Bodl. 264

Chapter 32
158A Dr Terence Armstrong, Scott Polar Research Institute
159B The British Library. Maps 982(9)
160C Library of the Academy of Sciences of the USSR, Leningrad
D Dr Terence Armstrong, Scott Polar Research Institute
161E The British Library. 10460.ee.15
161 panel
A Dr Terence Armstrong, Scott Polar Research Institute
B Julian Dowdeswell, Scott Polar Research Institute
C Dr Terence Armstrong, Scott Polar Research Institute
D Maria Pia Casarini, Scott Polar Research Institute
E Peter Wadhams, Scott Polar Research Institute

Chapter 33
165A Courtesy of The John Carter Brown Library at Brown University
B The Beinecke Rare Book and Manuscript Library, Yale University, New Haven
C By courtesy of Mr Charles Boxer
D Biblioteca Reale, Turin. MS O XVI/2
166E The British Library, Maps C.2.b.4
F The Newberry Library, Chicago. Novacco Map. 7c. G9250
167G The British Library. 682.b.14
168 panel
A The British Library. Maps C.7.e.2
B Museo Naval, Madrid
C Archivo General de Indias, Seville. M. y P. Mexico 34
D Courtesy of The John Carter Brown Library at Brown University
168H The British Library. Maps 147.d.26.(3)
169I The British Library. Add. MS 31,317
J Archivio di Stato, Florence. Misc. Medicea n.97.ins.91
K The British Library. OIOC Or.75.g.25

Chapter 34
170A The British Library. Maps C.3.c.8
171B Österreichische Nationalbibliothek, Vienna. Atlas Blaeu, Bd 41
C The British Library. Add. MS 21,593.c
D Algemeen Rijksarchief, The Hague. VEL.284
E The British Library. Maps 150.e.30
172F The British Library. MS Sloane 46A
173G The British Library. G.7366-69
174 panel
A The British Library. Add. MS 15,513
B From the Castle Howard Collection
C National Maritime Museum, Greenwich
175H The British Library. C.28.1.10

Chapter 35
176A National Maritime Museum, Greenwich
177B By kind permission of the Trustees of the Parham Park Estate, West Sussex
C The British Library. Add. MS 7085
D By Courtesy of the Natural History Museum
178 panel
A National Maritime Museum, Greenwich
B National Maritime Museum, Greenwich
C National Maritime Museum, Greenwich
D National Maritime Museum, Greenwich
179E National Maritime Museum, Greenwich
F By Courtesy of the Natural History Museum

Chapter 36
180A National Maritime Museum, Greenwich
181B National Library of Australia, Canberra
182C Mitchell Library, State Library of New South Wales
183D The British Library. 10491.d.26
E La Trobe Collection. State Library of Victoria, Melbourne
184F Art Gallery of South Australia, Adelaide
185 panel
A The Royal Geographical Society
B La Trobe Collection. State Library of Victoria, Melbourne
C La Trobe Collection. State Library of Victoria, Melbourne

Chapter 37
188A Aberdeen University Library
189B Aberdeen University Library
C Aberdeen University Library
D Aberdeen University Library
190E The British Library. Maps K. Top 117.24.1
F Aberdeen University Library
G National Portrait Gallery, London
191H Aberdeen University Library
I The British Library. 792.1.21
191 panel
A Aberdeen University Library
B National Portrait Gallery, London
C Aberdeen University Library
D Aberdeen University Library
192J Aberdeen University Library
K Aberdeen University Library
193L The British Library. 10095.i.3

Chapter 38
194A The British Library. 10095.d.12
195B Aberdeen University Library
C The British Library. 984.e.20
D Aberdeen University Library
196 panel
A Aberdeen University Library
B The Royal Geographical Society. Photo The Bridgeman Art Library
C Aberdeen University Library
D The David Livingstone Centre, Blantyre
E Aberdeen University Library
197E The Royal Geographical Society
F The Royal Geographical Society
G The David Livingstone Centre, Blantyre

Chapter 39
198A Aberdeen University Library
199B The British Library. Maps, RGS Journal XV
C Aberdeen University Library
D The British Library. Maps, RGS Journal XXVI
E The British Library. 10696.e.30
200F The Royal Geographical Society
201G The Trustees of the National Library of Scotland
202 panel
A The Trustees of the National Library of Scotland
B Aberdeen University Library
C Private Collection
D The David Livingstone Centre, Blantyre
E The Royal Geographical Society. Photo The Bridgeman Art Library
203H Aberdeen University Library
I The Trustees of the National Library of Scotland. On deposit from a private collection

Chapter 40
204A Aberdeen University Library
205B Aberdeen University Library
C Aberdeen University Library
206 panel
A Aberdeen University Library
B Aberdeen University Library
C The Hulton Picture Company
D Aberdeen University Library
207D The Royal Geographical Society
E Aberdeen University Library
F Aberdeen University Library

Chapter 41
208A Aberdeen University Library
B Aberdeen University Library
209C Aberdeen University Library
D National Archives of Zambia
E By courtesy of Oxford University Press

Chapter 42
213A The British Library. 796.ff.27
B The Bodleian Library, Oxford. 38.973
C The British Library. TAB 488.A.
214D The British Library. 10076.d.17
E The British Library. 10077.dd.21
215F The British Library. 563.d.21
G The British Library. 10076.dd.18
H The Royal Geographical Society

Chapter 43
216A The British Library. OIOC Prints and Drawings
217B The British Library. OIOC Persian MS 4380
C The British Library. G 3079
D The British Library. OIOC MS Orme 334, Maps 4
218 panel
A The British Library. OIOC Ad. Or.770
B The British Library. OIOC X/ 2314/3
C The British Library. OIOC Prints and Drawings
219E The British Library. Maps Ref.K.5
F The British Library. OIOC T.38698
G The British Library. 12907.v.

Chapter 44
220A Musée Guimet, Paris
221B The British Library. Maps, RGS Journal XXXVIII
222 panel
A Nicolas Roerich Museum, New York
B Nicolas Roerich Museum, New York
C Nicolas Roerich Museum, New York
222C The British Library. 1077.dd.14
223D The British Library. 10077.k.5
E The British Library. 10077.k.5
F The British Library. LR.80.d.11
G The British Library. PP 4273(1)

Chapter 45
224A The British Library. 10057. AAA.28
225B The British Library. 19957.T.5

Chapter 46
228A The British Library. 978.1.1
B Mariteim Museum Prins Hendrik, Rotterdam
231C The British Library. Maps C.2.c.4
D National Archives of Canada, Ottawa. NMC8099
F Scott Polar Research Institute
232G Scott Polar Research Institute
H Scott Polar research Institute
233 panel
A British Antarctic Survey. G. Sommers 39/5
B Scott Polar Research Institute
C The British Library. 2370.e.2
D Scott Polar Research Institute

Chapter 47
234A Michael Holford, London
B NASA/Science Photo Library, London E250/008NASO1L
235C Dr Richard Legeckis/Science Photo Library, London E265/001RLG04U
D Planet Earth Pictures 76/993R-230C
E Dr Gene Feldman, NASA GSFC/ Science Photo Library, London E250/ 029NAS09T
236F Telegraph Colour Library, London 0301031011
G NASA/Science Photo Library, London S540/063NAS07U
237H Earth Satellite Corporation/Science Photo Library, London E780/ 220ESC08G
I Earth Satellite Corporation/Science Photo Library, London E780/ 222ESC07J
J Dr Gene Feldman, NASA GSFC/ Science Photo Library, London E050/ 157NAS14D
238K ESA/PLI/Science Photo Library, London E050/139LI18C
L **NASA/Science Photo Library, London S380/110USA18U**
M NASA/Science Photo Library, London R360/039NAS04B
239N NASA/Science Photo Library, London R420/013NAS03M
O NASA/Science Photo Library, London R390/006NAS03P

The Ceque route map in Chapter 5 is based on material from R Tom Zuidema, 'Bureaucracy and Systematic Knowledge in Andean Civilization', in G A Collier, R I Rosaldo and J D Wirth, eds., *The Inca and Aztec States, 1400-1800: Anthropology and History* (Academic Press, New York and London, 1982), pp.440-41, figs. 16.4 and 16.5.

The map of Columbus's landfall in Chapter 9 is based on material from Robert H Fuson, *The Log of Christopher Columbus* (Ashford Press Publishing, Southampton, 1987), pp.204-7.

GLOSSARY OF TECHNICAL TERMS

Names printed in **bold type** within entries have their own entries.

AERIAL PHOTOGRAPHY, photography taken from any form of aircraft, including balloons. 'Vertical photography' is the name given to aerial photography taken with the camera axis vertical. 'Oblique photography' is the name when the axis of the camera is inclined away from the vertical. An assembly of photographs joined together is known as a 'mosaic'. *See* **photogrammetry, photomap**.

ALIDADE, an instrument of ancient origin for taking a sighting of an object with a view to determining or plotting its position. In its simplest form it is no more than a straight edge. In its more complex form the alidade carries a form of telescope.

ANTI-MERIDIAN, the other half of a **great circle** from a **meridian**. The anti-meridian is, therefore, at 180° **longitude** from the **meridian**.

ASTROLABE, an astronomical instrument originally designed to determine the rising and setting of stars without resort to calculation. When used for solar, lunar or planetary observations, an almanac was necessary. The principles of the astrolabe were known to the Greeks by, at latest, the 2nd century BC. Arab astronomers developed many astrolabes from the 7th century AD to the 17th century. Various metal plates (tympans) formed a kind of star-map for each of several latitudes. On the back of the astrolabe was a graduated circle with an **alidade** pivoted on its centre for the purpose of measuring the angle to a star or the Sun or for measuring vertical or horizontal angles on the ground. It was, however, primarily an astronomical instrument.

ASTROLABE, MARINER'S, a simplified form of **astrolabe** consisting of the graduated circle and the **alidade**.

BATHYSCAPE, a submersible vessel comprising an airtight flotation compartment with an observation capsule; used for deep-sea exploration and capable of reaching depths of over 5,000 fathoms. *See* **submersible**.

CABOTAGE, trade or transport in coastal waters.

CARAVAN, in Asia and Africa, a company of merchants and others travelling together with pack animals, especially where the journey is of long duration.

CARAVANSERAI (or **CARAVANSERA, CARAVANSERY**), a stopping place for a caravan. Originally a Persian inn with a large courtyard to accommodate the pack animals and merchandise.

CARAVEL (or **CARVEL**), types of light, fast, decked vessels with flush hull planks and with, usually, three masts with **lateen rig**. The rig was, sometimes, changed to **square rig** on the first two masts when sailing the oceans. Spanish and Portuguese caravels could sail against the wind, removing the need for oarsmen and the provisions to feed them. That made the caravel a ship suitable for the long voyages across oceans that began the Age of Discovery. The corresponding Flemish vessel was the karak.

CELESTIAL NAVIGATION, navigation by the Sun and other heavenly bodies; literally, navigation by the heavens. *See* **navigation**.

CEQUE, an Inca pilgrimage route linking **huaca** shrines as directly as possible.

CHRONOMETER, an accurate timepiece designed for determining **longitude** at sea. This is done by comparing local time observed astronomically with the corresponding time at the port of embarkation as given by a timepiece. The first such chronometer was made by Harrison in 1762. *See* **longitude**.

COG, a single-masted ship with a single square sail, developed in the Low Countries about 1200 and often with open frame fore- and stern-castles. Oars were needed in adverse winds. These vessels were the principal ships of north-east Atlantic trade in medieval times.

COMPASS, GYROSCOPIC, a compass whose principal element is a rapidly spinning vertical wheel which is always aligned to true north (geographic north) as opposed to magnetic north. By the nature of the gyroscope the north direction is maintained regardless of the motion of a ship or of magnetism.

COMPASS, MAGNETIC, the primary aid to navigation since the 13th century. In its first form a piece of **lodestone** served to indicate the direction of north. Then magnetized steel (the needle) replaced the lodestone. In the mariner's compass, a compass card, with a magnet attached to its underside, floats on the surface of a liquid so that the card maintains its horizontal position. The card is marked with 32 points (each point is 11¼°). In early compasses, there were 4 points, then 8, 16 and finally 32. *See* **lodestone**.

COSMOGRAPHY, strictly speaking, study of the universe but, more generally, study of the Earth as a whole and of the observable universe in relation to the Earth.

DEAD RECKONING, navigating without reference to the Sun or stars and solely by estimated course and estimated distance travelled along that course. In dead reckoning, account may be taken of drift due to wind or currents.

DECLINATION, the angle of the Sun or other heavenly bodies above the equator.

DHOW, Arabian **lateen-rigged** ship of traditional design, usually single-masted.

DOLDRUMS, the equatorial belt of low atmospheric pressure where the north-east and south-east **trade winds** converge, nowadays called the Inter-Tropical Convergence Zone. Calms and light variable winds prevail but there are frequent squalls, heavy rain and thunderstorms. The belt moves north or south of the **equator** in keeping with the Sun's motion but lagging behind the Sun by one or two months. Hurricanes are generated in this zone.

EMPORIUM, a centre of commerce.

ENTREPÔT, a centre for trade where goods are received from one part of the world for export to other parts. An entrepôt is often a **free port**.

EQUATOR, the great circle around the Earth at **latitude** 0°, being equidistant from the North and South Poles.

EQUINOCTIAL LINE (or **CELESTIAL EQUATOR**), an imaginary line on the celestial sphere formed by the intersection of a plane through the centre of the Earth and perpendicular to the axis of rotation of the Earth. It therefore corresponds to the Earth's equator.

FORE-AND-AFT RIG, in which the sails are aligned along the length of the ship as opposed to across the ship – the opposite of **square rig**.

FREE PORT, a port where goods are exempt from customs duty.

GEO-SYNCHRONOUS ORBIT, an orbit in which a **satellite** crosses the **equator** at exactly the same instant of time in each pass, thereby keeping in time with the Sun.

GLACIER, a mass of ice that moves downwards from above the snowline under the force of gravity and pressure due to the depth of snow. The pressure causes melting and the formation of granular ice which, in turn, is transformed into clear ice that facilitates the motion downwards.

GNOMON, a rod or pillar used to calculate the **meridian** altitude of the Sun from the length of shadow cast. Also the rod, pin or plate which casts the shadow on a sundial.

GREAT CIRCLE, the line traced out on the globe by a plane passing through the centre of the globe. A great circle divides a sphere into two equal hemispheres. A great-circle distance is the shortest distance between two points. A **meridian** and its **anti-meridian** together make a great circle, as does the **equator**.

GULF STREAM, a fast-flowing, warm, surface current which is a major part of the North Atlantic gyre. Leaving the Gulf of Florida at 140 miles a day it loses speed on its northward progression to the Grand Banks of Newfoundland. Some water continues its north-eastward passage as the North Atlantic Drift, flowing round the British Isles and on to the Arctic Ocean north of Norway.

HUACA, an Inca shrine or idol.

HYDROGRAPHY, the general study of the water bodies of the Earth; also, and more usually, the actual processes of charting the oceans, seas and navigable waters.

HYPSOMETER, an instrument for measuring or determining altitudes. The boiling-point hypsometer measures, very accurately, the boiling point of water. Since the boiling-point varies with atmospheric pressure and atmospheric pressure varies with altitude, the altitude can be obtained from the boiling-point.

ICEBERG, a mass of ice which has detached itself (or 'calved') from an ice barrier or the end of a glacier.

ICE-FLOE, an expanse of ice detached from an ice-field. The limits of an ice-floe are normally within visual range of a person standing on a floe.

JUNK, a Chinese sailing vessel of ancient and unknown origin. A junk is a flat-bottomed boat with a large rudder in place of a keel and square sails of linen or matting, flattened by bamboo strips which can be spread or closed at will. Chinese junks sailed as far as East Africa and the Red Sea by the early 15th century.

KNORR, a ship developed by Norsemen, very well adapted to Atlantic Ocean travels and designed to carry cargo.

LATEEN RIG, rig with a triangular (lateen) sail, bent on to a yard or gaff, hoisted to the head of a short mast.

LATITUDE, of a point on the Earth's surface, the angular distance of the point north or south of the equator. The **equator** is at latitude 0°.

LEEWAY, the sideways drift of a vessel in the direction away from the wind.

LODESTONE (or **LOADSTONE**), naturally occurring magnetic rock consisting of more or less pure magnetite (an oxide of iron).

LOG, a detailed record of a ship's voyage; also, a means of measuring the speed of a ship. The word comes from the practice of throwing a log overboard and timing its passage from bow to stern. Later the log was secured to a knotted line which was paid out over the stern. The knots were counted over an interval of time and the speed of the ship so calculated. Modern speed-measuring devices are still referred to as a log.

LONGITUDE, of a point of the Earth's surface, the angular distance of the point east or west of a **prime** (or standard) **meridian**. The prime meridian is at 0° longitude.

LOXODROME, *see* **rhumb line**.

MAGNETIC POLE, the Earth acts as a bar magnet whose axis is not coincident with the Earth's axis of rotation. The ends of the magnetic axis are the north and south magnetic poles. These are not fixed, but migrate around the North and South (geographic) Poles. A **compass** needle aligns itself with one or other of the magnetic poles, thereby indicating the direction of magnetic north or magnetic south.

MALARIA, a variety of intermittent fevers caused by the bite of the anopheles mosquito. The symptoms are high fever associated with ague. Malaria remains the greatest single cause of human mortality and invalidism.

MAP PROJECTION, the means of representing the spherical (or spheroidal) Earth on a flat sheet of paper. This can not be done without distortion of some kind. Map projections create a mesh of lines on paper corresponding to the imaginary graticule of **latitude** and **longitude** on the Earth's surface.

MERIDIAN, one half of a **great circle** passing through the poles and intersecting the **equator** at right angles. The other half of the **great circle** is the **anti-meridian**.

MIZZEN, the mizzen mast is the aftermost mast of a sailing ship, for example the third from the bow of a **square-rigged** three-masted ship.

MONSOON, a wind-system in which the direction of the prevailing wind is completely reversed or nearly so.

NADIR, the point directly below our feet – the opposite of **zenith**.

NAVIGATION, originally, determining the position and course of a ship. Now the term applies to submarines, aircraft, land vehicles, and even space vehicles. Navigation includes finding one's way with reference to local landmarks as in coastal navigation or desert navigation. Navigation at sea was first by reference to the Sun, then to the Pole Star. In the Pacific, navigation was by means of wave fronts and islands. Discovery of the properties of terrestrial magnetism led to the **magnetic compass** and the beginning of navigation as a science. The **astrolabe**, the **quadrant** and the cross-staff were all instruments of navigation in the 14th and 15th centuries. Navigation by the Sun was a crude procedure until **solar tables** were prepared. Almanacs and logarithmic tables were important aids. The octant and the **sextant** replaced successively the cross-staff and the astrolabe after the invention of the telescope. Invention of the **chronometer** was a great advance. So was the publication of the *Nautical Almanac* in 1767. However, navigation owes much to the Mercator Projection, which has been used for navigation at sea for almost four centuries. Radio-assisted navigation introduced a new era of precision in navigation for ships and aircraft. **Satellite navigation**, the United States Navstar (GPS) and the Russian equivalents promise greater precision with less effort in determining both position and heading.

OSTROG (plural **OSTROGI**), nowadays, one of the Russian words for prison; the word originally meant a stockaded frontier post.

OUTRIGGER, a boat equipped with a framework for supporting a pontoon outside the hull to provide stability.

PACK-ICE, large blocks of ice resulting from the breaking-up of an ice-field from the action of wind and waves. The blocks are larger than **ice-floes**.

PARALLEL (of LATITUDE), an imaginary line on the Earth's surface connecting all points equidistant from the **equator**. *See* **latitude**.

PHOTOGRAMMETRY, literally, making measurements on photographs; specifically, measurement made on a three-dimensional view obtained stereoscopically by simultaneous viewing of overlapping photographs. Such methods used with vertical **aerial photography** are the means by which modern mapping is produced. From the 3-D image exact positions can be plotted and contours and spot heights defined. Terrestrial photogrammetry applies the same technique to photography taken on the ground with the axis of the camera in the horizontal plane.

PHOTOMAP, a map that has an aerial photograph or a mosaic as its background.

PIROGUE (or **PIRAGUA**), any of various dug-out canoes.

PORTAGE, the transportation of boats, supplies, etc., overland between navigable waterways or the route overland used for such transportation.

PORTOLAN CHART, developed in Europe in the 13th century, the first charts intended specifically for mariners. Though much detailed coastal information is shown, inland features rarely appear. Most have complex sets of **rhumb lines**.

PRIME MERIDIAN, a meridian acting as the zero meridian from which all **longitudes** are reckoned.

PROJECTION, *see* **map projection**.

QUADRANT, a device consisting of a graduated arc of 90° and a sighting mechanism on a movable arm, formerly used to measure the altitude of stars in **navigation**.

QUIPU, an Inca means of recording or measuring; a knotted cord in which the intervals and colours of the knots signified various forms of information, including distances and locations.

REMOTE-SENSING, in its true sense, examining something without touching it, now specifically study of the Earth (or a planet) by artificial Earth **satellites**. Various sensors are used to obtain the reflectances and emissions of the Earth in various parts of the electromagnetic spectrum. From such sensing, assessments may be made of vegetation, agriculture, soils, geology, minerals, urban development, pollution, ocean temperatures, weather and climate, the atmosphere and a host of other phenomena.

RHUMB LINE, a compass bearing; a line that cuts all **meridians** at the same angle.

RIG, the arrangement of a ship's masts and sails.

ROARING FORTIES, the strong prevailing westerly winds of the southern hemisphere between about 40°S and 60°S, where, with the absence of intervening land masses, the winds are constant and strong. Also the ocean where the winds prevail.

SATELLITE NAVIGATION, *see* **navigation**.

SATELLITES, more properly artificial satellites, man-made carriers of instruments powered by solar or other energy placed in orbit around the Earth or a planet to collect and transmit various types of sensing data. Satellites are also used as a navigation aid, as a platform for the exploration of space and as a means of building space-stations. When placed at an appropriate altitude above the Earth, a satellite will remain permanently over that point on Earth. It is then in geo-stationary orbit. *See* **geo-synchronous orbit**.

SCURVY, a disease characterized by anaemia, weak gums, bleeding under the skin; caused by lack of vitamin C. It was prevalent among seamen and armies especially in winter and spring, due to lack of fresh fruit and vegetables in their diet. By the 19th century it had been largely eradicated from the Royal Navy and Mercantile Marine by the provision of fruit juice.

SEXTANT, a navigational instrument made up of a telescope through which a heavenly body is sighted, with protractors to determine its angular distance above the horizon or from another body.

SMALL CIRCLE, a line traced on the globe by a plane that does not pass through the centre of the globe. All parallels of **latitude** except the **equator** are small circles.

SOLAR TABLES, tables of the declination of the Sun throughout the year, essential for **navigation** by observation of the Sun.

SONAR, equipment used to locate underwater objects, to examine the sea-bed or measure depths and distances, all by the use of sound waves.

SQUARE RIG, an arrangement of sails in which the principal sails are spread by horizontal yards disposed at right angles to the mast and aligned athwartships – the opposite of **fore-and-aft rig**.

STANDARD MERIDAN, *see* **prime meridian**.

STEPPES, temperate, level grasslands extending from the lower Danube, through the south-east parts of European U.S.S.R. and into south-west Siberia, corresponding nearly to the Prairies of North America and the Pampas of South America.

SUBMERSIBLE, vessel capable of operating under water, often a small research vessel capable of descending to considerable depths. Many accommodate crews, others are unmanned. *See* **bathyscape**.

TRADE WINDS, winds that blow from the sub-tropical high-pressure belts towards the Inter-Tropical Convergence Zone. They blow from the north-east in the northern hemisphere and from the south-east in the southern hemisphere. Over ocean areas, they tend to blow with regularity. For most of the year the weather is fine but tropical cyclones (hurricanes in the Atlantic, typhoons in the Pacific) occur seasonally.

TRIANGULATION, a method of surveying or for determining the position of a point in relation to two others using trigonometry. In surveying, triangulation provides the frame-work for mapping, in the past by plane-table, nowadays by **photogrammetry**. From a carefully measured base-line a series of large triangles is developed in which only the angles are measured. Smaller triangles are then observed within the large triangles and still smaller triangles within those, and so on until the whole area is covered to a sufficient density. Then the detailed mapping can begin. Triangulation was replaced by electronic distance-measuring in the 1960s. The system, known as trilateration, involves the measurement of the sides of a triangle. In the late 1980s satellite position-fixing increasingly came to replace trilateration for surveying. It is quick and extremely accurate and it does not involve occupying high ground.

ZENITH, the point directly overhead – the opposite of **nadir**.

ZENITHAL DISTANCE, the angle from the **zenith** to a body under observation – the Sun; a star; a planet. Zenithal distance of the Sun plus or minus the **declination** of the Sun gives the latitude of the place from where the observation was made. When the Sun is north of the **equator** the **declination** is added for an observer in the northern hemisphere.

BIOGRAPHICAL GLOSSARY

These biographical entries are intended to provide supplementary information about the explorers and cartographers and some of the sponsors of exploration treated in the main text. Only names mentioned in the atlas proper are included. Names printed in **bold type** within entries have their own entries. The numbers at the end of entries refer to the chapter(s) in which the subject appears.

ABBOT, HENRY LARCOM (1831–1927), U.S. army officer and explorer. On graduation from West Point in 1854 Abbot was ordered to work on the Pacific Railroad Surveys. In spite of hostile Indians, he and Lieutenant **Robert Stockton Williamson** located two routes from California north into present-day Oregon and Washington. Abbot's career as an engineer continued until 1895 when he retired with the rank of colonel; Congress voted him the rank of brigadier-general, retired, in 1904. 22

ABRUZZI, LUIGI AMEDEO DE SAVOIA, Duke of the (1873–1933), Italian aristocrat, mountaineer and explorer. He qualified as a naval officer at 16, and was also a keen mountaineer from an early age. In 1897 he led the first successful ascent of Mount St. Elias, Alaska. In 1899–1900 he was leader of an Italian attempt on the North Pole from Zemlya Frantsa-Iosifa (Franz Josef Land). Severe frostbite forced him to hand over leadership of the final leg to **Umberto Cagni**, who reached a record 86°34′N. Abruzzi later led mountaineering expeditions to East Africa (1906) and the Himalayas (1909). He served as vice-admiral commanding the Adriatic fleet in the First World War. He resigned from the navy in 1917. 46

ABREU, ANTÓNIO DE, early 16th-century Portuguese explorer and diplomat. Born in Madeira, he accompanied **Afonso de Albuquerque** to India. In 1511 he commanded the expedition of three ships and 120 men with which Albuquerque hoped to open direct commerce with the Spice Islands. Leaving Malacca in November 1511 the expedition eventually reached Amboina after coasting Sumatra, Java, Bali and part of New Guinea. Meanwhile the direct route to Ternate had been sailed by **Francisco Serrão**, a captain of the expedition, as a captive aboard a pirate ship. After periods in Malacca and Portugal, Abreu was appointed governor of Malacca in 1526, where he served until his death at an unknown date. 29

AFONSO, DIOGO, 15th-century Portuguese navigator. A member of the households of the Infante Dom Fernando of Portugal and of his uncle, Prince **Henry the Navigator**, he was sent by the latter in 1446 to command a caravel in search of the explorer **João Fernandes**, lost in the region of Rio de Oro the previous year. His subsequent missions included a voyage in 1446 which added the central and western islands of the Cape Verde archipelago to those known as a result of the voyages of **Antoniotto di Usodimare** and of **Diogo Gomes** and Antonio da Noli. 12

AGNESE, GIOVANNI BATTISTA (1514–64), Italian mapmaker of Portolan charts. Active from 1536 onwards, he worked mainly in Genoa, although some charts are dated from Venice. About 70 manuscript chart atlases by him are known today. 33

AGUIRRE, FRANCISCO DE (1508–81), Spanish *conquistador*. A veteran of the Italian wars, who had witnessed the Sack of Rome in 1527, Aguirre left an office of some profit as crown representative on the town council of his native Talavera de la Reina to join the conquest of Peru. He accompanied **Valdivia** into Chile where he founded San Bartolomé de la Serena in 1549. In 1551 he was put in charge of the exploration and settlement of the Tucumán area, where he founded Santiago del Estero. Failing in a *putsch* on Valdivia's death in 1553, he was arrested and sent to Lima in 1557 but, after exoneration, returned in 1559 and was made governor of Tucumán in 1563. The achievements of his first two years in office were promising; the Indians were pacified and San Miguel de Tucumán was founded. In 1566, however, his men mutinied. He was obliged to purge himself of charges of heresy, but these were

renewed in 1570, when he was arrested, to be released five years later. He had lost three sons in the course of duty and made no more than a modest fortune on which he retired, spending the remainder of his life in San Bartolomé. 24

ALAMINOS, ANTÓN DE, 16th-century Spanish navigator. After serving on Columbus's last voyage, he was next recorded as pilot on the expedition of **Juan Ponce de León**, which discovered Florida in 1513 and in the course of which Alaminos made the first recorded observation of the Gulf Stream, on 21 April. After a period of residence in Cuba, he probably took part in the voyage of Francisco Hernández de Córdoba to Yucatán in 1517. He returned to Yucatán with **Juan de Grijalva** in 1518, reconnoitering the coasts of Mexico as far as the Ulúa. In 1519 he piloted **Cortés** to Mexico and took the news to Spain using the Gulf Stream. He later fell out with Cortés, joining those who accused him of exceeding his authority and misdirecting royal revenues. 10

ALARCÓN, HERNANDO DE (b.1500), Spanish *conquistador*. Born in Trujillo, he sought his fortune in New Spain. On 9 May 1540 Alarcón departed from Acapulco in command of the fleet supporting **Coronado's** expedition to Cíbola and Quivirá. He produced a remarkable map of California and made elevations of the coast. However, his discovery of the peninsular nature of California was ignored until confirmed about 160 years later by **Kino**. 17, 20

ALBUQUERQUE, AFONSO DE (1453–1515), Portuguese soldier and diplomat. Of a provincial noble house, with a tradition of royal service, he took part in King Afonso I's North African crusade in 1471 and served at court or in North Africa during the two succeeding reigns. In 1503 he was sent to India to supervise the defence of Cochin and in 1507 commanded the expedition that raised Hormuz. He returned to India in 1508 and took over the government of the Portuguese establishment there the following year after a severe altercation with the outgoing viceroy, Francisco de Almeida. He adopted an aggressive policy, designed to seize control of the spice trade by force. He took Goa in 1510, establishing the basis of an enduring Portuguese colony there, and Malacca in 1511. He became increasingly interested in crusading projects of millenarian resonance, planning the destruction of Mecca, the reconquest of Jerusalem and the diversion of the waters of the Nile. In 1512 he seized Socotra, attacked Aden and established Portuguese hegemony over Calicut. During the same period he encouraged the voyages of exploration that led the Portuguese to the Spice Islands. In 1515 he embarked on a renewed attempt to conquer Hormuz, which would have enabled him virtually to seal one of the traditional routes of the spice routes, but in September of that year he died at sea. 28

ALEXANDER THE GREAT (356–323 BC). The most famous conqueror of the ancient world. The son of Philip II of Macedon, he was taught by Aristotle. Succeeding his father in 336, he reaffirmed Macedonian dominance in Greece, and between 334 and 323 led his armies all but 'through to the ends of the earth', penetrating as far as Bactria and the Hindu Kush. He died at Babylon aged 32. His victories, though never consolidated into a world empire, spread Greek thought and culture throughout Egypt, northern India, Central Asia and the eastern Mediterranean. His body, sealed in a glass tomb and encased in gold, was preserved in Alexandria, the city he founded as his own memorial. The tomb has never been located. 2

ALFINGER, AMBROSIUS or **AMBROSIO** (d. 1533), German explorer of South America. In 1526 he was in charge of the interests of the Welzer banking house in Santo Domingo. In 1528 he was appointed to command the expedition to Venezuela of 300 colonists, organized by a German syndicate, largely financed by the Welzer. From Coro he quickly undertook the exploration of the shores of Lake Maracaibo, apparently in the hope of finding a short overland route to the Pacific, which was believed to lie to the south. After some expeditions of reconnaissance, in September 1531 he launched a major effort which reached the Magdalena valley, but he was

killed, reputedly by a poisoned arrow, in one of many battles with Indians on the way back in the valley of Chinácota. 25

AL-IDRISI (d. c.1165), Islamic physician and geographer. Though he has been claimed as a native of Ceuta in North Africa, nothing is known of his early life – except his own assertion that he travelled in Spain and North Africa – until he settled at the Christian court of Sicily, where he joined a group of Muslim savants. His main surviving work, known as *The Book of Roger* after its patron, King Roger II of Sicily, was completed in 1154 and seems to have been conceived as a commentary on a silver planisphere made for the king. The coloured maps which illustrate some manuscripts of the work reproduce this planisphere, which follows Ptolemaic models and shows each of the seven 'climates' of the world. 5

AL-ISTAKHRI, 10th-century Muslim geographer. Presumed a native of Fars, who may have settled in Baghdad, he was among the initiators of a new geographical tradition in Islam, substituting the study of 'countries' for that of the 'climates' into which **Ptolemy** had divided the world. His surviving work, the *Kitab al-Masalik wa'l-mamalik*, written towards the end of the first half of the 18th century, is an atlas of Islam, inspired by the work of the pioneering Persian geographer, al-Babkh. 5

AL-QAZWINI (d. 1283), Muslim geographer. Born in Persia of Arab ancestry, he was a magistrate until the Mongol conquest of Baghdad in 1258, after which he retired to concentrate on scholarship. His two great compilations, known respectively as *Cosmography* and *Geography*, synthesised, with methods of classification borrowed from Ptolemy, the information of most texts available to him. His *Cosmography*, which deals with the seen and unseen heavens, the elements, the climates of the earth, hydrography, geology, and flora and fauna, was the most comprehensive treatment of the universe produced in Islam up to the time. 5

ALVARADO, PEDRO DE (c.1485–1541), Spanish *conquistador*. He was born in Extremadura but was in Santo Domingo by 1510, before moving to Cuba. He took part in **Juan de Grijalva's** expedition to Yucatán and the Gulf of Mexico and later served as second-in-command to **Cortés**, who left him in command of the Aztec capital, where his sanguinary methods helped to provoke hostilities that resulted in Spanish evacuation on 30 June 1520. Alvarado was wounded but recovered to take part in the final recapture of the city in 1521. In 1524, he added most of highland Guatemala and El Salvador to the tally of Spanish conquests, founding the city of Santiago de los Caballeros on 24 June, and rejoined Cortés in Honduras in 1526. After a brief period of imprisonment in 1529, during an attempt by a civilian governor to assert civil authority over that of the *conquistadores*, he resumed his career in exploration and conquest, obtaining royal permission for a Pacific expedition in 1532. In January 1534 he diverted his efforts to an attempt to conquer Quito, where, however, he found other *conquistadores* had preceded him. Thereafter, while fighting to retain and enlarge his governorships in Guatemala and Honduras, he prepared further Pacific expeditions but none came to fruition. The last was prevented by the Indian uprising of 1541 in Nueva Galicia, western Mexico, where he died of wounds on 4 July. 24

ÁLVARES, FRANCISCO (c.1490–1540), Portuguese explorer of Ethiopia. A priest from Coimbra, he was appointed to the Portuguese embassy to Ethiopia in 1515 under Duarte Galvão, continuing in 1520 under Rui da Lima when the former ambassador died on the Red Sea. Returning to Italy in 1527 he went to Rome to report to the pope in 1533. He published a renowned account of his travels, *The Prester John of the Indies*, in the last year of his life. 11, 27, 28

ÁLVAREZ MALDONADO, JUAN, 16th-century Spanish *conquistador*. A citizen of Cuzco, Peru, from 1542, with an *encomienda* in Carabaya, he was commissioned in August 1567 by the viceroy to undertake an expedition of exploration to the little-known province of Moxos, beyond Opatari. On the banks of the River Amarumayo his force of 200 men encountered a rival band of would-be *conquistadores*. Most of the survivors of the ensuing affray were massacred by Indians in the summer of 1568, but Álvarez Maldonado survived to report on the topography of the region of the upper River Madre de Dios. 27

AMUNDSEN, ROALD (1872–1928), Norwegian polar explorer. He served as first mate on an Antarctic expedition (1897–99), and commanded the *Gjöa* which completed the first successful navigation of the Northwest Passage and fixed the position of the magnetic pole (1903–6). He acquired **Nansen**'s ship *Fram* and planned to reach the North Pole by northward drift, completing the journey by sledge. His ambition to become the first to locate and reach the North Pole was frustrated by **Robert Peary** (1908); he then turned his attention to the South Pole, which he reached on 14 December 1911, after a two-month dash by dog sleigh and skis from the Bay of Whales in the Ross Sea and pioneering a route up the Axel Heiberg Glacier to the polar plateau; he preceded the arrival of Scott's expedition by 35 days. In 1918–20 he commanded an expedition through the Northeast Passage to Nome, Alaska (a feat performed only once before, by **Nordenskiöld**). His final achievement was to complete a flight, by the airship *Norge*, across the North Pole from Vardö in Norway to the Canadian shore of the Bering Strait in 1926. A similar attempt, with Lincoln Ellsworth in 1925, had proved unsuccessful. Amundsen disappeared whilst attempting to rescue Nobile, the designer of the *Norge*, who had crashed in another airship. Amundsen's contribution to geological and geographical knowledge was substantial, as were his popular accounts of his expeditions. 23, 46

ANDAGOYA, PASCUAL DE (*c.* 1495–1548), Basque-born explorer of South America. He accompanied Pedrarias Dávila to Castilla del Oro in 1514 and took part in expeditions in relief of **Francisco de Becerra** and, under **Nuñez de Balboa**, to the Gulf of San Miguel. In 1521 he was a councillor of the fledgling Panama City, of which he became major in 1527. In 1522 he claimed to have discovered 'Birú' in a voyage south along the Pacific coast of South America, and that this was the inspiration for **Francisco Pizarro**'s search for 'Peru'. In 1529, for unknown reasons, his property was confiscated and he was expelled from Panama, but he obtained restitution from the superior tribunal at Santo Domingo. In 1536 he was arrested, again for unexplained motives, and sent to Spain for trial. Exonerated in 1537, he was appointed governor of the San Juan Valley region in 1538, arriving in 1540. He set about the establishment of Spanish power energetically, but became embroiled in disputes with neighbouring governors over the limits of jurisdiction. In 1541 he was ordered to Spain for a review of the case. In 1546 he returned to the New World in the expedition led by Pedro de la Gasca to enforce royal authority in Peru. He served in the royal campaign and died in Cuzco in 1548. 24

ANDRADE, ANTONIO DE (1580–1634). An Italian Jesuit of the Indian mission, he penetrated southern Tibet across the Himalayas in 1624 to gather information on Lamaism and to search for Christian communities thought to have been founded by St. Thomas. From Delhi through Badrinath and the Mana Pass he reached Tsaparang. In further journeys of 1625 and 1627 he and his coadjutors established a mission at Tsaparang, which lasted only until 1631 when its success provoked a violent local reaction. From 1630, Andrade was Jesuit provincial of India, based at Goa, where he died. 8

ANSON, GEORGE (1697–1762), British admiral. Between 1740 and 1744 he made a remarkable circumnavigation of the world. Sent by the Admiralty to harass Spanish colonies in South America and foment resistance against Spain in Peru and Chile, he led his fleet of ill-financed, under-manned ships across the Pacific. Despite losing all but one ship, he captured the annual Spanish treasure galleon from Acapulco to the Philippines. He returned to England with £500,000 in bullion. His account of his exploits – *Voyage around the World* (1748) – was a powerful polemic against the endemic naval corruption of the period. Coupled with the success of his circumnavigation, it also did much to alert British interests to the potential of the still largely unexplored Pacific. It contained, too, a recommendation that Britain colonize the Falkland Islands in the South Atlantic, which Anson saw as a strategic key to the Pacific. Anson was promoted rear-admiral in 1744 and granted a peerage in 1747 after defeating the French fleet off Cape Finisterre. He became a full admiral in 1761. 34

ANVILLE, JEAN-BAPTISTE BOURGUIGON D' (1697–1782), French geographer and cartographer, who was born and worked in Paris, and compiled over 200 maps that reflected the most up-to-date geographical knowledge of his day. He also wrote some 78 scholarly works covering both modern and historical geography. Among his most influential works was *Géographie Ancienne* (1768, with successive editions and translations up to 1815), and an historical atlas that reflected the antiquarian interests of his contemporaries and sought to outline the development of world history on a geographical basis. Many of his works were republished posthumously. His library of over 100,000 maps is held by the Bibliothèque Nationale.

ANZA, JUAN BAUTISTA DE, (1735–88), Spanish explorer of North America. In 1760 he was commander of the garrison of Tubac in Arizona. In 1769 he sought leave to explore a new overland route from Sonora to the new colonies in Upper California. He departed from Tubac in 1774, accompanied by the Franciscan missionary, Father Garcés, and reached the San Gabriel Mission after crossing the Gila and Colorado Rivers. Their second expedition in 1775–76 reached Monterey and set up both Garcés's mission amongst the Yumas and the colony of San Francisco. Anza was made governor of New Mexico – a role in which he achieved a great reputation as a pacifier of unsubdued Indian tribes, and developed new routes between his own territory and Sonora. 17, 20

ANZHU, PYOTR FEDOROVICH (1796–1869), Russian naval officer and Arctic explorer. Anzhu was of French ancestry and is sometimes known by the old family name of Anjou. He was educated at the naval academy of St. Petersburg, and then served for several years in the Baltic fleet. In 1820–24 he led a naval expedition to survey the New Siberian Islands, improving on earlier surveys by **Gedenshtrom** and **Pshenitsin**. Much of his subsequent career was spent as a commander of warships in the Baltic. He was promoted rear-admiral in 1844 and later advanced to the rank of admiral. 46

ARELLANO, ALONSO DE, 16th-century Spanish navigator of the Pacific. He was captain of the 40-ton pinnace *San Lúcas* in the expedition of **Urdaneta** of 1564–65 across the Pacific. He took advantage of the swiftness of his ship to part company from the fleet, reaching the Philippines on 29 January 1565. Apparently unable to find his former companions, he decided to proceed with Urdaneta's main mission – the discovery of a return route from the Philippines to New Spain. He set off on 22 April, heading north to find the westerlies. He claimed to have gone as far as 43°N and reached Navidad on 9 August, two months ahead of his commander. He was arraigned for desertion but acquitted. 33

ARMSTRONG, NEIL ALDEN (b. 1930), American astronaut. Armstrong was the first man to walk on the surface of the Moon. He made one previous space flight, as commander of *Gemini 8* in 1966, before commanding the *Apollo 11* mission that landed on the Moon on 20 July 1969. Armstrong and his co-pilot, 'Buzz' Aldrin, spent 21½ hours on the Moon. 47

ARTHUR, GABRIEL, 17th-century explorer of North America. Thought to have been a servant of **Abraham Wood**, the trader of Fort Henry, he was sent in 1673 with **James Needham** on a south-westward journey of exploration across what is now North Carolina and the Blue Ridge Mountains to Cherokee country, where he was captured by Indians and wandered with them beyond the Cumberland Gap for about 3,300 miles. 19

ASTORIANS (1810–13), U.S. fur-traders representing John Jacob Astor. To expedite trade with the Orient, Astor founded the Pacific Fur Company and planned a fur-trading post in Oregon. His traders on the sailing vessel *Tonquin* reached the Columbia River estuary and established Fort Astoria in 1811. (The *Tonquin* was subsequently attacked by Nootka Sound Indians and was blown up.) Meanwhile an overland party of 62, led by businessman Wilson Price Hunt, straggled into Fort Astoria in early 1812. The fort was subsequently taken by the British. Seven Astorians led by Robert Stuart returned overland, discovering South Pass in the process. With the failure of Astor's Pacific Fur Company, Astor abandoned plans for business in the far Northwest. 22

AYORA, JUAN DE, 16th-century Spanish explorer of South America. He accompanied Pedravias Dávila to Castilla de Oro in 1514 and led an expedition into the interior of Panama, notorious for expropriating and enslaving natives on flimsy pretexts. According to the most circumstantial account, he began his reconnaissance at or near the Río Ailigandi, crossing the Tubanama and Pocorosa country and sending a detachment as far as the Pacific shore. Leaving a garrison at Pocorosa that was massacred soon after, Ayora took his share of the booty and returned to Spain. 10

BACK, SIR GEORGE (1796–1878), English sailor and Arctic explorer. He served in the Royal Navy during the Napoleonic Wars and accompanied **Sir John Franklin** on his expeditions (1818, 1819–22, 1825–27) to Arctic Canada. He explored the Great Fish (Back) River in 1833–35, and the Arctic coast in 1836–37. 23

BAFFIN, WILLIAM (1584–1622), English navigator and explorer. In 1612, he was chief pilot on a voyage to search for the Northwest Passage, and in 1615 was pilot of the *Discovery* under **Robert Bylot** to Hudson Bay with the same object. During these voyages he explored parts of the Greenland coast. He again accompanied Bylot in the following year, when he explored Baffin Bay and Baffin Island, which are named after him. Baffin obtained, in 1615, the first longitude known to have been accurately measured by lunar observation at sea. His outline map of Baffin Island was deemed absurd by contemporaries but was confirmed in 1821. Having taken service with the East India Company, he was killed in 1622 on the island of Qishm in present-day Iran in the Anglo-Persian attack mounted to drive the Portuguese out of the Persian Gulf. 16

BAKER, SIR SAMUEL WHITE (1821–93). Adventurer, hunter and explorer, he worked in Ceylon and Asia Minor where he found the lady who accompanied him into Africa in 1860 and who was to become his wife. Hoping perhaps to find its source, he travelled up the Nile, explored some of its Abyssinian tributaries in 1861–62, and then went on south to Gondokoro where, in 1863, he met **Speke** and Grant. They were returning north after Speke's discovery of the source in Lake Victoria, but told Baker of another lake through which the Nile waters ran. Baker went on to see and name this as Lake Albert in 1864. But his overestimate of its size and southward extent was to cause confusion for a dozen years or more.

Baker was physically large, courageous and determined but also tactless and overbearing. His relations with Africans tended to be poor, sometimes disastrous. After his great expedition, which was rewarded with a knighthood in 1866, he took service with the khedive of Egypt, who hoped to found an empire in the upper Nile regions revealed by the explorers. Baker's shortcomings became more obvious as, in return for an enormous salary, he tried to end the slave trade and set up an administration in the years 1869–73. He claimed far more than he actually achieved and left a legacy of distrust, especially in the kingdom of Bunyoro. 39

BALBOA, VASCO NÚÑEZ DE (*c.* 1475–1519), Spanish explorer and *conquistador*, the first European to see the Pacific Ocean from its eastern shore and one of the main founders of Spain's empire in the New World. He sailed to the West Indies in 1500 and settled in Hispaniola. He fell heavily into debt and, to escape his creditors, stowed away on an expedition taking supplies to a newly founded colony on the east side of the Gulf of Urabá. The original settlers were found to have abandoned the settlement, but Balboa, a man of striking personality, convinced all on the expedition that they should found a settlement themselves; the site he chose was on the Panamanian side of the Gulf of Darién. In 1511, King Ferdinand appointed him interim governor of Darién.

By this time Balboa had heard rumours of gold in the south. In 1512 he became the first European to see the Colombian Andes. Reports of the proximity of a vast ocean encouraged attempts to cross the Isthmus of Panama. Balboa led the first in September 1513 and saw the Pacific Ocean on the 25th of the month. When he reached the shore, Balboa strode into the sea in full armour and claimed it for the king of Spain. This act enhanced his popularity with Ferdinand and the area of his governorship was enlarged. However, the king appointed Pedrarias Dávila, a man of excessive jealousy, to a superior position. Suspecting his loyalty, Dávila charged Balboa with fictitious transgressions and had him beheaded in January 1519. 10, 24, 25

BARENTS, WILLEM (d. 1597), Dutch navigator and Arctic explorer. Little is known of his life except that he was chief pilot on three Dutch expeditions in search of a Northwest Passage. On the first two, 1594 and 1595, he crossed the Barents Sea and charted parts of Novaya Zemlya. On the third, 1596–97, Barents chose a more northerly course, discovered Bear Island (Bjørnøya) and Spitsbergen, then crossed the Barents Sea, made the first recorded passage around the northern extremity of Novaya Zemlya, and was forced to winter nearby in Ledyanaya Gavan' (Ice Haven). The expedition set off for home in June 1597, but Barents, who had been seriously ill during the winter, died at sea soon after. 32

BARRETO, FRANCISCO (1520–73), Portuguese diplomat and explorer of East Africa. Born to a leading family of Faro, he became governor of the fortress of Baçaim (Bassein) in 1547. In 1555 he succeeded Viceroy Pedro de Mascarenhas as governor of Portuguese India, serving with distinction until his return to Portugal in 1559. In 1564 he commanded the Portuguese squadron that assisted the Spanish capture of a pirate's nest on the Moroccan coast. In 1567 he was appointed prospective governor of Monomotapa, the gold-rich East African empire that the Portuguese proposed to conquer. He arrived in Mozambique with a force of 1,000 men in May 1570 but the conquest proved arduous, its progress impeded by lack of intelligence and by differences between the military men and their Jesuit advisers as to the best route of approach. Barreto died in mid-campaign on 9 July 1573, bequeathing to his successor, Vasco Fernandes Homem, an impossible task. 27

BARROW, JOHN (1764–1848), British geographer and promoter of exploration. He was secretary to Earl Macartney, and accompanied the earl on his embassy to China and during his period as governor of the Cape of Good Hope colony. He published *Travels in China* (1804) and *Travels into Southern Africa* (1806). From 1806 until his death he was second secretary of the Admiralty, in which position he promoted many voyages of discovery, notably those of **John Ross** and **William Parry** to the polar regions. He was author of *Voyages of Discovery and Research in the Arctic Regions* (1846) and was one of the principal founders of the Royal Geographical Society. 38, 46

BARTH, HEINRICH (1821–65). One of the most scholarly of Africa's explorers, he was educated at the University of Berlin, learned Arabic in London and then travelled in North Africa before being invited to join the British Government's Central African Expedition in 1849. With **Richardson** and **Overweg**, he crossed the Sahara from Tripoli and sailed a boat they had transported with them on Lake Chad. But Richardson and Overweg died, leaving Barth in sole charge of the expedition in 1852. Having explored the Chad basin and established the separateness of the Benue, he travelled westward into the Fulani empire. Next he followed the Niger valley to Timbuktu, where he discovered the *Tarikh al Sudan* (History of Sudan), did work on languages and established the ethnography of a vast region. Barth returned to Europe in 1855. He published five volumes on his travels but never became as famous as he deserved to be, as popular attention switched to East Africa. 37

BATTS, THOMAS (d. 1698), 17th-century explorer of North America. He was in Virginia as early as 1667. With his brother Henry he was granted 5,878 acres of land in the Appomattox Valley in 1668. In 1671, with **Robert Fallam** he was sent on one of the expeditions sponsored by **Abraham Wood** in search of the 'South Sea', and got well beyond the head of the Roanoke River. 19

BAUDIN, THOMAS-NICOLAS (1754–1803), French navigator and explorer of Australia. Born at St. Pierre de Ré, he became a naval cadet in 1774 after a period as a merchant seaman and was commissioned in 1786. Despised by the French naval service, he accepted employment with Archduke Francis of Austria, commanding a frigate on a scientific mission to India, where he collected specimens for the archduke's botanical garden. A second such voyage from 1793 to 1796 took him to the south coast of China; owing to the state of war between France and Austria, the French Republic was the beneficiary of this venture and the recipient of its collections. In 1800 Napoleon chose Baudin to lead a major French scientific expedition to New Holland (Australia). He approached round the Cape of Good Hope and the Indian Ocean, arriving off Cape Leeuwin on 19 June 1801. Sickness and mutiny among his men and damage to his ships almost destroyed the expedition, but he was fortunate to reach Sydney in June 1802 at a time of peace between France and England. He completed a detailed inspection of the east, west and south coasts. He was prevented by adverse weather from extending his work along the north coast, and sailed for home in July 1803. Broken in health, he died on the way to Mauritius. His scientific colleagues, whose collaboration on the voyage had been grudging throughout, omitted his name from the official accounts. 35

BECERRA, FRANCISCO DE (d. *c.*1517), Spanish *conquistador*. A lieutenant of **Balboa**, he made two recorded expeditions, the first in the footsteps of **Garavito** and beyond to Garachiné on the Gulf of San Miguel. From there he reconnoitred the coast north almost as far as the present site of Panama City in 1514. A further expedition took him east from Darién by sea to the far side of the Gulf of Urabá, where he found smelting equipment said to come from a gold-rich culture, which he sought along the Sinú valley. He was never heard of again and Balboa declared that exploring the Sinú valley was 'like sending cattle to the slaughterhouse'. 10

BEHAIM, MARTIN (1459–1507), geographer of Nuremberg. He may first have visited Portugal in the 1480s. He claimed to have sailed down the west coast of Africa between 1485 and 1486 with **Diogo Cão**. He had returned to Nuremberg by 1490, where he began the work for which he is famous – constructing his terrestrial globe, the oldest still in existence. The globe was completed in 1492 and appears to have been designed to promote the idea of a navigable Western Ocean, which Behaim proposed in Portugal – apparently unaware of Columbus's achievement – in 1493. The globe is now in the collection of the Germanisches Nationalmuseum in Nuremberg. 9

BELLINGSHAUSEN, FABIAN GOTTLIEB BENJAMIN (1770–1852), Russian explorer. Bellingshausen is best remembered as having made the first sighting of the Antarctic continent, in January 1820. A small section of Princess Martha Coast was discovered and mapped by Bellingshausen's expedition during a three-year circumnavigation of the globe. The following year, Bellingshausen also discovered Peter I and Alexander Islands in Antarctica. 46

BENALCÁZAR, SEBASTIÁN MOYANO DE (*c.*1495–1550), Spanish *conquistador*. He went to the New World in 1514, took part in the conquest of Nicaragua in 1542 and served in Peru under **Francisco Pizarro**. He led a detachment to the conquest of Quito in 1533 and then seized present-day Ecuador. He sent out expeditions in various directions and, receiving rumours of 'El Dorado', marched north into Colombia in 1536, reaching the headwaters of the Rivers Cauca and Magdalena. Early in 1539 he marched on Bogotá to obtain a share of the spoils of the conquest by **Jiménez de Quesada**. His disputes with other *conquistadores* were settled by the crown, largely in his favour, in 1541, when he was made governor of a large part of the Magdalena valley and of what is now Colombia. He supported the crown in the Peruvian civil wars of the 1540s but his conduct was arbitrary and his loyalty suspect. In 1550 he was arrested, to be released only on appeal to the crown. He died on arrival in Spain late that year. 24, 25

BERING, VITUS (*c.*1680–1741), Danish navigator in the service of Tsar Peter the Great's navy. In 1724 the tsar ordered him to find whether there was water between Asia and North America or whether the continents were connected by land. Russia was interested not only in expansion but also in finding, if it existed, a sea route around Siberia to China. Bering set sail in July 1728 and in August passed through the strait which bears his name into the Atlantic, though bad weather prevented his sighting North America. Later Bering prepared to undertake a second expedition, but it was enlarged into what came to be called Russia's Great Northern Expedition (1733–43), during which much of Siberia's Arctic coast was mapped. With **Chirikov**, the expedition reached Alaska, though permanent Russian settlements in the Territory were not established until the 1790s. Bering, who commanded one ship in the expedition, was able to chart only the south-western coast of Siberia, the Alaskan peninsula and the Aleutian Islands before succumbing to scurvy, from which he died. 20, 32

BERRÍO, ANTONIO (*c.*1520–98) and **FERNANDO**, his son (1577–1622). Antonio served in his youth in the Spanish army in Italy and the Low Countries. He was the nephew by marriage and chosen heir of **Jiménez de Quesada**. Moving to Colombia to claim his inheritance in 1581, he became titular 'governor of El Dorado' the following year, with rights in the enormously valuable tribute of the Indians of Chita and the right to conquer the area between the Rivers Pauto and Papamene. Between 1581 and 1584 he made three journeys of reconnaissance, culminating in his great Orinoco journey of 1584, which convinced him that the fabled land lay in the Guiana highlands. A further expedition in 1587–89 ended in a mutiny that forced him reluctantly to cut short the search. He returned in 1590, however, with his son, Fernando, exploring the southern tributaries of the Orinoco and continuing in 1591 to Trinidad to seek help. Here he recruited Domingo de Vera, who established what they believed was a route to El Dorado along the Caroní in 1593. While awaiting further reinforcements from Spain in April 1595, Berrío briefly fell prisoner to English raiders under **Sir Walter Raleigh**, whose own fantasies about El Dorado were fed by those of his captive. In December 1595 Berrío founded Santo Tomé near the mouth of the Caroní as a base for continued exploration. On his death there in 1598, Fernando continued his efforts with renewed vigour, making 18 expeditions along southern tributaries of the Orinoco. In 1612 he was obliged to return to Spain because of his illicit dealings with foreign traders at Santo Tomé. Restored to favour in 1619 Fernando resumed his explorations, getting close to the source of the Orinoco. In 1622, he was captured by Barbary pirates on his way to Spain to recruit more help, and died a captive in Algiers. 26

BÉTHENCOURT, JEAN DE (1360–1422), Lord of Grainville in Normandy and conqueror of the Canary Islands. With **Gadifer de la Salle** he landed on the island of Lanzarote in 1402 and established a permanent settlement, also occupying Fuerteventura and Hierro by 1405. Though a subject of the king of France, he confided his islands to Castilian sovereignty, perhaps because his efforts depended on the help of a nearby power, before returning home. 8

BIANCO, ANDREA, 15th-century Venetian cartographer. Between 1437 and 1451 he appears ten times in Venetian records as an officer or adviser in commercial galley fleets sailing to Flanders, Barbary, Tana, Alexandria and Beirut. The Flanders run was a speciality of his, while in 1448 he was in London. In the 1450s he assisted **Fra Mauro** in Venice in the production of a great world map. Two important surviving works are signed by Bianco: an atlas of 1436 containing ten maps, in the Biblioteca Marciana; and a portolan chart made in London in 1448, now also in the Biblioteca Marciana. The latter records with great fidelity the discoveries made by Portuguese explorers along the west coast of Africa to the mid-1440s. 8, 12

BIEDMA, MANUEL DE (d. 1687), Franciscan explorer of South America. From 1658 he served the Franciscan missions in the Huallaga and Ucayali valleys. In 1673 Indians from along the River Pangoa arrived in Andamarca seeking conversion. Biedma was able to accompany them home, but the route was too difficult to ensure permanent communications. From 1676 he devoted himself to a wide-ranging search for a better route, failing in this task but contributing enormously to the exploration of the area. In 1684–85, for instance, a road was hacked open along the River Perené to near the River Tambo. In 1685–86 communications were opened with the Jesuit mission at San Miguel de los

Cunibos. Biedma was martyred by recalcitrant Cunibo Indians in July 1687. 26

BINGER, LOUIS (1856–1936), French Marine infantry officer, explorer and administrator. He explored into Senegal and along the Niger River and then to the Ivory Coast between 1887 and 1889. In 1893–95 he was governor of the Ivory Coast and in 1896–1907 director of African Affairs in the Ministry of Colonies. 37

BLAND, EDWARD (d. 1653). An English merchant trading with Spain, he went to Virginia in 1643, where he founded an estate of 8,000 acres at Kimages in Charles City County. In August 1650 he led an expedition from Fort Henry, accompanied by **Abraham Wood**, to reconnoitre to the south-west and as far as the Roanoke Falls. The journey contributed to the systematization of known routes rather than to the inauguration of new ones. On 20 October 1650 the Virginia Assembly granted him the right to colonize the territory he had traversed and he published *The Discovery of New Brittaine* to publicize the venture, which was cut short by his death in 1653. 19

BLAXLAND, GREGORY (1778–1853), English-born explorer of Australia. Born into a family of prosperous farmers, in 1805–7, with the promise of extensive grants of land there, he and his brother John sold their farms and migrated with their families to New South Wales, where they traded and pursued pastoral interests. In 1813, Gregory joined **William Lawson** and **William Charles Wentworth** in seeking a way over the Blue Mountains, in the hope of locating additional grazing lands. 36

BLUNT, WILFRED SCAWEN (1840–1922), English poet and traveller who, with his wife Anne, in 1879 travelled across Arabia, chiefly for reasons of his health. The journey is notable principally for the vivid diary left by Anne Blunt. Her unselfconscious upper-class elan and brio swept aside potential obstacles – she described her husband and herself as 'persons of distinction in search of other persons of distinction'. When published, her accounts of such incidents as visiting the harem of the emir of Hayil, of eating locusts and of the varied ways of the desert enjoyed great popularity. Her husband subsequently became a leading champion of the cause of Arab independence. 42

BODEGA Y QUADRA, JUAN FRANCISCO (1744–92), Spanish *conquistador* of North America. He accompanied the 1775 expedition of **Bruno de Hezeta**, discovering a bay that bears his name in California, and made a further surveying voyage of his own, producing a much improved map of the coast from 17°N to 58°N. He was the author of a further memoir of a surveying expedition of 1792. 20

BORCHGREVINK, CARSTEN (1864–1934), Norwegian explorer of the Antarctic. As a young man he emigrated to Australia, and first sailed into the Antarctic waters on a whaling ship in 1895. He succeeded in finding British sponsorship and on the *Southern Cross* travelled to Cape Adare. His expedition was the first to winter in the Antarctic (1899–1900), having reached the furthest point south, latitude 78°50', yet navigated. He explored the Ross Sea and surveyed the Ross Ice Shelf. 46

BOUGAINVILLE, LOUIS-ANTOINE DE (1729–1811), French soldier, diplomat and explorer. In 1756 he served under Montcalm in Canada, and in 1761 campaigned in Germany. Between 1767 and 1769 Bougainville completed the first French circumnavigation of the world, visiting Tahiti, discovered the year before by **Wallis**, and confirming its reputation as an earthly paradise – Bougainville changed its name to New Cythera. On the same voyage he revealed that Espiritu Santo (the New Hebrides) was an island, not, as **Quiros** had claimed in the 17th century, part of the imagined Terra Australis. His account of his journey – *Voyage autour du Monde* – was widely read. Bougainville subsequently returned to his military career, serving with the American army in the War of Independence; in 1780 he was promoted field-marshal. He gave much of the rest of his life to scientific pursuits, winning many honours from Napoleon. 34

BOURGMONT, ÉTIENNE VENIARD (active 1706–25), French explorer of North America. In Canada from about 1685, Bourgmont was made acting commander of Detroit. An Indian uprising in 1706 led him to flee the post and he took to the wilderness, spending five

years around the lower Missouri. He subsequently offered to help form alliances between France and the Indians he had encountered. The offer was accepted, and in 1714 he travelled up the Missouri to the mouth of the Platte. He was sent back to France in 1719 to report his discoveries. He returned to America the following year with instructions to stop Spanish incursions from the Southwest. A further journey to present-day Kansas to forge an alliance with the Comanche followed in 1724. He left the New World for France in 1725. 21

BRAZZA, PIERRE SAVORGNAN DE (1852–1905), originally Italian, he became a French citizen and naval officer in 1874. Brazza was sent by a group of unofficial enthusiasts to explore the Ogowe in West Africa (1875–77). Having reached the river, he went on to the Alima, a tributary of the Congo. He returned in 1879–82, now working for the French National Committee of the International Association, hoping to develop the Ogowe as a route to the Congo valley and thence to the lakes region in the centre of the continent. He soon came into rivalry with the Belgian King Leopold's agent, **Stanley**.

Brazza's treaty of 1880 with Makoko was a key development in the history of 19th-century Africa. Recognized by the French government in 1882, it became the basis of French sovereignty over the French Congo. Brazza developed the Ogowe route in a further expedition of 1883–85. From 1887 to 1897 he was governor of the French Congo and also undertook further exploration. Known as the 'pacific' explorer, he was a patient and generous friend of Africans. Conditions in French Equatorial Africa deteriorated after he left, and in 1905 he was called upon to report on the problems. He died in Senegal on his way back to France. 40

BRIEVA, DOMINGO DE, 17th-century Spanish explorer of South America. A Franciscan lay brother from Quito, he took part in the first Franciscan mission on the Amazon in 1632 and the 1634–35 expedition along the Río San Miguel. On a further mission in 1636, on the Río Napo, he decided with a colleague, Andrés de Toledo, to attempt to follow the river to its confluence with the Amazon. Driven on by hunger, they sailed all the way to the mouth of the Amazon, inspiring the Portuguese authorities to attempt an upriver route from Pará to Quito. Brieva accompanied this expedition, led by **Pedro de Teixeira**, while Andrés de Toledo went to Spain to report. 26

BROUWER, HENDRIK (1580–1643), Dutch mariner and explorer of the Far East and South America. His voyage from 1611 in the service of the Dutch East India Company exploited the new route round the Cape of Good Hope in the path of the Roaring Forties of the Southern Ocean. In 1613 he visited Siam and Japan. In 1617 he returned to Holland to serve for 15 years in the company's headquarters in Amsterdam or on intelligence-gathering missions in London. For three years from 1632 he was governor of Batavia, and in 1641 the Dutch West India Company sent him to Chile with the title of 'governor-general of America'. If the purpose of his mission was to secure a permanent base in South America for trans-Pacific trade, it was wildly over-ambitious. Brouwer died in the course of the expedition, off Valdivia, on 7 August 1643. 29

BROWNE, WILLIAM G. (1768–1813), English explorer of North Africa. Hoping to go on to Ethiopia, Browne reached Egypt in 1792 but was forced to travel west of the Nile Valley into the kingdom of Darfur. Here he was detained for three years until 1796. His account of that region was the first by a European explorer. Browne later travelled in Turkey and Persia, where he was murdered in 1813. 37, 42

BRUCE, JAMES (1730–94), Scottish explorer of Africa. He had been a wine merchant in London and in 1763 became consul at Algiers, where he studied Arabic. In 1768 he set out from Cairo via the Red Sea to Ethiopia, which he reached in 1770, where he became embroiled in Ethiopian politics. He travelled to the headstream of the Blue Nile in 1772, before returning along the Nile to Egypt. Rebuffed in London, he returned to Scotland. Not until 1790 did he write his book, *Travels to Discover the Sources of the Nile*, which revealed Bruce to be a remarkable traveller who ranks as the first modern scientific explorer of Africa. 27, 28, 37

BUACHE, PHILIPPE (1700–73). Son-in-law of the leading French geographer and cartographer **Guillaume de Lisle**, Buache did much work on the theoretical cartography of the oceans, including the development of bathymetric contours (isobaths) shown on the first accurate chart of the English Channel (1752). 20, 21

BURCHELL, WILLIAM (1782–1863). A botanist, Burchell worked in St. Helena between 1805 and 1810 before going on to South Africa, where he travelled north from the Cape into regions beyond the Orange River in 1811–15. His botanical, zoological and illustrative records of his experiences, which are outstanding, appeared in 1822. 38

BURCKHARDT, JOHANN LUDWIG (1784–1817), Swiss explorer of the Middle East. Born in Lausanne, Burckhardt studied in England from 1806. In 1809 the Association for Promoting the Discovery of the Interior Parts of Africa chose him to undertake a mission across the Sahara. As a preliminary, he spent a period studying Islam in Syria and learning Arabic. On his journey from Syria in 1812 he discovered the site of Petra in Jordan. Delayed in Cairo, he travelled up the Nile, making a further discovery of archaeological importance, the temple of Abu Simbel. Unable to proceed with the trans-Saharan project he crossed to Arabia and visited Mecca in Muslim guise. He died in Cairo on 15 October 1817, waiting for an opportunity to resume his mission to the Sahara, and leaving three volumes of *Travels*, all of which made significant contributions to knowledge. 42

BURKE, ROBERT O'HARA (1821–61), was born in Ireland, and migrated to Australia in 1853. In 1860, he was appointed to lead an expedition sponsored by the Royal Society of Victoria and the government of that colony, intended to anticipate other attempts to cross the continent from south to north. The venture turned out disastrously. With seven companions, Burke set out from Menindee on the Darling River, and established a base camp on Cooper's Creek. From this, Burke, Wills, Gray and King walked up to the Gulf of Carpentaria, reaching the tidal waters of the Flinders River, but not the sea itself. Gray died of starvation and exhaustion just before they reached the base camp again, which the others had left only hours before. Leaving Wills at the camp, Burke and King tried to reach an outstation at Mt. Hopeless, but Burke died two days later. King returned to the camp, to find Wills had died. Aborigines kept King alive until a search party found him in September 1861. 36

BURTON, SIR RICHARD FRANCIS (1821–90), British explorer of Arabia and Africa, one of the most idiosyncratic of the period and a gifted linguist. Burton joined the British Indian Army in 1842, partly to learn local languages and customs. This enabled him, in 1853, to disguise himself as a Muslim pilgrim and journey to Mecca and Medina, holy cities forbidden to non-Muslims. In 1854 he led an expedition into the Somali territory of East Africa penetrating as far as Harar, the 'forbidden city'. Shortly afterwards he and his companions, **Speke** and Stroyan, were involved in a skirmish with Somalis which led to their all being wounded. In 1857, Burton, again travelling with Speke, led an expedition to seek the lakes believed to exist in East Africa. Its most notable discovery was Lake Tanganyika, though Speke, making a detour to the north on his own, also discovered the southern shores of Lake Victoria, which, on little evidence, he claimed as the source of the Nile. Burton was later to resent bitterly the fame gathered by Speke as the discoverer of the Nile source. In 1861 Burton became the first European to climb Mount Cameroon in West Africa. In the same year, Burton left the Indian Army and joined the British Consular Service. Nevertheless, he continued his explorations, notably in the Gold Coast (Ghana) and in Dahomey, and in 1865 in Brazil, where he travelled up the Amazon and Plate rivers. His last appointment was as British Consul in Trieste, Italy. Burton was a prolific writer, and in addition to numerous accounts of his journeys (he published more than 50 books) he translated, among other works, the *Book of a Thousand Nights and a Night* (the 'Arabian Nights'). 29, 39, 42

BUTTON, SIR THOMAS (d. 1634), English navigator, naval officer and early explorer of Canada. He entered the navy in 1612, when he was given command of an expedition to search for the Northwest Passage and find the explorer Henry Hudson, who after a mutiny had been put adrift in a small boat with his son and seven loyal seamen. His two ships – *Resolution* and *Discovery* – entered Hudson Strait, where he named Resolution Island for his own ship. He then crossed Hudson Bay southwestwards to Nelson River, where he anchored during a particularly cruel winter. From the spring of 1613, Button and his men continued their explorations, before sailing for England in August. Button never returned to Canada but, remaining in the naval service, took part as a rear-admiral in the campaign (1620–21) against the pirates of the Algerian coast. 16

BYLOT, ROBERT (active c. 1610), British explorer of Hudson Bay. He sailed on **Henry Hudson**'s voyage of 1610, which discovered and partially explored Hudson Bay in that year and the next. It was Bylot who brought the ship and seven survivors home to England after the mutiny in June 1611. He returned to the Hudson Bay area in 1615 and 1616 in search of the supposed Northwest Passage. 16

BYRD, RICHARD EVELYN (1888–1957), American airman and polar explorer. He graduated as a naval officer in 1912, but injury interrupted his career and in 1917 he retrained as a naval aviator; soon after he was an acknowledged aviation pioneer. He was a pilot on an expedition to Greenland in 1925, and in 1926 he flew across the North Pole. His first Antarctic expedition, 1928–30, made much use of aircraft, discovered Marie Byrd Land and included the first flight over the South Pole (1929). He led three more expeditions to the Antarctic, in 1933–35, 1939–41 and 1946–47, each time using aircraft to explore and map the continent and to carry out scientific investigations. On his last visit to the Antarctic, 1955–56, he made his third flight over the South Pole. By the end of his life he was the world's leading figure in Antarctic exploration, and when he died was planning America's role in the International Geophysical Year (1957–58) and working towards a treaty to provide for international cooperation in Antarctica. 46

BYRON, JOHN (1723–86), British explorer and vice-admiral. With **George Anson** he circumnavigated the world (1740–44). In 1764, following belated recognition by the government in London of the long-term benefits of British exploration in the Pacific, he was given command of an expedition to the Pacific. He made no discoveries of significance, though before passing through the Strait of Magellan he laid claim to the Falkland Islands in the South Atlantic. 34

CABEZA DE VACA, ÁLVAR NÚÑEZ (1507–59). Spanish explorer of the Americas. In 1528 **Pánfilo de Narváez**, who had been granted rights to colonize territory between Florida and Mexico, landed his expedition, of which Cabeza de Vaca was treasurer, at Tampa Bay, Florida. He then abandoned his ships and explored northwards on foot. At Apalachee Bay, harassed by Indians, the expedition built vessels to enable it to return to its ships by sea. The journey proved a disaster. The expedition was shipwrecked off Texas; many drowned and the rest were taken as slaves by the Indians. Only Cabeza de Vaca and three others survived, to trudge to Spanish settlements in Sinaloa, which they reached in May 1536, accompanied by 600 native guides who had become Cabeza de Vaca's followers, enthralled by his charisma and his reputed sanctity.

In 1542, in South America, Cabeza de Vaca marched overland to relieve explorers trapped in Asunción. Under his command, most of the course of the River Paraguay was explored but his men were mutinous. He returned to Spain in the following year and was later appointed governor of the Río de la Plata province in Paraguay. However, the Spaniards under his command rebelled and in 1545 he was dismissed. Tried in Spain and found guilty of misrule, he was sentenced to banishment in Africa but pardoned after eight years. He ended his life as a judge in Seville. He wrote two books about his exploits. 10, 17, 26

CABOT, JOHN (c. 1450–c. 1499), Genoese-born navigator, who received Venetian nationality in 1476. He traded extensively in the eastern Mediterranean and claimed to have visited Mecca. He moved to Spain about 1490 and put plans to the authorities in Portugal and Spain for a westward voyage to Asia, perhaps in partnership or rivalry with **Columbus**. From Valencia in 1493, after he learned of Columbus's successful voyage, he came to Bristol, with his wife Mathea and

sons, Ludovico, **Sebastian** and Sanci. He convinced the Bristol men there was land in the west, but his first voyage failed (dates are uncertain). In March 1496 Henry VII authorized a western voyage, promising lavish grants if he succeeded. Sailing in the *Mathew*, he left Bristol in May 1497, reaching land near Cape Breton on 24 June. He coasted Newfoundland to Cape Bauld by mid-July and arrived back in Bristol on 6 August. He reached London on 10 August to report that he had found the land of the Great Khan (Cathay). A follow-up voyage was put in hand. London merchants fitted out a ship for him; those of Bristol four more. The fleet set out in May 1498. One ship turned back to Ireland; one seems to have returned to Bristol; the other three disappeared, and Cabot with them. 14

CABOT, SEBASTIAN (1474–1557), son of **John Cabot**, also a navigator. Sebastian Cabot was probably born in Venice but grew up in Bristol. He served the English and Spanish monarchs at various times. In 1508 he made a voyage, probably from Bristol, in search of a passage north of the American continent to the Orient. How far north he sailed is disputed, though he may have reached the entrance to Hudson Bay. He then sailed south along the coast of North America, wintering at an unknown place. The following summer he continued south along the coast before returning to England in May. In 1511, Cabot accompanied the English army sent by Henry VIII to support Ferdinand II of Aragon against the French and made a map of Gascony and Guyenne. Recruited into Spanish service between 1512 and 1530, and between 1532 and 1547, he held the important post of pilot major from 1518 – effectively chief examiner of pilots – at the Casa de la Contratación, the body in Seville that supervised navigation to the New World. In 1526 he commanded a Spanish expedition of four ships to develop trade with the Far East. He was resolved to find a strait to the Pacific Ocean by sailing westwards, but on reaching the River Plate met members of an expedition led by **Juan de Solís** and was told of the riches of the region. He therefore changed his plans and explored the area, but three years of search yielded little silver. Native resistance obliged him to return to Spain in 1530. There he was judged responsible for the expedition's failure and was banished to Oran in Algeria. Cabot was pardoned two years later and restored to his old post of pilot major. After Edward VI ascended the English throne in 1547, Cabot was offered a naval post in England, to which he moved, and, from 1549, a pension. In 1551 he helped to found, and became governor of, the Company of Merchant Adventurers for the discovery of Cathay, in which capacity he organized expeditions to search for a Northeast Passage to the Orient. The expeditions of 1553, 1555 and 1556 led to English trade with Russia by the northern route. In 1544, Cabot published a celebrated, engraved map of the then known world, now in the Bibliothèque Nationale, Paris. 12, 14, 16, 32

CABRAL, PEDRO ÁLVARES (1467–1520), Portuguese navigator. In 1500 he was given command of 13 ships by King Manuel I to continue **Vasco da Gama**'s work and take possession for Portugal of the western parts of the Indies. He sailed west from the Cape Verde Islands and in Easter week reached Brazil. Cabral took possession of the area for the king of Portugal and named it 'Land of the True Cross' before continuing to the Indies and then returning to Portugal, which he reached in June 1501. Later disagreements between the king and Cabral led to the latter's being replaced as head of the next Indies expedition (1502–3) by Vasco da Gama. Cabral then withdrew from royal service and retired to Santarém, where he died. 13, 29

CABRILLO, JUAN RODRÍGUEZ (d. 1543), Portuguese explorer of the Californian coast. He accompanied **Narváez** to Mexico in 1520 and took part in the conquest of the Aztec empire. Later he joined an expedition to Guatemala. In June 1542 he sailed, with two ships, from Navidad, a port in northwest Mexico, to explore the Californian coast. He discovered San Diego Bay, Catalina Island, Santa Monica, Monterey Bay and other areas, but died in San Miguel after a fall. The voyage, which continued after his death, reached the limits of modern Oregon in March 1543. 20

CÀ DA MOSTO, ALVISE DA (1432–88). A Venetian of distinguished family, he accompanied voyages made in the service of **Henry the Navigator** under **Antoniotto di Usodimare** in 1455–56, in the course of which the lower Gambia was explored for perhaps 200 miles and contact was made with the outposts of the empire of Mali. The Cape Verde Islands, according to an account published under Cà da Mosto's name, were also discovered by him. The details he recorded of Wolof peoples marked him out as a remarkable early ethnographer. 12

CAGNI, UMBERTO (1853–1932), Italian naval officer and explorer. Cagni made his name as an explorer under the patronage of the **Duke of the Abruzzi**. In 1897, he was a member of Abruzzi's mountaineering party which made the first ascent of Mount St. Elias, Alaska. He was second in command of Abruzzi's expedition towards the North Pole on *Stella Polare*, 1899–1900. After an injury had incapacitated Abruzzi, Cagni was given the leadership of the Pole party, which sledged to a record 86°34'N from Franz Josef Land. In 1906, he accompanied Abruzzi on an exploring and mountaineering expedition to equatorial Africa. He then resumed his naval career, rose to the rank of vice-admiral in the First World War, and later commanded the Italian Adriatic fleet. 46

CAILLIÉ, RENÉ-AUGUSTE (1799–1838), French explorer of North Africa. His great ambition was to reach, and be the first European to return from, Timbuktu. When the Société Géographique of Paris offered a prize of 10,000 francs for the first person to do so, he resigned his job and set out. He had earlier spent a year with a Moorish tribe and had studied Arabic and the religion of Islam, allowing him to travel disguised as an Egyptian. He reached Timbuktu in 1828, after many privations. Fearing murder, the fate of other European visitors, he then joined a caravan moving north from the city. He finally reached France, won the 10,000 franc prize and was awarded the Légion d'Honneur. He retired and published his *Journal*, but died aged only 38 from fevers contracted in Africa. 37

CAMERON, VERNEY LOVETT (1844–94), a British naval officer in the East African Anti-Slave Trade Patrol. In 1873 he was appointed by the Royal Geographical Society to take supplies to Livingstone. Travelling inland from the Zanzibar coast, he met Livingstone's followers bringing back his body. Cameron went on to explore Lake Tanganyika. Finding its outlet in the Lukuga, he reached Nyangwe on the Lualaba, but was unable to follow the river. Instead he continued westwards to complete the first European east–west crossing of Africa. Cameron's belief in the economic potential of tropical Africa influenced King Leopold. 39, 40

CANTINO, ALBERTO (active about 1502). The 'Cantino' manuscript world map was obtained surreptitiously in October 1502 by Alberto Cantino, agent of Duke Ercole d'Este of Ferrara, in Lisbon. It is preserved in the Biblioteca Estense in Modena and testifies to Italian anxiety at the Portuguese encroachment on the Far Eastern trade by using the new sea routes. Comparison with the traditional, or Ptolemaic, outlines in the **Henricus Martellus** map demonstrates a considerable improvement in the delineation of areas such as Africa and India. South Africa no longer curves eastwards, and the peninsular form of India becomes apparent, with Ceylon in true proportion. Madagascar, discovered in 1500, is shown for the first time. 10, 14

CÃO, DIOGO (active c. 1480), Portuguese explorer of Africa. He was sent by King John II on two voyages of discovery (1482, 1484–86) to the African coast. On the first he reached Cabo de Santa Maria; on the second he explored the lower reaches of the River Congo and the coast to Walvis Bay. He claimed all the areas he discovered for Portugal. Hitherto, Portuguese explorers had merely marked the area appropriated with wooden crosses or indentations made on trees. Cão erected *padrões*, stone columns surmounted by a cross and with lettering giving the King's name, his own and the date of discovery. Some have survived to this day. 12

CAPELLO, HERMENEGILDO (1841–1917), Portuguese sailor and explorer, he travelled in the hinterland of Luanda, especially the Cuango Valley between 1877 and 1880. Here he helped to lay the foundations of what would become Portuguese territory a few years later. 40

CARTERET, PHILIP (d. 1796), English navigator of the Pacific. Carteret, an officer in the Royal Navy, accompanied **John Byron** on his 1764–66 circumnavigation. In 1766 he was placed in command of the *Swallow*, the small and poor-sailing consort vessel of **John Wallis** on his Admiralty-sponsored voyage to the Pacific. After a painfully slow passage through the Strait of Magellan, Carteret became separated from Wallis. His subsequent crossing of the Pacific was made farther to the south than any yet attempted, in the process shifting southward yet again the location of the presumed southern continent, Terra Australis. Carteret's voyage revealed Pitcairn Island and the St. George's Channel between New Britain and New Ireland, though the Solomon Islands, which Carteret sailed through, were not identified by him as the islands discovered by **Mendaña** in 1568. Carteret reached England in March 1769. He was later promoted rear-admiral. 34

CARTIER, JACQUES (1491–1557), French navigator and explorer. Little is known of his early life, but he certainly made a voyage to the New World some time before 1534 and is thought to have landed in Brazil. In 1534, the French king, Francis I, sent Cartier, who had studied navigation at Dieppe, a centre for French navigators, to North America to search for gold and other precious metals. Cartier sailed from St. Malo with two ships. He probed into what is today called the Gulf of St. Lawrence, which he named, and landed on the Gaspé Peninsula. Before returning home, he claimed the area for France, thereby laying future French claims to Canada.

In 1535, Cartier was commissioned to make a second voyage, this time with three ships, with the same object. He returned to the Gulf of St. Lawrence, where he discovered the entrance to the St. Lawrence River and proceeded up it to near the site of modern Quebec city. In September he took a small party as far as the island of Montreal, where rapids prevented further progress. The local Iroquois were warm in their welcome but after a few hours Cartier and his party returned to their winter base. However, the Indians had told him of two rivers that led farther west and into areas where there were, so they said, gold, silver and spices. The severity of the winter took the expedition wholly by surprise. Scurvy killed 25 of his men and discipline deteriorated, while some of the sailors offended the Iroquois, who became hostile. In May, as soon as the river was free of ice, Cartier sailed for France.

Francis I sent another expedition in 1541, this time not only to look for gold but to secure France's title to the area against Spanish claims. He appointed a nobleman, Jean-François de La Rocque de Roberval, to command with Cartier as his subordinate. Cartier, however, sailed in May before Roberval was ready. He again moved up the St. Lawrence River to Cape Rouge, near modern Quebec city, where he established a settlement. Cartier then went farther west in search of precious stones and found, as he thought, gold and diamonds in abundance. In the spring, he set sail for France, but stopped at Newfoundland, where he encountered his superior, Roberval, who ordered him back to Quebec. Cartier slipped away at night and returned to France, where his 'gold' and 'diamonds' were found to be valueless. Roberval stayed in Canada for one winter, then abandoned plans to found a colony and also returned to France. French disappointment at these poor results led to a gap of some 50 years before they showed renewed interest in the area. 15, 16, 18

CARVER, JONATHAN (1710–80), explorer of North America. Raised in Massachusetts and Connecticut, of good family and education, he served in the militia and in a regiment of his native state until 1766, when **Robert Rogers** sent him along the Minnesota. In 1769 he removed to England and devoted the rest of his life to writing – most notably, his *Travels*. His work proved unremunerative and he died in misery. 19

CASARRUBIA, JUAN OR LORENZO DE, 17th-century Franciscan explorer of South America. A Franciscan missionary, he led the first Franciscan mission to the Amazon in August 1632, following the River Putumayo for 11 days, before the defection of his interpreter obliged him to return to Pasto. 26

CERMEÑO, SEBASTIÁN RODRÍGUEZ, 16th-century mariner and explorer of North America. Of Portuguese birth, but known always by the Castilian version of his name, he was ordered to sail from Manila in the 200-ton galleon *San Agustín* in July 1595 to investigate the North American coast for a harbour of refuge for shipping from the far shores of the Pacific. The loss of his ship in San Francisco Bay frustrated his mission. 20, 28, 29

CHAMPLAIN, SAMUEL DE (1567–1635). The most influential 17th-century French explorer of North America, Champlain was largely responsible for the foundation of Nouvelle France. In addition to journeys of exploration and fur-trading undertaken by himself, he sponsored many French expeditions in North America. After a three-year voyage to the Caribbean, Champlain made his first journey to Nouvelle France in 1603. He returned the following year, founding a colony which, in 1605, was re-established on the west coast of Nova Scotia and named Port Royal. Champlain made detailed explorations of the coast as far south as Cape Cod before being obliged in 1608 to abandon the colony. He established a new base – Quebec – the following summer, intending that it should become the capital of a great colony.

Over the next six years, Champlain made extended journeys, discovering Lake Champlain, exploring the Saguenay and St. Maurice Rivers and pushing west as far as Lake Huron. During this period, his routing of the Iroquois contributed greatly to the poor relations that thereafter existed between the French colonists and the Iroquois. Abandoning exploration after being wounded by Onondaga Indians in 1615, he devoted much of the rest of his life to furthering the interests of Nouvelle France, championing its fur-trading potential, collating information for a series of magnificent maps and dispatching expeditions to and beyond the Great Lakes. The fall of Quebec to Britain in 1629 led to four years' exile in Britain for Champlain. He returned to Nouvelle France in 1632 and died shortly afterwards. 15, 18, 21

CHANCELLOR, RICHARD (d. 1556), British navigator and explorer. Most of his early seafaring career was spent on voyages to the Mediterranean. In 1553–54 he was captain of *Edward Bonaventure* and pilot major of the fleet on **Sir Hugh Willoughby**'s expedition to seek a Northeast Passage. Willoughby and the crews of two ships perished on the expedition, but Chancellor made his way to the White Sea and overland to Moscow, where he negotiated the first trading relations between Britain and Russia. The Muscovy Company was founded in London to carry out the trade, and it sent Chancellor back to the White Sea in 1555. He died during his homeward voyage in 1556 when his ship was wrecked off the coast of Scotland. 32

CHANG CH'IEN (d.c. 112 BC), Chinese explorer, the earliest recorded. In 138 BC he was sent by the Chinese emperor to seek allies in Central Asia against the Huns, who were threatening the empire. Captured, he did not escape for ten years. After reaching Bactria, his intended destination, he tried to return to China via Tibet but was again captured by the Huns. He finally reached home after an absence of 12 years. He is chiefly remembered for helping forge the caravan route from China across the Gobi Desert – the Silk Road. 1

CH'ANG CHUN (1148–1227). He was a Taoist sage whom Genghis Khan commanded to attend his court in 1219. After a period of reluctant progress to the border, he departed in 1221 on a journey of 14 months which took him from Peking to Pervan, just south of Kabul, via the Tien Shan and Altai Mountains and Samarkand. Among the 19 disciples who accompanied him was Li Chih-ch'ang, who recorded the journey and described in detail a route that had only recently been reopened by Mongol armies after a long period of disuse. 1

CHENG HO (1371–1435), Chinese mariner of Southeast Asia and the Indian Ocean. Born in Yunnan of a Muslim family, he became a eunuch at the age of 10 in order to enter the imperial household. During military service against the Mongols in the 1390s he became an aide of the future emperor Ch'eng Tsu, who, on ascending to the throne in 1403, reversed the isolationist policies of his predecessor. In six expeditions up to 1424, and in defiance of convention, Cheng Ho, although a court official, was sent by sea to Southeast Asia, Ceylon, India, the Persian Gulf, Arabia and the African coast from Somaliland to Zanzibar. His patron's death interrupted the work of exploration and Cheng Ho was made garrison commander of Nanking, but in a last voyage, permitted in 1433, he united almost all the routes he had previously sailed. He returned to his duties in Nanking, where he died in 1435. 1, 27

CHIRIKOV, ALEXEI (1703–48), Russian naval officer and Arctic explorer. He was deputy to **Vitus Bering** on his 1741 navigation of the Bering Strait, commanding Bering's consort vessel, *St. Paul*. Having become separated from Bering, who died when his ship, *St. Peter*, was wrecked on Bering Island, Chirikov landed on one of the Aleutian Islands. He returned to north Russia in October the same year. 20, 32

CHRISTENSEN, LARS (1884–1965), Norwegian shipowner and Antarctic explorer. Christensen was born into a shipowning family; he entered the business in 1899 and started his own firm in 1907. In 1910 he began to send whaling factory ships to the Antarctic. Between 1927 and 1937 he made an important contribution to Antarctic exploration by sending out (and sometimes taking part in) a series of nine expeditions which were intended primarily to seek out new whaling grounds, but which also discovered and charted vast areas, including much of Queen Maud Land, Lars Christensen Coast, Ingrid Christensen Coast, and King Leopold and Queen Astrid Coast. 46

CHU-SSU-PEN (1273–1337), Chinese map-maker during the Mongol dynasty. He prepared a large map in the early 14th century in the form of an atlas, describing China and the surrounding countries, which includes a definite outline of Africa with place names, suggesting that Chinese knowledge had absorbed the sources of the Nile, the correct orientation of the Guinea coast, and the location of the Congo and of several of the Indian Ocean island groups. 1

CLAPPERTON, HUGH (1788–1827), Scottish sailor and explorer of west Africa. He made two journeys. In 1824 he joined an expedition which crossed the Sahara from Tripoli and which attempted to discover the course and termination of the lower Niger. He revealed the great kingdoms of Bornu and the Fulani empire centred on Sokoto, but was not allowed to proceed to the river. On his return to England in 1825, he was at once sent on another expedition to the same destination, this time from the south via the Bight of Benin. He reached the Niger overland with only his servant, **Richard Lander**, after the other members of his party had quickly succumbed to the unhealthy climate. He went on to Sokoto, but died there of dysentery. 37

CLARK, WILLIAM (1770–1838), U.S. soldier, explorer and public official. Clark, like his fellow Virginian **Meriwether Lewis**, served in the army in the 1790s, resigning as a lieutenant in 1796. At one time Lewis had served under Clark, and the two were close friends. When Lewis was appointed by President Thomas Jefferson to lead an expedition up the Missouri, over the mountains and west to the Pacific, Lewis chose Clark as his co-leader. (Lewis was the nominal leader and Clark his immediate subordinate, but their relations were clearly those of partners.) Both men kept journals of the expedition, which left Wood River, across from St. Louis, on 14 May 1804. Clark was the more personable, diplomatic and outgoing; he was also more adept at managing the boats. He was the expedition's geographer, making surprisingly accurate estimates of miles traversed, and sketching maps which even today identify portions of the route. After the expedition's return to St. Louis in September 1806, Clark was appointed Indian Agent for Louisiana Territory, then governor of Missouri Territory and finally superintendent of Indian Affairs for tribes of the Missouri and upper Mississippi. For the rest of his life he was busy with Indian matters. 22

COCKING, MATTHEW (1743–99), English explorer of Canada. An employee of the Hudson's Bay Company, in 1772 he undertook an inland probe to the Forks of the Saskatchewan to report on the activities of French fur traders, who, since the expulsion from Canada of the French, had monopolised much of the trade. His account lead directly to the decision of the Hudson's Bay Company to abandon its long-established policy of maintaining trading posts only on Hudson Bay. Cocking served as master of Fort Severn and York Fort before returning to England in 1772. 21

COELHO, GONÇALO, 16th-century Portuguese mariner. In 1501 he was appointed to command a fleet of six ships bound for India via the Brazilian coast, of which he wrote a detailed description. Vespucci's account of his first voyage under Portuguese colours is generally presumed to have been based on this expedition. On 10 June 1503 he led what may have been intended as a colonizing expedition, perhaps financed by Fernão de Noronha, who had a contract for dye-wood from the crown; the island which bears his name was discovered in the course of the voyage, probably in August 1503. 13

COLUMBUS, BARTHOLOMEW (d. 1514), brother of **Christopher Columbus**. He was the companion of Columbus in Lisbon from at least 1480. Between 1489 and 1492, according to early traditions, he attempted to find patrons in France and England for Columbus's transatlantic project. He arrived in Spain late in 1493, to be sent to join his brother in Hispaniola in June 1494. He played a major role in the government and exploration of the island, founding Santo Domingo on 5 August 1496 and crossing the island from north to south in the course of campaigns to suppress Indian resistance. He was arrested, with his brother, in October 1500 and sent to Spain to answer charges of exceeding his authority, but was released and rehabilitated to take part, reluctantly, in Columbus's last voyage in 1502–4. He then lobbied on behalf of his family at court until 1509 when he returned, with his nephew Diego, to resume duties in Hispaniola. He solicited, unsuccessfully, for a commission to conquer Cuba but was awarded the right to colonize Veragua. He died in Santo Domingo while attempting to organize an expedition. 10, 13

COLUMBUS, CHRISTOPHER (1451/2–1506), Genoese explorer, generally credited with the European discovery of the Americas. The son of a weaver, Columbus had minimal formal education, but took to the sea, as he said, 'at a young age'. By 1477 he had moved to Lisbon, from where he sailed widely in the Mediterranean and Atlantic trading worlds. In 1478, a recorded voyage took him to Madeira as purchasing agent for a Genoese firm. Probably in 1479 or 1480 he improved his social standing by marrying Dona Felipa Perestrello, daughter of the governor of Porto Santo, an island in the Madeiras group. Shortly after this, Columbus made at least one voyage to the Portuguese trading post of São Jorge da Mina on the Gold Coast of West Africa.

His project for attempting a crossing of the Atlantic may first have been offered to his adopted country, Portugal, which at that time led European nations in discovery and exploration. King John II is said to have submitted Columbus's plan to his maritime committee, which rejected it, allegedly because it was sceptical of the existence or exploitability of Japan. Columbus took his plan to the Spanish monarchs, Ferdinand and Isabella, in April 1486. His scheme gradually gathered support at their court and in January 1492 a consortium emerged to finance it. In April the monarchs endorsed Columbus's extravagant demands–which included a considerable share in any trade generated, the governorship of all lands he discovered, noble rank and the title of admiral. Columbus was provided with three ships – the *Niña*, the *Pinta* and the *Santa Maria* – for what was to prove the first of his four Atlantic crossings. The crews in total amounted to some 90 sailors. On 3 August 1492, the flotilla sailed from Palos, in Spain, for the Canary Islands, where repairs and modifications were made. On 6 September course was set due west, from San Sebastián de la Gomera. On 12 October land was sighted, an island which Columbus named San Salvador. Columbus thought he was on the edge of Asia and continued in search of China and Japan. Indeed, so certain was he of this that, in Cuba, he sent emissaries to seek the emperor of China. Attracted by rumours of gold, Columbus then sailed along the north coast of Hispaniola, where he founded the first European settlement in the New World, before returning to Spain. He had two ships only remaining to him, the *Santa Maria* having gone on a reef. The return journey was plagued by storms, but Columbus reached the port of Palos on 14 March 1493. This was Columbus's moment of triumph; the monarchs confirmed his titles and commissioned a second voyage, with the purpose of colonizing Hispaniola and exploring further.

On 5 September 1493, Columbus set sail with 17 ships carrying a 1,000 men and seeds, plants, tools and animals for colonization. The Atlantic crossing was made in the good time of 21 days, when the island of Dominica was reached. The fleet then sailed along the line of islands, discovered Puerto Rico and shortly afterwards reached Hispaniola. On landing, Columbus found that natives had killed the garrison and destroyed the fort. Columbus then turned eastwards and, on the north coast of Hispaniola, founded the settlement of Isabella. He left his brother, Diego, in command and then took the *Niña* and two caravels to explore and map the southern coast of Cuba, during which expedition he discovered Jamaica. In June 1496, having supressed disorders among the settlers and resistance among the Indians, he sailed again for Spain.

Columbus was then commissioned to undertake a third voyage and set sail, on 30 May 1496, on a more southerly route than hitherto. About 9°N the flotilla became becalmed in intense heat in the doldrums. After eight days, however, the wind revived and carried the ships to the island of Trinidad. Sailing along the shore of the island, Columbus, on 1 August, caught his first sight of the mainland, which he mistakenly thought to be an island. On the coast of Venezuela, he made his first recorded landing on the American continent. Now, for the first time, he came to believe that he had found 'a very great mainland'. He then sailed to the Hispaniola colony, which he found in revolt, partly owing to the paucity of discovered gold. In 1500, Ferdinand and Isabella sent Francisco de Bobadilla to restore order. His first act was to put Columbus and his two brothers in chains and ship them back to Spain. Released on arrival, Columbus was nonetheless in disgrace. To regain his fortune and good name, he asked for, and was granted, ships to make a new voyage.

On 9 May 1502, he set out with four caravels, apparently to discover a passage to the Indian Ocean between Cuba and the continent he had found in 1498. He believed, as did most people until Magellan's ship returned from circumnavigating the globe in 1522, that South America lay a short distance south-east of China. From Azua, having survived a hurricane, the four ships sailed past Jamaica to southern Cuba and crossed the Caribbean to the Bay Islands off the coast of Honduras. They then sailed along the coast of Central America, still looking for the strait. On New Year's Day 1503, he anchored off Panama, nearer to the Pacific Ocean than he realized. Now, however, having failed to find a strait, he concentrated on searching for gold and tried to establish a garrison in the province of Veragua (modern Panama). The Indians, at first friendly, turned hostile when they realised a permanent settlement was to be established, and Columbus was obliged to abandon the project and sail for home. His ships were rotten from *teredos*; they were finally beached at St Ann's Bay on the north coast of Jamaica. Columbus was marooned there for a year before a reluctant and jealous Governor Ovando allowed help to be sent from Hispaniola. On 29 June 1504, Columbus, with the 100 survivors of the 135 who had set out with him, set sail in a caravel for Spain, arriving on 7 September 1504. His remaining time was characterized by painful ill health, embitterment and the consolations of religion. He died in Valladolid on 20 May 1506. 8, 9, 10, 13, 47

CONTARINI, GIOVANNI MATTEO (d. 1506), Venetian or Florentine cartographer. The only known copy of his fan-shaped world map, engraved by Francesco Rosselli, was discovered in 1922, and is now in the British Library. For the first time on any printed map, the relationship between the Old World and the New World is shown, even though the Pacific Ocean is too small in comparison with the rest of the world. North America is assumed to be an eastward extending promontory of Asia. No other maps by Contarini are known, although he refers to himself on his map as 'Famed in the Ptolemaean art'. 9

CONTI, NICCOLÒ DI (c. 1395–1469), Venetian merchant and traveller. There is evidence that he was in Damascus in 1419, from where he seems to have embarked on a number of journeys in Asia, lasting some 25 years, during which he crossed Arabia to Baghdad and visited Persia and parts of India, before travelling to Burma and the East Indies. He had to abjure Christianity and embrace Islam as a condition of being allowed to return to Europe. In Europe again from 1444, he returned to Christianity. Thereafter he lived as a respected merchant. His journeys were recorded by Poggio Bracciolini in an account published in 1439. 28

COOK, FREDERICK (1865–1940), American explorer, who claimed to have been the first, in 1908, to reach the North Pole but was accused of fraud. Later business malpractices earned him a jail sentence (1925–30). 46

COOK, JAMES (1728–79), English naval officer and explorer of the Pacific. He was born in Yorkshire, the son of a farm labourer. Apprenticed to a Whitby ship owner, he studied mathematics and navigation and in 1755 was offered command of a North Sea trader; this he declined, probably to enlist as an able seaman in the Royal Navy, where he judged greater opportunities lay. Promotion came rapidly. In 1757 he was appointed master (navigator) of the *Pembroke*, in which he saw action during the Seven Years War – notably in the amphibious assault against Quebec, where his charting of the hazardous reaches of the St. Lawrence contributed to the brilliant success of General Wolfe's landing before his storming of the French citadel. He subsequently spent five summers (1763–67) charting the intricate shoreline of Newfoundland.

In 1768, having been hastily promoted lieutenant, Cook was appointed to command of the *Endeavour*, a Whitby collier, and dispatched on a scientific expedition to Tahiti. In April of the following year he reached the island, where scientists in the expedition observed the planet Venus pass between the Earth and the Sun, the principal object of the voyage. Cook, however, had further Admiralty orders, namely to seek the 'unknown continent' – Terra Australis – postulated by academic geographers to lie in the South Pacific. The leader of the botanical party was Joseph Banks (1743–1820), then aged 26, a natural historian of later renown and first president of the Royal Society. Following Admiralty instructions, Cook sailed to New Zealand, which had been discovered in 1642 by Abel Tasman, the Dutch mariner. Cook circumnavigated the two islands, surveying their coasts to produce the first reliable chart of New Zealand. He then turned westwards again to the eastern coast of Australia, which he annexed for Britain under the name of New South Wales, before turning northwards. Surviving near shipwreck on the Great Barrier Reef, which necessitated beaching the *Endeavour* after she struck the reef, Cook sailed for home, arriving in June 1771. Almost at once, the Admiralty organized a second, more ambitious voyage, this time with two ships – the former Whitby vessel, the *Resolution*, and a similar ship, *Adventure* – to undertake the first circumnavigation and penetration of the Antarctic Circle. The two ships left England in July 1772. Cook penetrated farther south in the Pacific than any previous European, despite the many hazards of Antarctic waters, including mountainous ice formations, ferocious winds, and freezing fog. But though he circled Antarctica he was unable to approach it closely enough to sight land. He did, however, push significantly to the south the existence of the presumed continent. On the same voyage, Cook became in 1773 and 1774 the first European to visit a number of Pacific islands; he charted Tonga and Easter Island and discovered New Caledonia. He then returned home by way of Cape Horn, discovering the South Sandwich Islands and South Georgia in the Atlantic. By great care over diet, he lost only one man to scurvy. On reaching England, he was promoted captain and elected a member of the Royal Society.

In June 1778, Cook set out on his third – and what was to prove last – great voyage of discovery. In the *Resolution*, accompanied by the *Discovery*, he determined to find the Pacific end of the hoped-for Northwest Passage, long sought by explorers. He again visited the mid-Pacific islands and discovered a number of the Cook Islands and the Hawaiian group. In March 1778 he finally reached the coast of present-day Oregon. He followed the coastline north and west – in the process mistaking the Aleutian Islands for a mainland – and sailed through the Bering Strait. At 70°44' he was repulsed by ice. He then turned south-east to the Hawaiian Islands, where he anchored in January 1779. The inhabitants were at first well disposed, but when a damaged mast forced him to return they were less accommodating. Then, in February, a native stole a cutter. Cook went to investigate the incident at Kealakekua Bay, but was stabbed to death during the ensuing fracas. His legacy included the conquest of scurvy (though through instinct rather than systematic study of the disease: scurvy continued to afflict mariners until well into the 20th century), the perfection of knowledge of the limits of the Pacific, and the accurate mapping of his discoveries, assisted by the use of Harrison's chronometer to determine longitude. 20, 21, 34, 35

COOLEY, WILLIAM DESBOROUGH (1795–1883) A historian of discoveries, founder of the Hakluyt Society and theoretical geographer, Cooley was regarded as an authority on the unexplored regions of Africa in the 1830s and 1840s. But his reluctance to modify his maps when practical exploration was carried out, and his denial that snow existed on the summit of Kilimanjaro, earned him scorn as the epitome of the 'armchair geographer' and he died in poverty. 39

CORONADO, FRANCISCO VÁSQUEZ DE (b. 1510). Spanish explorer of North America. At about the age of 25, he went to Mexico and was appointed governor of the New Galicia province. In 1540 Antonio de Mendoza, the viceroy, sent Coronado with 250 Spaniards and many Indian bearers to search for what were rumoured to be seven cities with enormous treasure situated to the north. He discovered the Grand Canyon and heard rumours of the wealth of Quivira, which he set out to discover in April 1541 with a party of 30 light horsemen. His 42-day search took him beyond the River Arkansas without yielding any treasures, but represented an enormous advance in knowledge of the interior of North America. Denied further preferment, he lived on the profits of vast estates in northern New Spain until his death at an uncertain date after 1549. 17

CORTE-REAL, GASPAR (d. 1501) and MIGUEL (d. 1502), Portuguese brothers and explorers. Gaspar set out from Terceira in 1500, sailing north to Greenland and then westward to Labrador and down the North American coast. The following year King Manuel granted him ships with which to undertake a new voyage, and privileges in any new lands discovered. Gaspar's ship was lost, though the other ship returned to Portugal, bringing with it a number of enslaved native Americans. Miguel set out from Lisbon in 1502 with two ships to search for his brother but he, too, was lost at sea; the second ship returned, but with no new information. Spain, however, recognized Portugal's right to lands discovered by the Corte-Reals. This was the basis for the great Portuguese fishery on the Newfoundland Banks. 14

CORTE-REAL, JOÃO VAZ (d. 1496). A gentleman of the household of the Portuguese Infante Don Fernando, he received the southern portion of the island of Terceira in the Azores in fee from the crown in 1474, adding that of São Jorge in 1483. He has been claimed as the protagonist of a pre-Columbian discovery of America in 1472 or 1473, as the accidental outcome of a Danish expedition from Iceland on which he is said to have served. No evidence earlier than the late 16th century, however, connects him with Atlantic exploration, though his son Gaspar had a celebrated role in that connection. 14

CORTÉS, HERNÁN (1485–1547), Spanish conquistador, the conqueror of Mexico and the explorer of much of southern North America. He was born at Medellín, Extramadura, of a noble but poor family. After legal studies which seem to have been quickly abandoned, he left for Santo Domingo in about 1501. In 1511 he fought under Diego de Velázquez and prospered. Then, in 1519, Velázquez gave him command of an expedition to reconnoitre the newly reported land of Mexico. With little more than 600 men, Cortés landed on the island of Cozumel, off Yucatán, conquered Tabasco and reached the site of present-day Veracruz, where, having decided to attempt the conquest of Mexico on his own account, he beached his boats to prevent retreat. He repudiated Velázquez's authority and his men elected him to an independent command. He then advanced towards the Aztecs, recruiting help from the Tlaxcalteca, a Nahua confederacy who resented Aztec hegemony. On 8 November 1519, he entered Tenochtitlán, on the site of present-day Mexico City. At first, the Spaniards were received peacefully, but while Cortés was away fighting a punitive force sent by Velázquez, hostilities broke out. Though defeated on 30 June 1520 ('the 'Sad Night'), Cortés raised many communities of the valley of Mexico against Tenochtitlán. After a long siege, assisted by havoc wrought in the Aztec ranks by a European disease

– probably smallpox – on 13 August 1521 he entered Tenochtitlán for the second time. Over the next five years he not only pacified the area formerly dominated by the Aztecs, but also conquered Honduras in person and much of Guatemala and El Salvador through subordinates. He organized Indian labour and introduced European crops and livestock, while also laying the foundations of a flourishing colony in what he called 'New Spain'. The acquisition of vast wealth and of the title of marquis failed, however, to compensate for his loss of power from 1526, when the Spanish crown began to build up a client-bureaucracy of its own in the lands he conquered. From the late 1520s his energies were absorbed by schemes to open access from Mexico to Pacific trade, while his values became intensely religious. In 1540 he returned to Spain, and took part in the Algerian campaign the following year. He resented criticism voiced in Spain of the sanguinary excesses and doubtful legitimacy of his conquests, and felt cheated of his just deserts and recognition. He was preparing to return to New Spain when he died in Seville on 2 December 1547. 6, 10, 17

COSA, JUAN DE LA (d. 1509), Spanish cartographer and navigator who accompanied Columbus's second expedition in 1493 and those of Ojeda and Vespucci (1499) and Bastidas (1500) as well as leading his own to Urabá in 1504. He served with other leading experts on a junta convened in 1507 in Burgos to plan the further exploration and exploitation of the New World. As promoter or participant he contributed to several colonization projects in Urabá, where he fell to a poisoned arrow in 1509. In 1500 he composed a map recording Columbus's discoveries, which survives in a later copy. 9, 10, 13

COVILHÃO or COVILHÃ, PEDRO or PÊRO DE (d. c.1524), Portuguese explorer of Africa. First recorded in the service of the duke of Medina Sidonia in Seville in the late 1460s, in about 1475 he entered the household of King Afonso V of Portugal, for whom he fought in the war of succession for the throne of Castile (1475–79). After diplomatic missions in Castile and the Maghrib, he was chosen for a mission to the mythical 'Prester John' – supposed to be the ruler of Ethiopia – apparently with the intention of verifying the navigability of the route around Africa to the Indian Ocean. Accompanied by Afonso de Paiva he departed in May 1487, adopting in Rhodes the disguise of a honey merchant. Arriving in Aden via Alexandria and Cairo, the fellow-travellers parted company. Of Paiva no more was heard. Covilhão's travels cannot be reconstructed with confidence from the surviving sources, but they took him to various parts of the west coast of India and East Africa as well as to Hormuz. He was able to report favourably on the accessibility of the Indian Ocean, around Africa, via Sofala or Madagascar, in a letter of 1492. He reached the court of the Negus of Abyssinia in 1494. He may have visited Portugal in 1514–15 but was still residing in Ethiopia in honourable estate when the next Portuguese mission arrived in 1520. 28

CRESQUES, ABRAHAM, (active 14th century). Jewish Catalan chartmaker, presumed to be the author of the Catalan Atlas of c.1375, an accumulation of travellers' reportage and Islamic knowledge showing a richly imagined view of the peri-Saharan world. This attribution is based on a similarly detailed map he created for the French royal library, c.1380. 11, 31

CROGHAN, GEORGE (d. 1782), Irish-born explorer of North America. He arrived in Pennsylvania in 1741 and became an Indian trader near Carlisle, Pennsylvania. His business was wrecked by French hostilities in 1752–54. From 1756 he was employed by the government as an Indian agent and served in the captures of Fort Du Quesne and of Detroit. In 1764 he was in England, lobbying for a more aggressive western policy. The following year he led an important expedition into Illinois country. In 1772 he retired with an immense fortune from the sale of land acquired from the Indians or by government concession, and devoted himself to more such speculations. His investments were wrecked by the American War of Independence and he died in poverty, unjustly accused of clandestine loyalty to the British crown. 19

CUNNINGHAM, ALLAN (1791–1839), British botanist and explorer of Australia. After training at Kew Gardens, he was sent by Sir Joseph Banks to collect

plants in Australia, arriving in Sydney at the end of 1816. In 1817, he accompanied John Oxley in his exploration of the Lachlan River area. The next year, he went with P.P. King on the surveying voyage of the north and north-western coasts of the continent. In 1819, he made further voyages with King, this time to Tasmania and up the east coast. He was back on the north-west coast in 1821. In 1822–23, he explored and botanized behind the Blue Mountains, up to the Liverpool Plains. In 1823, he went with Oxley to Port Curtis and Moreton Bay. He visited New Zealand in 1826, and in 1827 he travelled north from the Hunter River valley, inside the Great Dividing Range, discovering the Darling Downs and Cunningham's Gap, which offered access to them from Brisbane. He further explored this area in 1818 and 1829. After some years in England in the 1830s, he returned briefly to New South Wales in 1837. 36

DAMPIER, WILLIAM (c.1650–1715), English explorer who visited Newfoundland and the Caribbean before, in 1679, crossing the Isthmus of Darién to the Pacific, where he pillaged along the coasts of Spain's American empire. In 1688 he crossed the Pacific to the west coast of New Holland, returning in 1691 to England. Though brutal and piratical by nature, Dampier was a shrewd and sympathetic observer. His New Voyages (1697) sparked wide interest in the Pacific and led to a government appointment as leader of a naval expedition in 1699. Navigating to the north of Australia, its principal discovery was the islands of New Britain. Dampier returned to the Pacific in 1703; in the course of this voyage Alexander Selkirk, the model for Robinson Crusoe, was marooned on the island of Juan Fernández. Dampier returned to rescue Selkirk in 1708. The last years of Dampier's life were passed in poverty and bitterness at the eclipse of his fame as a pioneer of Pacific discovery. 34

DAS, SARAT CHANDRA, 19th-century surveyor of Tibet. Das was permitted to visit the centre of Lamaist learning, Tashilhunpo, in 1879. He explored the country north and northeast of Kanchenjunga while gathering texts. On a further journey in November 1881 he followed the Tsangpo (Brahmaputra) River from Sakya east to Samye and Tsetang. He visited Lhasa and returned to India in 1883, where he published narratives of his journeys. 43

DAVIS, JOHN (c. 1550–1605), English navigator, one of many who tried to find a Northwest Passage through the Canadian Arctic to the Pacific. He is thought to have proposed his first expedition to Sir Francis Walsingham, principal secretary to Queen Elizabeth, in 1583; two years later, he started on the first of his three northwestern expeditions. He came upon the east coast of Greenland, then headed south, round Cape Farewell, and northwards along Greenland's western coast. Then turning, as he thought, in the direction of China, he sailed up part of Cumberland Sound. On the last of these voyages, he passed through Davis Strait (named after him), entered Baffin Bay and sailed northwards along the western coast of Greenland as far as Disko Island. Davis fought against the Spanish Armada (1588), and in 1591 he made an attempt to find the elusive passage from the Pacific, via the Strait of Magellan. Davis accompanied expeditions to the East Indies in 1598 and 1601, but on a third voyage to the area he was hacked to death by Japanese pirates off the coast of Sumatra. Davis wrote The Seaman's Secrets (1584), a work on navigation, and The World's Hydrographical Description (1595), which deals with the Northwest Passage. 16

DEASE, PETER WARREN (1788–1863), Canadian fur trader and Arctic explorer. Dease was raised in Montreal and entered the fur trade with the XY Company at the age of 13. In 1821 he was appointed chief trader in the Hudson's Bay Company, working mainly in northern Canada. Between 1825 and 1827 he was seconded to John Franklin's expedition to explore the Arctic coast of North America. In 1837–39, he was leader of the company's own expedition to complete Franklin's survey of the north coast, and with Thomas Simpson achieved great success in tracing the coast along most of its length. He retired and settled near Montreal in 1843. 23

DE BRY, THEODORE (1528–98), Flemish engraver, publisher of the illustrated travel books known as The Great Voyages in 1590, followed by The Lesser Voyages.

He also brought together in a uniform series the illustrated accounts of, for example, Hariot's *Virginia* (which published John White's drawings for the first time), Jacques Le Moyne de Morgues's account of the French expedition in Florida; Benzoni's *History of the New World*; and Hans Staden's account of the Tupinambá cannibals of Brazil. His works were published in Latin, German and French editions. 25

DE LONG, GEORGE WASHINGTON (1844–81), American naval officer and Arctic explorer. He first visited the Arctic in 1873 as a member of a naval party searching for missing members of an expedition towards the North Pole. Six years later he secured backing for his own expedition towards the pole, but his ship *Jeannette* became trapped in ice in the Arctic Ocean and was crushed. The expedition had discovered Bennett, Jeannette and Henrietta Islands to the north of Siberia, but De Long and most of his party died of starvation after retreating in boats to the Lena River delta. 46

DENHAM, DIXON (1786–1828), English soldier and explorer of West Africa. He served under Wellington in Spain and at Waterloo. He then joined **Hugh Clapperton** in his expedition to the Sudan. On his return to England, he was appointed (1825) superintendent of the liberated slaves in West Africa, and in 1828 was made lieutenant-governor of the colony of Sierra Leone. He died of fever shortly afterwards. 37

DEZHNEV, SEMEN IVANOV (1608–72), Russian government agent and explorer. He entered government service about 1630 and worked in Siberia, where one of his main tasks was collecting dues, or tribute, from subjugated natives. In 1643 he was one of the first Russian settlers on the Kolyma River, and in 1647 he took part in an unsuccessful attempt to explore the Arctic coast east of the Kolyma. He tried again in 1648, and this time he reached the easternmost extremity of Siberia on the Bering Strait and, continuing round the coast, located the mouth of the Anadyr River. He established a post and settled on the river until 1662, when he returned west to Yakutsk. The importance of Dezhnev's discovery of the Bering Strait was not fully recognized until the 19th century; in 1898 the easternmost point of Asia was named Mys Dezhneva (Cape Dezhnev) in his honour. 32

DIAS, BARTOLOMEU (*c.*1450–before 1499), Portuguese navigator and explorer. Little is known of his early life, but in 1482 Dias commanded one of the ships in an expedition to the Gold Coast. In 1487, the king gave Dias command of three ships with the express purpose of turning the southern tip of Africa. According to a late tradition, shortly after reaching the mouth of the Orange River in southern Africa a storm erupted and blew the ships from sight of land. Dias and his crews did not again see land for some 13 days for, on again turning to port, no land at first appeared. It was only on his sailing north that he once more saw the coast. He had, in fact, rounded Africa's southern tip without having sighted it. 12, 13

DIAS, DIOGO, 15th-/16th-century Portuguese mariner. He was a captain in the first expedition of **Pedro Álvares Cabral** in 1500. He became separated from the main fleet and discovered Madagascar, to which he gave the name Ilha de São Lourenço. He has been uncertainly identified as the brother of **Bartolomeu Dias**. 29

DÍAZ, MELCHOR (d. 1540), Spanish *conquistador* and explorer of North America. He was in command at Culiacán in 1536 when **Álvar Núñez Cabeza de Vaca** returned from his long trek in the north. In 1539 he was ordered by the viceroy to reconnoitre the route to be taken by the projected expedition of **Francisco Vázquez de Coronado** in search of Cíbola. Leaving Culiacán on 17 November 1539, he followed the Indian trail into Sonora, across the desert of south-east Arizona, probably along the San Pedro valley, to the Magellan River. His report was discouraging but failed to deter the main expedition. He met Coronado at Chiametla in southern Sinaloa and guided the force for as long as his knowledge lasted. When Cíbola, in Zuni country, was reached, Díaz was sent back to Sonora with the news and then, on instructions from Coronado, made for the mouth of the Colorado River in the hope of meeting the supporting fleet under **Hernando de Alarcón**. He succeeded, by an arduous route partly along the Gila River, in finding a message that Alarcón had preceded

him at Yuma by about two months. He then explored the desert coast, perhaps as far as the Gulf of Santa Catalina, where he died of an accidentally self-inflicted lance-wound, probably in November 1540. 17

DORTAL or **DE ORTAL, JERÓNIMO**, 16th-century Spanish *conquistador*. His early military service included the Navarrese campaign of 1511. He is documented in the New World from 1531, when he accompanied Diego de Ordás on the Orinoco. As governor of Paria, in eastern Venezuela, from 1534, he devoted himself to the search for an overland route to the Orinoco. On his first attempt, in 1536, he was abandoned by his men but survived to make a second and successful effort in 1540. The route was unexploitable, however, and Dortal retired to Santo Domingo where he died at an uncertain date soon afterwards. 25

DOUDART DE LAGRÉE, ERNEST-MARC-LOUIS-DE-GONZAGUE (1823–68), French diplomat and traveller. His father was a lawyer and member of the parliament of Dauphiné. Educated partly by Jesuits, he was commissioned in the navy in 1845. He saw action in the Crimea but was troubled by ill health, which a hot climate was thought to favour. He applied for a post in Indo-China, where, from 1863, he was able to exercise his diplomatic talents and pursue his archaeological interest. He administered Cambodia as French resident in 1864–65, and set the study of Angkor on a scientific basis. In 1866 he was appointed to command the Mekong River Expedition with **Francis Garnier**. He reached Yunnan in January 1868, before a recurrence of his old throat trouble obliged him to hand over to Garnier. He made the last stages of the journey on a litter. His complaints, compounded by liver failure, increased, and he died at Hui-tse on 12 March. 45

DOUGHTY, CHARLES MONTAGU (1843–1926), English scholar, poet and traveller in Arabia. In 1875, while in Syria, he learned of ancient monuments in north-western Arabia and reached them in disguise after joining a caravan of pilgrims travelling to Mecca. After leaving the caravan at Mada'in Salih, he spent two years exploring Arabia alone, suffering many privations including assault and imprisonment by Arabs. On returning to England, he devoted himself to writing, notably his *Travels in Arabia Deserta* (1888), deliberately composed in archaic prose. 42

DRAKE, SIR FRANCIS (*c.*1540–96) English privateer and navigator. Sent to sea when still young, he was given command of his own ship in 1567 on a slave-trading voyage. Much of his subsequent career was spent in combat with Spain, the leading sea-power of the time. In 1572, Drake undertook a piratical mission against Spanish holdings in the New World. He sacked the harbour of Nombre de Dios on the Isthmus of Panama, crossed the Isthmus itself to see the Pacific and captured a mule train transporting 30 tons of silver. In 1577 he embarked on a further mission to raid Spanish New World settlements, this time on the Pacific coast. Of the five ships that began the expedition, two were abandoned on the River Plate. The remaining three then made the first English navigation of the Strait of Magellan, emerging into the Pacific to be met by a storm. One ship was lost, one returned to England. Drake meanwhile, having established that there was no landmass immediately south of Tierra del Fuego, as speculative geographers had predicted, and that the Atlantic and the Pacific met south of the American landmass, sailed north along the west coast of South America, plundering Spanish settlements. He continued north along the coast of North America searching for a strait that would lead him back the Atlantic. Failing to find one, he sailed south again and refitted in or near San Francisco Bay, which he named New Albion. The territory he saw he claimed for England. He returned to England across the Pacific.

Drake's voyage, the first English circumnavigation (and only the second ever made), was a triumph of seamanship and leadership; it was a remarkable financial success, too, repaying its backers many times over and making Drake immensely wealthy. Nonetheless, its contributions to exploration were limited and today, with various theories as to the location of his New Albion, a source of controversy. Drake was knighted for his feat in 1580. His subsequent career saw a further series of successful raids against Spanish possessions in the Atlantic and the New World and, in 1585, the

relief of Roanoke, the first English colony in North America (subsequently abandoned). Drake's raid on the Spanish fleet in Cadiz in 1587 and service against the Spanish Armada the following year did much to end the supremacy of Spanish naval power. He died at sea in 1596 after the only major failure of his piratical career – a disastrous raid against Spanish Caribbean settlements. 20

DULCERT, ANGELINO (active early 14th century). Majorcan or Genoese mapmaker whose work reflects the early discoveries of Atlantic island groups such as the Canaries. He created a world map in 1339. 8

DULHUT, DANIEL GREYSOLON (1636–1710), French explorer of North America. In Nouvelle France from the early 1670s, in 1678 he explored beyond Lake Superior in a mission to end a war between Ojibwa and Sioux Indians and reached Mille Lacs, claiming much of the upper Mississippi region for France. In 1683, having returned from France to answer charges of illegal fur-trading, he explored to Lake Nipigon, but his attempts to find the mythical 'Western Sea' were twice interrupted by wars with the Iroquois. He established Fort St. Joseph on the St. Clair River in 1686. In 1688 he was again exploring and trading around Lake Superior. 18

DUMONT D'URVILLE, JULES-SÉBASTIEN-CÉSAR (1790–1842), French naval officer and explorer. He entered the navy in 1807, and in his early career he developed skills in botany and entomology. The breadth of his talent enabled him to secure appointments as officer and naturalist on three important naval surveying and scientific expeditions to the Pacific. In 1822–25 he was a lieutenant on L.I.Duperrey's expeditions on the ship *Astrolabe*. On the latter, he entered Antarctic waters, surveyed in the Antarctic Peninsula region, and discovered Terre Adélie. He was promoted rear-admiral on his return, but two years later he was killed in a railway accident. 46

EANES, GIL 15th-century Portuguese explorer of the West African coast. A household servant of **Henry the Navigator**, he was credited with the rounding of Cape Bojador in 1434. This was probably not, however, the cape now so called, but Cape Juby, which had long been familiar to navigators from Europe. The following year he made a further voyage, skirting perhaps 200 more miles of coastline to the south. 11

ERATOSTHENES (*c.*276–*c.*194 BC). The first systematic geographer. He directed the library at Alexandria, *c.*255 BC; wrote on astronomy, ethics and the theatre; compiled a calendar, showing leap years, and a chronology of events since the Siege of Troy; and calculated the Earth's circumference with remarkable accuracy. He was known as Beta, because he was good in many fields without being supreme. He is said to have starved himself to death after going blind. 2, 24

ERHARDT, JACOB (d. 1901) With **Krapf** in East Africa from 1849 to 1853, Erhardt made a minor journey to Usambara. He is more famous as the author of the 'slug map', made on the basis of hearsay about the Great Lakes in 1855 and which postulated one immense lake in the interior of Africa in the shape of what came to be dubbed a 'great slug'. The map created widespread interest in Europe. He later worked as a missionary in India. 39

ERIC THE RED (*c.*950–*c.*1010). Norse explorer. He grew up in Iceland, but was exiled for three years. Sailing west to land sighted about AD 860, he explored and named southern Greenland, returning to Iceland to convey a colony to southwestern Greenland in 986, the Eastern Settlement, or Brattahlid. On a visit to Norway, he adopted Christianity and returned to Greenland to introduce it to the settlers. At his home at Brattahlid, he heard a report of lands farther west, which one of his sons, **Leif Eriksson**, went to explore in *c.*1000, as did others of his family in subsequent years, retaining ownership of the base they found, Leifssbudir. Eric remained at Brattahlid where he died early in the 11th century. 14

EIRIKSSON, LEIF (b.*c.*970), Norse explorer, son of **Eric the Red**, the first settler in Greenland. If legend is correct Leif may have been the first European to set foot in North America. After a visit to Norway, he was converted to Christianity and returned to Greenland to convert the settlers. About the year 1000, according to sagas written down three centuries later, he sailed from

Greenland and named Baffin Island 'Helluland', Labrador 'Markland' and Newfoundland 'Vinland', basing himself at L'Anse-aux-Meadows in Newfoundland. From there he may have voyaged south to where grapes grew, though this may only be legend. Grazing and timber (Newfoundland) and timber (Labrador) were his main economic objectives. 14

ESCALANTE, SILVESTRE, 18th-century Franciscan missionary and explorer of North America. Escalante set out from Santa Fe in 1776 with his colleague, Fr. Anastasio Domínguez, in the hope of finding a route to California. They covered ground never before traversed by white men, reaching the Utah valley and describing, by report, the Great Salt Lake. Escalante's diary, published in 1950, is the most vivid explorer's account of the Great Basin. 17

ESPEJO, ANTONIO DE, Spanish 16th-century explorer of North America. Born in Córdoba at an uncertain date, he sought his fortune in New Spain, where he was successful in commerce. In 1582 he was persuaded by Franciscan missionaries to support their endeavours on the northern frontier. On 10 November 1582 he set off from San Bartolomé with a large force, including 150 horses. He entered Paratabuzo country, where he found presumed evidence of Christian preaching, and followed the River Norte. He was enormously impressed by the buildings and markets of Cia, in Cunama country, and, without success, pursued rumours, picked up among the Zuni Indians, of a distant land rich in gold. He returned to San Bartolomé in July 1583 with booty which included 40,000 blankets. 17

ETZLAUB, ERHART (c. 1460–1532). German compass-maker and cartographer, based at Nuremberg. Among his publications is *Roma Weg* (The Way to Rome) c. 1492, showing details of pilgrimage routes to the Holy City, in effect an early road atlas. This and similar publications combined the written itinerary, detailing shrines, stopping places and hazards to be found en route, with the relatively new tradition of topographically accurate cartography. 7

EVANS, LEWIS (c. 1700–56). A Welshman who found employment with Benjamin Franklin in the American colonies. His two outstanding maps – *Pennsylvania, New Jersey, New York and the Three Delaware Counties* (1749, revised 1752) and *The Middle British Colonies in America* with an accompanying *Analysis* (1755) – were printed in London. The accurate plotting of roads and settlements of the former led to its being used extensively by settlers. The latter proved essential to British forces during the French and Indian wars. Between 1750 and 1778 he produced an *Atlas of North America*. 19

EVEREST, SIR GEORGE (1790–1866), British East India Company army officer and pioneer of the great Trigonometrical Survey of India. In 1823, as superintendent of the Indian Survey, he inherited from **William Lambton** the task of triangulating the whole subcontinent on a gridiron plan, and drove the project through with great rigour and efficiency. Everest insisted on strict accuracy and checked ground measurements with precise astronomical bearings. Mount Everest, whose height was first measured according to his methods, was named after him. 43

EYRE, EDWARD JOHN (1815–1901) British-born Australian explorer. He migrated to New South Wales in 1833. For some years, he engaged in pastoralism, before turning to overlanding stock to the new settlements at Melbourne and Adelaide. In 1839, he explored north from the head of Spencer's Gulf to Lake Torrens and the Flinders Range, and round the Eyre Peninsula. In 1840, he went north again, as far as Lake Eyre and Mt. Hopeless. The next year, he set out to follow the coast from Fowlers Bay to King George Sound. He and his Aboriginal companion Wylie endured great privation, before being succoured by a whaling vessel near Esperance. Late in 1841, Eyre was appointed Protector of Aborigines at Moorundie, where he had notable success in establishing good relations between then and the white pastoralists who came in ever-increasing numbers. This success sits oddly with his harsh treatment of blacks in Jamaica in 1865, whence he had gone after terms as lieutenant-governor of the New Zealand and St. Vincent colonies. 36

FAGUNDES, JOÃO ÁLVARES, 16th-century Portuguese explorer of Newfoundland. Only cartographic evidence remains of his colonizing activities near Cape Breton

Island in the early 1520s. He held a fishing concession at that time from the Portuguese crown in the Newfoundland Banks. 15

FA HSIEN (4th–5th century AD). A Buddhist monk, born in Shansi province, who made the first recorded journey overland from China to India and back by sea between 399 and 414. The purpose of his journey was to gather religious texts, but his account of his experiences enormously enriched Chinese geography. 1

FALLAM, ROBERT, 17th-century explorer of North America. An educated trader, he was the companion of **Thomas Batts** in the great expedition of September 1671 from Appomattox in search of the 'South Sea', which he reported finding, apparently misled by the tides of the Tug Fork River. 19

FEDERMANN, NIKOLAUS (d. 1542), German *conquistador*. He entered the service of the German Welser banking family before going to Venezuela in 1530, where he led the first European expedition into the interior. In 1537 he led a further expedition, this time climbing the Andes into present-day Colombia, where he met the expeditions of **Jiménez de Queseda** and **Sebastián de Benalcázar** in Bogotá in 1539. Obliged to return to Spain to counter, with claims to rewards, accusations of fraudulent misuse of royal revenues, he died in custody in Valladolid on 21 or 22 February 1542. 25

FERNANDES, ANTÓNIO, 16th-century Portuguese explorer of Africa. He was a carpenter by trade who went to Africa in commutation of a sentence of death for an unknown crime. He was in Kilwa by 1501, presumably left by Cabral. By 1505 he was established at Sofala, from where he made his pioneering journeys into the Zambezi basin, first recorded in a document of October 1514, which reported that he had gone to investigate the sources of the gold of Monomotapa. 14, 27

FERNANDES, JOÃO, 15th-century Portuguese navigator. A resident of Terceira in the Azores, he received a commission to discover unknown islands in the Atlantic in 1499. With two fellow-Azoreans, Francisco Fernandes and João Gonçalves, and in association with a group of English merchants from Bristol, he undertook a voyage which had been credited with the discovery of some part of the North American mainland, but which is generally regarded as having reached no further than Greenland. 14

FERNÁNDEZ, JUAN (c. 1529–99). The three or four pilots of this name who served in Peru and Chile in the 16th century are easily confused, but the Juan Fernández in question here seems to have arrived in Peru in about 1550. He is credited with the discovery of a relatively fast sea route from Peru to Chile, outflanking the adverse current by sailing well out into the Pacific and returning with the aid of the westerly current and winds in the southern part of the ocean. This method, which he essayed in 1574, reduced the sailing time from 90 to 30 days. In November 1574, he gave his name to the Juan Fernández Islands. 14

FERNÁNDEZ DE OVIEDO Y VALDES (1478–1557), Spanish historian and geographer whose *History of the West Indies* (1535) was an account of the discovery and settlement of the region, supplemented by a number of draft maps. 26

FERRER, or **FERRELO, BARTOLOMÉ**, 16th-century Spanish explorer of the Pacific. He accompanied **Cabrillo** on his expedition of 1542–43 to California, and, after Cabrillo's death in 1543, continued northwards, discovering the coast of present-day Oregon. 20

FIELD, DARBY, 17th-century explorer of North America. Of Irish origin, Field was a servant of the Laconia Company, established in 1629 to open a route from Maine to Lake Champlain. In 1642 he was the first European explorer in the White Mountains. With two Indian guides he ascended the mountains at a point where he could see the Gulf of St. Lawrence from the summit. His misleading reports of diamonds encouraged further exploration along the Saco River. 19

FILCHNER, WILHELM (1877–1957), German explorer who led the German expedition (1911–12) to the Antarctic. In later life he resumed the work begun in his 1903–3 expedition through north-eastern Tibet, taking scientific expeditions to the Himalaya regions in 1926–28, 1935–37 and 1939. His *Route-Mapping and*

Position-Locating in Unexplored Regions (1957) was a major contribution to the literature of exploration and cartography. 46

FINDLAY, ALEXANDER GEORGE (1812–75). Findlay was a maker of maps, sea charts and atlases who had an influence on debates about the Nile when he published maps in 1867 designed to show that **Speke** had not reached the ultimate source and that **Burton** might be the true discoverer, if not **Livingstone**. He was wrong. 39

FLINDERS, MATTHEW (1774–1814) was born at Donington, Lincolnshire, and entered the navy in 1789. In 1791 he was a midshipman on the *Providence* during Bligh's second breadfruit voyage; and in 1795 he sailed out to New South Wales on the *Reliance*. From 1796, with George Bass he examined sections of the coast south of Sydney; and in 1798–99 the pair circumnavigated Tasmania, thus proving it to be an island and opening the way for ships to reach Sydney via Bass Strait. Flinders returned to England in 1800. Having come to the notice of the Admiralty and Sir Joseph Banks, in 1801 he was appointed to the *Investigator* to carry out a precise survey of the continent's coasts. With a party of scientists among his company, Flinders worked at this task in stages over the next three years. When the *Investigator* proved unseaworthy, he determined to obtain a replacement in England. His first attempt to do so ended in the wreck of the *Porpoise* on a reef off the coast of Queensland; his second in his six-year detention at Mauritius, where he arrived at the end of 1803. Flinders's circumnavigation gave rise to accurate delineations of the continent's coasts, and to striking natural history collections. It and **Baudin**'s parallel voyage effectively mark the end of the last great period of European exploration of the Pacific Ocean, which began in the 1760s. His narrative of his explorations gave currency to the name 'Australia'. 35, 36

FLORES DE LEÓN, DIEGO, 17th-century Spanish explorer of South America. In 1621, lured by the old legend of the city of 'Los Césares', he led a force of 46 men along the Río Peulla and discovered Lake Nahuel Huapí, turning south until obliged by hunger and hostile Indians to return to Chile. The route he had found was gradually exploited by missionaries. 24

FORREST, JOHN (1847–1918) and **ALEXANDER** (1849–1901), were members of a numerous family who lived near Bunbury, Western Australia. In 1863, John qualified as a surveyor, a profession that Alexander also pursued. In 1869, John searched for the missing **Ludwig Leichhardt** inland towards Lake Moore and Lake Barlee. The following year, he and Alexander led a party west to east along the edge of the Great Australian Bight, establishing the course of the telegraph line from Adelaide to Perth, built in 1877. In 1874, the pair took another party from Geraldton to the Overland Telegraph Line. In 1879, Alexander and his younger brother Matthew spent six months exploring the Kimberley region in the northwest, finding extensive pastoral lands about the Fitzroy and Ord Rivers. When John became the colony's surveyor-general in 1883, the opening of this region was one of his first tasks, and he and Alexander acquired extensive interests there. Alexander became member for Kimberley in 1887, and was mayor of Perth in the 1890s while John was the colony's premier from 1890 to 1891. 36

FOX or **FOXE, LUKE** (1586–1635), English explorer. Sea-bred from boyhood, he was bent on Arctic exploration from the time of his participation in John Knight's Greenland voyage of 1606. In 1631, in emulation of **Thomas James**'s expedition to find the Northwest Passage, he sailed along the western and southern coasts of Hudson Bay, making a valuable hydrographic survey. Convinced that no passage existed in that area, and with his crew debilitated by scurvy, he returned to England. He gave names to many features, including Foxe Basin and Foxe Peninsula. In 1635 he published *Northwest Fox; or Fox from the North-West Passage*. 16

FRANKLIN, SIR JOHN (1786–1847), English sailor and Arctic explorer. He joined the Royal Navy as a midshipman and served on **Matthew Flinders**'s hydrographic survey of the coast of Australia. He later fought under Nelson at the battles of Copenhagen and Trafalgar. His Arctic experience began in 1818 on a Royal Navy expedition to Spitsbergen. Its divided aims, inadequate technology and reliance on traditional naval virtues of discipline in the face of a hostile environment established a pattern of British polar exploration that persisted for almost a century and that, whatever its claims of *esprit de corps*, achieved negligible results at huge cost.

Between 1819 and 1827 Franklin made a number of overland journeys in the Canadian Arctic. In 1834 he was appointed governor of Tasmania. In 1845 Franklin was given command of an expedition to trace the Northwest Passage. Beset in pack-ice in Victoria Strait, the expedition members quickly fell prey to the Arctic winter. Franklin died the following summer; others of the expedition attempted to reach the Great Fish River (Back River), site of a Hudson Bay Company trading post. Though surrounded by Inuit living off the land, they all perished, many of lead poisoning from tinned food, others from scurvy. The many rescue missions sent to search for Franklin added significantly to knowledge of the Canadian Arctic. Franklin himself, when news of his epic failure was confirmed, was perversely elavated to the ranks of great British explorers. 23

FRASER, SIMON (1776–1862), Canadian trader and explorer. In the service of the North West Company from 1792, and a partner from 1801, from 1805 Fraser pioneered routes to the regions west of the Rocky Mountains, establishing trade posts as he did so around the northern reaches of the Fraser River, which he had discovered and named. In 1808, in the expectation that the Fraser River would prove to be the Columbia River, the mouth of which was aleady known, he descended it to the Pacific. 21

FRÉMONT, JOHN CHARLES (1813–90), American soldier, explorer and politician. After attending the scientific department of the College of Charleston (South Carolina) and teaching mathematics aboard a U.S. naval vessel, Frémont was commissioned in 1838 second lieutenant in the Topographical Engineers. With the scientist Joseph Nicolas Nicollet he made reconnaissances into the territory between the upper Mississippi and Missouri rivers. After eloping with Jessie Benton, Senator Thomas Hart Benton's daughter, in 1842 Frémont was sent up the Platte and North Platte rivers to South Pass. His report was published and widely distributed, establishing Frémont's fame. Shortly thereafter he was on his way West again. This time he made an enormous circuit of the West. His widely distributed report included a map which clarified concepts of the vast region. On a third expedition he participated in the Bear Flag Revolt in California, was court-martialled and resigned his commission. In 1848–49 a private expedition ended disastrously in the San Juan Mountains of Colorado; he made a fifth and last expedition in 1853–54. Frémont's career included his unsuccessful presidential candidacy as a Republican in 1856, disastrous participation in the Civil War, and failed attempts to make a fortune from his California properties. His real contribution was in popularizing knowledge of the great migration trails into the American West. 22

FRÉZIER, AMÉDÉE-FRANÇOIS (1682–1773), French cartographer, scientist and builder. A lawyer's son from Chambéry, he abandoned theology for scientific studies and became a military engineer in charge of the defences of St. Malo, where his scientific papers drew his superiors' attention. In 1712 he was sent to South America to report on Spanish defences. Departing on 23 November, he sailed west of the Falkand Islands, of which he produced the first authentic chart, and round Cape Horn. In three years of espionage in Chile and Peru he compiled a vast amount of botanical, zoological and ethnographic information. Among the specimens he gathered was the ancestor of most modern cultivated strawberries. In 1719–25 he worked on the fortifications of Haiti. Steady promotion took him to the post of inspector-general of the defences of Brittany in 1739. His interests veered progressively towards the study of building techniques and architecture, which occupied his retirement from 1763 to his death in 1773. 13

FRITZ, SAMUEL (*c.*1659–1725), German Jesuit explorer and missionary in South America. Born in Tratenau, he was sent to Quito in 1684 to join the Jesuit mission to the Omaguas region of the middle Amazon, where he served from 1686. He extended the bounds of his mission for 400 or 500 leagues between the Rivers Napo and Negro, distinguishing himself not only in preaching the faith but in protecting Indians from secular exploitation and in defending the rights of the Spanish crown against Portuguese encroachments on Spanish territory. His contributions to the ethnography, geography and cartography of the Amazon region were a notable by-product of the mission, which he headed from 1704 until his death in 1725. 26

FROBISHER, SIR MARTIN (*c.*1535–94), English navigator. Frobisher was one of the first to search for the Northwest Passage to the Orient. In 1553, he made his first voyage to Guinea and, during the next decade, undertook annual expeditions to northern Africa and the Levant. Frobisher made three attempts to reach Asia by sailing westward. In 1576, during his first voyage, he rounded the southern tip of Greenland and sailed into a deep inlet on the east coast of Baffin Island (today's Frobisher Bay). On this and his second voyage he took back to England quantities of rock supposed to contain gold ore, but which proved valueless. On his second trip (1577) he annexed Baffin Island to the English crown. During his third voyage, in 1578, he commanded 15 ships, entered Hudson Strait by mistake, without realizing its significance, and explored the upper part of Frobisher Bay. Frobisher was vice-admiral in **Drake**'s expedition (1585–86) to the West Indies and, in 1588, commanded the *Triumph* against the Spanish Armada, for which he was knighted. In 1592, **Sir Walter Raleigh** gave him a squadron to plunder the coast of Spain, from which expedition he returned with much booty. In 1594 he was mortally wounded while fighting a Spanish force near Brest, France. He died at Plymouth. 14, 16

FUCHS, SIR VIVIAN (b. 1908), British Antarctic scientist, explorer and adminstrator. Fuchs trained as a geologist and led several scientific expeditions to Africa during the 1930s. In 1947–50 he was leader of the Falkland Islands Dependencies Survey's expeditions to Antarctica, and he remained in charge of the Survey's activities after his return home. In 1955–58 he led the Commonwealth Trans-Antarctic Expedition, which made the first surface crossing of Antarctica. From 1958 he was director of the Falkland Islands Dependencies Survey, which in 1962 became the British Antarctic Survey. He resigned from the directorship in 1973, but has remained active in Antarctic science and administration. 46

GAGARIN, YURI ALEXSEYEVICH (1934–68), Russian cosmonaut. A Soviet test pilot, Gagarin was the first man in space. He made his flight in the space-capsule *Vostok* in April 1961. It consisted of one orbit of the Earth and lasted just short of 90 minutes. Gagarin was killed in a helicopter crash. 47

GALLEGO, HERNANDO, 16th-century Spanish explorer of the Pacific. A veteran of the voyages of Ulloa and **Ladrillero** in the Strait of Magellan, he sailed as chief pilot in **Mendaña**'s Pacific expedition in November 1567. While the other expert aboard, **Pedro Sarmiento de Gamboa**, was intent on finding islands reported in Inca legend, Gallego hoped to find a new route across the ocean to New Guinea. When they discovered the Solomon Islands in February 1568, Gallego conducted a detailed survey of substantial parts of the coasts of six islands in a brig of his own construction. However, he grossly underestimated the archipelago's distance from Peru, helping to create the misleading impression of the extent of the Pacific. He persuaded Mendaña to return home while they still had supplies for the journey, and reached Callao in September 1569. 33

GAMA, CRISTÓVÃO DA (*c.*1516–42). The fourth son of **Vasco da Gama**, he made his first recorded voyage to India in 1532, returning to become a gentleman of the royal household. From 1538 he served his brother **Estevão da Gama**, who succeeded Garcia de Noronha as viceroy of Portuguese India. In 1540 he accompanied the Portuguese punitive expedition to the Red Sea and led a volunteer force from among the members of the expedition to the defence of Christian Ethiopia against Muslim invaders, during which he fell in battle in the late summer of 1542. His expedition was important, however, in consolidating and extending Portuguese knowledge of the interior of Ethiopia, and ultimately, instrumental in the defeat of the Muslims. 27

GAMA, ESTEVÃO DA (d. 1575), Portuguese diplomat and mariner. He served as a naval commander in India when his father, **Vasco da Gama**, was viceroy (1524–38). In 1538 he was appointed governor of Malacca and in 1540 was chosen as governor of Portuguese India. His expedition to destroy hostile shipping in the Red Sea in 1541 was noteworthy for leaving a volunteer force which, under the command of his brother **Cristóvão da Gama**, helped save Ethiopia from Muslim conquest. In 1542 he returned to Portugal but removed to Venice to avoid a marriage arranged by the king. Refusing subsequent preferment, except as nominal commander of the garrison of Lisbon, he lived until 1575. 28

GAMA, VASCO DA (*c.*1460–1524), Portuguese navigator. He was born in Sines, then educated in Évora; subsequently he was trained in nautical science. In 1492 he became a naval officer. Another Portuguese navigator, **Bartolomeu Dias**, had discovered a possible route to India by sailing around the Cape of Good Hope in 1488. In 1497, the Portuguese king, Manuel I, ordered da Gama to follow that route and continue to India, there to establish trading links. The expedition was given urgency by Portugal's need to reach the Indies – which had been allocated to Portugal by the pope under the Treaty of Tordesillas of 1493 – before the Spanish could pre-empt their claim. Da Gama commanded four ships, the crews numbering 170 in all, and left Lisbon on 8 July 1497. After reaching the Cape Verde Islands, he took advantage of the prevailing winds, veered far out into the Atlantic and then swung back eastwards to the Cape of Good Hope. Whether this was fortuitous or deliberate is uncertain, but his course is followed by sailing ships to this day. Da Gama then sailed northwards, stopping at trading centres along the east coast of Africa. He next turned north-east to India, reaching Calicut on 20 May 1498. There trade was largely controlled by Muslim merchants, who resented European interference. Thus, when he sailed for home, he was able to take with him only samples of Indian goods, though from more friendly trading posts he obtained a handsome cargo of spices. Many of his crew died of disease on the voyage, only 55 surviving.

Da Gama made a second voyage to India in 1502, again with the object of establishing trade links. This time he was more successful, for in 1500 the Portuguese king had sent a fleet to India to break the Muslims' monopoly of trade. Da Gama returned to Portugal in 1503 and retired from naval service. He had already been rewarded by the king with the title 'admiral of India'; then, in 1524, King John III named him viceroy. Da Gama sailed to India to govern the colonies but died shortly after arriving. 13, 29

DE GAMBOA, PEDRO SARMIENTO (d. 1596), 16th-century Spanish navigator, surveyor and scientist. Born in Alcalá de Henares, Sarmiento was in New Spain by 1555, from where, for unknown reasons, he was obliged to flee to Peru. In 1564, he was arraigned before the Inquisition in Lima, accused of conjuration, but was exonerated with his reputation for astronomical and historical learning intact. In 1567–69, he accompanied the voyage, which he helped inspire, of **Alvaro de Mendaña** to the Solomon Islands. Under the patronage of the viceroy of Peru, Sarmiento played a major role in the suppression of Inca resistance both in the field and in writing his history of the Incas, which impugned the legitimacy of the pre-colonial regime. Despite renewed harrassment by the Inquisition, he continued his scientific work, producing among many other observations an improved calculation of the longitude of Lima in 1578. In 1579, provoked by **Drake**'s raid on Callao, the viceroy sent him to the Strait of Magellan to plan defences against further pirate incursions. His survey and passage of the Strait took him 16 months. In 1581 he was sent back to the region from Spain with 350 potential settlers, of whom only 64 completed the journey to establish the communities of Rey Don Felipe and Nombre de Jesús in 1584. On his way back to Spain to obtain supplies for the settlers, Sarmiento was captured by the English and taken to Queen Elizabeth's court (where he conversed with the queen in Latin). Borrowing his ransom, he departed in October 1586 after a few weeks' detention but was imprisoned on his way through France. By the time his ransom was paid by the Spanish Crown in 1590, the colonists he had left at the Strait had perished or fled. In 1591, he was appointed to accompany a fleet to New Spain, but died in Lisbon the following year while planning the expedition. Among his many surviving works, his account of his voyages to the Strait of Magellan is outstanding for its moving descriptions and detailed surveying information. **24, 33**

GARAVITO, ANDRÉS, 16th-century Spanish *conquistador*, a lieutenant sent by **Balboa** in 1515 to find a direct route west across the Isthmus from Santa María la Antigua in Darién to the Pacific. With 80 men, he followed the Río Tanela over the Serranía de Darién by Indian trail to a river which flowed west, probably the Río Tuira, along which he reached the sea. The route was too steep to be commercially useful. Nothing is known of Garavito's subsequent career. **10**

GARAY, FRANCISCO DE (d. 1523). A friend and shipmate of **Columbus**, he served with **Bartolomé Columbus** in Hispaniola and, after 1509, compiled a considerable fortune in Jamaica. In 1519 he financed the reconnaissance of the coasts of the Gulf of Mexico by **Alonso Álvarez de Pineda**. He made repeated efforts between 1520 and 1523 to conquer the Pânuco Valley, which brought him into conflict with **Cortés** over the limits of their respective spheres. On Christmas Day, 1523, the two leaders achieved an amicable settlement, but Garay fell suddenly ill and died within a few days. **10**

GARAY, JUAN DE (*c.*1528–83), Spanish *conquistador*. He went to Peru at the age of 14 and in the early 1560s was among the settlers of Santa Cruz de la Sierra in south-east Bolivia. In 1568, when the colony failed, he led the survivors to Asunción. In 1573 he was sent to find an exploitable route through the Paraná valley to the ocean. In 1574 he rescued the incoming governor Ortiz de Zárate, shipwrecked in the River Plate; in 1578, Zárate's heir made Garay deputy governor and ordered him to re-found Buenos Aires, which had been abandoned in 1541. The formal act of foundation took place on 11 June 1580. In 1581 Garay explored the coast of Mar del Plata in the hope of finding news of the fabled riches of the city of 'Los Césares'. He was killed in a skirmish with Indians, at the confluence of the Coronada and Carcaraña, in March 1583. **26**

GARICA, ALEJO or **ALEIXO** (d. *c.*1526), Portuguese explorer of South America. Marooned on or near the island of Santa Caterina, almost certainly by the expedition of **Juan Diaz de Solís**, Garcia made a remarkable if ill-documented journey, probably between 1522 and 1526, during which he travelled inland and along the Paraguay River possibly as far as the Andes. According to the story told by Indians to later explorers, Garcia was returning with great riches when, beyond the upper reaches of the Paraguay, he was killed by Indians. His objective was said to be a 'White King' who ruled mountains of silver. This rumour helped inspire his successors in the exploration of the River Plate and its drainage. **26**

GARCÉS, FRANCISCO (1738–81), Spanish Franciscan, explorer of North America. After studying in the college of his Franciscan Order in Querétaro, he worked for 12 years in the mission of San Javier del Bac in Arizona, making a spectacular series of journeys of exploration, evangelization and peaceful extension of the limits of the king of Spain's authority. In 1769 he undertook a mission to the Apache; in 1770 he went north to Los Gileños. In 1771 he reached the Californian mountains and in 1773–74, with **Juan Bautista de Anza**, led the expedition that opened an overland road to California from Tubac to Monterey. In 1775 he undertook the epic journey – much of it unaccompanied – that generated, in the form of his diary, one of the classics of exploration literature. He travelled from San Francisco along the Colorado and into the Nevada desert, reaching Yuma country in September 1776, where he later returned to establish a mission. He was killed during the Yuma uprising of July 1781. **17**

GARNIER, MARIE-JOSEPH-FRANÇOIS 'FRANCIS' (1839–73). Born the son of an engineer, he studied in Montpellier and entered naval college in 1855. In 1860 he was sent to China, where he witnessed the siege of Peking before being transferred to Saigon. Invalided home after action at Ki-Hoa and Mytho on the Mekong, he supplicated for a post in the civil adminstration of Indo-China. Appointed an inspector of native affairs in 1863 he published pseudonymous works calling for an extension of French power along the Mekong. In 1866 the French government responded by commissioning the Mekong River Expedition under **Captain Doudart de Lagrée**; Garnier was charged with the expedition's astronomical, meteorological and geographical work. During the course of the expedition, Lagrée sickened and died, but Garnier reached the River Yangtze in 1868 and after a diversion to Tibet, emerged at Shanghai on 12 June of that year, after a journey of more than 6,000 miles. A life of honour and profit at home was interrupted by the war of 1870, in which he served with distinction in the defence of Paris. Disenchantment with the terms of the peace led him to enter politics and journalism. He was in China as a correspondent in 1873, when he was called urgently to Indo-China to help save Hanoi from blockade by insurgents. He led with panache a successful operation, in the course of which he was killed on 21 December. **45**

GASTALDI, GIACOMO (*c.*1500-*c.*1565), Venetian cartographer, native of Villafranca in Piedmont, cosmographer to the Serene Republic of Venice. Highly influential, Gastaldi's maps were copied by many later cartographers and publishers, among them **Abraham Ortelius**, Giovanni Battista Ramusion and **Gerard Mercator**. Gastaldi's large, separately published maps number more than 200 in the 20 or so years between 1544 and 1565, and it was he who was largely responsible for the establishment of Italian cartographic supremacy during the middle decades of the 16th century. His maps include Spain (1544), Europe (1546), World (1546, 1561 – now lost, and 1564), Germany (1552), Asia (1559–61), Europe (1559), Africa (1564), America (undated), and an influential edition of **Ptolemy** in 1548 which provided the basis for most subsequent Italian editions up to the 1590s. **17**

GEDENSHTROM (HEDENSTRÖM), MATVEY MATVEYEVICH (1780–1843), Swedish/Russian explorer. He was born in Sweden but was educated at university in Russia and spent the rest of his life there. In 1808 he was exiled to Siberia for alleged smuggling. Soon after his arrival in Irkutsk, he was commissioned by Count N. P. Rumyantsev to survey the New Siberian Islands, which had been known to hunters since 1770 but had never been properly mapped. He worked on the survey until 1810, and the project was concluded by **Pshenitsin** in 1811. Gedenshtrom continued to travel and conduct research in Siberia until 1827, when he was allowed to return to European Russia. **32**

GILBERT, SIR HUMPHREY (*c.*1537–83), English navigator. In common with many Englishmen of his time, he was confident that there was a northwest passage by water that would lead to the East Indies and, to support his views, he wrote in 1575 his celebrated *Discourse on a North-West Passage to India*. Two years later Elizabeth I gave him authority to search for such a passage and 'discover and possess' lands not already taken by a Christian prince. **Raleigh**, his half-brother and lifelong friend, was of his company, but the expedition (1578–79), of which little is known, proved fruitless. Gilbert mounted a second expedition in 1583, landed in Newfoundland and took possession of the island in the name of Queen Elizabeth. On the return journey, Gilbert sailed on the frigate *Squirrel*, the smaller of the two vessels remaining to him, and perished with her crew when she capsized and sank off the Azores on 9 September 1583. **16**

GILES, ERNEST (1835–97) was born in Bristol, England. He arrived at Adelaide in 1850. In 1872, he explored central Australia west from the Overland Telegraph Line. In 1873–74, he made a second westward probe; and in 1875 he crossed from South Australia to Western Australia through the Great Victoria Desert, making the return journey the following year. **36**

GIST, CHRISTOPHER (*c.*1706–59), soldier and explorer of North America. A native of Maryland, son of a surveyor, he was appointed by the Ohio Company in 1750 to explore the Ohio River. From Shannopin's Town (now Pittsburgh) he crossed the Ohio to the mouth of the Scioto and continued into Kentucky. The following year he resumed his efforts, from the Monongahela to the Kanawha. From 1753 to 1755 he served with George Washington, twice saving his life. In 1756 he was sent as an agent to the Cherokee in East Tennessee, but failed to enlist them in the service of the crown. He died of smallpox soon after withdrawing from this service. **19**

GÓES, BENTO DE (1562–1607). A Jesuit at the Mughal court in Agra, he was sent in 1603 to find the best route overland to China and verify whether, as the Chinese Jesuits believed, it was to be identified with the Cathay of **Marco Polo**. From Lahore, disguised as a Muslim, he joined a caravan to Kabul, thence making his way to Yarkand, where his disguise was discarded and from where he visited the jade mines of Khotan. Another caravan took him over the Hindu Kush to join Marco Polo's route at Taliqan, about 300 miles east of Bukhara. At Kara Shahr his conversations with caravan traders convinced him of the identity of China and Cathay. He pressed on to Su-chou before his health collapsed. A messenger from the Chinese Jesuit mission reached him just before he expired and 'seeking Cathay, found heaven'. **Section VIII**

GOMES, DIOGO, 15th-century Portuguese mariner. He has been credited with a voyage or voyages to the Cape Verde Islands and Lower Gambia similar to that of **Antonio di Usodimare**, whom he can be presumed to have accompanied or followed at an uncertain date between 1456 and 1458. He was a squire of the household of **Henry the Navigator**, of whose world and work he gave a circumspect account to **Martin Behaim** in the 1490s. **12**

GOMES, FERNÃO (active *c.*1469–74), Portuguese explorer of the African coast. King Afonso V of Portugal had no interest in exploration and in 1469 leased government rights to Gomes, who paid an annual fee and agreed to explore some 400 miles of African coast every year. The arrangement was hugely successful: Gomes explored roughly 2,000 miles of coast and amassed a fortune. Details are sparse, as the voyages, no longer in the king's hands, were not chronicled in the Portuguese royal archives. According to the only surviving account, in João de Barros's 16th-century chronicle, *Asia*, Axim on the Ivory Coast was reached in 1470, Elmina in 1471, the Cameroons and Fernando Po in 1472, the Equator in 1473 at Cabo de Santa Catarina, and the islands of São Tomé and Príncipe in 1474. Gomes's contract was not renewed in 1474, when the king placed his son, later João II, in command of exploration. **12**

GÓMEZ or **GOMES, ESTEBAN** or **ESTEVÃO** (*c.*1484–1538). A Portuguese pilot in Spanish service, he sailed with **Magellan**, but deserted in November 1520 when his commander ordered him to explore the southerly arm of the great strait. Having secured a pardon, he advised on the problem of longitude-finding in the Pacific and served against French pirates. Ordered to seek a northerly strait, he sailed from Corunna on 24 October 1524 and searched the length of the North American coast from about Nova Scotia south to Florida, making detailed observations that had an immediate impact on cartography. Until 1528 he supervised shipbuilding in Corunna, and in 1533 received an abortive commission to build the long-projected Guadalquivir canal. In 1535 he sailed as chief pilot on the ill-starred expedition to the River Plate of **Pedro de Mendoza**. He died during the ascent of the River Paraguay in a skirmish with Indians. **15**

GOSSE, WILLIAM CHRISTIE (1842–81), English-born explorer of Australia. He reached Adelaide with his parents in 1850, where he subsequently trained as a surveyor. From 1859 into the 1870s, he worked in widely separated parts of South Australia. In 1873, the colonial government employed him to explore west from Alice Springs, a task that led him to the discovery of Ayers Rock. **36**

GREGORY, SIR AUGUSTUS (1819–1905) was born at Farnsfield, Nottinghamshire. In 1829 he came with his family to the newly founded Swan River colony, where he became a cadet surveyor. In 1846, together with two brothers, he explored inland to the north of Perth. In 1848 he traced portions of the Murchison River, a move that led to the opening of the Geraldton district. In 1855–56 he headed the North Australian Exploring Expedition, examining the Victoria River basin, and travelling eastwards across the Northern Territory and Barkly Tableland to the east coast at Port Curtis. In 1858, on behalf of the New South Wales Government, he led a search for the missing **Leichhardt**, through the Channel Country down to Adelaide. The following year, the new Queensland government appointed him commissioner of lands and surveyor-general. In the decades following, he oversaw the surveying of this large colony, and reported in detail on its geology. 36

GRIJALVA, HERNANDO DE, 16th-century Spanish *conquistador* and navigator of the Pacific. Documented in New Spain from 1532, he accompanied **Diego Becerra**'s expedition from Manzanillo in 1533. Striking off on his own, he discovered the islands of Socorro and San Benedicto and explored the Tehuantepec coast. He was then sent from New Spain by **Cortés** to assist in the suppression of Inca resistance in Peru in 1536. Perhaps on his own initiative, perhaps on secret instructions from Cortés, he decided to explore the Pacific for exploitable islands and/or a route to the Spice Islands from Peru. He sailed from Paita in April 1537, heading south-west, but, finding only the discouraging emptiness of the ocean, aborted the mission and turned north, intending to make New Spain or California. His crew demanded that he should make for the Moluccas and, on his refusal, killed him and turned west. The mutineers, at the cost of most of their lives, completed the most southerly crossing of the Pacific so far recorded, close to the equator, before being shipwrecked on the coast of New Guinea, from where Portuguese missionaries rescued them. 33

GRIJALVA, JUAN DE (*c*.1480–1527), 16th-century Spanish *conquistador*. He arrived in the New World in 1508 and served in the conquest of Cuba. In January 1518, he was sent to follow up the reconnaissance of Yucatán. At Ulúa, on 19 June, he received reports, the first known to Europeans, of the existence of the Aztec state. After reaching Cape Rojo, he returned to Cuba in September. In 1523 he joined an abortive expedition of conquest to the Pánuco Valley under **Francisco de Garay** and then took service in Central America with the forces of Pedrarias Dávila. He was killed in a skirmish with Indians in Villahermosa, Nicaragua, on 21 January 1527. 26

GROSEILLIERS, MEDARD CHOUART, SIEUR DES (*c*.1632–1710), French fur-trader and explorer in North America. The companion and brother-in-law of **Radisson**, doubt exists as to where he and Radisson penetrated on their early ventures in and around the Great Lakes in the mid- and late 1650s. The quantities of furs illegally traded by Groseilliers and Radisson led to conflict with the French authorities and persuaded him to offer his services to English traders. In 1668, with the patronage of Prince Rupert, Groseilliers founded Fort Charles in James Bay. His success in fur-trading in the region was instrumental in the establishment of the English Hudson's Bay Company. 18

GRUEBNER, JOHANN or **JOHN** (1623–80), with **ALBERT D'ORVILLE** (1621–62) a member of the Jesuit mission to China commissioned in 1661 to reopen overland communications to Europe because of the blockade of the Dutch ports. Departing from Peking in April, in October they became the first European travellers to make a verifiable visit to Lhasa. They continued via Shigatse across the Himalayas to Kathmandu, where they arrived on Christmas Eve. D'Orville died at Agra in March 1663 but Gruebner continued along the Indus valley and thence by sea to reach Rome in February 1664. He campaigned for a mission to Nepal, but the effect of his journey was to deter rather than to encourage similar efforts. 44

GUERRA, CRISTÓBAL and **LUIS** (d.1504). Merchants of Triana. Suppliers of hard tack for the fleets bound for the New World, they took advantage of the relaxation of **Columbus**'s monopoly in 1499 to finance a profitable voyage to Venezuela with **Pero Alonso Niño**. They also participated – financially and in person – in the expedition of Luis Vélez de Mendoza to Brazil in 1501. Their last voyage ended in their deaths in the region of Cartagena – Cristóbal in combat with Indians and his brother in a shipwreck. 10

GUNNISON, JOHN WILLIAMS (1812–53), U.S. army officer and explorer. In 1848–50 Gunnison, a West Point graduate and topographical engineer, surveyed parts of Utah and the Great Salt Lake with Captain Howard Stansbury. When Congress authorized the Pacific Railroad Surveys Captain Gunnison was ordered to survey a route near the 38th Parallel through southern Colorado by way of the Huerfano River and Cochetopa Pass into Utah. In October 1852 his party was attacked by Paiute Indians on the Sevier River in southern Utah, and Gunnison was killed. Lieutenant E.

G. Beckwith, who escaped, completed the survey. 22

HAKLUYT, RICHARD (*c*.1552–1616), English geographer, born in or near London. Editor of the great collection of voyages published as *The Principall Navigations, Voiages and Discoveries of the English Nation*, later expanded into three volumes between 1598 and 1600. It is an important source work of geographical knowledge and is an insight into the nature of the Elizabethan age. Hakluyt not only collected and edited material on English voyages, but also sought out and translated travel literature of other countries. 16, 17

HALL, CHARLES (1821–71), American explorer of the Arctic. He made two expeditions (1860–62, 1864–69) in search of the missing British explorer **John Franklin**. Then in 1871, he commanded a ship on an expedition to the North Pole and reached 82°11′N, the highest latitude to that date. 16

HATSHEPSUT or **HATSHOPSITI** (*c*.1503–*c*.1482 BC). As ruler of Egypt in her own right, equipped with a false beard, she sent a seaborne expedition to the Land of Punt, generally thought to have lain in the Horn of Africa. Despite an impressive building programme, she seems to have lost prestige towards the end of her reign and to have been supplanted by her erstwhile favourite, Thutmose III. 27

HAYDEN, FERDINAND VANDIVEER (1829–87), U.S. geologist and survey director. In 1867 he was appointed geologist in charge of the Geological Survey of Nebraska; Hayden subsequently enlarged this into the United States Geological and Geographical Survey of the Territories. Operating under Interior Department control and cultivating influential men of Congress, Hayden's Survey received increasingly large annual appropriations. It mapped Colorado and made the cliff dwellings and the Mount of the Holy Cross known to the world. The Survey also conducted the first scientific exploration of Yellowstone, and the park was created partly because of Survey publicity. Hayden Survey annual reports are voluminous compilations of the natural history of the American West, and hundreds of supplementary monographs were issued under the Survey's aegis. Ultimately the competition of the Hayden Survey with three other surveys operating in the West led to their consolidation into the United States Geological Survey in 1879. 22

HAYES, ISSAC (1832–81), American explorer of the Arctic. A physician, he served on **Kane**'s second expedition to the Arctic as surgeon. In the course of the expedition, he led a party across Kane Basin to the east shore of Ellesmere Island. Convinced by this experience that there was an open Arctic sea, he led his own Arctic expedition in 1860, reaching a new farthest north of 81°35′. 46

HEARNE, SAMUEL (1745–92), British explorer of Canada. Hearne joined the Hudson's Bay Company in 1766, serving at Fort Churchill as mate of the sloop *Churchill* for two years. In 1769 he led the first of two unsuccessful attempts to confirm rumours gathered from Indians of a sea-passage to the Pacific and of important copper deposits. He made a third attempt in 1770, this time penetrating to the Arctic Ocean, which he reached at the mouth of the Coppermine River in Coronation Gulf. Although his reports laid to rest for good hopes of a navigable Northwest Passage, and though the copper deposits found were disappointing, Hearne had nonetheless pioneered a route across a huge expanse of previously unknown territory and fixed the northernmost limits of the American continent (despite reporting a position almost five degrees too far to the north). The journey also helped confirm the company in its belated realization of the importance of establishing inland posts: in 1774 the first Hudson's Bay Company post away from Hudson Bay – Cumberland House – was founded by Hearne. Between 1775 and 1782, when it was captured by France, Hearne was commander of Fort Churchill. In 1795, Hearne published an account of his expedition to the Arctic, *Journey from Prince of Wales Fort on Hudson's Bay to the Northern Ocean*. 21

HEDIN, SVEN ANDERS VON (1865–1952), Swedish explorer of Central Asia. From 1885, Hedin undertook a series of arduous journeys across Central Asia. His most important achaeological finds included the Silk Road oasis of Lou-lan in the Lop Nor desert, a region long assumed incapable of sustaining life on any scale, which, as Hedin demonstrated, had been thriving and

productive until about the 4th century AD. He made two unsuccessful attempts to penetrate Lhasa in 1900–1. In 1906–8, Hedin succeeded in making extensive journeys in Tibet, for which he received considerable acclaim, not least in Britain. Pro-German sympathies in the First World War and later suspected Nazi sympathies greatly harmed his reputation, though his voluminous published works, in particular *My Life as an Explorer* (1925), enjoyed considerable popularity. 44

HENDAY (or HENDEY), ANTHONY (active 1750–62), English explorer of Canada. He made only one major journey, travelling south-west from the Hudson's Bay Company's York Fort in 1754–55 to report on the activities of French fur-traders. In the company of Cree Indians, Henday journeyed almost to within sight of the Rocky Mountains, though his reports on where he had been were never less than vague. Nonetheless, he was able to confirm the degree of penetration achieved by the French and the threat they posed to the Hudson's Bay company. He retired from Company service in 1762. 21

HENRY THE NAVIGATOR (INFANTE DOM HENRIQUE OF PORTUGAL) (1394–1460). The third son of King João I and Philippa of Lancaster, he acquired an early addiction to chivalric values. In 1415 he was present at the capture of Ceuta, and in 1418 led an expedition in relief of the garrison. Though these – with two similar later ventures – were his only known excursions from Portugal, he became important as a patron of navigators. His unruly household could be profitably employed on voyages of piracy, slaving and exploration, and its expenses defrayed by the gold he hoped to find along the west coast of Africa. His long military and diplomatic efforts to secure a forward base in the Canary Islands were a failure, but under his patronage, and that of other Portuguese princes, the Madeira group and seven islands of the Azores were colonized; the Cape Verde Islands were discovered; the lower reaches of the Rivers Gambia and Senegal were explored; and the latitude of Sierra Leone was reached. Slaves and small quantities of gold seem to have produced a return from what began as a financially precarious undertaking. Meanwhile, the death of senior members of the royal house made Henry's role in domestic politics increasingly important. He never ceased to advocate 'great deeds', generally with a crusading flavour, consistent with his role as master of the chivalric Order of Christ since 1420. The only projects that came to fruition, however, were the 'crusades' against Tangier in 1437 – a disaster that cost the life of the Infante Fernando and left Henry with abiding feelings of guilt – and in 1458 against Ksar es-Sghir. Though pious and scientific motives have commonly been alleged for Henry's contributions to exploration, his personal chronicler seems to have been right in saying that Henry acted to fulfil his horoscope. 12, 13

HERBERSTEIN, SIGISMUND, FREIHERR VON (1486–1566), imperial ambassador to Moscow 1517, born in Styria. He travelled twice to Moscow, in 1517 and 1526, where his knowledge of Slavonic languages enabled him to collect first-hand information on Russia and adjacent territories then little known in western Europe. In the 1540s he began assembling his collected materials into a book, the *Rerum Moscovitarum commentarii*, published at Vienna in 1549 with a map of Muscovy. Herberstein destroyed the old belief in the existence of mountain ridges in central Russia. 32

HERODOTUS (*c*.484–*c*.420 BC), Greek writer known as 'the father of history'. He travelled widely in Asia, Egypt and eastern Europe; his *Histories*, an account of the Greco-Persian wars and the events preceding them, is one of the world's first major prose works, incorporating many vivid and, to contemporaries, almost incredible travellers' tales; modern research has sometimes shown even the wildest of them to contain an element of truth. 2, 39

HEZETA, BRUNO DE (1751–1807), Spanish soldier and surveyor of North America. A native of Bilbao, he joined the marine corps of the Spanish navy at the age of 14. His early actions were against Algerian corsairs. In 1733 he was put in charge of the station at San Blas on the California coast. In 1775 he led a surveying expedition along the north-west coast of what is now the United States. After service in the Philippines and Cuba, he returned to Spain in 1787. He distinguished himself in action as commander of the naval base at

Roses in the French revolutionary war and in the defence of Algeria against the English in 1797. 20

HOHERMUTH, GEORG or **JORGE** (d. 1540), German-born explorer of South America. He arrived in Venezuela in 1535, nominated to the governorship by the Welser family, which ran the colony as a concession from the Spanish crown. He at once organized an expedition in search of the reputed riches of the region of Los Llanos. By about the time he reached the River Meta, he had gathered reports of the wealth of the Colombian highlands but was unable to find a route of ascent. When he returned to Coro in May 1538, only 90 men survived of his original complement of more than 400. Disgraced and deposed, he died two years later. 25

HOMEM, DIOGO, 16th-century Portuguese cartographer. The son and pupil of **Lopo Homem**, he was exiled from Portugal before 1547 for complicity in a murder. Between 1557 and 1576 he executed a large number of maps for patrons in England and Venice. Though some attributions are doubtful, he can confidently be credited with, among other works, a Mediterranean map in Rome, a planisphere in the British Library and part of the *Atlas Miller* in the Bibliothèque Nationale, Paris. His work was said to have contributed towards the first edition of the *Theatrum Orbis Terrarum* of **Ortelius** in 1584. A third cartographer of the name of Homem – André – exiled for murder, was working in Paris in 1565, but his relationship to Diogo and Lopo is unknown. 13

HOMEM, LOPO (d. 1565), 16th-century Portuguese cartographer. A cartographer of this name is recorded in Portugal from 1517. In 1524 he served on the commission established by the Portuguese and Spanish crown to fix the limits of their respective spheres of navigation. Frequent remittances in Portuguese royal records suggest the scale of his work under royal patronage. Among surviving maps known to have been executed by him, only one, a planisphere of 1554 in Florence, is signed. 13

HORNEMANN, FRIEDRICH (1772–1801), German explorer of Africa, employed by the African Association of London. He travelled to the continent in 1797 and made his way from Cairo to Murzuk before following the caravan route across the Sahara to Bornu. His journey was the first European scientific expedition in north-west Africa. His notes and journals were never recovered after his early death. 37

HOUGHTON, DANIEL (1740–91), British soldier and explorer in West Africa, employed by the African Association of London. In 1790 he followed the course of the Gambia River but died 400 miles inland. His journey nonetheless provided invaluable information for **Mungo Park**. 37

HOVELL, WILLIAM HILTON (1786–1875), English-born explorer of Australia. He migrated with his family to New South Wales, where first he traded, then took up land. In 1824, he joined **Hume** to explore south-west from Lake George to Port Phillip; and in 1826 he was one of a party that travelled by sea to Western Port, where he explored further. In the 1830s, he took up extensive pastoral holdings on the Goulburn Plains. 36

HSÜAN TSANG (AD 596–664) Chinese explorer of Central Asia and India. In 629 he departed from Ch'ang-an for India in the hope of finding reliable Buddhist texts. His journey took him across the Gobi Desert, Turkestan, Bukhara and Bactria to Kashmir and the Punjab. After a period of study in Buddhist monasteries, he travelled down the Ganges valley. Rather than take the customary sea-route home he returned overland around the Takla Makan desert. His account of the geographical discoveries of his 16 years' absence, *Hsi-yu-chi*, was written at the emperor's command. 1

HUC, EVARISTE REGIR (1813–68). With Joseph Gabet, he set off from north of Peking in 1844, hoping to secure admission to the closed kingdom of Tibet in order to open a Catholic mission. By a circuitous route, they reached Kumbum, where a caravan took them to Lhasa, arriving in January 1846. Preaching was not permitted, but they were able to supplement Western knowledge of Central Asia in the *Recollections of a Journey* published by Huc in 1850. 44

HUDSON, HENRY (d. 1611), English navigator and explorer. Little is known of his early life but he must have attained some distinction in his profession for, in 1607, the Muscovy Company, which had been founded by **Sebastian Cabot**, appointed him to find a northwest sea route to Asia. Hudson sailed from England in the *Hopewell* with his young son, John, and a crew of ten men. He sailed along the coast of Greenland and reached Spitsbergen, about 700 miles from the North Pole, where ice-floes, hitherto unsuspected, obliged the party to return to England. Nevertheless, Hudson had sailed farther north than any European before him. He made a second attempt to find a northern route to the Orient in 1608, but again ice blocked his passage.

In the following year, the Dutch East India Company gave him a ship, the *Half Moon*, and a crew of 20 men to lead a further expedition, this time taking an eastern route. Hudson sailed north-east but the crew became rebellious because of the intense cold; he therefore changed course to North America. He crossed the Atlantic and sailed down the east coast as far as present-day North Carolina. He then explored Chesapeake Bay and Delaware Bay and sailed up what is now known as the Hudson River as far as modern Albany, before returning home. This achievement led to Dutch claims to territories in the New World. In 1610, Hudson undertook his last voyage, this time sponsored by a group of English merchants. He crossed the Atlantic in the *Discovery* and arrived in America off the northern coast of Labrador. Still sailing westwards, the ship reached turbulent waters in what is today Hudson Strait. Hudson, believing that he had finally come to the Pacific Ocean, passed on into Hudson Bay. He then sailed south into James Bay, but could find no outlet and was obliged to winter there. Cold, hunger and disease caused mounting discontent among the crew. Hudson intended, in the following spring, to search again for a western outlet from the bay. The crew mutinied, however, and before sailing back to England cast Hudson, his son and seven loyal sailors adrift in a small, open boat. None of his party was ever seen again. 15, 16

HUMBOLDT, FRIEDRICH WILHELM HEINRICH ALEXANDER VON (1769–1859). The son of a wealthy Prussian officer, he received a strict Calvinist upbringing at the University of Göttingen in 1789–90, he became devoted to the study of natural science, especially geology, and embarked on the profession of a mining engineer. His record in the inspectorate of mines of Ansbach-Bayreuth commended him to the Spanish government when he applied to undertake a scientific expedition to Spanish America. From 1799 to 1804, accompanied by Aimé Bonplaud, he covered more than 6,000 miles of territory. Among the important features of their work were the mapping of the Casiquiare River, the ascent of Mount Chimborazo to 19,280 feet, and the collation and publication of a vast amount of topographical, botanical and geological data which local savants shared with the travellers. Humboldt made new observations on his peculiar interests – the measurement of the Earth's geomagnetic field, the mapping of isotherms and isobars and the history of the Earth's crust. He formed radical views on the social, political and economic problems of the Spanish empire, and revolutionary views on the relationship between plants, creatures and habitats. From 1804 to 1827 Humboldt lived in Paris, seeing through the press his 30 volumes of data and commentary. In 1828, the exhaustion of his private fortune obliged him to return to the court of Berlin, as household tutor and privy councillor. In 1829 he inspected the mines of the Ural Mountains and made meteorological and geological observations in Central Asia comparable to those he had reported from America. The last 25 years of his life were dominated by the writing of *Kosmos*, an investigation of the nature and structure of the universe that had extended to five volumes by the time of his death. 26

HUME, HAMILTON (1797–1873), was born near Parramatta, New South Wales, where his father held land. Learning bushcraft from Aborigines, he undertook the first of a series of explorations to the south-west of Sydney in 1814 when only 17. In 1818 he and James Meehan pushed as far as Lake Bathurst and the Goulburn Plains. The following year he, Meehan and **John Oxley** explored between this area and the coast at Jervis Bay. In 1821 or 1822, he found the Yass Plains; and in 1824–25, he and **William Hovell** travelled south-west to Port Phillip. Rewarded with grants of land, Hume thereafter pursued pastoralism. With **William Charles Wentworth**, Hume was one of the most distinguished of the first generation of native-born colonists; and his efforts also underwrote the subsequent pastoral expansion, for all his explorations revealed rich grazing lands. 36

HURTADO DE MENDOZA, GARCÍA (1535–1609). After military service in Italy and Germany he went to Peru on his father's appointment as viceroy in 1556. His father chose him to take command of the forces that had been sent to subdue Chile and had been left leaderless and divided by the deaths of **Pedro de Valdivia** and his successor. Thanks to dauntless energy and considerable reinforcements, he carried the conquests south of the River Bíobío, explored in person as far as the Gulf of Reloncaví, and sent **Juan Ladrillero** to explore the islands of Chilóe and the western approaches to the Strait of Magellan. Relieved of his command under the shadow of the usual complaints from subordinates of abuse of his authority, he returned to Spain and to pardon in 1561. He served in the occupation of Portugal in 1580 and in 1589 returned as viceroy to Peru, where he spent seven years of outstanding achievement, measured by the increase of revenues and growth of educational foundations. Still abused by resentful subordinates, he spent the rest of his life in honourable retirement and was vindicated by a eulogy published after his death by Cristóbal Suárez de Figueroa. 24

HUTTEN, PHILIP VON (1511–46), cousin of the humanist Ulrich von Hutten, he joined the Welzer establishment in Venezuela with **Hohermuth** in 1534 and took part in the expedition to the Llanos in 1535. His own expedition, commissioned in 1540, was the first to designate 'El Dorado' as its objective. He left Coro on 1 August 1541, initially following routes pioneered by Hohermuth and **Pérez de Quesada**. During three years of wanderings in the Llanos he made contact with a people of allegedly impressive material civilization, whom he called the Omagha – a name also assigned by **Francisco de Orellana** to a prosperous and sedentary culture on the middle Amazon. He found nothing exploitable, however, and his prestige was low when he eventually got back to Barquisimeto in February 1546. Caught up in a dispute over the office of governor he was murdered by one of the contenders in April. With his death, the series of German-led expeditions in Spanish South America ceased. 25

IBN BATTUTA (MOHAMMED IBN ABDULLAH IBN BATUTA) (1304–1368/9), a Moroccan and possibly the greatest of all Muslim travellers. On a pilgrimage to Mecca in 1325 he conceived an ambition to travel 'through the Earth'. Though he rarely ventured beyond the Muslim world he nonetheless reached the Niger in West Africa and Kilwa in East Africa. His Asian travels took him across Transoxiana, Afghanistan, India, the Maldives, Ceylon and Sumatra to China. He left a reputation as the most-travelled man on Earth; though received with stupefaction in Fez, his accounts of his journeys are almost entirely convincing. 5, 11

IBN MAJID OR MAJID, SHIHAB AL-DIN AHMAD (active later 15th century). His father and grandfather were both 'masters of navigation' expert in the sailing conditions of the Red Sea. In a series of works on the subject in the second half of the 15th century he collected and extended the knowledge he gained from family tradition, providing a set of sailing directions, or at least indications, from the southern tip of Africa to China, and, in detail, from Sofala to the Bay of Bengal. He died, probably, after 1501. The story that he guided **Vasco da Gama** across the Indian Ocean should not be taken literally. 5, 28, 29

INCE, JONATHAN, 17th-century explorer of North America. With **John Sherman**, he was among the frontiersmen commissioned by the Massachusetts colony to explore the area between the source of the Merrimack and the coast in order to fix the boundary of the state. They claimed to have found the source of the river on 1 August 1652, at Aqueldalian, inspiring Massachusetts to attempt to annex Maine. 19

IRARRAGA, IGNACIO DE, a Franciscan missionary of the Huallaga region of Peru. In 1644 he led an expedition on foot along the right bank of the river Huallaga to determine its course and assess the prospects of evangelization of tribes who could not be reached from the south. 26

JACKSON, FREDERICK GEORGE (1860–1938), British adventurer, soldier and explorer. After education at Edinburgh University, Jackson visited the Arctic on a sailing vessel in 1887; this inspired in him a wish to lead his own Arctic expedition. He tested his plans and equipment with a journey to northern Russia in 1893–94, and under the patronage of newspaper proprietor Alfred Harmsworth (Lord Northcliffe), he explored a large part of the Russian Arctic archipelago of Franz Josef Land. After his return he enlisted as an army officer and served in the Boer War and the First World War. He was later an adventurer and big-game hunter in Africa. 46

JAMES, THOMAS (1593?-1635?), English explorer of James Bay, which is named after him, who was searching for the Northwest Passage in the same year as **Luke Fox**. James, financed by Bristol merchants, sailed in the *Henrietta Maria* in 1631. He wintered in Charlton Island and in the following year (1632) continued to search for the passage. He then returned to England in the following year and published his book *The Strange and Dangerous Voyage of Captain Thomas James in his Intended Discovery of the North-West Passage into the South Sea*, which subsequently inspired Samuel Taylor Coleridge. 16

JOHN OF PIANO CARPINI (*c.*1180–1252), Franciscan friar and explorer of Mongolia. He set out from Lyon in April 1245, on a mission from the pope to the Great Khan, and later wrote an extensive account of his journeys in Asia. He ended his life as bishop of present-day Bar in Yugoslavia. 31, 44

JOLLIET, LOUIS (1645–1700), Canadian-born explorer of North America. The discoverer with **Jacques Marquette** of the Mississippi River, and, with Marquette in 1673, the first to navigate the river, descending to within 400 miles of the Gulf of Mexico. Jolliet's account of the descent was lost, though a later report written by him agrees substantially with that made during the journey by Marquette. Jolliet was granted Anticosti Island in the Gulf of St Lawrence as a reward; this was subsequently seized by the British. He was made royal professor of hydrography in 1697. 18

JÖRGENSÖN, JÖRGEN (1780–1841), was born in Copenhagen. Becoming a seaman, he found himself at Sydney in 1801, and seems to have sailed with **Flinders** between 1801 and 1804. In 1805–6, he returned to Europe, and for the next 20 years led an adventurous and dissolute life, commanding privateers, 'liberating' Iceland, and being repeatedly imprisoned in England for debt and other offences. In 1826, he was transported for life to Tasmania, thus finding himself at Hobart again after 23 years. In 1827, he was granted a ticket-of-leave, and in the service of the Van Diemen's Land Company he explored the central and northern areas of the island. 36

KANE, ELISHA KENT (1820–57), American polar explorer. In 1850 he was appointed senior medical officer of a ship sent to search for the lost British polar explorer, **John Franklin**. Three years later he commanded a second expedition, which navigated the head of Baffin Bay and Smith Sound, before entering and exploring Kane Basin. Expeditions by sledge led to the sighting of Humboldt Glacier and a farthest north of 80°10'. His vessel became frozen in the ice, and Kane set off overland to Upernavik in Greenland – a journey, by boat and by sledge, of some 1,800 miles. His published accounts of his journeys earned him considerable sums. 46

KELSEY, HENRY (*c.*1670–1729), English explorer and fur-trader in Canada. His significance as an explorer lies in the journey he made between 1690 and 1692 with a party of Cree Indians trading with the Hudson's Bay Company. The exact course of his journey is the subject of some dispute; similarly, despite its trail-blazing nature, it seems to have done little to encourage further expansion by the Hudon's Bay Company. Kelsey nonetheless penetrated farther west than any other 17th-century European explorer in Canada, crossing the Saskatchewan and Red Rivers and reaching the great plains of western Canada. He returned to England in 1722, having served the Hudson's Bay Company in a variety of positions, including, from 1718–22, governor of all the company's posts. 18

KENNEDY, EDMUND (1818–48), was born on Guernsey in the Channel Islands. After training as a surveyor, he migrated to New South Wales in 1840, where he was quickly employed in the new Port Phillip pastoral district. After a period of inactivity, in 1845 he was appointed **Sir Thomas Mitchell**'s deputy for the expedition into central Queensland. In 1847, on a second expedition into that area, he disproved Mitchell's idea that the Barcoo River was the great inland waterway predicted by theoretical geography. The following year, Kennedy headed an expedition up the eastern coast of Queensland from Rockingham Bay to Cape York. His party suffered greatly in the arduous terrain. Kennedy was forced to leave eight men at Weymouth Bay, of whom only two survived. Subsequently, he left three others at a camp farther to the north, of whom none survived; and he himself was speared by Aborigines when within reach of his supply ship. This expedition is notable for the role of the Aboriginal Jackey Jackey, who showed great skill and concern for his white companions, and who alone reached Port Albany, where the ship *Ariel* was waiting for the party. 36

KING, CLARENCE (1842–1902), American geologist and explorer. King graduated from Yale's Sheffield Scientific School in 1862 and then joined the California Geological Survey. In 1867 he became Director in Charge of the United States Geological Exploration of the Fortieth Parallel. For the next decade he and his small, competent staff explored scientifically and mapped a strip of land from present-day Cheyenne, Wyoming, to the eastern base of the Sierra Nevada, working approximately within a 100-mile strip of land through which ran the 40th parallel. The Fortieth Parallel Survey Reports in seven volumes and an atlas set high standards for scientific reporting. King was also the first director of the United States Geological Survey. 22

KINO, EUSEBIO FRANCISCO (*c.*1645–1711), Jesuit explorer of North America. A native of Segno (Trentino) and of German ancestry, he joined the Jesuits in 1665 and, after studying in Fribourg, became a professor of mathematics at Ingolstadt. He went to Spain in 1678 to prepare for the New World mission, which he joined in 1681. In 1683–84 he served as surveyor on expeditions into California. In 1687 he began his mission to the Pima and other peoples of northern Sonora and southern Arizona, to which he devoted the rest of his life, founding missions and building magnificent churches. His tireless journeys involved detailed exploration of the Gila country and of Lower California and the confirmation, in 1702, of the peninsular nature of California. 17, 20

KNIGHT, JAMES (d. *c.*1720), English explorer of Canada. Employed by the Hudson's Bay Company, by 1692 he was in charge of all its posts. In 1719 he led an expedition to search for the Northwest Passage and to prospect for gold, which the Indian reports had convinced him could be found to the north-west. The expedition was wrecked in either 1719 or 1720. Its loss reinforced the company's reluctance to establish trading posts away from its existing establishments in the south of Hudson Bay. 21

KRAPF, JOHANN LUDWIG (1810–81). A German from Tübingen who studied at Basle Seminary and then joined the (English) Church Missionary Society, Krapf worked and travelled in Ethiopia from 1837 to 1843. He found out much about Shoa, and, trying to reach it from the south, landed at Mombasa in 1844. His subsequent missionary work, expert linguistic enquiries and rather less expert geography in East Africa made him an important pioneer. He made journeys into Ukambani, from where he saw Mount Kenya in 1849, and Usambara. Though there were later brief visits to Ethiopia and Mombasa, his active missionary work ended in 1853. 39

LACERDA E ALMEIDA, FRANCISCO JOSÉ DE (1753–98). The Portuguese governor of Sena on the lower Zambezi and a considerable geographer and mathematician, Lacerda was anxious to find ways of linking his country's establishments on the east and west of Africa. But his journey ended in the Cazembe's kingdom on the shores of Lake Mweru when he died of fever in October 1798. His was the first visit by an expert traveller to the region. 38

LADRILLERO, JUAN, 16th-century *conquistador* and mariner. First recorded with **Andagoya** in the San Juan valley in 1540, he fought on the royalist side against the Peruvian rebels at Xaquixaguana and served in Chile with **García Hurtado de Mendoza**, who ordered him to explore the southern extremities of the country by sea. He sailed from Valdivia on 17 November 1557. With **Hernán Gallego** among his pilots, he charted a course through the Chiloé archipelago and entered the Strait of Magellan in March 1558. His exploration was cut short by cold and want of food in August, but he had followed the strait to within sight of the Atlantic. 24

LA FORA, NICOLÁS, 18th-century Spanish military engineer. He accompanied the **Marqués de Rubí** on an inspection of the northern frontier of New Spain between 1766 and 1768. In 23 months they covered 7,600 miles, through hostile Apache country to Santa Fe, then into Texas, returning via the coast. Lafora wrote an account of the expedition with many surveying details. In 1770 he published a map of New Spain on the basis of a survey he conducted himself. 17

LAING, ALEXANDER GORDON (1793–1826) After education at Edinburgh University Laing joined the West India regiment, and when it was posted to West Africa took the opportunity to explore the hinterland of Sierra Leone in 1822. Chosen therefore to lead an expedition from Tripoli inland towards Timbuktu, Laing set out in 1825, having fallen in love with, and married, the British consul's daughter. Laing became involved in the intense hostility between the Fulani and the desert Tuareg peoples. He barely survived one attack on him before becoming the first European in modern times to reach Timbuktu. He was murdered as he tried to make his way to the west coast in 1826, and his records and journals were destroyed. 37

LAMBTON, WILLIAM (1756–1823), British East India Company engineer officer, who collaborated with **Colin Mackenzie** in the trigonometrical mapping of the conquered south Indian state of Mysore after 1799. In 1812 he became superintendent of the Indian Survey, but lived to complete only part of the 'great arc' of triangulations that was to bisect India and form the starting point for later measurements. 43

LANDER, RICHARD (1804–34), English explorer of West Africa with his brother John (1807–39). He accompanied **Hugh Clapperton** on his second expedition; after Clapperton's death (1827), he returned to England and published his journal. The British government, impressed, sent Lander to explore the course of the lower Niger. He set out with his brother in 1830 and travelled from Badagry to Bussa where he reached the Niger, which he then followed south to its outlet, so solving a problem that had baffled the geographical world. The brothers returned to England before returning again to Africa. On Fernando Po they were attacked by tribesmen and Richard was killed. 37

LANDSBOROUGH, WILLIAM (1825–89), was born in Ayrshire, Scotland, and migrated to New South Wales in 1841. Between 1858 and 1861, he explored the area of the Comet and Nogoa Rivers in central Queensland. In 1861–62, he searched for the **Burke** and **Wills** expedition from the Gulf of Carpentaria southwards, reaching Melbourne in October 1862, to complete the first north to south crossing of the continent. These journeys revealed many areas suited to pastoralism, and Landsborough took up substantial holdings before failing financially in the hard times of the late 1860s. 36

LA SALLE, GADIFER DE (14th/15th centuries), French navigator. He was a cadet member of a noble family of Poitou who served in the households of Philip the Bold of Burgundy and of the king of France. He took part in a Prussian crusade and in the duke of Bourbon's expedition to Al-Mahdiya in 1390. In 1402 he sailed with **Jean de Béthencourt** to the Canary Islands in an attempt to conquer the archipelago and find the fabled 'River of Gold' in mainland Africa. He later quarrelled with his partner and withdrew from the enterprise, probably in 1412, but in 1402–3 explored the outline of the archipelago by sea and much of the islands of Lanzarote and Fuerteventura on overland expeditions. 8

LA SALLE, ROBERT CAVELIER SIEUR DE (1643–87), French explorer in North America. He first went to Canada in 1666 and in 1673 became commandant of Fort Frontenac. He returned to France in 1675 and 1677, when he was granted rights to explore and trade in New France. Between 1679 and 1681 he crossed the Great Lakes and built a number of trading forts in the face of hostility from the Iroquois before, with a small party, descending the length of the Mississippi. He reached its mouth in 1682. There he formally took possession of the river valley for France, naming the vast region Louisiana (after Louis XIV). In France again from 1684, La Salle was granted rights to colonize the regions he had explored. Reaching the Gulf of Mexico by sea from France, La Salle was unable to find the mouth of the Mississippi. His party grew restless after repeated attempts to march overland to the river and killed him. **17, 18**

La Vérendrye, Pierre Gaultier de Varennes (1685–1749), French explorer of North America. La Vérendrye, the last of the great French path-finding explorers of North America, was born in Canada, at Trois Rivières. His principal concern throughout his career was to further the French fur trade, with much of his exploratory work taken up by the search for the *mer de l'ouest*, or Western Sea, speculated by French geographers and assumed, once found, to offer easy access to the Pacific. Between 1727 and 1728 he pushed the frontiers of New France to the west. In 1731, with three of his sons – Jean-Baptiste, Pierre and François – he established fur-trading posts at the Lake of the Woods on the Red River south of Lake Winnipeg. He returned to the West in 1734 with a further son, Louis Joseph. His sons continued to undertake exploration of the West, most notably in 1742–43 as far as the Black Hills, though attempts to reconstruct their route have been hampered by the unreliability of their reports. La Vérendrye's most celebrated feat was his 1738–39 journey from the Assiniboine River to the Mandan villages of the Missouri, in the process demolishing almost entirely the prospect of finding the Western Sea. Further expeditions promoted by La Vérendrye included that in 1741 to the Saskatchewan River, later one of the most important of the fur-trade rivers. **21**

Lawson, William (1774–1850), English-born explorer of Australia. After training as a surveyor, he joined the New South Wales Corps as an ensign, reaching Sydney at the end of 1800. For the next decade, he served at the outposts of Norfolk Island and Newcastle. In these years, he began to acquire extensive pastoral and agricultural holdings on the Cumberland Plain. In 1813 when, in common with other pastoralists, he was hard-pressed to maintain his herds and flocks on existing lands, he joined **Gregory Blaxland** and **William Charles Wentworth** in pioneering a route over the Blue Mountains to the west, a development which foreshadowed the great pastoral expansion of the 1820s and 1830s. Granted more land by Governor Macquarie as a reward, Lawson was commandant of the new settlement at Bathurst from 1819 to 1824, when he undertook further explorations. In the 1820s, he vastly expanded his holdings, which became among the largest in the colony. **36**

Laycock, Thomas (*c.*1786–1823), reached Sydney in 1791. Joining the New South Wales Corps, he served on Norfolk Island, and was then posted to the new settlement at Port Dalrymple, Tasmania, in 1806. In February 1807, with a small party he followed the river valleys south, making the first overland crossing to Hobart, then repeated his steps north. In 1810, he accompanied the Corps when it was recalled to England, returning to New South Wales in 1817, where he prospered in trade and pastoralism. **36**

Lederer, John, 17th-century explorer of North America. He arrived in Virginia from Germany in 1668, and was commissioned to find a passage westward through the mountains. His first effort, in March 1669, took him to the crest of the Blue Ridge Mountains. On his second, in May and June 1670, he penetrated North Carolina from the James River Falls. On his third, in August 1670, he explored the upper Rappahannock for the first time on record, continuing with his Indian guides when his companions deserted him. In 1671 he fled to Maryland from charges of peculation. His account of his discoveries (published in 1672) was important in drawing attention the vast breadth of the North American continent. **19**

Leichhardt, Ludwig (1813–*c.*1848), was born at Trebatsch, Prussia, and studied medicine and natural sciences at various institutions in Germany, England and France. After a number of field trips in Europe, he decided to pursue his interests in Australia, reaching Sydney early in 1842. After investigating fauna, flora and geology about Sydney, he travelled overland from Newcastle to Brisbane. Ever ambitious, in 1844 he organized a privately sponsored expedition to explore north-eastern Australia. Departing from Jimbour Station on the Darling Downs on 1 October, his party reached Port Essington in the Northern Territory on 17 December 1845, after a trek of almost 3,000 miles. Now determined to cross the continent from east to west, Leichhardt first attempted this in December 1846 from the Darling Downs, but this effort ended in failure after six months, due mostly to an excessively wet season. He made his second attempt in February 1848, again from the Darling Downs, only for his party to disappear utterly. Leichhardt made important collections, and his journal of his first expedition is a classic of Australian exploration. His disappearance is one of the enduring mysteries of Australian history. **36**

Le Maire, Jacob (d.1616). Son of Isaac Le Maire, organizer of the South Sea Company of Amsterdam, he obtained a commission in 1614 to discover the 'Unknown Southern Land' and a new route to it, other than through the Strait of Magellan. With **Willem Schouten** as pilot, he left Texel in June 1615. They discovered the Le Maire Strait and Cape Horn in January 1616. The expedition's surviving ship was impounded in Batavia by the Dutch East India Company, and Le Maire died on the homeward passage in the Indian Ocean. **13, 33**

Lemos, Gaspar de. This late 15th-/early 16th-century Portuguese sea-captain is unrecorded in known documents, save as the bearer of the news of the discovery of Brazil by **Pedro Álvares Cabral** in 1500. **13**

Lepe, Diego de (d. *c.*1513), Spanish *conquistador*. Like **Vicente Yáñez Pinzón**, he was a citizen of Palos, who attempted to exploit the relaxation of Columbus's monopoly of navigation in 1499, closely following Pinzón, with two ships, to a landfall probably in the vicinity of Cabo São Agostinho. After coasting a short distance to the east, he returned home in the summer of 1500. On 15 November of that year he contracted to make a second voyage, in three caravels, and in 1501 a third. He disappears from Spanish records after 1504, but has been tentatively identified with Diego de Lepe, slaver, hanged for smuggling in Portugal in 1513. **13**

Lewis, Meriwether (1774–1809), U.S. soldier, explorer and public official. President Thomas Jefferson chose Lewis, a fellow Virginian, to lead a 'Corps of Discovery' across the Louisiana Purchase and on to the Pacific. He brought Lewis to Washington as his private secretary, and for nearly three years prepared him for the task. This included instruction in Philadelphia from members of the American Philosophical Society. On 14 May 1804, after having chosen a former army officer and friend, **William Clark**, to accompany him, and with about 40 others, he set out from Wood River, across from St. Louis. Lewis and Clark kept meticulous journals as the expedition laboriously made its way up the Missouri. Lewis, a naturalist, especially recorded the flora and fauna. They wintered at the Mandan villages and in April 1805, joined by a Shoshone squaw, Sacagawea, headed on up the Missouri. They arrived on the shores of the Pacific in early November 1805, and dubbed their winter quarters Fort Clatsop. On 23 March 1806 they headed for home, arriving at St. Louis on 23 September. Their expedition was crucial in establishing the westward thrust of American expansion, and revealed in detail the scale and variety of the Northwest. More than 8,000 miles were traversed; hundreds of natural specimens were collected; detailed maps were prepared. Lewis was rewarded with appointment as governor of Louisiana Territory. He was unsuccessful in this endeavour, however, and on a trip to Washington died at a tavern on the Natchez Trace. The exact cause of his death, whether by his or another hand, is not known. **20, 21, 22**

Lima, Manuel Félix de. A failed merchant and mining prospector in Brazil in the early 18th century, in 1742, at the age of about 50, he opened a route from the Mato Grosso in a journey which began in São Paolo, continuing along the Paraguay to the River Alegre. From Cuiabá he descended the Rivers Guaporé, Mamoré and Madeira, following the Amazon to Belém. **26**

Linschoten, Jan Huyghen van (1563–1610), Dutch traveller and historian, born at Haarlem. He spent six years in Goa in Spanish service as a clerk to the East India fleets (Spain and Portugal at this time were united, and Spain controlled the Portuguese trade east of the Cape). He returned to the Netherlands in 1592, becoming a propagandist for the Far Eastern trade. His work, the *Itinerario*, appeared in Amsterdam in 1595–96. Much of Linschoten's information on China was gathered from Dirck Gerritszoon, who was the first pilot in the Dutch fleet to the East. In 1594–95 Linschoten accompanied **Barents**, as supercargo, on his first two voyages in search of the Northeast Passage. **29**

Lisle, Guillaume de (1675–1726), French geographer and cartographer. He was geographer to Louis XV, and published a world map (1700) which was based on accumulated empirical knowledge, finally rejecting many of the errors of the Ptolemaic system. Often regarded as the founder of modern cartography, de Lisle produced a number of atlases, including an early historical atlas of classical antiquity, which reflect an astonishing depth of knowledge of relatively remote regions such as Arabia, Persia and India.

Livingstone, David, (1813–73), Scottish missionary and explorer of Africa. He attended classes at Glasgow University and Anderson's College (Strathclyde University) before becoming a licentiate of the Faculty of Physicians and Surgeons in London. He also became a congregational minister with the London Missionary Society, and at their instigation went to South Africa in 1841. Livingstone's youthful interest in field sciences, combined with a belief that his calling was to be an itinerant missionary to tribes living north of Kolobeng, led him to make the first of three journeys of exploration. This was to verify reports that there was a large lake somewhere north of the Kalahari Desert. He discovered Lake Ngami in 1849 and reached the Zambezi in 1851. During a second expedition (1850) to Lake Ngami and the upper reaches of the Zambezi River, he first encountered the slave trade and decided to devote his life to fighting it.

In the period 1853–56, he made his great series of journeys from the centre of Africa to the west coast and then right across the continent to the east. He travelled up the Zambezi River, but the dense tropical rain forests induced repeated bouts of fever, reducing him to near collapse by the time he reached Luanda in Angola. He returned to Linyanti, and then undertook further exploration to see if the Zambezi could provide a route to the east coast. The party set off in November 1855, travelling down the Zambezi until they came to a waterfall, called by the Makololo the 'Smoke that Thunders', which Livingstone named the Victoria Falls after the British Queen. He reached Quelimane on the east coast. He returned to Britain a national hero. The British government appointed Livingstone in 1853 to command an expedition which would use a steamboat on the Zambezi in the hope of finding a route into the African interior. Such a route, developing British trade and interests, i.e. 'legitimate trade', would help lead to the extinction of the illegitimate trade in slaves. However, the Quebrabasa Falls blocked his progress, as did rapids farther up its course. Nevertheless, during travels through the region north of the Zambezi, he discovered lakes Chilwa and Nyasa in 1859. The British government recalled Livingstone in 1863. In 1865 he returned to Africa, at the prompting of the Royal Geographical Society, to look for the source of the River Nile, still in dispute despite **Speke**'s 1862 discovery. In 1867 or 1868 he reached lakes Bangweulu and Mweru. He reached Nyangwe on the Lualaba River in March 1871, where further progress was prevented by the antagonism of the slave traders and the desertion of his followers. The following November found him at Ujiji on Lake Tanganyika, but now weak and without financial resources. For almost three years no certain word had been heard of him in Britain, and he was generally feared dead. The *New York Herald* sent **Henry Morton Stanley**, a journalist, to find him. This he did at Ujiji, with Stanley uttering the immortal phrase 'Dr Livingstone, I presume'. Together they explored the northern end of Lake Tanganyika, but Livingstone declined to leave Africa with Stanley, remaining convinced that he would still find the headwaters of the Nile. He died, ultimately of dysentery, in a small village on Lake Bangweulu on 1 May 1873. His body was preserved in salt and carried to the coast, from where it was taken to England and, in 1874, interred in Westminster Abbey.

One of the great figures in the history of exploration,

Livingstone took enormous trouble to establish correct positions by taking astronomical observations and provided excellent data on geology, botany and zoology. His first book, *Missionary Travels and Researches* (1857), was one of the century's best sellers; two other principal books recording his later expeditions appeared in 1865 and posthumously in 1874. **38, 37, 39, 40**

LOAISA, GARCÍA JOFRE DE (d. 1526), Spanish *conquistador* and explorer of the Strait of Magellan. A knight of St. John, of distinguished family, he was chosen in April 1525 to command the venture to the Moluccas by the route opened by Magellan. His appointment as 'Governor of the Moluccas' shows the great expectations aroused by the voyage, which attracted investment from spice-dealers and bankers, including the Fugger. The fleet of seven ships departed from Corunna on 24 July 1525. The most advanced vessels arrived off the Strait of Magellan on 14 January 1526. In the ordeal of navigating the Strait, which they attempted three times, three ships were lost or deserted and two others separated from the flagship by a storm shortly afterwards. Loaisa died in mid-Pacific on 30 July, convinced that the Strait could never offer a viable route to Asia. **13, 33**

LONG, STEPHEN H. (1784–1864), U.S. army engineer and explorer. In 1819–20 Long led a disastrous expedition up the Missouri River on a steamboat, the *Western Engineer*, hoping to reach the mouth of the Yellowstone. The expedition reached Council Bluffs, where many men died of scurvy. Hardly had he returned before he was ordered to lead an expedition west along the Platte and South Platte rivers to the Rockies, south to the Red River, and then east back to the white settlements. From this expedition came a map labelling the region as the Great American Desert. In 1823 Long explored the Red River of the North and along the 49th Parallel. Engineering activities occupied the rest of his long career. **22**

LÓPEZ DE CÁRDENAS, GARCÍA, 16th-century Spanish explorer of North America. A captain in the expedition to Quivira of **Francisco Vázquez de Coronado**, he saved his commander's life in battle against the Zuni Indians in 1540. In the same year he discovered the Grand Canyon. He led the campaign against the Tiguex Indians during the winter of 1540–41, and returned to New Spain with a booty of buffalo skins. **17**

MACKENZIE, SIR ALEXANDER (*c.* 1764–1820), fur-trader and explorer, born in Scotland, possibly at Inverness. His mother died when he was a child and he was taken by his father to New York. Mackenzie later joined a fur-trading company, in which he subsequently became a partner when it was absorbed into the North West Company, formed in competition to the Hudson's Bay Company. He operated from Fort Chipewyan at the head of Lake Athabasca. His first expedition on behalf of his company in 1789 was made in search of a waterway to the Pacific. This took him to the Great Slave Lake and down the river, now named after him, to the Arctic Ocean. He named it the River of Disappointment, since it did not lead to the Pacific. In 1792 he set out on his second expedition to reach the Pacific, this time going westwards from Lake Athabasca along the Peace River. This took him up to its confluent, the Parsnip River, and then across to the Fraser, which he mistook for the upper course of the Columbia. He abandoned this river when he correctly judged its course, briefly turned north and then west across the mountains by following the Dean River, reaching the Pacific at Dean Channel. Mackenzie thus became the first white man to cross the continent north of Mexico. More important, his two journeys greatly encouraged European settlement of the American northwest. He was knighted and later returned to Scotland, where he died. **20, 21**

MACKENZIE, COLIN (*c.* 1753–1821), British Engineers officer in the service of the East India Company's Madras Army and antiquarian. He mapped the territories conquered from Tipu, sultan of Mysore, after the wars of 1790–99, being among the earliest to introduce trigonometrical methods. In 1807 he was appointed surveyor-general of Madras, and in 1819 became surveyor-general of India. He collected an invaluable archive of indigenous religious, historical and topographical texts. **43**

MCCLINTOCK, SIR FRANCIS LEOPOLD (1819–1907), British naval officer and Arctic explorer. He entered the Royal Navy in 1831 and served in the Americas and the Pacific. In 1848–49 he was lieutenant on HMS *Enterprise* on **Sir James Ross**'s expedition to the Canadian Arctic, during which he developed the man-hauled sledging technique that the navy later adopted for most of its polar expeditions. He took part in the Franklin search in 1850–51, on *Assistance*, and again in 1852–54 as commander of *Intrepid* (during which he completed a sledge journey of over 1,000 miles and discovered Prince Patrick Island). In 1857–59 he commanded *Fox* on an expedition sent to the Canadian Arctic by Lady Franklin to find conclusive evidence of the Franklin expedition's fate. He retired from the navy with the rank of admiral in 1884. **23**

MCCLURE, SIR ROBERT JOHN LE MESURIER (1807–73), British naval officer and Arctic explorer. He entered the navy in 1824. He had his first experience of the Arctic in 1836–37 as mate on **George Back**'s *Terror* expedition to Hudson Bay. He returned to the Canadian Arctic in 1848–49 as first lieutenant on *Enterprise* during **Sir James Ross**'s expedition in search of **Sir John Franklin**. Soon after his return home, he was given command of *Investigator* for another Franklin search expedition which entered the Arctic through Bering Strait in 1850. *Investigator* became beset in the ice off Banks Island in the Canadian Arctic and was eventually abandoned. McClure and his crew were rescued by other search expeditions and were taken home by way of Baffin Bay in 1854, thus becoming the first men to travel through the Northwest Passage. McClure later served in the Pacific and in England, and retired with the rank of admiral in the year of his death. **23**

MCQUEEN (or **M'QUEEN**), **JAMES** (1778–1870). 19th-century geographer and commentator on African affairs. On the basis of information received from slaves in the West Indies, McQueen correctly predicted in 1821 where the outlet of the Niger would be found. While a journalist and political writer in Glasgow and later London, he took a full part in debates about African geography and published several books and maps. **37**

MAGELLAN, FERDINAND (*c.* 1480–1521), Portuguese explorer. His parents, members of the nobility, died when he was some ten years old, and shortly afterwards he became a page at the royal court, where he received his education, including that in navigation. Magellan went to East Africa in 1505 and, for the next eight years, was in virtually constant action in the Indian Ocean theatre. In 1512 Magellan volunteered for cavalry service in Morocco, where he sustained a wound that left him with a life-long limp. King Manuel I of Portugal refused his request for increased wages and gave him leave to seek service elsewhere. Magellan therefore moved to Spain, perhaps in 1516, where he married in 1518. With other Portuguese exiles, he successfully sought royal patronage. On 22 March 1518, he was appointed captain-general of a fleet to explore a route westwards to the East Indies. The fleet – five ships, with a total complement of 241 men – sailed from southern Spain on 20 September 1519. The ships crossed the Atlantic to Brazil and then followed the coast southwards, searching for a passage into the Pacific Ocean until March 1520. After winter quarters and the suppression of a mutiny in what is now southern Argentina, the voyage was resumed on 18 October 1520. A few days later, a polar tempest drove two of his ships into the hidden strait for which they were searching, now called the Strait of Magellan. He now had three ships only (one had been grounded and another detached by deserters) but these he led down the strait, despite massive tides. Emerging on 27 or 28 November, he began the first recorded crossing of the Pacific – 90 days of deprivation and anxiety under sail until Guam was reached on 6 March 1521. Despite the vast size of the Pacific as revealed by Magellan, 16th-century navigators continued to underestimate its extent, a process compounded by the difficulties of establishing longitude with accuracy. On 16 March he reached Samar and on 7 April Cebu, where he offered the services of his men to the ruler in a regional war, in which he was killed on 27 April. Only one ship of the five which had begun the voyage – the *Victoria* – returned to Europe, in the process completing the first circumnavigation. Her cargo of spices was nonetheless deemed to have justified the venture. **9, 13, 16, 26, 33, 34**

MAGYAR, LÁSZLÓ (1818–64). The illegitimate son of a Hungarian landowner, Magyar joined the Austrian navy and then explored in Brazil before moving to West Africa in 1848 and then to Angola, where he married an African princess. From 1850 to 1855, he carried out some potentially important journeys among the southern tributaries of the Congo River and then visited Linyanti on the Zambezi, in the course of which journey he met **Livingstone**. Perhaps because Livingstone did not acknowledge the work of someone he saw as a rival explorer, more probably because his results were published much later and in Hungarian, Magyar has remained an underrated figure. **38**

MALASPINA, ALEJANDRO (1754–1809). Born in Palermo, he joined the Spanish marines in 1774 and served with distinction, particularly in the siege of Gibraltar in 1781. In 1782 he was sent to the Philippines, and in the course of his mission made his first cicumnavigation, returning in 1784. In 1789 he was given command of two frigates to conduct a scientific expedition to South America and the Pacific. Despite the brilliant success of the venture, which reached 60°N and recorded exact longitudes for many new locations as well as collecting sixty crates of natural history specimens for the Madrid museum, Malaspina's recognition did not last for long. The liberal recommendations he made for the reform of the government of Spanish America, which had been fashionable when he departed, seemed dangerous to conservatives in the climate created by the French Revolution. In 1796 his enemies exploited this reactionary mood to have him arrested for sedition. He was released in 1803 at Napoleon's request but refused service with the French puppet-state in northern Italy and retired to poverty in Sicily. **35**

MALOCELLO, LANZAROTTO (13th–14th centuries), Genoese explorer of the Canary Islands. He gave a corrupt version of his name to the island of Lanzarote, where he established a short-lived garrison. The date, though uncertain, was first recorded on a map dated 1339. **8**

MARIGNOLLI, JOHN OF. He led a papal mission to the Great Khan in 1339, arriving in Peking in 1342. He served the see established by Franciscans there until 1345, when he embarked at Hangchow. He reached Quilo on the Malabar coast in April 1346, but did not return to Avignon until 1353. According to the account he later interpolated in his *Bohemian Chronicle*, he made a voyage in the interim to Java and Sumatra. He became a chaplain to the Emperor Charles IV. **31**

MARQUETTE, JACQUES (1637–75), French Jesuit explorer of North America. Sent to North America in 1666, he engaged in missionary work among the Ottawa Indians of Lake Superior. In 1673, accompanied by **Louis Jolliet**, he discovered the upper waters of the Mississippi River. Marquette and Jolliet descended the river to beyond the confluence with the Arkansas River, at which point they were able to confirm that the southward-flowing Mississippi would not provide a route to the Pacific. **18**

MARTELLUS, HENRICUS (active 1480–96), German cartographer and geographer working in Florence. The *Insularum*, or description of islands, written by Martellus in Florence in about 1490 contains a world map, Ptolemaic in design. In his representation of Asia, Martellus follows **Ptolemy**, but he also had knowledge of **Dias**'s voyage of 1487–89, and the traditional land-bridge between southern Africa and south-east Asia is no longer apparent. Africa is labelled 'the true modern form of Africa from the description of the Portuguese', with mention of Dias's farthest eastern point, and place names indicating the limit of his explorations. **13**

MARTÍNEZ DE IRALA, DOMINGO (*c.* 1512–56). Born in Guipúzcoa, he was among the gentlemen who sailed with **Pedro de Mendoza** to the River Plate in 1535. He accompanied Juan de Ayolas along the Paraguay as far as Candelaria and succeeded to the command in June 1539. In 1540 his expedition into the Chaco verified his predecessor's death. In mid-1541, he abandoned the outpost at Buenos Aires and concentrated the expedition's surviving strength upriver at Asunción. In 1543, having been supplanted in control by the arrival of the relief force of **Alvar Núñez Cabeza de Vaca**, he was sent to explore the upper reaches of the river. A mutiny restored him to command in March 1544 but he continued the policy of exploration, believing that rich lands would be discovered north and west of the Paraguay basin. In November 1547, he launched a great march across the Chaco, which opened a fragile route to Peru. Violence among the settlers of Asunción obliged him to return in April 1549. In 1552 his authority was at last confirmed by the crown. He made exploration of the Chaco region his personal monopoly, but achieved nothing further there by the time of his death on 3 October 1556. 26

MASCARDI, NICCOLÒ (1624–74), Italian Jesuit explorer of South America. Born in Sarzana, he joined the Jesuits in 1638 and the mission to Chile in about 1650, after studies in Rome that included a period under the aegis of Athanasius Kircher, with whom he corresponded from the New World. His missionary work was interrupted by a series of commissions to undertake exploration into the unknown territory towards the Strait of Magellan, where rumours of the city of 'Los Césares' persisted and where Spaniards who had formerly searched for its fabled riches were supposed to have founded surviving communities. In four years of wandering alone, he was said to have baptized 60,000 Indians. His work, which finally dispelled remaining myths about the cone of South America, ended with his martyrdom in Poya on 15 February 1674. 24

MASSA, ISAAC (1586–1643), Dutch cartographer and traveller to Moscow, born at Haarlem. Massa first arrived in Russia in 1601 as a merchant trainee, remaining there until 1609 when he returned home with a collection of ethnographic and cartographic materials which he made available to Hessel Gerritszoon: a description of Siberia; the map of the northern coast of Russia from the White Sea to the Ob; a plan of Moscow; and possibly a manuscript of Russia by Crown Prince Fyodor Godunov. Gerritszoon published a map based on Massa's materials in 1612. 32

MATTHEW (OF) PARIS (d. 1259), English historian and monk at St. Albans. His world history, *Chronica Majora*, represented a summary of high medieval ecclesiastical history, historiography and geography, and included a number of manuscript maps of major pilgrimage routes. 7

MAURO, FRA (d. 1459). He was a Camoldensian, a member of the community of San Michele, on Murano, from at least 1433, and may be identified with a Venetian religious of the same name recorded in 1409. At some time he can be presumed to have resided at San Michele al Leme in Istria, for which he made an estate map. From 1448, at the latest, he was primarily engaged in the mapping of the world, with **Andrea Bianco** among his assistants. An elaborate world map was commissioned by King Afonso V of Portugal and received by the patron early in 1459. The surviving work from Fra Mauro's hand is a richly painted and gilded, roughly circular mappamundi commissioned by the Signoria of Venice, measuring more than six feet in diameter: its finishing touches, on 26 August 1460, were applied only after his death, which can be fixed to between March and October 1459. 27, 28, 30

MAWSON, SIR DOUGLAS (1882–1958), Australian geologist and Antarctic explorer. Mawson spent most of his career as a geologist at the University of Adelaide. He was a member of the scientific staff of **Shackleton**'s Antarctic expedition of 1907–9. In 1911–14 he led the Australasian Antarctic Expedition, which discovered and explored George V Land and Queen Mary Land. In 1929–31 he was leader of the British, Australian, New Zealand Antarctic Research Expedition, and discovered Mac Robertson Land and Princess Elizabeth Land. In addition to his distinguished record as an Antarctic scientist (for which he was knighted in 1914), he was also recognized as an authority on Australian geology. 46

MENDAÑA DE NEIRA, ÁLVARO DE (*c.* 1542–95). A Galician by birth, he went to Peru in 1567, accompanying his uncle who was embarking on an official career which would culminate in the governorship. On arrival, he was fired by Inca legends of rich islands in the Pacific to undertake a search which cost 60,000 pesos and led, in 1568, to the discovery of the Solomon Islands. The islands produced little evidence of exploitability, and though Mendaña was appointed their prospective governor in 1574 it was not until 1595 that he was able to organize a follow-up expedition. The six ships, with 378 colonists and 280 soldiers, left Callao on 9 April. On 21 July the Marquesas Islands were discovered, and on 7 September the little Santa Cruz group. The Solomon Islands, however, could not be found and Mendaña died in Graciosa Bay on 18 October, leaving his widow in command and his pilot, **Pedro de Quiros** to find the way to safety in the Philippines. 33

MENDOZA, ANTONIO DE (1490–1552), Spanish viceroy of New Spain from 1535. A cadet member of one of Spain's most illustrious families, he ruled Mexico with conspicuous success during a period marked by the Indian rebellions of 1541 and 1547, the struggle over the 'New Laws' in favour of the Indians of 1542, the epidemic of 1545, frequent *conquistador* unrest and protracted demographic crisis. Yet he presided over an increasingly prosperous and civilized colony. During his term, exploring achievements included the journeys of **Cortés** and **Ulloa** to California, of **Niza** and **Coronado** into the interior of North America, of **Alarcón** and **Rodrigues Cabrillo** to the Colorado and Upper California, and of **Villalobos** across the Pacific. He died in office after a protracted illness on 23 July 1553. 17

MENDOZA, FRANCISCO DE (d. 1545), 16th-century Spanish *conquistador*. As a young captain he took part in the expedition to Tucumán of **Diego de Rojas**, on whose death from a poison arrow in January 1544 he was elected to command. He left his mutinous subordinate, Nicolás de Heredia, in charge of a garrison in the Calamuchita valley, while he marched on to the banks of the Paraná. On his return to the camp he was murdered, probably at the instigation of Heredia, who assumed command. 26

MENDOZA, GARCIA HURTADO DE *see* **Hurtado**

MENDOZA, PEDRO DE (*c.* 1499–1537), Spanish *conquistador*. Of the family of the Duques del Infantado, he served as a page at the court of Charles V and as a soldier in the Pavia campaign of 1526. In the early 1530s the danger of Portuguese infiltration from the north made colonization of the River Plate seem urgent; when Mendoza was appointed to the prospective command in May 1534 he was the most aristocratic individual yet to have confided his future to the New World. His orders were to fortify the mouth of the River Plate and seek inland for the fabled realm of the 'White King', reported as a result of the exploration of **Alejo Garcia**. He invested his own fortune in the expedition of 16 ships and attracted further funds from German bankers. With more than 1,500 men, he set off from Sanlúcar de Barrameda on 24 August 1535, arriving early in 1536, when the settlement of Buenos Aires was founded. The expedition proved unwieldy. Hundreds died from starvation and Indian attacks. Mendoza, who had sickened on the voyage out, died on his attempted return in mid-Atlantic on 23 June 1537. Buenos Aires was abandoned in 1541, but survivors of the expedition founded a thriving colony in Paraguay. 26

MERCATOR, GERARD (1512–94), Flemish geographer, cartographer, mathematician and calligrapher. Born at Rupelmonde and schooled at 's Hertogenbosch in Brabant, Mercator later studied at Louvain under Gemma Frisius, an astronomer and theoretical mathematician. Mercator produced a double cordiform woodcut world map in 1538, then in 1569 the world map on the projection that still bears his name. He also made globes with Frisius in 1537, 1541 and 1551. He produced maps of Palestine in 1537; of Europe in 1554; of the British Isles in 1564; of Flanders in 1540; and prepared an edition of **Ptolemy** in 1578. The individual parts of his *Atlas* were first published complete, posthumously, in 1595. He died of a cerebral haemorrhage at Duisburg. 34

MIDDLETON, CHRISTOPHER (*c.* 1690–1770), English naval officer. Employed by the Hudson's Bay Company since 1721, in 1740 Middleton was commissioned into the Royal Navy to lead an expedition to the west coast of Hudson Bay to search for the Northwest Passage. His expedition spent the winter of 1741–42 at Fort Churchill on Hudson Bay and sailed north the following summer. Though turned back by ice at what Middleton called Repulse Bay, the expedition nonetheless undertook useful survey work of Hudson Bay. 21

MITCHELL, SIR THOMAS (1792–1855), was born at Craigend, Scotland. After becoming proficient in languages and science he joined the army, seeing duty in the Peninsular campaign. In 1827, he took up the position of assistant surveyor-general in New South Wales, then succeeded to the senior position on **Oxley**'s death. With his teams, he refined the boundaries of the colony's 19 counties, which were redeclared in 1829 and, with a 20th added, again in 1836. Mitchell had enlarged views of his abilities and destiny, and in the 1830s he turned to the exploration of inland Australia. Searching for a great river that theoretical geography said should traverse the continent, he traced sections of the Gwydir, Barwon, Bogan, Darling and Lachlan Rivers. In 1836, he went south from the Murray across Victoria to Portland, discovering the rich pastoral lands he named 'Australia Felix', and by his return journey to Sydney establishing the 'Major's Line', the route that pastoralists were soon following in the rush to occupy the Port Phillip district. In 1837 Mitchell returned temporarily to England, publishing an account of his explorations the following year. He returned to New South Wales in 1841; and at the end of 1845 led another expedition in search of the illusory continental waterway, this time up into central Queensland. Mitchell was given to exaggeration, and was frequently in trouble with his superiors, but he did explore widely in inland Australia; his reports of his explorations were very influential in the rapid spread of pastoralism. 36

MOFFAT, ROBERT (1795–1883). Moffat was a gardener in Scotland but joined the London Missionary Society and was sent to South Africa in 1816. He made a journey over the Orange River into the semi-desert country of the Namaquas in 1817, but found his true vocation in the mission station he founded at Kuruman among the Tswana north of what was then Cape Colony. He also established contact with the Ndebele as they migrated north over a long period of years. As a result, Moffat made significant journeys to the north in 1829, 1835 and especially in 1854, 1857 and 1859, when he reached what is now Zimbabwe. He was not as expert a geographer and scientist as the man who married one of his daughters, **David Livingstone**, but was a greater figure in the conventional missionary sense. 38

MOOR, WILLIAM (d. 1765), English sailor and explorer of Canada. Moor served on ships of the Hudson's Bay Company from 1730, making repeated Atlantic crossings. In 1742, he sailed with **Middleton**, a cousin, on a voyage north from York Fort searching for the Northwest Passage. In 1747, Moor commanded an expedition of his own in Hudson Bay. Though further knowledge of the west coast of the Bay was gathered, a navigable Northwest Passage, now an increasingly forlorn hope, remained as elusive as ever. 21

MÜNSTER, SEBASTIAN (1498–1552), cosmographer, scholar and Hebraist, born at Basel. His best-known works are the editions of **Ptolemy** (first edition in 1540), and his great *Cosmographia Universalis* (first edition in 1544), both with many woodcut maps after Ptolemy together with early maps of the modern world and published by his son-in-law Heinrich Petri. He also published commentaries on Caius Julius Solinus and Pomponius Mela in 1538, illustrated with woodcut maps. Münster's *Cosmographia* maps remained the most influential maps prior to the first edition of **Abraham Ortelius**'s *Theatrum* atlas in 1570. 15, 46

MYLIUS-ERICHSEN, LUDWIG (1872–1907), Danish explorer of the Arctic. He led the Danish Greenland expedition (1902–4), and in 1906 explored much of north-east Greenland. 46

NACHTIGAL, GUSTAV (1834–85), German physician and explorer of West Africa. He explored parts of Algeria and Tunisia, and from 1869 to 1874 much of the Sahara, becoming the first European to penetrate the Tibesti highlands and to reach Lake Chad. Nachtigal crossed into Darfur in 1874, and then, by way of Khartoum, reached Cairo in November. Ten years later he was appointed German imperial commissioner to West Africa, in which capacity he was ordered in 1884 to annex as colonies the Cameroons and Togoland. 37

NANSEN, FRIDTJOF (1861–1930), Norwegian polar explorer, scientist and diplomat. Nansen developed a taste for polar exploration on an Arctic voyage in 1882 on a Norwegian sealing vessel. In 1888, while keeper of the Natural History department of Bergen Museum, he made the first crossing of Greenland, from east to west. His account of the journey (1890) had an immediate impact, establishing him as one of the foremost polar explorers of the day and highlighting in particular his intelligent adaptation of Lapp and Inuit methods to modern polar travel. His reputation was confirmed further by his Arctic expedition of 1893–96. Attempting to prove the existence of the circulation of Arctic currents and of a permanent ice-cover in the Arctic Ocean, he deliberately beset his ship, *Fram*, in the pack-ice off the New Siberian Islands. The *Fram* was released three years later off Svalbad. In the course of the drift, Nansen and a fellow expedition-member, Johansen, made an attempt on the Pole itself, reaching a new farthest north of 86°14′. Though he undertook no further major expeditions, and for a period returned to his scientific work, Nansen thereafter was regarded as the *éminence grise* of polar travel, without whose help and approval few polar expeditions were thought complete. **Roald Amundsen** in particular was his protégé, Nansen lending him the *Fram* for his successful attempt on the South Pole (1910–12). Though consulted equally eagerly by British polar explorers of the period, notably **Scott** and **Shackleton**, he was unable to overcome their prejudice in favour of man-hauling. His eminence embraced a field far larger than polar exploration, however. He was the first ambassador for the newly independent Norway in London (1906–8), a role in which his dignity and calm, emphasised by his impressive physical presence, won him enormous international respect. He later became an avid champion of the League of Nations. In 1922 he was awarded the Nobel Peace Prize for his relief work after the Russian Revolution. 46

NARES, SIR GEORGE STRONG (1831–1915), Scottish naval officer and Arctic explorer. He was mate on board *Resolute* in the Arctic expedition of 1852–54 before serving in the Crimean War. Between 1866 and 1867 he surveyed much of the coast of Australia. In 1875–76 he commanded two ships on a British naval attempt to reach the North Pole; one of his sledge parties penetrated to 83°10′N. Three years later he surveyed the Strait of Magellan. 46

NARVÁEZ, PÁNFILO DE (*c.* 1470–1528), Spanish *conquistador*. He took part in the conquests of Jamaica in 1509 and Cuba in 1512–14. The governor of Cuba, Velásquez, sent Narváez in 1520 to Mexico to supersede **Hernán Cortés**, who defeated him at Cempoala and kept him virtually under arrest until 1523. Returning to Spain, Narváez received a commission to conquer Florida in 1526. His expedition left Sanlúcar de Barrameda in June 1527. The voyage was disastrous, with many men lost to desertion or shipwreck. Florida was reached in April 1528 but the unwieldy expedition broke up for want of food and Narváez died on the Texas coast in November. Part of his force returned along the shore of the Gulf of Mexico to Pánuco, completing the map of an imperfectly known stretch of coast. 10, 17

NEALE, WALTER, 17th-century explorer of North America. He was a governor of the Laconia Company who took part in efforts in the early 1630s to open access from New England to Lake Champlain. He claimed to have explored the course of the Piscataqua River and to have found a possible approach to the lake towards the west. 19

NEARCHUS (4th century BC), Greek sailor and explorer. A Macedonian general and friend of **Alexander the Great**, Nearchus commanded the sea-borne expedition from the Indus to the Tigris that carried back to the Middle East much of Alexander's army. Its importance to exploration lay principally in the systematic records compiled by Nearchus of the territories visited in the course of the voyage. Nearchus also published influential accounts of India. 2

NEEDHAM, JAMES (d. 1673), 17th-century explorer of North America. Needham arrived in South Carolina from Barbados in September 1670 and quickly became established as a respectable planter. After he had gained experience of the frontier with **Henry Woodward**, **Abraham Wood** chose him to make an expedition with **Gabriel Arthur** in the course of his elusive campaign to find a short route to the 'South Sea'. Leaving Fort Henry in May 1673, Needham and Arthur crossed the Blue Ridge Mountains of North Carolina and the New River to Cherokee country near the source of the Tennessee River. Leaving Arthur as virtual prisoner of the Indians, Needham returned to Fort Henry for supplies but was murdered by his Occaneechee guide. 19

NEWPORT, CHRISTOPHER (d. 1617), 17th-century English explorer of North America. He fought with **Drake** at Cadiz in 1587, and was operating as a privateer in the Atlantic between 1592 and 1605. In 1606 he took service with the Virginia Company, whose settlers he conveyed to Jamestown in a series of voyages from 1607 to 1610. In 1611 he moved to the service of the East India Company, bringing Sir Robert Sherley home from Persia and taking Sir Thomas Rowe to the Mughal court. He died at Bantam (East Indies) in August 1617. 19

NICHOLAS OF CUSA (1401–64). He was a native of the diocese of Trieste, which he served for a long period in minor orders in administrative and legal affairs. In 1432, at the Council of Basle, he attracted attention by his arguments in favour of conciliarism. By 1437, however, he had become a strong ultramontanist and in 1440 was ordained priest and made a cardinal by Nicholas V, serving as Bishop of Bressanone, and in a number of diplomatic and legative posts. He made original contributions in astromony, botany and humanism as well as a series of maps of parts of Europe, including some of eastern Europe that incorporated the results of exploration by 'crusading' expeditions. 7

NICOLLET, JEAN (*c.* 1598–1642), French explorer in Canada. Nicollet went to the New World in 1618 and, in 1634, under the direction of **Samuel de Champlain** made an important westward journey, hoping to find a navigable route to the Pacific. His major achievement was the discovery of Lake Michigan. He also identified the Fox River. He was drowned on a later journey. 18

NIEBUHR, CARSTEN (1733–1815), German-born traveller in the Middle East. Born in Hanover, he trained as a surveyor and worked in Denmark. In 1760 he was appointed to accompany the Danish scientific mission to Arabia. The deaths of colleagues left him largely in command during the detailed survey of the area from al-Mocha to San'a in Yemen in 1763–64. The expedition proceeded by sea to Bombay, where more deaths left Niebuhr alone. After 14 months in India he returned via Muscat, reaching Copenhagen in 1767. His *Description of Arabia* and *Travels through Arabia* inaugurated the modern tradition of scientific travel-writing about the peninsula. 42

NIÑO, PERO ALONSO, 15th- and 16th-century Spanish navigator. He was a seaman of Moguer who sailed with his brother, Juan, on **Columbus**'s first Atlantic crossing aboard their ship *Niña*, and on other voyages with Columbus. In association with the brothers **Guerra** he attempted to follow up the discoveries of Columbus's 1498 voyage to the mainland of South America in May 1499. After visiting Margarita and parts of the Venezuelan coast, the expedition departed in February 1500, returning to Spain with pearls and some gold, obtained by truck. Niño was arrested for embezzling part of the revenue due on the profits but soon released. Nothing is known of his subsequent life. 10

NIZA, MARCOS DE, 16th-century Spanish explorer of the Americas. He was serving in the Franciscan mission of New Spain in 1539 when Governor **Antonio de Mendoza** sent him to assure the Indians of Tucuyán of Spain's benevolent intentions. He reached Abra and sent home exaggerated reports of the wealth of Cíbola, where he had sent his black slave, Estebanico, to reconnoitre. He guided the follow-up expedition of **Vázquez de Coronado** in 1540 and was said to have made a further expedition, of which no known records have survived. 17

NORDENSKIÖLD, ADOLF (1832–1901), Swedish scientist and explorer born in Finland, the first man to sail through the Northeast Passage. He took part in five scientific expeditions to Spitsbergen between 1858 and 1872, being in command of the last three. He then twice (1875, 1876) crossed the Kara Sea to the outflow of the Yenisei. The experience he gained now gave him the confidence to search for the Northeast Passage to find a sea route to northern Siberia. Nordenskiöld left Tromsö, in Norway, in July 1878. He was delayed by ice and frozen in near the Bering Strait, but in July of the following year he was able to proceed and reached the Pacific on 20 July 1879. He received many honours and then made one last Arctic trip (1883), an expedition to Greenland, before abandoning exploration for a life of writing and service in the Swedish parliament. 32

OCHOGAVIA, MIGUEL DE, 17th-century Spanish explorer of South America. From his *conquistador* grandfather he inherited a valuable estate in his native Barinas. In 1636 he led an expedition at his own cost into the region of the Rivers Apure and Carare, returning with 500 natives who seem to have been used, if not as slaves, as forced labour. After a spell commanding the defences of Lake Maracaibo against pirate attack, he was exiled from Barinas, for unknown reasons, for six years. In 1645, however, he was chosen to command the Apure navigation expedition, which it was hoped would open a navigable route across the continent by way of the Orinoco. The success of the 48-day expedition in 1647 brought Ochogavia considerable acclaim and a knighthood of the Order of St. John. Nothing is known of his subsequent career. 26

OGILBY, JOHN (1600–76), born in Edinburgh, died in London. Geographer, historian, publisher of geographical descriptions of the continents, Cosmographer Royal in 1671, and Master of the King's Revels. He compiled the first book of road maps of England and Wales in 1675, utilizing the statute mile of 1,760 yards as the standard unit of measurement. He issued a large map of London in 20 sheets with William Morgan. He translated Arnold Montanus's *Africa*, and published *America* in 1670; *China*, *Japan* and *Asia* followed in 1673 with a number of newly engraved maps and views. These were the first English illustrated works on several of the countries described. 19

OJEDA or HOJEDA, ALONSO DE (*c.* 1468–*c.* 1516), Spanish *conquistador* of noble family. From the household of the Duke of Medina Sidonia, he went with **Columbus** on his second voyage and made a vital contribution to the conquest of Hispaniola. In 1499 he commanded an expedition that broke Columbus's monopoly of the previous year, and discovered parts of the coasts of Guiana and Venezuela. His companion, **Vespucci**, made an excursion along the Brazilian coast. A follow-up expedition in 1502 was barren of results, as was an attempt to organize another in 1504. In 1507, however, Hojeda was granted a mainland governorship in the Urabá region, where, arriving in November 1509, he founded the colony of San Sebastián in February 1510. Hunger, dissension and native hostility obliged him to abandon it the following May, and he spent his last years in poverty in Santo Domingo. 10

OLDHAM, JOHN (*c.* 1600–36), British explorer of North America. Oldham arrived in America in 1623, but his attempts to set up an independent trading venture and an independent church at Plymouth led to his expulsion in 1624. From 1628 to 1630 he was in England, unsuccessfully seeking a land-grant in Massachussets. Scorning a grant in Maine, he established himself on a prosperous footing in Watertown by May 1631, serving in the General Court from 1632. In 1633 he made an expedition up the Connecticut River, pioneering the overland route from Boston to Hartford. In July 1636 he was murdered by Indians while on a trading venture to Block Island. 19

OÑATE, JUAN DE (*c.* 1550–after 1625), Spanish *conquistador*. Son of the *conquistador* Cristóbal de Oñate, he inherited a vast fortune from his father's speculations in the silver mines of Zacatecas, to which he added by new mining ventures farther north at San Luis Potosí. On 21 September 1595 he was commissioned to lead the conquest of New Mexico. Political intrigues delayed his departure until 1598. Establishing settlements as far north as San Gabriel, he explored westward in person as far as Moqui country, and sent expeditions deep into the Great Plains. In 1601 he led a search for Quivira in Kansas – the fabled city that had drawn **Coronado** across the Arkansas 60 years before. In 1604 he led his last expedition westwards, reaching the mouth of the Colorado in January 1605. He resigned the thankless job of governor of New Mexico in 1608. He was still alive in 1625 when he was made a knight of the Order of Santiago. 17

ORELLANA, FRANCISCO DE (1511–46), Spanish *conquistador*. He went to Peru in 1535 and fought under **Gonzalo Pizarro**, a friend from his childhood. In 1541 Orellana was appointed second-in-command of an expedition led by Pizarro to explore the unknown land east of the Andes. When it reached the Coca River Pizarro, exhausted and starving, ordered the construction of a brig to sail in search of food. Orellana was given command of the vessel. Shortage of food forced him to the waters of the Amazon, which he reached on 11 February 1542. There he found sufficient food for his own party only. Whether he abandoned the others, or whether he was unable to return upstream to them because of the current, is uncertain. He reached the Atlantic Ocean in August 1542, returned to Spain and was granted permission to colonize the territory he had seen. He returned in May 1545 to lead a war expedition. A series of disasters culminated in his death the following year. **26**

Ortelius, Abraham (1527–98), cartographer and publisher, the 'father of modern geography'. He was born, worked and died in Antwerp. He began as a colourist of maps and engravings in 1547. In 1564 he compiled and published maps of the world. An historical map of Egypt was produced in 1565, followed by historical maps of Asia (1567) and Spain (1570). In 1570 he also published the first uniformly conceived modern atlas, the *Theatrum Orbis Terrarum*, which remained continuously in print up to 1612, with new maps and an historical supplement, the *Parergon*, added in subsequent editions. It was translated into French, German, Dutch, English, Italian and Spanish. **33, 46**

D'Orville, Albert *see* **Gruebner, Johann**

Overweg, Alfred (1822–52). A German geologist who joined **Richardson** and **Barth** on the Central African Mission in 1850, Overweg died in 1852 after having carried out some useful exploration in the Lake Chad region. **37**

Oxley, John (*c.*1785–1818), was born in Yorkshire, England. Joining the navy, he acquired skills that were to stand him in very good stead in New South Wales, where he made coastal surveys between 1802 and 1806. In 1812, he was appointed the colony's surveyor-general. Joining exploration to this work, he journeyed behind the Blue Mountains in 1817 and 1818. In 1823 he surveyed sections of the coast of what is now Queensland, between Port Curtis (Gladstone) and Moreton Bay (Brisbane). In the mid-1820s, he commenced the systematic surveying of the colony that led to the declaration of 19 counties and a limit of location in 1826. **36**

Pacheo Pereira, Duarte. His origins are uncertain but his attainments in arms, letters and navigation suggest a noble and well-educated background. In 1503 he sailed with **Afonso de Albuquerque** to India, where he distinguished himself in the defence of Cochin (1504). He returned to a hero's welcome in Lisbon in July 1505. He gained further distinction commanding a naval squadron against corsairs but, as governor of the establishment of São Jorge da Mina at Elmina in West Africa from 1510, he incurred suspicion of plotting against the crown and was imprisoned for several years before clearing his name. He never regained royal favour but his great work, the *Esmeraldo de Situ Orbis*, provided a detailed guide for navigation around the coast of Africa, and is a major source of knowledge of the routes of early Portuguese maritime explorers. **12**

Paez, Pedro (1564–1622), Spanish Jesuit explorer and missionary in Ethiopia. Born in Olmedo and educated by Jesuits, he joined the order in 1582 and was appointed to the Indian mission in 1588, from where he was sent to join the mission in Ethiopia. Captured by Turkish pirates en route, he was enslaved until his escape in 1596. He then served in Goa until his mission to Ethiopia was resumed in 1603. His part in converting the court and a substantial part of the clergy was fundamental. His exploration of the Lake Tana region enabled him to discover and map the source of the Blue Nile. The route was described soon after in the *Itinerario* of Jeronimo Lobo but remained little known. Páez died in Gondar on 20 May 1622. **27, 37**

Palgrave, William Gifford (1826–88), British Jesuit explorer of Arabia. He became fluent in Arabic while serving as a missionary in Syria. He then resolved to cross Arabia, which in 1862–63 he accomplished, disguised as a Syrian doctor; intended as a missionary reconnaissance, his journey was also in part a secret mission at the orders of Napoleon III to gather intelligence about Arabia for French policy-makers. In 1864 he left the Jesuit order. The following year, by then in the British diplomatic service, he was sent on a mission to Ethiopia. He later served as consul in many parts of the world, including Bulgaria, Siam and Uruguay, where he died. **42**

Palmer, Nathaniel Brown (1799–1877), American seafarer and Antarctic explorer. Palmer went to sea in 1813 and made his first voyage to the Antarctic on a sealing vessel in 1819. In 1820–21 he commanded *Hero* on a sealing voyage to the Antarctic, during which he made one of the first sightings of the Antarctic continent on the coast of the Antarctic peninsula, Palmer Land. He returned to the Antarctic as commander of the *James Monroe* in 1821–22, and participated in the discovery of the South Orkney Islands. He made his last voyage to the Antarctic in 1829–21, but continued his seafaring career as a captain of trading ships until 1856. **46**

Pardo, Juan, 16th century. He was captain in the expedition of Pedro Menéndez de Avilés to thwart French colonial plans in Florida in 1565. In 1566 he was ordered to explore inland from Santa Elena (between modern Savannah and Charleston) 'to discover and conquer the interior country from there to Mexico'. He persevered for 150 leagues and left a garrison in a stockade at the foot of the Appalachians. **17**

Park, Mungo (1771–1806), Scottish surgeon and explorer of Africa. He began his travels as a ship's surgeon in the service of the East India Company and made a voyage to Sumatra. Park then offered his services to the African Association in London, which in 1795 sent him to explore in West Africa, his principal commission being to trace the Niger. This he reached near Segu, Mali, on 20 July in the following year, conclusively proving the easterly direction of its flow. He returned to England where his account of this exploit, *Travels in the Interior Districts of Africa* (1799), became immediately popular. He returned to medical practice but was asked by the British government to return to Africa and discover the termination of the Niger. He arrived at the Gambia in 1805 with 40 Europeans. The ensuing rainy season severely depleted the expedition, many of whom had succumbed to malaria and dysentery by the time the Niger was reached. At Sansanding Park built a boat and set off down the river, probably on 19 November, with the four surviving members of the expedition, a guide and some African slaves. In April of the following year the party was ambushed at Bussa; the only surviving member, a slave, reported that Park drowned while trying to escape. Park's records were lost. The problem of the termination of the Niger remained unsolved for another 24 years. **37**

Parke, John Grubb (1827–1900), U.S. army officer and explorer. Within four years of his graduation from West Point in 1849, Lieutenant Parke was ordered to run the western half of the 32nd Parallel route for the Pacific Railroad Surveys. His activities took him from Dona Ana, near El Paso, west to the Pimas Indian villages along the Gila River in southern Arizona. Then he worked on the survey for railroad routes inland from San Francisco Bay to Los Angeles. Park also wrote an essay on the zoology of the 32nd Parallel for the Pacific Railroad Reports. He rose to the rank of major-general in the Union Army; he was later appointed the 22nd superintendent of West Point. **22**

Parry, Sir William (1790–1855), British explorer of the Arctic. He joined the Royal Navy at 13 and rose to the rank of Admiral. In 1819 he was given command of two ships, the *Heda* and the *Griper*, to find the Northwest Passage. Sailing west through Lancaster Sound he discovered and named Melville Island, Barrow Strait and a number of the Parry Islands. Two further expeditions (1821–23, 1824–25) failed to find the passage, but did identify the Fury and Hecla Strait between Baffin Island and the Canadian mainland, thus identifying an alternative route into the passage, and a way to the magnetic pole. His explorations also revealed major new whaling grounds. In 1827 he attempted to reach the North Pole by sledge from Spitsbergen, reaching 82°45'N. **23, 46**

Paterson, William (1755–1810). A Scottish botanist and explorer, Paterson made four major journeys in South Africa through the Karroo and on to the sources of the Orange River in 1777–79. He later became lieutenant governor of New South Wales. **38**

Payer, Julius von (1842–1915), Austrian army officer and Arctic explorer. Payer qualified as a lieutenant in the Austrian army in 1859, and soon after was assigned to the Military Geographical Institute in Vienna, in which he was mainly concerned with mapping the Austrian Alps. In 1869–70 he was cartographer on the German Arctic expedition of Karl Koldewey, which explored parts of east Greenland. Soon after, he met the Austrian naval officer **Karl Weyprecht**, and together they planned a major Austro-Hungarian Arctic expedition. After a preliminary expedition to the Barents Sea in 1871, they undertook the main expedition on *Tegetthoff* in 1872–74, discovering and exploring the archipelago of Franz Josef Land (Zemlya Frantsa-Iosifa). After the expedition he retired from the army and devoted his life to painting. **46**

Peary, Robert Edwin (1856–1920), American naval engineer and Arctic explorer, probably the first explorer to reach the North Pole or its near vicinity. He led his first expedition in 1886 when he explored part of the Greenland ice cap. He led two more expeditions to north Greenland, in 1891–92 and 1893–95, when he twice crossed the ice cap from west to east, discovering the north-east coast. He later turned his attention towards the North Pole, and between 1898 and 1909 led three expeditions with the Pole as his main objective. His moment of triumph came on 6 April 1909 when he and his party became the first to stand at the North Pole (though his achievement has subsequently often been questioned). He was promoted to rear-admiral in 1911 and retired from naval service soon after. **46**

Pecador, Pedro de, 17th-century Spanish explorer of South America. A Franciscan lay brother from Quito, he took part in the first Franciscan mission to the Amazon under **Juan de Casarrubia** and played a leading part in that of 1634 along the Río San Miguel; thanks to his knowledge of medicine he was able to cure his colleagues' wounds when the Becaras Indians turned against the missionaries. He journeyed to Popayán, vainly seeking help, and then down the River Aguarico to the lands of the Encabellados Indians, with whom he negotiated a treaty of peace. He took the news to Quito by a trail-blazing route upriver along the River Napo. **26**

Pérez, Juan, 18th-century Spanish explorer of North America. He was said to be a native of Majorca. In 1773 he was appointed by the viceroy of Mexico to lead a naval expedition to verify rumours of Russian infiltration of northern California. He set sail in the frigate *Nueva Galicia* from San Blas on 24 January 1774, reaching Nootka before being forced back by bad weather. He arrived in Monterey in August. **20**

Petermann, August (1822–78), German geographer. In 1855 he founded *Petermann's Mitteilungen*, a periodical for many years regarded as the most reliable account of contemporary exploration. He was noted for his vigorous promotion of Arctic exploration, particularly in association with his theory of an ice-free Arctic ocean or 'open Polar Sea'. However erroneous, his ideas nonetheless influenced the planning of several important expeditions between the 1850s and the 1880s. **46**

Philby, Harry St. John (1885–1960), English explorer of the Middle East. Son of a Ceylon tea-planter, he was educated at Westminster and Trinity College, Cambridge, before joining the Indian Civil Service. In 1915 he accompanied the British Expeditionary Force to Iraq and spent almost the whole of the next 25 years in Arabia, converting to Islam in 1930 and contributing in particular to the study of the Empty Quarter. In 1940 he was arrested for opposition to the war, but was soon exonerated. In 1945 he returned to Arabia and renewed his intimacy with King Saud. On the latter's death in 1955, finding himself unwelcome in Saudi Arabia, he removed to Beirut where he devoted himself to scholarship and writing until his death on 30 September 1960. **42**

Piccard, Auguste (1884–1962). A Swiss physicist, Piccard pioneered the use of high-altitude balloons, ascending to the stratosphere in a series of flights made in 1930–31. He subsequently developed the first deep-sea vessel that could operate independently of a mother-ship on the surface. In 1953, with his son Jacques, Piccard descended to 10,400 feet in his bathyscape *Trieste* off the Atlantic coast of West Africa. In 1960 Jacques, in company with Donald Walsh of the U.S. Navy, descended in *Trieste* to the bottom of the Mariana Trench, at 35,800 feet the deepest ocean floor in the world and never subsequently reached. **47**

PIGAFETTA, ANTONIO (before 1491–after 1525). Born in Vicenza, he reputedly served the Knights of Rhodes before 1519, when he was in the household of Francesco Chiericati. During a visit to Barcelona he obtained leave to enlist as a gentleman volunteer in the flagship of the fleet that **Magellan** was assembling in Seville, bound for the Moluccas. By surviving the voyage and using his literary gifts to record it, Pigafetta acquired renown in Europe, where he was received at the Spanish, Portuguese, French, Mantuan, Venetian and papal courts. His account of the voyage, finished in 1524 and first printed in 1525, became and remained the most influential source on the first circumnavigation of the world. **13, 33**

PIKE, ZEBULON MONTGOMERY (1779–1813), U.S. army officer and explorer. At 15 Pike enlisted in the army and saw service with Mad Anthony Wayne in the Old Northwest. He was promoted lieutenant in 1799 and served at frontier posts. In 1805 he conducted a reconnaissance of the upper Mississippi. His map was the first reasonably accurate one of the region, but Pike failed to identify the true source of the great river. Three months after his return (in 1806) General Wilkinson ordered Pike to lead a party southwest from St. Louis and up the Arkansas River. By late autumn Pike was into the Colorado mountains, where he tried unsuccessfully to climb the peak that bears his name. He crossed the Sangre de Cristo Mountains and in February built a stockade on the Conejos River, a tributary of the Rio Grande. There he was captured by a Spanish force, taken to Mexico and eventually released near Natchitoches, Louisiana, on 30 June 1807. His narrative of the expedition was published and gained him some fame, but there has always been some mystery about the real purpose of the expedition. He was promoted brigadier-general and was killed during the war of 1812 when he led an attack on Toronto (April 1813). **20, 22**

PINZÓN, MARTIN ALONSO (d. 1493), Spanish navigator, one of three brothers. He commanded the *Pinta* and helped supply men and equipment for **Columbus**'s first voyage to the New World (1492). There remains dispute concerning his part in the voyage, in which he challenged Columbus's choice of route and mysteriously abandoned the expedition for more than six weeks during the exploration of Cuba and Hispaniola. Separated again by storms on the way home, Pinzón died shortly after reaching port in Bayona in 1493, accused by Columbus of treachery but later hailed by his family and friends as more deserving of the glory of discovery. His brother, Francisco Martin Pinzón, was pilot of the *Pinta*, and another brother, **Vicente Yánez**, commanded the *Niña* on the same expedition.

PINZÓN, VICENTE YÁNEZ (d. before 1519), Spanish navigator. Brother of **Martin Alonso** and Francisco Martin, and captain of the *Niña* on **Columbus**'s first Atlantic voyage (1492). In 1499, Vicentè Yánez led an expedition which, in the following year, reached the coast of Brazil, where he reported the mouth of the River Amazon. In 1505, as governor, he was granted permission to colonize Puerto Rico, but he did not take possession of it. It was probably on his last recorded voyage, which departed in March 1508, that he explored the coasts of Honduras and Yucatán with **Juan Díaz de Solis**. **9, 10, 13**

PIRES, TOMÉ (*c.* 1468–*c.* 1540), Portuguese apothecary and diplomat. Son of King João II's apothecary, he was apothecary to the Infante Afonso from 1490. In 1511 he left for India, with a large salary from the King, probably to gather medicinal specimens. **Afonso de Albuquerque** used his expertise in the spice trade of Malacca between 1512 and 1516, when he was appointed to head Portugal's projected diplomatic mission to China. Records are missing after his arrival in Peking in 1520, but tradition maintained that he survived for 20 years at the Chinese court. **29**

PITTS, JOSEPH (1662–1735). An English seaman, captured by pirates and sold into slavery in Algiers in 1678, he was forcibly converted to Islam and accompanied his master on a pilgrimage to Mecca, of which he published, after his escape, the first account since that of **Varthema**. **42**

PIZARRO, FRANCISCO (1476–1541), Spanish *conquistador*, the explorer and conqueror of Peru. He was the illegitimate son of a captain of infantry and a farmer's daughter. From 1498 to 1501 he served in Spain's Italian wars. In 1502 he emigrated to Hispaniola. He took part in a number of expeditions on the Caribbean coast, and in 1513 accompanied **Balboa** across Panama to discover the Pacific Ocean. In these expeditions he played minor though important roles; in 1524, with Diego de Almagro and capital from an independent backer, he launched a project for the conquest of Peru. After a series of setbacks on the Peruvian coasts, he obtained a commission from the crown in 1529, and early in 1531 he sailed from Panama with his three brothers, 185 men and 27 horses in three ships. After a long period of indecision, they marched inland in September 1532, profiting from the Inca empire's internal conflicts. In Cajamarca on 15 November 1532 Pizarro treacherously seized the Inca Atahualpa, who was garrotted after collection of a huge ransom. On 15 December Pizarro entered Cuzco, but Inca resistance remained formidable and the *conquistadores* were split by their own rivalries. These led to open hostilities between followers of Pizarro and Almagro from 1538. In the course of these squabbles, Pizarro was murdered by rioters in Lima – the capital he had founded for Peru in 1535 – on 26 June 1541. **24**

PIZARRO, GONZALO (1512–48), Spanish *conquistador*, youngest of **Francisco**'s brothers. He took part in the conquest of Peru and was appointed by his brother to lead an expedition in search of a fabled 'Land of Cinnamon' in 1541. He marched across the Andes to the Napo River, and sent **Francisco de Orellana** downriver on a foraging trip which was to end in the first navigation of the River Amazon. In 1544, incensed by royal efforts to ease Indian burdens at the *conquistadores'* expense, he launched a rebellion which ended with his defeat at the battle of Jaquijaguana on 9 April 1548 and execution the following day. **24**

PIZARRO, HERNANDO (*c.* 1501–78), Spanish *conquistador*, the only legitimate Pizarro brother. He took part, under his brother **Francisco**, in the conquest of Peru, leading an exploratory force to Pachácamac and the advance guard in the march on Cuzco. He played a leading role in the Pizarros' war against Diego de Almagro and ordered the latter's judicial murder in 1538. On returning to Spain in 1539 he was imprisoned in the castle of La Mota at Medina del Campo, while a huge fortune accumulated from the brothers' conquests. Released in 1561, he retired to his native Trujillo where he built a sumptuous palace. **24**

POLO, MARCO (*c.* 1254–1324). Venetian traveller in the East. In 1260, his father and uncle, Niccolò and Maffeo Polo, undertook a successful trading venture to the Mongol province on the lower Volga. Their immediate return to Venice was blocked by a war and they journeyed eastwards instead. They reached Kublai Khan's capital at Shang-tu in 1265. The khan took kindly to the western travellers and entrusted them with letters to the Pope, asking him to send 100 wise men, possibly with a view to teaching Christianity to the Chinese. The brothers returned to Venice in 1269. On a second journey, made with the authority of the Pope Gregory X in 1271, they took Marco Polo. Joining the main Silk Road via Kashgar, they reached the khan's court by 1275, where Marco quickly became a favourite, whom the khan employed as a sort of male sheherazade to relate strange tales of remote parts of the empire. The khan sent Marco on numerous business expeditions, including journeys to Yunnan and Hangchow (Quinsay) and perhaps beyond.

The Polos remained in China until about 1292, when they were given the task of escorting the intended bride of a Persian ruler by sea from Ch'üan-chou (Zaitun) to Hormuz. After two years, they arrived at their destination. The ruler of Persia had died in the meantime and the young bride was given to his son. The Polos then continued by way of Constantinople to Venice, where they arrived in 1295. Marco Polo then joined Venetian forces fighting Genoa, and in 1290 was taken prisoner. He was held captive for two years, during which time he dictated an account of his travels to a fellow prisoner, one Rustichello (or Rusticiano), a writer of chivalric romances. The resulting manuscript – popularly known as *Il milione* – introduced its readers to paper currency, asbestos and coal ('a kind of black stones which ... maintain the fire better than wood'). Widely regarded as fantastic and unreliable, the work stimulated exploration by conveying rumours of the vastness of the Orient, the wealth of Japan and the habitability of regions south of the equator. When the author died at the age of 70, he is said to have been asked to retract his inventions and replied that he had not recorded the half of all he had seen. **9, 28, 30, 31, 34, 44**

'POMBEIROS'. The word means slave agents. The two famous in exploration, Pedro João Baptista and Antonio Nogueira da Rocha, were sent from Cassange in Angola across the continent to Sena on the lower Zambezi in the years 1806–11. Baptista was literate enough to keep a simple journal. The two slaves visited the Mwata Yamvo, the Cazembe and other African potentates. **38**

PONCE DE LEÓN, JUAN (*c.* 1460–1521), Spanish *conquistador* who took part in the pacification of Hispaniola from 1502 and governed Puerto Rico in 1510–11. On 23 February 1512 he was commissioned to seek the rumoured island of Bimini, where, he professed to believe, the fountain of eternal youth would be found. On 27 March 1513 the expedition discovered Florida and, on 21 April, the Gulf Stream – a discovery that greatly speeded the homeward voyage of transatlantic shipping. He died of wounds inflicted by natives during a return expedition, delayed until 1521. **10, 15, 17**

POND, PETER (1740–1807), American fur-trader and explorer of the Northwest, born in Milford, Connecticut. After service in the French and Indian war, he became a trader in Detroit (1765). Thence he moved west to Mackinac, and made a series of journeys along the upper Mississippi (1773–75); he travelled via Lake Superior to the Saskatchewan River, and in 1778 established a post on the Athabasca River. Tried and acquitted of the murder of a rival trader, he was involved in the creation of the North West Company (1783–84). He created a number of maps of the territories he travelled, and created a manuscript map of North America (1784), which he presented to Congress. **21**

POPE, JOHN (1822–92), U.S. army officer and explorer. After graduating from West Point in 1842 Pope was assigned to the Topographical Engineers. From 1851 until 1853 he served with the Department of New Mexico. When Congress authorized the Pacific Railroad Surveys Pope was assigned the survey of the 32nd Parallel route, along with Lieutenant **John G. Parke**. Pope worked eastward from Dona Ana (near El Paso) across the Staked Plain to Big Spring, thence north-east to Fort Washita on the Red River. He explored the Guadalupe Mountains of New Mexico in search of a suitable pass. After the survey Pope rose steadily in rank, with both successes and failures, and retired in 1886 with the rank of major-general. **22**

POPPLE, HENRY (d. 1743). English geographer and surveyor notable for his mapping of the British colonial holdings in North America (published in 1733). **19**

PORTOLÁ, GASPAR DE (*c.* 1722–84), Spanish explorer of North America. He served in the Spanish army and in 1767 was appointed governor of Lower California. Two years later he led an expedition to California to seize the northern parts of the present American state of California to arrest the spread of Russian posts from the north. He established overland routes to San Francisco and Monterey, where he helped to found the missions of **Junípero Serra**. **17, 20**

POVEDA, MARTÍN DE, 16th-century Spanish *conquistador*. With fellow-citizens of Chachapoyas he set off in 1566 to continue the search for El Dorado beyond the reach of previous expeditions. After a march of over 900 miles, which took them through the recently founded settlement of San Juan de los Llanos, the survivors arrived in Bogotá, having demonstrated that no rich land lay between the areas explored by **Gonzalo Pizarro** and **Pérez de Quesada**. **24**

POWELL, JOHN WESLEY (1834–1902), U.S. scientist and explorer. Powell came from a humble background, growing up on a farm in southern Wisconsin. Ambitious, intelligent and interested in natural history, he determined to break away from farming. From 1852 until he went off to war in 1861 Powell was a schoolmaster, attending college as and when he could afford it. As a labour of love he also made natural history trips down mid-Western rivers. He lost his right arm at Shiloh in the Civil War, married and, after the war, accepted a professorship of geology at Illinois Wesleyan University. In 1867 he led a natural history group into western Colorado. By the end of the season he had made up his mind to float down the Green and Colorado Rivers. On 24 May 1869 Powell and nine crew members in four boats cast off from Green River Station on the Union Pacific Railroad. More than three months later the crew (minus three who had climbed out of the Canyon and had been killed by Indians) came ashore near the Mormon village of Callville, just below the Grand Canyon. Through his writings, lectures and personal contacts Powell became well known. He soon had his own survey, the United States Geographical and Geological Survey of the Rocky Mountain Region. In 1872 he descended the Green and Colorado Rivers a second time. His geologic theories have withstood the test of time, while his interest in ethnology assured the retention of Indian languages and mythology. As an administrator he brought about the consolidation of the Western surveys into the United States Geological Survey in 1879, and was its second director; he was also instrumental in establishing the Bureau of American Ethnology. He ranks as the foremost scientist exploring the American West after the Civil War. 22

PRZHEVALSKY, NIKOLAI MIKHAILOVICH (1839–88), Russian soldier and explorer of Central Asia. He led five expeditions, all of great scientific interest, in which despite enduring great privation he trekked across huge areas of Central Asia and collected substantial numbers of botanical and zoological specimens. His first expedition (1867–69) took him to the Far East. His second (1870–73) covered Mongolia and China to the headwaters of the Yangtze River. On his third (1876–77) he crossed the Tien Shan range to the River Tarim and surveyed the lake of the Lop Nor. He made a series of attempts to reach Lhasa, the capital of Tibet, but was rebuffed by Tibetan forces. Among his many discoveries was *Equus przevalskii*, the last breed of wild horse known to exist. 44

PSHENITSIN, P. Russian scientist. Little is known of his life. In 1808–10 he was geodesist on M. M. Gedenshtrom's expedition to explore the New Siberian Islands. In 1811 he took over the leadership of the expedition and completed the survey. 46

PTOLEMY, CLAUDIUS (c. AD 87–c. 150) of Alexandria, geographer and mathematician. Compiled the geographical description (the *Geographia*) of the known world or *oikumene* in c. 125, but the oldest extant manuscript with maps on his projection are from 12th and 13th century codices. A manuscript was brought to Italy and translated into Latin by Jacopo Angelo in 1406, and was first printed, without maps, in 1475; the first illustrated edition appeared at Bologna in 1477. The first modern maps for comparison were added in 1482 in the Ulm edition; 20 maps were added in Martin Waldseemüller's edition in 1513; Gastaldi's new translated edition added 60 new maps in 1584; Mercator's edition included an interpretation of the Classical maps in 1578; the last important edition was Girolamo Porr's in 1598. Ptolemaic concepts exerted a strong influence on Renaissance geographical thought and remained influential long after the Columbian discoveries. 2, 5, 7

PYNCHON, WILLIAM (c. 1590–1662). A rich and well-connected merchant, one of the founder patentees of the Massachusetts Bay Company, he arrived with the Winthrop fleet in 1630; he established himself as a trader, chiefly in furs, and played a prominent part in the government in Massachusetts and Connecticut until 1651. His trading post at Springfield, where the fur trade of Connecticut was gathered for shipping to London, became a centre for the exploration of the tributaries of the Connecticut River from its establishment in 1635. In 1650 the publication of his tract, *The Meritorious Price of our Redemption*, scandalized Boston society, and Pynchon decided to retire to England, where he devoted himself to theology until his death on his estate at Wraysbury. 19

PYTHEAS. A Massiliot Greek, he undertook a voyage of conscious exploration in the Atlantic waters towards the end of the 4th century BC, probably in order to investigate the sources of Carthaginian trade. He

claimed to have circumnavigated the British Isles, reported its approximate shape and gathered reports about Arctic regions. His observations of tides and latitudes passed into Greek geographical tradition. 2

QUADRAMITO or QUADRAMIRO, ANTONIO DE, 16th-century missionary. Between 1574 and 1581 he was active in the Chiloé archipelago, with his companion Cristóbal de Mendo or Mérida, exploring the area at the orders of the governor, Hurtado de Mendoza, and seeking sites for missions for his order, the Franciscans. He died at an unknown date, during a subsequent mission among the Huelches. 24

QUESADA, GONZALO JIMÉNEZ DE (1509–79), Spanish *conquistador*. A lawyer, he was made chief justice of the colony of Santa Maria in 1536 but almost at once obtained a commission to explore the course of the River Magdalena in the hope of finding a route to Peru. The arduous journey took him to the Opón valley, where a route opened to the Colombian highlands. Evidence of the area's wealth convinced him to turn aside. After a brief respite at Barranco Bermeja, he began the approach to the highlands on 28 December 1536 and reached them at La Grita in the Vélez region, on 9 March 1537. Despite the rigours of the march and the weakness of his men, fewer than two hundred in number, he conquered the valley of Bogotá in an efficient summer's campaign, extorting from the defeated chief Sagipa a huge booty in gold and emeralds. He called the land Nueva Granada and the capital, founded on 27 April 1538, Santa Fe de Bogotá.

Early in 1539 two independent Spanish expeditions under Federmann and Benalcázar converged on the region from the east and south respectively. The three commanders agreed on the re-foundation of the capital on 27 April 1539, and to submit their rival claims to the arbitration of the crown. Jiménez de Quesada left in May 1539 to press his suit. Passed over for the governorship of the territory he had discovered and conquered, he returned in 1549 to occupy a series of largely honorific positions until 1568, when he obtained a commission to conquer part of Los Llanos. The expedition was an expensive disaster, of three years' duration, which obliged him, after further brief service in a frontier command, to retire to Huesca with what he could salvage of his fortune. His brilliant secondary career as a writer produced *El Antijovio*, a classic of *conquistador* literature. 25

QUESADA, HERNÁN PÉREZ DE, 16th-century Spanish *conquistador*. He accompanied the expedition of his brother Gonzalo Jiménez de Quesada to Bogotá. In 1538 he made an unsuccessful attempt to locate a reported Amazon realm near the Papamene River and commanded the scouts who made contact with the expedition of Sebastián de Benalcázar. In 1540 he launched a search for an Inca temple irrationally supposed to lie north of the Chibcha country, and on 1 September 1541 led a numerous force into unknown territory beyond the River Bermejo in an attempt to find the fabled El Dorado. After many hardships and the loss of 80 men and 110 horses, he managed to fight his way through to the Spanish outpost at Pasto. His conviction that he had come close to his goal inspired more disastrous expeditions in his wake, in particular that of Philip von Hutten. 25

QUIROS or QUIRÓS or QUEIROS, PEDRO FERNÁNDEZ or FERNANDES DE (c. 1565–1615). Spanish navigator of the Pacific. Born in Évora, he was a ship's scrivener who acquired profound knowledge of Pacific navigation aboard the trading galleons that plied between Acapulco and Manila. He served as pilot aboard Mendaña's 1595 voyage in search of the Solomon Islands. After his commander's death he safely piloted the fleet, through terrible privations, to the Philippines. Unable to secure patronage in Peru for a projected Pacific voyage of his own, he made a pilgrimage to Rome in the Holy Year 1600, securing approval of his plans from the Spanish ambassador and Pope Clement VIII. In 1603, with the endorsement of King Philip III of Spain, he returned to Peru and obtained three ships with the apparent aim of finding and settling the mythical continent of Terra Australis Incognita. Quirós consciously modelled himself on Columbus, affecting the same mystical language and clothing himself in a Franciscan robe. His fleet left Callao in December 1605, but the following month an apparent failure of nerve made him revert to

tested routes after an initial attempt to plunge into the entirely unknown regions of the South Pacific south-west of Chile. His modest haul of newly discovered islands included the New Hebrides, called by Quirós Espíritu Santo. He took it for the imagined continent, but abandoned an initially enthusiastic attempt at colonization. In 1607 he returned to Madrid to plead for another chance, tiring the court with vividly penned memoranda. He was at last granted leave in 1614 and hastened back to Peru, but died exhausted and broken in health soon after arriving. 33, 34

RABBAN SAUMA. A Nestorian Christian of Peking he began a pilgrimage to Jerusalem, reaching Armenia in 1280. Entering the service of the Persian Khan Arghun, he led an embassy to the Pope in 1287, visiting Constantinople, Naples, Rome, Genoa, Paris and Bordeaux. His account, written on his return to Persia, mirrored that of Marco Polo's travels in the opposite direction. He was never able to get back to China. 1

RADISSON, PIERRE ESPRIT (c. 1630–1710), French explorer of North America. He was a fur-trader in Nouvelle France from 1651; considerable doubt exists as to where exactly in Canada Radisson explored: his accounts of his journeys are consistently vague. It seems probable, however, that with his brother-in-law Groseilliers he travelled on a fur-trading expedition in 1659–60 to present-day Minnesota, from where they returned with a substantial quantity of furs. These were confiscated by the French authorities at Montreal for having been collected without the appropriate approval. Radisson and Groseillers then transferred their loyalties to Britain and in 1668 sailed for Hudson Bay, where Groseilliers established Fort Rupert. In 1670, having returned to England and won further backing for more fur-trading ventures, Radisson established Port Nelson on Hudson Bay. These efforts effectively led to the founding that year of the English Hudson's Bay Company. Despite subsequently turning against the English and raiding their Hudson Bay trading posts, Radisson eventually won a pension from the company. 18

RAE, JOHN (1813–93), Scottish surgeon, fur-trader and explorer. Rae qualified as a surgeon at Edinburgh in 1833; immediately afterwards he entered service with the Hudson's Bay Company and sailed to Canada. After ten years at Moose Factory trading post on James Bay, Ontario, he was appointed leader of a company expedition to complete the survey of the Arctic coast of North America, from Hudson Bay to the Boothia Peninsula. In 1847–49 he returned to the Arctic coast with Sir John Richardson's Franklin search expedition. After Richardson's return home, Rae continued the search in the same region until 1851. In 1853–54 he resumed the survey of the Arctic coast; during this expedition he accidentally discovered the fate of the Franklin expedition. He retired from Company service in 1856, but he continued to travel and carry out surveys for another ten years before settling in London. 23

RALEIGH, WALTER (c. 1554–1618). The son of a Devonshire gentleman, he volunteered to fight on the Protestant side in the French Wars of Religion in 1569. He studied law and saw service in Ireland, making recommendations on policy that attracted the attention of Queen Elizabeth I. Royal favour brought him a series of offices of profit and lucrative monopolies from 1582. He used his influence in favour of an aggressive maritime and colonial policy. In 1584–89 he promoted the unsuccessful Roanoke Island colonial venture in North America. In 1592 he fell from royal favour when his secret marriage and the birth of his son became known to the Queen. Among his efforts to recover standing, his expedition to Guiana in 1595, while adding nothing to the extent of exploration, helped to spread the legend of El Dorado. In 1596–97 he accompanied the Earl of Essex's raids on Cadiz and the Azores. His militant policies were detested by King James I, who came to the throne in 1603. Suspected of plotting the King's overthrow, he was imprisoned under sentence of death. He spent his time writing and lobbying for a further voyage to Guiana. When he was allowed to undertake one, in 1616, it proved a costly failure and a provocation to Spain. Raleigh was returned to prison and beheaded in 1618. 15, 26

REBMANN, JOHANN (1820–76). Also from the Basle Seminary, Rebmann joined **Krapf** in East Africa in 1846. He made a journey inland towards Kilimanjaro, and saw the snow on its summit in May 1848, a discovery that created interest and argument in Europe. He continued his missionary work near Mombasa until 1875. 39

REIS, PIRI (d. 1554), admiral of the Turkish fleet in Egypt, nephew of the pirate Kelam Reis. Piri Reis distinguished himself at the battles of Modon and Lepanto. He remained with the Ottoman fleet during the reigns of Selim I (1512–20) and Suleiman the Magnificent (1520–66). He is best known today for his *Kitab-i Bahriye* (Things Pertaining to the Seas), a portolan chart and textual description of 1513 generally held to have been based on a lost map of **Columbus**'s. 5, 9

RENNELL, JAMES (1742–1830), British naval officer and East India Company engineer officer who was known as the 'father of Indian geography'. He became surveyor-general of Bengal in 1764 and carried out much of the earliest mapping of eastern India. After retiring from India in 1777, he published a '*Bengal Atlas*' (1779) and a '*Memoir of a Map of Hindostan*' (1783). In 1797 he constructed an African map based on the materials collected by **Mungo Park**. 37, 43

RIBAUT, JEAN (*c.* 1520–65), French explorer of North America. In 1562, he established a colony in present-day South Carolina at Paris Island; the settlement failed and he tried to establish another in Florida, but was killed by Spaniards. 15

RIBEIRO, DIOGO (active 1510–35), Portuguese royal cosmographer in Spanish service at Seville from about 1519, becoming cosmographer and chartmaker at the Casa de la Contratación. Three world maps have survived – one of 1527, two of 1529 – regarded as copies of the Spanish *padrón real*. Ribeiro's maps show the tracks of **Magellan**'s circumnavigation in 1519–20, and the place-names in Patagonia record his passage along the coast. Ribeiro presents the width of the Pacific as 125°, from Peru to the Moluccas, only some 25° short of the true width. 10, 15

RICCI, MATTEO (1552–1610), Italian Jesuit missionary in China and cartographer. The son of a prominent pharmacist of Macerata in the Papal States, he was admitted to the Society of Jesus in 1571. After joining the Jesuit mission at Macao in 1582, he obtained leave to establish a mission within Chinese territory, first at Shiuhing in Kwantung province, later working his way gradually north until he was allowed to settle in Peking in 1601. His methods of evangelization, based on scrupulous respect for Confucian tradition, scandalized some other missionaries, but he was able to compile and transmit to the outside world scientific data and maps about China in unprecedented quantities. He remained in Peking until his death. 1

RICHARDSON, JAMES (1806–51). The original leader of the British government's Central Africa Mission of 1850, Richardson had already investigated the Saharan slave trade in the 1840s. In 1851 he reached the Lake Chad region from Tripoli and, while separated from **Barth**, died. 23

RIVERA VILLALÓN, PEDRO DE (*c.* 1664–1744), Spanish explorer and surveyor of North and Central America. Born in Antequera, he served in the Netherlands in the late 1670s. He was probably in the New World by the 1690s, serving as an engineer and, before 1710, as a colonel of infantry. In 1710 he became governor of Tlaxcala and in 1713 commanded the fleet from Veracruz to Spain, where he took part in the siege of Barcelona of 1714–15. Returning to the governorship of Tlaxcala, and after an interlude campaigning against pirates in Yucatán, he was appointed in 1724 to inspect the northern defences of the Spanish empire. The inspection of three-and-a-half years' duration covered 9,000 miles and produced a detailed survey, meticulously mapped by Rivera's assistant, Francisco Álvarez Barreiro. In 1731 Rivera was made governor of Veracruz, but was able to transfer the following year to the more remunerative governorship of Guatemala where he served until retirement in 1542, removing to Mexico City, where he died. 17

ROBINSON, GEORGE AUGUSTUS (1788–1866), seems to have been born in London, where he entered the building trade, and developed a religious disposition. In January 1824 he reached Hobart, and in 1829 was appointed to 'civilize' and Christianize the Tasmanian Aborigines. Believing that he needed to become better acquainted with their languages and customs, in 1830–34 he travelled extensively through the island, then supervised the removal of survivors to Flinders Island in Bass Strait, where he sought to replace Aboriginal culture with a pseudo-European one. The attempt ended disastrously, with the death of almost all the Aborigines. Subsequently, Robinson served as Protector of the Aborigines in the Port Phillip district. 36

RODRÍGUEZ CERMEÑO, SEBASTIÁN *see* **Cermeño, Rodríguez Sebastián.**

ROERICH, NICOLAS (1870–1947), Russian traveller and painter in Central Asia, and member of the Russian Academy of Arts. Accompanied by his wife Elena and son George, he undertook a pioneering three-year journey (March 1925 to May 1928) across Central Asia. His belief that a common cultural bond linked many of the nomadic peoples from the Russian Steppes to the Himalayas was largely confirmed by his discovery of the Tibetan concept of *Shambhala* – a legendary kingdom of of Righteousness – and the mythical White Water Lands, or *Belovodye*, of the Russians of the Altai mountains. Roerich also identified examples of day-to-day life that were shared by otherwise apparently different nomads. He subsequently produced a large number of powerfully painted canvases of Himalayan and Central Asian scenes, and a series of scholarly philosophical essays. 44

ROGERS, ROBERT (1731–95). An Indian trader born in Methuen, Massachusetts, he was a recruiting officer for William Shirley's expedition to Nova Scotia in 1755. To escape prosecution for counterfeiting, he joined the New Hampshire Regiment in the same year, serving as a captain and distinguishing himself in scouting and skirmishing. In 1756 he was appointed to command a ranger company and was promoted major in 1758, acquiring considerable renown for prowess against French and Indian opponents. In peace he reverted to disreputable habits in his trading ventures and got into debt. In 1765 he removed to England, where his writings about frontier life were acclaimed and he secured appointment as fort commander at Michilimackinac. From there, he commissioned **Jonathan Carver** to explore Minnesota. His self-interested conduct in his command led to his arrest on suspicion of treasonable dealings with the French in 1766, but he was released for want of evidence and again went to England, where he was imprisoned for debt. Freed by the intervention of his brother, James, he returned to America in 1775, attempting a double game between the rebels and the authorities, which led to his dismissal by the latter and imprisonment by the former. In 1780 he fled to England, where he eked out a wretched existence on half pay until his death in cheap lodgings. 19

ROGGEVEEN, JACOB (1659–1729), Dutch explorer. He studied law and theology and in 1706 went to the Dutch East Indies to work in the justice department. He returned to Holland, and in 1722 led an expedition to the Pacific. Its route westwards around Cape Horn took Roggeveen farther south than any previous navigator. The huge icebergs he sighted confirmed to him the existence of Terra Australis, the great southern continent. Roggeveen's major discoveries in the Pacific were Samoa, Easter Island and the Society Islands. 34

ROHLFS, GERHARD (1831–96), German physician and explorer of North Africa. He joined the French Foreign Legion in 1855 and then travelled in Morocco disguised as an Arab. Between 1865 and 1867, he crossed from the Mediterranean coast to the Gulf of Guinea. He traversed other parts of the Sahara three times and in 1868 joined the British expedition to Ethiopia. In 1878–79 he led an expedition to Wadai. In 1884 he was briefly German consul in Zanzibar. 37

ROJAS, DIEGO DE, 16th-century Spanish *conquistador*. Commissioned by Governor Vaca de Castro in 1542 to undertake the exploration and conquest of the regions to the south-east of the former Inca empire in the direction of the River Plate, Rojas departed with 200 men in early summer 1543, and had reached Jurí territory in the region of Santiago del Estero by January 1544 when he died of wounds received in conflicts with the Indians. 24

ROSEBOOM, JOHANNES, 17th-century explorer of North America. He was among the traders of Albany, New York, employed by Governor Thomas Dongan in the last quarter of the 17th century to enhance the range of the fur trade by opening routes to Indian tribes rich in pelts. In 1685 he reached Michilimackinac at the junction of Lakes Huron and Michigan in a journey of three months. In a return venture in 1687 he was captured by French scouts, and did not return to Albany until the late 1690s. 19

ROSS, SIR JAMES CLARK (1800–62), British naval officer and polar explorer. Ross entered the Royal Navy in 1812. Six years later he set out on the first of eight expeditions which made him the most experienced polar explorer of his time. He was a junior officer on the naval Northwest Passage expeditions of his uncle John Ross (1818) and of **William Parry** (1819–20, 1821–23, 1824–25). In 1829–33 he was on John Ross's private Northwest Passage expedition on *Victory*, during which he discovered the North Magnetic Pole. After promotion to captain in 1834, he led an expedition to relieve icebound whalers in Baffin Bay (1836). In 1839–43, he commanded the navy's first major Antarctic expedition, on *Erebus* and *Terror*, during which he discovered the Ross Sea, Ross Ice Shelf, Ross Island and Victoria Land. His last expedition was to the Canadian Arctic on *Enterprise* and *Investigator*, 1848–49, in search of **Sir John Franklin**'s missing expedition of 1845. He spent the rest of his life in retirement. 23, 46

ROTZ, JEAN (active 1534–60), Dieppe chartmaker and hydrographer to King Henry VIII, to whom Rotz dedicated in 1542 a *Book of Idrography* (now in the British Library). The charts are famous for their depiction of the outline of the northern coat of Terra Australis – ('The londe of Jaua' and 'the lytil Jaua') which bears more than a passing resemblance to the shape of Australia and shows Portuguese place-names. This has been held by several commentators to prove a Portuguese discovery, or at least a landfall, of Australia before 1550. Rotz's chart of 1542 marks the island of Sumatra as 'trapobana' (the Ptolemaic name for Ceylon, transferred after the Portuguese had reached Sumatra itself, Ceylon being called 'Ceilon'). The American map, covering the West Indies, is the first map to depict Indian wigwams. 13

RUBÍ, PEDRO JORDÁN DE URRIÉS Y PIGNATELLI, MARQUÉS DE, 18th-century Spanish surveyor of North America. As a young man he served in New Spain as nominal commander of the inspection of the fortifications of the northern frontier undertaken by **Nicolás La Fora** in 1766–68. On his return to Spain in 1778 he became involved with the economic reform movement and founded the Real Sociedad Económica de Amigos del País de Zaragoza in 1789. He inherited the title of Marqués de Ayerbe (that of Marqués de Rubí was a courtesy title obtained from his mother's family) and became a grandee of Spain in 1789. 17

SAAVEDRA CERÓN, ÁLVARO DE (d. 1529), Spanish explorer of the Pacific whose voyage of 1527–28 discovered the best east–west route from New Spain directly across the north Pacific. He left, at **Cortés**'s orders, from Sihuatanejo (Zacatula) on 31 October 1527, losing two of his three ships on the voyage out, and arrived at Tidore the following March. After succouring the Spanish garrison he attempted to return to New Spain first via New Guinea (1528) and then by a northerly route (1529). Saavedra died at about 28°N; the expedition battled on to about 31°N but without finding winds to take them home. 33

SAAVEDRA, HERNANDARIAS or **HERNANDO ARIAS DE** (1561–1634). Born in Asunción, he took part in his first expedition, in search of the city of 'Los Césares' under Gonzalo de Abreu, governor of Tucumán, at the age of 15. He became a settler of Buenos Aires at the time of its re-foundation by **Juan de Garay**, whose daughter he married; he played a major role in the military expeditions launched from the colony to control the hinterland until 1589, when he returned with his family to Asunción, where he was acting governor from 1592 to 1594. After a series of military commands in the region, he became temporary governor of Río de La Plata in 1598, and permanent governor from 1602. During a governorship remarkable for the expansion of the colony he launched a series of expeditions of exploration between 1604 and 1608, including, in 1604, a renewed attempt to find 'Los Césares' and marches into unknown territory along both banks of the River Plate. His term of office expired in 1609, but he was re-appointed for a further term in 1614 until 1618, when, in accordance with his proposals, the government of Paraguay was separated from that of Río de La Plata and Hernandarias again retired, this time for good. **26**

SANTA CRUZ, ALONSO DE (1500–72). Spanish geographer and cosmographer whose globe (1542) and manuscript *Atlas* (1545) reflected the contribution of Spanish navigators in defining the shape and extent of the New World. **10**

SCHMIDT, OTTO (1891–1956), Russian Arctic explorer. A scientist by training, he became vice-president of the Academy of Sciences of the U.S.S.R. He made several explorations, notably to Franz Josef Land (1928, 1930) and another from Archangel to the Pacific (1932). **32**

SCHMIDT, ULRICH or **ULRICO**, 16th-century German explorer of South America. He was among at least 80 Germans who shipped to the River Plate in 1535 with the expedition of **Pedro de Mendoza**. He took part in all the campaigns and major exploratory expeditions along the River Paraguay with Juan de Ayolas and Domingo Martínez de Irala. In 1552 he obtained permission to return home, where he converted to Protestantism. His account of his experiences in South America was published in 1567 and has remained popular ever since. **26**

SCHÖNER, JOHANN (1477–1547). German map-maker and geographer, working in Nuremberg. His succession of revised globes (1515, 1520, 1523, 1533) reflected the growing knowledge of the continental disposition of the globe. **9**

SCHOUTEN, WILLEM (d. 1625). In 1601–3 he was in the West Indies with Wolfhaart Harmansen. In 1615 he was made pilot of a Dutch expedition under the command of **Jacob Le Maire** to find a safer route around the south of America than the perilous one discovered by **Magellan** in 1520 and to evade the trade restrictions of the Dutch East India Company. The expedition embarked with some 90 men in two small ships, one of which was accidentally set on fire in a South American port. The remaining vessel battled through storms to round (and name) Cape Horn, entering the Pacific in January 1616. In Java, however, the ship was confiscated by representatives of the Dutch East India Company, which claimed exclusive trading rights in the area. When released, the remaining crew (some 20 men) returned home as passengers in 1617. **13, 33**

SCOTT, ROBERT FALCON (1868–1912), British naval officer and polar explorer. A regular officer of the Royal Navy, Scott was appointed by the Royal Geographical Society in 1900 to lead an expedition to the Antarctic on the ship *Discovery*, despite having no experience of polar travel. From the expedition's base at McMurdo Sound, Scott with Edmund Wilson and **Ernest Shackleton** made the first extended penetration of Antarctica, painfully reaching 82°S. The journey exposed Scott's shortcomings as a polar explorer – not least his rejection of dogs in favour of man-hauling as his principal means of transport – while his desperate struggle to return to his base with food running short and in deteriorating weather was an experience repeated fatally in his second journey. Nonetheless, Scott returned to England with a burgeoning reputation as a polar explorer. In 1910, he led a second expedition on the *Terra Nova*. This, a larger and more ambitious undertaking, aimed to carry out a substantial body of scientific work as well as reach the Pole. Scott, with a party of four others, following almost exactly the route pioneered by Shackleton in 1908, reached the South Pole on 17 January 1912, one month after the Norwegian party of **Roald Amundsen**. The disappointment of defeat, an insufficient diet, incipient scurvy and the hardships of man-hauling slowed the party on its return, leading to the illness and subsequent death of one of them, Evans. By mid-March, a further expedition member, Lawrence Oates, had also died. Scott and his two surviving companions struggled to within 150 miles of their base before dying, too; their bodies were discovered by other expedition members the following spring. The epic endeavours of Scott and his party and stoic acceptance of their fate, as recounted in Scott's diary, ensured immediate fame and a posthumous knighthood. He is commemorated, too, in the Scott Polar Research Institute in Cambridge. **46**

SENEX, JOHN (*c.*1700–40), surveyor, engraver, publisher and geographer to Queen Anne. He published Seller's *System of Geography*; a *General Atlas* (1708–12); *New General Atlas* (1721) and numerous separately published maps such as Mayo's *Barbados* (1722) and Budgen's *Sussex* (1724). Senex was elected to the Royal Society in 1728. **34**

SERPA PINTO, ALEIXANDRE ALBERTO DE LA ROCHA (1846–1900), Portuguese explorer of Africa. Serpa Pinto joined the Portuguese army in 1864 and served in Mozambique. In 1877 he joined **Capello** and **Ivens** on an expedition, but parted from them to go south along the line of the Zambezi River to the Victoria Falls. From here he continued south to Pretoria, and emerged on the Natal coast in 1879 having completed a north-west–south-east crossing of the continent. In 1889 Serpa Pinto became governor of Mozambique. He attempted to secure the Shire Valley area for Portugal, but a British ultimatum thwarted him (and brought down the Portuguese government) in 1890. **40**

SERRA, FRAY JUNÍPERO (1713–84), Spanish explorer of North America. Born and educated in Majorca, he joined the Franciscans at the age of 16. In 1749 he was sent to serve in the order's Mexican missions. In 1768 he took over the mission to Lower California from the expelled Jesuits, but the following year was sent to Upper California by the secular authorities as part of the effort to prevent Russian infiltration from the north. He founded nine missions, including San Diego, where he narrowly escaped martyrdom. He died at San Carlos mission on 28 August 1784. **17**

SERRÃO, FRANCISCO (d. *c.*1516), Portuguese explorer of the Spice Islands. Documented in Portuguese India from 1505, he took part in the defence of Cananor in 1507 and in the voyage of Diogo Lopes de Sequeira to Malacca of that year. The ship he captained on **Abreu**'s voyage of discovery in 1511 was wrecked and he was taken by pirates to Ternate, becoming the first Portuguese in the Spice Islands and claiming, in his request for rewards, to have equalled the services of **Vasco da Gama** and **Afonso de Albuquerque**. His reports on the islands of the East Indies exaggerated their extent, helping to influence Magellan's belief that the richest of them lay within Spain's sphere of navigation. Serrão died in Ternate, apparently of poison administered by order of the rajah at a time of disaffection with Portugal. **29**

SHACKLETON, SIR ERNEST HENRY (1874–1922), British merchant naval officer and Antarctic explorer. He served as third lieutenant on *Discovery* during **Scott**'s first Antarctic expedition, 1901–4. In 1907–9 he led his own expedition to the Antarctic on the ship *Nimrod*. He and three companions explored towards the South Pole; they discovered the Beardmore Glacier and the great ice sheet of the Polar Plateau, and sledged to within 97 miles of the Pole before being forced to turn back because of depleted supplies. On his second expedition, 1914–17, he took *Endurance* to the Weddell Sea, intending to make the first crossing of Antarctica. The plan failed after *Endurance* was crushed by ice in the Weddell Sea; Shackleton then made an 800-mile open-boat voyage across the Southern Ocean to South Georgia over which he and two others made the first crossing to ensure the rescue of his men. Though none of the expedition's goals was reached, Shackleton, an impetuous misfit in civilian life, showed himself a leader of resource and courage, capable of inspiring great loyalty in his men. In 1921 he set out on his third Antarctic expedition with *Quest*, but on 5 January 1922 he died suddenly of a heart attack at South Georgia. **46**

SILVA PORTO, ANTONIO FRANCISCO DA (1817–90), Portuguese explorer of Africa. Originally from Oporto, Silva Porto became a slave- and ivory-trader from Benguela who explored the interior and tried to extend Portuguese influence. He met **Livingstone** in 1853 near the upper Zambezi, but Livingstone was inclined unfairly to dismiss his achievements as an explorer of the region. In 1890, disillusioned by Portugal's failure to hold its own in the scramble for Africa, he surrounded himself with barrels of gunpowder, wrapped himself in his national flag and applied a match. **38**

SILVEIRA, GONÇALO DA (1521–61), Portuguese Jesuit missionary in India and Africa. The tenth son of an aristocratic family, he was educated for a clerical career. While at the University of Coimbra he joined the fledgling Jesuit Order, attaining priestly orders in 1545. After further studies in Gandía and Rome he continued his ministry in Lisbon until 1556, when he sailed with a group of Jesuits bound for Goa. Until 1559 he served as Jesuit Provincial in India, resigning to join the mission to Monomotapa organized by the bishop of Cochin. Departing in January 1560 he was obliged to leave his companions, ministering to new Christian communities on the way, and arrived alone at the court of the ruler of Monomotapa in Africa on 26 December. Initial success was crowned next month when the ruler and many of his subjects were baptized, but the ruler turned against Silveira, perhaps incited by Muslims at his court, and the Jesuit was put to death, allegedly by garrotting or strangling on the altar of his chapel, on 3 March 1561. **27**

SILVES, DIOGO DE, 15th-century Portuguese explorer of the Azores. He is known only from an annotation on a map by Gabriel Vallseca of 1439, on which he is credited with the exploration of the Azores in 1427. As a result, the archipelago, of which previous recorded knowledge was vague, came to be represented and located on maps with enhanced accuracy. **8**

SINGH, NAIN, 19th-century Indian surveyor. He made the first successful foray into Tibet for the Survey of India in 1866. In a journey of 1,200 miles, made entirely in disguise, he surveyed in secret the whole route from the Nepalese frontier to Lhasa and a long stretch of the Tsangpo (Brahmaputra) River. Even this achievement was dwarfed by his journeys of 1867 and 1874, when he mapped the upper branches of the Indus, surveyed 18,000 square miles of territory around the upper Sutlej, and discovered major hydrographic and topographic features of Tibet. **43**

SIMPSON, THOMAS (1808–40), Scottish fur-trader and explorer. In 1829 he travelled to Canada to enter service with the Hudson's Bay company as protégé of his cousin Sir George Simpson, the company's resident governor-in-chief. In 1837–39 he was second in command to **Peter Dease** on a successful company expedition to explore the Arctic coastline of North America from Point Barrow in the west to the Boothia Peninsula in the east. A few months after his return to southern Canada he was shot and killed in mysterious circumstances; whether he was murdered or committed suicide has never been resolved. **23**

SMITH, JOHN (1580–1631), English explorer of North America. After armed service against France and Turkey, Smith journeyed to Virginia in 1605. Extensive surveys undertaken under his leadership of The James, Rappahannock and Potomac Rivers and to the head of Chesapeake Bay showed that they would not, as hoped, provide access to the 'South Sea' – the Pacific. Smith was elected leader of the English Virginia colony in 1608. He returned to England the following year but between 1610 and 1617 was again in North America. **15, 19**

SMITH, JEDEDIAH STRONG (1799–1831), U.S. fur-trader and explorer. From 1822 until his death at the hands of Comanche Indians along the Cimarron River in 1831 Smith was active as a trail blazer. In 1826–27 he penetrated the American Southwest from Cache Valley in northeastern Utah to the San Gabriel Mission in southern California. He then advanced north through the San Joaquin Valley, before turning east to surmount the Sierras and the Great Basin to the trappers' rendezvous at Bear Lake in northeastern Utah. He was the first white man to accomplish this. He remained in the Far West until 1830. His writings did much to make known the American West to a wider audience. **22**

SOARES DE ALBERGARIA, LOPO (b. *c.*1460), Portuguese navigator and diplomat. He was the son of King João II's chancellor. In 1504, on his first mission to India, he led a fleet of 13 sail against Calicut and Cannanore. He returned in 1505 to Portugal, where he intrigued against **Afonso de Albuquerque**. In 1514 King Manoel appointed him governor of Portuguese India. In order to check Egyptian and Turkish plans to renew attacks on Portuguese positions, he entered the Red Sea in 1517, devastating Muslim shipping, attacking Jedda and firing Zeila. On his return to Portugal in June 1519 he retired to Tôrres Vedras, where he died at an unknown date. 28

SOLÍS, JUAN DIAZ DE (*c.* 1470–1516), Spanish explorer. His origins and early life have been extensively and inconclusively debated. From March 1508 to August 1509, with **Vicente Yánez Pinzón**, he reconnoitred much of the Caribbean coast of Central America. After a spell of imprisonment, perhaps occasioned by explorers' rivalries, he was restored to favour and succeeded **Vespucci** as pilot major in 1512. On 8 October 1515 he departed on a search for a westward route to the Pacific and early in 1516 reached and penetrated the River Plate, where he was killed and eaten. 10, 13

SOTO, HERNANDO DE (*c.* 1499–1542), Spanish explorer and *conquistador*. He fought in Panama with Pedrarias Dávila in 1514, and in Nicaragua with Hernández de Córdoba in 1524, before joining the conquest of Peru at his own expense. He fought intrepidly and grew rich on the booty, but, falling out with his fellow *conquistadores*, he went to Spain in 1535 and obtained a commission to conquer Florida. From Havana, his huge expedition reached Tampa on 25 May 1539, then wandered lost in what are now parts of the southern United States for three years. Soto died on the banks of the Mississippi on 21 May 1542. The survivors eventually escaped in ships they built themselves. 10, 17

SPEKE, JOHN HANNING (1827–64), British Indian Army officer and explorer of Africa, the discoverer of Lake Victoria and the source of the Nile. As a young soldier he served in the Punjab and explored the Himalayas. He subsequently travelled with **Burton**, first to Somaliland, then to East Africa. In 1858 they discovered Lake Tanganyika. In the same year, Speke, travelling without Burton, found Africa's largest lake, which he named Lake Victoria. He was certain this was the principal source of the Nile, although many disputed his claim. The Royal Geographical Society asked him to undertake another expedition to confirm his discovery; this he did in 1860–63 with Grant. Speke, having left Grant in camp nursing an ulcerated leg, reached the source of the Nile in July 1862, having spent several months in the remarkable kingdom of Buganda, which he now revealed to the world. Speke returned to Britain to confront Burton and other doubters with his new discoveries, but before he could do so he accidentally killed himself when shooting game in Somerset. However, his two books are a mine of information. 38, 39, 40

STANLEY, SIR HENRY MORTON (1841–1904), British-American journalist and explorer of Africa. He was born in Wales and raised in a workhouse. He ran away to sea, reaching America where he was adopted and took American citizenship. He fought in the Civil War, first on the Confederate side, then on the Union side. After the war he became a journalist; in 1868 he was sent to Africa by the *New York Herald* to report the Abyssinian campaign, and in 1871 to search for **David Livingstone**, of whom nothing had been heard for many months. He found Livingstone at Ujiji. His achievement, together with his account of his journey, *How I Found Livingstone* (1872), made him world-famous. With Livingstone he then explored the northern end of Lake Tanganyika. Financed by the *Herald* and the *Daily Telegraph*, Stanley returned to Africa in 1874 to accomplish a remarkable feat of exploration. He circumnavigated Lake Victoria, confirmed that **Speke** was right to claim it as the source of the Nile, and then went on to explore more of Lake Tanganyika before going west to Nyangwe on the Lualaba. By sailing down the river he confirmed that it was the Congo, and in August 1877 emerged on the west coast after 999 days in the interior. From 1879 to 1884, often in rivalry with **Brazza**, he worked to establish roads around the cataracts on the lower Congo, thus in effect creating Leopold II's Congo Free State. Between 1886 and 1889, Stanley returned to Africa at the prompting of Leopold to 'rescue' Emin Pasha, the Austrian-born Muslim and governor of the Upper Nile province of Equatoria, then cut off from Egypt by the Mahdists. He went up the Congo and then through the near-impassable Ituri Forest to Lake Albert. Linking up with Emin Pasha, Stanley and his party discovered the Ruwenzori massif and Lake Edward before making the journey to the east coast. The expedition was highly controversial but confirmed Stanley's ruthless effectiveness as a traveller through Africa. 39, 40

STEFÁNSSON, SIGURDUR (d. *c.* 1594/5). Icelandic mapmaker who published an original map of the known northern climes in *Terrarum Hyperboreaum* (1570). His work included the earliest extant map showing the discoveries of the Norsemen (the *Skalholt* map), postulating a great northern continent from which projected Greenland and, farther south, Helluland, Markland and Vinland. His maps do not indicate any possibility of a Northwest Passage, but show the possible existence of a Northeast Passage. 14, 23

STEVENS, ISAAC INGALLS (1818–62), U.S. army officer and public official. When Congress authorized the Pacific Railroad Surveys, Stevens, a West Point graduate who had resigned his commission to become governor of Washington Territory, accepted the appointment to direct the exploration of a northern railroad route. He divided his survey into two sections. Stevens led the one west from Fort Union on the Yellowstone River, while Captain George B. McClennan moved east from Washington Territory. Stevens was the more successful, locating five passes over the Continental Divide and suggesting two possible railroad routes. In his later career, Stevens campaigned against the Northwest Indians, was a territorial delegate to Congress and major-general of volunteers in the Civil War. He was killed at Chantilly, Virginia, in September 1862. 22

STOBNICZA, JAN (active 16th century). Polish cartographer whose world map (1512) indicated the existence of the Americas, but not their continental nature; it was the first map to be printed in Poland. 9

STRELECKI, SIR PAUL (1797–1873), was born near Poznan into Prussian citizenship. Teaching himself the principles of geology, he made field trips in North and South America in the mid-1830s, before seeing Hawaii, the Marquesas, Tahiti and New Zealand on his way to New South Wales, where he arrived in 1839. Undertaking a geological survey of the colony, he travelled widely through the interior, on one southern trip discovering Mount Kosciusko. Subsequently, he reported on the geology of Tasmania, before returning to live in England. In 1845 he published his *Physical Description of New South Wales and Van Diemen's Land*, the first significant account of Australia's geology. 36

STUART, JOHN MCDOUALL (1815–66), Scottish-born explorer of Australia. After being educated at the Scottish Naval and Military Academy, he migrated to South Australia, arriving in January 1839. In 1844, he accompanied **Sturt** on his expedition into central Australia, in the course of which he learned the need to travel in stages and to follow water-holes. Between 1846 and 1858, Stuart practised as a surveyor. In mid-1858 he explored north of Lake Torrens as far as Coober Pedy. Then, between 1859 and 1862, in a series of expeditions sponsored by pastoral interests and the colonial government, he became the first European to cross the continent from south to north, reaching the Indian Ocean to the east of present-day Darwin, on the way discovering the Macdonnell Ranges and Central Mt. Stuart. In 1871–72 the Overland Telegraph Line, linking Australia to Singapore (and thus to Europe), was built largely along his route. 36

STUART, WILLIAM (*c.* 1678–1719), English explorer of Canada. Sent by **James Knight** inland from York Fort in 1715 to report on the activities of French fur-traders, Stuart, a Hudson's Bay Company servant since 1691, made an extended westward journey. His account of the journey is unreliable but he may have reached a point close to Great Slave Lake. Stuart later succumbed to violent bouts of insanity, after one of which, in 1719, he died. 21

STURT, CHARLES (1795–1869), was born in Bengal, where his father was a judge. Educated in England, he joined the army in 1813, and saw duty in the concluding stages of the Napoleonic War. In December 1826 he sailed with his regiment to New South Wales, reaching Sydney in May 1827. Late in 1828, Sturt commenced the first of his exploring expeditions, when he set out to trace the course of the Macquarie River. This led him into a series of detailed investigations of the Murray-Darling system, which culminated in his tracing the Murray to the sea in 1830. After a brief stint as commandant of Norfolk Island, Sturt returned to England, where he published a narrative of his journeys. He returned to New South Wales in 1835, then, in 1838, accepted the position of surveyor-general in South Australia, only to lose it shortly afterwards and to be given a series of lesser ones in compensation. Like **Mitchell**, taken with the idea of a vast inland waterway, Sturt led an expedition into central Australia in 1844. He could scarcely have chosen a worse time and place. For six months, intense heat and drought kept his party confined to Depot Glen, and when they were at last able to move outwards, the sand and stones of the Simpson and Sturt deserts destroyed the illusion of an inland sea. After suffering grievously from scurvy, the party returned to Adelaide in January 1846. Failing eyesight forced Sturt to return to England in 1853. Like **Mitchell's**, Sturt's journeys were important in revealing the geography of inland Australia. 36

SVERDRUP, OTTO (1855–1930), Norwegian explorer of the Arctic. He took part in Nansen's expedition between 1893 and 1896 and later (1898–1902) led an expedition that reached the west coast of Grant Land. He commanded subsequent expeditions, notably that in 1921 to the Ob River area of Siberia. 46

TASMAN, ABEL JANSZOON (1603–59), entered the service of the Dutch East India Company in 1632 or 1633, and by 1634 was mate and then captain of ships trading about the islands of the East Indies. He returned to Europe briefly in 1637–38. In 1639, he captained one of the two ships the Company sent to search for the 'Rica de Oro' and 'Rica de Plata' islands supposed to lie somewhere to the east of Japan. In 1642, Governor-General Anthonio van Diemen sent him to explore New Holland (Australia), and to look for a feasible route across the Pacific to Chile, in the hope of expanding the company's trade. During this voyage, he discovered Van Diemen's Land (Tasmania) and Staten Land (New Zealand). He returned to Batavia via Tonga and the Fiji Islands and north around New Guinea. In 1644, van Diemen sent Tasman on another voyage to see if Australia and New Guinea were joined, and if Australia was one continuous landmass. In this voyage, he came to the western edge of Torres Strait (without finding it), and sailed westwards about the Gulf of Carpentaria, Arnhem Land and the north-west coast, with Visscher charting. In 1647 the Company sent Tasman on a mission to Siam; and in 1648 he commanded a squadron of eight ships sent to capture the Spanish treasure galleon sent annually from Mexico to Manila, an expedition which ended in failure and disgrace. He subsequently set himself up as a merchant in Batavia, and prospered. While Tasman was not an ever-enquiring explorer such as Cook, his voyages added considerably to European knowledge of the Indian and Pacific Oceans, and, especially, of New Holland. 34

TEIXEIRA, PEDRO DE (d. 1641), 17th-century Portuguese explorer of South America. Born in Castaneda, near Coimbra, he was present at the foundation of Pará, where, from 1616, he distinguished himself in warding off Dutch attacks. In 1625 he expelled the Dutch from the Xingu River and the English interlopers from the left bank of the Amazon. In 1626 he led an expedition up the Tapajós and in 1629 recaptured the fortress of Tocujós from pirates. Various efforts to ascend the Amazon from Pará failed in the course of the 1630s, but in 1638 the downriver journey of the Franciscan lay brothers, **Brieva**, Andrés de Toledo and Las Llagas, inspired a further effort, which Teixeira was appointed to lead, returning from Quito the following year to become governor of Pará. In May 1641 he died when about to return to Portugal. 26

TELEKI, SAMUEL (1845–1916), Hungarian explorer of Africa, where (1886–9) he and his party discovered Lakes Rudolf and Stefanie. 39

THESIGER, WILFRED PATRICK (b. 1910), English soldier, writer and explorer of Arabia. Having served and explored in Ethiopia and the Sudan in the 1930s, in 1946–47 and 1947–49 Thesiger twice crossed the Empty Quarter, or Rub' al-Khali, of southern Arabia. His journeys were notable less as feats of exploration – the region had been traversed by other European explorers, notably **Philby** and **Thomas**; moreover Thesiger relied on native guides – than for the finely observed accounts of desert life they inspired him to write, chief among them *Arabian Sands*. 42

THOMAS, BERTRAM SYDNEY (1892–1950), English explorer of Arabia. A former political officer in the Middle East, Thomas made the first crossing of the

Empty Quarter, the Rub' al-Khali, of southern Arabia. Though using native guides and taking probably the easiest route across the Quarter, Thomas was the first to record systematically the topography of the region. He also provided valuable accounts of its inhabitants; winning their co-operation was his principal achievement, according to a later traveller of the Empty Quarter, **Wilfred Thesiger**. 42

THOMPSON, DAVID (1770–1857), English-born Canadian explorer and geographer. Though not generally achnowledged in his lifetime, Thompson was among the most influential 19th-century explorers of Canada, largely as a result of his painstaking survey work and remarkably detailed maps. From 1784 to 1797 Thompson worked for the Hudson's Bay Company as a fur-trader, perfecting largely self-taught skills in navigation and position-fixing. From 1797, when he joined the North West Company, he travelled down the Missouri and surveyed around the northern reaches of the Mississippi. From 1807, he turned his attentions to the regions west of the Rocky Mountains, travelling to the source of the Columbia River; by 1811 he had travelled the length of the river to the Pacific. The map he made of the region was the most detailed and accurate available for much of the 19th century. From 1816 to 1826 he served with the U.S.–Canadian boundary commission. 21, 22

THOMSON, JOSEPH (1858–95), Scottish explorer and cartographer of Africa. The maps he published after his first expedition showed Lake Tanganyika and the relationship of the Great Rift Valley lakes and their drainage system. In 1882–83 he travelled through, and mapped, Masailand, Kenya and Uganda. In 1885 he explored much of northern Nigeria, securing British interests there (in the face of German competition) by concluding treaties with native chiefdoms, and in 1890 he explored the Zambezi river, similarly gaining a number of concessions for the British South Africa Company. Among his memoirs are *To the Central African Lakes and Back* (1881) and *Through Masai Land* (1887). 39

THORNE, ROBERT (d. 1527). A Bristol merchant and member of an Anglo-Azorean syndicate formed in 1501 to promote exploration of the North Atlantic, who played a part as publicist and propagandist in the promotion of English seafaring, particularly recommending the search for short routes to the Orient by the presumed Northeast and Northwest Passages, and even by way of the North Pole. He died in 1527 in Seville, where he helped to organize backing for the voyage to the River Plate of **Sebastian Cabot**. 32

TOMISON, WILLIAM (c. 1739–1829), Scottish fur trader and explorer. In 1760 he became a labourer with the Hudson's Bay Company, stationed at York Fort and Fort Severn. On two occasions (1767, 1769) he was sent to join the Indians inland to promote the fur trade. On the first expedition he stayed on the eastern shore of Lake Winnipeg; on the second he travelled south and west of Lake Manitoba. Tomison was now in high favour with the company and he prospered. For the next six years he remained at Fort Severn, implementing the committee's new policy of building company posts near to those of the rival Canadian traders. He opened direct trade links with Indians to the west and by 1786 had secured an almost exclusive trade arrangement with them. He was then promoted chief at York Fort and thereafter made several return visits to Great Britain. But his later years in Canada were marred by acrimony, largely because of his difficult personality. He returned to Great Britain in 1799 but, finding himself averse to retirement, went back to Canada for one further term; in 1803 he retired. He returned to Canada again, however, in 1806, where he remained for four years in a variety of minor posts. In 1810 he returned to the Orkneys. 21

TORRES, LUIS VÁEZ DE (d. c.1615), Spanish navigator. Little is known of his life, save that he discovered the strait that is named after him between Australia and New Guinea, and that he proved the latter to be an island. 33

TOSCANELLI, PAOLO DAL POZZO (1397–1482), Italian physician. Toscanelli was well regarded in his day as an astronomer and geographer. His only surviving work is on the intervals of Halley's comet. He was consulted by the Duke of Ferrara as an authority on Ptolemy. A strong tradition attributes the inception of **Columbus**'s plan to his influence. In a letter of 1474, of which a copy survives in Columbus's hand, Toscanelli projected a westward passage to Asia. 9

TOVAR, PEDRO DE His father, Fernando, was steward of the household of Juana, the titular queen of Spain, of suspect sanity, who lived in seclusion. He can therefore be presumed to have had a courtly upbringing. In New Spain, where he settled from before 1540, he enjoyed gentlemanly status and was made ensign-bearer in the expedition to Quivira of **Francisco Vásquez de Coronado**, who sent him from Cíbola to explore Tusayan in north-east Arizona. His month-long mission gathered reports of wealthy Indian communities farther afield, which inspired the journey of **López de Cárdenas**, during which Tovar was wounded. 17

TSYBIKOV, GOMBOZHAB (1873–1930), Russian scholar and traveller in Tibet. Born in Buryatia, Tsybikov joined the Oriental Department of St. Petersburg University in 1895. In 1899 he was proposed by the university to the Russian Imperial Geographical Society as a suitable candidate to travel to Tibet. Though motivated in part by the need to counter successful British attempts to penetrate Tibet, the purpose of the journey, at least for Tsybikov, seems to have been as much scholarly as political. In the guise of a Buddhist pilgrim, Tsybikov set off in late November 1899 from Urga in Mongolia. After reaching Lhasa the following year, in the process joining the handful of those who successfully journeyed to the forbidden land, Tsybikov spent almost two years in Tibet, visiting all the principal monasteries in and around Lhasa and collating extensive information on Tibetan religious institutions and history. This, much of it today held at the Institute of Oriental Studies in Leningrad University, made a major contribution to Tibetan studies in Russia and the wider Western world. Tsybikov subsequently pursued his academic career at Vladivostok and Irkutsk universities until his death in 1930. 44

TUCKEY, JAMES K. (1776–1816). A Royal Navy commander who fought in the Napoleonic wars and was a prisoner in France for ten years, in 1816 Tuckey was chosen to lead an expedition to explore the Congo river from its mouth, for the first time using a steamboat in Africa. The breakdown of the steamboat, the rapids of the lower Congo and malaria led to the failure of the expedition and Tuckey's own death, though he did leave a short account of his experiences. 40

URDANETA, ANDRES DE (1498–1568), Spanish navigator of the Pacific. He was both a soldier (he fought for Charles V in Italy and Germany) and, from 1553, a member of the Augustinian Order. Urdaneta took part in **Loaisa**'s voyage to the Moluccas, where he served until 1536. Having transferred to Mexico, via Spain, he refused command of a transpacific expedition and embraced religion, but was summoned from the cloister in 1559 to guide a new attempt. When the fleet at last sailed in 1564, it was intended to conquer and colonize the Philippines, much to Urdaneta's dismay, as he hoped for a voyage to New Guinea. His most important task – the discovery of a viable route across the Pacific – was accomplished between June and October 1565. After returning to Spain to report, he was refused permission to found a mission in the Philippines, owing to his advanced age. He died in the Augustinian house in Mexico City. 33

USHAKOV, GEORGIY ALEKSEYEVICH (1901–63), Russian explorer. He was born and raised in the Siberian far east. In 1926–29 he was the first head of a polar research station on Ostrov Vrangelya (Wrangel Island) in the Russian Arctic. His best-known achievement was as leader of a four-man expedition that explored and mapped the Russian Arctic archipelago of Severnaya Zemlya in 1930–32. From 1932, he was assistant director of the Northern Sea Route administration. In 1935, he led a high-latitude expedition on the icebreaker *Sadko*, during which a small island was discovered in the northern Kara Sea and named Ostrov Ushakova in his honour. 46

USODIMARE, ANTONIO or **ANTONIOTTO DI**, 15th-century Italian navigator. Of a far-flung Genoese trading family he took service with **Henry the Navigator** in the mid-1450s and made two recorded voyages which extended the limits of navigation under sail along the west coast of Africa and explored the lower reaches of the Rivers Senegal and Gambia. His discovery of the Cape Verde Islands – or, at least, of some of them – is disputed on behalf of **Diogo Gomes**. His voyages were recorded by **Alvise da Cà da Mosto**. 12

VACA, CABEZA DE *see* **Cabeza de Vaca**.

VADILLO, JUAN, 16th-century Spanish governor in the New World. Early in the 1530s he was a magistrate in Santo Domingo, where he was instrumental in suppressing native rebellions and conducting a census. Transferred to Santa Marta, he encouraged exploration southwards towards Colombia and Peru. 25

VALDIVIA, PEDRO DE (1497–1553), Spanish *conquistador*. He served in the Spanish army in Italy before going to the New World and playing an important part in the conquest of Venezuela, joining **Francisco Pizarro** in Peru by 1535. He began the conquest and colonization of Chile in 1548. He extended his conquests to beyond the River Biobio, initiated exploration beyond the Andes and founded six towns, but fell fighting the indomitable Araucano Indians of the extreme south on Christmas Day 1553. 24

VALSECA, GABRIEL (active 1439–1447), Majorcan portolan chartmaker. Four examples of his work survive, three of which were made in Majorca. The fourth (of which only a fragment remains), presumably also made in Majorca, shows early Portuguese voyages along the north-west coast of Africa. The 1439 chart is an early example of the transformation of inter-section points in the network of rhumb-lines drawn on a chart into elaborate compass roses. The chart is preserved at the Biblioteca de Catalunya in Barcelona. 8

VANCOUVER, GEORGE (c. 1750–98), English navigator and surveyor of the Pacific. Having accompanied **Captain Cook** on his second and third voyages to the Pacific, and after service in the West Indies, Vancouver, a Royal Navy officer, was given command of an expedition to the Pacific in 1791. Its purpose was both to do further survey work along the north-west coast of America and to take possession of the region around Nootka Sound for Britain. After preliminary surveys along the coasts of New Zealand and Australia, Vancouver arrived off the North American coast in 1792 having sailed via Tahiti and Hawaii. Three years of painstaking surveys ensued. Though he died before the results of his work were published in 1798, his efforts did much to establish British claims to the region, largely at the expense of Spain. Vancouver Island, which Vancouver circumnavigated, is named after him. 20, 35

VARTHEMA, LODOVICO (d. 1517). Born probably in Bologna or Rome, perhaps in the late 1460s, he may have been a soldier in his youth in the papal forces. In 1500 he left Venice and, passing through a series of Levantine ports, established himself in Damascus in 1502 in order to learn Arabic. He joined a caravan bound for Mecca, becoming the first recorded Christian visitor. From Mecca, he travelled on with pilgrims returning to Persia but in Aden was seized as a Christian spy. Imprisoned in Raudha, he exerted his charm with the sultan's wife to obtain his release. He made his way to India, where he served with the Portuguese. In 1508 he was in Lisbon and later returned to Rome where he died in June 1517. His *Itinerary*, which though corroborated in many details has something of the flavour of a picaresque novel, contains the first accounts of Mecca and of Aden by a Christian eye-witness. 42

VÁZQUEZ DE AYLLÓN, LUIS or **LUCAS** (d.c.1528), Spanish *conquistador*. Of good family in Toledo, with legal training behind him, he was appointed a magistrate in Santo Domingo in 1511. He accompanied the expedition in pursuit of **Cortés**, under **Pánfilo de Narváez**, from whom he parted on terms of enmity. In 1521, he took part in a slaving expedition which touched the North American coast, probably in North Carolina. Fired with enthusiasm, he went to Spain to obtain a commission to conquer the territory. The terms of the contract he obtained on 12 June 1523 committed him to search for a strait to the Pacific Ocean and establish a colony. He set off with 600 potential settlers in July 1526, and after the wreck of his flagship founded San Miguel de Gualdape, probably on the Georgian or South Carolina coast. With most of his fellow-settlers Vázquez de Ayllón died of disease or wounds sustained fighting Indians. The 150 survivors fled to Santo Domingo. 15

Vélez de Mendoza, Alonso, 16th-century Spanish navigator. An impecunious nobleman, knight of the Order of Santiago, he collaborated with the **Guerra** brothers of Triana to raise finance for a voyage to the New World in two caravels in 1500. Commissioned on 5 June of that year, the expedition sailed from Seville on 18 August. Taking a route farther south than that pioneered by **Christopher Columbus** on his third Atlantic crossing, he went via São Tiago in the Cape Verde Islands and reached the Brazilian coast probably not far south of the landfall of **Vicente Yánez Pinzón**. He continued south, probably discovering the Rio de San Francisco, which he called Rio de Cervatos, but found little that was commercially exploitable apart from logwood and unsatisfactory slaves. 13

Veniard, Bourgmond de *see* **Bourgmond, Veniard de**.

Vera, Gaspar de, 17th-century Spanish missionary in South America. A Franciscan in the Huallaga valley in 1643, he made a journey with two colleagues, Juan Cabezas and the lay brother Agustín de Mendía, of over 23 days to the lands of the Comanahua Indians to open communications between the mission country on the western slopes of the Andes and the upper Amazon. 26

Verazzano, Giovanni da (*c.*1480–*c.*1527), Italian mariner and explorer of the New World. Commissioned by François I of France to explore the unknown regions between Newfoundland and Florida with the hope of finding a sea passage between them to 'the happy shores of Cathay', in 1524 Verazzano sailed north from approximately Cape Fear to Maine, in the process revealing the continuous eastern coastline of North America. Verazzano nonetheless remained convinced he had found an easy passage to the East, having persuaded himself that the waters of Pamlico Sound, seen by him across the Carolina Outer Banks, were the Pacific. Chiefly through the map produced by his brother Gerolomo, which portrayed North America narrowing dramatically at the latitude of present-day South Carolina, this mistaken view was widely accepted by many in Europe for almost 100 years. The voyage was notable also for revealing what is now New York harbour. Verazzano made a further voyage to the New World in 1526 or 1527, but was killed by natives in the Caribbean. 15

Verendrye, Pierre Gaultier de Varennes, Sieur de la *see* **La Verendrye**.

Vesconti, Pietro (active 1311–27) of Genoa. Vesconti drew portolan charts from 1311 to 1327, the *Carta nautica* of 1311 being the oldest extant example. He is thought to have made maps for Sanudo in *c.*1320. 7

Vespucci, Amerigo (1454–1512), Florentine navigator after whom America is named. A notary's son with good social connections, Vespucci became an agent of the Medici bank in 1479 and, towards the end of 1491, was sent to Seville where he became a business associate and friend of **Columbus**. His first recorded transatlantic voyage in his own right was made with **Alonso de Ojeda** in 1499–1500, when in an excursion of his own he saw the mouth of the Amazon. Vespucci's next voyage was made in Portuguese service, under **Gonzalo Coelho**, leaving Lisbon on 13 May 1501. The purpose was to explore further the coast of Brazil and to find a passage farther south. It is not known how far it reached: an account under Vespucci's name claimed the expedition sailed beyond 50°S. The narratives, attributed to Vespucci, of these and other unverified voyages so impressed **Martin Waldseemüller** that in 1507 he proposed that the New World be called 'America'. By 1513, when Waldseemüller revised his view, the name had become ineradicable. In 1508, Vespucci was appointed pilot major – effectively, chief examiner of pilots – for Spain's New World trade. He held the position until his death in Seville in 1512. 9, 10, 13

Viele, Aernout, or Arnout, Cornelissen, (1640–*c.*1704). Born in New Amsterdam, he was established in Albany by 1659. In 1660 he signed a petition against white traders in Indian country. His skill in Indian languages, especially those of the Iroquois, among whom he lived at intervals, made him sought after as an interpreter from 1682. From 1691 until at least 1699 he was often at Quondaga Castle, playing an instrumental role in the government's efforts to preserve the peace of the frontier of New York State. Between 1692 and 1694 he led an expedition north of the Great Lakes into the Ottawa country and on to the Upper Ohio and Indiana. After 1704 his name disappears from the registers of the Dutch congregation in Albany. 19

Villagra, Francisco de (1511–63), Spanish *conquistador*. After service in Tunis and Peru he joined **Valdivia**'s expedition to Chile in 1540, becoming deputy governor by Valdivia's choice in 1547. He explored the Cuyo region after a visit to Peru in 1551 and effectively replaced Valdivia in command on the latter's death in 1553. His lack of success in the war in the south against the indomitable Araucanos Indians undermined his authority, and in 1557 he was arrested and expelled by the incoming governor, **García Hurtado de Mendoza**. He retained, however, the loyalty of many of Valdivia's old comrades and was appointed to take over the government again between 1561 and 1563. He renewed the war against the Araucanos with vigour, losing his son, Pedro, in the campaign. He died in office, to be succeeded by his cousin, also called Pedro. 24

Villagra, Pedro de (b. *c.*1508–77), Spanish *conquistador*. Born in Mombeltrán in León, he went to seek his fortune in Peru in 1537. He joined the expedition to Chile of **Pedro de Valdivia** and became garrison commander in Imperial by 1555. In 1563 he succeeded his cousin Francisco as governor of Chile. 24

Villalobos, Ruy López de (d. 1546). Having trained in law, he was in Mexico by 1540 when he was given a rôle in **Antonio de Mendoza**'s plans for Pacific exploration. The death of **Pedro de Alvarado**, who had overall responsibility, delayed the expedition, but a fleet under Villalobos sailed from Navidad on 1 November 1542, via the Revillagigedo Islands, reaching the Marshall Islands in January 1543, and Mindanao on 2 February. Villalobos gave the name of 'Filippina' to the island of Leyte – a name that came to be extended to the entire Philippine archipelago. He reached the Moluccas in April 1544 but, after heroic efforts, found the Portuguese occupants too well entrenched, and left Ternate in February 1546. A reconnaissance party under Iñigo Ortiz de Retes made one unsuccessful attempt to find a way back to New Spain between May and October 1545, by which point Villalobos was demoralized and exhausted. He died in Amboina shortly after beginning an attempt of his own, leaving the survivors of his expedition to depend on Portuguese shipping by way of the Indian Ocean for their ultimate repatriation. 33

Vivaldi, Ugolino and **Guido**, 13th-century Genoese merchants. They left Genoa in May 1291 in two ships to search for a route to India 'through the ocean', the first European explorers to attempt this. Their unknown fate attracted expeditions in search of them and encouraged European navigation to Africa. 8, 12

Vizcaíno, Sebastián 16th-/17th-century Spanish navigator. Having served in the occupation of Portugal (1580), he sailed regularly on the Manila treasure galleon across the Pacific from 1586. In 1596 he was ordered to renew the search for safe harbours in northerly latitudes on the Pacific coast of North America. His first expedition was distracted by an attempt to inaugurate a pearl-fishery in the Gulf of California. Campaigns against pirates prevented him from resuming the task until 1602–3, when he sailed from Acapulco as far as about 43°N, making a detailed survey of the coast and identifying a useful harbour at Monterey. After serving as a magistrate in Tehuantepec, from where, in 1608, he opened a new and improved route to Coatzacoalcos, he was commissioned in 1611 to search the north Pacific for the fabled islands of Rica de Oro and Rica de Plata, and to open diplomatic contacts with Japan. Departing on 22 March, he reached Japan on 10 June. He never established cordial relations with his hosts and, after building a new ship, he left on 27 October 1612, arriving back at Zacatula early the following year. He was recorded for the last time in action against pirates off Acapulco in 1616. 20

Waldseemüller, Martin (1470–1521), professor of geography at St. Dié in Lorraine. In his *Cosmographiae introductio*, the essay accompanying his new edition of **Ptolemy** in 1513, he discussed the adoption of **Amerigo Vespucci**'s name rather than that of **Columbus** for South America. This was later used for the northern continent as well. Adopting the appellation on his large world map of 1507, he saw 'no reason why we should not call this ... America after the sagacious discoverer Americus'. However, on the map of America in the 1513 edition of Ptolemy, Waldseemüller reverts to the idea that his information was supplied from the maps of 'the Admiral' (Columbus). The 1513 edition was the most influential edition of Ptolemy during the first 40 or so years of the 16th century. 9, 13

Wallace, Alfred Russell (1823–1913), English naturalist. After travelling in the Amazon Basin from 1848 to 1852, in 1854, after losing all his specimens from the Amazon and his notes, Wallace journeyed to the Far East, spending the next eight years in the Malay Archipelago. In 1858, he first formulated a belief in natural selection; his writings on the subject profoundly influenced Charles Darwin at the moment that Darwin was himself formulating similar theories, and hastened the publication in 1859 of Darwin's *Origin of Species*. Wallace's voluminous writings and huge collection were similarly crucial in the formation of many other aspects of modern zoology. The Wallace Line in the Malay Archipelago, a division between faunas, is named after him. 45

Warburton, Peter (1813–89), was born in Cheshire, England and migrated to Australia in 1853, finding work in Adelaide. In 1858, he explored north to Lake Torrens and Lake Eyre; and in 1866, he went north of Lake Eyre into what is now southern Queensland. In 1872, he made a harrowing journey from Alice Springs through the Great Sandy Desert to the west coast. 36

Wedge, John Helder (1793–1872) was born in England, where he trained as a surveyor. In 1824 he migrated to Tasmania. In the next dozen years, he explored the island's interior extensively; in 1825 he was associated with John Batman in the opening of the Port Phillip district (Victoria), where he took up land. 36

Wentworth, William Charles (1790–1872) was seemingly born either at Sydney or en route to Norfolk Island, where his father was for a time assistant surgeon. After being educated in England, he returned to the colony, where he helped work his father's estates on the Cumberland Plain to the west of Sydney. In 1813, when sheep and cattle numbers and drought had made it imperative that pastoralists locate new grazing areas, Wentworth, **Gregory Blaxland** and **William Lawson** succeeded in finding a route over the Blue Mountains, thus opening the way for the colony's westward expansion. Wentworth then studied law in England, returning to the colony in 1824, where he founded the *Australian* newspaper, and was active in politics, supporting the causes of the emancipists and the native-born, and arguing for representative government. From the mid-1850s, he lived in England, apart from a period back in New South Wales in 1861–62. His 1819 account of the colony was among the first to praise the society emerging there. 36

Weyprecht, Karl (1838–87). An Austrian army officer, he was deputed in 1871 with **Julius von Payer** to test **August Petermann**'s theory of an ice-free route to the North Pole. In 1872 he started north from Cape Nassau on Novaya Zemlya aboard the reinforced vessel *Tegethoff*, but soon became trapped in ice and drifted for nearly a year before encountering Franz Josef Land, where the expedition remained until April 1874. Weyprecht then attempted to return by boat, from which he was rescued by a Russian trawler in August. In 1882 he helped to co-ordinate the first International Polar Year. 46

Wheeler, George Montague (1842–1905), U.S. army officer and explorer. Wheeler, who graduated from West Point in 1866, was ordered to duties in California. By 1868, these included survey activities in the American Southwest. In 1869 he surveyed the region east of the Sierras searching for a feasible military route from Oregon south to Arizona. When he submitted his report, Wheeler suggested the creation within the War Department of an organization that would survey, for military purposes, the entire American West. He was summoned to Washington, where his suggestion received favourable attention. In 1871 Wheeler was in the field with his own organization: the United States Geographical Surveys West of the One-Hundredth Meridian. Wheeler hired scientists and artists, and valuable scientific work was undertaken. Much of the mapping, however, was poor. Competing with the simultaneous surveys of **Hayden**, Wheeler's men found themselves drawn into rivalry with their civilian counterparts, each contesting the other's territories. When the United States Geological Survey was created in 1879, the Wheeler Survey was vigorously criticized by scientists. Yet though Wheeler's was the weakest of the four surveys, its work over thousands of square miles of the arid West remains impressive. 22

WHIPPLE, AMIEL WEEKS (*c*.1816–63), U.S. army officer and explorer. Whipple graduated from West Point in 1841 and shortly thereafter joined the Topographical Engineers. From 1849 to 1853 he was with the U.S.–Mexican boundary commission. He was then assigned to run a railroad survey along the 35th Parallel. Beginning at Fort Smith, Arkansas, in July 1853, Whipple's route followed the Canadian River, ran west to the Zuni villages, down the Bill Williams Fork to the Colorado, up to Needles and across the Mojave Desert to San Bernadino, California. It is now recognized as having been the most feasible route to the Pacific at the time. Whipple continued his topographical duties until the Civil War, when, as a major-general, he was mortally wounded at Chancellorsville and died on 7 May 1863. 22

WILKES, CHARLES (1798–1877), U.S. naval officer and explorer. Wilkes entered the U.S. Navy in 1818, and saw service in the Mediterranean and the Pacific before being appointed head of the Depot of Charts and Instruments in 1834. In 1838–42, he was lieutenant commanding the United States Exploring Expedition which, among other achievements in the southern oceans, discovered parts of Wilkes Land, Antarctica. On his return home, Wilkes was court-martialled and reprimanded for illegally punishing some of his men. He later served with distinction in the American Civil War, and retired in 1866 with the rank of rear-admiral. 46

WILLIAM OF RUBRUCK (*c*.1212–95), explorer of Central Asia and Franciscan friar. He accompanied Louis IX's crusade in 1248, and attempted a mission to the Mongols in 1253–55. His hosts insisted on treating him as an ambassador from Louis but he was able to debate with Nestorians at the Mongol Court, to confront the Great Khan Möngke face to face, to visit Karakorum in person and to make detailed geographical and ethnographic observations, which were unsurpassed by subsequent travellers, including **Marco Polo**, for 600 years. 31

WILLIAMSON, ROBERT STOCKTON (1824–82), U.S. army officer and explorer. It fell to Williamson, who graduated from West Point in 1848, to search out feasible railroad passes across the southern Sierras for the Pacific Railroad Surveys. No such passes were found, forcing him to recommend railroad routes using Cajon or San Gorgonio passes to Los Angeles. This left out San Diego. Even today the railroad to that city has to dip briefly into Mexico. He also worked with Lieutenant **Henry Abbot** in surveying two routes from California to Oregon. 22

WILLOUGHBY, SIR HUGH (d.1554), British military officer and explorer. He was a son of Sir Henry Willoughby of Middleton, from whom he inherited extensive estates. He was knighted for his role in the military campaign in Scotland of 1544; subsequently he had a commission on the Scottish border. In 1553 he was appointed captain general of a fleet of three ships fitted out by London merchants to seek a Northeast Passage. One of the ships, commanded by **Richard Chancellor**, reached the White Sea. The other two, under Willoughby, were forced to winter on the coast of Lapland, where the entire company died, reportedly of cold or starvation, but possibly of carbon monoxide poisoning caused by attempts to heat the ships. 32

WILLS, WILLIAM (1834–61), was born in Devon, England, and reached Victoria in 1853. He joined the expedition being led by **Burke** to cross Australia from south to north in 1860, being promoted to second in command when one of the original members of the expedition, Landells, left it. After accompanying Burke to the Gulf of Carpentaria, he died at the base camp on Cooper's Creek *c*.29 June 1861. 36

WINSLOW, EDWARD (1595–1655). Born in Worcestershire, he was a prosperous printer of Leyden who joined the Pilgrim Fathers in 1620. He helped make the colony's first treaty with the Indians in 1621 and wrote the first published account of the 'plantation', which appeared in 1622. In 1623 he introduced a bull and heifers to Massachusetts, and during a visit to England in 1625 defended the colony against its detractors and raised loans in its support. From 1625 to 1632 he was instrumental in setting up the trading posts that made the Plymouth settlement prosperous, exploiting parts of Maine and Connecticut in the process. From 1629 he served as the colony's agent, making several trips to England, where his Puritan zeal caused him to be briefly imprisoned in 1634 for illicit preaching. Meanwhile, and for many years subsequently, he was prominent in the government of Massachusetts. From 1646 his work on the colony's behalf kept him in England, until 1654, when Cromwell appointed him a commissioner of the abortive expeditionary force to Hispaniola, which seized Jamaica instead. He died on the voyage home, on 8 May 1655. 19

WOOD, ABRAHAM, 17th-century explorer of North America. He has been identified as the indentured servant of that name who first came to Virginia in 1620. By 1638, at least, he seems to have been a freeman and landowner. In 1644 he represented Henrico County in the Virginia assembly and sat for Charles City in 1654 and 1656, when he served as a militia colonel in the Indian wars. His career as an explorer centred on his command at Fort Henry (at present-day Petersburg), where he operated a thriving trading establishment. In 1650 he accompanied **Edward Bland** on his expedition to Occaneechee Island, and from 1671 organized a series of expeditions in search of the 'South Sea' that revealed the vastness of North America. He was still alive in March 1680, when he was conducting negotiations with hostile Indians. 19

WOODWARD, HENRY (d. *c*.1686), 17th-century explorer of North America. In 1664 he joined the Carolina settlement begun near Cape Fear. In 1666 he accompanied Robert Sandford to Port Royal, where he remained among the Indians with an extensive grant as 'tenant at will' of the Lords Proprietors of Carolina. Captured by Spaniards, he professed Catholicism and was employed as a surgeon in San Agustín. In 1668, however, he escaped and soon became the leading figure in the internal exploration of the Carolinas, travelling, for instance, in 1674 alone along the Savannah River to the warlike Westo Indians. Hostilities between the Westo and the settlers in 1677 caused him to remove to England, where the Proprietors commissioned him to explore beyond the Savannah. In 1685 he opened communications between the Charleston colony and the Lower Creek Indians, creating a buffer against Spanish expansion; but the journey broke his health and he probably died soon after his return in 1686. 19

WYTFLIET, CORNELIS VAN (d. 1597), geographer and secretary to the Council of Brabant. He is best known for his *Descriptionis Ptolemaicae augmentum*, published at Louvain in 1597. This was the first atlas devoted exclusively to the Americas, despite the mention of the name of **Ptolemy** in the title. Wytfliet's work is as important in the study of the history of the cartography of the New World as Ptolemy's maps are in the study of the Old World. 17

YERMAK, TIMOFEYEVICH (d. 1585), Russian cossack. Yermak was leader of a band that lived by plundering on the Volga River, until they were driven out by government forces. In 1581, probably at the instigation of the powerful merchant family of Stroganov, he led a force of over 800 men over the central Urals in a campaign against the Tartar khanate ruled by Kuchum. After overthrowing Kuchum, he established the first Russian stronghold in Siberia in the town of Sibir' on the Irtysh River. Kuchum's subjects fought back, and in 1585 Yermak was killed and his men retreated. Although Yermak had failed, other Russians renewed his campaign in 1585, and the systematic conquest of Siberia followed soon after. 32

YOUNGHUSBAND, FRANCIS (1863–1942). An Indian Army cavalry officer addicted to exploration, he made his first major expedition in 1887 across the Gobi Desert from Peking to Kashgar via Kumul in the Karlik Tagh mountains, accompanied only by a cook and an interpreter. On his way to India he investigated the hydrography of the Karakoram range, discovering the Mutagh Pass. In following years he made surveying expeditions to Hunza and the Pamirs. In 1904 he commanded the military expedition to Lhasa that reversed the encroachments of Russian influence in Tibet. The opportunity was taken to extend the area surveyed by **Nain Singh** along the Tsangpo (Brahmaputra) River. 44

INDEX OF PLACE NAMES

There has necessarily been compromise in the choice and spelling of geographical names in this Atlas. To use exclusively contemporary forms would confuse the reader and hamper geographical understanding; to use exclusively modern names and spellings would offer no help to the reader of contemporary explorers' accounts and would not properly portray the continuing sense of exploration and discovery which the Atlas reflects. To this end, the following general principles have been applied:-

1. In order to convey this sense of discovery some countries *are* given their early names on appropriate maps, e.g. Cathay (China), Cipangu (Japan), New France (Quebec), New Holland (Australia), New Spain (Mexico).

2. The names of all other countries, major features and inhabited places are spelled in accordance with English conventional usage of about 1900, thus avoiding the inevitably anachronistic ring of some modern names, e.g. Siam (not Thailand), Formosa (not Taiwan), New Hebrides (not Vanuatu), Ladrone Islands (not Marianas).

3. For lesser places and features, particularly in the New World and the Pacific, the names first given by their discoverers are shown, followed by the modern name in brackets, e.g. Espiritu Santo (Tampa), Conigi (Terceira), Dradate (Port Sudan), Dampier Island (Karkar).

4. Other early names which are peripheral to the main story are shown in brackets following the English conventional name, e.g. Chinese names in India and Africa.

The spelling of present-day names follows that found in *The Times Atlas of the World* though in the interests of simplicity there has been a general omission of diacritics in spellings derived by transliteration from non-Roman scripts, e.g. we use *Sana* rather than *Ṣanʿāʾ*.

The index includes every name shown on the maps other than those added to the periphery for locational purposes. Following the main entry name the modern name or spelling, if different, is given in brackets, as are any variant forms that may be pertinent. All such alternative names are cross-referenced in the index.

Places are located generally by reference to the country in which they lie or to island groups or sea areas, narrowed down as necessary by location as *E* (east), *N* (north), *C* (central), etc. The modern political boundaries of most of Africa being particularly inappropriate in the context of early exploration, the location of places there is given simply as *C Africa*, *NE Africa*, *W Africa*, etc.

Reference is to the page on which the relevant map will be found, unless the place or subject is dealt with in a chapter as a whole, when the reference will be to the pages of that chapter. Where there are two or more maps on a page, reference is to the page/map number, e.g. 229/2. Legendary and fabled lands, named within quotations marks (e.g. 'El Dorado'), are of their nature difficult to show on maps and the reference in these cases is to the page where the name occurs in the text.

The following abbreviations are used:

a/c	also called	*Jap.*	Japanese
Afr.	Afrikaans	*mod.*	modern
Amh.	Amharic	*Mong.*	Mongolian
anc.	ancient	*N*	North(ern)
Ar.	Arabic	*n/c*	now called
a/s	also spelled	*Nor.*	Norwegian
C	Central	*n/s*	now spelled
Chin.	Chinese	*Per.*	Persian
Dan.	Danish	*Port.*	Portuguese
E	East(ern)	*Russ.*	Russian
Eng.	English	*S*	South(ern)
f/c	formerly called	*s/c*	sometimes called
Fr.	French	*Som.*	Somali
f/s	formerly spelled	*Sp.*	Spanish
Ger.	German	*Viet.*	Vietnamese
Ind.	Indian	*W*	West(ern)
It.	Italian		

Glossary of geographical terms occurring in names in the index:

-baai	*(Afr.)*	bay
Baie	*(Fr.)*	bay
Bahía	*(Sp.)*	bay
Baía	*(Port.)*	bay
Bugt	*(Dan.)*	bay
Cabo	*(Sp., Port.)*	cape
Cap	*(Fr.)*	cape
-gunto	*(Jap.)*	archipelago
Daryacheh	*(Per.)*	lake
Hayk'	*(Amh.)*	lake
Île(s)	*(Fr.)*	island(s)
Isla(s)	*(Sp., Port.)*	island(s)
Kyst	*(Nor.)*	coast
Lago	*(Sp., Port.)*	lake
Monte	*(Sp., Port.)*	mountain
More	*(Russ.)*	sea
Mys	*(Russ.)*	cape
Ostrov(a)	*(Russ.)*	island(s)
Ozero	*(Russ.)*	lake
Poluostrov	*(Russ.)*	peninsula
Ponta	*(Port.)*	point
Proliv	*(Russ.)*	strait
Punta	*(Sp.)*	point
Raas	*(Som.)*	cape
Ras	*(Ar.)*	cape
-retto	*(Jap.)*	chain of islands
Rio	*(Port.)*	river
Río	*(Sp.)*	river
Serra	*(Port.)*	mountains
Serranía	*(Sp.)*	mountains
Shamo	*(Chin.)*	desert
Shan	*(Chin.)*	mountain
Sierra	*(Sp.)*	mountains
Tanjung	*(Ind.)*	cape
Zaliv	*(Russ.)*	bay
Zemlya	*(Russ.)*	land

Sarmiento 123
CHATTAHOOCHEE RIVER *SE USA* Arthur 99
CHELYUSKIN, CAPE *N Siberia* Great Northern Expedition 159; Nordenskiöld 160
CHEN-LA *see* CAMBODIA
CHEPO *Panama 52/*
CHESAPEAKE BAY *NE USA* Sebastian Cabot 78; Newport 98
CHESTERFIELD INLET *N Canada* Christopher 108; Rae 114/1
CHIAHA *SE USA* de Soto 55/6, 90
CHIANG KHAN *N Siam* Mekong River Expedition 225
CHICAMA *Panama* F. Pizarro 119
CHICASA *SE USA* de Soto 55/6
CHICHILTICALE *NW Mexico* Coronado 90
CHICKAHOMINY RIVER *E USA* John Smith 98
CHICOANA *NW Argentina* Rojas 121
CHIEN-SHUI *SW China* Mekong River Expedition 225
CHIHUAHUA *N Mexico* Espejo 90; Rubí, La Fora and de Rivera 93; Pike 110
CHIH-TI-CHIANG *see* CHITTAGONG
CHIKUGO *W Japan* early province 26
CHIKUZEN *W Japan* early province 26
CHILAPA *Guatemala* Cortés 54/5
CHILE Inca empire 35; early Spanish exploration 121; Sarmiento 123
CHILLICOTHE *see* LOWER SHAWNEE TOWN
CHILOÉ, ISLA DE *S Chile 121*
CHIMÁN *see* THEVACO
CHINA early embassies from Japan 26; Portuguese visits 146; Marco Polo 154; Przhevalsky and Tsybikov 221; Mekong River Expedition 225; *see also* CATHAY
CHINCHA *C Peru* H. Pizarro 120/2
CHIN-CH'ENG *C China* Chang Ch'ien 19
CHINDE *C Mozambique* Silveira 138; Lacerda 194; Livingstone 201/3
CHINESE TURKESTAN (*a/c* Sinkiang) *region of W China* Marco Polo 154; Przhevalsky and Roerich 221
CHINGUETTI *W Africa* Saharan trade 59, 60
CHIOS *island of Aegean* Genoese colonization 36; visited by Christopher Columbus 44
CHIPEWYAN Indian tribe of N Canada 97
CHIRA *river of NW Peru* F. Pizarro 120/3
CHIRAMBIRÁ, PUNTA *see* CHARAMBIRÁ
CHITA *E Colombia* Antonio de Monteverde 132
CHITTAGONG (*Chin.* Chih-ti-chiang) *E India* Cheng Ho 22; early trade 144; *see also* SUDKAWAN
CHOLULA *Mexico* native centre 34; Cortés 54/4
CHOTANO *river of N Peru* 120/3
CH'ÜAN-CHOU *SE China* Marco Polo 154
CHUBUT *river of S Argentina* 70
CHUCUITO *S Peru* Inca empire 35
CHUCUNAQUE, RIVER *see* BALSA, RIVER
CHUKCHI PENINSULA (*Russ.* Chukotskiy Poluostrov) *NE Siberia* Great Northern Expedition 159
CHUKCHI SEA (*Russ.* Chukotskoye More) *NE Siberia* 160; Bering 229/2
CHUKOTKA *region of NE Siberia* Nordenskiöld 160
CHUKOTSKIY POLUOSTROV *see* CHUKCHI PENINSULA
CHUKOTSKOYE MORE *see* CHUKCHI SEA
CHURCHILL *river of NE Canada* fur trade route 97
CHURCHILL (*f/c* Fort Churchill, *n/c* Churchill) Munk 85; Pond 106
CIGANTES (*n/c* Curaçao) *SE Caribbean* Niño and Guerra 51/1
CILICIA Roman province of SE Anatolia 24
CINCO HERMANAS (*a/c* Yef Pelee) *W New Guinea* Torres 168
'CINNAMON LAND' *Ecuador* 122
CIPANGU (*mod.* Japan) Christopher Columbus's map 45
CITLATÉPETL *mountain of Mexico* Cortés 54/4
CIUATECPAN *Guatemala* Cortés 54/5
CIUDAD GUAYANA *see* SANTO TOMÉ
CIUDAD JUÁREZ *see* EL PASO DEL NORTE
CLARKSVILLE *see* OCCANEECHEE ISLAND

COATS ISLAND *NE Canada* 85
COBRE, RIO DO *SE Africa* da Gama 145/1, 3
COCA *Ecuador* G. Pizarro 119
COCANADA (*n/s* Kakinada) *E India* early trade 144
COCHETOPA PASS *SW USA* Gunnison 112
COCHIN (*Chin.* Ko-chih) *SW India* Cheng Ho 22; 145/2,3; Marco Polo 154
COCHIN CHINA *country of S Indochina* Mekong River Expedition 225
COD, CAPE *NE USA* Champlain 95; Winslow 100/3
COFAQUI *SE USA* de Soto 91
COFITACHEQUI *SE USA* de Soto 55/6, 91
COLBECK, CAPE *Antarctica* Ross 232
COLHUÉ HUAPÍ, LAGO *S Argentina* Mascardi 121
COLIGUA *S USA* de Soto 55/6
COLLIOURE *SW France* visited by Christopher Columbus 44
COLLO *Algeria* Aragonese protectorate 36
COLOMBI (*n/c* São Jorge) *island of Azores* 42
COLOMBIA early Spanish exploration 119, 125–129; Berrio and Missionary explorers 132
COLOMBO (*Chin.* Kai-lang-pu) *W Ceylon* Cheng Ho 22; early trade 144, 145/3
COLONEL HILL *Bahamas* possible landfall of Christopher Columbus 46/3
COLORADO *state of W USA* the Great Surveys 113
COLORADO PLATEAU *SW USA* Oñate 90; Domínguez and Escalante 93; Powell 113
COLORADO RIVER *SW USA* Smith 110; Powell and Wheeler 113
COLUMBIA RIVER *NW USA* Hezeta 104; Thompson 106; Lewis and Clark 110; Frémont 111; railroad survey 112
COLUMBUS (Georgia) *see* COWETA
COMODO (*n/s* Komodo) *island of E Indies* Wallace 224
COMOGRE (*n/c* Ailigandi) *Panama* Ayora 52
COMORO ISLANDS (*Fr.* Îles Comores) *E Africa* early trade 114; Diogo Dias 145/3; Livingstone 201/3
CONCEPCIÓN *NW Mexico* Anza and Garcés 93
CONCEPCIÓN *C Chile* Fernández 121
CONCEPCIÓN, CANAL *S Chile* Sarmiento 123
CONCEPCIÓN DE LA VEGA *Hispaniola* Colón 51/2
CONCEPTION ISLAND *Bahamas* possible landfall of Christopher Columbus 46/3
CUSCO *see* CUZCO
CONCHOS *river of N Mexico* early Spanish explorers 90, 93
CONCORD *NE USA* Willard 100/3
CONGO (*a/c* Zaire) *river of C Africa* Cão 63; Stanley 203/7, 204, 206
CONGO FREE STATE (*a/c* Belgian Congo, *n/c* Zaire) 204–206
CONIGI (*n/c* Terceira) *island of Azores* 42
CONNECTICUT RIVER *NE USA* Winslow and Pynchon 100/3
CONSOLACIÓN, CABO *NE Brazil* Pinzón 69
CONSTANTINOPLE (*anc.* Byzantium, *mod.* Istanbul) Ibn Battuta 32/1
CONTWOYTO LAKE *N Canada* Hearne 108
COOK INLET *SE Alaska* Cook 104
COOK ISLANDS *S Pacific* Cook 176
COOPER CREEK (*a/c* Cooper's Creek) *C Australia* Gregory, Burke and Wills 183
COOSA *SE USA* Amerindian tribe 90
COOSA RIVER *SE USA* Arthur 99
COPACABANA *N Bolivia* Inca shrine 35/inset
COPIAPÓ *C Chile* Inca empire 35; Almagro 121
COPILCO-ZACUALCO *Guatemala* Cortés 54/5
COPPER Inuit group of N Canada 84
COPPERMINE RIVER *N Canada* Hearne 108; Franklin 114/1
CORAL SEA *SW Pacific* Cook 176
CORDILLERA DE MÉRIDA *N Colombia* Federmann 125
CORDILLERA ORIENTAL *mountains of Bolivia and Colombia* Federmann 125; early exploration 132
CORDOBA (*Sp.* Córdoba) *SW Spain* visited by Christopher Columbus 44

CORNWALLIS ISLAND *N Canada* Richardson 114/1
CORO *W Venezuela* Hohermuth 125; Alfinger and Federmann 129
CORONATION GULF *NW Canada* Hearne 108; 114/1
CORONGO *N Peru* Pizarro 120/2
CORRENTES, CABO DAS *SE Africa* da Gama 145/3
CORRIENTES *N Argentina* Aguirre 121
CORUMBÁ *see* CANDELARIA
CORUNNA (*Sp.* La Coruña) *NW Spain* Loaisa 66
CORVO *island of Azores* 42
COSA *SE USA* de Soto 55/6, 90
COSTE *SE USA* de Soto 55/6, 90
COTAGAITA *S Bolivia* Rojas 121
COUNCIL BLUFFS *C USA* Lewis and Clark 110
COUNTESS OF WARWICK ISLAND *see* KODLUNARN ISLAND
COWETA (*n/c* Columbus) *SE USA* Arthur and Woodward 99
COZUMEL, ISLA DE *NE Mexico* Aztec trade route 34
CREE Indian tribe of C Canada 97
CRETE acquired by Venetians 36
CROOKED ISLAND *Bahamas* possible landfall of Christopher Columbus 46/3
CRUZ, CABO de *S Cuba* Christopher Columbus's 4th voyage 51/1
CUANDO, RIVER (*a/s* Kwando) *Angola* 194, 197
CUANGO, RIVER (*a/s* Kwango) *Angola* 194, 197; 204
CUANZA, RIVER *Angola* 194, 197, 204
CUAUHPILOAYAN *C Mexico* native centre 34
CUAUHTEPEC *S Mexico* native centre 34
CUAUHTOLCO *S Mexico* native centre 34
CUBA Christopher Columbus's voyages 46/3, 51/1
CUBANGO, RIVER (*a/c* Kavango) *Angola* 194, 197; 204
CÚCUTA *N Colombia* 125; 129
CUCHIVERO *river of W Venezuela* Berrio 132
CUENCA *see* TUMIBAMBA
CUILO, RIVER *C Congo* 204
CUITO, RIVER *Angola* 194, 197
CULIACÁN *NW Mexico* early Spanish explorers 90, 93
CUMBERLAND GAP *E USA* Arthur 99; Walker 101
CUMBERLAND HOUSE (*a/c* The Pas) *N Canada* Hudson's Bay Company 106
CUMBERLAND SOUND *NE Canada* Davis 85; 115
CUNENE, RIVER *Angola* 194, 197; 204
CURAÇAO (*f/c* Cigantes) *island of SE Caribbean* Niño and Guerra 51/1; 129
CUTTACK *E India* early trade 144
CUVO, RIVER *NW Angola* 204
CUYUNI *river of E Venezuela* 129
CUZCO (*n/s* Cusco) *S Peru* Inca empire 35; F. Pizarro 120/2; Almagro 121
CYPRUS Latin kingdom 36
CYRUS W. FIELD BAY *NE Canada* 86
CYZICUS *NW Anatolia* Alexander the Great 25

D

DACIA INFERIOR AND SUPERIOR Roman provinces of Romania 24
DAGOMBA people of W Africa 190
DAHOMEY kingdom of W Africa; Binger 192
DAIBOL *see* DAYBUL
DALMATIA *region of W Yugoslavia* Venetian traders 36
DAMASCUS (*Ar.* Dimashq or Ash Sham, *Fr.* Damas) *W Syria* Ibn Battuta 32/1; Blunt and Guarmani 212
DAMOT kingdom of Ethiopia 188
DAMPIER, CAPE *New Britain, W Pacific* Dampier 172
DAMPIER ISLAND (*n/c* Karkar) *New Guinea* Dampier 172
DAMPIER STRAIT *New Guinea/ New Britain* Dampier 172
DANGER ISLAND *see* SAN BERNARDO
DANGHE NANSHAN *see* HUMBOLDT RANGE
DANKAZ (*n/s* Denk'ez) *C Ethiopia* Fernandes 139
DANUBE, RIVER *C Europe* German and Latin traders 36
DARBAT *S Arabia* Thesiger 212
DAR ES SALAAM *E Africa* 198; Thomson 203/8
DARFUR kingdom of NE Africa; Browne 188; Nachtigal 193
DARIÉN (*f/c* Santa María la Antigua del Darién) *Panama* Christopher Columbus's 4th voyage 51/1; 119
DARIEN, GULF OF *Panama/ Columbia* 51/1, 52
DARJEELING (*n/s* Darjiling) *NE India* Roerich 221
DARLING DOWNS *E Australia* Cunningham 181
DARLING RIVER *SE Australia* Mitchell 181
DARNLEY, CAPE *Antarctica* Mawson 232
DARUR *NE Sudan* Ibn Battuta 32/1; *see also* DOROO
DARWIN *N Australia* stock route 185
DARYACHEH-YE ORUMIYEH *see* URMIA, LAKE
DAULATABAD *C India* Ibn Battuta 32/2
DAVIS STRAIT *Canada/Greenland* 85; Leif Eiriksson 75; Parry and Ross 115
DAWSON, ISLA *S Chile* 71
DAWSON RIVER *E Australia* Mitchell 183
DAYBUL (*a/s* Debal, Daibol) *NW India* Ibn Battuta 32/2
DE GREY RIVER *NW Australia* Warburton 184
DE WIT'S LAND *NW Australia* 171
DEAD SEA *Palestine* 212
DEBAL *see* DAYBUL
DEBARUA (*n/s* Dibarwa) *N Ethiopia* Christovão de Gama and Da Lima 139
DEHRA DUN *NW India* Nain Singh 221
DELAGOA BAY (*Port.* Baia de Lourenço Marques) *S Mozambique* Portuguese shipwreck survivors 141
DELAWARE BAY *E USA* Hudson 80
DELGADO, CAPE *N Mozambique* da Gama 145/1; British coastal survey 198
DELHI *N India* Ibn Battuta 32/2
DELICIAS *Cuba* possible landfall of Christopher Columbus 46/3
DELIVERANCE ISLAND *SE New Guinea* Torres 168
DELLY, MOUNT *S India* da Gama 145/2
DENGZHOU *see* TENG-CHOU
DENK'EZ *see* DANKAZ
DERWENT RIVER *S Tasmania* Wedge 182
DESEADO, CABO *S Chile* Loaisa and Magellan 71
DESOLACIÓN, ISLA *S Chile* 71
DEVON ISLAND *NE Canada* 85;

114/1; Sverdrup 230/5
DEWA *N Japan* early province 26
DEZHNEV, CAPE (*a/c* East Cape, *Russ.* Mys Dezhneva) *E USSR* Cook 104; Dezhnev 159; Nordenskiöld 160
DHOFAR (*n/s* Zufar) *region of S Arabia* Cheng Ho 22; Thesiger 212
DIAMANTINA RIVER *C Australia* Burke and Wills 183
DIAMOND CREEK *W USA* Wheeler 113
DIARA *W Africa* Saharan trade 59, 60
DIBARWA *see* DEBARUA
DIMASHQ *see* DAMASCUS
DINAWAR *S Ceylon* Ibn Battuta 32/2
DIU *NW India* Conti and Covilhão 144
DJENNÉ *see* JENNE
DJIBOUTI *see* FRENCH SOMALILAND
DJIDJELLI (*n/s* Jijel) *Algeria* Aragonese protectorate 36
DMITRIYA LAPTEVA, PROLIV strait between Siberia and New Siberian Islands Gedenshtrom and Pshenitsin 229/1
DOAR, RAS EL *E Sudan* De Castro 142
DOBO *Aru Islands, E Indies* Wallace 224
DOHA (*n/s* Ad Dawhah) *SE Arabia* 212
DOMASHNIY, OSTROV *island of Severnaya Zemlya* Ushakov 230/4
DOMINICA *island of SE Caribbean* Christopher Columbus's 2nd voyage 46/4, 51/1
DOMINICA (*n/c* Hiva Oa) *S Pacific* Mendaña 167/7
DOMINICAN REPUBLIC *see* HISPANIOLA
DONA ANA *SW USA* Pope 112
DONGOLA *N Sudan* Nachtigal 193
DOREY *NW New Guinea* Wallace 224
DOROO (*mod.* Darur) *E Sudan* De Castro 142
DRADATE (*mod.* Port Sudan) *E Sudan* De Castro and Rodrigues 142
DRAKENSBERG *mountains of S Africa* 194
DRAKES BAY *W USA* Drake 105
DRONNING MAUD LAND *see* QUEEN MAUD LAND
DUBAWNT LAKE *C Canada* Hearne 108
DUCIE ISLAND *see* LA ENCARNACIÓN
DUKE OF GLOUCESTER ISLANDS *S Pacific* 175
DUNGENESS, PUNTA *S Argentina* 71
DUNHUANG *see* TUNHWANG
DURANGO *C Mexico* Rubí, La Fora and de Rivera 93
DZHEKSONA, OSTROV *see* JACKSON ISLAND
DZUNGARIA *region of C Asia* Ch'ang Chun 19

E

EAST CAPE see DEZHNEV, CAPE
EAST CHINA SEA Japanese routes to China 26; La Pérouse 179
EAST INDIES early Chinese exploration 22; 144; Brouwer 145/3; Serrão 146; Tasman 171; Roggeveen 174
EAST RIVER MOUNTAIN (n/c Narrows) E USA Batts and Fallam 99
EAST SIBERIAN SEA NE Siberia Great Northern Expedition 159; Nordenskiöld 160; early exploration 229
EASTER ISLAND (Sp. Isla de Pascua) SE Pacific Roggeveen 175; Cook 176
EASTERN FRONTIER REGION S Africa 195
EASTERN SETTLEMENT (a/c Brattahlid, mod. Julianehåb) S Greenland Eric the Red 75
EASTMAIN C Canada English trading post 97
ECHIGO N Japan early province 26
ECHIZEN C Japan early province 26
ECUADOR Inca empire 35; early Spanish exploration 119
EDDYSTONE POINT NE Tasmania Robinson 182
EDEL'S LAND SW Australia 171
EDWARD, LAKE E Africa Stanley 203/7; 206
EENDRACHT'S LAND W Australia 171
EGYPT Alexander the Great 25; Ibn Battuta 32/1; Portuguese exploration 142; Bruce and Browne 188; partition of Africa 208
EL BIRKAH (n/s Al Birkah) W Arabia Burton 212/1
'EL DORADO' fabled land of S America 124, 126
EL FASHER S Sudan Browne 188
EL PASO SW USA Parke 112
EL PASO DEL NORTE (n/c Ciudad Juárez) N Mexico early Spanish explorers 90, 93
EL TUR see TORO
ELEPHANT ISLAND Antarctica Shackleton 232
ELLEF RINGNES ISLAND N Canada Sverdrup 230/5
ELLESMERE ISLAND N Canada 114/1; Sverdrup 230/5
ELLICE ISLANDS (n/c Tuvalu) SW Pacific 175
ELLSWORTH LAND Antarctica 232
ELMINA see SÃO JORGE DA MINA
EMPTY QUARTER (Ar. Rub'al Khali) SE Arabia Thesiger 212
ENDEAVOUR RIVER NE Australia Cook 176
ENDERBY LAND Antarctica Mawson 232
ENDERE Sinkiang, W China Silk Road 151
EPIRUS Roman province of NW Greece 24
EQUATORIAL GUINEA see RIO MUNI
ERIE, LAKE Canada/USA French exploration 95; Roseboom 100/4; Rogers 101
ERITREA (now part of Ethiopia) partition of Africa 208
ERIVAN (n/s Yerevan) Armenia 212
ERZURUM E Anatolia Ibn Battuta 32/1
ESFAHAN see ISFAHAN
ESPERANCE SW Australia Eyre 184
ESPERANZA, ISLA S Chile Sarmiento 123
ESPIRITU SANTO (n/c Tampa) SE USA de Soto and Narváez 55/6
ESPÍRITU SANTO, CABO S Argentina 71
ESPIRITU SANTO, CAPE E Philippines Anson 173
ESPIRITU SANTO ISLAND New Hebrides, SW Pacific Quiros 166/4; Bougainville 175
ESTRELLA, BAÍA DE LA Solomon Islands Mendaña 166/3
ESTRELLA, PONTA DA S Africa da Gama 67
ETAH NW Greenland Ross 115
ETCHU C Japan early province 26
ETHIOPIA (f/c Abyssinia) Portuguese exploration 139; 142; 144; 188, 193
EUROPE Latin Christendom 36; satellite map of plant life 237
EYRE, LAKE S Australia Eyre 182

F

FADDEYEVSKIY, OSTROV island of E Siberian Sea Anzhu 229/1
FAEROE ISLANDS Norwegian Sea Norse voyages 75
FAIAL island of Azores 42
FAIS W Pacific Saavedra 164
FALKLAND ISLANDS S Atlantic Byron 175
FALSE CAPE S Argentina Magellan 70
FANG-PAN see BOMBAY
FAREWELL, CAPE S Greenland Gaspar Corte-Real 76
FATU HIVA see MAGDALENA
FENI ISLANDS W Pacific Dampier 172
FERGHANA region of C Asia Chang Ch'ien 19
FERNANDO PO (Sp. Fernando Póo, mod. Bioko) island of W Africa 63
FERRO see HIERRO
FEZ (Fr. Fès) Morocco Ibn Battuta 59; Saharan trade 60, 188; Caillié 192
FEZZAN region of S Libya Hornemann 188; Rohlfs and Nachtigal 193
FIJI SW Pacific Tasman 171; Cook 176
FILCHNER ICE SHELF Antarctica Filchner 232
FITZROY RIVER NW Australia Forrest 184
FLINDERS RANGE S Australia Eyre 183
FLINDERS RIVER NE Australia Leichhardt 183
FLORA, CAPE (Russ. Mys Flora) Franz Josef Land Jackson 230/2
FLORENCE (It. Firenze) N Italy visited by Christopher Columbus 44
FLORES island of Azores 42
FLORES island of East Indies Abreu and Rodrigues 146
FLORES SEA E Indies Wallace 224 see also BANDA, STRAITS OF
FLORIDA state of SE USA Ponce de León 51/1; Narváez and de Soto 55/6, 91; early settlements 80
FOGO Cape Verde Islands 64
FORMOSA (n/c Taiwan) E Pacific La Pérouse 179
FORT ALBANY (Fr. Fort Sainte-Anne) C Canada English trading post 97
FORT BENTON W USA railroad survey 112
FORT BOISE NW USA Frémont 111
FORT BOURBON see YORK FORT
FORT BRIDGER W USA Frémont 111; railroad survey 112
FORT CAROLINE SE USA French colony 80
FORT CHURCHILL see CHURCHILL RIVER
FORT CLATSOP NW USA Lewis and Clark 110
FORT COLVILE NW USA Smith 110; railroad survey 112
FORT ENTERPRISE NW Canada Franklin 114/1
FORT FRANKLIN NW Canada Franklin 114/1
FORT-GOURAUD see IDJIL
FORT HALL W USA Frémont 111
FORT HENRY (n/c Petersburg) E USA Bland and Wood 98, 99
FORT LARAMIE W USA Frémont 111
FORT LEAVENWORTH C USA railroad survey 112
FORT MANDAN NW USA Lewis and Clark 110
FORT NELSON see YORK FORT
FORT PRINCE OF WALES NE Canada English trading post 97
FORT RESOLUTION NW Canada Franklin 114/1
FORT RUPERT see RUPERT HOUSE
FORT SAINT-JACQUES see RUPERT HOUSE
FORT SAINT-LOUIS see MOOSE FACTORY
FORT SAINTE-ANNE see FORT ALBANY
FORT SAINTE-THÉRÈSE see FORT SEVERN
FORT SEVERN (Fr. Fort Sainte-Thérèse) N Canada Tomison 106; see also SEVERN FACTORY
FORT SMITH C USA Whipple 112
FORT UNION C USA railroad survey 112
FORT VANCOUVER NW USA Lewis and Clark 110; railroad survey 112
FORT WALLA WALLA NW USA railroad survey 112
FORT WASHITA C USA Pope 112
FORT YUMA SW USA Parke 112
FORTE VENTURA (n/s Fuerteventura) island of Canaries 42
FORTÍN LAVALLE NW Argentina Aguirre 121
FORTUNE ISLAND (a/c Long Cay) possible landfall of Christopher Columbus 46/3
FOULWEATHER, CAPE NW USA 104
'FOUNTAINS OF THE NILE' E Africa 201/6
FOUTA DJALLON see FUTA JALLON
FOX RIVER N USA Jolliet and Marquette 95
FOXE BASIN NE Canada 85; Parry 115
FRAGOSO, PONTA S Africa da Gama 67
FRANTSA-IOSIFA, ZEMLYA see FRANZ JOSEF LAND
FRANZ JOSEF LAND (Russ. Zemlya Frantsa-Iosifa) W Arctic Ocean 159, 160; Payer and Jackson 230/3
FREETOWN Sierra Leone Laing 190; Caillié 192
FRENCH EQUATORIAL AFRICA partition of Africa 208
FRENCH SOMALILAND (n/c Djibouti) partition of Africa 208
FRENCH WEST AFRICA partition of Africa 208
FROBISHER BAY NE Canada Frobisher 85–86
FROWARD, CAPE S Chile 71
FUENTERRABÍA NW Spain visited by Christopher Columbus 44
FUERTEVENTURA (f/s Forte Ventura) island of Canaries 42
FURY AND HECLA STRAIT NE Canada Parry 114/1
FUTA JALLON (Fr. Fouta Djallon) region of W Africa 190

G

GABRIEL ISLAND NE Canada Frobisher 86
GAIRDNER, LAKE S Australia Giles 184
GALATIA Roman province of C Anatolia 24
GALLA see OROMO
GALLEGOS, RÍO S Argentina Loaisa 66; Magellan 70
GALLYA, OSTROV see HALL ISLAND
GALVESTON BAY S USA de Vaca 90
GALWAY NW Ireland visited by Christopher Columbus 44
GAMBIA partition of Africa 208
GAMBIA, RIVER W Africa 59, 60; Park 190
GANDO Canary Islands Gadifer de la Salle 43/3
GANGES (n/c Ganga) river of N India Hsüan Tsang 20; Conti 144
GAO W Africa Ibn Battuta 59; Saharan trade 59, 60
GARACHINÉ Panama Beccera 52
GASCOYNE RIVER W Australia Giles 184
GAUR NE India Cheng Ho 22
GAZZARIA S Russia Genoese settlement 36
GEESH C Ethiopia Bruce 188
GENOA (It. Genova) NW Italy birthplace of Christopher Columbus 44
GEORGA, ZEMLYA see GEORGE LAND
GEORGE, LAKE C Africa Stanley 206
GEORGE LAND (Russ. Zemlya Georga) Franz Josef Land Jackson 230/3
GEORGE V LAND Antarctica Mawson 232
GEORGIA state of SE USA early exploration 99
GEORGIA, STRAIT OF W Canada Vancouver 104
GEORGIAN BAY C Canada Champlain 95
GERALDTON W Australia Giles 184
GERMAN EAST AFRICA (n/c Tanzania) partition of Africa 208
GERMAN SOUTHWEST AFRICA (n/c Namibia) partition of Africa 208
GERMANIA INFERIOR AND SUPERIOR Roman provinces of NW Germany 24
GHADAMÈS (n/s Ghudamis) SW Libya Saharan trade 59, 188; Rohlfs 192
GHAIL (n/s Al Ghayl) C Arabia 212
GHANA see GOLD COAST
GHARNATA (mod. Granada) S Spain Ibn Battuta 59
GHASSANA SW Arabia Ibn Battuta 32/1
GHAT SW Libya Saharan Trade 59, 60; Barth, Overweg and Richardson 192
GHIR, CAP see GUER, CABO DE
GHUDAMIS see GHADAMÈS
GIBARA Cuba possible landfall of Christopher Columbus 46/3
GIBRALTAR, STRAIT OF (f/c Strait of Hercules) 42
GIBSON DESERT W Australia Forrest and Giles 184
GILA RIVER SW USA Parke 112
GILBERT ISLANDS (n/c Kiribati) C Pacific Grijalva 164; 175; La Pérouse 179
GILBERT RIVER NE Australia Leichhardt 183
GILOLO (n/c Halmahera) island of Moluccas, E Indies Wallace 224
GJOA HAVEN N Canada Amundsen 114/1
GLADSTONE see PORT CURTIS
GLENELG RIVER SE Australia Mitchell 181
GOA W India Portuguese trade 144, 145/3 see also SINDABUR
GOBI DESERT EC Asia Ch'ang

H

I

J

JACKSON ISLAND (*Russ.* Ostrov Dzheksona) *Franz Josef Land* Jackson 230/3
JACMEL *Hispaniola* Ojeda 51/1
JAHUACAPA *Guatemala* Cortés 54/4
JAKARTA *see* BATAVIA
JALAPA *Guatemala* Cortés 54/5
JALAPA *Mexico* Cortés 54/4
JAMAICA Christopher Columbus, Bastida and de la Cosa 51/1
JAMES BAY *NE Canada* Hudson, James 85; French exploration 95; English trading posts 97
JAMES RIVER *E USA* Newport 98
JAMES ROSS ISLAND *Antarctica* 232
JAMESTOWN *E USA* English colony 80; John Smith 98
JANOS *NW Mexico* de Rivera 93
JAPAN early embassies to China 26–27; La Pérouse 179; *see also* CIPANGU
JAQUIJAHUANA (*n/c* Anta) *S Peru* F. Pizarro 120/2
JAUF (*n/s* Al Jawf) *N Arabia* Blunt, Guarmani and Palgrave 212
JAUJA *C Peru* Pizarro 120/2
JAVA (*Ind.* Jawa) *E Indies* Fa Hsien 20; Cheng Ho 22; Abreu 146; Cook 176; Wallace 224
JAVA MAJOR (*n/c* Borneo) *SE Asia* Christopher Columbus's map 45
JAVA MINOR (*n/c* Sumatra) *SE Asia* Christopher Columbus's map 45
JAVA SEA *E Indies* Wallace 224
JAVHLANT *see* ULIASSUTAI
JAWA, RIVER *W Africa* 190
JEDDA (*Ar.* Jiddah) *W Arabia* Cheng Ho 22; Ibn Battuta 32/1; Rodrigues 142; Covilhão 144; Bruce 188; Burckhardt and Burton 212/1; Doughty 212/2
JENNE (*Fr.* Djenné) *W Africa* Saharan trade 59, 60; Caillié 192
JEQUETEPEQUE *river of N Peru* 120/3
JERUSALEM *C Palestine* Ibn Battuta 32/1
JESÚS, ISLA DE (*n/c* Nui) *SW Pacific* Mendaña 166/5
JETAVANA MONASTERY *N India* Fa Hsien 20
JIDDAH *see* JEDDA
JIJEL *see* DJIDJELLI
JORDAN *see* TRANSJORDAN
JUAN DE FUCA, STRAIT OF *Canada-USA* Vancouver 104
JUAN FERNÁNDEZ ISLANDS *SE Pacific* 175
JUBBA (*n/s* Jubbah) *N Arabia* Blunt, Guarmani and Palgrave 212
JUDAEA Roman province of Palestine 24
JULIANEHÅB *see* EASTERN SETTLEMENT
JULIMES *N Mexico* Rubí, La Fora and de Rivera 93
JUNÍN, LAGO DE *C Peru* Pizarro 120/2
JUVENTUD, ISLA DE LA *see* PINES, ISLE OF
JYEKUNDO (*Chin.* Yü-shu) *W China* 20

K

KAAPSTAD *see* CAPE TOWN
KAFFA (*n/s* Kefa) *region of S Ethiopia* Fernandes 139
KAFFA *S Russia* Ibn Battuta 32/1; Genoese settlement 36
KAFUE, RIVER *S Africa* 194, 197; 204
KAGA *C Japan* early province 26
KAGERA (*a/c* Alexandra Nile) *river of E Africa* 200; 207
KAI *C Japan* early province 26
KAI ISLANDS *E Indies* Wallace 224
KAIROUAN *C Tunisia* Saharan trade 59
KAKINADA *see* COCANADA
KALAHARI DESERT *S Africa* Livingstone 194
KALBA *SE Arabia* Ibn Battuta 32/1
KALINGANAGARA *E India* Hsüan Tsang 20
KAMARAN *island of S Red Sea* Soares 142
KAMBATTA *S Ethiopia* Fernandes 139
KAMCHATKA *peninsula of E USSR* Bering and Chirikov 104; Great Northern Expedition 159; La Pérouse 179
KAMPALA *E Africa* Speke 200
KANAUJ *N India* Ibn Battuta 32/2
KAN-CHOU *NW China* Marco Polo 154
KANEM *city and kingdom of W Africa,* trade routes 59, 60; 188; 192
KANIN NOS *NW Russia* 158/1
KANO *W Africa* Saharan trade 59, 60; 188; Clapperton 190; Barth, Overweg and Richardson 192
KANSAS RIVER *C USA* Frémont 111
KANTIN, CAPE *see* CANTIM, CABO DE
KAO-LANG-PU *see* COLOMBO
KAOUAR *see* KAWAR
KAPUAS, RIVER *Borneo* 224
KARA SEA *N Russia* Great Northern Expedition 159; Nordenskiöld 160; 229, 230/4
KARACHI *Pakistan* early trade 144
KARAKHOJA *Sinkiang, W China* 151
KARAKOL (*n/c* Przheval'sk) *Russian C Asia* Przhevalsky 221
KARAKORAM *mountains of NW India* 221
KARAKORUM *Mongolia* William of Rubruck 154
KARANGWE *E Africa* Grant 200
KARBALA' *C Mesopotamia* Ibn Battuta 32/1 *see also* KERBALA
KARIBOU Inuit group of N Canada 84
KARKAR ISLAND *see* DAMPIER ISLAND
KARSH (*mod.* Kerch) *S Russia* Ibn Battuta 32/1
KASAI, RIVER *C Africa* 194, 197; Cameron 204
KASHAN *NW Persia* Browne 212
KASHGAR (*Chin.* Kashi) *Sinkiang, W China* Chang Ch'ien 19; Fa Hsien 20; Marco Polo 154
KASHMIR *region of NW India* Hsüan Tsang 20
KATHERINE RIVER *N Australia* Stuart 182
KATHMANDU *C Nepal* 221
KATIF (*n/s* Al Qatif) *E Arabia* Palgrave 212
KATONGA *river of E Africa* 200
KAVANGO, RIVER *see* CUBANGO
KAWACHI *C Japan* early province 26
KAWAR (*Fr.* Kaouar) *W Africa* Saharan trade 59, 60
KAWLAM (*n/c* Quilon) *S India* Ibn Battuta 32/2
KAYAK ISLAND *SE Alaska* Bering 104
KAZAN-RETTO *see* VOLCANO ISLANDS
KAZARUN (*a/s* Kazerun) *SW Persia* Ibn Battuta 32/1

KAZEMBE *see* CAZEMBE
KAZUSA *C Japan* early province 26
KAZVIN *NW Persia* Browne 212
KEALAKEKUA BAY *Hawaiian Islands* Cook 179
KEBBI kingdom of *W Africa* 188, 192
KEBRABASA FALLS *see* QUEBRABASA RAPIDS
KEFA *see* KAFFA
KEMP LAND *Antarctica* Mawson 232
KENEH *NE Egypt* 144
KENGTUNG *C Burma* Mekong River Expedition 225
KENKEK *C Asia* William of Rubruck 154
KENNEBEC RIVER *NE USA* Winslow 100/3
KENYA *see* BRITISH EAST AFRICA
KENYA, MOUNT *E Africa* 198, 203/8
KERBELA (*n/s* Karbala') *C Iraq* Blunt 212
KERCH *see* KARSH
KERMAN *see* KIRMAN
KESH *C Asia* 151
KHAIBAR (*n/s* Khaybar) *NW Arabia* Guarmani 212
KHAJURAHO *N India* Ibn Battuta 32/2
KHAMBHAT *see* CAMBAY
KHANBALIK (*n/c* Peking, *Chin.* Beijing) *N China* Ch'ang Chun 19; Marco Polo 154
KHAN TENGRI *mountain of C Asia* Fa Hsien 20
KHARFA *C Arabia* Palgrave 212
KHAYBAR *see* KHAIBAR
KHEMMARAT *NE Siam* Mekong River Expedition 225
KHETA *river of N Siberia* 17th-century hunting parties 159
KHOIKHOI people of *S Africa* 195
KHOLEYS (*n/s* Khulays) *W Arabia* Burckhardt 212/1
KHOMAS HIGHLAND *see* PARDA, SERRA
KHOTAN (*n/s* Hotan, *Chin.* Ho-t'ien) *Sinkiang, W China* Chang Ch'ien 19; Fa Hsien and Hsüan Tsang 20; Silk Road 151; Marco Polo 154; Roerich 221
KHULAYS *see* KHOLEYS
KII *C Japan* early province 26
KILIMANJARO *mountain of E Africa* Rebmann 198; 203/8
KILWA *E Africa* Cabral 145/3; slave trade port 198
KIMBERLEY PLATEAU *N Australia* Gregory 182; Forrest 184
KING WILLIAM, CAPE *New Britain, W Pacific* Dampier 172
KING WILLIAM ISLAND *N Canada* Franklin and McClintock 114/1
KIRIBATI *see* GILBERT ISLANDS
KIRMAN (*n/s* Kerman) *S Persia* Marco Polo 154; Browne 212
KIVU, LAKE *C Africa* 204, 206 *see also* RUZIZI, LAKE
KLAMATH RIVER *W USA* Frémont 111
KO-CHIH *see* COCHIN
KODLUNARN ISLAND (*a/c* Countess of Warwick Island) *NE Canada* Frobisher 86
KOKSOAK RIVER *NE Canada* 85
KOLA PENINSULA *NW Russia* Willloughby 158/1
KO-LAN *see* QUILON
KOLGUYEV ISLAND *NW Russia* 158/1
KOLI *C Ethiopia* Fernandes 139
KOLOBENG *S Africa* Livingstone 194; Bantu migration routes 195
KOLYMA *river of NE Siberia* 17th-century hunting parties 159
KOLYUCHKIN BAY *NE Siberia* Nordenskiöld 160
KOMODO *see* COMODO
KOMSOMOLETS, OSTROV *island of Severnaya Zemlya* Ushakov 230/4
KONG *W Africa* Saharan trade 188; Binger 192
KORDOFAN *region of S Sudan* 188, 192
KORLA *Sinkiang, W China* Silk Road 151
KOSSEIR (*n/s* Quseir) *E Egypt* De castro 142; 144
KOTEL'NYY, OSTROV *island of Laptev Sea* Anzhu 229/1
KOUKLA *W Africa* Saharan trade 59, 60
KOZHIKODE *see* CALICUT
KOZUKE *N Japan* early province 26
KRONPRINSESSE MÄRTHA KYST *see* PRINCESS MARTHA COAST
KRUNG THEP *see* BANGKOK
KUANG-CHOU *see* CANTON
KUCHA (*n/s* Kuqa) *Sinkiang, W China* Hsüan Tsang 20; Silk Road 151
KUCHING *NW Borneo* Wallace 224
KU-LI-KO *see* CALICUT

KUMUL (*Chin.* Ha-mi) *Sinkiang, W China* early trade 151
KUNDUZ *see* QUNDUZ
KUNLUN MOUNTAINS *W China* Silk Road 151; 154, 221
KUNMING *SW China* Mekong River Expedition 225
KUPANG *W Timor, E Indies* Wallace 224
KUQA *see* KUCHA
KURILE ISLANDS *N Pacific* La Pérouse 179
KURUMAN *S Africa* Campbell 194; Bantu migration routes 195
KUWAIT 212
KWA, RIVER *W Congo* 204
KWANDO, RIVER *see* CUANDO
KWANGO, RIVER *see* CUANGO
KYAKHTA *E USSR* Przhevalsky 221
KYOGA, LAKE *E Africa* 198, 200
KYOTO *see* HEIAN-KYO
KYUSHU southern island of *Japan* 26

L

LA AUSTRIALIA DEL ESPÍRITU SANTO (*n/c* Espiritu Santo) *island of New Hebrides* Quiros and Torres 166/4, 167/6
LA BANDA *NW Argentina* Aguirre 121
LA CONVERSIÓN DE SAN PABLO (*n/c* Hao) *S Pacific* Quiros 167/8
LA CORUÑA *see* CORUNNA
LA ENCARNACIÓN (*n/c* Ducie Island) *S Pacific* Quiros 167/8
LA FLORIDA *SE USA* Ponce de León 80
LA GRAN ALDEA (*n/c* Teguise) *Canary Islands* Gadifer de la Salle 43/2
LA GRANDE RIVIÈRE *NE Canada* 85
LA HABANA *see* HAVANA
LA PALMA *island of Canaries* 42; Gadifer de la Salle 43/3
LA PAYA *N Argentina* Inca empire 35
LA PAZ *Bolivia* Inca empire 35; 121
LA SERENA *C Chile* Aguirre 121
LA TORA (*n/c* Barrancabermeja) *N Colombia* 125
LABRADOR *region of NE Canada* Corte-Reals 76; Bristol trading voyages 78; Inuit expansion 84; *see also* MARKLAND
LACHLAN RIVER *SE Australia* Oxley 181
LADAKH *region of NW India* Roerich 221
LADRONE ISLANDS (*n/c* Mariana Islands) *W Pacific* Saavedra 164; Byron 175
LAIAS (*a/c* Ayas) *SE Anatolia* Marco Polo 154
LAI-CHOU *E China* Ch'ang Chun 19
LAILA (*n/s* Layla) *C Arabia* Thesiger 212
LAMBAYEQUE *river of N Peru* F. Pizarro 120/3
LANCASTER SOUND *NE Canada* Baffin 85; Franklin 114/1,2
L'ANSE-AUX-MEADOWS *Newfoundland* Norse trading base 75
LANZAROTE (*f/c* Lanzarotus Marocelus) *island of Canaries* 42, 43/2, 3
LAOS Mekong River Expedition 225
LAPTEV SEA *N Siberia* Great Northern Expedition 159; Nordenskiöld 160; early exploration 229, 230/4
LA'SA *S Arabia* Cheng Ho 20
LAS PALMAS *Canary Islands* Christopher Columbus's 1st voyage 47/5
LAUNCESTON *N Tasmania* Laycock 182
LAYLA *see* LAILA
LE MAIRE STRAIT *S Argentina* 66
LEBANON 212
LEBRIJA *river of N Colombia* 125
LECHE *river of N Peru* 120/3
LEMHI PASS *NW USA* Lewis and Clark 110
LENA *river of E Siberia* Great Northern Expedition 159
LENA DELTA *N Siberia* De Long 229/2
LESSER ANTILLES *islands of E Caribbean* Niño and Guerra 51/1
LEVANT Latin states 36
LHASA *S Tibet* 20; Nain Singh and Tsybikov 221
LIANG-CHOU (*a/c* Wuwei) *NW China* Marco Polo 154
LIBERIA partition of Africa 208
LIBYA partition of Africa 208
LIMPOPO, RIVER *S Africa* Campbell 194
LINCOLN SEA *N Canada/N Greenland* Markham 230/5
LINDI, RIVER *N Congo* 206
LINGES (*n/s* Lingga) *Sumatra* Wallace 224
LINYANTI *S Africa* Livingstone 194, 197; Porto 197
LISBON (*Port.* Lisboa) *C Portugal* expeditions to Canaries and

Azores 42; visited by Christopher Columbus 44; Christopher Columbus's 1st voyage 47/4; da Gama 66; Corte-Reals 76
LISBURNE, CAPE *N Alaska* McClure 114/1
LITHUANIA Polish evangelization 36
LITTLE MIAMI RIVER *N USA* Croghan 101
LIVERPOOL PLAINS *SE Australia* Oxley 181
LIVONIA *region of the Baltic* Teutonic conquest 36
LLANOS *region of W Venezuela* 125; 129; 132
LOACH *SE Asia* Christopher Columbus's map 45
LOANDA *see* LUANDA
LOBO, CABO DO (*mod.* Cabo de Santa Maria) *SW Africa* 63
LOBOS *island of Canaries* 43/2
LOBOS, ISLAS *S Chile* Sarmiento 123
LOK'S LAND (*f/c* Hall's Island) *NE Canada* Frobisher 86
LOMANI, RIVER *E Congo* 204, 206
LOMBOK *island of E Indies* Wallace 224
LONG CAY *see* FORTUNE ISLAND
LONG ISLAND *Bahamas* possible landfall of Christopher Columbus 46/3
LONG ISLAND *New Guinea* Dampier 172
LONG ISLAND SOUND *NE USA* Winslow 100/3
LONG REEF *see* VOLCÁN QUERNADO
LONGREACH *NE Australia* stock route 185
LOOKOUT, CAPE *E USA* Verrazano 80
LOP NOR (*n/s* Lop Nur) *marshy depression of Sinkiang, W China* Silk Road 151; Przhevalsky 221
LOPBURI *C Siam* Cheng Ho 22
LOPEZ, CAP *see* LOPO GONÇALVEZ, CABO DE
LOPO GONÇALVEZ, CABO DE (*mod.* Cap Lopez) *WC Africa* 63
LOPORI, RIVER *N Congo* 206
LORD HOWE ISLAND *see* BAJOS DE LA CANDELARIA
LORETO *NW Mexico* Portola and Serra 93
LOS ANGELES *W USA* Spanish mission 103; railroad survey 112
'LOS CÉSARES, CITY OF' *S America* 121
LOS VILOS *C Chile* Almagro 121
LOU-LAN *NW China* Silk Road 151
LOURENÇO MARQUES (*n/c* Maputo) *S Mozambique* portugese shipwreck survivors 141; da Gama 145/1
LOWER CALIFORNIA (*Sp.* Baja California) *NW Mexico* Portola and Serra 93; Spanish exploration 103; Mendaña 167/5
LOWER SHAWNEE TOWN (*n/c* Chillicothe) *NE USA* Croghan 101
LOZI people of C Africa 195
LUALABA, RIVER *C Africa* 194, 197; 198; Livingstone 201/6; Stanley 203/7; Cameron 204; 206
LUANDA (*f/s* Loanda, *f/c* São Paulo de Loanda) *N Angola* Livingstone 197; Capello and Ivens 204
LUANG PRABANG *N Laos* Mekong River Expedition 225
LUANGWA, RIVER *S Africa* 194, 197; 198; 203; 204
LUAPULA, RIVER *S Africa* 194, 197, 204
LUCIPARA REEFS *East Indies* Serrão 146
LUDAMAR *region of W Africa* 190
LUEMBE, RIVER *C Africa* 197
LUGDUNENSIS Roman province of NW France 24
LUITPOLD COAST *Antarctica* Filchner 232
LUKUGA *river of E Africa* 198; Thomson 203/8; Cameron 204
LULUA, RIVER *S Congo* Cameron 204
LUNDA people of E Africa 198
LURIO, RIVER *E Africa* 194, 197
LUSITANIA Roman province of Portugal/Spain 24
LUVUA, RIVER *C Africa* 197; 198; 203/7
LYAKHOVSKIYE OSTROVA *islands of E Siberian Sea* Gedenshtrom and Pshenitsin 229/1
LYCIA Roman province of SW Anatolia 24

M

MABILA (*a/s* Mauvilla) *SE USA* de Soto 55/6, 90
MACAO (*Port.* Macau) *S China* 145/3; Pires 146; Anson 173; La Pérouse 179
MACASSAR (*a/s* Makassar, Makasar; *n/c* Ujung Pandand) *S Celebes, E Indies* Wallace 224
MACASSAR STRAIT *E Indies* Wallace 224
MCCLINTOCK CHANNEL *N Canada* Franklin 114/2
MCCLINTOCK ISLAND (*Russ.* Ostrov Mak-Klintoka) *Franz Josef Land* Payer 230/3
MACDONNELL RANGES *C Australia* Stuart 182; Warburton and Gosse 184
MACEDONIA Roman province of SE Europe 24
MACHAME *E Africa* Rebmann 198
MACHAR *N Caucasus* Ibn Battuta *32/1*
'MACHIPARO' fabled land of S America 129
MACHU PICCHU *C Peru* Inca empire 35
MACKENZIE Inuit group of N Canada
MACKENZIE BAY *NW Canada* 114/1
MACKENZIE RIVER *NW Canada* Mackenzie 108; Franklin 114/1
MACKINAC ISLAND AND STRAITS *N USA* Roseboom 100/4; Rogers 101
MACKINAW CITY *see* MICHILIMACKINAC
MACQUARIE RIVER *SE Australia* 181
MACQUARIE RIVER *E Tasmania* Laycock 182
MACROBERTSON LAND *Antarctica* Mawson 232
MACTAN ISLAND *C Philippines* Magellan 165
MADAGASCAR (*f/c* Ilha de São Lourenço) early trade 144; Diogo Dias 145/3; partition of Africa 208
MADEIRA *river of C Brazil* Felix de Lima 135
MADEIRA ISLANDS *N Atlantic* early exploration 42–43; visited by Christopher Columbus 44
MADRAS *S India* Hsüan Tsang 20
MADRE DE DIOS, ISLA *S Chile* Sarmiento 123
MADURA *island of E Java* Wallace 224
MADURA *S India* (*n/s* Madurai) *S India* Ibn Battuta 32/2
MAFIA ISLAND *E Africa* 198, 203/7
MAGDALENA (*n/c* Fatu Hiva) *S Pacific* Mendaña 167/7
MAGDALENA *river of Colombia* Benalcázar 125; Alfinger 128
MAGELLAN, STRAIT OF *S Chile* Magellan 71; de Ulloa 121; Loaisa and Magellan 164; Byron 175
MAGHRIB (*a/s* Maghreb) *the Arabic areas of NW Africa* Ibn Battuta 59; Saharan trade 59, 60
MAGNA MARGARITA (*n/c* New Guinea) Torres 168
MAHDIA *see* AL MAHDIYA
MA-I-MAI *see* PHILIPPINE ISLANDS
MAINE *state of NE USA* early exploration 100/3
MAIO *Cape Verde Islands* 64
MAJORCA (*Sp.* Mallorca) *island of W Mediterranean* conquered by Catalans 36
MAKASAR, MAKASSAR *see* MACASSAR
MAKKAH *see* MECCA
MAKOLOLO people of S Africa - migration 195
MALABAR COAST *SW India* Ibn Battuta 32/2
MALACCA *S Malaya* Cheng Ho 22; Pires 146; Wallace 224
MALACCA, STRAIT OF *Malaya/Sumatra* Pires 146
MALANDANZA (*n/c* Umuda Island) *SE New Guinea* Torres 168
MALAWI, LAKE *see* NYASA, LAKE
MALAYA Pires 146; Marco Polo 154; Wallace 224
MALDIVE ISLANDS (*Chin.* Tien-kan Islands) *Indian Ocean* Cheng Ho 22; Ibn Battuta 32/2; early trade 144
MALEBO POOL *see* STANLEY POOL
MALI *W Africa* Ibn Battuta 59; trade routes 59, 60
MALINDI *E Africa* Cheng Ho 22 *see also* MELINDE
MALLORCA *see* MAJORCA
MALUCO *see* SPICE ISLANDS
MALUKU *see* SPICE ISLANDS
MALYY LYAKHOVSKIY, OSTROV *island of E Siberian Sea* Gedenshtrom and Pshenitsin 229/1
MANADO *see* MENADO
MANDAN VILLAGES *N USA* La Vérendrye 106
MANDELEY *N Ethiopia* Da Lima 139
MANGAZEYA *W Siberia* 17th-century hunting parties 159
MANGAZEYA SEA (*a/c* Gulf of Ob) *W Siberia* Great Northern Expedition 159
MANGI *country of China* Christopher Columbus's map 45
MANICA *C Mozambique* Fernandes 138
MANILA *N Philippines* Spanish port 173
MANITOBA, LAKE *C Canada* Indian fur trade 97; L Vérendrye and Tomison 106
MANTA *Ecuador* Alvarado 119
MANTARÓ *river of C Peru* F. Pizarro 120/2
MANÚ *river of S Peru* Maldonado 121
MANYIKA tribe of Mozambique 138
MAPACHTEPEC (*n/s* Mapastepec) *S Mexico* native centre 34
MAPUTO *see* LOURENÇO MARQUES
MAPUTO RIVER *S Mozambique* Portuguese shipwreck survivors 141
MARACAIBO *NW Venezuela* Alfinger 129
MARACAIBO, GULF OF (*n/c* Golfo de Venezuela) Ojeda 51/1; 125; 129
MARACAIBO, LAKE *N Colombia* 125
MARAÑÓN *river of E Peru* de Póveda 119; F. Pizarro 120/2; early exploration 134
MARBLE ISLAND *N Canada* Knight 108
MARDIN *SE Anatolia* Ibn Battuta 32/1
MARGARITA *island of SE Caribbean* Niño and Guerra 51/1; 129
MARIANA ISLANDS *see* LADRONE ISLANDS
MARIAS RIVER *NW USA* Lewis and Clark 110
MARIE BYRD LAND (*a/c* Byrd Land) *Antarctica* Byrd 232
MARKLAND (*mod.* Labrador) *E Canada* Leif Eiriksson 75
MARQUESAS ISLANDS *S Pacific* Mendaña 167/7; Cook 176
MARRAKESH (*Fr.* Marrakech) *Morocco* Saharan trade 59, 60, 188; 192
MARSA HALI *W Arabia* Ibn Battuta 32/1
MARSEILLES (*Fr.* Marseille) *S France* visited by Christopher Columbus 44
MARSHALL ISLANDS *W Pacific* Byron 175
MARTINIQUE *island of E Caribbean* Christopher Columbus's 4th voyage 46/4
MARYLAND *state of E USA* early exploration 98
MASAI people of E Africa 198; Thomson 203/8
MASCARENE ISLANDS *SW Indian Ocean* route to East Indies 145/3
MASHONALAND *E Africa* Portuguese exploration 138
MASQAT *see* MUSCAT
MASSACHUSETTS *state of NE USA* early exploration 100/3
MASSACHUSETTS BAY *NE USA* Norse trading voyages 75
MASSAWA (*n/s* Mits'iwa) *NE Ethiopia* Christovão da Gama and Da Lima 139; Soares and De Castro 142; Bruce 188
MASSINA *region of W Africa* 190
MATABELELAND *S Africa* Bantu migration routes 195; 197
MATAGORDA BAY *S USA* de Rivera 93
MATANZAS *W Cuba* 51/1
MATLATZINCO *N Mexico* native centre 34
MATO *river of W Venezuela* Berrio 132
MATOCHKIN SHAR *NW Russia* 158/1
MATO GROSSO *region of S Brazil* Felix de Lima 135
MATSUMAE *N Japan* 26
MATTAPONI RIVER *E USA* John Smith 98
MAUMEE RIVER *N USA* Rogers 101
MAURETANIA Roman province of NW Africa 24
MAURITIUS *SW Indian Ocean* route to East Indies 145/3
MAUVILLA *see* MABILA
MAYA early empire of C America 34
MECCA (*Ar.* Makkah, *Chin.* T'ien-t'ang) *W Arabia* Cheng Ho 22; Ibn Battuta 32/1; Burckhardt and Burton 212/1; Doughty 212/2
MEDELLÍN *N Colombia* 125; 128
MEDINA (*Ar.* Al Madinah) *W Arabia* Burckhardt and Burton 212/1
MEDITERRANEAN SEA European expansion 36
MEHERRIN RIVER *E USA* Bland and Wood 98
MEKONG *river of SE Asia* Mekong River Expedition 225
MELANESIA *islands of SW Pacific* 175; Cook 176; Malaspina 179
MELBOURNE *SE Australia* stock route 185
MELINDE (*n/s* Malindi) *E Kenya* da Gama 145/1,3
MELLI *river of C Ethiopia* 139
MELVILLE BUGT *NW Greenland* Ross 115
MELVILLE ISLAND *N Canada* 114/1
MELVILLE PENINSULA *NE Canada* 85; 115
MELVILLE SOUND *see* VISCOUNT MELVILLE SOUND
MEMPHIS *N Egypt* Alexander the Great 25
MENADO (*n/s* Manado) *NE Celebes, E Indies* Wallace 224
MENAM (*n/c* Chao Phraya) *river of SE Asia* 225
MENDAWAI, RIVER *Borneo* 224
MENDOZA *N Argentina* Inca empire 35; Villagra 121
MENINDEE *SE Australia* Burke and Wills 183
MERRIMACK RIVER *NE USA* Willard, Sherman and Ince 100/3
MESOPOTAMIA Roman province 24; Ibn Battuta 32/1
META *river of E Colombia* 125; 129; Alonso de Herrera 132
META INCOGNITA PENINSULA *NE Canada* Frobisher 86
MEXICO (*f/c* New Spain) early Indian states 34; de Solis and Pinzón 51/1; Cortés 54/4, 5; early Spanish explorers 90–93
MEXICO, GULF OF satellite chart of water temperature 235
MEZARIB *SW Syria* Guarmani 212
MICHIGAN, LAKE *C USA* Nicollet 95
MICHILIMACKINAC (*n/c* Mackinaw City) *N USA* Roseboom 100/4
MICRONESIA *islands of W Pacific* 175; 176; 179
MIDDLE EAST early exploration 212–215
MIKAWA *C Japan* early province 26
MIKINDANI *E Africa* Livingstone 203/7
MILLE LACS *N USA* Dulhut 95
MIMASAKA *W Japan* early province 26
MINA *C Ethiopia* Fernandes 139
MINDANAO *island of C Philippines* Loaisa 165
MING-CHOU *E China* embassies from Japan 26
MINNESOTA RIVER *N USA* Carver 101
MINO *C Japan* early province 26
MIRAN *Sinkiang, W China* Silk Road 151
MISOOL *W New Guinea* Torres 168; *see also* MYSOL
MISSISSIPPI RIVER *C USA* de Soto 55/6, 90; Jolliet, Marquette and La Salle 95; Carver 101
MISSOURI RIVER *C USA* Vial 93; Bourgmont and La Vérendrye 106; Lewis and Clark 110
MISTASSINI, LAKE *C Canada* French exploration 95
MISURATA *N Libya* 188, 192
MITCHELL RIVER *NE Australia* Leichhardt 183
MITS'IWA *see* MASSAWA
MIXTEC early native state of Mexico 34
MOABAR *S Asia* Christopher Columbus's map 45
MOÇAMBIQUE *N Mozambique* Silveira 138; da Gama 145/1,3
MOCOSO *SE USA* Narváez 55/6
MOESIA INFERIOR AND SUPERIOR Roman provinces of E Europe 24
MOGADISHU (*Som.* Muqdisho) *S Somaliland* Ibn Battuta 32/1; Covilhão 144; da Gama 145/3
MOHOTANI *see* SAN PEDRO
MOJAVE DESERT *SW USA* Garcés 93
MOLLOBAMBA *S Peru* Inca shrine 35/inset
MOLUCCAS Wallace 224; *see also* SPICE ISLANDS
MOMBASA (*Port.* Mombaça) *E Africa* Ibn Battuta 32/1; early trade 144; da Gama 145/3; Burton, Speke and Krapf 198; Thomson 203/8; route to Lake Victoria 205
MONCURE *see* USHERY
MONGOLIA Marco Polo 154; Przhevalsky, Roerich and Tsybikov 221
MONOMOTAPA, EMPIRE OF (*a/c* Mwene Mutapa) *E Africa* Portuguese contact 138
MONTAGU HARBOUR *New Britain, W Pacific* Dampier 172
MONTANA TERRITORY *NW USA* the Great Surveys 113
MONTEREY *W USA* early Spanish explorers 93; Vizcaino 103
MONTREAL (*Fr.* Montréal) *E Canada* Champlain 95; *see also* HOCHELAGA
MOORE, LAKE *W Australia* Forrest 184
MOOSE FACTORY (*a/c* Moose Fort, *Fr.* Fort Saint-Louis) *C Canada* English trading post 97
MOOSE RIVER *C Canada* French exploration 95; Indian fur trade 97
MOQUI *SW USA* Amerindian tribe 90, 93
MORETON BAY *E Australia* 181
MOROCCO Caillié and Rohlfs 192; partition of Africa 208
MOSSEL BAY (*Afr.* Mosselbaai, *f/c* Golfo dos Vaqueiros) *S Africa* 63, 65
MOSUL (*Ar.* Al Mawsil) *N Iraq* Ibn Battuta 32/1; Marco Polo 154
MOTANE *see* SAN PEDRO
MOTUPE *NW Peru* F. Pizarro 119, 120/3
MOYOWOSI *river of E Africa* 200
MOZAMBIQUE Portuguese exploration 138; 144, 145/1,3; Lacerda 194; Bantu migration routes 195; partition of Africa 208
MU US SHAMO *see* ORDOS DESERT
MUISCA Indian tribe of C Colombia; Quesada 125
MULLER RANGE *mountains of C Borneo* 224
MULTAN *NW India* Ibn Battuta 32/2
MUQDISHO *see* MOGADISHU
MURCHISON FALLS *E Africa* 200; 207
MURCHISON RAPIDS *E Africa* route to Lake Nyasa 205
MURCHISON RIVER *W Australia* Forrest and Giles 184
MURCIA *S Spain* conquered by Catalans 36
MURDERERS BAY (*n/c* Golden Bay) *S New Zealand* Tasman 171
MURMANSK *N USSR* Peary 229/2
MURRAY RIVER *SE Australia* Sturt 181, 183
MURRUMBIDGEE RIVER *SE Australia* Sturt 181
MURZUK (*Ar.* Murzuq) *S Libya* Hornemann 188; Rohlfs 192; Barth, Overweg and Richardson 192
MUSASHI *C Japan* early province 26
MUSCAT (*Ar.* Masqat) *SE Arabia* early trade 144; Palgrave 212
MUSTERS, LAGO *S Argentina* Mascardi 121
MUTSU *N Japan* early province 26
MWENE MUTAPA *see* MONOMOTAPA
MWERU, LAKE *C Africa* Lacerda 194; 198, 201; Livingstone 203/7; 204
MYSOL (*n/s* Misool) *W New Guinea* Wallace 224

N

NACAJUCA *Guatemala* Cortés 54/5

NACO *Honduras* 55/5

NACOGDOCHES *S USA* Pike 110

NAFUD *region of N Arabia* Blunt and Guarmani 212

NAGATO *W Japan* early province 26

NAGCHU (*n/s* Nagqu) *C Tibet* Przhevalsky 221

NAHUEL HUAPÍ, LAGO *S Argentina* de León 121

NAJD *see* **NEJD**

NAMIBIA *see* **GERMAN SOUTHWEST AFRICA**

NAMOI RIVER *SE Australia* Mitchell 183

NANTUCKET SOUND *NE USA* Winslow 100/3

NAPITUCA *SE USA* de Soto 55/6

NAPLES (*It.* Napoli) visited by Christopher Columbus 44

NAPO *river of Ecuador and Peru* G. Pizarro 119; 125; early exploration 134

NARA *C Japan* early Japanese capital 26

NARBONENSIS Roman province of S France 24

NARES STRAIT *Canada/Greenland* Nares 230/5

NARRAGANSETT BAY *NE USA* Winslow 100/3

NARROWS *see* **EAST RIVER MOUNTAIN**

NATAL *region of S Africa* routes of Portuguese shipwreck survivors 140; Bantu migration routes 195

NATCHITOCHES *S USA* de Soto 90; Rubí and La Fora 93; Pike 110

NAVIDAD *S Mexico* Saavedra 164

NAVIGATORS' ISLANDS (*n/c* Samoa) *S Pacific* Roggeveen 175; Cook 176

NAZWA (*a/s* Nizwa) *SE Arabia* 22; Ibn Battuta 32/1

NDEBELE people of *S Africa* - migration 195

NDENI (*a/c* Santa Cruz) *New Hebrides* Mendaña 166/4

NEACURAM *SE Asia* Christopher Columbus's map 45

NEBRASKA *state of C USA* the Great Surveys 113

NEEDLES *SW USA* Smith 110; railroad survey 112

NEGRO, MONTE (*mod.* Monte Canjombe) *SW Africa* 63

NEGRO, RÍO *S Argentina* 70; 121

NEGRO, RÍO *N Brazil* 135

NEIVA *S Colombia* Benalcázar 125

NEJD (*n/s* Najd) *region of W Arabia* Doughty 212

NELSON HEAD *NW Canada* 114/1

NELSON RIVER *N Canada* Kelsey 97

NEMOCÓN *C Colombia* Quesada 125

NEPTUNE satellite picture 239

NETSILIK Inuit group of *N Canada* 8

NEVADA *state of W USA* the Great Surveys 112

NEW ALBION *land north of New Spain* (Mexico) Drake 105

NEW ANDALUSIA *region of N Colombia* 119

NEW BRITAIN (*f/c* Nova Britannia) *W Pacific* Tasman 171; Dampier 172; Carteret 175

NEW BRUNSWICK *province of E Canada* Champlain 95

NEW CALEDONIA *SW Pacific* Cook 176; La Pérouse 179

NEW ENGLAND *NE USA* early exploration 100/3

NEW ENGLAND RANGE *SE Australia* Cunningham 181

NEW FRANCE (*Fr.* Nouvelle France) early French territory of *E Canada* 95–97

NEW GRANADA Spanish viceroyalty of northern South America 132

NEW GUINEA (*f/c* Magna Margarita) Torres 168; Tasman 171; Dampier 172; Cook 176; Wallace 224

NEW HANOVER *W Pacific* Dampier 172

NEW HEBRIDES (*n/c* Vanuatu) *SW Pacific* Mendaña and Quiros 166/4; Bougainville 175; Cook 176; Malaspina 179

NEW HOLLAND *see* **AUSTRALIA**

NEW IRELAND *W Pacific* Tasman 171; Dampier 172; Carteret 175; Malaspina 179

NEW JERUSALEM (*mod.* Vera Cruz) *New Hebrides* Quiros 167/6

NEW MEXICO *state of SW USA* the Great Surveys 113

NEW PLYMOUTH (*n/c* Plymouth) *NE USA* English colony 80; Winslow 100/3

NEW RIVER *E USA* Batts and Fallam 99

NEW SIBERIAN ISLANDS (*Russ.* Novosibirskiye Ostrova) *E Siberian Sea* 159, 160; early exploration 229/1

NEW SOUTH WALES *province of SE Australia* Cook 176; early exploration 181

NEW SPAIN (*n/c* Mexico) early Spanish explorers 90–93

'NEW TOLEDO' *S America* 121

NEW ZEALAND *S Pacific* Tasman 171; Cook 176

NEWCASTLE *SE Australia* stock route 185

NEWCASTLE WATERS *N Australia* stock route 185

NEWFOUNDLAND called Terra Verde by Gaspar Corte-Real 76; Cartier 80; 85; *see also* **VINLAND**

NEYSHABUR *see* **NISHAPUR**

NGAMI, LAKE *S Africa* Livingstone 194; Bantu migration routes 195

NGOMBA, LAKE *see* **RUKWA, LAKE**

NGONI people of *E Africa* - incursions 198

NGUNI people of *S Africa* 140; 195

NIAGARA FALLS *USA/Canada* Roseboom 100/4

NICAEA *see* **IZNIK**

NICHOLAS II LAND *see* **SEVERNAYA ZEMLYA**

NICOBAR ISLANDS (*Chin.* Tsui-lan-shih) *NE Indian Ocean* Cheng Ho 22; early trade 144

NIGER, RIVER *W Africa* 59, 60, 63; Park and Lander 190; Barth, Overweg and Richardson 192

NIGERIA partition of Africa 208

NIKUNAU *see* **BYRON ISLAND**

NILE, RIVER *Egypt* Browne and Bruce 188; *see also* **BLUE NILE**, **WHITE NILE**

NIPIGON, LAKE *C Canada* French exploration 95; Indian fur trade 97

NISHAPUR (*n/s* Neyshabur) *NE Persia* Ibn Battuta 32/1

NITO *Honduras* Cortés 55/5

NIYA *Sinkiang, W China* Silk Road 151

NIZHNE-KAMCHATSK *E Siberia* Great Northern Expedition 159

NIZWA *see* **NAZWA**

NOOTKA SOUND *W Canada* Cook 104, 179

NORDBRUK, OSTROV *see* **NORTHBROOK ISLAND**

NORFOLK ISLAND *SW Pacific* Cook 176; Malaspina 179

NORICUM Roman province of *C Europe* 24

NORTH BAY *Tasmania* Tasman 171

NORTH ISLAND *New Zealand* Cook 176

NORTH LAND *see* **SEVERNAYA ZEMLYA**

NORTH POLE Peary 229/2

NORTHBROOK ISLAND (*Russ.* Ostrov Nordbruk) *Franz Josef Land* Jackson 230/3

NORTHEAST PASSAGE *Siberia* 158–161

NORTHERN RHODESIA (*n/c* Zambia) partition of Africa 208

NORTHERN TERRITORY *N Australia* early exploration 182, 184

NORTHWEST PASSAGE 84–87; 114–115

NORVEGIA, CAPE *Antarctica* Bellingshausen 232

NORWAY Norse voyages 75

NOTO *N Japan* early province 26

NOUVELLE BRETAGNE *region of NE Canada* 97

NOUVELLE FRANCE *see* **NEW FRANCE**

NOVA BRITANNIA *see* **NEW BRITAIN**

NOVA SCOTIA *island of E Canada* Gaspar Corte-Real 76; 80; Champlain 95

NOVAYA SIBIR', OSTROV *island of*

O

E Siberian Sea Anzhu, Gedenshtrom and Pshenitsin 229/1

NOVAYA ZEMLYA *islands of N Russia* Willoughby 158/1; 160

NOVOSIBIRSKIYE OSTROVA *see* **NEW SIBERIAN ISLANDS**

NUBIAN DESERT *NE Africa* Bruce 188

NUELTIN LAKE *C Canada* Hearne and Stuart 108

NUESTRA SEÑORA DEL SOCORRO *New Hebrides* Quiros 166/4

NUEVA CANTABRIA (*n/c* Parmana) *C Venezuela* Berrio 132

NUEVO, GOLFO *S Argentina* 70

NUEVO LEÓN *Guatemala* Cortés 54/5

NUI *see* **JESÚS, ISLA DE**

NULLARBOR PLAIN *S Australia* Eyre 184

NUMIDIA Roman province of *N Africa* 24

NUPE people of *W Africa* 190, 192

NUREMBERG (*Ger.* Nürnberg) *S Germany* visited by Christopher Columbus 44

NUYT'S LAND *SW Australia* 171

NYAMWEZI people of *E Africa* 198, 200

NYANGORE *E Africa* Livingstone 203/7

NYANGWE *E Africa* Stanley 203/7; Cameron and Stanley 204

NYASA, LAKE (*s/c* Lake Malawi) *C Africa* 194, 197; 198; Livingstone 201/3; 203/7; Thomson 203/8; access from coast 205

NYASALAND (*n/c* Malawi) partition of Africa 208

OAKOVER RIVER *W Australia* Warburton 184

OB *river of W Siberia* 158/1; 17th-century hunting parties 159

OB, GULF OF *see* **MANGAZEYA SEA**

OCALA *SE USA* de Soto 55/6, 91

OCCANEECHEE ISLAND (*n/c* Clarksville) *E USA* Lederer 99

OCCANEECHEE NECK *E USA* Bland and Wood 99

OCITA *SE USA* de Soto 91

OGASAWARA-GUNTO *see* **BONIN ISLANDS**

OGOWE (*Fr.* Ogooué) *river of W Africa* de Brazza 204; 205

OHIO RIVER *N USA* Viele 100/4; Croghan and Gist 101

OKHOTSK *E Siberia* Great Northern Expedition 159

OKHOTSK, SEA OF *E Siberia* Great Northern Expedition 159

OKTYABR'SKOY REVOLYUTSII, OSTROV *island of Severnaya Zemlya* Ushakov 230/4

OKI *W Japan* early province 26

OKINAWA *island of S Japan* on early route to China 26

OLGA, MOUNT *C Australia* Giles 184

OLIFANTS RIVER *S Africa* 194

'OMAGUA' fabled land of *S America* 132

OMAN *region of SE Arabia* Ibn Battuta 32/2

OMI *C Japan* early province 26

OMOTO *S Peru* Inca shrine 35/inset

OMSK *E Russia* Roerich 221

ONTARIO, LAKE *Canada/USA* French exploration 95; Roseboom 100/3; Rogers 101

OODNADATTA *C Australia* Giles and Forrest 184; stock route 185

OPÓN *river of C Colombia* Quesada 125

ORANGE, CABO *see* **SANTO DOMINGO, CABO DE**

ORANGE FREE STATE *S Africa* 194

ORANGE RIVER *S Africa* 65; Gordon and Patterson 194

ORDOS DESERT (*Chin.* Mu Us Shamo) *NW China* Przhevalsky 221

ORFORD, CAPE *New Britain, W Pacific* Dampier 172

ORINOCO, RIVER *Venezuela* Christopher Columbus and Ojeda 51/1; 129; early exploration 132

ORIZABA *Mexico* Cortés 54/4

ORMUZ *see* **HORMUZ**

OROKOLO BAY *SE New Guinea* Torres 168

OROMO (*a/c* Galla) people of *Ethiopia* 188

OSAGE RIVER *C USA* Pike 110

OSHIMA PENINSULA *N Japan* 26

OSORNO *S Chile* de León 121

OSUMI *W Japan* early province 26

OTTAWA RIVER *C Canada* Champlain 95; Indian fur trade 97

OUADANE *see* **WADAN**

OUALATA *see* **WALATA**

OUBANGUI *see* **UBANGI**

OWARI *C Japan* early province 26

OXUS (*n/c* Amu Darya) *river of C Asia* Chang Ch'ien 19

OYÓN *C Peru* Pizarro 120/2

P

PACAHA *SE USA* de Soto 55/6

PACHÁCAMAC *W Peru* Inca empire 35; H. Pizarro 120/2

PACIFIC OCEAN reached overland by Mackenzie 106; exploration 1520–1565 164; exploration 1567–1606 166–167; Cook 176–179; La Pérouse and Malaspina 179; radar picture of ocean floor 234; satellite picture of microscopic surface plants 235

PACIFIC OCEAN, NORTH exploration 1728–1794 104; Cook, La Pérouse and Vancouver 179

PACIFIC OCEAN, SOUTH exploration 1721–1768 175

PADRONE, CABO (*mod.* Great Fish Point) *S Africa* Dias 63,65

PAEKCHE early Korean state 26

PAGAN *C Burma* Marco Polo 154

PAITA *W Peru* F. Pizarro 119; Grijalva 164; Mendaña 167/5

PALAWAN *island of W Philippines* Magellan 165

PALESTINE 212

PALMAS, CABO DAS (*mod.* Cabo Palmas) *W Africa* 63

PALOS *SW Spain* visited by Christopher Columbus 44

PAMIRS *mountains of C Asia* Marco Polo 154, 221

PAMLICO SOUND *E USA* the 'Sea of Verrazano' 80

PAMPHYLIA Roman province of *S Anatolia* 24

PAMUNKEY RIVER *E USA* John Smith 98

PANA (*n/c* Poopó) *W Bolivia* Rojas 121

PANAMA Christopher Columbus's 4th voyage 51/1; early Spanish exploration 119

PANAMÁ (*Eng.* Panama City) F. Pizarro 119

PANAMA, ISTHMUS OF early exploration 52

PANNONIA INFERIOR AND SUPERIOR Roman provinces of *C Europe* 24

PAPUA (*f/c* Tierra de San Buenaventura) *SE New Guinea* Torres 166/5

PARAGUA *river of S Venezuela* Berrio 132

PARAGUAY *river of N Argentina* Aguirre 121

PARANÁ *river of N Argentina* Aguirre 121; Cabot 131

PARDA, SERRA (*mod.* Khomas Highland) *mountains of SW Africa* 63

PARIA *N Bolivia* Inca empire 35

PARMANA *see* **NUEVA CANTABRIA**

PARRAL *N Mexico* de Rivera 93

PARRY ISLANDS *N Canada* Sverdrup 203/5

PARUCITO *river of W Venezuela* Berrio 132

PARWAN *SE Afghanistan* Ibn Battuta 32/2

PAS, THE *see* **CUMBERLAND HOUSE**

PASCUA, ISLA DE *see* **EASTER ISLAND**

PASTO *SW Colombia* Benalcázar 125; 134

PATAGONIA *region of S Argentina* exploration by Magellan 70

PATAPSCO RIVER *E USA* Newport 98

'PATITI' fabled land of *S America* 123

PATIVILCA *river of W Peru* Pizarro 120/2

PATRICK ISLAND *N Canada* 114/1

PAWNEE villages *C USA* Astorians 110

PEACE RIVER *N Canada* Mackenzie 106

PEARCE POINT *N Australia* Gregory 182

PEARL ISLANDS (*Sp.* Archipiélago de las Perlas) *Panama* F. Pizarro 119

PEGU *S Burma* Conti 144; 145/3
PEKING *see* KHANBALIK
PELLY BAY *N Canada* Rae 114/1
PEMBA *island of E Africa*
198, 203/7
PENNSYLVANIA *state of NE USA*
early exploration 100/4
PENTAM *SE Asia* Christopher
Columbus's map 45
PERIM *island of S Red Sea* Soares
and De Castro 142
PERROS, ISLA DE (*n/c* Bristow
Island) *SE New Guinea*
Torres 168
PERSEPOLIS *S Persia* Alexander the
Great 25
PERSIA (*n/c* Iran) Alexander the
Great 25; Ibn Battuta 32/1;
Marco Polo 154; early
exploration 212
PERSIAN GULF Ibn Battuta 32/1;
Conti 144; Marco Polo 154;
Palgrave 212
PERTH *W Australia* Forrest and
Giles 184; stock route 185
PERU Inca empire 35; Pizarro
119, 120
PERWALI *NW India* Ch'ang
Chun 19
PESHAWAR *NW India* Fa Hsien
and Hsüan Tsang 20
PETERSBURG *see* FORT HENRY
PETRA *S Transjordan* Doughty
and Palgrave 212
PHILIPPINE ISLANDS (*Chin.* Ma-i-
mai) *W Pacific* 22; exploration
1521–1565 165; Anson 173;
Malaspina 179
PHNOM PENH *see* PNOM PENH
PHOENICIA Roman province 24
PICKAWILLANY (*n/c* Piqua) *N
USA* Croghan 101
PICO (*f/c* Ventura) *island of
Azores* 42
PIKES PEAK *W USA* Pike 110
PINAS, PUNTA *N Colombia* F.
Pizarro 119
PINES, ISLE OF (*Sp.* Isla de Pinas,
n/c Isla de la Juventud) *W Cuba*
Christopher Columbus's 2nd
voyage 51/1
PIONER, OSTROV *island of
Severnaya Zemlya* Ushakov 230/4
PIQUA *see* PICKAWILLANY
PISCATAQUA RIVER *NE USA*
Neale 100/3
PITCAIRN ISLAND *S Pacific* 175
PIURA *river of NW Peru* F. Pizarro
120/3
PLATE, RIVER (*Sp.* Río de la Plata)
N Argentina early exploration
131
PLATTE RIVER *W USA* Long
110; Frémont 111
PLYMOUTH *see* NEW PLYMOUTH
PNOM PENH (*n/s* Phnom Penh) *S
Cambodia* Mekong River
Expedition 225
POCOMOKE RIVER *E USA*
Newport 98
POCOROSA (*n/c* Santa Cruz)
Panama Ayora 53
POLAND evangelization in
Baltic 36
POLAR Inuit group of N
Canada 84
POLYNESIA *islands of C Pacific*
175; Cook 176, 179
P'O-NI *see* BORNEO
PONTUS Roman province of N
Anatolia 24
POOPÓ *see* PANA
POOPÓ, LAKE *C Bolivia* Inca
empire 35
POPAYÁN *SW Colombia*
Benalcázar 125
POPOCATEPETL *mountain of Mexico*
Cortés 54/4
POROLISSENSIS Roman province
of E Europe 24
PORT AUGUSTA *S Australia*
Eyre 184
PORT CURTIS (*n/c* Gladstone) *E
Australia* Gregory 183
PORT DES JARDINS (*n/c* Puerto de
la Peña) *Canary Islands*
Béthencourt and La Salle 43/2,3
PORT ESSINGTON *N Australia*
Leichhardt 182
PORT HEDLAND *W Australia*
Warburton 184; stock
route 185
PORT HOWE *Bahamas* possible
landfall of Christopher
Columbus 46/3
PORT LINCOLN *S Australia* Eyre
182, 184
PORT MACQUARIE *SE Australia*
Oxley 181
PORT NELSON *NE Canada*
Button 85
PORT OBALDIA *Panama* 52
PORT ROYAL (*n/c* Annapolis
Royal) *E Canada* French colony
80; Champlain 95
PORT ROYAL SOUND *SE USA*
80; Arthur 99
PORT SUDAN *see* DRADATE
PORTLAND BAY *SE Australia*
Mitchell 181
PORTO SANTO *Madeira Islands* 42

PORTOBELO *see* PUERTO BELLO
PORTUGAL Portuguese voyages
across North Atlantic 76
PORTUGUESA *river of W
Venezuela* 125
PORTUGUESE GUINEA (*n/c*
Guinea-Bissau) partition of
Africa 208
POSESIÓN, BAHÍA *S Chile*
Magellan 71
POTOMAC RIVER *E USA*
Newport 98
POTOSÍ *S Bolivia* Rojas 121
PRAIA *Cape Verde Islands* Diogo
Afonso 64
PRAIRIE DU CHIEN *N USA*
Carver 101
PRINCE CHARLES ISLAND *NE
Canada* 85
PRINCE EDWARD ISLAND *E
Canada* Norse trading voyages
75; Cartier 80
PRINCE OF WALES ISLAND *N
Canada* McClintock 114/1;
Franklin 114/2
PRINCE OF WALES STRAIT *N
Canada* McClure 114/1
PRINCE REGENT INLET *N Canada*
McClintock 114/1
PRINCESS ELIZABETH LAND
Antarctica 232
PRINCESS MARTHA COAST (*Nor.*
Kronprinsesse Märtha Kyst)
Antarctica Bellingshausen 232
PRUSSIA conquests in the
Baltic 36
PRZHEVAL'SK *see* KARAKOL
PUCARÁ *S Peru* Inca shrine
35/inset
PUEBLA *Mexico* Cortés 54/4
PUEBLO DE LA CALLE *N Brazil*
Orellana 135
PUEBLO DEL CORPUS *N Brazil*
Orellana 135
PUEBLO DE LOS BOBOS *N Brazil*
Orellana 135
PUEBLO DE LOS QUEMADOS *N
Brazil* Orellana 135
PUEBLO VICIOSO *N Brazil*
Orellana 135
PUERTO BELLO (*n/s* Portobelo)
Panama 52
PUERTO BERMEJO *S Chile*
Sarmiento 123
PUERTO CARREÑO *W Venezuela*
Diego de Ordas 132
PUERTO CORTÉS *Honduras* 55/5
PUERTO DE CARENAS (*n/c*
Havana, *Sp.* La Habana) *W
Cuba* 51/1
PUERTO DE LA ESTACA *Canary
Islands* Béthencourt and La
Salle 43/3
PUERTO DE LA PEÑA *see* PORT
DES JARDINS
PUERTO DE ROSARIO *Canary
Islands* 43/3
PUERTO DE TAZACORTE *see*
TAZACORTE
PUERTO DESEADO *S Argentina*
Magellan 70
PUERTO ROSARIO *S Chile*
Sarmiento 123
PUERTO SAN JULIÁN *S Argentina*
Magellan 70
PUMPU *N Peru* Inca empire 35
PUNA, ISLA *Ecuador* F.
Pizarro 119
PUNA DE ATACAMA *plateau of N
Chile* 121
PUNO *S Peru* Inca shrine 35/inset
'PUNT' fabled land of E Africa
144
PURÉN *C Chile* Valdivia 121
PUTUMAYO *river of Colombia/Peru/
Brazil* 125; 134

Q

QALHAT *SE Arabia* Ibn
Battuta 32/1
QU'APPELLE RIVER *C Canada*
Indian fur trade 97
QUEBEC (*Fr.* Québec) *city and
region of E Canada* Champlain 95
QUEBRABASA RAPIDS (*a/c*
Kebrabasa Falls) *SE Africa*
Lacerda 194; Livingstone 197,
198, 201/3
QUECHOLAC *Mexico* Cortés 54/4
QUEEN CHARLOTTE ISLANDS *W
Canada* Pérez 104
QUEEN ELIZABETH ISLANDS *N
Canada* 114/1; early
exploration 230/5
QUEEN MARY LAND *Antarctica*
Mawson 232
QUEEN MAUD LAND (*Nor.*
Dronning Maud Land)
Antarctica Christensen 232
QUEENSLAND *province of NE
Australia* early exploration 183
QUELIMANE *C Mozambique*
Silveira 138; Livingstone 201/3
QUEMADO *W Colombia* F.
Pizarro 119
QUIAHUITZTLAN *Mexico* native
centre 34; Cortés 54/4
QUIGUATE *S USA* de Soto
55/6, 90
QUILON (*Chin.* Ko-lan) *S India*
Cheng Ho 22 *see also* KAWLAM
QUIMISTÁN *Honduras* 55/5
QUINSAY (*n/c* Hangchow, *Chin.*
Hangzhou) *E China* Marco
Polo 154
QUIRAUK MOUNTAINS *see*
APPALACHIAN MOUNTAINS
QUISPICANCHA *S Peru* Inca shrine
35/inset
QUITO *C Ecuador* Inca empire 35;
G. Pizarro and Benalcázar 119;
Benalcázar 125
QUIVIRA *C USA* Coronado 90,
Vial 93
QUIZQUIZ *S USA* de Soto
55/6, 90
QUNDUZ (*n/s* Kunduz)
Afghanistan Ibn Battuta 32/1
QUSEIR *see* KOSSEIR

R

RABEGH (*n/s* Rabigh) *W Arabia*
Burckhardt 212/1
RADFORD *see* TOTERO
RAIATEA *island of S Pacific* 175
RAKAHANGA *S Pacific*
Mendaña 166/5
RANGOON *S Burma* 145/3
RANKIN INLET *N Canada*
Moor 108
RAPPAHANNOCK RIVER *E USA*
Newport 98
RECIFE, CABO DO (*mod.* Recife
Bay) *S Africa* da Gama 67
RED DEER RIVER *C Canada*
Kelsey 97
RED RIVER (*Viet.* Song Ca, *Fr.*
Fleuve Rouge) *N Indochina* 225
RED SEA Cheng Ho 22; Ibn
Battuta 32/1; Portuguese
exploration 142, 144; Bruce
188
REINA ADELAIDA, ARCHIPÉLAGO
DE LA *S Chile* Sarmiento 123
RELONCAVÍ, GULF OF *S Chile* 121
REPUBLICAN RIVER *C USA* Pike
110; Frémont 111
REPULSE BAY *N Canada*
Middleton 108; Rae 114/1
RHAETIA Roman province of W
Europe 24
RHIR, CAP *see* GUER, CABO DE
'RICA DE ORO' fabled land of NW
Pacific 172
'RICA DE PLATA' fabled land of
NW Pacific 172
RICHE ROQUE *Canary Islands*
Gadifer de la Salle
RIO DE LA TRINIDAD *N Brazil*
Orellana
RIO DE ORO (*n/c* Western Sahara)
partition of Africa 208
RIO GRANDE *river US/Mexico*
early Spanish explorers 90, 93
RIO MUNI (*n/c* Equatorial Guinea)
partition of Africa 208
RIPON FALLS Speke 200, 201/5;
Stanley 203/7
RITTER MOUNTAINS (*n/c* Tergun
Daba Shan) *W China*
Przhevalsky 221
RIYADH (*Ar.* Ar Riyad) *C Arabia*
Palgrave 212
ROANOKE *E USA* English
colony 80
ROANOKE RIVER *E USA* Bland
and Wood 98
ROBESON CHANNEL *Canada/
Greenland* Nares 230/5
ROCA, GOLFO DA *S Africa* da
Gama 67
ROCKINGHAM BAY *NE Australia*
Kennedy 183
ROCKY MOUNTAINS *W Canada-
USA* Domínguez and Escalante
93; first crossing 106; Lewis
and Clark and Pike 110;
Frémont 111; railroad survey
112; the Great Surveys 113
ROES WELCOME SOUND *N
Canada* Middleton and Moor
108; Rae 114/1
ROMAN EMPIRE 24
ROME (Georgia) *see* TOMAHITAN
RONNE ICE SHELF *Antarctica*
Shackleton 232
ROOKE ISLAND *New Britain W
Pacific* Dampier 172
ROPER RIVER *N Australia*
Stuart 182
ROSARIO *C Argentina*
Mendoza 121
ROSS ICE SHELF *Antarctica* route
to South Pole 232
ROSS SEA *Antarctica* Ross 232
ROUGE, FLEUVE *see* RED RIVER
ROVUMA, RIVER *see* RUVUMA
ROXO, CABO *Mexico* 51/1
RUB'AL KHALI *see* EMPTY
QUARTER
RUBI, RIVER *C Africa* 206
RUBICÓN *Canary Islands* 43/2
RUDOLF, LAKE *E Africa* Teleki
and Höhnel 203/8
RUDOLF ISLAND (*Russ.* Ostrov
Rudol'fa) *Franz Josef Land*
Payer 230/3
RUFIJI, RIVER *E Africa* 194,
197; 198

RUKWA, LAKE (*n/c* Lake
Ngomba) *E Africa* 198
RÚM CAY *Bahamas* possible
landfall of Christopher
Columbus 46/3
RUPERT HOUSE (*a/c* Fort Rupert,
Fr. Fort Saint Jacques) *N
Canada* English trading post 97
RUPERT RIVER *N Canada* French
exploration 95
RURUCACHI *S Peru* Inca shrine
35/inset
RUVUMA, RIVER (*a/s* Rovuma) *E
Africa* 194, 197; Livingstone
201/3, 203/7
RUWENZORI *mountains of C Africa*
Parke and Jephson 206
RUZIZI, LAKE (*n/c* Lake Kivu) *E
Africa* Baker 201/5
RYUKYU ISLANDS *S Japan* early
Japanese routes to China 26

S

Sabi, River *see* Save
Sabta (*mod.* Ceuta) *NW Morocco* Ibn Battuta 59
Saco River *NE USA* Field 100/3
Sacramento *W USA* railroad survey 112
Sacramento River *W USA* Frémont 111
Sadlermiut Inuit group of N Canada
Sado *N Japan* early province 26
Safaga Island *see* Suffange, Ilha
Safi (*a/c* Asfi) *Morocco* Saharan trade 188
Safra (*n/s* As Safra') *W Arabia* Burckhardt 212/1
Sagami *C Japan* early province 26
Sagamoso *river of N Colombia* Alfinger 125
Saguenay River *E Canada* French exploration 95; Indian fur trade 97
Sahara Ibn Battuta 59; Saharan trade 59, 60; early exploration 188, 192
Saigon *S Indochina* Conti 144; 146; Mekong River Expedition 225
St. Albany *SW Australia* Eyre 184
St. Ann's Bay *Jamaica* Christopher Columbus marooned 51/1
St. Augustine *SE USA* Spanish colony 80
St. Croix *E Canada* Champlain 80
St. Francis, Cape *see* Serras, Cabo de
St. George *SE Australia* Mitchell 183
St. George, Cape *W Pacific* Dampier 172
St. George's Channel *New Britain/New Ireland* Dampier 172; Carteret 175
St. Helena *island of S Atlantic* 66
St. Helena Bay *see* Santa Elena, Angra de
St. John, Cape *see* San Juan, Cabo
St. Lawrence, Gulf of *E Canada* Norse trading voyages 75; Cartier 80
St. Lawrence Island *Bering Sea, N Pacific* 104
St. Lawrence River *E Canada* Cartier 80; Champlain 95
St. Louis *C USA* Vial 93; Pike 110
St. Matthew Island *Bering Sea, N Pacific* 104
St. Maurice River *E Canada* Champlain 95
St. Paul *N USA* Carver 101; railroad survey 112
St. Vrain Fort *W USA* Frémont 111
Sairam *C Asia* 151
Saka *S Ethiopia* Fernandes 139
Sakaka (*n/s* Sakakah) *N Arabia* Guarmani 212
Sakhalin *island of NW Pacific* La Pérouse 179
Sal *Cape Verde Islands* 64
Salado *river of NW Argentina* 121
Salala (*n/s* Salalah) *S Arabia* Thesiger 112
Saldanha *S Africa* Dias 63, 65
Salé *NW Morocco* Ibn Battuta 59; Saharan trade 60
Salisbury Island (*Russ.* Ostrov Salisburi) *Franz Josef Land* Jackson 230/3
Salm Island (*Russ.* Ostrov Sal'm) *Franz Josef Land* Payer 230/3
Salt Lake City *W USA* railroad survey 112
Salto, Cabo do *S Africa* da Gama 67
Samana Cay *Bahamas* possible landfall of Christopher Columbus 46/3
Samar *island of C Philippines* Magellan 165
Samarkand *C Asia* Chang Ch'ien and Ch'ang Chun 19; Hsüan Tsang 20; Ibn Battuta 32/1; 151
Samarra *N Mesopotamia* Ibn Battuta 32/1
Samoa *see* Navigators' Islands
Samogitia *region of the Baltic* Polish evangelization 36
San Antonio *W USA* Spanish mission 103
San Antonio, Cabo *W Cuba* Christopher Columbus's 2nd voyage 51/1
San Bartolomé *N Mexico* Espejo 90
San Bartolomé *W Pacific* Loaisa 164
San Bernardino *SW USA* railroad survey 112
San Bernardino Strait *C Philippines* galleon route 173
San Bernardo (*n/c* Danger Island) *S Pacific* Mendaña 166/5
San Cristobal *Solomon Islands* Mendaña 166/3
San Diego *SW USA* Portola and Serra 93; Cabrillo 103; railroad survey 112
San Fernando de Velicata *NW Mexico* Portola and Serra 93; Spanish mission 103
San Francisco *W USA* Anza and Garcés 93; Spanish mission 103; Drake 105; Smith 110; railroad survey 112; satellite images 237
San Gabriel *SW USA* early Spanish explorers 93; Spanish mission 103; Smith 110
San Germán *Puerto Rico* Christopher Columbus's 2nd voyage
San Geronimo *NW Mexico* Coronado and Díaz 90
San Joaquin River *SW USA* Garcés 93; Frémont 111
San Jorge *Solomon Islands* Gallego 166/3
San Jorge *river of N Colombia* 125
San Jorge, Golfo *S Argentina* Magellan 70; 121
San Juan *W Argentina* Villagra 121
San Juan *river of N Colombia* Balboa 125
San Juan, Cabo (*f/c* Cape St. John) *W Africa* 63
San Juan Batista (*n/c* Yule Island) *SE New Guinea* Torres 168
San Juan de los Llanos *C Colombia* Hohermuth and Federmann 125
San Juan de Prado *W New Guinea* Torres 168
San Juan Mountains *W USA* Gunnison 112
San Julián, Cabo *E Brazil* de Lepe 69
San Lucas, Cabo *W New Guinea* Torres 168
San Luis Obispo *W USA* early Spanish explorers 93; Spanish mission 103
San Matías, Golfo *Argentina* 70; 121; Magellan 131
San Miguel *SW USA* Domínguez and Escalante 93
San Miguel (*n/c* Amotape) *NW Peru* Benalcázar 119; F. Pizarro 119, 120/3
San Miguel de Gualdape *SE USA* Spanish colony 80
San Miguel de Tucumán (*n/c* Tucumán) *NW Argentina* Aguirre 121
San Miguel, Golfo de *Panama* 52; 119
San Pablo, Cabo (*n/c* Tanjung Vals) *S New Guinea* Torres 168
San Pablo Bay *W USA* Drake 105
San Pedro (*a/c* Motane, *n/s* Mohotani) *S Pacific* Mendaña 167/7
San Pedro Sula *Honduras* 55/5
San Román, Cabo *Venezuela* Ojeda 51/1
San Sebastián (de la Gomera) *Canary Islands* Christopher Columbus's 1st voyage 47/4, 5
Sana (*a/s* Sanaa) *SW Arabia* Ibn Battuta 32/1; 212
Sandwich Islands (*n/c* Hawaiian Islands) Cook 179; Vancouver 179
Sangha (*a/c* Sanga) *river of C Africa* 204
Sannikova, Proliv *channel in New Siberian Islands* Gedenshtrom and Pshenitsin 229/1
Santa *W Peru* F. Pizarro 119
Santa Barbara *SW USA* early Spanish explorers 93; Spanish mission 103
Santa Catarina, Cabo de *WC Africa* 63
Santa Catarina, Ilha de *S Brazil* Cabot 131
Santa Cristina (*n/c* Tahuata) *S Pacific* Mendaña 167/7
Santa Cruz (Panama) *see* Pocorosa
Santa Cruz (New Hebrides) *see* Ndeni
Santa Cruz, Río de *S Argentina* Magellan 70
Santa Cruz Islands *SW Pacific* La Pérouse 179
Santa Elena *SE USA* Pardo 91
Santa Elena, Angra de (*mod.* St. Helena Bay) *S Africa* 63, 65
Santa Fe *SW USA* early Spanish explorers 90, 93; Pike 110
Santa Fé *C Argentina* Aguirre 121
Santa Fé de Bogotá *see* Bogotá
Santa Helena, Bahia de (*a/c* Angra de Santa Elena, *mod.* St. Helena Bay) *SW Africa* da Gama 67
Santa Inés, Isla *S Chile* Loaisa 71
Santa Isabel *Solomon Islands* Mendaña 166/3
Santa Lucía, Cabo *S Chile* Sarmiento 123
Santa Maria *Azores* Christopher Columbus's 1st voyage 47/5
Santa Maria, Cabo de *see* Lobo, Cabo de
Santa María de Bogotá *C Colombia* Quesada 125; *see also* Bogotá
Santa María la Antigua *Colombia* Balboa and Garavito 52
Santa Marta *N Colombia* Colón 51/2; Jiménez de Quesada 125; 128
Santee River *SE USA* Lawson 99
Santiago *C Chile* Inca empire 35; Valdivia 121
Santiago *Hispaniola* 51/2
Santiago, Cabo *S Chile* Sarmiento 123
Santiago de Cuba 51/1
Santiago del Estero *NW Argentina* Aguirre and Rojas 121
Santo Agostinho, Cabo *E Brazil* Vespucci 69
Santo Antão *Cape Verde Islands* Diogo Afonso 64
Santo Domingo *Hispaniola* Christopher Columbus and Colón 51/1, 2
Santo Domingo, Cabo de (*mod.* Cabo Orange) *NE Brazil* Vespucci 68
Santo Tomé (*n/c* Ciudad Guayana) *E Venezuela* Berrio 132
Sanuki *W Japan* early province 26
São Brandão, Ponta de *S Africa* da Gama 67
São Francisco, Rio *E Brazil* Pinzón 69
São Jorge *see* Colombi
São Jorge da Mina (*mod.* Elmina) *W Africa* visited by Christopher Columbus 44; Portuguese trading factory 63
São Lourenço, Ilha de *see* Madagascar
São Miguel (*f/c* Brazil or Capraria) *island of Azores* 42
São Nicolau *Cape Verde Islands* Diogo Afonso 64
São Paulo de Loanda *see* Luanda
São Roque, Cabo *E Brazil* Magellan 66; Vespucci 69
Sao Thomé, Isla do (*mod.* São Tomé) *island of W Africa* 63
São Tiago *Cape Verde Islands* Christopher Columbus's 3rd voyage; Diogo Afonso 64
São Tomé *see* Sao Thomé, Isla do
São Tomé, Cabo de *E Brazil* Loaisa 66
São Vicente *Cape Verde Islands* Diogo Afonso 64
São Vicente *S Brazil* Schmidl 131
Sarai *see* Al Sara
Sarawak *region of N Borneo* Wallace 224
Sardinas, Río *S Chile* Magellan 71
Saskatchewan River *C Canada* Kelsey 97; Cocking, Henday and de Niverville 106
Satsuma *W Japan* early province 26
Saturn satellite image 239
Sault Ste. Marie *C Canada* Groseilliers and Radisson 95; Indian fur trade 97
Savage Islands *NE Atlantic* 42, 43/3
Savannah River *SE USA* Narváez 55/6; Arthur 99
Save, River (*a/c* Sabi) *SE Africa* 194, 197
Savona *NW Italy* home of Christopher Columbus 44
Say *W Africa* Saharan trade 188; Barth, Overweg and Richardson 192
Saylac *see* Zeila
Saylan *see* Ceylon
Scandinavia evangelization 36
Scioto River *NE USA* Croghan and Gist 101
Scotia Sea *S Atlantic* Cook, Bellingshausen and Shackleton 232
Seal, Cape *see* Talhado, Cabo
Segu (*Fr.* Ségou) *W Africa* Saharan trade 188; Park 190
Seilan (*n/c* Ceylon) Christopher Columbus's map 45
Selima *NW Sudan* trade route 188
Seminole, Lake *SE USA* Arthur 99
Semliki, River *C Africa* Stanley 206
Sena *C Mozambique* Lacerda 194; Livingstone 201/3
Senegal (*Fr.* Sénégal) *river of W Africa* 59, 60
Senegambia *region of W Africa* early exploration 190; French railway 192
Seram *see* Ceram
Seringapatam (*Chin.* Sha-li-pa-tan) *S India* 22
Serra Lyoa (*mod.* Cape Sierra Leone) *NW Africa* 62
Serrán *see* Zarán
Serranía de Majé *mountains of Panama* 52/3
Serras, Cabo das (*mod.* Cape St. Francis) *S Africa* da Gama 67
Sesheke *S Africa* Livingstone 194, 197
Settsu *C Japan* early province 26
'Seven Cities of Cíbola' fabled place of SW USA 91, 102
Severnaya Zemlya (*f/c* Nicholas II Land, *s/c* North Land) *C Arctic Ocean* 160; Ushakov 230/4
Severn Factory (*a/c* Fort Severn) *C Canada* English trading post 97
Severn River *C Canada* Indian fur trade 97; Tomison 106
Sevier River *W USA* Gunnison 112
Sevilla (Mexico) *see* Cempoala
Seville (*Sp.* Sevilla) *SW Spain* reconquered 36; expeditions to Canary Islands 42/1; visited by Christopher Columbus 44; Magellan 66
Seychelles *islands of Indian Ocean* early trade 144
Sha-chou (*a/c* Tunhwang) *NW China* Chang Ch'ien 19; Fa Hsien 20; Buddhist centre 151; Marco Polo 154
Shadwan Island *see* Xedua
Sha-li-pa-tan *see* Seringapatam
Shammar, Jabal *N Arabia* Guarmani and Palgrave 212
Shanghai *E China* Marco Polo 154
Shang-tu *N China* Marco Polo 154
Shari, River (*Fr.* Chari) *C Africa* Nachtigal 193
Sharja (*n/s* Sharjah, *Ar.* Ash Shariqah) *E Arabia* Palgrave 212
Sharja *SW Arabia* Ibn Battuta 32/1
Shendi *Sudan* Bruce 188
Shetland Norse voyages 75
Shibam *S Arabia* Thesiger 212
Shigatse (*n/s* Xigazê) *S Tibet* Nain Singh 221
Shikoku *island of S Japan* 26
Shima *C Japan* early province 26
Shimosa *C Japan* early province 26
Shimotsuke *N Japan* early province 26
Shinano *C Japan* early province 26
Shiraz *SW Persia* Ibn Battuta 32/1; Marco Polo 154; Browne 212
Shire, River *SE Africa* 197; Livingstone 201/3; route to Lake Nyasa 205
Shoa kingdom of Ethiopia 188
Sholkal'skogo, Proliv *strait in Severnaya Zemlya* Ushakov 230/4
Siam (*n/c* Thailand, *Chin.* Hsien-lo) early Chinese exploration 22
Siargao *see* Arcon
Siberia early exploration 158–161
Siem Reap *C Cambodia* Mekong River Expedition 225
Sierra Leone early exploration 190, 192; partition of Africa 208
Sierra Leone, Cape Schouten and Le Maire 66; *see also* Serra Lyoa
Sierra Nevada *W USA* Smith 110; Frémont 111; railroad survey 112
Sijilmassa *C Morocco* Ibn Battuta 59; Saharan trade 60
Silk Roads *C Asia* 150–153; 154–157
Silla early Korean state 26
Simpson Desert *S Australia* Stuart 182
Simpson Strait *N Canada* 114/1
Sinai Peninsula *Egypt* 212
Sinaloa *NW Mexico* de Rivera 93
Sind (*n/s* Sindh) *region of NW India* Ibn Battuta 32/2
Sindabur (*n/c* Goa) *W India* Ibn Battuta 32/2
Sindh *see* Sind
Singapore *S Malaya* Conti 144; 145/3; Byron and Wallis 174; Wallace 224
Sinkiang (*Chin.* Xinjiang) early Chinese exploration 18–20; *see also* Chinese Turkestan
Sinope *N Anatolia* Ibn Battuta 32/1
Sinú *river and region of NW Colombia* 53
Siraf *SW Persia* 22; Ibn Battuta 32/1
Slave Coast *W Africa* 190
Slave River *C Canada* Mackenzie 108
Smith Sound *NE Canada* Bylot and Baffin 85; Ross 115; Nares 230/5
Smith's Falls *E USA* John Smith 98
Smyrna (*n/c* Izmir) *W Anatolia* Ibn Battuta 32/1
Snake River *W USA* Astorians 110; Frémont 111
Society Islands (*Fr.* Iles de la Société) *S Pacific* Roggeveen 175; Cook 176
Soconusco early native state of Guatemala 34
Soemba *see* Sumba
Soembawa *see* Sumbawa
Soerabaja *see* Surabaya
Sofala (*n/c* Nova Sofala) *C Mozambique* Fernandes 138; Covilhão 144; da Gama 145/1,3
Sogdiana *region of C Asia* Chang Ch'ien 19
Sohar (*n/s* Suhar) *SE Arabia* Palgrave 212
Sokoto *W Africa* Clapperton 190
Solomon Islands *SW Pacific* Mendaña and Gallego 166/3; Carteret 175; Malaspina 179
Somaliland (*n/c* Somalia) Ibn Battuta 32/2; early trade 144
Somerset Island *N Canada* Amundsen and Ross 114/1
Song Ca *see* Red River
Sotho people of S Africa 195
Sonora *district of NW Mexico* Oñate and Díaz 90; Garcés 93; Kino 103
South Africa, Union of partition of Africa 208
South China Sea Pires 146; Byron and Wallis 174
South East Cape *S Tasmania* Robinson 182
South Georgia *S Atlantic* Cook 176; Cook and Shackleton 232
South Island *New Zealand* Cook 176
South Park *W USA* Hayden and Wheeler 113
South Pass *W USA* Astorians 110; Lander 112
South Pole Amundsen and Scott 232
South Sandwich Islands *S Atlantic* Cook 232
'South Sea' or 'Southern Sea' 100; 126
South Shetland Islands *Antarctica* Bellingshausen 232
Southampton Island *NE Canada* 85
Southern Ocean Cook 176; Cook and Bellingshausen 232
Southern Rhodesia (*n/c* Zimbabwe) partition of Africa 208
Spain reconquest 36
Spanish Morocco (now part of Morocco) partition of Africa 208
Speke Gulf *Lake Victoria* 200
Spencer Gulf *S Australia* Eyre 182
Spice Islands (*a/c* Maluco, *Eng.* Moluccas, *Ind.* Maluku) *East Indies* Portuguese exploration 146; Loaisa and Magellan 165
Spitsbergen *see* Svalbard
Springfield *NE USA* Pynchon 100/3
Sri Lanka *see* Ceylon
Stanley Falls *NE Congo* Stanley 204
Stanley Pool (*n/c* Malebo Pool) *W Congo* Stanley 204
Stefanie, Lake *S Ethiopia* 203/7
Stolbovoy, Ostrov *island of Laptev Sea* Anzhu 229/1
Suakim (*n/s* Suakin) *E Sudan* Ibn Battuta 32/1; De Castro 142; Covilhão 144
Sudan *name formerly given to Africa south of the Sahara from the*

U

V

W

X

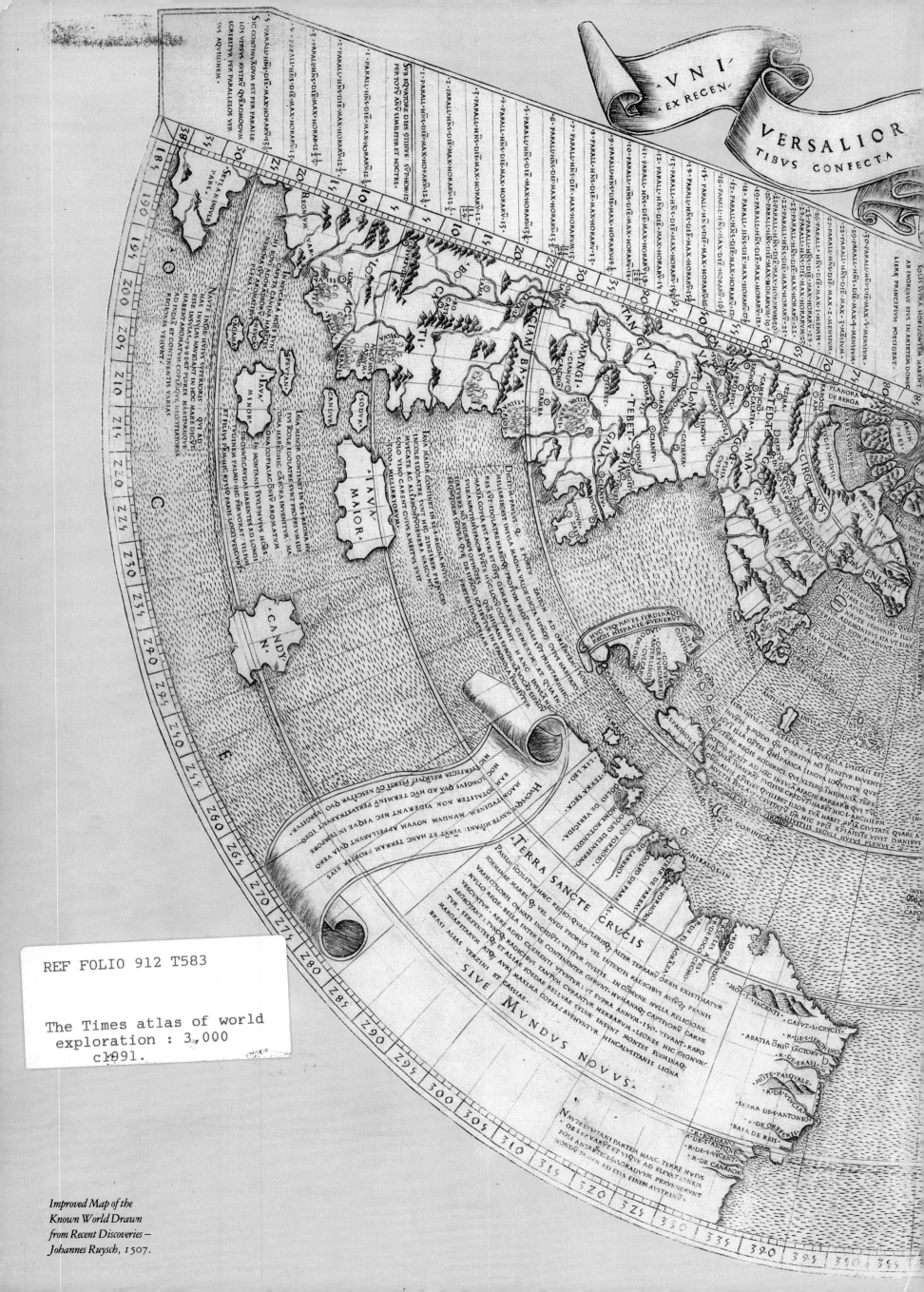

*Improved Map of the
Known World Drawn
from Recent Discoveries —
Johannes Ruysch, 1507.*